THE LOEB CLASSICAL LIBRARY

FOUNDED BY JAMES LOEB, LL.D.

EDITED BY

G. P. GOOLD, PH.D.

LIBANIUS

II

452

LIBANIUS

SELECTED WORKS

WITH AN ENGLISH TRANSLATION,
INTRODUCTION AND NOTES BY

A. F. NORMAN

THE UNIVERSITY OF HULL

IN THREE VOLUMES

II

SELECTED ORATIONS

CAMBRIDGE, MASSACHUSETTS
HARVARD UNIVERSITY PRESS
LONDON
WILLIAM HEINEMANN LTD
MCMLXXVII

American
ISBN 0-674-99497-3

British
ISBN 0 434 99452 9

Printed in Great Britain

CONTENTS OF VOLUME II

L. 1

LIBANIUS

PREFACE

THE speeches in this volume are selected from those of the Theodosian age, and arranged in chronological order as far as possible. The choice of material is an individual one, dictated by a combination of considerations of length and relative ease of access to translations and studies elsewhere. Hence most of the orations which deal with matters specifically educational do not appear, and the reader is directed to the studies of P. Wolf and Festugière where translations are already available.

Two works of major importance for the study of Libanius have appeared in the interval since the appearance of Volume I. Of these, *Antioch* by J. H. W. G. Liebeschuetz, takes its place among the standard works on later Roman society, while the first volume of the *Prosopography of the Later Roman Empire* (cited throughout as *PLRE*) is an invaluable reference work for the major personalities of the 4th century. This, however, does not entirely supersede the work of Seeck, which remains the chief source of information for the correspondents of Libanius as a whole. It is also assumed that the reader will have access to Jones' *Later Roman Empire* for more detailed discussion of the problems canvassed by Libanius. The edition of *Libanius, Discours moraux* by Schouler appeared too late to be used in this volume.

As in Volume I, the text is based on Foerster's collation of manuscripts. Reference to readings of Foerster (F.) and Reiske (Re.) is accompanied by indication of manuscript support, for which see Vol. I, pp. lv f., and the introductions to the various orations in this volume.

A. F. N.

BIBLIOGRAPHY

For the manuscripts, see Vol. I, Introduction, pp. lv f. and introductions to the separate orations. The following works are relevant to the present volume :

Libanius : Editions

F. Morel : *Libanii Orationum Tomus* II, Paris, 1627.
J. A. Fabricius : *Bibliotheca Graeca*, VII 145-378, Hamburg, 1715.
D. Gothofredus : *Opera Juridica Minora*, Leiden, 1733.
A. Bongiovanni : *Libanii Sophistae Orationes* XVII, Venice, 1754.
J. J. Reiske : *Libanii Sophistae Orationes et Declamationes*, Altenburg, 1791.
R. Foerster : *Libanii Opera*, 12 vols. (Teubner), Leipzig, 1903–1924 (repr. 1963).
H. Bouchery : *Themistius in Libanius Brieven*, Antwerp, 1936.
L. Harmand : *Libanius, Discours sur les patronages*, Paris, 1955 (*Or.* 47 with translation and commentary).
A. F. Norman : *Libanius' Autobiography* (*Or.* 1), Oxford, 1965 (*Or.* 1 with translation and commentary).
B. Schouler, *Libanius, Discours moraux*, Paris, 1973.

LIBANIUS

Translations

E. Monnier : *Dix Discours choisis de Libanius* (Sorbonne, unpublished), *c.* 1860.

L. Petit : *Essai sur la vie et la correspondance du sophiste Libanius* (with translation of *Or.* 1), 1866.

R. van Loy : " Le ' Pro Templis ' de Libanius," *Byzantion*, viii (1933), pp. 7-39 (translation), 389-404 (comment).

R. A. Pack : *Studies in Libanius and Antiochene Society under Theodosius*, Ann Arbor, 1935 (includes translation of *Or.* 45, and comment).

J. Festugière : *Antioche païenne et chrétienne*, Paris, 1959 (includes translation and comment on *Or.* 3, 34, 35, 36, 43, 55, 58).

G. Downey : " Libanius' Oration in Praise of Antioch (*Or.* XI)," with commentary, *P.A.Ph.S.* ciii (1959), pp. 652-686.

G. Downey : *A History of Antioch in Syria*, Princeton, 1961 (includes translation of *Or.* 5 and 10).

P. Wolf : *Libanios, Autobiographische Schriften*, Zürich, 1967 (translation of *Or.* 1-5, with comment).

Sources

Ammianus Marcellinus : *Histories*, 3 vols., ed. Rolfe (Loeb).

Ausonius : *Poetical Works*, 2 vols., ed. White (Loeb).

Chrysostom (John) : *Opera*, Migne, *Patrologia Graeca* (=*P.G.*), vols. xlvii-lxiv.

Chrysostom (John) : *Homilies on the Statues*, *P.G.* xlix.

Codex Theodosianus : ed. Mommsen, 3 vols., Berlin, 1905 (repr. 1954) = *C. Th.*

Codex Theodosianus : translated C. Pharr, Princeton, 1952.

BIBLIOGRAPHY

Eunapius : *Lives of the Sophists*, ed. Wright (Loeb) = *V.S.*

Himerius : *Orations*, ed. Colonna, Rome, 1951.

Julian : *Works*, ed. Wright, 3 vols. (Loeb).

Julian : *Epistulae, Leges, Fragmenta*, ed. Bidez and Cumont (Paris and London), 1922 = *E.L.F.*

Julian : *Œuvres complètes*, ed. Bidez, Rochefort, Lacombrade, 2 vols. in 4, Paris, 1924–1964.

Malalas : *Chronographia*, Migne, *P.G.* xcvii.

Malalas : *Die römische Kaisergeschichte bei Malalas*, ed. A Schenk von Stauffenberg, Stuttgart, 1931.

Salvian : *De Gubernatione Dei*, Migne, *Patrologia Latina* (=*P.L.*), vol. liii.

Socrates : *Historia Ecclesiastica*, Migne, *P.G.* lxvii.

Sozomen : *Historia Ecclesiastica*, Migne, *P.G.* lxvii.

Symmachus : *Orationes et Epistulae*, ed. Seeck, *M.H.G.* (*A.A.*), vi, Berlin (repr.), 1961.

Themistius : *Orationes*, ed. Dindorf, 1832 (repr. 1961).

Themistius : *Orationes*, ed. Downey and Norman, 3 vols. (Teubner), Leipzig, 1965–1974.

Theodoret : *Historia Ecclesiastica*, Migne, *P.G.* lxxxii.

Zosimus : *Histories*, ed. Mendelssohn, 1887 (repr. 1963).

Selected Modern Literature

J. Bidez : *La Vie de l'empereur Julien*, Paris, 1930.

C. Bonner : " Witchcraft in the lecture room of Libanius," *T.A.P.A.* lxiii (1932), pp. 34-44.

R. Browning : " The riot of A.D. 387 in Antioch," *J.R.S.* xlii (1952), pp. 13-20.

J. Declareuil : *Quelques Problèmes d'histoire des institutions municipales au temps de l'Empire romain*, Paris, 1911.

G. Downey : *A History of Antioch in Syria*, Princeton, 1961.

G. Downey : " The Olympic Games at Antioch in the 4th century A.D.," *T.A.P.A.* lxx (1939), pp. 428-438.

R. Foerster and K. Muenscher : Pauly-Wissowa, *R.E.* xii. 2. 2485 ff., *s.v.* " Libanius."

R. Goebel : *De Johannis Chrysostomi et Libanii orationibus quae sunt de seditione Antiochensium*, Göttingen, 1910.

H. Grégoire : " Le préfet du prétoire, Fl. Eutolmius Tatianus," *Anatol. Stud. in honour of W. Ramsay*, 1923, pp. 151-154.

R. A. Hug : *Antiochia und der Aufstand des Jahres 387*, Winterthur, 1863.

L. Jalabert and R. Mouterde : *Inscriptions grecques et latines de la Syrie*, vol. III (2 parts), Paris, 1950–1953.

A. H. M. Jones : *Cities of the Eastern Roman Provinces*, Oxford, 1937 (2nd ed. 1971).

A. H. M. Jones : *The Later Roman Empire*, 3 vols., Oxford, 1964 = *LRE*.

A. H. M. Jones (and others) : *Prosopography of the Later Roman Empire*, vol. I, Cambridge, 1972 = *PLRE*.

D. Levi : *Antioch Mosaic Pavements*, 2 vols., Princeton, 1947.

J. H. W. G. Liebeschuetz : *Antioch*, Oxford, 1972.

J. H. W. G. Liebeschuetz : " The finances of Antioch in the 4th century A.D.," *Byz. Z.* lii (1959), pp. 344-356.

J. H. W. G. Liebeschuetz : " The Syriarch in the 4th century A.D.," *Historia*, viii (1959), pp. 113-126.

BIBLIOGRAPHY

H. I. Marrou : *Histoire de l'éducation dans l'antiquité*, Paris (2nd ed.), 1950.

F. Martroye : " Les patronages d'agriculteurs et de vici aux ive et ve siècles," *Rev. hist. droit fr. et étr.* (ser. 4), vii (1928), pp. 201-248.

J. F. Matthews : " Maternus Cynegius and his family," *J.T.S.* N.S. xviii (1967), pp. 438-446.

S. Mazzarino : *Aspetti sociali del quarto secolo*, Rome, 1951.

J. Misson : *Recherches sur le paganisme de Libanios*, Louvain, 1914.

A. F. Norman : " The family of Argyrius," *J.H.S.* lxxiv (1954), pp. 44-48.

A. F. Norman : " Gradations in later municipal society," *J.R.S.* xlviii (1958), pp. 79-85.

R. A. Pack : " *Curiales* in the correspondence of Libanius," *T.A.P.A.* lxxxii (1951), pp. 176-192.

P. Petit : *Libanius et la vie municipale à Antioche au ive siècle après J.-C.*, Paris, 1955.

P. Petit : *Les Étudiants de Libanius*, Paris, 1957.

P. Petit : " Recherches sur la publication et la diffusion des discours de Libanius," *Historia*, v (1956), pp. 476-509.

P. Petit : " Les sénateurs de Constantinople dans l'œuvre de Libanius," *Antiquité Classique*, xxvi (1957), pp. 347-383.

P. Petit : " Sur la date du *Pro Templis* de Libanius," *Byzantion*, xxi (1951), pp. 285-310.

A. Piganiol : *L'Empire chrétien*, Paris, 1947.

F. Schemmel : " Der Sophist Libanius als Schüler und Lehrer," *Neue Jahrbb. für kl. Alt. und Pädag.* xx (1907), pp. 52-69.

F. Schemmel : " Die Hochschule von Konstantinopel im ivten Jahrhundert," *ibid.* xxii (1908), pp. 147-168.

O. Seeck : *Die Briefe des Libanius zeitlich geordnet,* Leipzig, 1906 (repr. 1966) = *B.L.Z.G.*

O. Seeck : *Geschichte des Untergangs der Antiken Welt,* Berlin, 1897–1921 (repr. 1967).

O. Seeck : " Libanius gegen Lucianus," *Rh.M.* lxxiii (1920), pp. 84-101.

G. R. Sievers : *Das Leben des Libanius,* Berlin, 1868 (repr. 1967).

J. H. W. Walden : *The Universities of Ancient Greece,* New York, 1912.

P. Wolf : *Vom Schulwesen der Spätantike, Studien zu Libanius,* Baden-Baden, 1960.

F. de Zulueta : " De patrociniis vicorum," *Oxford Studies in Social and Legal History* i (1909), pp. 1-78.

ORATION 2

TO THOSE WHO CALLED
HIM TIRESOME

INTRODUCTION

This oration was composed by Libanius in his 67th year, *i.e.* in A.D. 380/1, and refutes criticisms currently made against him in Antioch of his tiresome and cantankerous attitude. Such comments, duly reported to him by candid friends, appear to have come as a sudden shock to him, since they flatly contradict that reputation for affability and humanity which he had long enjoyed and for which Eunapius provides confirmation. An almost contemporary account by Libanius himself of his situation at this time is provided in those sections of the *Autobiography* which are appended to his original oration of A.D. 374. In these there is significant duplication of incidents referred to in the present oration[a]; and the circumstances whereby Libanius found himself suddenly deprived of the support which he had previously enjoyed among the upper classes in Antioch may be explained by the series of deaths there related,[b] and by the hostility of *principales*, of whom Sabinus, a connection by marriage and his friend twenty years before, is now the clearest example.[c]

In this speech, Libanius indignantly rejects such

---

[a] *i.e. Or.* 1. 155-204 : for the visit of Archelaüs *cf.* 1. 166 ; the battle of Adrianople, 1. 179.

[b] *Or.* 1. 182 ff. ; 188. [c] *Or.* 1. 190 ff.

criticisms. He points out his genuine affability towards the working class and the scrupulous punctilio he has always shown in his dealings with individuals of the administrative classes. He may, admittedly, have dilated upon his family background and his scholastic success, but his purpose had always been to stimulate and encourage friends and pupils. He confesses himself to be a staunch adherent of order in society, and therefore, in view of his open disapproval of the divisive tendencies of the age, naturally to be regarded as a *laudator temporis acti*, but his unpopularity on this account is confined to the *parvenu* and the *nouveau-riche*. The social criticisms which he has presented, upon the ruinous condition of the pagan religion, of the peasantry, or of the decurionate, and upon the corruption and incompetence revealed in both military and provincial administration, are only too clear from the facts. The last straw, of course, is the decline of the prestige of his Hellenic system of education, and the prominence currently given to the studies of Latin, law and shorthand. The studies of the classics naturally imbue the student with a genuine concern for the distress of suffering humanity, which is extended to cover the circumstances of the present day, and the scholar is bound to deplore the upsetting of the balance of society, unless and until some effort be made to remedy current abuses. In any case, his own criticisms have always been made with a practical end in view, that they should be transmitted to court for the emperors' attention, but his efforts to publicize the need for reform have always been frustrated by the self-interest or indolence of the notables at court. For example, his recent approach to the praetorian prefect upon the matter of recruitment to the *curia* had produced no reaction other than hostility. Since human support has failed, the sole recourse remaining is to intercede with the gods for the relief of present abuses.

These arguments mark a significant recognition by Libanius of his growing insecurity. The underlying theme of the whole oration is that of the comparison of the present with the prosperous order of the reign of Julian, but the call for avenging the murder of Julian, with which he had welcomed the accession of Theodosius barely two years before (*Or.* 24), had fallen on ears that were either obstinately deaf or increasingly hostile, as is clear from the bitter tones of § 58/9. His natural morbidity was not diminished by the personal griefs and afflictions suffered in A.D. 380, and his lowness of spirit is clearly revealed in his *Autobiography*. Even the recent triumph over the sophist Gerontius, who had aspired to his official chair, had proved a hollow one (*Or.* 1. 186 ff.), since for the first time in nearly twenty years his tenure of the sophistic chair at Antioch had been challenged, with ominous backing from the provincial governor. The immediate threat to his position had been evaded, but the incident clearly had served to concentrate upon him the increasingly hostile regard of many of the upper classes, from whom he singles out for attack those *honorati* and serving officials, whom he here describes with the unflattering innuendo normally reserved for Christians. The bitterness of this oration is matched by that of his reaction to the criticisms voiced by individuals at this time. In reproving an acquaintance named Heortius who had written to

4

him criticizing him for arrogance, he retorts with allegations of ignorance, lack of sympathy and dislike, remarking that he has already punished, by the composition of an oration, a whole city which had passed such a judgement upon him.[a] The reference is obviously to the present oration.

The " punishment " is here reserved for those sections of Antiochene society who have arrogated to themselves undue influence over the direction of the city's affairs, and consists primarily of a catalogue of grievances of the down-pressed— workers, decurions, peasants, rank-and-file soldiery and provincials. The point of departure for the development of his argument is his refusal of the honorary quaestorship offered by Julian, acceptance of which would have given him *entrée* into the class of *honorati*. Among pagan intellectuals there evidently existed deep suspicion of such distinctions, for Eunapius speaks with approval of Libanius' correctness here,[b] and Themistius, lampooned by Palladas upon his elevation to the prefecture, has recourse to an elaborate oration of apology.[c] *Honorati, principales*, military commanders, governors and the varied hotch-potch of imperial agents and secre-

[a] *Ep.* 12. 3 : ὑπεροψίας δὲ μνησθείς, εἰ μὴ δώσεις δίκην, Ἡρακλεῖ χάριν ἔχειν ἀλεξικάκῳ. ἐγὼ δὲ ἤδη πόλιν ὅλην τοῦτο φθεγξαμένην τετιμώρημαι λόγῳ.

[b] *V.S.* 496 : Eunapius confuses the honorary prefecture, offered by Theodosius and accepted in A.D. 383/4, with the quaestorship refused in A.D. 363, but his commendation of Libanius' motives remains valid : οὐκ ἀπεδέξατο φήσας τὸν σοφιστὴν εἶναι μείζονα. καὶ τοῦτό γέ ἐστιν οὐκ ὀλίγος ἔπαινος, ὅτι δόξης ἐλάττων ἀνὴρ μόνης ἥττητο τῆς περὶ τοὺς λόγους, τὴν δὲ ἄλλην δημώδη καὶ βάναυσον ὑπελάμβανεν.

[c] Palladas (*Anth. Pal.* 11. 292) : Themistius, *Or.* 34.

taries, whose presence made Antiochene society more incoherent and unbalanced, have used such distinctions for their own elevation to undermine the established system of local organization. Throughout the speech there is implicit a strong protest against the incompetence and corruption which are symbolized by the uses made by such gentry of the practice of private audience (εἴσοδοι). This was something of long standing and, in palmier days, had been employed by Libanius himself, not without arousing prejudice against him (*Or.* 1. 107 ff. ; 125). The general odium aroused by the practice had resulted in a curb imposed by imperial decree (*C. Th.* 1. 16. 13 of A.D. 377), and was to be followed in the next few years by a total ban by the prefect (*Or.* 52. 46), and limitations even upon official audiences (*cf. Or.* 10. 3 ; 26. 13 ff. ; 27. 12 ff. ; 56. 2 ff.). Courtesy calls by officials which Libanius deplores (§ 9 ; *cf. Or.* 1. 166) were also forbidden by legislation in A.D. 383. The practice however was so deeply rooted that, even after such curbs, expressly designed to remove corruption, he felt called upon to deliver two orations against its continuance (*Orations* 51 and 52) in A.D. 388.

The oration also throws important light upon his purpose in composing such propaganda speeches, and upon their methods of publication. In addition to the explicit statement of his intentions in this oration (§§ 70 ff.), a comparison of its arguments with that portion of the *Autobiography* which he had composed in A.D. 374 is not without significance for his practice.[a] That narrative of his sophistic suc-

---

[a] *Cf.* P. Petit, "Recherches sur la publication et la diffusion des discours de Libanius," *Historia* (1956), pp. 478 ff.

ORATION II

cesses, which figures so prominently in the *Auto-biography* (1. 81 ff.), he here asserts has been reserved for his students only (§§ 12 f.), and has became general knowledge at second-hand and not through any information direct from him (§§ 14 f.). The implication is that an oration like the *Autobiography* had received no general distribution in the years following its composition. Discretion and selectivity distinguish the methods of disseminating such works. Certain orations were too contentious to be widely published without great risk to the author, as is proved by his remarks in *Ep.* 916. Such is the case even with the monody upon his uncle, Phasganius, as he confesses himself,[a] and the circumstances of date of composition and of content would certainly place the *Autobiography* in this category. Even for declamations, the current practice was, as often as not, the use of the private auditorium and carefully selected audience (*cf.* § 25 ; *Or.* 1. 101), and there was a consistent attempt by the author to control the publication of his works, cf. *Ep.* 33. The successful insistence upon publication by Strategius is marked as exceptional (*Or.* 1. 113), and even Julian had much difficulty in persuading Libanius to consent to a general distribution of *Or.* 12.[b] In the case of the present oration, such deliberate restriction

---

[a] *Ep.* 283. 2 ff : ἃ μὲν οὐκ εἶχε κίνδυνον εἰς πολλοὺς ἐκφέρεσθαι ἐν πολλοῖς εἴρηται· τοῦ λόγου δὲ ἡ τρίτη μοῖρα φίλων ἐδεῖτο σαφῶν, οὓς ὀλίγοις δεξάμενος τοῖς βάθροις κλείσας τὰς θύρας ἀνέγνων δεόμενος αὐτῶν, εἴ τι φαίνοιτο καλόν, σιγῇ θαυμάζειν μηδὲ τῇ βοῇ πολλοὺς ἐγείρειν . . . ὅστις οὖν οὐκ ἐπιθυμεῖ βαράθρου, κρύψαι λόγον αἱρήσεται μᾶλλον ἢ διδοὺς τρέμειν.

[b] *Ep.* 785. 2 : λόγος δὲ ὁ μὲν εἰς τὴν πανήγυριν ἔτι μέλλει κρύπτεσθαι μὲν ἐθέλων, ἑλκόμενος δὲ εἰς μέσον παρὰ τοῦ βασιλέως καὶ ἴσως φανεῖται, δεῖ γὰρ ἐκεῖνον κρατεῖν.

7

seems to have been essential, and the actual audience confined to a handful of intimate friends behind closed doors. It is through the agency of these friends, and of their connections at court, that the practical purpose of these controversial orations is achieved. Passed from lip to lip, these arguments could penetrate the centres of power with less risk to their author, and create a climate of opinion from which action might follow, more effectively than from any personal intervention, such as had had so little success with the praetorian prefect.

MANUSCRIPTS AND BIBLIOGRAPHY

Manuscripts number twenty-nine in all, and include the major codices utilized in Vol. I (*viz.* CAPUVIBM). In establishing his apparatus, Foerster, as Reiske had done before him, also made use of Monacensis gr. 101 (= Mo.). The divergent traditions are indicated by the broad groupings of the codices into (i) CAPBM and (ii) VUI Mo. For the history of the publication of the text, however, a Bodleian MS. (Barocc. 219, of the 14th century) is of importance, since from it stems a copy, dated A.D. 1629, in the Gale Collection in Trinity College, Cambridge, and another in the Bodleian (Langbain. Advers. 20), itself transcribed first by Olearius and then by J. C. Wolf, to form the basis of the edition first published by Fabricius (*Bibl. Gr.* VII, 179 ff., Hamburg, 1715), with Olearius' Latin translation. This text was utilized by Reiske in his edition, supplemented by the readings of A and Mo. The speech formed part of Monnier's unpublished collection, in

French translation (*cf.* Vol. I, p. lvii). For Foerster's work on the MSS. *cf.* his edition, vol. I, pp. 208-238. A German translation, with notes, by P. Wolf appears in Libanios, *Autobiographische Schriften*, Zürich, 1967, pp. 123 ff.

ΠΡΟΣ ΤΟΥΣ ΒΑΡΥΝ ΑΥΤΟΝ
ΚΑΛΕΣΑΝΤΑΣ

R 171   1. Ὡς δὲ βαρύς, ὡς δὲ ἐπαχθής, εἴρηταί τισι F i.
περὶ ἡμῶν. ὁ δ᾽ ἀπαγγέλλων Ἀνδρόμαχος ἦν
ὀμνύς, ἐπιστεύετο δ᾽ ἂν καὶ οὐκ ὀμνύων καλός τε
ὢν κἀγαθὸς καὶ ἡμῖν ἑταῖρος καὶ οὐχ ἡδέως τὰ
R 172 τοιαῦτα ἀκούσας· οὕτω πλεῖστον ἀπεῖχε τοῦ | τὰ
οὐκ εἰρημένα πλάσαι ἄν ποτε κατ᾽ ἐμοῦ. προκαλοῦμαι τοίνυν αὐτοὺς εἰς ἔλεγχον καὶ ἀξιῶ δεῖξαι τοῖς εἰρημένοις ἀληθείας τι μετόν· ἀλλ᾽ οὐχ
ἕξουσι. |

   2. Καὶ πρῶτον μὲν ἐκεῖνο θαυμάσαι τις ἂν δι- F 2
καίως πῶς εἰς τὸν παρελθόντα χρόνον οὕτως ὄντα
μακρὸν οὐκ ἦλθε ταυτὶ τὰ ἐγκλήματα. ἕτερα μὲν
γὰρ εἴρηται πολλὰ ψευδῆ μὲν καὶ αὐτὰ καὶ παρὰ
ἀνθρώπων ἐχθρῶν οἷς αἰσχύνεσθαί τε ὕστερον συν-
έβη καὶ μόνον οὐκ εἰς γόνυ κατενεχθεῖσιν ἱκετεύ-
ειν συγγνώμην ἔχειν αὐτοῖς μωράνασι, καὶ ἔσχον,
τουτὶ δὲ νῦν εἰσῆλθεν ἀναμεῖναν ἕβδομον καὶ ἑξη-
κοστὸν ἔτος. 3. οὐ γὰρ δὴ ἔστιν εἰπεῖν ὡς λεγόμενον ἐλάνθανεν, ὥσπερ οὐδὲ τἄλλα. τῆς τε γὰρ
τῶν λεγόντων ἀσελγείας ἦν μὴ κρύπτειν, εὐνοί τε
R 173 ἡμῖν πολλοὶ παρ᾽ ὧν ἂν ἐπυνθανόμην. | 4. τί οὖν;

---

[a] For the date of birth of Libanius *cf.* Sievers, pp. 207 f.

10

ORATION 2

TO THOSE WHO CALLED HIM TIRESOME

1. Tiresome and overbearing! That is how I have been described by some people. Andromachus told me so, and gave me his solemn word, though I would believe him without it, for he is a gentleman, a pupil of mine, and one who did not enjoy hearing such remarks. So he was the most unlikely person ever to have fabricated such comments against me if they had not been made. Well, I challenge those to prove it, and I require them to show some truth in their remarks. They will not be able to!

2. First of all, it might justifiably be a matter for surprise how it is that these criticisms have not been aired during all this long time past. Plenty of other criticisms have been made, falsely of course and by my personal enemies, but later on they came to feel sorry and almost fell on bended knee to beg for the pardon, which they got, for their utter stupidity. And now this crops up, after waiting for my 67th year to do it.[a] 3. It cannot be said, for instance, that it was an accidental remark : nor were the others, either. Such openness was a sign of the impudence of those responsible for it, and I have plenty of friends to keep me informed. 4. Well? Am I to

11

LIBANIUS

χρὴ[1] νομίζειν ὅτι νεώτερος μὲν ὢν ἠπιστάμην σωφρονεῖν, προϊούσης δὲ τῆς ἡλικίας διεφθάρην; ἀλλὰ
τοὐναντίον εἰκὸς ἦν, λῆξαί με νῦν, εἰ καὶ πρότερον
ἐπαχθὴς ἦν. δεινὸς γὰρ παιδεύειν καὶ ἐπανορθοῦν
ὁ χρόνος. 5. ἀλλ᾽, οἶμαι, τοιοῦτόν ἐστιν· ἅπαντα
τἄλλα διεξεληλυθότες, καθ᾽ ἕκαστον αὐτῶν ἐρυθ-
ριάσαντες, ἐπειδὴ σιγᾶν οὐ δύνανται, φροντίσαντες
οὐδὲν εἰ μηδὲν ἐροῦσι πιθανόν, ἐπὶ τοῦτο ἐξηνέχ-
θησαν ὅπως αὐτοῖς φεύγουσι τὰς ἐμὰς συνουσίας
εἴη λόγος.

6. Βαρὺς ἐγώ; τί οὖν ἔστιν ἀκούειν τῶν ἐπὶ τῶν
ἐργαστηρίων ὁπότε παρίοιμι λεγόντων; οὐχ ὁ |
μέτριος; οὐχ ὁ κοινός; οὐχ ὁ καὶ τὰς τῶν πενε- F 24
στάτων προσρήσεις ἀμειβόμενος τοῖς ἴσοις; ἔστιν
οὖν ὅστις ἂν ἐκείνοις αὐτὸν ἴσον ἐν οἷς ἔξεστι
ποιῶν τῶν ἐν τέλει καὶ δυνατῶν κρείττων ἂν ἀξιώ-
σειεν εἶναι; οἳ φιλοῦσι μέν μου καὶ ὀφθαλμοὺς
καὶ κεφαλὴν καὶ χεῖρας, εἰ καὶ μὴ σφόδρα φιλοῦ-
σιν αὐτόν, ἔχοντες δ᾽ οὐδὲν ἔλαττον ἀπέρχονται.
7. ποῦ τοίνυν ὁ βαρύς; ἐν τοῖς πρὸς τοὺς ἄρχοντας;
ἀλλ᾽ ἴσασιν ἅπαντες οἵ τε εἰσιὼν καθιζάνω παρὸν
ἔς τι[2] κάλλιον, καὶ μεθ᾽ ὧν ἀπαντῶ καὶ προπέμπω,
καὶ τίνων ἀποσχιζόμενος, ὧν ἑλκόντων με παρ᾽ |
R 174 ἑαυτοὺς πολλάκις οὐδὲν μᾶλλον ὑπακούσας φαί-
νομαι. 8. καὶ τί ταῦτα λέγω, λέγειν ἔχων τὸ
γραμματεῖον ἐκεῖνο ὃ διεωσάμην, ὅπως μὴ σε-

[1] τί οὖν χρή mss. Corrected Re.
[2] παρὸν Re., F. (UIMo.): παρ᾽ ὧν (CAPBMV): παρὼν
Fabr. | ἔς τι Re., F.: ἐστι CAPBMV: εἴς Fabr. (UIMo.).

---

[a] For the metal-working industry in Antioch cf. Or. 31.
12. Unusually enough, the factories were there centres of
social intercourse (cf. Or. 1. 87, 8. 4). Libanius takes a
personal and sympathetic interest in the welfare of the

12

believe that when I was younger I knew how to behave decently, but now, with advancing years, I have fallen from grace? The opposite is more likely, that even if I was overbearing in the past, I have stopped being so now; for time is a fine teacher and corrector. 5. The case, I imagine, is as follows. After having had recourse to every other shift, and having been made to blush at every one, they still cannot keep quiet; without concerning themselves about the conviction of any of their assertions, they have been reduced to this, so as to have some justification for avoiding association with me.

6. I tiresome? Then what can you hear people say in the workshops whenever I go by?[a] "Decent and polite, isn't he? He replies in kind to the greetings even of the penniless." Is there any who puts himself on a par with them, where possible, and yet could claim to be superior to the authorities and the leading townsfolk? Yet they like the sight and sound of me and what I do, and even if they don't like me personally, they come off none the worse for that. 7. Where am I tiresome, then? In dealings with the governors? But everyone knows where I seat myself when I attend them, though I could go higher. They also know those whose company I keep when I go to meet and to escort people, and those from whom I dissociate myself, to whom, despite all their inducements to join them, I am never seen to show any deference. 8. And what need is there to mention this when I need only adduce those credentials that I refused, so as not to seem to

workers (*e.g. Or*. 36. 4; 58. 4 f., 22), in this differing greatly from Themistius, who regards them merely as the material for uplifting discourse (*e.g. Or*. 21. 254 b-c).

μνότερος γεγενῆσθαι δόξαιμι; καίτοι γε ὑπῆρχε
λαβόντι δεινὰ πάσχειν λέγειν οὐχὶ βαδιζόντων παρ᾽
ἐμὲ τῶν τὰς ἀρχὰς ἐχόντων καὶ θορύβου γε ἐμπι-
πλάναι τὰς τῶν ἀρχόντων καταγωγὰς ὁπότε παρ᾽
αὐτοὺς ἐρχοίμην. ἀλλ᾽ οὐδέτερον ἐβουλήθην οὐδέ
γε ἡγησάμην μέγα οὐδὲ ταῖς διὰ τὸν τρόπον μου
R 175 τιμαῖς | ἠξίωσα προσθεῖναι τὰς ἀπ᾽ ἐκείνων τῶν
γραμμάτων. 9. ἠθέλησεν Ἀρχέλαος ὁ γέρων ἐλθεῖν ὡς ἐμέ, διεκώλυσα· Δομνίκος μετ᾽ ἐκεῖνον,
καὶ τοῦτο ἐκώλυσα προαισθό|μενος. ἦλθεν Ἀρ- F 24
χέλαος ὁ ἀδελφιδοῦς Ἀρχελάου λαθών γε καὶ ἐλύ-
πησεν ἐλθὼν καὶ τοῦτ᾽ ἤκουσεν αὐτὸ καὶ εἶξε.
Σαπῶραι δὲ καὶ Ἰούλιοι καὶ Βίκτωρες ἀρρωστοῦν-
τος οὐκ ἔχοντος φυγεῖν ἧκον, ἐγὼ δὲ εἰς γῆν ὑπ᾽
αἰσχύνης ἔβλεπον ἔργῳ δῆλον ποιῶν ὅτι τῇ τιμῇ
βαρυνοίμην.

10. Ἀλλὰ βαρύς εἰμι τοῦ γένους μεμνημένος.
ἐμοὶ δὲ ὑπῆρχε μὲν πλὴν ὀλίγων κομιδῇ λέγειν
πρὸς ἅπαντας ὡς ἕνεκα γένους οὐδ᾽ ἀντιβλέπειν
ἔχοιεν ἂν πρὸς ἐμέ, εἶπον δὲ οὐδεπώποτε οὐδὲ
ἐπήρθην ταῖς εἰκόσιν αὐτῶν οὐδὲ ταῖς λειτουργίαις,
ἀλλ᾽ ἀρκεῖν ἡγησάμην τὸ ταῦτα ἡμῖν συνειδέναι
τὴν πόλιν, τοῖς δ᾽ ἄλλοις ὡς οὐδὲν φαυλοτέροις εἰς

---

a The acceptance of Julian's offer of the honorary position
of *quaestor* (*sacri palatii*) would have given Libanius the
status and privilege of *honoratus*, with right of entry to the
governor. Eunapius (*V.S.* 495 f.) wrongly asserts that the
offer of honorary status made by Julian and refused by
Libanius was that of prefect. Julian himself (*E.L.F.* No. 98)
addresses Libanius as "Sophist and *Quaestor*." The
honorary prefecture was offered by Theodosius and accepted
only in A.D. 383/4. Seeck (*Untergangs*, v, p. 527) and Petit
(*Byzantion*, xxi, p. 293) agree that Julian's offer was that of
quaestor and that Eunapius confused the two offers.

have become too high and mighty ? But if I had accepted them, I could have said that I was affronted at imperial officials when they do not come to see me, and I could fill the governors' headquarters with turmoil whenever I went to see them.[a] But I had no wish for either, nor yet did I set much store by it, nor did I think it proper to add the distinction conferred by these credentials to that which I had gained through my own personality. 9. The elder Archelaüs wanted to visit me, and I stopped him.[b] Next Domnicus[c] had the same idea, but I got wind of it and put a stop to this too. Archelaüs, nephew of Archelaüs, did pay me a visit, unexpectedly, and annoyed me by doing so, was told just that and went away again. People like Sapor, Julius and Victor[d] came when I was ill and could not avoid them, but in my distaste I kept my eyes fixed on the ground and made it clear by so doing that I was embarrassed at the compliment.

10. " But you are tiresome," I may be told, " because you are always talking about your family." I could say to all but a very few that, as far as families go, they couldn't even look me straight in the face, but I never have done so, and never have I exalted myself because of their portraits[e] or public services ; I thought it enough that the city should be equally aware of them, but I continue my association with the others as being in no way my inferiors in

---

[b] *Cf. Or.* 1. 165 f. *PLRE* 100. Seeck (I, II) 83 f.
[c] *PLRE* 265.
[d] Three generals of the reign of Valens. *PLRE* 803, 481 (2), 957 (4).
[e] Portraits of civic notables could be hung in the City Hall, as was that of Libanius himself, *cf. Or.* 42. 43 f.

γένους λόγον ὁμιλῶν διατελῶ. 11. πάππου δὲ καὶ
ἐπιπάππου μνησθῆναι μὲν ὁμολογῶ καὶ πολλάκις,
μνησθῆναι δὲ οὐκ ἐπὶ τούτοις, ἀλλ' ὅτι τῷ μὲν καὶ
μαντικὴ γένοιτο τέχνη πρὸς ἑτέροις ἀγαθοῖς παρ'
ἧς προμάθοι τὸ βιαίως αὐτῷ τοὺς υἱεῖς ἀποθανεῖ-
R 176 σθαι | τοὺς καλούς, θατέρου δὲ τὴν περὶ τοὺς
παῖδας ἐπιμέλειαν πολλάκις διηγούμην· δι' ἣν ἦλθε
μὲν εἰς Ἀπάμειαν αὐτός, ἤγαγε δὲ πείσας πολλοῖς
χρήμασι σοφιστοῦ σθένος, ἀπέφηνε δὲ θαυμα-
στοὺς | οὓς ἐγέννησε τοὺς τῆς ἐμῆς μητρὸς ἀδελ- F 2
φούς. καὶ ταῦτα διεξῄειν οὐ ψιλῆς χάριν εὐφημίας
ἀλλ' ὅπως πατήρ τις ἀκούσας ζηλώσειεν.
   12. Ἐν τοίνυν τῇ νεότητι διεφύγομεν ἃ μὴ πάνυ
ῥᾴδιον, καὶ τούτου μάρτυρες πρὸς τοῖς πάντα ἐπισταμένοις θεοῖς εἰσί μοι τῶν ἡλικιωτῶν οἱ ζῶντες
ἔτι, νῦν μὲν σαπροί, τότε δὲ ἠνθοῦμεν. ἠνώχλη-
σα οὖν ἐγὼ τῇ μνήμῃ τῆς σωφροσύνης; εἶπον
ἄξιος εἶναι διὰ τοῦτο τιμῶν; ἢ οὓς ἐξῆν μάρτυρας
καλεῖν ἐκάλεσα; 13. εἰ δὲ μὴ τοῦτο, τῶν περὶ
τοὺς λόγους ἐμνημόνευσα πόνων ἢ τῶν ἐνταῦθα ἢ
τῶν ἑτέρωθι; ἢ ὡς ἀγόμενος Ἀθήνησιν ὑπὸ τῆς
ἀρχῆς ἐπὶ τὸν θρόνον ἔφυγον; τούτων οὐκ οὔσης
ἀνάγκης ἐμνημόνευσα λαμπρύνων ἄλλως ἐμαυτόν;
οὐκ ἔστι, παρακλήσεως δὲ εἵνεκα τοῖς νέοις πολλάκις. ᾧ τοὔνομα τοῦτο ὁ βαρὺς ἥκιστα ἂν προσ-
ήκοι.

---

   [a] Cf. Or. 1. 3. Libanius' family, one of the most prominent in Antioch, was punished and suffered confiscation of
property in c. A.D. 303, as part of the general repression
following the revolt of Eugenius at Seleuceia (for which cf.
Or. 11. 158 ff., 19. 45 f., 20. 18 ff.).
   [b] Panolbius and Phasganius (cf. PLRE 665 (1), Seeck
234 f.).

the matter of birth. 11. I do admit that I have mentioned my grandfather and great-grandfather, and frequently too ; but this mention was for no such reason as this, but, in addition to his other accomplishments, because of my great-grandfather's skill in divination, in consequence of which he had foreknowledge of the violent death of his fine sons.[a] As for my grandfather, I often discoursed upon his care for his children, which was the reason why he personally went to Apamea, brought back a teacher of high ability, using the persuasion of a high fee, and made his sons, my mother's brothers, men of note.[b] This account I would give, not for the sake of empty compliments, but so that any parent who heard it might be moved to emulate him.

12. Now, in my youth I succeeded in avoiding what it was not particularly easy to avoid,[c] and besides the omniscient gods I have as witnesses for it those of my contemporaries who still survive, now frail, but then we were in our prime. Well! Have I been a nuisance in calling to mind my own probity ? Have I claimed to deserve respect on this account ? Have I called those whom I could call as witnesses ? 13. Leaving this aside, have I ever mentioned my labours in rhetoric either here or abroad ? or that I was invited to Athens by the governor,[d] and escaped to take up the chair here ? Did I ever mention such things unnecessarily, and take vain pride in them ? No ! I have mentioned them to my students often enough, but to encourage them, and to this the term " tiresome " is the last that should be applied.

[c] Cf. Or. 1. 12, 20 ff.
[d] For this invitation by Strategius in A.D. 353 cf. Or. 1. 81 ff., 62. 61.

14. Ἀλλὰ τοὺς παρ' ἑτέρων λόγους ὄντας ἢ σπουδαίους ἢ οὐ τοιούτους ἐκβάλλω ταῖς εἰς ἐμαυτὸν εὐφημίαις· ἐγὼ τὸν δεῖνα σοφιστὴν ἐνί|κησα F 2 καὶ τὸν δεῖνα ἐπεστόμισα καὶ τὸν δεῖνα κατέβαλον καὶ τὸν δεῖνα κατεπάλαισα καὶ τὸν δεῖνα φεύγειν ἠνάγκασα καὶ τοὺς ἐν Αἰγύπτῳ τοὺς πολλοὺς καὶ τοὺς Ἀθήνησι τοὺς τρεῖς εἰς φόβον κατέστησα καλούμενος ὑπὸ τῆς ἐν ἑκατέρᾳ βουλῆς; 15. οὐχ ἑτέρων ταῦτα ἀπαγγελλόντων μεμαθήκατε; εἰ δ' οὐκ ἀπήγγελλον, ἠγνοεῖτ' ἂν ἕνεκά γ' ἐμοῦ τὰς νίκας. ἐπεὶ καὶ περὶ τῶν εἰκόνων καὶ ὧν ὑπὲρ αὐτῶν ἔγνωσαν οὐ μικραί τινες οὐδὲ ὀλίγαι πό-
R 177 λεις, οὔπω μὲν | ἀκηκόατε, πεύσεσθε δ' ἴσως, οὐ μὴν ἐμοῦ γε λέγοντος. 16. καίτοι τούτου[1] γε οἷόνπερ οἶδε φασὶν ἀνθρώπου τί ποτ' ἦν; πάντα τόπον καὶ καιρὸν ἐμπιπλάναι τῶν τοιούτων ῥημάτων καὶ ἡμέρας γε ἑκάστης, τοτὲ[2] πρὸ μεσημβρίας, τοτὲ[2] μετ' ἐκείνην.

17. Καὶ μὴν καὶ ὅστις γε εὖ ποιήσας πολλάκις μνημονεύει τῆς χάριτος, βαρύς,[3] εἴπερ ἐγγὺς μὲν τοῦτο τοῦ ὀνειδίζειν, λυπηρὸν δὲ ἐκεῖνο. σκοπῶμεν τοίνυν εἰ μὴ εὖ πεποίηκα τὴν ἐμαυτοῦ, δεσμὸν μὲν ἰσχυρὸν ἀπορρήξας ᾧ με κατέδησε βασιλέως ψῆφος οὗ πάντες | ἴστε, δραμὼν δὲ ὡς ὑμᾶς οὐκ F 2 ἀκίνδυνον δρόμον, ἐναντίον[4] τῇ τοῦ βασιλέως ἐπιθυμίᾳ, ἐπίδοσιν δὲ λαμπρὰν τοῖς λόγοις ἐνεργασάμενος. ταύτην οὖν προφέρων τῇ πόλει τὴν εὐ-

---

[1] τούτου Norman : τοῦτο Fabr. (mss.) : τοιούτου F. : τοῦ Re. [2] τοτὲ F. (I ; το τὲ U) : τό τε Re. (other mss.).
[3] βαρύς F., Re., Fabr. : βαρὺ mss.

18

14. " Ah ! but by your own self-praise you damn other people's oratory, whether it be good or bad," I may be told. "You have defeated such and such a teacher, reduced so and so to silence, brought down another, floored another, caused the retirement of another. Your many opponents in Egypt,[a] those three in Athens, you set all of a flutter when you were invited by the council there." 15. Haven't you learnt this from other sources ? If it weren't for them, you would be unaware of my triumphs, as far as I am concerned. Of the statues of me and the decrees passed about them by many great cities, you have never heard a word, though you may perhaps do so —but certainly not by my telling. 16. Yet what was to be expected of me, if I were such as these people say I am ? Every place, every occasion would reecho such a tale, every day, morning, noon and night.[b]

17. However, I suppose that any benefactor who keeps harping on his kindness is tiresome, for his attitude is akin to reproach, and that causes discomfort. Still, let us consider whether I have been a benefactor to my country, by breaking the strong bond imposed on me by the emperor's decree, as you all well know, and by hastening to return to you, at no small risk to myself[c] since it was contrary to the emperor's desire, and by effecting a remarkable improvement in oratory. Did I leave anything at all

[a] Possibly referred to in *Ep.* 1274 (A.D. 364) when he is invited by Maximus (*praef. Aegypt.*). There is no other reference in Libanius. For the Athenians *cf. Or.* 1. 25.

[b] For the implications of this passage for the publication of his speeches *cf.* Petit, *Historia*, v (1956), pp. 478 ff.

[c] *Cf. Or.* 1. 94 ff. Here Libanius concocts or adapts a line of tragedy to make his point.

---

[4] δρόμον repeated before ἐναντίον (MSS.) : cancelled F.

R 178 ἐργεσίαν οὐδοτιοῦν | ἀνῆκα; καὶ τίς οὕτως ἀναιδὴς
ὅστις εἰπεῖν τολμήσειεν ἄν;

18. Ἀλλ' ἡ βάδισις φορτική. ποία, πλὴν εἰ τὴν
παρὰ τοῦ νοσήματος λέγοι τις; ἀλλὰ τὸ βλέμμα,
ἀλλ' αἱ ὀφρύες, ἀλλ' ἡ φωνή. οὐ τὸν ἐπίχαρίν με
καλεῖν εἰώθατε; ταῦτ' οὖν οἷόν τε τὰ ὀνόματα συν-
ελθεῖν ὥστε τὸν αὐτὸν τοῦτό τε καὶ βαρὺν ἐν δίκῃ
καλεῖσθαι; 19. εἰσὶ τοίνυν τινὲς οἳ τῷ τὸν γέλωτα
καθάπαξ φυγεῖν ταύτην ἠνέγκαντο τὴν προσηγορίαν. πότ' οὖν ἢ διεκώλυσα γελῶντας ἢ νέφος
ἐπήγαγον εὐφροσύνῃ; ποσάκις δὲ αὐτὸς ἡγεμὼν
ἐγενόμην γέλωτος ἐν οἷς ἐξῆν; ἐπεὶ σπουδῆς γε
καὶ προνοίας πραγμάτων ἐπιστρεφούσης πρὸς ἑαυ-
τὴν πονηρὸν ἂν ἦν γελᾶν τε αὐτὸν καὶ γελᾶν ἑτέρους ποιεῖν. 20. τοσοῦτον δὲ ἀπέχω ταύτης τῆς
αἰτίας ὥστ' οὐδὲ πρὸς τοὺς φοιτῶντας τοιοῦτος
γεγένημαι, ἀλλ' ἡδονήν τινα τὴν ἀπὸ τῆς ἡμερότητος καταμιγνύω τῷ πράγματι δι' ἣν οὐδὲν δέομαι πληγῶν ἑκόντων ἅπαντα ποιούντων, ἑτέρους
δὲ ἴσμεν μυρίας ῥάβδους ἀνηλωκότας οἳ οὔτε τοσ-
οῦτον ἐδυνήθησαν οὔτ' ἐκλήθησαν ὃ νῦν ἐγώ. |

21. Τί δ'; ἐν ταῖς ἀρρωστίαις ἔστιν εἰπεῖν ὡς F
τοὺς μὲν ἄλλους δι' ἑκάστης ἡμέρας ἠξίουν παρ'
ἐμὲ βαδίζειν, τοὺς δὲ καὶ νυκτός, ἐνίους δὲ μηδ'
ἀπαλλάττεσθαι τῆς κλίνης, αὐτὸς δὲ ταύτην ἐλ-
λείπων τὴν φορὰν εἰκός τι ποιεῖν ἐνόμιζον; τοῖς
μὲν γὰρ πρέπειν τὴν λειτουργίαν, ἐμαυτῷ δὲ τὴν
περὶ ταῦτα ἀτέλειαν. 22. καὶ μὴν πάλαι μὲν ἑω-

───────────

[a] Gout, Or. 1. 140 ff., 243 f.

[b] As did Eunapius also, V.S. 495-496.

[c] Libanius claims to be punctilious in the social duty of
sick visiting, cf. Or. 1. 105, 63. 4. He complains bitterly
when his son Cimon does not receive such attentions.

undone when I proffered such service for my country? Who is so bare-facedly impudent as to dare assert such a thing?

18. "Ah! but we find your walk is offensive." Indeed? unless of course you refer to the effects of my illness.[a] "And your glance, your haughty airs, your tone!" But you used to describe me as "charming"![b] Can there be any consistency in these terms? Can you properly describe the same man as both "charming" and "tiresome"? 19. Some people have applied the term to me, asserting that I absolutely eschew laughter. But when have I ever stopped people from having a laugh or when have I cast a cloud over mirth? I myself have often raised a laugh on occasions that warrant it: but when serious matters and consideration are required, it would be wrong to burst into laughter oneself or to cause others to do so. 20. So far from being liable to this charge am I that I have never comported myself so even towards my pupils, but I impart into the subject an element of genteel pleasantry. That is the reason why I have no cane to beat them, for they do everything willingly. But others I know have broken hundreds of canes without winning the influence and reputation that I have now.

21. Well, then? Can it be said that in my times of illness I expected others to visit me every day, at night even, and some never to leave my bedside, and yet thought I was behaving properly if I failed to return such services, my idea being that it was all right for them to perform such a duty and for me to be exempt from it? 22. No, indeed![c] In times long

21

ρώμην θέων ἐπὶ τὰς θύρας τῶν ἀσθενούντων καὶ
R 179 κλίμακας, | νῦν δὲ φερόμενος τὰ μὲν ἵππῳ, τὰ δὲ
χερσὶν οἰκετῶν. καίτοι τίς οὐκ ἂν ἱκανὴν ἔχειν
ἀπολογίαν ἡγησάμενος τό τ' ἐν τοῖς ποσὶ κακὸν τό
τε γῆρας ταύτης αὐτὸν ἀφῆκε τῆς ταλαιπωρίας;
ἀλλ' οὔτε τοῖς ⟨οὐκ⟩[1] ἐπισκεψαμένοις με κάμνοντα
τοῦτο πώποτε ἐμεμψάμην αὐτός τε καὶ παρὰ δύναμιν πολλάκις ἧκον ἐπισκεψόμενος.

23. Τί λοιπόν; ἐν ταῖς ἐπιδείξεσιν εἰμὶ βαρύς,
τὸν μὲν ἀεὶ γιγνόμενον κρότον κἂν ᾖ πολὺς ὡς
ἐλάττω τοῦ δέοντος αἰτιώμενος, ταῖς δ' εἰωθυίαις
φωναῖς προστιθέναι καινὰς ἀξιῶν, τὰς δὲ εὐφημίας ὥσπερ λίθινος δεχόμενος καὶ οὔτε ὀφθαλμοῖς
οὔτε χειρὶ τοὺς ἐπαινέτας οὔτε μειδιάματι τιμῶν;
24. ἐγὼ δὲ αὐτοὺς οἶδα καὶ ῥήμασιν ἐπισχὼν δεόμενος μὴ οὕτω λίαν κόπτειν αὐτοὺς μηδ' ἐν οἷς
ἐμὲ κοσμοῦσι ταλαιπωρεῖν. ἃ δ' ἠγανάκτησα πολ-
λάκις ὑπὲρ Πλάτωνος καὶ Δημο|σθένους ὁπότε F 2
ἀδικοῖντο ὑπὸ τοῦ θεάτρου, τὰ πολὺ διεστηκότα συν-
αγόντων ταῖς βοαῖς, οἶμαι πάντας εἰδέναι, καὶ γὰρ
δὴ καὶ προλόγῳ ταῦτα ἔπαυσα, μᾶλλον δὲ ἐβου-
R 180 λήθην μέν, ἔτι δὲ ταὐτὸν ἔστιν οὗ[2] | τολμᾶται.

25. Αὐτὸ τοίνυν τὸ πλῆθος τῶν ἐπιδείξεων ἐπειδή
δή τινας ᾐσθόμην δυσχεραίνοντας, ᾤμην δέ γε αὐτοῖς ὁ ἠλίθιος χαρίζεσθαι τῇ πυκνότητι, κατέλυσα
καὶ ἃ πρότερον ἐν πλείοσι ταῦτ' ἐν τοῖς φοι-

---

[1] οὐκ F. (inserted Fabr.) : μὴ inserted in I.
[2] οὗ F., Re. (CB, A before correction to ὅ, PM after
correction from ὅ) : ὅ VUIMo.

---

[a] By implication Libanius means himself and his own com-
positions. The audience interrupt his speech, exclaiming that this is the real Demosthenes, and he stops them. *Cf.
Or.* 3. 18, where both Demosthenes and himself receive

past I could have been seen hurrying on foot to the doors and stairways of the sick, though nowadays I am taken there on horse-back or by the hands of my slaves. Yet everyone would think gout and age excuse enough and would rid himself of this burdensome obligation. But I have never made this reproach against those who did not come to visit me as I lay sick, and I have often gone visiting in person and when I was not fit to do so.

23. What next, then? I am tiresome in my declamations : I have no good word for the applause that greets them on each occasion, however great it may be, since I regard it as less than it deserves to be ; I demand fresh compliments above and beyond the normal ; I receive their acclamations like a graven image and honour the plaudits with never a glance, gesture or smile. 24. I know that I have restrained them, and verbally too, and begged them not to weary themselves too much or to exhaust themselves in their applause for me. Everyone, I am sure, realizes the discomfort I have often felt for Plato and Demosthenes, when they have not had a fair reception from the audience,[a] who by their applause link together subjects that are quite distinct. In fact, I even put a stop to this in my prologue, or rather I wished to do so, but the wish is father to the thought !

25. As for the actual number of my declamations, when I saw people becoming restive at them—for, like a fool, I used to think that I was doing them a favour by their frequency—I put a stop to that, and now I give to my regular pupils the declamations that

a less flattering reception. Later scholars nicknamed Libanius " Demosthenes the Second " or, simply, " Demosthenes," *cf.* Foerster, vol. I, p. 74.

LIBANIUS

τῶσι δεικνύω. οὕτω πάνυ δέδοικα τὸ¹ δοκεῖν εἶναι
βαρύς.

26. Νὴ Δί᾽, ἀλλὰ τούτων μὲν οὐδὲν οὐδεὶς αἰ-
τιᾶται, ἐκεῖνο δὲ τὸ τὰ πάλαι μὲν ὄντα ποθεῖν τε
καὶ ἐπαινεῖν τῶν παρόντων δὲ κατηγορεῖν, καὶ
τότε μὲν φάσκειν εὐδαίμονας εἶναι τὰς πόλεις νυνὶ
δὲ δυστυχεῖν, καὶ τοῦτον ἀεί τε καὶ πανταχοῦ καὶ
καθ᾽ ἡμέραν λέγεσθαί μοι τὸν λόγον. 27. εἰσὶ δὲ
οἱ ταῦτα μεμφόμενοι καὶ οἱ τοῖς λόγοις ἀνιώμενοι
τούτοις, οἷς τὰ παρόντα συνήνεγκεν· οἷς δ᾽ ἐλυμήνατο, τῶν ἐπαινούντων. γεγόνασι δὲ οὗτοι μὲν
ἐξ ἐνδόξων ἄδοξοι καὶ ἐξ εὐπόρων ἄποροι, ἐκεῖνοι
δὲ τοὐναντίον ἐν δόξῃ καὶ πλούτῳ καὶ δυνάμει, ὧν
τοσοῦτον ἀπεῖχον ταῖς ἐλπίσιν ὅσονπερ τοῦ πτή-
σεσθαι. 28. οὐκοῦν τοῖς μὲν εὖ | πράττουσι παρὰ F
R 181 τὴν ἀξίαν ἀηδής εἰμι καὶ βαρὺς ταῦτα λέγων | τοῖς
δ᾽ ἐξ εὐδαιμόνων κατενεχθεῖσι κεχαρισμένος, οἷα
δὴ συναχθόμενός τε καὶ πεπληγμένος ταῖς ἐκείνων
συμφοραῖς. διὰ τί οὖν, ὅταν με βαρὺν καλῶσιν,
οὐ προσδιορίζουσι μικρόν τι προστιθέντες τὸ σφί-
σιν· οὐ γὰρ ἅπασί γε ἐγὼ βαρὺς ἀλλ᾽ οἷς τὰ κακὰ
τῶν πολλῶν ἀγαθά. πᾶσι μὲν οὖν ὢν βαρὺς ᾐσχυ-
νόμην ἂν τοῖς λεγομένοις, εἰ δὲ τοῖς οὕτως εὐ-
τυχηκόσι σεμνύνομαι· 29. οὓς ἡδέως ἂν ἐροίμην
πότερά με ψεύδεσθαί φασι τοῖς ἐπαίνοις τουτοισὶ
καὶ τοῖς ψόγοις ἢ οὔ. εἰ μὲν γὰρ ψεύδεσθαι, δει-

¹ ⟨καὶ⟩ τὸ F. (V).

ᵃ For the " regular " declamations cf. Or. 3 passim. The
practice of declaiming before a select audience was popular

24

I used to give before a wider audience,—so afraid am I of the appearance of being tiresome.[a]

26. No one, however, makes any accusation like that. The complaint is that I am constantly praising and longing for what is dead and gone, denouncing the present day, harping on the past prosperity and the present misery of the cities, and that this is my tale, everywhere, every day. 27. Some complain about this and are annoyed at my comments, but they are those who have benefited from the present situation. People who have been hard hit are among those who applaud them, and these are the people who have lost the prestige and the wealth they once enjoyed : on the other hand, those others enjoy prestige, wealth and influence, though they used to have as little expectation of them as they had of flying in the air. 28. So to these *nouveaux-riches* I am inordinately displeasing and tiresome with these remarks, but with those who have been brought low from their affluence I am in high favour, in so far as I am filled with sympathy and alarm at their misfortunes. So then, when people call me " tiresome," why are they not more precise in their definition, and simply add the rider, "to themselves"? For I am certainly not tiresome to everybody, only to those who batten on the misery of the majority. No ; if I were tiresome to everybody, I would be ashamed of such comments, but if to those who enjoy a prosperity of this sort, I pride myself on them. 29. I would like to ask them if their assertion is that I am a liar in using such commendations and reproofs or not. If they say that I am, let them

among pagan sophists at this time, *cf.* Eunap. *V.S.* 483 ; Lib. *Or.* 1. 101, *Ep.* 1075.

ξάτωσαν ὡς οὐκ ἀμείνω ταῖς πόλεσι τὰ πρόσθεν·
εἰ δ' ἀληθεύειν, τί χαλεπαίνουσι; τί δ' οὐχὶ τὴν
ἀλήθειαν βαρεῖαν καλοῦσιν, ἀλλὰ τὸν ἑπόμενον
ἐκείνῃ βαρύν; οὐ γὰρ ὁ ἐμὸς λόγος τὰ πράγματα
πεποίηκεν ἀλλ' ὑπὸ τῶν πραγμάτων οἱ λόγοι τοιοῦτοι γεγένηνται. 30. εἶπον ὅτι πάλαι πολλαὶ
θυσίαι καὶ μεστὰ τῶν θυόντων τὰ ἱερὰ καὶ θαλίαι
καὶ αὐλοὶ καὶ ᾠδαὶ καὶ στέφανοι καὶ πλοῦτος ἐν
ἑκάστῳ κοινή τις οὗτος τοῖς δεομένοις ἐπικουρία.
τί οὖν ἐψευσάμην; καὶ νῦν τοὺς νεὼς ἴδοι τις ἂν
τοιούτους; μᾶλλον δέ, ἴδοι τις ἂν πενίαν ἑτέρωθι
τοσαύτην; 31. εἰσὶ μὲν οἳ ὡς ἥδιστ' ἂν θεοὺς
ἀναθήμασι τιμήσαιεν, ἴσασι δ' ὡς εἰ κομίσαιεν
ἐκεῖσε ταῦτα ἑτέρων ἐστίν, ὅπου γε καὶ τὴν πολ-
λὴν ἑκάστου τῶν θεῶν γῆν | ἕτεροι γεωργοῦσι καὶ F 9
τῆς προσόδου μέτεστι τοῖς βωμοῖς οὐδοτιοῦν.
32. εἶπον ὅτι τοῖς περὶ τὴν γῆν πονοῦσιν ἦν καὶ
κιβώτια πάλαι καὶ ἐσθὴς καὶ στατῆρες καὶ μετὰ
προικὸς οἱ γάμοι. νῦν δὲ διὰ πολλῶν μὲν ἐρήμων
R 182 ἥξεις ἀγρῶν οὓς τὸ πιέζεσθαι | ταῖς¹ εἰσπράξεσιν
ἐκένωσε προστεθέντος ἑτέρου κακοῦ μείζονος, τῶν
τὰ ἄντρα σφῶν αὐτῶν ἐμπεπληκότων, τῶν μέχρι
τῶν ἱματίων σωφρόνων. ὅσοι δὲ καὶ μένουσιν ἐν

¹ ταῖς F., Re., Fabr. : τε MSS.

ᵃ Under Julian's reforms, cf. Or. 1. 119, 17. 9, 18. 286 ff.
Temple properties had previously been confiscated by Constantine, Or. 30. 6, 62. 8.

ᵇ Julian intended that his newly reorganized pagan church
should engage itself not merely in religious but also in
social and welfare activities : Julian, E.L.F. Nos. 84, 89.
Libanius approved of this and deplores the attacks on pagan
temples on this account, cf. Or. 30. 20.

prove that the cities were no better off before ; if that I am telling the truth, what are they complaining about ? If they don't call the truth tiresome, why do they call me, who follow the truth, tiresome ? My comment is not the cause of the present situation : such comments are caused by it. 30. I have said that in the past there were sacrifices in plenty [a] : the temples used to be full of worshippers, there was good cheer, music, songs, garlands, and the treasure in every one was a means of assistance to those in need. [b] What lie did I tell, then ? Can you find the temples like this nowadays ? Indeed, can you find such dire poverty anywhere else ? 31. There are some who would gladly honour the gods with offerings but know that, if they take them there, they fall into some one else's hands, to judge by the cases where others farm the great estates of every one of the gods and not a penny of the revenue reaches the altars. [c] 32. I have said that in the past the workers of the land used to have money chests, clothes, and cash, and marriages with dowry. Nowadays, though, you can go through miles of deserted farmland. The burden of taxation has emptied it, and there is another and worse trouble besides,— that crew who pack themselves tight into the caves, those models of sobriety, only as far as their dress is concerned. [d] Those who do stay on the farms have no

[c] Julian's religious reforms were immediately rescinded by Jovian and the temple lands again confiscated. *C. Th.* 5. 13. 3, 10. 1. 8 (A.D. 364).

[d] The Christian monks, who made the caves of Mt. Silpius their hermitage, accused by Libanius and pagans generally of every kind of anti-social excess. *Cf. Or.* 30. 8 ff. See also Festugière, *Antioche.*

ἀγροῖς οὐδὲν δέονται κλείειν θύρας· οὐδεὶς γὰρ φόβος ἀπὸ λῃστῶν τῷ γε οὐδὲν ἔχοντι.

33. Ἀλλὰ τὰς βουλὰς ἐρεῖς. ἀλλ' εἰ καὶ μηδὲν
ἄλλο διέκειτο κακῶς, τοῦτό γ' ἂν ἔπειθε μόνον
λέγειν οἷάπερ λέγω. ἀντὶ μὲν ἑξακοσίων τῶν τότε
οὐδὲ ἑξήκοντα νῦν. ἑξήκοντα εἶπον; οὐδὲ μὲν οὖν
ἓξ παρ' ἐνίοις. 34. ἀλλ' εἰσὶ τῶν πόλεων ἐν αἷς ὁ
αὐτὸς εἰσπράττει, λούει καὶ πάλιν λούει. τί τοῦτό
ἐστι τὸ αἴνιγμα; λούει τε τῇ χορηγίᾳ τῶν ξύλων
καὶ τὸν ἀμφορίσκον λαβὼν βαλανεὺς ὁ λειτουργῶν
γίγνεται. εἶθ' ὁ μὲν θερμὸν ὁ δὲ ψυχρὸν ὕδωρ
ἐζήτησε, τῷ δέ, οὐκ ἔνι γὰρ μερισθῆναι, τὴν θα-
F 250 τέρου φέρειν ὀργὴν ἀνάγκη. | 35. ἀλλ' οὐ παρ' |
ἡμῖν ταῦτα. μηδέ γε, ὦ Ζεῦ, γένοιτο, ἀλλ' οὐ R
τοῦτο δεῖ σκοπεῖν οὗ ταῦτα οὐκ ἔστιν, ἀλλ' ὅτι οὗ
ταῦτα ἔστιν ἔνι. καὶ μὴν αἷς μὲν τῶν βουλῶν ἡ
γῆ πονηρά, τῷ μεγέθει τῶν φορτίων ἀπολώλασιν
οὐδενὸς τῆς τοιαύτης ἐρῶντος γῆς οὐδὲ ὠνουμένου,
παρ' οἷς δὲ βελτίων, ἀντὶ τῶν κεκληρονομηκότων
ἔχουσι τοὺς πρίασθαι δυναμένους δεσπότας. εἶθ'
οἱ μὲν πολιτευόμενοι ταπεινοὶ καὶ ὀλίγοι καὶ οὐ
πένητες μόνον ἀλλ' ἤδη καὶ πτωχοί, οἱ δ' οὐκ
οἶδ' ὁπόθεν εἰσπεσόντες θέντες τιμήν, τὸ γὰρ ἀληθὲς εἰρήσεται, τρυφῶσιν ἐν τοῖς ἐκείνων, οἱ μὲν

ᵃ On the flight from the councils cf. Jones, LRE, pp.
740 ff., Liebeschuetz, Antioch, pp. 174 ff., Petit, Vie municipale, pp. 321 ff. On the decline in curial numbers indicated by
Libanius' figures cf. Or. 48. 3 ff., 49. 8. See also Or. 32. 8,
Ep. 851.
    ᵇ Cf. Or. 49. 31. The curial's task of collecting the taxes
for his locality was one of his most important duties in the
eyes of the imperial administration. The provision of heating

need to bar their doors : beggars have no need to fear bandits.

33. You will mean our city councils, then. If there were nothing else amiss, this at least should induce you to say what I say. Instead of the 600 of days gone by, there aren't even sixty now. Sixty, did I say ? In some places there aren't even six.[a] 34. There are some cities where the same person collects the taxes,[b] becomes a bathman and then becomes a bathman once again. What is the answer to this riddle ? He acts the bathman by his duty of providing the fuel, and then the performer of this service becomes the bath attendant by getting hold of the bucket. Then there is a call for hot water here, for cold water there, and he has to put up with the bad temper of one or the other, for he cannot be in both places at once. 35. "But that doesn't happen here." Good Lord ! I hope not ! But what we have to consider is not the places where it does not happen, but that there are places where it can. In fact, the councils where the land is poor are ruined by the size of their burdens, for nobody has any desire for such land or purchases it. Where the land is better, instead of the hereditary occupants, they have as landlords those people who can buy it up. Then the councillors are depressed and depleted ; they are not just poor ; they are beggared, while these newcomers from heaven knows where suddenly descend, put down the money—let's give the devil his due !—and luxuriate in their property,

for the civic baths is one of the highest and most expensive liturgies, reserved for the *principales.* For any such to undertake personally the " vulgar " task of bath attendant would be unheard of.

LIBANIUS

οἰκίας οἱ δὲ ἀγροὺς οἱ δὲ ἀμφότερα κεκτημένοι. 36. καὶ τὸ μὲν τῆς βουλῆς ἀξίωμα οὐδαμοῦ, σοβοῦσι δὲ οἱ ξένοι καὶ γαμοῦσιν, ἡμεῖς δὲ ὁρῶμεν καὶ συνδειπνοῦμεν καὶ συνευχόμεθα γῆρας, βουλεύοντι δὲ οὐδεὶς ἂν δοίη κόρην· οὐχ οὕτω μισεῖ τὴν ἑαυτοῦ. μηνὸς ἂν δέοι τῷ γε δι᾽ ἀκριβείας εἰπεῖν βουλομένῳ τὰς τῶν ἐν ταῖς βουλαῖς συμφοράς.

37. Οἶδα καὶ ὑπὲρ τῶν στρατιωτῶν ὥσπερ ὑπὲρ τῶν βουλευόντων στενάξας, οὐδὲ τούτων ἴσως ἀδίκως, πεινώντων καὶ ῥιγούντων καὶ οὐδ᾽ ὀβολὸν ἐχόντων διὰ τὴν τῶν λοχαγῶν καὶ στρατηγῶν δικαιοσύνην, οἳ τοὺς μὲν ἀθλιωτάτους ποιοῦσιν αὐτοὺς δὲ πλουσιωτάτους. πεινῶσι δὲ καὶ οἱ τῶν ἱππέων ἵπποι, ὁ δὲ | λιμὸς οὗτος χρυσὸς ἐκείνοις F πρὸς τῷ | παρὰ τοῦ βασιλέως ὃς διὰ τῶν χειρῶν τῶν στρατιωτῶν εἰς τὰς ἐκείνων ἔρχεται. 38. καὶ καλὸν μὲν ἐμέσαι καὶ μεθυσθῆναι καὶ συνάψαι τούτοις εὐθὺς ἐδωδὴν ἑτέραν καὶ πόσιν, αἰσχρὸν δὲ αἱ μελέται καὶ τὸ ἐν τῷ πεδίῳ πρέπουσι πόνοις αὐτὸν γυμνάσαι. τοιγαροῦν ἐν ταῖς μάχαις ἀρκεῖ βοῆσαι τοῖς πολεμίοις καὶ οἱ μὲν ᾤχοντο ἀπιόντες, ὁ δὲ μένων πεισόμενος ἔμεινε. καὶ περιδεεῖς μὲν αὐτοῖς αἱ ψυχαί, σκιῶν δὲ οὐ πολὺ διαφέροντα τὰ σώματα. 39. πικρὰ δὲ καὶ ἡ γῆ τοῖς ποσὶν ὑποδημάτων ἀπορίᾳ· δεῖ γὰρ δὴ καὶ εἰς γύναιον ἀνα-

R 184

---

[a] There was no legal restriction on the sale of curial land until A.D. 386, *C. Th.* 12. 3. 1.

[b] Officials and the military, aided by the *principales*, were some of the chief offenders in promoting this flight of councillors from the curia. Libanius, with his customary prejudice against the military (*e.g. Or.* 48. 30), here conveniently forgets that one of his own aunts had married a military officer (*Or.* 47. 28).

gaining possession of their estates, their houses, or both.*a* 36. Nowhere is there any respect for the council : outsiders swagger in and contract marriages, and we look on, join their banquets and wish them long life : but nobody would let his daughter get married to a councillor—he doesn't loathe her as much as that !*b* I would need a month if I wanted to give an accurate description of the misfortunes of the members of the councils.

37. I know that I have complained on the soldiers' behalf too, as well as for the councillors, and here too perhaps not without good reason. They starve and shiver, and haven't a penny to their name—all through the probity of their colonels and generals who feather their own nests and make the lives of their men a misery.*c* The cavalrymen's horses starve too, and such starving means gold for the officers, above and beyond the pay from the emperor which passes through the soldiers' hands into their own. 38. Their glory is to get drunk, fetch up their food and start off at once on another round of eating and swilling : it is a disgrace for them to practise or to school themselves with proper exercises on the training field. As a result, all the enemy needs to do in action is to set up a yell, and they are off and away, and any who stays, stays but to be beaten : their souls are fearful, their bodies little better than shadows.*d* 39. Even the ground is hard to their feet for lack of footwear ; for they are obliged, of course,

---

c Cf. Or. 47. 32.
d Cf. Or. 18. 209 ff. The contrast here is between the high morale of Julian's armies and the shock following the disaster of Adrianople. Criticism of army efficiency was widespread at this time, cf. Or. 24. 3 ff., Zosimus, 4. 23.

LIBANIUS

λίσκειν καὶ παῖδας, ἔστι δὲ ἑκάτερον ἑκάστῳ καὶ
οὔτε τοὺς γάμους κωλύουσιν οὔθ' ἥ τις ἂν γένοιτο
τροφὴ καὶ ταῖς τικτούσαις καὶ τοῖς τικτομένοις
σκοποῦσι. τεμνομένου τοίνυν εἰς τοσαύτας τομὰς
τοῦ σίτου τῷ στρατιώτῃ πόθεν ἐκείνῳ κόρος; ἡ δὲ
ἀπὸ τούτου βλάβη ζημία τῷ πολέμῳ καθίσταται.
40. ἀλλ' οὐκ ἐν ἐκείνοις τοῖς καιροῖς οὓς ἐπαινῶ
ταῦτα ἦν, ἀλλ' εὐδοξίας μὲν ἀντὶ χρημάτων ἤρων
οἱ ἡγούμενοι, τὰ δὲ τῶν στρατιωτῶν οὐδεὶς ἦν ὁ
ἀφαιρησόμενος. οἱ δ' αὐτοὶ καὶ ἰσχυροὶ καὶ ἀν-
δρεῖοι καὶ τεχνῖται πολέμων καὶ οὐκ | ἐγάμουν, F 2
ἀλλ' ὅπως μηδὲ δεήσονται γάμων εὕρητο. οἱ δέ γε
ἵπποι φέροντες τοὺς ἱππέας ἥδιστον μὲν τοῖς[1] οἰ-
R 185 κείοις θέαμα φοβερὸν δὲ τοῖς ἀντιπάλοις, καὶ | ἦν
εἰρήνη παραινούντων ἑαυτοῖς τῶν βαρβάρων τὴν
ἡσυχίαν ἄγειν. 41. εἰ δὲ δεῖ καὶ περὶ τῶν τὰ ἔθνη
διοικούντων ἀρχόντων εἰπεῖν, ἦρχον μὲν οἱ βέλτιστοι κριθέντες, τούτων δὲ οἱ μὲν ἐμμείναντες τῷ
τρόπῳ κατεγήρων ἐν τοῖς θρόνοις, οἱ δὲ ἐκπε-
σόντες ἑαυτῶν ἀπέθνησκον καὶ οὐκ ἦν παραίτησις.
τοῦτ' οὖν ἐποίει τοὺς νόμους κρατεῖν. 42. ἀλλὰ
νῦν τρέχει μὲν ἐπὶ τὴν ἀρχὴν ὁ πρίασθαι δυνηθείς,
μεταστρέφεται δὲ περισκοπῶν μὴ οὐ πολλοὺς ἀπέχει[2] σταδίους ὁ διαδεξόμενος. ὁμολογεῖ δὲ εὐθὺς
ὡς ἧκε ληψόμενος, καὶ τοῦτο τῆς ἀρχῆς τὸ προ-
οίμιον, ἐν δὲ τοῖς ἁπάντων ὀφθαλμοῖς τὰ πρότερον
ἐν σκότει γιγνόμενα τολμᾶται, κἂν ἐξέλθῃ τῆς
ἀρχῆς, μικρόν τι τοῦ παντὸς ἐξεμέσας τὸ πλέον
32

to spend their money on the wife and children—for every one of them has both. Nothing stops them getting married and they don't concern themselves with what the mothers and the children will have to live on. So when soldiers' rations are so sub-divided, where can the man get his fill? The harm resulting from this is a loss of military efficiency. 40. This was not the case in those good old days which I commend. Then the officers hankered after glory, not cash, and no one would rob the soldiery of what was theirs. And the men themselves were sturdy and brave, specialists in warfare, and they remained unmarried : it was ensured that they would even have no need of marriage. And the horses on which the cavalry were mounted were a fine sight for our folk to see, and a fearsome one for the foe, and there was peace, and the barbarians counselled themselves to keep it. 41. And if mention must be made also of the governors who administer the provinces, then the best were selected for office, and those of them who behaved consistently with their character grew old in their chairs of office, while those who lapsed were put to death, and there was no appeal. That then is what used to produce the rule of law. 42. Nowadays, though, it is the man who has been able to buy it who scurries into office and keeps turning round to see, in case his successor is hard on his heels. He agrees straightaway that he is there for what he can get ; and this is the prelude to his term, and what previously used to be done under cover is now ventured upon in full view of all and sundry, and, even if he leaves office, he fetches up some small part of the

---

[1] τοῖς inserted F., conj. Re.
[2] ἀπέχει F., Cobet, Fabr. : ἀπέχῃ Re. (mss.).

κατέπεψε. βαρὺς οὖν ὁ τὰ μὲν μισῶν τὰ δὲ θαυμάζων;

43. Εἶεν· εἰ δὲ δὴ καὶ τἄλλα με πάντα φίλον ἐποίει τοῖς παροῦσιν, οὐκ ἄν με καὶ μόνα τὰ περὶ τοὺς λόγους εἰκότως ἐξεπολέμωσεν; οἳ πάλαι μὲν ἤστραπτον νῦν δ᾽ εἰσὶ σκοτεινοί, καὶ πάλαι μὲν | εἷλκον τὴν πανταχόθεν νεότητα νῦν δ᾽ οὐδὲν εἶναι κέκρινται. 44. ἀλλ᾽ οἱ μὲν ἐοικέναι δοκοῦσι πέτραις εἰς ἃς ὁ σπείρων μαίνεται προσαπολλὺς τὴν σποράν. καρποὶ δ᾽ ἑτέρωθεν ἀπὸ τῆς Ἰταλῶν R 186 φωνῆς, ὦ δέσποινα Ἀθηνᾶ, καὶ τῶν νόμων. | οὓς ἔδει πρότερον φέροντας τοὺς ἐπισταμένους ἑστάναι πρὸς τὸν ῥήτορα βλέποντας ἀναμένοντας τό· ὦ οὗτος ἀναγίνωσκε. ἤδη δὲ καὶ ὑπογραφεῖς ἐν ταῖς μεγίσταις ἀρχαῖς, ὁ δὲ τὸ λέγειν ἀντ᾽ ἐκείνου μαθὼν ὑπ᾽ ἐκείνων τε καταγελᾶται καὶ αὐτὸς ὀδύρεται. 45. πολλοὶ δὲ πολλοῖς οὐσίας ἐκ συνηγοριῶν σεσωκότες ἐκπηδήσαντες ἐκ τῶν δικαστηρίων ὁπλῖται γεγένηνται, οὐ τῆς ἐκ τῶν χειρῶν δόξης ἐπιθυμοῦντες ἀλλ᾽ εἰδότες ὅτι δόρυ λέγουσιν[1] εὐθὺς ὑπάρξει γαμεῖν καὶ τὰ τῆς γυναικὸς ἐσθίειν, πολεμίου δὲ ἐπελθόντος ἐν ἀκμῇ μάχης ῥᾷστον ἀντὶ τῶν

F 2

---

[1] δόρυ λέγουσιν Re. (MSS.) : δόρυ ἑλοῦσιν F. : δεῦρο ἥκουσιν Gasda : δόρυ λαβοῦσιν Fritz (commended by F. vol. III. xxvii), cf. Plat. Resp. 374 D.

[a] For examples of the purchase of office cf. Or. 4. 28 ; 28. 22 ; 48. 11 ; Zosimus, 5. 2. The succession of governors in the Theodosian age was extraordinarily rapid, cf. Or. 1. 251 ff. Between A.D. 380 and 393 there were at least eleven Comites Orientis. Between A.D. 353 and 364, despite three changes of emperor, there were only six: v. Downey, Comites Orientis and Consulares Syriae.

total and digests the greater part. So am I tiresome in hating all this and admiring the past?[a]

43. Well! even if everything else reconciled me to the present situation, would not the state of oratory alone be enough to set me at odds with it? Rhetoric, that in the past used to flash like lightning, is now under a cloud: it used to attract young students from far and wide, but now it is considered a mere nothing. 44. It is held to be like the stony ground on to which the sower scatters seed and then is enraged to lose his crop also. It is from other sources that the yield comes—from Latin, by all that is holy, and law.[b] Previously, if they had any training, they had to bring in their law books and stand, with eyes fixed on the orator, waiting for the words, "You, read that, please." But now they are even secretaries[c] in the highest offices of state, while the student of eloquence, rather than of that stuff, is a laughing-stock for them and laments his own plight. 45. Many people, who have saved many a man's property in consequence of their advocacy,[d] have decamped from the courts and enlisted as soldiers, not from any desire for the fame to be gained in combat, but in the knowledge that if they claim acquaintance with arms, they will be able to marry straightaway and live on what the wife has, and that in the event of any enemy attack, in the heat of battle

[b] For the competition of Latin and law cf. Or. 1. 154, 213 ff.; 40. 5; 48. 29 f. Liebeschuetz, pp. 243 ff.

[c] For the competition provided by shorthand, with hopes of preferment to the *schola notariorum*, cf. Or. 62. 8 ff., 51. Julian in his appointments consciously reacted against Constantius' preference for notaries, cf. Or. 18. 158. Cf. Wolf, pp. 80 ff., Liebeschuetz, pp. 242 f.

[d] For decurions as advocates v. Petit, *Étudiants*, 179 ff.

χειρῶν χρήσασθαι τοῖς ποσὶν ὡς οὐκ ἐσομένων
εὐθυνῶν. 46. τῶν τοίνυν καλουμένων σημείων τρε-
R 187 ψαμένων μὲν τὸν Ἑρμῆν | τρεψαμένων δὲ τὰς Μού-
σας, τὴν δ' οὖσαν τοῖς περὶ ἐκείνας εὐδαιμονίαν
εἰς αὐτὰ μεταθέντων, καὶ τῶν μὲν τεταπεινωμένων, τῶν δὲ τὰς γνάθους φυσώντων, ἀγανακτεῖ
τις εἰ τῆς τέχνης ἀχρήστου μοι γεγενημένης ἀλγῶ; |
47. Ἀλλ' οὐχ ὑπὲρ ταύτης, φησί, μόνον ἀλγεῖς F 2.
ἀλλ' ὅλως ἐπιλαμβάνῃ μὲν τῶν νῦν, ὑμνεῖς δὲ τὰ
πρότερα καὶ περιεργάζῃ. τίνα, ὦ βέλτιστοι, παρα-
βαίνων νόμον, τίνας ὑπερπηδῶν ὅρους τῇ περὶ
ταῦτα λύπῃ; πῶς ἀδίκημα γίγνεται τὸ τοῖς πράττουσι κακῶς συνάχθεσθαι; ἐγὼ μὲν γὰρ χρηστό-
τητος εἶναι νομίζω τὸ μὴ μόνον ὑπὲρ τῶν οἰκείων
ἀνιᾶσθαι κακῶν ἀλλὰ κἂν τοῖς ἑτέρῳ συμβαίνουσι
ταὐτὸ ποιεῖν. 48. καὶ οἶδα πολλοὺς οὐ μόνον τοὺς
καθ' αὑτοὺς εἰ ἀτυχοῖεν ἐλεοῦντας ἀλλὰ κἂν ταῖς
τῶν τραγῳδιῶν ἀναγνώσεσι δάκρυα κατὰ τῶν βι-
βλίων ἀφιέντας. πῶς οὖν οὐχὶ καὶ τούτους κακί-
ζετε; 49. ῥᾴδιόν γέ τοι πρὸς αὐτοὺς λέγειν· τί δὲ
ὑμῖν μέλει τῶν Νιόβης τέκνων, ἢ εἴ τις Κάδμου
θυγάτηρ τὸν αὑτῆς ἀπέκτεινε; Λάιος δὲ ὑμῖν
πατήρ; Οἰδίπους δὲ ἀδελφός; Ἑκάβη δὲ μήτηρ;
Κρέων δὲ ὁ Κορίνθιος θεῖος; Γλαύκη δὲ ἀνεψιά;
πρῴην Ἱππόλυτον τὸν Εὐριπίδου θρήνων οὐκ ἠξί-
ωσα τοσούτων ὅσωνπερ ἄν, εἰ παρῆν καὶ ἑώρων
R 188 τὸ πάθος; τί | οὖν οὐκ ἐγκαλοῦμαι ταῖς | πρὸ τῶν F 2.

ᵃ The tutelary deities of learning and of literature are
Hermes, and the Muses led by Apollo Musegetes.
ᵇ The tragic stories referred to are those of Niobe (who
boasted of her numerous family as compared with that of
Leto, and had her children slain by Apollo and Artemis in

it is the simplest matter to use one's feet instead of one's hands, for there will be no questions asked. 46. And this so-called shorthand has put learning and literature[a] to flight and has monopolized the rewards that devotees of those subjects used to possess, either reducing them to poverty or causing them to gnash their teeth : so is it taken amiss that I complain now that my art has been rendered useless ?

47. "Oh!" comes the rejoinder, "your complaints are not just about that. You are never satisfied with carping at the present and fussing about, singing the praises of the past." Well, my friends, what law have I broken, what limits have I overstepped in my grief on this account ? How does sympathy with the unfortunate become a crime ? I regard it as perfectly proper to be upset by not just the troubles of one's own, but by those of others too. 48. And I know plenty of people who don't confine themselves to pitying themselves in their misfortunes, but who, even in their readings of tragedies, let their tears fall upon their books. Do you abuse these people, too ? 49. It is easy to say to them, "What concern of yours are the children of Niobe ? or that a daughter of Cadmus killed her own son ? Is Laïus your father ? Oedipus, your brother ? What's Hecuba to you—your mother ? Have you got Creon of Corinth for an uncle, or Glauce for a cousin ? " Only just recently haven't I regarded the Hippolytus of Euripides as deserving my laments as much as if I were present and witnessed his fate ?[b] Why then don't they accuse

consequence) dramatized by Aeschylus ; of Agave and Pentheus, Euripides' *Bacchae* ; of the *Oedipus* by Sophocles ; of the *Hecuba*, *Medea* and *Hippolytus* of Euripides. Libanius had evidently composed a declamation on the Hippolytus

Τρωικῶν συμφοραῖς πληττόμενος; 50. ὑμεῖς δέ,
ὦ πρὸς Διός, νέων ἐκφερομένων καὶ πατέρων ἀκολουθούντων συνεκφέροντες οὐ θρηνεῖτε, καὶ ταῦτα
οὐδεμιᾶς ἀναγκαζούσης συγγενείας; τοὺς ἐπιτι-
μῶντας οὖν εἰκότως ἂν ἔχοιτε. καὶ μὴν ἐν εὐερ-
γέταις οἷς ταῦτα εἰσενηνόχατε γονεῦσιν ἠρίθμησθε.
51. εἰ δ' οὐδὲν δεινὸν τὸν οὐ προσήκοντα ἀπο-
θανόντα δακρύειν, πῶς δεινὸν τοὺς ζῶντας ἐν
ὀδύναις, ὃ πολὺ τοῦ θανάτου πικρότερον; εἰ δ'
ἄξιον ἀθυμεῖν κακῶς φερομένης πόλεως, διὰ τί μὴ
καὶ ἔθνους; εἰ δὲ ἑνός, διὰ τί μὴ καὶ πλειόνων;
52. ἀλλ' ἐμοὶ μὲν τοὺς συναχθομένους εἰ καὶ πλεῖστον ἀπέχοιεν τῶν περὶ λόγους φιλῶ, τοὺς δ' ἐν
ἑτέροις ζῶντας εἰ μὴ τῶν αὐτῶν ἀξιοίην οὐκ ἀδι-
κήσω; οὐκ ἐσμὲν Κύπριοι οὐδέ, σὺν Ἀδραστείᾳ
δὲ εἰρήσεται, τῷ σεισμῷ κατενεχθεῖσαν ἐπείδομεν
R 189 τὴν πόλιν, ἀλλ' ὅμως οἰμωγαὶ | καὶ ὀδυρμοί, καὶ
ὦ πόλεις, ποῦ ποτε ἄρ' ἐστέ; πολλῶν ἦν ἀκούειν
λεγόντων, καὶ οὐδεὶς ἐπέπληξεν εἰ τοσαύτῃ τῆς
νήσου διειργόμενοι τῇ θαλάσσῃ μετέχειν τῆς συμ-
φορᾶς ἐνομίζομεν. 53. τί οὖν αὐτοῖς | ἡ περιεργία F 25
βούλεται; οὐκ εἰμὶ μὲν τῶν δυνάμεων ἡγεμὼν οὐδὲ
ἐκοινώνησα τῶν ἐν Θράκῃ παρατάξεων οὔτε ὡς
στρατηγὸς οὔτε ὡς στρατιώτης ἀλλ' οὐδ' ἂν ἀπὸ

---

story only just recently. For his progymnasmata on Medea
and Niobe *cf.* vol. viii, pp. 373, 391 F.

  [a] For this morbidity of outlook in Libanius, increased in
part by the depression produced by gout and migraine, *cf.*
Or. 1. 151, 35. 25, 62. 53.

  [b] Cited from Plato, *Resp.* 451 A. *Cf.* also *Or.* 1. 158.
Adrasteia is Nemesis, whose cult, connected with the Olympia, enjoyed much popularity in Syria : *cf.* Seyrig, *Syria*,
xiii (1932), pp. 30 ff.

me of being affected by events that happened before
the Trojan War? 50. Good heavens! when young men
are carried out to burial and their fathers follow the
bier, don't you join the cortège of mourners, though
no bond of kinship demands it? You can expect to
be reproved for it, then, even though the parents to
whom you have extended this token of sympathy
count themselves in your debt.[a] 51. If there is
nothing wrong in bewailing one who is not a relative,
when he dies, how is it wrong to bewail those who
live a life of agony, which is a far harsher fate than
death? And if it is proper to feel despondency when
a city is in sore straits, why not for a province, too?
And if for one province, why not for more besides?
52. Those who sympathize with me in my grief,
however far removed they may be from the world of
learning, receive my affection. Will I not be doing
injustice to people in other walks of life, if I refuse to
accord them the same? We are not Cypriotes, not
yet—and may Heaven forfend[b]—have we beheld our
city laid low by earthquake, but still you could hear
many people moaning and lamenting, "Alas, poor
cities! Where on earth are you now?" and no one
has reproved us for thinking that we shared in the
disaster, though separated from the island by such a
stretch of sea.[c] 53. What is the point of this un-
necessary fuss? I am no leader of armies, nor did I
participate in the fighting in Thrace, either as general
or as private[d]: I could never have borne the sight of

[c] Severe earthquakes afflicted Cyprus in A.D. 343 and
365, but these seem to be too early for a reference here. The
most likely is that recorded in A.D. 374/5 by Zosimus (4. 18).
[d] The battle of Adrianople, A.D. 378, when Valens was
killed, cf. Or. 1. 179; 24. 3 f.; Amm. Marc. 31. 13.

LIBANIUS

δένδρου ποθὲν ὑψηλοῦ τὴν θέαν ἤνεγκα ἂν τῆς μεγάλης ἐκείνης μάχης, ἀλλ' ὅμως ἀκούσας τῆς συμβολῆς τὸ πέρας τό τε μέτωπον ἔπληξα καὶ τῶν τριχῶν ἔτιλα καὶ τὰς αἰτίας πρὸς ἐμαυτὸν ἐξήτασα[1] τῶν κακῶν ὧν τῆς ὑστεραίας καὶ πρὸς ἄλλους ἐμνήσθην. ἡμάρτανον οὖν τούτοις; καὶ τίς ὁ τοῦτο φήσων;

54. Οὐ βουλεύω μέν, ἀλλ' ἀφεῖμαι ταῖς περὶ τοὺς λόγους φροντίσιν, ἄχθεσθαι δὲ ἔξεστί μοι καὶ τῇ τῶν βουλευόντων πενίᾳ καὶ τῷ τῶν τοῖς ἄρχουσιν ὑπηρετούντων πλούτῳ, ὧν ἔνιοι πέρυσι κρέα πωλοῦντες οἱ δὲ ἄρτους οἱ δὲ λάχανα ταῖς ἐκείνων οὐσίαις μεγάλοι γεγένηνται περὶ τιμῆς οὐδὲν δι-
R 190 ενεχθέντες· τοσοῦτος | αὐτοῖς ἐστιν ὁ χρυσός. 55. οἱ δὲ καὶ τῷ μεγέθει τῶν οἰκιῶν λυποῦσι τοὺς γείτονας οὐκ ἐῶντες τῆς ἡμέρας ἀπολαύειν καθαρῶς. εἶτ' ἐκεῖνοι μὲν οὐδὲν ἀδικεῖν σοι δοκοῦσι τῇ μεταβολῇ καὶ ταῖς τῶν πραγμάτων διορυχαῖς, εἰ δέ τις ἐπὶ τούτοις οὐ δύναται σιωπᾶν φορτικὸς οὗτός ἐστι καὶ βαρύς; 56. ἀλλὰ σὺ | μὲν εἴ σοί F 2 τις τῶν συγγενῶν ἴσος γένοιτο κατὰ πλοῦτον ἀποπνίγῃ, καὶ τὸ πρᾶγμα οὐκ ἀνεκτὸν καὶ ἥδιστ' ἂν δίκην ἔλαχες τῇ Τύχῃ, ἐμὲ δὲ αὐτὴν ὡς δίκαια ποιοῦσαν ἐπαινεῖν ἠξίους οὕτω πολλῇ περὶ τοὺς ἀνθρώπους ἀδικίᾳ κεχρημένην καθ' ἑκάτερον, καθελοῦσαν μὲν οὓς εὖ ποιεῖν ἐχρῆν, δοῦσαν δὲ τὰ παρ' αὐτῆς τοῖς καθάρμασιν. 57. ἢ καὶ τὸν τῶν ἡνιόχων πλοῦτον ἐπαινεῖν με προσήκει καὶ ὅς ἐστιν ἑτέροις τισὶν ἐπί τινι γέλωτι καὶ τὸ πρόχειρον εἶ-

---

[1] ἐξήτασα F. (CAPBM) : ἐζήτησα Re. (VUI).

---

[a] His immunity from curial liturgies came to him as sophist of the city.

[b] Private building in Antioch was very much the fashion

40

that great battle even from some coign of vantage in a tree-top, but still, when I heard the result of the engagement, I beat my brow, tore my hair and pondered on the causes of the disaster, and next day imparted them to others too. Was I at fault in this, then ? Who will tell me so ?

54. I am no councillor : I have immunity because of my concern with rhetoric,[a] but I can still be upset at the poverty of the councillors and the wealth amassed by the lackeys of the governors. Some of these, only recently hawkers of meat, bread or vegetables, have grown great on the property of the councillors and enjoy just as much respect as they, so great is the wealth they possess. 55. Others, just by the size of their houses, are a nuisance to their neighbours, for they do not allow them the enjoyment of full clear daylight.[b] Isn't it the case, then, that you can see nothing wrong with them in this change and undermining of their fortunes, whereas anyone who cannot keep silent on this matter is vulgar and tiresome ? 56. But in your case, if one of your relatives becomes your equal in wealth, you are green with envy ; the situation is intolerable, and you would cheerfully put Lady Luck in the dock. Yet you expect me to commend her for fair dealing, though she has used men so unfairly both in ruining those on whom she should have smiled and in granting her favours to guttersnipes. 57. Or do you think I should also commend the fortunes made by the racing drivers,[c] or those won by certain other in-

at this time (*Or.* 11. 227) and ostentatious town houses were built both by *honorati* and by *principales*.

[c] Libanius thought as little of the races and the theatre as did Julian. *Cf. Or.* 16. 41 ff. Jul. *Misop.* 340 a, 343 d ff.

ναι ζώνης τυχεῖν καὶ τὸ τοὺς νεανίσκους ἀναι-
σχυντεῖν, καὶ τὸ τοὺς πατέρας ταῦτα ὁρῶντας
ἀνέχεσθαι, καὶ τὸ τῆς μὲν ἡμέρας τὸ πλέον καθεύδειν, τῆς δὲ νυκτὸς ἐν τῷ μέλλειν λοῦσθαι δα-
πανᾶν; ἐν ᾧ δὲ μέλλουσιν, ὅ τι καὶ ὅπου δρῶσιν οὐ
λέγω.

58. Τέτταρες ἦσαν ὑπογραφεῖς ἐκείνῳ περὶ οὗ
λέγων τι καλὸν οἶδα λυπῶν, καὶ τὰς ἀγγελίας οἱ
φέροντες ἑπτακαίδεκα, καὶ ὁ τούτοις ἐφεστηκὼς
ἆθλον εἶχε πολλῶν ἐτῶν τὴν περὶ τὸν χαλκὸν
R 191 ἀρχήν, οἱ δ' ἄλλοι | τὰς πόλεις ἐποίουν λαμπράς.
τὰ δὲ νῦν, οἱ μέν εἰσιν εἴκοσι καὶ πεντακόσιοι, οἱ
δὲ τῶν μυρίων πλείους, ᾧ δὲ μέλει τούτων ὁπότ'
αὐτῷ δόξειεν | ὕπαρχος ἀνεφάνη.   59. τούτοις F 2.
κεντοῦμαι τὴν ψυχήν, περὶ τούτων οὐ δύναμαι μὴ
τὰ δίκαια λέγειν καὶ ἔχω γε τοὺς ἀποδεχομένους,
ὥσπερ ὑμεῖς ἀλλήλους ἐν τοῖς καλοῖς συμποσίοις
ἐν οἷς πολλὴ μὲν ἡ χιών, πολλὴ δὲ ὕβρις, αἰσχραὶ
δὲ ἅμιλλαι, πονηραὶ δὲ νῖκαι, ὑμνοῦνται δὲ ἀντὶ
τῶν θεῶν οἱ τῶν κακῶν τῶν παρόντων αἴτιοι.

60. Τῷ πολλάκις γάρ, φησί, τοῦτο ποιεῖν βαρὺς
εἶ. τὸ πολλάκις δὲ λέγειν ἃ καλῶς ἔχει λέγειν, τῷ
λέγοντι μέμψιν[1] ἐνεγκεῖν δίκαιον; καὶ πῶς; ἢ γὰρ

---

[1] μέμψιν ἂν Re. (mss. except BMV) : [ἂν] F.

[a] The baldric (ζώνη) is the symbol of the στρατιώτης
(officialis); similarly ἀναξυρὶς καὶ ζωστήρ, Or. 62. 14: cf.
R.E. xvii. 2047, s.v. " Officium."

[b] The innuendo is again that of pederasty.

[c] Julian. For his purge of the civil service cf. Or. 18.
131 ff. (Vol. I, pp. 365 ff.)

[d] The precise nature of this supervision of coppersmiths

dividuals by reason of the amusement they provide, and their easy passage to service posts[a] ; and the way mere lads are debauched and their fathers look on complacently, and how they sleep for the greater part of the day and spend their nights waiting to bathe ? And what they do in this period of waiting, and where they do it, I forebear to mention.[b]

58. My emperor—and I know that any commendations I make of him will cause offence—my emperor had four secretaries and seventeen couriers only[c] : the minister in charge of them held the job as reward for the long years of service as superintendent of the armouries,[d] and the rest made the cities prosperous. But nowadays there are 520 secretaries and more than 10,000 couriers,[e] and the minister in charge of them turns up as prefect whenever he likes. 59. At this I am smitten to the heart : I cannot help but speak the truth about it, and I have my supporters, just as you have each other at your fine parties, where there is plenty of iced water laid on and plenty of misconduct, and where there is competition in vice and winning is a disgrace, and where not the gods but those responsible for our present woes receive hymns of praise.[f]

60. " Yes," comes the reply, " it is by harping so often on this that you are tiresome." But is it right for the speaker to be reproved for harping upon what he is justified in saying ? How can it be ? Either

is unclear. It seems to be connected with arms manufacture, which was a state monopoly, controlled by the *magister officiorum* (*Not. Dign. Or.* XI. 18 ff.).

[e] *Agentes-in-rebus* or στρατιῶται.

[f] This jibe is directed against the Christians influential at court and in Antioch. According to him, they are drunkards (hence the snow to cool the wine, *cf. Or.* 1. 76) and sexual perverts.

οὐ δίκαια[1] ἃ μὴ χρῆν, ἢ καὶ πολλάκις, ἃ προσῆκεν. |

R 192 61. ὁρᾷς ὡς τοῖς αὐτοῖς κατὰ τὴν ἡμέραν ἑκάστην ἀλλήλους προσαγορεύομεν καὶ οὐκ ἐσμὲν βαρεῖς οὐδὲ λυποῦμεν τοῖς ῥήμασιν ἀλλ᾿ ἡδίους ποιοῦμεν, ὁ δ᾿ οὐ προσειπὼν ἠτίμασεν. οἱ δὲ περὶ τὰς τραπέζας ὑμῖν ᾄδοντες νέοι καὶ ὑφ᾿ ὧν τοῖς ᾄσμασι πίνετε, οὐ τοῖς αὐτοῖς ὑμῖν παραπέμπουσι τὰς κύλικας καί εἰσιν ἡδίους αὐτοῦ τοῦ πόματος; πῶς οὖν ἐκεῖνο μὲν οὐ βαρύ, τοῦτο δέ; εἰ γὰρ ἐκεῖνο τοῖς πότοις πρέπει, καὶ τοῦτο ταῖς συμφοραῖς. 62. οἶδα δὲ ἔγωγε | πολλοὺς ἐπὶ δεινοῖς τισιν ἐν F 2 θρήνοις ἀποθανόντας ὧν οὐδεὶς κατηγόρησεν ὅτι μὴ προεπαύσαντο, ἀλλὰ καὶ καλῶς ἔδοξαν ᾐσθῆσθαι τῶν κακῶν αὐτῷ τῷ συνεκβεβιωκέναι[2] τῇ λύπῃ. 63. στῆσον τὴν λύμην τὴν περὶ ἕκαστον καὶ στήσεις μοι τοὺς περὶ αὐτῆς λόγους. εἰ δὲ ἐκείνη χωρεῖ, τί μοι τὴν γλῶτταν ἀποστρέφεις[3]; αὐτὰ γάρ με κινεῖ τὰ πράγματα πρὸς τὰ ῥήματα· σὺ δ᾿ ὅμοιόν τι ποιεῖ ὥσπερ ἂν εἴ τις ἰατρὸς οὐκ ἔχων ἕλκος ἰάσασθαι τὸν ὀδυνώμενον ἐκέλευε μὴ στένειν. 64. ἀπόδος τὴν παλαιὰν ἰσχύν τε καὶ ὥραν ταῖς πόλεσι, καὶ τῆς παλινῳδίας ἀκούσῃ. κατάστησον εἰς τὴν ἔμπροσθεν τάξιν τοὺς λόγους, καὶ τότ᾿ αὐτοὺς ἀπαίτει τοῦ καιροῦ τὴν εὐλογίαν. εἰ δὲ ἡ νόσος βαδίζει καὶ τὸ κακὸν ἀεὶ μεῖζον[4] γί-
R 193 γνεται καὶ μικρὰ | τὰ πρὸ τοῦ πρὸς τὰ νῦν καὶ τι-

---

[1] ἢ γὰρ F. (mss.) : καὶ γὰρ Re., Fabr. | δίκαια Re. (mss.) : λεκτέα F. : δίκαιον Gasda.

[2] συνεκβεβιωκέναι F., Re. (ACPBM) : συμβεβιωκέναι Fabr. (VUIMo.).

[3] ἀποστρέφεις Re. (mss.) : ἀποφράττεις F.

improper statements should not be made or justifiable ones should—and often. 61. You see us addressing each other in the same words every day without being tiresome or annoying in what we say. In fact, we give pleasure by it, and anyone who fails to greet us, slights us. And those youngsters who sing to you round the table and to the accompaniment of whose songs you drink—don't they pass you your cups with the same refrain and provide more pleasure than the actual drink?[a] So how is it that that is not tiresome, while this is? If that suits your drinking, this suits our misfortunes. 62. I know many people who have died of grief at some disaster, but nobody has ever reproached them for not having put a stop to it before that, but they were even thought to have had a proper appreciation of their troubles by dying and so taking leave of their grief. 63. Put an end to all the indignities I have mentioned, and you will put a stop to my comments about them. If they continue, why do you try to divert my tongue? The very facts induce me to speech. Your behaviour is like that of a doctor who is incapable of curing a wound and yet tells the agonized patient to stop moaning. 64. Restore to the cities their vigour and glory of old and you will hear my recantation. Place oratory back in its former place, and then you can require it to sing the praises of the present. But if the ailment progresses and the trouble waxes ever greater, if the past is of little account as compared

[a] A typical pagan misrepresentation of Christian religious ceremonial.

---

[4] ἀεὶ ⟨μεῖζον⟩ F.: ἀεὶ γίγνεται ⟨μεῖζον⟩ Fabr.: κακὸν ⟨κάκιον⟩ ἀεὶ Gasda. Read κακὸν περιγίγνεται?

μιώτερα τὰ φαυλότερα καὶ ἀτιμότερα τὰ κρείττω,
τί με τὴν φθορὰν ἀναγκάζεις ἐγκωμιάζειν;

65. Μάλιστα μὲν οὖν τὰ τῆς οἰκουμένης ἁπάσης
ἐμαυτοῦ νενόμικα βελτίω τε καὶ χείρω, καὶ γίγνομαι τοιοῦτος οἷον ἄν με ποιῶσιν αἱ ἐκείνης τύχαι,
μισεῖσθαι δὲ ὁ φιλῶν τὴν οἰκουμένην οὐκ ἄξιος.

66. εἰ δ᾽ οὖν | καὶ κατακλείοι μέ τις εἰς τὴν ὑπὲρ F
τῆς ἐνεγκούσης πρόνοιαν, ἀτυχεῖν μοι δοκεῖ ταῖς
μετοικίαις αὕτη πολλῶν τινῶν οἳ τὰς αὑτῶν καταλιπόντες πόλεις καὶ οἴκους, εἰ δὴ καὶ οἴκους καὶ
R 194 οὐδ᾽ ἂν ὄναρ ἡδέως ἰδόντες οὗπερ ἔφυσαν, | ξένοι
πολιτῶν κρατεῖν οἴονται δεῖν τρέμοντες[1] μὴ νόμον
θῇ βασιλεὺς εἶναι τῶν παραδόξων πλούτων εὐ-
θύνας. 67. οἷς οὐκ ἐξαρκεῖ τὰ ἡμέτερα ἔχειν,
ἀλλὰ κἂν αἰτιάσηταί τις τὴν Τύχην θυμοῦνται, καὶ
βαρὺς ὁ μεμψάμενος· τὸ γὰρ εἰς τοῦθ᾽ ὑμᾶς ἥκειν
παρρησίας ὄντας οἷοίπερ ἐστέ, πῶς οὐ πάνδεινον;

68. εἰ δὲ γεωργὸς ὢν ἀεὶ σπείρων οὐδὲν κομιζό-
μενος κατεβόων τῶν ἐτῶν τῶν τὸ μὲν λαβόντων τὸ
δὲ οὐ δεδωκότων, ὀχληρὸς ἂν ἦν τοῖς ταῦτα καθ᾽
ἕκαστον ἔτος ἀκούουσι; καὶ πῶς ἐνῆν μὴ θρηνεῖν
ἐν αὐχμοῖς καὶ ἐπομβρίαις καὶ νοσήμασιν ἄλλοις
καὶ τῇ περὶ τὴν σπορὰν αὐτὴν ζημίᾳ; 69. ἀλλὰ
μητρὸς μὲν τηκομένης μήκεσι νόσων ἔδει κλάειν,
πατρίδος δὲ ἢ καὶ πρὸ τῆς μητρὸς ἂν εἴη κακῶς

---

[1] ⟨οὐ⟩ τρέμοντες Re., Fabr.

[a] A fair example of the *philanthropia* professed by Libanius and Themistius, reminiscent of Terence, *Heauton.* 77.

[b] For immigration into Antioch, previously commended
in *Or.* 11. 163 ff., *cf.* Liebeschuetz, p. 99. Libanius in the
Theodosian period is very critical of this development, *cf.*
Or. 10. 25, 41. 6. His special target here is the *honorati* who
settle in Antioch.

with the present, if things of little worth are held more precious, and the better is of less repute, why do you force me to speak in praise of our loss?

65. So when I have particularly considered the state of the whole world, good and bad alike, to be my own concern, and my attitude is such as its fortunes make it,[a] one who so loves the world does not deserve to be an object of hatred. 66. So, even if I should be confined just to consideration for the city that bore me, her I regard as ill-used in the immigration of many persons : these leave their native towns and their homes,—if indeed they have homes to leave and if it were not the case that the last place they would pluck up courage to see, even in their dreams, was their own birthplace—and, outsiders as they are, they regard it as their right to ride rough shod over citizens, and they are all of a tremble in case the emperor should decree an investigation into their unexpected wealth.[b] 67. They are not satisfied with possessing what is ours, but if there is any word of blame for Fortune, they are up in arms, and anyone who complains is tiresome. For you, being the people you are, to be brought to such a pass with regard to your freedom of expression, that is a most dreadful thing. 68. If I were a farmer, sowing my seed all the time and getting no return, if I grumbled at the years that took all and gave nothing, would I be a nuisance to those who heard it year after year? How could I help complaining in times of drought, flood, and agricultural diseases also, and in the losses made upon the actual sowing? 69. If it is right to grieve when one's mother is wasted by long illnesses, should a man make merry when his

47

διακειμένης ἑορτάζειν ἐχρῆν; ἤδειν ἀρέσκοντα
ποιῶν τοῖς λαχοῦσιν αὐτὴν δαίμοσι, τοῦτο δὲ ἠπιστάμην δίκαιον ὄν. δίκαια τοίνυν ποιῶν οὐκ ἠδί-
κουν. |

70. Ἕν μὲν τοῦτο τοσοῦτον ἔπειθε λέγειν, ἕτερον F
δὲ οὐκ ἔλαττον· ἤλπιζον δράσειν τι τὸν λόγον καὶ
R 195 ἰάσεσθαι καὶ ἐπανορθώσειν | ἑτέρων πρὸς ἑτέρους
αὐτὸν φερόντων, ἕως εἰς ὦτα τοῖς βασιλεῦσιν
ἀφίκοιτο. 71. δεδυστύχηται δέ μοι καὶ τοῦτο τὸ
μάτην με ταῦτα ἐλπίσαι. περὶ παντὸς γὰρ μᾶλλον
διαλέγονται τοῖς βασιλεῦσιν οἷς τούτου μέτεστιν
ἢ τῶν τηλικούτων, καὶ τὰ συμφέροντα ὑπερβάντες
ἀφ' ὧν χαριοῦνται λέγουσι. 72. καὶ τί δεῖ τοῖς
ἄλλοις ἐπιτιμᾶν; οὐδ' αὐτὸν ἐκίνησα τὸν ὕπαρχον
εἰς φροντίδα τῶν βουλῶν εἰπών (ὃ τίνα οὐκ ἂν
ἐπεσπάσατο;) ὅτι τὸ γένος τοῦτο ἐκλείψει παίδων
βουλευταῖς οὐκ ἐσομένων, γάμων αὐτοῖς οὐ γιγνομένων, τοῦ βουλεύειν κακῶν εἶναι δοκοῦντος
ἐσχάτου. 73. ὁ δ' ἐλέγχειν μὲν οὐκ εἶχέ μοι τὸν
λόγον, εἰπὼν δὲ κακῶς τρεῖς ἢ τέτταρας τῶν πολιτευομένων σὺν ὀργῇ μεγάλῃ πᾶν ὃ προσῆκεν ᾤετο
πεπληρωκέναι καὶ τῷ τρυφᾶν[1] πάλιν αὐτὸν ἔδωκε.
74. Τί οὖν λοιπόν; εὔχεσθαι τοῖς θεοῖς χεῖρα

[1] τρυφᾶν F., conj. Re. : γράφειν Re. (edit.), Fabr. (mss.).

---

[a] A commonplace with Libanius.
[b] Especially the tutelary goddess of Antioch, the Muse
Calliope (Or. 1. 102 ; 31. 40).
[c] The emperors are Theodosius and Gratian, not (as
Foerster, vol. I, p. 208) Arcadius. Arcadius did not become
emperor until A.D. 383.
[d] The prefect is usually identified with Domitius Modestus,
praefectus praetorio Orientis (=ppO), A.D. 369–377. Liban-
48

country is in sore straits, for she should mean more to him than his mother, even?[a] I knew that my conduct was pleasing to the deities who took her under their protection,[b] and this I knew to be right. So if my behaviour was right, I did no wrong.

70. This then is the sum of one matter that induced me to speak, but there is another, no less weighty. I hoped that my remarks would have some effect, and would serve as a cure and corrective, transmitted from person to person until it reached the emperors' ears.[c] 71. This has been a vain hope and I have not succeeded. Those who have the ear of our rulers converse with them on any matter but this, neglecting things of importance and reporting only what will win them favour. 72. And what need to reproach all and sundry? Not even the prefect himself did I move to concern himself with the local councils, though I said what would convince anybody, that this class of person would die out, since councillors would have no children, they remain unmarried and their status is regarded as the worst of all possible evils. 73. He could not refute what I had to say, but flew into a temper and abused three or four of the councillors, thought that he had done his whole duty, and took himself to his flesh-pots again.[d]

74. What recourse have we, then? Pray the gods

ius' intervention, which was certainly made in person, would then have occurred at least four years before the composition of this oration, and under a different emperor. A nearer date in the reign of Theodosius seems more appropriate, and the most likely candidate would be Neoterius (ppO, A.D. 380–381), who had apparently sponsored the consular Carterius (for whom cf. PLRE 182 (3)). This incident would account for the unflattering picture of the prefect, which is unlike anything Libanius wrote about Modestus.

ὀρέξαι καὶ τοῖς ἱεροῖς καὶ τοῖς γεωργοῖς καὶ ταῖς
βουλαῖς καὶ τῇ τῶν Ἑλλήνων φωνῇ καὶ τὰ μὲν
οὐ δικαίως | ηὐξημένα μικρὰ ποιῆσαι, τὰ δὲ ἀδίκως F
καταφρονούμενα τὰ αὑτῶν κομίσασθαι δοῦναί τε
ἀφορμὰς ἐμοὶ χαρᾶς ἀντὶ τῆς νῦν ἀνίας.

to stretch their protecting hand over temples, farmers, councils and the language of the Greeks, to bring low all that has improperly been raised up, to allow what is unjustly despised to recover its due, and to grant me, in place of my present woe, full cause for joy.

ORATION 50

FOR THE PEASANTRY,
ABOUT FORCED LABOUR

INTRODUCTION

THE date of composition is shown by the reference to
C. Th. 15. 9. 1 (§ 12) to be after July A.D. 384.
Parallels with the first oration against Icarius (*Or.* 27.
14 ff.) place it firmly in Icarius' term of office as *Comes
Orientis*, in the winter or spring of A.D. 385.

The situation in Antioch was then embittered by
the prolongation of famine conditions, which had
existed since A.D. 382. Then Libanius had, by his
personal intervention with the *Comes*, averted the
risk of civil disorder, which usually accompanied such
crises, and had protected the bakers from excessive
victimization (*Or.* 1. 205 ff.). Now, however, under
Icarius, whom he had regarded as his protégé, he
found the offer of his services in a similar situation
rejected. Icarius, indeed, resorted to the extremes
of control—regimentation of the bakers' corporation,
supervision by his own nominees of both the bakeries
and the markets generally, the imposition of fixed
prices and of rationing for bread, not to mention the
more normal imposition of emergency demands upon
the city councillors for their services in maintaining
the food supply (the *sitegia* : *cf. Or.* 27-29 *passim*).
All such measures were applied by his agents with
the brutality and venality characteristic of the administration. Simultaneously, an influx of hungry
refugees into Antioch exaggerated the general

increase in the population of the city, which was a feature of this period (*Or.* 27. 6), so creating a problem of accommodation, which was almost totally ignored in the building projects then being instituted by the rich magnates resident in the city. Needless to say, the ordinary city councillor, in the face of such a combination of pressures, found himself squeezed between the increased demands of the administration and the growing discontent of the hard-pressed proletariate.

Libanius, piqued at personal slights and genuinely distressed at the situation in Antioch, resumed his rôle as the spokesman of the oppressed, and began a series of orations against the excesses of Icarius' administration. The personal attacks, which contrast so strongly with the oration of advice to Icarius upon his arrival (*Or.* 26), commenced in the late autumn of A.D. 384 with a speech of protest to him against the conduct of his nominees towards the bakers (*Or.* 29), moving on, early in A.D. 385, to the open attack upon him for neglecting to control these subordinates (*Or.* 27), all these orations being designed to influence opinion in Antioch, until he finally composed an oration, ostensibly addressed to the emperor, demanding Icarius' dismissal for the malpractices which he describes (*Or.* 28). At the same time, he composed, also for the attention of the imperial administration, the present oration, taking his stand upon considerations of natural justice and public utility. The same grievances, which are used in the narrowly personal attack upon the governor, are here deployed in the exposition of a point of principle in a spirit of genuine social reform, the two sets of arguments supplementing each other as doublets in the same way as those of *Or.* 33 and 45 are to do in the following year.

The point of principle upon which Libanius seizes here is the local custom of the casual requisitioning of forced labour.[a] According to Libanius, the practice was peculiar to Antioch and of long standing. Had it been imposed by the city council he might well have been less bitter in his complaints, but the authorization evidently came from the *Comes* alone, and there was a sharp contrast between the efforts of the central government to regulate the demands for the *angariae* in the *cursus publicus* from A.D. 382 onwards (*cf. C. Th.* 8. 5. 38-45) and the continuance of this casual requisitioning of services by the officials resident in Antioch. Icarius, indeed, upon entering office had proclaimed his disgust at this practice and had announced his intention of stopping it : instead, it had been applied more arbitrarily than ever (*Or.* 27 15 f.). Extensive demolitions and rebuilding in the city, both public and private, brought with them the problem of disposal of rubble and debris. Expenditure on this was avoided by obtaining a permit from the *Comes* through his officials to requisition the services of animals and their owners to perform the task. The victims of this practice were, without exception, the peasantry visiting the local market, whose social status was thus demonstrated as being inferior to that of the townsmen. Since the city itself possessed draft animals in large numbers, and

---

[a] The phrase περὶ τῶν ἀγγαρειῶν may well be a later intrusion into the title, since the term does not appear in the text of the oration. This type of local requisitioning is not to be confused with the general system of ἀγγαρεῖαι by imperial regulations (for which *cf. C. Th.* 8. 5).

yet refused to use them for its public services, the
inequality of treatment became the more glaring
(§ 5). Even worse was the extension of the practice
to the services of private individuals (§§ 16 ; 20 ff.).
The consequence was that both the public and
private interests in the city of Antioch were being
run on the cheap in crude monetary terms but that
the returning peasants suffered personal inconvenience and even danger, as well as economic loss, and
so began a boycott of the markets which in turn
affected the citizens by increasing the prevailing
scarcity and raising the cost of living.

The arguments deployed before the emperor are
those of justice and public utility. Whether they
affected the conduct of the administration in any
way is more than doubtful. In the next year Libanius
was to publicize yet another kind of administrative
abuse—that of prison conditions. However partial
he may be in the presentation of his arguments, he
certainly illuminates the growing social unrest and
economic depression which were to provoke the
violence of the riots against the statues in A.D. 387.
The oration also clearly reveals the growing impo-
tence of the city council. The influence of the *Comes*
is all-important, and this in turn is applied upon the
solicitation of various potentates, but the councillors
themselves, both as landlords and as agents responsible for collection of taxation demanded by the
central government, retain the odium attached to
their nominal authority. The abuses here listed contribute to that rift between urban and rural life which
is displayed in *Or.* 47 (*De Patrociniis*), and are a sharp
contrast to the rhetorical praises of country life
which appear both in Libanius (Foerster, vol. VIII

pp. 261 ff., 349 ff.) and in Themistius (*Or.* 30) and are a commonplace in the schools. Libanius here has the merit of indicating clearly that the economic basis of his urban society lies in the maintenance of the rural economy.

MANUSCRIPTS AND BIBLIOGRAPHY

Only four manuscripts (CAPI) survive for this oration. Although all have the same title, it is possible, as Foerster suggested, that the phrase περὶ τῶν ἀγγαρειῶν is an addition by a Byzantine scholar. A collection of excerpts compiled by Macarius Chrysocephalus in the 14th century preserves four passages from the speech under the title περὶ τοῦ ἐν τῇ πόλει πηλοῦ.

The *editio princeps* was that of Gothofredus, Geneva, 1631, with Latin version and notes (*Libanii Sophistae Orationes IV*), reproduced in his *Opera Juridica Minora*, Leiden, 1733. Reiske's edition, Altenburg, 1791, incorporates these notes. The latest editor was Foerster. Monnier translated the speech. Assessments of it appear in Pack, *Studies*, Petit, *Libanius et la vie municipale*.

L

ΥΠΕΡ ΤΩΝ ΓΕΩΡΓΩΝ ΠΕΡΙ ΤΩΝ
ΑΓΓΑΡΕΙΩΝ

1. Εἰ καὶ περὶ μικρῶν δόξω τισίν, ὦ βασιλεῦ, F iii
ποιεῖσθαι τοὺς λόγους, ἀλλὰ σοί γε οὐ περὶ μικρῶν
οἶμαι δόξειν λέγειν διὰ τὸ πᾶν ὅτιπερ ἂν ᾖ δίκαιον
μέγα κεκρίσθαι παρὰ σοί. συμβαίνει δὲ ταῦτα
ὑπὲρ ὧν ἀκούσῃ[1] σήμερον, ⟨ὃ⟩[2] εἰκότως σε καὶ
μόνον ἔπειθεν ἄν πως. οὗ μείζω μοι τὴν ἐλπίδα
ποιεῖ τὸ ταὐτὸ καὶ λυσιτελεῖν. ὅτι δὲ ἀληθῆ λέγω
παρ' αὐτῶν ὑπάρξει σοι τῶν πραττομένων, ὦ φιλ-
ανθρωπότατε βασιλεῦ, μαθεῖν. |

2. Πολλὰ ποιεῖ χοῦν ἐν ταῖς πόλεσιν, ὦ θεία F 4a
κεφαλή, πίπτουσαι οἰκίαι σαθραί,[3] αἱ δὲ τεκτόνων
τέχνῃ λυόμεναι, θεμέλιοι νέαις τιθέμενοι, περὶ οἰκοδομήματα δημόσια τὰ αὐτὰ ταῦτα γιγνόμενα.
τοῦτον δὴ τὸν ἀπὸ τούτων χοῦν δεῖ μὲν ἔξω φέρεσθαι τειχῶν ὅπως ἐφ' ὅτουπερ ἔκειτο τοῦτο δέ-
ξαιτό τι ἴδιον ἢ δημόσιον. 3. καὶ τὸ μὲν δίκαιον
ἦν ἀφ' ἧς οἰκοδομεῖται τὰ δημόσια δαπάνης, ἀπὸ
ταύτης καὶ τοῦτο πράττεσθαι τὸ μέρος. εἰ γὰρ τὰ

---

[1] ἀκούσῃ F. : ἀκούσειν Re. text (mss.) : ἀκούσεις conj. Re.
[2] ⟨ὃ⟩ conj. Re., F.
[3] σαθραὶ Cobet, F. : σαπραί Re. (mss.).

---

[a] Or. 50 F., 49 Re.

ORATION 50 [a]

FOR THE PEASANTRY, ABOUT FORCED LABOUR

1. Even if some believe that my orations deal with trivial matters, Sire, I think that you at least will not believe that I deal in trivialities, because every consideration of right has been adjudged of importance in your eyes. Such happens to be the subject of which you will hear today, and this of itself may well carry conviction with you, but what raises my hopes the more is the fact that it is also a subject that involves your interests also. And the truth of my statements, your most gracious majesty,[b] you will be able to gauge from the facts themselves.

2. In our cities, your majesty, there is much that produces rubble—the collapse of derelict houses, their demolition by workmen and the laying of foundations for new ones, and the very same thing happening with public buildings too. The rubble from them must be carted outside the walls so that the vacant site can receive some building, private or public. 3. The proper thing would be for the cost of doing this job to be included in the cost of the public building schemes, for if, in the case of timber,

---

[b] On the " philanthropy " of Theodosius *cf. Or.* 19. 16 f. ; 20. 16 f. Themist. *Or.* 19.

LIBANIUS

ξύλα καὶ τοὺς λίθους καὶ κεραμίδας καὶ ἐργάτας
καὶ τέκτονας καὶ πάντα ἁπλῶς δι᾽ ὧν ἄν τις ἢ
R ii. 552 κατασκευάσαιτό τι τῶν | οὐκ ὄντων ἢ ἐπισκευά-
σειε τῶν καμόντων, εἰ τούτων καὶ τῶν τοιούτων
δίκαιον μὴ φεύγειν τὴν δαπάνην τὴν πόλιν, ταὐτὸ
κρατείτω δίκαιον καὶ περὶ τὸν χοῦν. εἰ δὲ καλῶς
τὰ νῦν γιγνόμενα γίγνεται περὶ τὸν χοῦν, τί μὴ
διὰ πάντων τοῦτο ἔρχεται τῶν ποιούντων δημόσιον
οἰκοδόμημα; εἰ μὲν γὰρ ὠμὸν τοῦτο, κἀκεῖνο· εἰ
δ᾽ οὐ δεινόν,[1] οὐδ᾽ ἐκεῖνο. 4. ἀλλὰ δεινόν τε, ὦ
βασιλεῦ, καὶ ἄδικον καὶ κακὸν καὶ λόγου παντὸς
ἐπιεικοῦς ἐστερημένον. τί λέγεις; ἔθηκα τιμὴν
ὀρέων ἢ ὄνων ἢ καμήλων, ἐμισθωσάμην τοὺς ἐπι-
μελησομένους τούτων ἑκάστου, καὶ γέγονεν ἐντεῦθεν ἐμοί τε καὶ γυναικὶ καὶ παισὶν ἡ τροφή.
σὺ δ᾽ ἅπτῃ καὶ ἕλκεις καὶ τὸ ἐμὸν σὸν ποιεῖς, καὶ
δεῖ τὸ μὲν ἐργάζεσθαι | σοί, βλέποντα δὲ ἐμὲ σιω- F 4
πᾶν. ὅρα, ὦ βασιλεῦ, μὴ οὐ σφόδρα βασιλείας τοῦτο ᾖ ἐπὶ τὸ κτηθὲν ἐμοὶ τὸν ἄρχοντα βαδίζειν.
εἰ μὲν γὰρ ψῆφος ἀφαιρεῖταί με τὴν οὐσίαν καὶ
τοῦτ᾽ ἔστιν ἀδικημάτων δίκη, πάντα ἔστω τἀμὰ
τῆς πόλεως· εἰ δ᾽ οὐδὲν τούτων ἔγνωσται, πῶς ἃ
παρὰ τῶν νόμων ἔχω ταῦτά με οὐκ ἐᾷς ἔχειν;
5. Ἔστι τῇ πόλει χωρία παρὰ παλαιῶν ἀνδρῶν
R ii. 553 ἐν διαθήκαις | δεδομένα τῇ πόλει. ταῦτα γεωρ-
γεῖται τῇ πόλει καὶ τούτων ἐστὶν ἡ πρόσοδος τῆς
κεκτημένης. ἐν τούτοις τοῖς χωρίοις ἔστι ταῦτα ἃ
νῦν ἔφην, ὀρεῖς, ὄνοι, κάμηλοι. τί ταῦτα ὑπερβαί-

[1] δεινὸν ⟨τοῦτο⟩ conj. Re., Monnier.

[a] Cf. Or. 27. 15: λέγω τὰ περὶ τὸν χοῦν ὃν ἐκφέρειν ἀλλοτρίοις
ἔδωκεν ὄνοις δέον οἰκείοις ἀναγκάζειν.
[b] On the question of the city estates of Antioch cf. Or.

bricks, tiles, builders and carpenters, in fact every-thing to do with the erection of a new structure or the renovation of one in disrepair,—if it is not the thing for the city authority to evade such and similar costs, then the same principle should also apply to the disposal of rubble.[a] If the present practice in disposing of rubble is correct, why does it not apply to all aspects of the construction of public buildings ? If this is oppressive, then that would be too, and if there is no harm in this, neither would there be in that. 4. But there is harm in it, Sire : it is wrong and wicked and without any reasonable justification. Why ! Suppose I pay a price for mules or asses or camels and hire people to look after them all, and the income from them maintains my wife and children and myself. Then suppose that you lay hands on them, take them off and make what is mine yours, and they must work for you while I must look on and hold my tongue. Observe, Sire, that it is quite unconstitutional for a magistrate to invade my property. If a verdict in law robs me of my possessions and this is a punishment for my misdeeds, then let all I have be confiscated to the city. But if no such verdict has been declared, then how do you forbid me possession of what I legally possess ?

5. The city has estates bequeathed to it by testa-ment from men of days gone by. These are farmed for the city and the income from them belongs to the city that owns them.[b] On these estates there are what I have just mentioned, mules, asses, camels.

31. 16 ff., Liebeschuetz, *Antioch*, pp. 149 ff., and in *B.Z.* lii (1959), pp. 344 ff. For a different view *cf.* Petit, *Vie muni-cipale*, pp. 96 ff.

LIBANIUS

νοντες οἱ τὴν ἀρχὴν ἔχοντες ἐπὶ τοὺς ἄλλους χω-
ροῦσι καὶ ποιοῦντες ἀτελὲς πᾶν ἐκείνοις ὧν ἐστιν
ὁ πόνος, τούτων ποιοῦσι τὸ ἔργον οἷς ἄδικον ἐνοχλεῖν; εἰ γὰρ ἐκείνοις ἔξω τοῦτο τῶν τεταγμένων,
καὶ ἡμῖν.   6. οὔκουν ἔχοι τις ἂν δεῖξαι νόμον οὔτε
σὸν οὔτε ἄλλου βασιλέως οὐδενὸς καθ' ὃν καὶ
τοῦτ' ἔστιν ἐν λειτουργίαις.   οὐδέ γε ἐν τοῖς καθ'
ἕκαστον ἔτος γράμμασιν ἐν οἷς ἃ δεῖ φέρειν ἔστιν
οὐδαμοῦ προσγέγραπται· τοῖς δὲ ἄρχουσι καὶ τοῦτο περὶ ὅτουπερ ὁ νῦν λόγος ἐξέστω ποιεῖν καὶ
R ii. 554 τοὺς ὄνους τοὺς οὐ τῆς πόλεως | ποιεῖν τῆς πόλεως.
καίτοι καὶ εἰ νόμῳ τοῦτο διώριστο,[1] κατὰ μὲν τὴν
ἐντεῦθεν ἀνάγκην ἐγίγνετ' ἄν, οὐ μὲν ἄνευ γε τοῦ
χαλεπῶς φέρειν, ἦν δ' ἂν ἴσως τι καὶ παραμυθίας
ἐξ αὐτοῦ τοῦ κεῖσθαι νόμον.   νῦν δὲ | νόμος μὲν F 4
οὐδαμοῦ, τοῦτο δὲ πολὺ τὸ ἔργον.   7. τοῦτο δὲ
ὅταν εἴπω, τὸ ἀδίκημα λέγω.   ἡδέως δ' ἂν αὐτοὺς
ἐροίμην διὰ τί μὴ καὶ οἰκέτας καὶ θεραπαίνας καὶ
στρώματα καὶ σκεύη καὶ ἁμάξας ἄγουσιν ἐκ τῶν
οἰκιῶν ἐπὶ τὴν πόλεως χρείαν.   εἰ γὰρ ὅτι οὐκ
ἔξεστι φήσουσιν, οὐδὲ ταῦτα ἔξεστι.   πῶς οὖν τὸ
μὴ ἐξεῖναι τιμῶντες οἷς τούτων ἀπέχονται τὸ αὐτὸ
τοῦτο δι' ὧν ποιοῦσιν ὑβρίζουσι; καὶ μὴν ὑπὲρ
πολλῶν αὐτοὺς οἶδα διὰ γραμμάτων ὑμᾶς ἐρομέ-
νους εἰ ποιητέον, ὡς οὐκ ὂν θέμις ποιεῖν ὃ μὴ τῆς
τοιαύτης ἐξουσίας ἔτυχε.   πῶς οὖν οὐ καὶ περὶ

---

[1] διώριστο F. (CP, γρ in marg. A) : διείρητο Re. (AI).

---

[a] " Indictiones . . . quibus modus canonicarum functio-
num, seu tributorum et munerum publicorum continebatur "
(Gothofred.).

[b] The magisterial *relationes* to the emperor (*e.g.* those of
Pliny to Trajan, *Ep.* x, and of Symmachus).   For regula-

Why do the magistrates ignore these and proceed against other people ? Why grant complete immunity to them whose task it is and impose the job on those whom it is wrong to burden with it ? If this lies outside their sphere of obligation, it is outside ours, too. 6. Nor could one point to a law of yours or of any other emperor whereby this also is part of the civic duties. Nor is it anywhere written into the annual list of obligations to be performed [a] that the governors should be allowed to indulge in the practice now under discussion and to confiscate to the city asses that do not belong to her. But if this had been defined by law, it would take place in accordance with the enforcement of the law, not without resentment, it is true, but there would perhaps be a measure of consolation to be derived from its legal enactment. As it is, there is no law at all, but the practice is frequent. 7. And when I say this practice, I mean this illegal practice. I would like to ask them why they don't take male and female slaves, bedding, furniture and carriages from private houses for the service of the city. If they say that it is illegal, this is illegal too. How comes it then that they show respect for legality by refraining from these actions and yet violate this very same principle by the actions that they do ? Moreover, I know that they will communicate with you on many questions to enquire whether such and such an action should be taken since it is not lawful to do anything not so permitted.[b] How is it then

tions concerning them *cf. C. Th.* 11. 29 (especially 29. 5 of A.D. 374, where both the governor and his staff are held to be criminally responsible for any dereliction of duty in presenting them).

τούτων ἤροντο καὶ τὰ παρ' ὑμῶν ἀναμείναντες
οὕτως ἢ ἔδρων ἢ οὔ; νῦν δ' αὐτῷ τῷ φυγεῖν τὸ
ἐρωτῆσαι τὸ μὴ τῶν δικαίων εἶναι τοὔργον δεδη-
λώκασιν.

8. Ἔτι τοίνυν, εἰ μὲν τῶν ὑφ' ὑμῶν τοῦτο ἦν
ἐγνωσμένων, κοινὸν ἂν ἦν τοῦτο τῶν ὑφ' ὑμῖν πόλεων ὥσπερ αὖ καὶ τὰ ἄλλα. νῦν δ' ἀπιστίᾳ τοὺς
ἄλλοθεν ὡς ἡμᾶς ἐρχομένους ἔχει πρᾶγμα τοιοῦτο
καὶ ἀκούοντας καὶ ὁρῶντας. ἔρχονται γὰρ ἐκ πόλεων ἐν αἷς τοῦτο οὐκ ἔστι, καὶ οὐχ ἡγοῦνται τὰς
R ii. 555 αὑτῶν | ὃ χρῆν ἔχειν οὐκ ἔχειν ἀλλ' εἶναι παρ' ἡμῖν
ὃ μὴ εἶναι βέλτιον.

9. Ἴδοις δ' ἄν, ὦ βασιλεῦ, καὶ αὐτοὺς τοὺς ἄρ-
χοντας οἷς οὐ ποιοῦσιν ὧν δρῶσι κατηγοροῦντας. |
οὗτοι γὰρ τῶν μὲν ἐν δυνάμει γεγενημένων καὶ F 47
στρατοπέδων ἡγησαμένων αἰδοῦνται τούς τε ὄνους
καὶ τἄλλα, καὶ παρέρχονται τὸν χοῦν οἱ ταῦτα
ἐλαύνοντες ἀνεσπασμέναις ταῖς ὀφρύσι καὶ ὀρθοῖς
τοῖς αὐχέσι, κἄν τις λάβηταί τινος παριόντος παρα-
νενόμηκε. τῶν ἄλλων δὲ οἱ μὲν μετὰ πόνου τὰ
σφῶν αὐτῶν ῥύονται, οἳ δ' ἂν ἀντιβλέψαι τολμή-
σωσι, τυπτόμενοι μανθάνουσιν ὅτι κρεῖττον ἦν σιω-
πῇ πάσχειν κακῶς. τοῦ τοίνυν μὴ δικαίως τούσδε
πιέζεσθαι τὸ μὴ καὶ πάντας τὰ τοιαῦτα πονεῖν
σημεῖον. εἰ γὰρ οὐδεὶς ὑπ'[1] ἐκείνων οὐ πονούντων
παραβαίνεται νόμος, οὐδ' οἶδε νόμῳ πρὸς τοῦτ'
ἄγονται.

10. Ἐρεῖ τοίνυν τις ὡς εἰ καὶ μὴ γεγραμμένον
τοῦτ' ἔστιν ἀλλ' εἰς ἔθος ἥκει. ἔθη δὲ εἰ μὲν ἀκί-
νητα πάντα ἔμεινεν, εἰκός τι καὶ οἶδε πεπόνθασι
δεδουλευκότες τοῖς ἔθεσιν· εἰ δὲ λέλυται πολλὰ διὰ
παντὸς τοῦ χρόνου τοῖς κρείττοσιν εἰξάντων τῶν

that they did not make enquiries on this matter too and, after awaiting your reply, act accordingly ? Simply by omitting to enquire they have shown their actions to be illegal.

8. Moreover, if this were one of your edicts, it would be of universal application to the cities under your sway, as are the other edicts also. But visitors to us from elsewhere are possessed by disbelief when they hear and see such goings-on. They come from cities where this practice does not exist, and their notion is not that their home town does not possess a privilege it should have, but that there exists here a practice we could better do without.

9. And you may observe, Sire, that the governors themselves by their omissions proclaim their sins of commission. They respect the asses et cetera of retired officials and military officers, and their drivers pass by the rubble with disdainful face and noses in the air, and if somebody claims any of them as they pass by, it is an outrage. But anybody else either rescues his animals with much trouble or, if he dares look askance, learns under the lash that he would do better to suffer in silence. So the fact that not everyone performs these duties is proof that these people are unjustly oppressed, for if no law is broken by those not doing the task, these here are not legally forced to do it either.

10. But it will be objected that even if this is not a matter of statute, it has passed into custom. If all customs remained inviolate, there is some sense in their slavish adherence to custom. But if many lapse with the passage of time, with the worse giving way

---

¹ ὑπ' F. (I): ἐπ' Re. (CAP).

χειρόνων, μὴ τὸ περὶ τῆς τοῦ πράγματος φύσεως διαλέγεσθαι φεύγοντες ἐπὶ τὸ πεπρᾶχθαι πολλάκις καταφευγόντων. ἄχθεσθαι γὰρ ἄξιον ὅτι γέγονε πολλάκις, ἀλλ᾽ οὐκ ἐπὶ τῶν αὐτῶν διὰ τοῦτο μένειν. 11. ἦσάν τινες οἳ πονηρὰν ἑορτὴν εἰσήγαγον R ii. 556 εἰς τὴν Δάφνην. | ἦν δὲ τὸ πάντα τρόπον ἀσχη- F 4 μονεῖν ἑορτὴν ποιεῖν. τοῦτό τις κατιδὼν βασιλεὺς ἐπιεικὴς καὶ σώφρων αἰσχυνθεὶς μὲν τοῖς πραττομένοις, ἀλγήσας δ᾽ ὑπὲρ τοῦ χωρίου παύει τὴν ἐπὶ τοιούτοις σύνοδον καὶ παύσας εὐδοκιμεῖ. καὶ οὐδεὶς πρὸς αὐτὸν τὰ τῆς ἑορτῆς ἔλεγεν ἔτη οὐδ᾽ ὡς τὰ κεκρατηκότα δεῖ κρατεῖν διὰ τέλους. ἀλλ᾽ ἐξεβέβλητο τοῦτο τῆς Δάφνης τὸ νόσημα χρόνον πολὺν ἕως αὐτὸ πάλιν ἄνδρες ἀξίως τοιούτων ἑορτῶν βεβιωκότες εἰσήγαγον. 12. αἱ κατὰ τῶν βουλευόντων πληγαὶ διὰ κακίαν ἀρχόντων εἰς ἔθος R ii. 557 ἧκον. τοῦτ᾽ αὐτὸς | ἀνήρηκας[1] νόμῳ κἂν τοῖς ἐπαίνοις τοῖς περὶ σοῦ τῶν μεγάλων καὶ τοῦτο ἔστιν. ἐπὶ τὰς διὰ τῶν θηρίων λειτουργίας ἀνάγκαις ἤγετό τις πρότερον. σὺ γνώμης[2] τοῦτο ἐποίησας οὔτε κωλύων βουλομένους οὔτε ἕλκων ἄκοντας. | R ii. 558 καὶ οὔτε ἐνόμιζες ἀδικεῖν ἔθει μαχόμενος οὔτε ἠδίκεις. μηδὲ ἔστωσαν ἀνεψιῶν γάμοι γέγραφας ἐν

---

[1] ἀνήρηκας conj. Re., F. : ἀνήρηκε Re. text (mss.).
[2] σὺ γνώμης Monnier, F. : συγγνώμης Re. (mss.).

---

[a] The Maiuma, *cf. Or.* 10. 14. The ban on this orgiastic ritual, which was associated with Dionysus and Aphrodite and notorious for its immorality, had perhaps been imposed by Julian, *cf. Or.* 41. 16. Julian certainly disapproved of the festival, *cf. Misop.* 362 d. Gothofredus, with less likelihood,

to the better, let them not, in evading discussion about the nature of the practice, have recourse to the argument of its prevalence in the past. Its long history should be cause for annoyance, and not reason for remaining as you are. 11. A disgusting festival was introduced by certain persons to Daphne : its ceremonial was that of utter and absolute licence.[a] This came to the eye of a good and prudent emperor, and he, ashamed at the behaviour and distressed for the sanctuary, put a stop to a gathering of this character, and won approval for doing so. And nobody told him how many years the festival had lasted,[b] or that what had been the fashion should forever be the fashion, but this plague was banished from Daphne for a long time until men whose manner of life was in keeping with such kind of festivals once again introduced it. 12. The flogging of city councillors has, through the failings of the governors, hardened into custom. You personally have banned this practice by law,[c] and in the recital of your praises this forms one of the cardinal points. In the past people were forced under compulsion to undertake the provision of the beast shows. You made this voluntary [d] ; you neither sought to hinder the willing nor to draft the unwilling. Neither did you think yourself wrong in going counter to custom, nor were you wrong. You also decreed that marriages between cousins be banned, though the

identified the emperor with Constantius. *V.* Julian, *E.L.F.* No. 102 ; *C. Th.* 15. 6.

[b] It had been organized by Commodus, *cf.* Malalas 284 ff.

[c] *C. Th.* 12. 1. 80, 85 (A.D. 380, 381).

[d] *C. Th.* 15. 9. 1 (July A.D. 384) : a later enactment, 12. 1. 109 (April A.D. 385).

ἐξουσίᾳ πολλῇ τοῦ πράγματος ὄντος. καὶ τῶν
φαινομένων σοι δικαίων οὐκ ἦν ὁ τοῦ ἔργου χρόνος
δυνατώτερος. πρὸς ταῦτα ἔδει βλέψαι τοὺς τῆσδε
τῆς πόλεως ἄρχοντας καὶ μὴ μᾶλλον αἰδεσθῆναι
τὸν τῶν ἀδικημάτων χρόνον ἢ τὸ δίκαιον εἶναι ταῦτα
πεπαῦσθαι. |

13. Καίτοι πόσους ἐποιησάμην, ὦ βασιλεῦ, περὶ F 47
τούτου λόγους πρὸς ἕκαστον. οὓς μέμφεσθαι μὲν
ὡς οὐκ ὄντας δικαίους οὐκ εἶχον, ἄγειν δὲ εἰς
ἔργον οὐκ ἐβούλοντο, οὐχ ἵν' ὁ σὸς οἶκός τι κερ-
δάνειε, κέρδος μὲν γὰρ οὐδ' εἴ τι χρυσίον ἐντεῦθεν
R ii. 559 ἐγίνετό | σοι, ὅτου γὰρ οὐχ ἡγεῖται τὸ καλὸν τοῦτο
ἅπαν ζημία, οὐ μὴν οὐδ' αὐτὸ τοῦτο ἐντεῦθεν ἐγίγνετο, ἀλλ' ὁ μὲν πόνος ἑτέρων, ὁ δὲ μισθὸς ὧν
εἰπεῖν οὐ βούλομαι. 14. ἀλλ' ὅπερ ἔφην, πολλάκις
μὲν ἐμεμφόμην τὸ τὰ τοιαῦτα περιορᾶν, ἤνυον δὲ
οὐδέν. καὶ ἦν λοιπὸν σοί τε, ὦ βασιλεῦ, διαλέγεσθαι καὶ διὰ τῆς σῆς ψήφου βοηθεῖν τοῖς ἀδικουμένοις, πρὸς ὃν ἢ οὐδεὶς τολμήσει μεμνῆσθαι τοῦ
ἔθους ἢ μάτην. ἐλαύνων γὰρ δὴ σὺ τοὺς πολεμίους καὶ νόμοις καινοῖς εὖ ποιεῖς τοὺς ἀρχομένους. ὧν ἕκαστος λύει τὸν πάλαι κείμενον εἰκότως
ἀμείνων δήπου δεικνύμενος. 15. εἰ δὲ γεγραμ-
μένους λύεις λογισμοῦ πείθοντος, πῶς τοῦτο ἐν
ἀγράφοις ὀκνήσεις τῆς αὐτῆς ἐνούσης αἰτίας; ὁρῶμεν δήπου καὶ τοὺς ἰατροὺς τοῦτο ἔργον ἔχοντας
ἐκβάλλοντας τὰ τοῖς σώμασιν ἐνοικοῦντα κακὰ καὶ
μᾶλλόν γε εὐδοκιμοῦντας τοὺς τοῦτο δυνηθέντας

---

^a Cf. Victor, *Epit.* 48, Ambrose, *Ep.* 60. 8. The decree
itself does not survive, though the wording of *C. Th.* 3. 12. 3
(A.D. 396) implies previous legislation on the matter.

practice was widely current.[a] Nor was the long period of this currency of more influence than what you felt to be right. It is the duty of the governors of this city to observe such examples and not have such regard for the long reign of misdeeds as for the rightness of ending them.

13. But oh ! the protests I have made, Sire, to every one of them on the matter ! They could not complain that these were not right ; they simply refused to translate them into action, not that the imperial house might profit thereby, for it would not profit you at all, even if any money resulted from it ; anything not directed by right is sheer loss. So far from any such result accruing, one set of people did the work while the payment for it went to people I forbear to mention. 14. As I have said, I have often reproved them for neglecting such matters, but with no success. The sole alternative was to address you, Sire, and to assist the injured parties by means of your decree, for no one will dare mention custom to you or, if he does so, it will be in vain. For you bless your subjects by the defeat of the enemy [b] and by new laws, every one of which annuls one of long standing, and rightly too, since it is seen to be the better. 15. And if, at the dictate of reason, you annul laws in the statute book, you will certainly not shrink from it in the case of unwritten laws, if they are open to the same objection. Indeed we see doctors also, whose job it is, getting rid of the ailments that reside in the bodies of their patients, and those who can do so in the case of illnesses of

[b] The first of Theodosius' military successes against the Goths was celebrated in A.D. 379 ; cf. Vol. I, p. 502 n.

κατὰ τῶν πολὺν ἐν τοῖς σώμασι δυναστευσάντων χρόνον. καὶ νῦν ὅσῳπερ ἄν τις ἐτῶν μνημονεύσῃ πλειόνων, τοσούτῳ μείζων ἀπὸ τῆς θεραπείας ἡ δόξα. |

16. Μάλιστα μὲν οὖν καὶ τὰ κοινὰ τῶν οἰκοδο- F 47 μημάτων σὺν τῷ δικαίῳ τὴν ἀρχὴν | λαμβανέτω, R ii. 560 τὸν κέραμον. εἰ δ᾽ οὖν δεῖ τι καὶ ἀδικεῖσθαι περὶ ταῦτα τοὺς ὄνους, περὶ ταῦτά γε ἀδικείσθωσαν μόνα. νῦν δὲ τίς ἄν, ὦ Γῆ καὶ Ἥλιε καὶ θεοὶ πάντες καὶ δαίμονες, ἐνέγκαι τὴν παροινίαν[1]; τοῖς ἰδιώταις, ὦ βασιλεῦ, ταῦτα καὶ δέδοται καὶ δίδοται. καὶ οἱ μὲν προσιόντες αἰτοῦσι πύλην ὀνομάζοντες, ὁ μὲν τήν, ὁ δὲ τήν, ὁ δὲ τὴν τρίτην, τῷ ῥήματι τούτῳ τὰ δι᾽ αὐτῶν ἐλαυνόμενα λαβεῖν ἀξιοῦντες, οἱ δ᾽ ὥσπερ ἁπάντων τούτων δεσπόται ταχέως ἐχαρίσαντο τὰ ὀλίγα γράμματα. ἐν δὲ τοῖς ὀλίγοις τούτοις πολλοὶ μὲν ὄνοι, πολλοὶ δὲ ὀρεῖς, πολλαὶ δὲ κάμηλοι. ὧν ἐπιλαμβάνονταί τε[2] καὶ πρὸς τὸν χοῦν ἄγουσι παίοντες τοὺς ἐλαύνοντας οἰκέται τῶν λαμβανόντων τὴν χάριν πρὸς τοῖς ὑπηρέταις τῆς ἀρχῆς. 17. εἰ δ᾽ οὐδὲ στρατηγοῖς οἰκοδομουμένοις ταῦτα δοτέον, πῶς σοι, ⟨ὦ⟩[3] φροντίδες ὑπὲρ | ὧν αὐτοὶ κέκτηνται μόνων, ἄλλου R ii. 561 δὲ οὐδενός; ὦ κάκιστε ἀνδρῶν, ἐπριάμην μὲν ἐγὼ καὶ τρέφω καὶ ἰατρὸν ἐπὶ τὰ χωλεύοντα καλῶ καὶ μισθὸν τούτου τελῶ, βαδιεῖται δὲ καὶ χρήσεται τοῖς ποσὶν οὐχ ὑπὲρ | ἐμοῦ μᾶλλον ἢ σοῦ; τί τού- F 47 του παρανομώτερον; τί δεινότερον; τί δ᾽ ἄλλο τὸ τῶν τυράννων ἢ τοῦτο ἔστιν, ἀφελέσθαι τοῦτον, ἐκείνῳ δοῦναι, τὸν μὲν ἀδικῆσαι, τῷ δὲ δι᾽ αὐτοῦ

---

[1] παροινίαν Re. (mss.) : παρανομίαν F.
[2] τε F. : μὲν Re. (mss.).

long standing enjoy the greater reputation. So now, the more the years that are recalled for the practice, the greater the fame to be gained from the cure.

16. If possible, let our public constructions have their right and proper foundation,—of tiles. Anyway, if our asses must be improperly burdened with this, then let the improprieties be confined to this alone. But now, by all that is holy in heaven and earth, who can endure the enormities ? The service of our asses, Sire, has been and is being given to private individuals. They seek an audience, put in their request, and name the gate, one this, one that, another yet a third, and simply by this naming they claim the impressment of everything that passes through, and the authorities, just as though they own it all, are quick to oblige them with the brief missive. But in this brief missive are involved many asses, mules and camels. And the slaves of those who obtain this favour, as well as the governor's lackeys, get hold of them and direct them to the rubble, belabouring their drivers with blows. 17. But if this concession is not to be granted even to military officers for their building projects, how is it allowable to you, whose concern is simply and solely for what they personally possess ? You utter rascal, I buy animals, feed them, call the veterinary if they go lame and pay cash for it, but when they walk and use their legs, are they not to do so for me more than for you ? Nothing is more illegal than this, nothing more shocking. This is sheer tyranny, to take from A and give to B, to wrong the one and,

---

³ σοι, ᾧ Norman : σοι Re. text (MSS.) : σοι οὖ conj. Re. : οἷς F.

LIBANIUS

τούτου χαρίσασθαι καὶ τὴν ἑτέρου βλάβην ἄλλου ποιῆσαι κέρδος. καὶ νῦν εἰ βουληθείην τὰ τῶν τοῦτο[1] λαβόντων ὀνόματα πάντα διελθεῖν, πολύ τε τοῦτο ἔσται καὶ ἀποκναίσει.

18. Κωλύσεις οὖν, ἐροῦσι, τὸν ἄρχοντα διδόναι χάριν; πάνυ γε, τὴν ἄδικον. ὡς δὲ οὐκ ἔνι τὸ δίκαιον ἐν ταύτῃ παντί που δῆλον καὶ αὐτοῖς τοῖς τε διδοῦσι τοῖς τε λαμβάνουσιν. ἢ πόθεν ἐφοβοῦντο καὶ οὗτοι κἀκεῖνοι πρὸς τὰς ἀπειλὰς ἃς ἐποιούμην, ὅτι ταῦτα οὐκ ἀγνοήσεις ἀλλ᾽ ἔσται τις ὁ μηνύσων; 19. ἀλλ᾽ ὅμως ἐρεῖ τις ὅτι δεῖ τι τοῖς ἄρχουσιν ἐξεῖναι. ἐγὼ δὲ ἐρῶ ταὐτὸ πάλιν ὅτι τὸ δίκαιόν σφισι μόνον ποιεῖ τὴν ἐξουσίαν, ἃ δέ ἐστιν ἔξω τούτου κεκώλυται. καὶ τοῦτο τοίνυν, οὐ γὰρ ἐν τοῖς δικαίοις ἐστί, κεκωλυμένον ἐστίν. οἱ δὲ ὥσπερ ἀντὶ τῶν νόμων αὐτοὶ γεγενημένοι καὶ τὰς ἀκροπόλεις σὺν δορυφόροις κατειληφότες καὶ τῆς Ῥωμαίων πολιτείας κεκινημένης οὕτω μέμνηνται τῆς ἐξουσίας καὶ ταῦτα εἰδότες ὡς οὐδὲ σοί πάντα
R ii. 562 ἔξεστιν, ὦ | βασιλεῦ. αὐτὸ γὰρ τοῦτ᾽ ἔστι βασιλεία τὸ μὴ πάντα τοῖς ἐπ᾽ αὐτῆς ἐξεῖναι. εἰ δὲ τοῦτο εἰς ἐξουσίαν ἀνοί|σομεν, οὐδ᾽ εἰ μάχοιντο τοῖς F ⟨ νόμοις αἱ γνώσεις, αἰτιασόμεθα οὐδὲ ἐγκαλέσομεν οὐδ᾽ εἰ τοὺς ὑστέρους τῷ σχήματι πρὸ τῶν προτέρων ἄγοιεν. τὸ γὰρ δὴ ἄρχειν ἀκουσόμεθα πανταχοῦ.

20. Φίλοις οὖσιν ἔδει τι παρὰ τοῦ φιλοῦντος

---

[1] τοῦτο Re., F. : τούτων Gothofred. (mss.).

[a] Libanius reverts to the more classical views (*e.g.* of Dio Chrysostom, *Or.* 1. 48 R) upon the limitations of sovranty. In this he contradicts the view put forward by Themistius, that the emperor is νόμος ἔμψυχος.

74

by this very wrong, to oblige the other, and to make one man's loss another man's gain. And now, if I were to recite the complete list of names of the recipients of this favour, it will be a very long job and will wear me out.

18. " So you will stop governors granting favours, will you ? " they will exclaim. Yes, certainly—when it is wrong. And that there is no question of right in this is surely clear to everyone, even to the donors and to the recipients. Or how was it that both these parties were alarmed at my threats that you would not be kept in ignorance of this but that there would be someone to inform you ? 19. Still, it will be suggested that the governors should be allowed some authority. My rejoinder is, once again, that right alone is the basis of their authority, and anything beyond it is forbidden. And this practice too, for it certainly is not one that is right, has been forbidden. But these people act as though they were laws to themselves : they behave as though they have occupied our citadels with their body-guards and the government of the Roman empire has broken down, and then they make their appeal to authority, though they know full well that not even to you, Sire, is all permitted. For it is the very essence of monarchy that its holders are not omnipotent.[a] But if we make this concession to authority, we shall proffer no complaint even if their dictates are at loggerheads with the law, nor any charge even though they promote the socially inferior over the heads of their betters, for in every case we shall be told, " I'm the governor ! "

20. " A friend should be able to get something

εἶναι. καλῶς. ἔστιν ἄργυρός σοι καὶ ἐσθὴς καὶ χρυσίον καὶ ἀνδράποδα καὶ βοσκήματα καὶ γῆ. τούτων, εἴ τι βούλει, δὸς καί, εἰ βούλει γε, πάντα. τὸ γὰρ δὴ κωλῦον οὐκ ἔσται. τῶν ἐμῶν δὲ ἕτερον μὴ ποίει δεσπότην. ἀλλ' ὅταν τις ἐλθὼν ἢ παρακαθήμενος ἢ καὶ παρεστὼς μνημονεύῃ τῆς τοιαύτης χάριτος καὶ χοῦ καὶ ὄνων, λέγειν πρὸς αὐτὸν ὅτι, ὦ ἄριστε, ἐγώ σε πάνυ μὲν φιλῶ καὶ βουλοίμην ἄν σοι πολλήν τε καὶ καλὴν γενέσθαι τὴν οἰκίαν, ἃ δὲ οὐ καλὸν δοῦναι, μὴ δοῦναι καλόν. |

R ii. 563 21. οὔπω μέν τις τῶν τοῦτο πεπονθότων ἐπὶ τὰς τῶν κρατούντων εἰκόνας κατέφυγε, δεῖσαι δὲ ἄξιον μὴ γένηται. τί οὖν χρή σε ποιεῖν; σοὶ μὲν ἔστι χρυσίον, ὄνους δὲ ὁρῶμεν πωλουμένους καὶ πρίασθαι ῥᾴδιον. οὕτω σοι βέλτιον οἰκοδομεῖσθαι. τὸ δὲ σὺν ἀραῖς, τοῦτο δὴ τὸ νῦν, παραινῶ σοι φυγεῖν. οὕτως ἂν ἦσαν ἄρχοντες ὡς ἀληθῶς, τοὺς μὲν οὐκ ἐπιτρίβοντες, τοὺς δὲ νουθετοῦντες καὶ τοὺς μὲν τοῦ κακῶς πάσχειν τοὺς δὲ τοῦ ποιεῖν ῥυόμενοι. κέρδος δὲ δήπου καὶ τοῦτο τὸ κωλυθῆναι ποιῆσαι κακῶς. |

22. Ὡς δ' οὐκ ἐν ἐξουσίᾳ τοῖς ἄρχουσι τὰ τοι- F αῦτα διδόναι, δῆλον ἐξ ὧν ἤδη τις ὃς παρὰ βασιλέως τοῦτο εὕρηται γεγένηται. τί γὰρ ἐνοχλεῖν ἔδει τῷ βασιλεῖ δοθέντος ἂν δικαίως καὶ παρὰ τοῦ δικάζειν τεταγμένου; ἀλλ', οἶμαι, ληψόμενος μὲν παρ' ἐκείνων ᾔδει τὴν χάριν, οὐ μὴν μετά γε τῆς τοῦ δικαίου μερίδος. τοῦτο δὴ δεδιὼς καὶ

---

[a] Legislation to regularize this practice was passed in A.D. 386, *C. Th.* 9. 44. 1.

from a friend." True enough ! you have silver plate, clothing, gold, slaves, cattle and land. Give them any of these, if you like ; yes, and if you like, give them all. There will be nothing to stop you. But don't make another man master of what is mine. When someone comes and sits or stands by your side and suggests a favour like rubbish disposal and claiming asses, just tell him, " My dear sir, I am very fond of you : I would like you to have a big, fine house, but what it is not right to give, it is right not to give. 21. None of the victims has yet sought sanctuary at the statues of the emperors,[a] but we ought to have some qualms about the possibility of this happening. What should your course of action be, then ? You have money : I see that there are asses for sale, and it is easy enough to buy them. Your building is better done this way. My advice to you is not to let it become an object of execration as it is now." In this way they would act as real governors, without oppressing the one party, but advising the other, and they would save the one from suffering harm, the other from doing it. And there is indeed some advantage in being prevented from doing harm.

22. And that such grants are not in the governors' sphere of authority is clearly revealed by the fact that one applicant secured it from the emperor. For what need was there to trouble the emperor if it could have been granted legally by the appointed governor ? He knew, I think, that though he would get the concession from them too,[b] it would have been without legal sanction, and so, alarmed at this and

[b] Indicative of the encroachment of the imperial administration upon the sphere of municipal authority.

θαρρεῖν οὐκ ἔχων ὡς οὐκ ἔσονταί ποτε τῶν τοιούτων εὐθῦναι, βασιλέως ἧκε κομίζων ἐπιστολήν.
ἣν ἐπαινεῖν μὲν οὐκ ἔχω, φημὶ δὲ πίστιν εἶναι τοῦ
μὴ τοῖς ἄρχουσι τούτοις τὰ τοιαῦτα ἐξεῖναι.

R ii. 564   23. Καὶ τί δεινόν, φησίν, | ἐξιόντα τὸν ὄνον φορ-
τίον ἕτερον οὐκ ἔχοντα τοῦτο φέροντα ἐξιέναι;
τοῦτ᾽ αὐτό, φαίην ἄν, τὸ ἐξὸν μὴ φέρειν φορτίον
ἀναγκάζεσθαι φέρειν. ὥσπερ γὰρ ἀνθρώπῳ τοῦ μὴ
φέρειν τὸ φέρειν βαρύτερον, οὕτως, οἶμαι, καὶ ὄνῳ.
καὶ διὰ τοῦτ᾽ αὐτοῖς τῆς ἐξ ἀγρῶν εἰς ἄστυ πορεί-
ας ἢ ἐξ ἄστεος ἐκεῖσε κουφοτέρα, ὅτι ἐν ἐκείνῃ
μὲν φορτία, ἐν ταύτῃ δὲ τοῦτ᾽ οὐκ ἔστιν, ἀλλ᾽ ἐλευ-
θερία βάρους. ὁ δὲ γεωργὸς ἐφιζάνων τε οὐχ οὕτω
λυπηρὸς καὶ φειδοῖ πολλάκις ἀκολουθεῖ. 24. ἀλλ᾽
οἱ κυρίους αὐτοὺς οὗτοι ποιοῦντες ὧν ἐκ τῶν νόμων
οὔκ εἰσιν, ἀποστεροῦσι τοὺς ταλαιπώρους τούτους
ὄνους ταυτησὶ τῆς παραμυθίας τὰ νῶτα αὐτῶν ὑπο-
τιθέντες τοῖς ὑψηλοῖς τούτοις χώμασιν. ἐφ᾽ ἃ δεῖ
χωρεῖν τοὺς γεωργούς, ὠθοῦντας ἐνίους τὸν ὄνον. |
καὶ πολλάκις ἧς δεῖται μὲν ἐπὶ τὸν ἀγρὸν πύλης, F
αὕτη[1] πλησίον, δεῖ δὲ ἐκ μέσης τῆς πόλεως ἢ τέρ-
ματός γε ἑτέρου λαβόντα τοῦ χοῦ τὴν αὐτὴν ἐλ-
θόντα πάλιν ὁδὸν οὕτως ἅψασθαι τῆς πύλης. 25.
καὶ τὸ ἔτι δεινότερον, τῶν ἀδικουμένων αὐτῶν
ἀγὼν ὑπὲρ τοῦ φορτίου σπεύδοντος ἑκάστου πρὸ
ἄλλου τυχεῖν τοῦ φορτίου. καὶ τοῦτο, ὦ Ζεῦ καὶ
θεοί, πωλεῖται τὸ κακόν. καὶ ὁ μὲν οὖ τυρὸν ἔμελ-

---

[1] αὕτη Re., F. : αὐτὴ Gothofred. (MSS.).

---

[a] Reiske points out that this passage proves that the
speech was delivered in Antioch. Thence it was presumably
to be despatched to court. The emperor here mentioned is
certainly not Theodosius, but probably Valens.

with no assurance that it would not be a matter for future investigation, he turned up here with a letter of permission from the emperor.[a] I cannot commend it, but I contend that it is evidence that such things are not permitted to the governors here.

23. " And what harm is done," I am asked, " if an ass that is leaving town with no other load should leave with this one ? " Just this, that it is forced to carry a load when it need not. Acting as porter is a heavier job for a man than not doing so. The case is the same, I think, for an ass, too. And because of this the journey from town to the farm is lighter work than that from the farm to town : on the way there, they are loaded, on the way back, they are not, but they enjoy freedom from burden. And if the farmer rides the way home, he is not such a heavy burden, and often he spares it by walking behind. 24. But these gentry who make themselves masters of what is not legally theirs rob these wretched beasts of this bit of respite by piling their backs high with masses of rubble. And the farmers must go and get it, some of them prodding their asses on. Often the gate through which he needs to pass to reach his farm is close by, but he has to collect his load from the middle of the city or right from the other end of it, and retrace his steps before getting to the gate.[b] 25. Worse still, there is competition among the victims themselves as each one struggles to get a load before some one else. And, by the powers above ! this sinful business becomes a matter of buying and selling. One offers the money that was to be the price of his cheese and

[b] The imposition is all the greater considering the extent of the city area of Antioch, described in *Or.* 11 (*Antiochikos*).

λεν ἕξειν ἀργυρίου, τοῦτο δοὺς ἀπῆλθεν, ὁ δ' οὐ
δυνηθεὶς ἔστηκε κλάων, ἐλεεῖ δὲ οὐδείς. καίτοι τί
τούτων ἐλεεινότερον οἷς ἐκ τῆς ἀπορίας ἡ βραδυ-
R ii. 565 τής; ὧν οἱ μὲν τοῦ χοῦ μετέλαβον | ⟨δείλης⟩,[1] οἱ
δ' ἡλίου μέλλοντος δύσεσθαι, οἱ δὲ δεδυκότος, οὓς
εἶναι χρῆν οἴκοι πρὶν ἥκειν μεσημβρίαν. 26. νυκτὸς τοίνυν ἐν ὁδῷ καταλαβούσης τοὺς ταῦτα πεπον-
θότας τί τούτοις ἢ πόθεν ἢ συμφορᾶς ἴαμα μήτ'
εἰς πανδοκεῖον αὐτοὺς εἰσάγοντος μηδενὸς βαλλαν-
τίου, πῶς γὰρ τοῦ γε οὐκ ὄντος; τήν τε ἐν νυκτὶ
πορείαν σφαλερὰν τῶν κακούργων ποιούντων τροφῆς τε οὐδαμόθεν φαινομένης οὔτ' αὐτοῖς οὔτε τοῖς
ὄνοις. καὶ νόσους τοίνυν καὶ θανάτους εἰκὸς ἐκ
τοῦ τοιούτου γεγενῆσθαι πολλάκις, εἰ δὲ καὶ μὴ
ταῦτα, λύπην γε[2] καὶ δάκρυα τούτων τε αὐτῶν καὶ
τῶν τούτοις οἰκείων ἐν τῷ μὴ ἔχειν ἀλλήλους ὀδυ-
ρομένων. 27. καίτοι ταῦτα | δεινὰ μέν, εἰ καὶ F
παρὰ τῶν πολεμίων γίγνοιτο, δεινότερα δέ, ὅταν
ὑπὸ τῶν ἐπὶ σωτηρίᾳ τε καὶ βοηθείᾳ παρ' ὑμῶν
πεμπομένων. καὶ πληγαὶ δέ, ὦ βασιλεῦ, γίγνονται παρὰ τῶν τούτοις ἐφεστηκότων στρατιωτῶν.
καὶ ἡ μὲν πρόφασις· οὐκ ὀξέως ἅπαντα ποιεῖς,
ἀλλ' ὕπτιος εἶ καὶ βραδύς, τὸ δ' ἀληθές· οὐκ ἔστιν
ἀργύριόν σοι οὐδὲ ἔνι μοί τι παρὰ σοῦ λαβεῖν.
δίδου τοίνυν ἀτυχίας δίκην. 28. καὶ οἷς μὲν ἔστιν,
ὦ βασιλεῦ, σακκία σῖτον ἢ κριθὰς ἤ τι τοιοῦτον
ἀγρόθεν ἐνηνοχόσιν, ἧττον τὸ κακόν· νῦν δὲ καὶ
τοῖς χιλὸν κεκομικόσιν ἴση τοῦ ταῦτα ὑπηρετεῖν

---

[1] δείλης supplied after μὲν Re., after μετέλαβον F.
[2] γε conj. Re., F. : τε Re. text (mss.).

[a] Banditry was only too common in rural areas, cf. their
activities after the Riot of the Statues, Or. 19. 58, 23. 18.

so gets away : another can offer nothing and stands there in tears, but no one has any pity for him. Yet there is nothing more pitiable than those whose delay is caused by their poverty. They get their load of rubble in late afternoon, or just before sunset, or after sunset, though they should have been home before midday. 26. So night overtakes these poor wretches on their way home, and what remedy is there for their plight, and where can it come from, for no purse secures them entry into an inn—how can it, when they have none ?—and criminals make travel by night dangerous,[a] and there is nothing to feed either their asses or themselves ? The natural consequences of all this are often illness and death, or at least sorrow and tears both on their part and on that of their relatives, as they lament their loss of each other. 27. This would be bad enough if it happened at the hands of our foes, but it is far worse when it is caused by those whom you send for their succour and protection. Floggings also occur, Sire, inflicted by the soldiery set to supervise them, the excuse being, " You are not doing things at the double. You are a slowcoach ! " But the real reason is, " You've got no money and I can get nothing out of you. So pay for your misfortune ! "[b] 28. Those who possess sacks, Sire, after carrying wheat or barley or the like from their farms, find their plight easier. But the carriers of fodder are equally compelled to perform these

Bandits were held to be in league with innkeepers, Or. 33. 40 ; 45. 6. The most notorious example of a bandit community was that of Marathocupreni, Or. 48. 36, Amm. Marc. 28. 2. 13.

[b] Libanius' prejudice against the " soldiery " is here obvious, but not unjustified, cf. Or. 27. 14.

LIBANIUS

ἀνάγκη, σακκίων δὲ οὐκ ὄντων τὸ τοῦ γεωργοῦντος
ἱμάτιον ἀντ᾽ ἐκείνου γίγνεται χεῖρον αὐτῷ καθ-
ιστάμενον, τό τε σαπρὸν τό τε οὐ σαπρόν. καίτοι
πῶς ἂν ταύτην ἐνέγκαι γεωργὸς τὴν ζημίαν, ᾧ μὴ
ἔστιν ἕτερον αἰτῆσαι παρὰ τῆς γυναικός, ᾧ τὰ
παιδία γυμνά; 29. ἐκ μὲν οὖν τοῦ τοῦτον τὸν
τρόπον ἐκφορεῖσθαί τι τοῦ χοῦ γηράσκει μὲν τῷ
ἀνθρώπῳ θᾶττον ἢ δεῖ θοιμάτιον, μένει δὲ ὅμως
R ii. 566 αὐτῷ. αἱ δὲ τῶν πυλωρῶν ἁρπαγαί, μικρὸν | εἰ-
πεῖν χαλινοὺς ὄνων καὶ ἱμάντας ἑτέρους καὶ σχοινία
καὶ ἄρτους κεκρυμμένους ἰχνευομένους, ἀλλ᾽ εἰ μὴ
καὶ τὸν χιτῶνα αὐτὸν προσαφέλοιτο, φιλανθρωπότερος ἀξιοῖ νομίζεσθαι. περὶ μὲν γὰρ τὸν εἰσ-
ιόντα ταῦτα ποιοῦσιν ὡς, εἰ φέρων ὀφθείη χοῦν,
ἀποδώσοντες, ἀναστρέφοντος | δὲ οἱ μὲν ἑαυτοὺς F
ἠφάνισαν, ὁ δ᾽ οἰμώξας καὶ πλήξας τῇ χειρὶ τὸ
μέτωπον ἀπῆλθε. καὶ ἔστι τοῖς ἀθλίοις ἐν εἰρήνῃ
πόλεμος χρῄζουσι μὲν τῆς πόλεως, ἀκούουσι δὲ
παρὰ τῶν ἔργων ὅτι χρὴ φεύγειν τὴν πόλιν.
30. Τοῦτο δὲ τὸ χαλεπόν, ὦ βασιλεῦ, γίγνεται
χαλεπώτερον προσθήκην ὑπὸ τοῦ καιροῦ λαβὸν ἐπὶ
τὸν χειμῶνα παρὰ τῶν ἀρχόντων ἐκταθέν. ὃς ἴστη
πρότερον ἐπελθὼν τοῦτο τὸ ἀδίκημα. ἀλλὰ νῦν
ψῦχος μὲν καὶ πηλὸς καὶ ὄμβρος, πολὺ τούτων
ἕκαστον, ἀναπνοὴ δὲ οὐδαμόθεν. οὐδὲ ἔστι σπον-
δῶν τυχεῖν, ἀλλὰ λέγεται μὲν ὑπὸ τῶν ὁρώντων
τοὺς πόνους[1] ὅτι ταῦτα οὐ κατὰ τὴν πολιτείαν, ἐκ-
φέρεται δὲ ὅμως ὁ χοῦς, μᾶλλον δὲ ὁ πηλός, ἔστι
δ᾽ οὗ καὶ βόρβορος. ὑφ᾽ ὧν ἀμφοτέρων ἄχρηστα

---

[1] πόνους F. (I) : ὄνους Re. (CAP).

services, and they have no sacks ; so the peasant's cloak does instead and deteriorates in consequence, whether it was tattered or not. But how can a peasant sustain this loss when he cannot ask his wife for another and his children run naked ? 29. As a result of this manner of disposing of rubble, the fellow's cloak wears out more quickly than it should, but for all that he still keeps it. As for the rapacity of the gate keepers, their ferreting out of donkey bridles, other straps and ropes and hidden loaves is hardly worth the mention [a] : if they do not rob the fellow of his very jerkin, they can claim to be thought generous ! For this is their method of dealing with him when he enters town : he will get it back, they say, if they see him coming out with his load of rubble, but when he does return, they are nowhere to be seen, and so he beats his brow in lamentation and departs. And war is waged in peace time against the poor devils who need the city but are schooled by events to avoid it.

30. This oppression, Sire, becomes the more oppressive since the season adds to it because the governors extend it into the winter. In times past the onset of winter used to put a stop to this injustice, but now there is cold, mud and rain—all in plenty—and no respite at all. No truce is made. The observers of the impositions say that the practice is unconstitutional, but still the export of rubble, or rather of mud, and at times even of muck, goes on. And in consequence of this combination, the corn

[a] In view of the continuing famine, the *Comes* Icarius proceeded to ration bread as well as to impose a price edict, *cf. Or.* 1. 205 ff. The ration that could be taken out of town was two loaves per man, *Or.* 27. 14.

τοῖς σιτηγοῦσι τὰ σακκία, κἂν ἐμβαλὼν εἰς οὕτω
διακείμενα σῖτον ἄγῃς διέφθειρας. τῆς δ᾽ ἐντεῦθεν
βλάβης ἐπὶ τὸν ἄρτον ἐρχομένης εἰς τὴν τοῦ σίτου
τιμὴν ὁ κομίσας ἐζημίωται. 31. ταυτὶ δὲ τὰ πάθη
καὶ τῇ πόλει τὴν περὶ τὴν τροφὴν συμφορὰν ἐπ-
έτεινε, καὶ τέταρτον προσετέθη κακόν. καὶ νῦν
ἀριθμοῦμεν τὰ τῶν μυῶν ἔθνη, τοὺς ὄφεις, τὰς ἀκ-
ρίδας, τὸν χοῦν. παιδεύονται γὰρ οἷς ζημιοῦνται
φεύγειν ὥσπερ τι βάραθρον τήνδε τὴν πόλιν καὶ
ζητεῖν οὗ ταῦτα οὐ πείσονται. ὥστε οἷς οὐ πᾶσα |
R ii. 567 ἀνάγκη δεῦρ᾽ ἰέναι, βαδίζουσιν ἄλλοσε παραινοῦν-
τες οἷς συντυγχάνοιεν ἀναστρέφειν. |

32. Καὶ τῆς περὶ ταῦτα ἐνδείας αἰτιάσαιτο μὲν F
ἄν τις καὶ ἄλλο τι, μέμψαιτο δ᾽ ἂν εἰκότως καὶ τὰς
τῶν ἀρχόντων χάριτας. παρ᾽ ὧν εἰ μὴ λάβοις
δίκην, δόξεις οὐ σφόδρα κήδεσθαι τῶν πόλεων, εἰ
ἃς ὅπλοις σώζεις ἐκδίδως ἀρχόντων κακίᾳ. οἷς
οὐκ ἂν μὲν ἦν λόγος οὐδ᾽ εἰ τοῖς πενεστέροις ταῦτα
ἐχαρίζοντο, ἥττων[1] δ᾽ ἂν ἦν ἡ κατηγορία τῆς τῶν[2]
χάριν λαμβανόντων ἐνδείας ἀφαιρούσης τι τοῦ μίσους.[3] νῦν δὲ ἐκείνους μὲν οὐδ᾽ ἴσασιν, ἀλλ᾽ ἐκ
τῶν ὄντων αὐτοῖς τῶν ὀλίγων ἐπανορθοῦσι τὰς οἰκίας, οἷς δὲ πάντα πολλὰ καὶ γέλως τὰ τοῦ Γύγου,
τούτοις οὕτω συνοικοδομοῦσιν, οἷς μυρίαι μὲν κάμηλοι, πολλοὶ δὲ ὀρεῖς καὶ ζεύγη, πλῆθος δὲ ἵππων
ταῖς τῶν ἱπποκόμων χερσὶ κοσμουμένων, οἳ δι-

---

[1] ἥττων Re., F. : ἧττον Gothofred. (mss.).
[2] τῶν ⟨τὴν⟩ Re., F.
[3] μίσους Re. (API) : μύσους F. (C).

---

[a] In sharp contrast with the praises of the amenities of
Antioch recited in *Or.* 11.
[b] King of Lydia, ancestor of Croesus, proverbially wealthy,

carriers' sacks become useless : if you put corn in
them in this condition, and bring it in, it goes bad.
The resulting damage affects the bread and the
carrier suffers loss in the price of his corn. 31. These
troubles also intensify the city's difficulties with the
food supply, but there is a fourth source of nuisance,
too. Now we catalogue the hordes of flies, the
snakes, the locusts and the rubble. People are
schooled by their afflictions to avoid this city as
though it were the pit, and to seek out a place where
they will not suffer so.[a] So those who are not absolutely obliged to come here go elsewhere and warn
any they meet to turn back.

32. And though various other complaints might
be made about the failings in this, favours granted
by the governors can be regarded with justified disapproval. Unless you punish them, it will be thought
that you are not greatly concerned for the cities, if
you protect them by force of arms and yet expose
them to the wickedness of governors. They would
not have a leg to stand on even if they distributed
these favours to the poorer classes, but the accusation would be less pointed, since the poverty of the
recipients of a favour detracts somewhat from its
odium. As it is, they simply ignore them. They
repair their houses from their own small possessions,
while those who have everything in plenty and who
would make mock of the wealth of Gyges [b] have the
governors providing such assistance for their building, though they have camels innumerable, mules
and carts in plenty, and numbers of horses that are
titivated at the hands of their grooms. These would

cf. Herod. 1. 8 ff. The target for Libanius' invective here
is once more the *honorati*.

καιότερον ἂν τοῖς δεσπόταις τὰ τοιαῦτα ὑπούργουν
ἢ οἱ μικρὸν τῶν τεθνεώτων διαφέροντες ὄνοι. 33.
νῦν δ᾽ ἐκεῖνα μὲν ἐν τρυφῇ τε καὶ φάτναις καὶ ὕβρει
καὶ θεραπείᾳ, οἷς δ᾽ ἀπὸ τῶν ὄνων ὁ βίος, τούτοις
ὃ μόνον ἔστιν αὐτοῖς ἀπόλλυται. ἡμεῖς δὲ τοῖς
αὐτοῖς ὀφθαλμοῖς ὁρῶντες τήν τε ἐν τούτοις ταλαι-
πωρίαν τήν τε ἐν ἐκείνοις ἀσέλγειαν σχετλιάζομεν
καὶ λέγοντες ἃ τοὺς ἀλγοῦντας εἰκὸς ληροῦμεν. ὁ
γὰρ προσέξων οὐκ ἔστιν οὐδὲ ὁ πεισόμενος. ἀλλὰ
R ii. 568 παρὰ σοῦ, | φιλανθρωπότατε βασιλεῦ, ταῦτα ἡμῖν
γενέσθω καὶ | φαίνου κηδόμενος μὴ τῶν πόλεων F 48
μόνον ἀλλὰ καὶ τῶν ἀγρῶν, μᾶλλον δὲ τῶν ἀγρῶν
ἢ τῶν πόλεων πλέον. ἐκεῖνοι γὰρ τούτων ὁ θεμέ-
λιος. 34. καὶ φαίη τις ἂν ἐπὶ τῶν ἀγρῶν ἐστη-
κέναι τὰς πόλεις κἀκείνους εἶναι κρηπῖδα ταύταις,
παρ᾽ ὧν πυροί, κριθαί, βότρυες,[1] οἶνος, ἔλαιον,
τροφὴ μὲν ἀνθρώποις, τροφὴ δὲ τοῖς ἄλλοις ζῴοις.
εἰ δὲ μὴ βόες ἦσαν μηδ᾽ ἄροτρον μηδὲ σπέρματα
μηδὲ φυτὰ μηδὲ ἀγέλαι βοσκημάτων, οὐδ᾽ ἂν ἐγέ-
νοντο τὴν ἀρχὴν πόλεις. καὶ γενόμεναι δὲ τῆς
ἐκείνων ἐξήρτηνται τύχης, καὶ τὸ εὖ τε καὶ χεῖρον
αὐταῖς πράττειν[2] ἐκεῖθεν ἔστι. 35. καὶ τὴν παροῦσαν ταύτην ἀκαιρίαν τὴν κοινὴν ὁ κείνων τόκος
ἀδικηθεὶς ἔτεκε. καὶ νῦν ἐν εὐχαῖς αἱ πόλεις ἅπα-
σαι μείζονές τε καὶ ἐλάττονες εὐμενῶν τὴν γῆν
ἀπολαῦσαι τῶν Ὡρῶν. ἣν δεομένην τῶν ἐργασο-
μένων ἴσμεν, οὓς ἅπαντας τοῦ Κελεοῦ μαθητὰς χρὴ
νομίζειν εἶναι. ὅστις οὖν τοῖς ἐκείνων πολεμεῖ

---

[1] βότρυες F. : βότρυς τε mss., Re. (who would omit τε):
βότρυς Macarius.
[2] αὐταῖς πράττειν Re. (mss.) : πράττειν αὐταῖς F.

---

[a] Celeus, king of Eleusis, welcomed Demeter exhausted

86

more properly provide such services for their masters than donkeys that are practically dying on their feet. 33. But those beasts live on the fat of the land in their mangers, arrogant and well-tended, while those who make a living from their donkeys lose the only thing they have. And we, with one and the same glance, see misery here and rapacity there and complain, but in expressing our natural feeling of dismay, we are wasting our time, for there is none who will pay any heed or yet believe us. But let us get it from you, your most kind Majesty : show your concern not just for the cities, but for the countryside too, or rather for the countryside in preference to the cities—for the country is the basis on which they rest. 34. One can assert that cities are founded on the country and that this is their firm footing, providing them with wheat, barley, grapes, wine, oil and the nourishment of man and other living beings. Unless oxen, ploughs, seed, plants and herds of cattle existed, cities would not have come into being at all. And, once in existence, they have depended upon the fortunes of the countryside, and the good and ill that they experience arise therefrom. 35. And the harm wrought to its offspring has given rise to the present distemper that affects all alike. Now in all cities, great and small, they pray that the land should enjoy the blessing of the Seasons. We know that it needs men to work it, and we should regard them all and every one as disciples of Celeus.[a] Any foe to their well-being—and in this even their

after her wandering in search of Persephone, Hom. *Hymn. Dem.* 96 ff. In return she instructed him in her mysteries, *ibid.* 475 ff., and he became, along with Triptolemus, a patron of agriculture.

πράγμασιν, ἐν οἷς εἶναι συμβαίνει καὶ τοὺς ὄνους,
οὗτος τῇ γῇ πολεμεῖ, ὅστις δὲ τῇ γῇ, οὗτος καὶ
ταῖς πόλεσι καί, νὴ Δία γε, καὶ τοῖς πλέουσιν αὐτοῖς, ἐκεῖ κἀκείνοις δεῖ τῶν παρὰ ταύτης. καὶ γὰρ
εἰ τὸ πλείω τὰ ὄντα ποιεῖν ἀπὸ τῆς θαλάττης αὐ-
τοῖς, ἀλλ' αὐτό γε τὸ δύνασθαι ζῆν ἀπὸ τῆς γῆς. |

36. Καὶ σοὶ δὲ ὁ φόρος ἐκεῖθεν, ὦ βασιλεῦ. δια- F 48
λέγῃ μὲν γὰρ περὶ αὐτοῦ ταῖς πόλεσιν ἐν τοῖς γράμμασι, ταῖς δὲ ἐκεῖθεν τὸ δοῦναι. ὅστις τε οὖν βοη-
θεῖ τοῖς γεωργοῖς, οὗτος τὰ σὰ συνέχει, καὶ ὅστις
ἐπηρεάζει, περὶ τὰ σὰ κακὸς γίνεται. ταύτην τε
R ii. 569 οὖν τὴν ἐπήρειαν ἐπισχετέον σοι, | βασιλεῦ, νόμῳ
καὶ τιμωρίᾳ καὶ γράμμασι, καὶ τῇ περὶ ὧν νῦν
ἀκούεις σπουδῇ παρακλητέον ἅπαντας εἰς τοὺς ὑπὲρ
τῶν γεωργῶν λόγους. 37. οἶμαι δέ σοι προσήκειν
μὴ νομίζειν ἱκανὸν εἰ μηδὲν ἔτι τοιοῦτον ἔσται,
ἀλλὰ καὶ δίκην ἐθελῆσαι λαβεῖν. δίκη δὲ πρέπουσα
τοὺς μὲν ἀρχιτέκτονας ὅσα τε χώματα καὶ ὅσων
ἂν μετετέθη χρημάτων εἰπεῖν, ταυτὶ δὲ τὰ χρήματα
γενέσθαι σοι μέρος τῆς ὑπὲρ τῶν ὅλων δαπάνης,
τοὺς δὲ τιθέντας ἀμφοτέρους εἶναι, τούς τε δόντας
τὴν χάριν τούς τε λαβόντας.

asses are included—is foe to the land, and the foe to the land is foe to the cities also, and indeed to mariners as well, for they too need the produce of the land. They may get from the sea increase of their store of goods, but the very means of life comes from the land.

36. And you too, Sire, obtain tribute from it. In your rescripts you hold converse with the cities about it, and their payment of it comes from the land. So whoever assists the peasantry supports you, and ill-treatment of them is disloyal to you. So you must put a stop to this ill-treatment, Sire, by law, punishment and edicts, and in your enthusiasm for the matter under discussion, you must encourage all to speak up for the peasants. 37. In my opinion, you should not regard it as sufficient that there should be no repetition, but you should also be ready to impose punishment. A suitable method would be for the architects to declare the quantity of rubble to be disposed of and the cost of such disposal, and for you to receive this sum to cover part of the expenses of government, and for its contributors to be both the donors and the recipients of the favour.

ORATION 30

TO THE
EMPEROR THEODOSIUS,
FOR THE TEMPLES

INTRODUCTION

THE *Pro Templis* stands as the most positive affirmation of Libanius' position in the religious controversies which follow the reign of Julian. His other statements in these years had been, almost without exception, nostalgic and backward-looking, vindications of either Julian or himself (as in the *Epitaphios* and the *Autobiography*), complaints and criticisms of contemporary society (as in *Oration* 2), or attempts to preserve the purity and exclusiveness associated with the festivals of paganism (as in *Oration* 10). In the present speech, however, he looks ahead, and presents on behalf of the institutions of his religion more urgent suggestions and demands which are destined ultimately for the emperor's ear. He demands for persecuted pagans toleration and freedom to worship inside the limits allowed by law, and concludes his demand for the maintenance of law and order with a minatory tone, unusual for the pagan propagandist of his day, emphasizing that, if the protection of the law is not to be available to his fellows, it must be expected that they will themselves take measures for their own protection. Conflicting attitudes are therefore visible here—the pagan respect for law, the ideal of *philanthropia*, which appears in contemporary pleas for toleration, and the final exasperation of persecuted pagans, such as erupts into action in the last defence of the Serapeum.

The oration begins with a summary of the history of religion until the reign of Constantine, who, despite his disastrous religious legislation, set strict legal limits upon the interference to which the institutions of paganism were to be subjected (§§ 4-7). A steady erosion of this protection in matters of religion followed thereafter, chiefly inspired by the illegal activities of predatory monks and their " pastor " in attacking rustic shrines (§§ 8-11). All this is the negation of law, contrary to imperial edict and detrimental to the social order, with ecclesiastical courts claiming summary jurisdiction, and Christian bigots preaching charity and yet ruining the temples and the amenities of the cities along with them (§§ 12-23). The rule of law must be paramount, and forcible conversion eschewed. The monopoly of the benefits which Christians claim to confer on mankind is false, since even now the continuance of sacrifice, both in Rome and in Alexandria, promotes the safety of empire. This was amply revealed by the fate of the family of Constantine and the fame of Julian (§§ 24-37). In any case the destruction of temples, which are integral to both urban and rustic society, and which, incidentally, belong to the emperor, is sheer stupidity. At least preserve them as works of art and put them to other uses (§§ 38-43). High officials at court have been guilty of conspiring to deceive the emperor for their suppression, and have illegally worked hand in glove with the ravaging monks, inducing them to claim the emperor as their supporter. In the face of such unsanctioned aggression, whereby Christians continue to oppress the institutions of paganism, the persecuted, in default of the legal protection to which they are entitled, have no other recourse than to meet force with force (§§ 44 ff.).

Various commentators have been tempted to interpret religious legislation of the Theodosian age as directly affected by the arguments of this oration, with the result that its form and dating have long been a matter of debate. The form of the address, as Petit, following earlier precedent, has fully shown,[a] is that of the " open letter," carefully restricted in circulation and presented to a very select audience. This was the practice in operation at Athens, with its private auditoria (Eunapius, *V.S.* 483), and consistently used by Libanius in Antioch (*e.g. Or.* 2. 25). The precautions taken in the case of such controversial orations as this are outlined in *Ep.* 283, where the funeral oration upon his uncle Phasganius is delivered to an audience of no more than four. Even so, such restricted circulation was utilitarian in purpose, since it directed propaganda to the right quarters at court in safety and with effectiveness, the orator's friends there acting as intermediaries (*cf. Or.* 2. 70 ff.). Hence the unexpected combination of social criticism and violent personal abuse here.

For this oration, the *terminus post quem* is A.D. 381, when Flavianus, mentioned as bishop of Antioch in the text (§ 15), was appointed, and when *Oration* 2 was composed (*cf. Or.* 1. 208). There he had plumed himself (*Or.* 2. 8) upon his consistent refusal of an honorary office, specifically mentioning the quaestor-

[a] " Recherches sur la publication et la diffusion des discours de Libanius" (*Historia*, v [1956], pp. 479-509).

ship granted by Julian. The implication is that, at
the time of composing that speech, he had received
no such recognition from Theodosius. The extreme
terminus ante quem is given as A.D. 391 by its reference to the continued existence of the Serapeum
(§ 44) ; so that the composition must antedate the
destruction of the temple in that year. A more
precise definition may be seen in the reference at the
beginning of the speech to the honorary office granted
him by Theodosius, and accepted by him. This is
the honorary prefecture referred to by Eunapius
(*V.S.* 496), who yet manages to confuse the issue
by stating that it was offered by Julian and refused
by Libanius. Libanius' acknowledgement, however,
is reproduced in almost identical terms in the proem
to the *De Vinctis* (*Or.* 45), which may be dated with
precision to A.D. 386. Such considerations rule out
Seeck's attempt to place the speech to the winter of
A.D. 388/9,[a] and some other explanation must be
given for the passage in the *Autobiography* (*Or.* 1.
257-258) which he identifies as Libanius' reference to
the grant of this honorary office. The similar dat-
ings given by Gothofredus,[b] Sievers [c] and Van Loy [d]
are also rendered invalid. Seeck's further suggestion
that the rescript of September A.D. 390 (*C. Th.* 16.
3. 1) was in direct response to the arguments given
in this speech must also fall.

Tillemont and Foerster, however, though for
different reasons, both date the speech to A.D. 384.
Tillemont rejects outright Gothofredus' identifica-

[a] *Geschichte des Untergangs der antiken Welt*, v, pp.
527 ff. [b] *Opera iuridica minora*, Leiden, 1733, pp. 469 ff.
[c] *Das Leben des Libanius*, Berlin, 1868 (repr. 1969), p.
192. [d] *Byzantion*, viii (1933), pp. 17 ff.

tion of the high official pilloried in this oration
(§§ 46 ff.) with Cynegius (ppO, A.D. 384–388) : and
Foerster [a] cannot bring himself to believe that the
violent condemnations of this oration could possibly
be applied to Cynegius in his lifetime, in view of the
otherwise favourable notices which the prefect receives in other orations. This argument, it must be
admitted, takes little account of the practice of
Libanius in his treatment of other high officials,
where he shows himself to be no respecter of persons,
nor yet of his habits in the publication of his more
controversial orations. Both agree in identifying the
pagan consul of § 53 with Richomer, and see in the
narrative of *Oration* 1. 219—where honours proffered
by both consul and emperor are mentioned—the occasion for the delivery of this oration. However, the
problems connected with the honorary prefecture
are explained by neither, the one denying the grant
altogether, the other merely ignoring it, despite the
indications here and in *Oration* 45. Both identify the
law which currently bans pagan sacrifice with *C. Th.*
16. 10. 7 of A.D. 381.

The most recent examination of the problem has
been conducted by Petit,[b] and he has succeeded in
explaining the difficulties already mentioned and
placing the oration in its social and historical context.
For him, the honours of A.D. 384 proffered by both
consul and emperor (*Or.* 1. 219) are the nomination
to the prefecture and its acceptance, so that the
speech must occur after that. The episode of *Or.* 1.
258 is concerned not with the grant of the prefecture

[a] Foerster, *Libanius*, vol. III, pp. 80-81.
[b] Petit, " Sur la date du ' Pro Templis,' " *Byzantion*, xxi,
pp. 293 ff.

but with the permission to transfer during Libanius' own lifetime his property to his illegitimate son Cimon.[a] The misguided prefect is to be identified with Cynegius, currently in office, the pagan consul with Eutropius (iv, Seeck ; cos. A.D. 387 and designate in late 386), and the ban on pagan sacrifices is that of *C. Th.* 16. 10. 9 of A.D. 385. From these and other indications the oration is to be allocated to A.D. 386, which, significantly enough, is the date of the *De Vinctis*, with its almost identical introduction.[b]

The oration thus falls into context as far as concerns both the career of Libanius and the development of imperial policy in social and religious affairs. Libanius presents his arguments as a propagandist of paganism from the social elevation of *honoratus*, a rank which he himself says he has held for some little time. The activities of Cynegius, criticized here and praised elsewhere, were at first concerned with curial recruitment, and only after the law of A.D. 385 does he appear to have diverged to the suppression of pagan temples, including that at Apamea (*cf.* Theodoret, *H.E.* 5. 21. 1), in this exceeding the mandate allowed him by the law. At the time of the composition of the *Pro Templis* Cynegius had moved to Egypt but had not yet extended his religious excesses to Alexandria (§§ 35 f.). The oration is therefore a protest against the recent religious purges in the

[a] Petit's recognition of this incident as prompted by Libanius' request for the property transfer is in no way vitiated by his misinterpretation of some of the manœuvres which ensured its success (*cf.* Libanius, *Autobiography*, ed. Norman, p. 224).

[b] A similar identity of treatment may be observed in passages composed about the same time upon the same topic in *Or.* 1. 171 and *Or.* 24. 13 f. (*cf.* Vol. I, p. 501, note *c*).

diocese of the East and a warning against extending a similar reign of terror to the pagan cults of Egypt. At the same time Theodosius is alerted to the damage, both social and economic, caused by this illegitimate encroachment upon the limits set by imperial decree. The urgency of tone in this speech indicates that he is conducting here a desperate, last-ditch defence of the institutions of his religion.

Manuscripts and Bibliography

Manuscripts which antedate the 17th century number thirteen, including the eight collections utilized by Foerster (CAPUVIBM). Of these, A shows a lacuna of one folium (from § 19 ὡς ἔχει to § 28 δέ σοι), —a lacuna which is reproduced both in the *editio princeps* of Gothofredus (Geneva, 1634), in his *Opera Juridica Minora* (Leiden, 1733) and in Reiske's edition (Altenburg, 1791). It reappears also in Orelli's edition of 1828, a work which also contains John Chrysostom's *In Eutropium* and (pseudo-)Themistius, *Or.* XII (*De Religionibus*). Mai (*Fronto* (ed. 2), Rome, 1823) first supplied the missing text, the oration being printed in its entirety for the first time by L. de Sinner (*Novus SS. Graecorum saec. iv delectus*, Paris, 1842, pp. 227 ff.). The oration was translated into English by Nathaniel Lardner (in *Arguments of Celsus etc. against the Christians* by Thomas Taylor (the Platonist), London, 1830) ; into French by Monnier (*cf.* Vol. I, p. lvii), and by Van Loy (*Byzantion*, viii (1933), pp. 19 ff.). Excerpts from the speech appear in Thomas Magister, Planudes and Macarius.

Comment upon the oration appears in Gothofredus (*loc. cit.*), Tillemont (*Histoire des empereurs*, V², note

ORATION XXX

16 on Theodosius I), Seeck, Foerster (*loc. cit.*), Pack, and—most recently and successfully—by Paul Petit, " Sur la date du ' Pro Templis,' " *Byzantion*, xxi, pp. 293 ff. A running commentary is given by Van Loy (*Byzantion*, viii (1933), pp. 389 ff.).

XXX

ΠΡΟΣ ΘΕΟΔΟΣΙΟΝ ΤΟΝ ΒΑΣΙΛΕΑ
ΥΠΕΡ ΤΩΝ ΙΕΡΩΝ

R ii. 155   1. Ἐπὶ πολλῶν πρότερον συμβουλῶν, ὦ βασι- F
λεῦ, δόξας σοι τοῦ προσήκοντος τετυχηκέναι καὶ
τῶν τἀναντία καὶ βουλομένων καὶ λεγόντων τῷ
R ii. 156 βελτίω παραινεῖν κεκρατηκὼς | ἥκω ταὐτὸ καὶ νῦν
ποιήσων ἀπὸ τῆς αὐτῆς ἐλπίδος. σὺ δὲ μάλιστα
μὲν καὶ νῦν πεισθείης· εἰ δὲ μή, μήτοι νομίσῃς τοῖς
σοῖς ἐχθρὸν εἶναι πράγμασι τὸν εἰρηκότα λογιζόμενος μὲν ἄνευ τῶν ἄλλων τὸ μέγεθος τῆς τιμῆς
ἧς με τετίμη|κας, ἐνθυμούμενος δὲ ὡς οὐκ εἰκὸς F
μὴ σφόδρα τὸν εὖ παθόντα φιλεῖν τὸν εὖ πεποιηκότα. τοῦτ' αὐτὸ γάρ ἐστι καὶ δι' ὃ συμβου-
λεύειν οἶμαι δεῖν περὶ ὧν ἂν ἡγῶμαι χρηστόν τι
λέξειν. ἄλλως μὲν γὰρ οὐκ ἂν τῷ βασιλεῖ δυναίμην ἀποδοῦναι χάριτας, λόγοις δ' ἂν ἴσως μόνοις
καὶ τοῖς ἀπὸ τῶν λόγων.

    2. Δόξω μὲν οὖν οὐκ ὀλίγοις κίνδυνον πολὺν
ἔχουσιν ἐπιχειρεῖν ὑπὲρ ἱερῶν σοὶ καὶ τοῦ μὴ δεῖν
κακῶς αὐτὰ πάσχειν ἧπερ νῦν, μέλλων διαλέγεσθαι,
δοκοῦσι δέ μοι πλεῖστον ἁμαρτάνειν τῆς σῆς φύ-

---

^a *Or.* 30 ed. F.   *Or.* 28 ed. Re.
^b *Or.* 45 begins with a similar profession of gratitude for

100

ORATION 30 [a]

TO THE EMPEROR THEODOSIUS, FOR THE TEMPLES

1. On many previous occasions, Sire, when I have tendered advice, you have felt that I have reached a proper conclusion, and I have prevailed over those whose words and wishes were opposed to mine because of the superior merits of my counsel. Now too I come on the same errand, inspired with the same hope, and now too especially lend me your ears. If, however, I fail to convince you, do not consider the speaker to be hostile to your administration. Apart from anything else, reflect upon the great distinction you have bestowed upon me and consider that the beneficiary cannot but reasonably feel the strongest affection for his benefactor.[b] Simply for this reason I feel that I must advise on matters where I believe I have something worth while to say. In no other way could I show my gratitude to my sovereign, only perhaps by my oratory and what follows from it.

2. To many people it will appear that I am courting much danger by embarking upon an address to you about the temples and the need for them not to be abused as they are now, but in my view such people,

honours received. For its importance *cf.* Introd. p. 95 and the article of Petit there cited.

R ii. 157 σεως | οἱ τοῦτο τὸ δέος ἔχοντες. ὀργίλου μὲν γὰρ
οἶμαι καὶ χαλεποῦ τὸ εἴ τι λέγοιτο τῶν οὐκ ἀρε-
σκόντων αὐτῷ, χωρεῖν εὐθέως ἐπὶ τὴν τῶν εἰρημένων δίκην, ἠπίου δὲ καὶ φιλανθρώπου καὶ πράου,
ταῦτα δὴ τὰ σά, τὸ μὴ δέχεσθαι μόνον τὴν οὐκ
ἐπαινουμένην ὑφ᾽[1] ἑαυτοῦ συμβουλήν. οὐ γὰρ τοῦ
πεισθῆναί τε καὶ μὴ κύριος ὁ τῶν λόγων ἀκροώ-
μενος, οὔτε φεύγειν τὴν ἀκρόασιν ἄξιον οὐκ οὔσης
βλάβης ἐντεῦθεν οὐδεμιᾶς, οὔτ᾽ εἰ μὴ κατὰ νοῦν
εἴη τὰ λεγόμενα, χαλεπαίνειν τε καὶ τιμωρίαν ζητεῖν, εἴ τις ἃ βέλτιστα ἔχειν ὑπελάμβανε ταῦτα
ἐθάρρησεν εἰπεῖν. 3. δέομαι οὖν εἰς ἐμέ τε τεί-
νειν τὸν λέγοντα τὴν ὄψιν, ὦ βασιλεῦ, | καὶ μὴ F 89
τοῖς διὰ πολλῶν ἐκκρούειν καὶ σὲ κἀμὲ βουλησο-
μένοις διδόναι τοὺς ὀφθαλμούς. ὡς πολλάκις γε
νευμάτων δύναμις πλέον τῆς ἀπὸ τῶν ἀληθῶν ἰσχύος ἠνέγκατο. φημὶ δὲ δεῖν κἀκείνους ἐάσαντάς
με καθ᾽ ἡσυχίαν τε καὶ χωρὶς ἐπηρείας διεξελθεῖν
τὸν λόγον ὕστερον αὖ πειρᾶσθαι καὶ αὐτοὺς λόγῳ
κρατῆσαι τῶν ἡμῖν εἰρημένων.

4. Οἱ πρῶτοι φανέντες ἐπὶ γῆς, ὦ βασιλεῦ, τὰ
R ii. 158 μετέωρα καταλαβόντες | σπηλαίοις τε καὶ καλύ-
βαις αὑτοὺς διασώζοντες θεῶν εὐθὺς ἔννοιαν λαβόντες καὶ γνόντες ὁπόσον ἡ ᾽κείνων εὔνοια τοῖς
ἀνθρώποις, ἱερά τε οἷα εἰκὸς τοὺς πρώτους φύντας
καὶ ἀγάλματα σφίσιν αὐτοῖς ἐποίησαν. τῶν πραγμάτων δὲ εἰς πόλεις προελθόντων ἤδη τῆς περὶ
ταῦτα τέχνης εἰς τοῦτο ἀποχρώσης πολλαὶ μὲν ἐν
ὑπωρείαις, πολλαὶ δὲ ἐν πεδίοις ἐφάνησαν, ἐν ἑκά-

---

[1] ὑφ᾽ F., conj. Re.: om. U : ἐφ᾽ other mss.

in entertaining these fears, are very much mistaken in their assessment of you. To my mind, it is the choleric, ill-tempered man who proceeds immediately to condemn the expression of opinions, when anything is said that is displeasing to him : the kindly, humane gentle character—your own qualities, Sire [a] —merely refuses the counsel of which he does not approve. For where it lies with the hearer of a discourse whether to be convinced by it or not, it is unjustified for him to refuse a hearing, since no harm can come of it, or to become angry and resort to punishment if he disagrees with any remarks when anyone has the courage to say what he conceives to be right. 3. I beg you then, Sire, to turn your gaze on me as I speak, and not to let your eyes light upon those who will wish by various means to delude both you and me, for often enough the influence of a nod has more effect than the force of truth. I submit that they too should allow me to develop my argument quietly and without abuse and afterwards attempt by argument themselves to refute what I have said.

4. The first men who appeared on earth, Sire, occupied the high places and protected themselves in caves and huts, and soon gained a notion of gods and realized how much their good will means to mankind. They raised the kind of temples to be expected of primitive man and made idols for themselves. As their culture advanced towards urbanization and building techniques became adequate for it, many cities made their appearance at the mountain's foot or on the plains, and in each and every one of them

[a] The customary notice of Theodosius' clemency, *cf. Or.* 45. 1 ; 50. 1.

στη δὲ μετὰ τὸ τεῖχος ἀρχὴ τοῦ λοιποῦ σώματος |
R ii. 159 ἱερὰ καὶ νεώ. παρὰ γὰρ δὴ τῶν τοιούτων κυβερ-
νητῶν ἡγοῦντο μεγίστην αὑτοῖς καὶ τὴν ἀσφάλειαν ἔσεσθαι. 5. κἂν ἐπέλθῃς τὴν γῆν ἅπασαν ἣν
οἱ Ῥωμαῖοι νέμονται, πανταχοῦ τοῦτο εὑρήσεις,
ἐπεὶ κἂν τῇ μετὰ τὴν μεγίστην πρώτῃ νεώ τινες
ἔτ᾽ εἰσίν, εἰ καὶ τῶν τιμῶν ἐστέρηνται, ὀλίγοι μὲν
ἐκ πάνυ πολλῶν, οὐ μὴν ἐξῆλθέ γε ἅπαν ἐξ αὑ|τῆς F 90
τοῦτο. καὶ μετὰ τῆς τῶν θεῶν τουτωνὶ συμμαχίας
ἐπιόντες Ῥωμαῖοι τοῖς ἐναντίοις μαχόμενοί τε ἐνί-
κων καὶ νενικηκότες βελτίω τοῖς ἡττημένοις τοῦ
R ii. 160 πρὸ τῆς ἥττης | τὸν ἐπ᾽ αὐτῇ χρόνον ἐποίουν φό-
βους τε ἀφελόντες καὶ πολιτείας τῆς αὑτῶν μετα-
δόντες.

6. Παίδων τοίνυν ἡμῶν ὄντων καθαιρεῖ μὲν τὸν
περιυβρίσαντα τὴν Ῥώμην ὁ Γαλατῶν ἐπ᾽ αὐτὸν
ἀγαγὼν στρατόπεδον, οἳ θεοῖς ἐπῆλθον πρότερον
R ii. 161 εὐξάμενοι, κρατήσας δὲ καὶ ἀνδρὸς | ἐπ᾽ ἐκείνῳ
ταῖς πόλεσιν ἀνθεῖν παρεσχηκότος ἡγησάμενος αὑτῷ λυσιτελεῖν ἕτερόν τινα νομίζειν θεὸν εἰς μὲν τὴν
R ii. 162 τῆς πόλεως περὶ ἣν ἐσπούδασε ποίησιν | τοῖς ἱεροῖς
ἐχρήσατο χρήμασι, τῆς κατὰ νόμους δὲ θεραπείας
ἐκίνησεν οὐδὲ ἕν, ἀλλ᾽ ἦν μὲν ἐν τοῖς ἱεροῖς πενία,
παρῆν δὲ ὁρᾶν ἅπαντα τἄλλα πληρούμενα. 7.

---

[a] Constantinople, " the first city next to the greatest "
(Rome) : a regular description, cf. Or. 1. 284 ; 18. 11 ; 59.
94. Christians (e.g. Euseb. Vit. Const. 3. 48, Augustine, Civ.
Dei, 5. 25) claimed that Constantine founded his new capital
with no temples or idols, but temples certainly survived
from the Byzantium which preceded it.

[b] An argument lately used by Symmachus concerning the
Altar of Victory, Symm. Rel. 3.

[c] For commendation of Roman generosity with grants of
citizenship cf. Dion. Hal. Ant. 1. 9. 4.

the first buildings to be erected after the wall were shrines and temples, for they believed that from such governance they would have the utmost protection also. 5. And if you travel the whole length of the Roman world, you will find this everywhere the case. Even in our second capital some temples still exist,[a] robbed of all honour, admittedly, but though they be but few out of very many, still they have not vanished from it completely. And it was with these gods to aid them that the Romans used to march against the foe, engage them in battle,[b] conquer them and, as conquerors, grant the vanquished a condition of life better than that which they had before their defeat, removing their fears and allowing them a share in their own civic life.[c]

6. While I was still a boy, the ruler who held a reign of terror in Rome was brought down by the leader of an army of Gauls—Gauls who, originally worshippers of the gods, turned against them and attacked them.[d] He, after overcoming the person who had infused new life into the cities,[e] thought it to his own advantage to recognize some other as a god, and he employed the sacred treasures on the building of the city upon which his heart was set.[f] For all that, he made absolutely no alteration in the traditional forms of worship, but, though poverty reigned in the temples, one could see that all the rest of the ritual

---

[d] Libanius was born in A.D. 314. In A.D. 312 Maxentius was defeated at the Milvian Bridge by Constantine, Caesar in Britain and Gaul, Zos. 2. 16.

[e] Licinius, Augustus in the East, defeated by Constantine, A.D. 323. Zos. 2. 28.

[f] Zosimus (2. 29) agrees that Constantine's adoption of Christianity occurred after the fall of Licinius.

κατάβασης δὲ τῆς ἀρχῆς ἐπὶ τὸν ἐξ ἐκείνου, μᾶλ-
R ii. 163 λον δὲ τοῦ σχήματος, | ὡς τό γε κρατεῖν ἑτέρων
ἦν οἷς ἡ ἐξ ἀρχῆς παιδαγωγία καὶ τὸ μέχρι παντὸς
ἴσον δύνασθαι παρέσχεν, οὗτος οὖν ἐν τῷ κελεύ-
εσθαι παρ' αὐτῶν βασιλεύων ἄλλα τε οὐ καλὰ πεί-
θεται καὶ μηκέτ' εἶναι | θυσίας. ταύτας ὁ 'κείνου F ς
μὲν ἀνεψιός, ἀρετὴν δὲ ἅπασαν κτησάμενος ἐπαν-
άγει καὶ τεθνεῶτος ἐν Πέρσαις, ὅ τι δεδρακὼς ἢ
μέλλων ἀφίημι νῦν, μένει μέν τινα τὸ θύειν ἱερεῖα
χρόνον, νεωτέρων δέ τινων συμβάντων ἐκωλύθη
παρὰ τοῖν ἀδελφοῖν, ἀλλ' οὐ τὸ λιβανωτόν. ἀλλὰ
τοῦτό γε καὶ ὁ σὸς ἐβεβαίωσε νόμος, ὥστε μὴ
R ii. 164 μᾶλλον ἀλγεῖν ἡμᾶς | οἷς ἀφῃρέθημεν ἢ χάριν εἰ-
δέναι τῶν συγκεχωρημένων. 8. σὺ μὲν οὖν οὔθ'
ἱερὰ κεκλεῖσθαι ⟨ἐκέλευσας⟩[1] οὔτε μηδένα προσ-
ιέναι οὔτε πῦρ οὔτε λιβανωτὸν οὔτε τὰς ἀπὸ τῶν
ἄλλων θυμιαμάτων τιμὰς ἐξήλασας τῶν νεῶν οὐδὲ
τῶν βωμῶν, οἱ δὲ μελανειμονοῦντες οὗτοι καὶ
πλείω μὲν τῶν ἐλεφάντων ἐσθίοντες, πόνον δὲ παρ-
R ii. 165 έχοντες τῷ πλήθει τῶν ἐκπωμάτων | τοῖς δι' ἀσ-

---

[1] ἐκέλευσας inserted F., conj. Re. Cf. schol. C : τὸ σχῆμα
ἀτελές· λείπει τὸ ἐκέλευσας.

---

[a] Zosimus (4. 36) implicitly agrees. Christians, however
(e.g. Socr. H.E. 1. 18), assert that he razed temples and forbade
sacrifices, the latter point confirmed by Constantius' edict
of A.D. 341 (C. Th. 16. 10. 2). Constantine's own edicts allowing pagan ritual (ibid. 9. 16. 1-3) are prior to A.D. 324.
[b] Constantius II (Augustus in East A.D. 337–361), notorious for his weakness in the face of his eunuchs and officials
of court, cf. Or. 18. 152 ff. ; 62. 8 ff. Amm. Marc. 21. 16. 16.
[c] Cf. Or. 1. 27. C. Th. 16. 10. 4-6 ; the breach of these
edicts was punishable by death.   [d] Julian ; cf. Vol. I.
[e] Van Loy identifies this with the law of Valentinian and
Valens, C. Th. 9. 16. 7 of A.D. 364 (cf. Zos. 4. 3). This does

was fulfilled.[a] 7. To his son passed the government, or rather the shadow of it, for the reins of power were held by others who, through their control of his earliest upbringing, had gained a supremacy absolutely equal to his own.[b] He, then, ruling under orders from them, was induced to adopt several misguided policies, in particular, the banning of sacrifices.[c] His cousin, a paragon of all virtue, restored them. Of his actions and intentions I make no mention here, but after his death in Persia,[d] the performance of sacrifice lasted for some little time until, after some untoward incidents, it was banned by the two imperial brothers,[e] an exception, however, being made in the case of offerings of incense. This particular exception has also been confirmed by a law of your own, so that we do not so much lament what we have lost as show gratitude for the concession we have obtained. 8. You then have neither ordered the closure of temples nor banned entrance to them. From the temples and altars you have banished neither fire nor incense nor the offerings of other perfumes.[f] But this black-robed tribe, who eat more than elephants and, by the quantities of drink they consume,[g] weary those that accompany their drink-

not provide room for the time lag or the unrest mentioned by Libanius, which should refer to Procopius' revolt. The edict is thus, in Libanius' narrative, that of *C. Th.* 9. 16. 8.

[f] Theodosius (*C. Th.* 16. 10. 7 of A.D. 381) had forbidden sacrifices to be made in temples, allegedly used for purposes of divination. This ban was reinforced by that of A.D. 385 (*ibid.* 10. 9). Turification is finally banned in A.D. 392 after the fall of Tatianus (*C. Th.* 16. 10. 12).

[g] For the anti-social activities of the monks *cf. Or.* 2. 32, 45. 26; Amm. Marc. 27. 3. 14, Eunap. *V.S.* 472, Zos. 5. 23, *C. Th.* 12. 1. 63 (*ignaviae sectatores*).

LIBANIUS

μάτων αὐτοῖς παραπέμπουσι τὸ ποτόν, συγκρύπτοντες δὲ ταῦτα ὠχρότητι τῇ διὰ τέχνης αὐτοῖς πεπορισμένῃ μένοντος, ὦ βασιλεῦ, καὶ κρατοῦντος

R ii. 166 τοῦ νόμου θέουσιν ἐφ᾽ ἱερὰ ξύλα φέροντες καὶ | λίθους καὶ σίδηρον, οἱ δὲ καὶ ἄνευ τούτων χεῖρας καὶ πόδας. ἔπειτα Μυσῶν λεία καθαι|ρουμένων ὀρο- F 9 φῶν, κατασκαπτομένων τοίχων, κατασπωμένων ἀγαλμάτων, ἀνασπωμένων βωμῶν, τοὺς ἱερεῖς δὲ ἢ σιγᾶν ἢ τεθνάναι δεῖ· τῶν πρώτων δὲ κειμένων δρόμος ἐπὶ τὰ δεύτερα καὶ τρίτα, καὶ τρόπαια τροπαίοις ἐναντία τῷ νόμῳ συνείρεται. 9. τολμᾶται μὲν οὖν κἀν ταῖς πόλεσι, τὸ πολὺ δὲ ἐν τοῖς ἀγροῖς.

R ii. 167 καὶ πολλοὶ μὲν οἱ καθ᾽ ἕκαστον πολέμιοι, | ἐπὶ δὲ μυρίοις κακοῖς τὸ διεσπαρμένον τοῦτ᾽ ἀθροίζεται καὶ λόγον ἀλλήλους ἀπαιτοῦσι τῶν εἰργασμένων καὶ αἰσχύνη τὸ μὴ μέγιστα ἠδικηκέναι. χωροῦσι τοίνυν διὰ τῶν ἀγρῶν ὥσπερ χείμαρροι κατασύροντες διὰ τῶν ἱερῶν τοὺς ἀγρούς. ὅτου γὰρ ἂν ἱερὸν ἐκκόψωσιν ἀγροῦ, οὗτος[1] τετύφλωταί τε καὶ κεῖται καὶ τέθνηκε. ψυχὴ γάρ, ὦ βασιλεῦ, τοῖς ἀγροῖς τὰ ἱερὰ προοίμια τῆς ἐν τοῖς ἀγροῖς κτίσεως γεγενημένα καὶ διὰ πολλῶν γενεῶν εἰς τοὺς νῦν ὄντας ἀφιγμένα. 10. καὶ τοῖς γεωργοῦσιν ἐν αὐτοῖς αἱ ἐλπίδες ὅσαι περί τε ἀνδρῶν καὶ γυναικῶν καὶ τέκνων καὶ βοῶν καὶ τῆς σπειρομένης γῆς καὶ τῆς πεφυτευμένης. ὁ δὲ τοῦτο πεπονθὼς ἀγρὸς ἀπολώλεκε καὶ τῶν γεωργῶν μετὰ τῶν ἐλπίδων τὸ

---

[1] οὗτος F., conj. Re., Cobet : τούτῳ Re. text (PU, corrections in VI) : τοῦτο other mss.

[a] For this denigration of Christian ritual cf. Or. 2. 59; and the monkish pallor, Or. 62. 10.

ing with the singing of hymns, who hide these excesses under an artificially contrived pallor [a]—these people, Sire, while the law yet remains in force, hasten to attack the temples with sticks and stones and bars of iron, and in some cases, disdaining these, with hands and feet. Then utter desolation follows,[b] with the stripping of roofs, demolition of walls, the tearing down of statues and the overthrow of altars, and the priests must either keep quiet or die. After demolishing one, they scurry to another, and to a third, and trophy is piled on trophy, in contravention of the law. 9. Such outrages occur even in the cities, but they are most common in the countryside.[c] Many are the foes who perpetrate the separate attacks, but after their countless crimes this scattered rabble congregates and calls for a tally of their activities, and they are in disgrace unless they have committed the foulest outrage. So they sweep across the countryside like rivers in spate, and by ravaging the temples, they ravage the estates, for wherever they tear out a temple from an estate, that estate is blinded and lies murdered. Temples, Sire, are the soul of the countryside : they mark the beginning of its settlement, and have been passed down through many generations to the men of today. 10. In them the farming communities rest their hopes for husbands, wives, children, for their oxen and the soil they sow and plant. An estate that has suffered so has lost the inspiration of the peasantry together

[b] Proverbial—of a prey to all and sundry ; cf. Or. 12. 40, 14. 26 ; and Vol. I, p. 59 n.

[c] Temples and altars in the countryside (mentioned in the ban of C. Th. 16. 10. 12 of A.D. 391) are finally doomed to demolition by Arcadius in A.D. 399 (ibid. 10. 16).

πρόθυμον· μάτην γὰρ ἡγοῦνται πονήσειν τῶν εἰς
δέον τοὺς πόνους ἀγόντων ἐστερημένοι θεῶν. τῆς
R ii. 168 γῆς δὲ οὐκέθ' ὁμοίων | πόνων ἀπολαυούσης οὐδ' ἂν
ἴσος ὁ τόκος | τῷ πρὶν ἀπαντώῃ. τούτου δὲ ὄντος F
τοιούτου πενέστερος μὲν ὁ γεωργός, ἐν βλάβῃ δὲ
ὁ φόρος. καὶ γὰρ ἂν σφόδρα ἐθέλῃ τις, τό γε μὴ
δύνασθαι κωλύει.

11. Οὕτως ἐπὶ τὰ μέγιστα τῶν πραγμάτων βα-
δίζει τὰ διὰ τὴν τούτων ἀσέλγειαν κατὰ τῶν ἀγρῶν
τολμώμενα, οἳ φασὶ μὲν τοῖς ἱεροῖς πολεμεῖν, ἔστι
δὲ οὗτος ὁ πόλεμος πόρος τῶν μὲν τοῖς ναοῖς ἐγκειμένων, τῶν δὲ τὰ ὄντα τοῖς ταλαιπώροις ἁρπα-
ζόντων τά τε κείμενα αὐτοῖς ἀπὸ τῆς γῆς καὶ ἃ
τρέφουσιν. ὥστ' ἀπέρχονται φέροντες οἱ ἐπελ-
θόντες τὰ τῶν ἐκπεπολιορκημένων. τοῖς δὲ οὐκ
ἀρκεῖ ταῦτα, ἀλλὰ καὶ γῆν σφετερίζονται τὴν τοῦ
R ii. 169 δεῖνος ἱερὰν εἶναι λέγοντες, | καὶ πολλοὶ τῶν πατ-
ρῴων ἐστέρηνται δι' ὀνόματος οὐκ ἀληθοῦς. οἱ δ'
ἐκ τῶν ἑτέρων τρυφῶσι κακῶν οἱ τῷ πεινῆν, ὥς
φασι, τὸν αὐτῶν θεραπεύοντες θεόν. ἢν δ' οἱ πε-
πορθημένοι παρὰ τὸν ἐν ἄστει ποιμένα, καλοῦσι
γὰρ οὕτως ἄνδρα οὐ πάνυ χρηστόν, ἢν οὖν ἐλθόντες ὀδύρωνται λέγοντες ἃ ἠδίκηνται, ὁ ποιμὴν
οὗτος τοὺς μὲν ἐπήνεσε, τοὺς δὲ ἀπήλασεν ὡς ἐν
τῷ μὴ μείζω πεπονθέναι κεκερδακότας. 12. καί-

---

^a Thus neglect of the gods is held to produce the famines
which had been prevalent since A.D. 382 ; cf. Symm. Rel.
3. 15 ff.

^b On temple properties, cf. Bidez, Vie de Julien, pp. 225 ff.

^c Zosimus 5. 23 supports this accusation.

^d See on § 8 above. Theodosius himself about this time
complained, " monachi multa scelera faciunt " (Ambrose, Ep.
41. 27).

with their hopes, for they believe that their labour will be in vain once they are robbed of the gods who direct their labours to their due end.[a] And if the land no longer enjoys the same care, neither can the yield match what it was before, and, if this be the case, the peasant is the poorer, and the revenue jeopardized, for whatever a man's willingness, surely his inability frustrates him.

11. So the outrages committed by these hooligans against the estates bear upon vital matters of state.[b] They claim to be attacking the temples, but these attacks are a source of income, for, though some assail the shrines, others plunder the wretched peasantry of what they have, both the produce stored from the land and their stock ; and the invaders depart with the loot from the places they have stormed. Others are not satisfied with this, but they appropriate the land too,[c] claiming that what belongs to this or that body is temple property, and many a man has been robbed of his family acres on this false title. Others, again, claim to worship their god with fasting, and yet grow fat on the misfortunes of other folk.[d] And if the victims of this looting come to the " pastor " in town—for that is the title they give to a fellow who is not all that he should be—,[e] if they come and tearfully recount their wrongs, this pastor commends the looters and sends the victims packing with the assurance that they are lucky to have got off so lightly. 12. Yet, Sire, these

[e] *i.e.* the bishop (at this time Flavianus, § 15), with his ecclesiastical court. The term was, of course, current in Christian circles, but arouses Libanius' ire because it was also one of his own expressions to signify his relation as sophist with his pupils ($\dot{\alpha}\gamma\acute{\epsilon}\lambda\eta$).

τοι τῆς μὲν σῆς ἀρχῆς, ὦ βασιλεῦ, καὶ οὗτοι, τοσούτῳ δὲ χρησιμώτεροι τῶν ἀδικούντων αὐτοὺς
ὅσῳ τῶν ἀργούντων οἱ ἐργαζόμενοι. οἱ μὲν γὰρ
F 94 ταῖς μελίτταις, οἱ δὲ | τοῖς κηφῆσιν ἐοίκασι. κἂν |
ἀκούσωσιν ἀγρὸν ἔχειν τι τῶν ἁρπασθῆναι δυναμένων, εὐθὺς οὗτος ἐν θυσίαις τέ ἐστι καὶ δεινὰ
ποιεῖ καὶ δεῖ στρατείας ἐπ᾽ αὐτὸν καὶ πάρεισιν οἱ
σωφρονισταί, τοῦτο γὰρ ὄνομα τίθενται ταῖς λη-
στείαις, εἰ μὴ καὶ[1] μικρὸν εἶπον. οἱ μέν γε πει-
R ii. 171 ρῶνται λανθάνειν καὶ ἃ τολμῶσιν ἀρνοῦνται, | κἂν
καλέσῃς λῃστήν, ὕβρισας, οἱ δὲ φιλοτιμοῦνται καὶ
σεμνύνονται καὶ τοὺς ἀγνοοῦντας διδάσκουσι καὶ
γερῶν ἀξίους εἶναί φασιν αὐτούς. 13. καίτοι τοῦτο
τί ἕτερόν ἐστιν ἢ ἐν εἰρήνῃ πολεμεῖσθαι τοὺς γεωρ-
γούς; οὐδὲν γὰρ αὐτοῖς ἐλάττους ποιεῖ τὰς συμφορὰς τὸ παρὰ τῶν οἰκείων πάσχειν κακῶς, εἰ μὴ
καὶ δεινότερον τὸ οὓς εἰκότως ἂν ἐν ταραχαῖς εἶχον
συμμάχους, ὑπὸ τούτων ἐν ἡσυχίας καιρῷ πάσχειν
οἷα διῆλθον.

14. Καίτοι τί μαθών, ὦ βασιλεῦ, τὰς δυνάμεις
συνέχεις καὶ ὅπλα κατασκευάζῃ καὶ στρατηγοῖς
κοινολογῇ καὶ τοὺς μὲν ἐκπέμπεις οἷ συμφέρει,
τοῖς δὲ ἐπιστέλλεις ὑπὲρ τῶν ἐπειγόντων, τοῖς δὲ
ἀντεπιστέλλεις ὑπὲρ ὧν ἐρωτῶσι; τὰ δὲ τείχη
ταῦτα τὰ καινὰ καὶ οἱ θερινοὶ πόνοι τί βούλεται
R ii. 172 ταυτὶ | πάντα καὶ ποῖ βλέπει; καὶ τί προξενεῖ
ταῖς τε πόλεσι καὶ τοῖς ἀγροῖς τὸ ζῆν τε ἐν ἀδείᾳ

[1] καὶ F. (V) : om. Re. (other mss.).

---

[a] The σωφρονισταί are a type of rural police, cf. Marc.
Diac. Vit. Porph. p. 22. Here their function is usurped by
the monks.

ORATION XXX, 12–14

victims are your subjects too, and as workers are
more useful than idlers, so are they more useful than
their oppressors. These are as the bees, those the
drones. And if they hear that an estate has something worth looting, it is straightaway involved in
sacrifices and is committing all manner of crimes :
an armed visitation is called for, and up come the
justices,[a] which is the term they use to describe
these—for want of a better word—footpads, for footpads at least try not to be found out and they deny
their misdeeds. Call one of them a footpad and
you insult him. But this crew flaunt their excesses,
boast of them, advertise them to those who are unaware of them, and claim that they should be re-
warded. 13. But it is nothing else than war in peace
time waged against the peasantry. Ill-usage at the
hands of their fellows is no alleviation for their misfortunes, except for the fact that it is even worse
that those allies they might normally have had in
times of trouble are responsible for their experiencing the above-mentioned outrages in time of peace.
14. Then what is your purpose, Sire, in maintaining
your forces, equipping your armies and conferring
with commanders ? Why send them to where they
are needed, post despatches to them on matters of
urgency, despatch replies to their queries ? What
is the point of these fresh fortifications, these labours
of midsummer ? [b] What is the object of all this ?
What is it that allows both town and country to live

[b] The fortifications and labours of midsummer were
identified by Seeck and Van Loy with the Balkan campaigns
of A.D. 390, and so held to indicate a late date for the speech.
Petit (op. cit. p. 305) identifies with the successful campaign
against the Gruthungi of A.D. 386.

113

καὶ καθεύδειν ἀκρι|βῶς καὶ μὴ θορυβεῖσθαι ταῖς F
ἀπὸ τῶν πολέμων ἐλπίσιν ἀλλ' εὖ εἰδέναι πάντας
ὅτι κἂν ἐπίῃ τις, λαβών τι κακὸν μᾶλλον ἢ λυπή-
σας ἄπεισιν; ὅταν οὖν σοῦ τοὺς ἔξωθεν πολεμίους[1]
ἀνείργοντος τῶν ὑπό σοι τινες ἐπί τινας τῶν ὑπὸ
σοι φέρωνται τῶν κοινῶν ἀγαθῶν οὐκ ἐῶντες μετέχειν, πῶς οὐ τὴν σὴν πρόνοιαν καὶ φροντίδας καὶ
πόνους ἀδικοῦσιν, ὦ βασιλεῦ; πῶς δὲ οὐκ ἐν οἷς
πράττουσι καὶ τῇ σῇ γνώμῃ πολεμοῦσι;

15. Παραβαίνοντας γάρ φησι τὸν οὐκ ἐῶντα
θύειν νόμον καὶ θύοντας ἐτιμωρούμεθα. ψεύδον-
ται, ταῦτα ὅταν λέγωσιν, ὦ βασιλεῦ. οὐδεὶς γὰρ
οὕτω θρασὺς τούτων δὴ τῶν τῆς ἀγορᾶς ἀπείρων
ὡς ἀξιοῦν εἶναι κυριώτερος νόμου, νόμον δὲ ὅταν
εἴπω, τὸν τεθεικότα λέγω. πιστεύεις οὖν ὡς οἱ

R ii. 173 μηδὲ τὴν τοῦ πράκτορος | χλαμύδα φέροντες οὗτοι
βασιλείας ἂν κατεφρόνουν; ταυτὶ δὲ τὰ παρὰ τούτων ἐλέγετο μὲν καὶ παρὰ Φλαβιανῷ πολλάκις,

R ii. 174 ἠλέγχθη δὲ οὐδεπώποτε. οὐδὲ | γὰρ νῦν. 16. ἰδοὺ
γὰρ δὴ προκαλοῦμαι τοὺς κηδεμόνας τοῦδε τοῦ
νόμου· τίς εἶδέ[2] τινας τούτων τῶν ἀναστάτων ὑφ'
ὑμῶν γενομένων τεθυκότας ἐπὶ τῶν βωμῶν, ὡς ὁ
νόμος οὐκ ἐᾷ; τίς νέος, τίς πρεσβύτης, τίς ἀνήρ,
τίς γυνή, τίς τῶν τὸν | αὐτὸν οἰκούντων ἀγρὸν οὐ F
συμφερόμενος τοῖς θύσασι τὰ περὶ τοὺς θεούς, τίς
τῶν ἐν τοῖς πλησίον; πολλὰ δ' ἂν καὶ δυσμένεια
καὶ φθόνος ἐμποιήσειε γείτοσιν, ἀφ' ὧν ἔλθοι τις
ἂν[3] ἡδέως ἐπ' ἔλεγχον, ἀλλ' ὅμως οὔτε τούτων οὔτε

---

[1] πολεμίους F. : πολέμους Re. (mss.).
[2] εἶδέ F. (M) : οἶδέ Re. (other mss.).
[3] ἂν inserted F. (V) : om. Re. (other mss.).

114

in security, to sleep soundly and not to quake with expectations of war, save the universal conviction that any invader will retire after suffering more damage than he has caused? So, while you keep external foes at arm's length, if one group of your subjects attacks another and prevents them sharing in the general prosperity, they inevitably do harm to your precautions, your policies and your task, Sire, and by their activities they rebel against your will also.

15. The assertion is, of course, that they were punishing those who offer sacrifice and so contravene the law that bans it. This assertion, Sire, is always a lie. None of these ignorant rustics is so impudent as to claim to be above the law, and when I say the law, I mean its formulator. Do you really believe that those who cringe even at the tax-collector's uniform would despise the emperor's majesty? Yet this was the argument so often put to Flavianus,[a] but it was never proved—nor is it now. 16. Now look! I challenge the guardians of this law. Who has seen anyone out of all the persons you have dispossessed who has sacrificed on the altars in the manner forbidden by the law, whether you be young or old, man or woman, a fellow-villager who disagrees with sacrifices to the gods, or any native of the neighbourhood? Spite and envy could provide reason enough for neighbours to start proceedings against them, but for all that neither from them nor from anywhere else has anyone come forward, nor

---

[a] Patriarch of Antioch A.D. 381–404. His activities are either disparaged or ignored by Libanius, but his journey to court after the Riots of the Statues to plead on behalf of the city was most successful (*cf.* Chrysostom, *Homilies on the Statues*, esp. Hom. 21).

ἐκείνων οὐδεὶς ἧκεν, ἀλλ' οὐδὲ ἥξει δεδιὼς ἐπιορ-
κίαν, ἵνα μὴ πληγὰς λέγω. τίς οὖν ἡ πίστις τῆς
αἰτίας ἢ τὸ λέγειν τούτους ὡς ἅπερ οὐκ ἐξῆν ἔθυσαν; ἀλλ' οὐκ ἀρκέσει τοῦτο τῷ βασιλεῖ.

17. Οὐκ ἔθυσαν οὖν; ἐρήσεταί τις. πάνυ γε,
R ii. 175 ἀλλ' ἐπὶ θοίνῃ καὶ ἀρίστῳ καὶ εὐωχίᾳ τῶν | βοῶν
ἀλλαχοῦ σφαττομένων, βωμοῦ δὲ οὐδενὸς τὸ αἷμα
δεχομένου οὐδὲ μέρους οὐδενὸς καομένου οὐδὲ οὐ-
λῶν ἡγουμένων οὐδὲ σπονδῆς ἀκολουθούσης. εἰ
δέ τινες συνελθόντες εἴς τι φαιδρὸν χωρίον μόσχον
ἢ πρόβατον ἢ ἄμφω θύσαντες τὰ μὲν ἑψήσαντες τὰ
δὲ ὀπτήσαντες κατακλιθέντες ἐπὶ τῆς γῆς ἔφαγον,
οὐκ οἶδ' εἴ τινας οὗτοι παρέβαινον τῶν νόμων.
18. οὐδὲ γὰρ κεκώλυκας ταῦτα, ὦ βασιλεῦ, νόμῳ,
ἀλλ' ἓν εἰπὼν δεῖν μὴ ποιεῖν τἆλλα πάντα ἀφῆκας.
ὥστ' εἰ καὶ μετὰ πάντων θυμιαμάτων συνέπινον,
οὐ παρέβαινον νόμον οὐδέ γε εἰ πάντες ἐν ταῖς
φιλοτησίαις ᾖδόν τε καὶ ἐκάλουν θεούς, εἰ μὴ καὶ
τὴν οἴκοι δίαιταν γιγνομένην | ἑκάστῳ συκοφαντή- F
R ii. 176 σεις. 19. ἦν[1] ἔθος πολλοὺς ἀγρότας[2] εἰς | τοὺς γνω-
ριμωτέρους συνιόντας ἐν ταῖς ἑορταῖς θύσαντας
εἶτα εὐωχεῖσθαι. τοῦθ' ἡνίκα ἐξῆν ποιεῖν, ἐποίουν.
μετὰ ταῦτα πλὴν τοῦ θύειν ἡ περὶ τἆλλα ἔμεινεν ἐξ-
ουσία. καλούσης τοίνυν τῆς εἰωθυίας ἡμέρας ὑπ-
ήκουον καὶ οἷς ἀκίνδυνον ἐτίμων αὐτήν τε καὶ τὸ
ἔδος. ὅτι δὲ καὶ θύειν ἄξιον, οὐδεὶς οὔτ' εἶπεν
οὔτ' ἤκουσεν οὔτ' ἔπεισεν οὔτ' ἐπείσθη. οὐδ' ἂν εἴ-

---

[1] ἦν F., conj. Re. : ἦν Re. text (MSS.).
[2] ἀγρότας F. (BM, C marg.) : ἀγροὺς Re. (other MSS.).

[a] This was a practice still allowed by law: cf. C. Th.
16. 10. 17 (of A.D. 399) where the occasions for such festivities
are *vota publica*.

will he, if he has any qualms about perjury—not to mention the flogging for it. So what basis is there for the charge, save the mere assertion that they have performed an illegal sacrifice? But this will not do for the emperor.

17. " They did not sacrifice, then ? " will be the comment. Of course they did, but for a banquet, a dinner, a feast, and the oxen were slaughtered elsewhere [a] : no altar received the blood offering, no single part of the victim was burned, no offering of meal began the ceremony, nor did libations follow it. If people assemble in some beauty spot, slaughter a calf or a sheep, or both, and boil or roast it, and then lie down on the ground and eat it, I do not see that they have broken the laws at all. 18. You, Sire, have put no legal ban on these acts. By banning the performance of one specific action you automatically permit everything else. So even if they were in the habit of drinking together amid the scent of every kind of incense, they broke no law, nor yet if in their toasts they sang hymns and invoked the gods, unless indeed you intend to use a man's private life as grounds for accusation. 19. It used to be the custom for country folk to assemble in large numbers at the homes of the village notables at holiday time, to make a sacrifice and then hold a feast. This they did while ever it was permitted to do so, and thereafter all the rest, with the exception of sacrifice, remained permissible. So, summoned on the usual day, they dutifully honoured it and the shrine in a manner that involved no risk. That they also thought fit to offer sacrifice no single person has ever said or heard, alleged convincingly or be-

ποι τις τῶν ἐκείνοις ἐχθρῶν ὡς ἢ αὐτόπτης θυσίας
γέγονεν ἢ ὡς ἔχει¹ τὸν μεμηνυκότα. εἰ δ᾽ ἦν ταῦτα
ἢ τὸ ἕτερόν γε, τίς ἂν ἤνεγκε τούτους ἕλκοντας καὶ
βοῶντας καὶ κατηγοροῦντας οὐκ ἐν τῷ Φλαβιανοῦ
δικαστηρίῳ, ἀλλ᾽ ἐν τοῖς ὡς ἀληθῶς δικαστηρίοις;
οὕτω γὰρ μᾶλλον ᾤοντο ἂν ἀναιρήσειν τὸ θύειν
ἀνελόντες τῶν τεθυκότων τινάς. 20. ἀλλ᾽ οὐκ αὐτῶν
ταῦτα εἶναι φήσουσι παραδιδόναι τοῖς ἀποκτενοῦ-
σιν ἄνθρωπον, οὐδ᾽ ἢν τὰ δεινότατα εἰργασμένος ᾖ.
ἐγὼ δὲ ὅσους μὲν ἐν στάσεσιν ἀπεκτόνασιν οὐδὲ τὴν
τῆς προσηγο|ρίας αἰσχυνόμενοι κοινωνίαν, παρίημι, F 9
μή τις εἰς τὸ ἀπερίσκεπτον τὰ τοιαῦτα ἀνενέγκῃ·
ἀλλ᾽ ἐν οἷς ἐξηλάσατε τοὺς ταῖς αὐτῶν ἐπιμελείαις
πενίᾳ βοηθοῦντας ἔν τε γραυσὶ καὶ πρεσβύταις οὔσῃ
καὶ παιδίοις ὀρφανοῖς καὶ τούτων τοῖς πλείοσι τὰ
πολλὰ πεπηρωμένοις τοῦ σώματος, ταῦτα οὐ φόνος;
ταῦτα οὐ θάνατος; ταῦτα οὐκ ἔστιν ἀποκτεῖναι,
καὶ πικροτέρω² γε θανάτῳ, διὰ τοῦ λιμοῦ; τοῦ
τρέφεσθαι γὰρ αὐτοῖς ἀπολωλότος τοῦτ᾽ ἐλείπετο
δήπου. εἶτ᾽ ἐκείνους μὲν ἀπολλύντες οὐδὲν αἰτια-
θέντας ἀπώλλυτε, τούτους δ᾽ ἂν παραβεβηκότας
νόμον ⟨οὔ⟩³· οὕτω τὸ τὰ δικαστήρια φυγεῖν τὸν
τοῦ μὴ τεθυκέναι τοὺς ἀνθρώπους ἔλεγχον ἔχει.

---

¹ ἔχει: A ends (gap of one folium); resumes § 28, δέ σοι.
Similarly Re.   ² πικροτέρῳ mss.: πικροτάτῳ F.
³ οὔ inserted F., conj. Monnier: om. mss.

ᵃ On the jurisdiction of episcopal courts cf. C. Th. 1. 27. 1
(A.D. 318), Const. Sirm. i (A.D. 333), Jones, LRE 491 f.
   ᵇ Libanius consistently criticizes those Christian governors
who, despite the brutality of their physical punishments, yet
profess to avoid the imposition of the death penalty (cf. Or.
4. 38, 45. 27 ff.), as either exceeding the bounds of their
duty or failing to perform it.

lieved. Nor yet could any of their enemies assert
that he either had personally witnessed a sacrifice
or could produce an informant about one. But
if he had these proofs, or even one of them, who
would have put up with arrests, a hue and cry, and
charges made by these people, not in Flavianus'
court but in a real court of law ?ᵃ For they might
expect more success in doing away with sacrifices if
they did away with some individuals who had performed them. 20. But it is not their way, they will
say, to hand a man over to execution, even though
he be guilty of the most heinous crime.ᵇ I forebear
to mention the numbers they have murdered in their
riotings in utter disregard of the name they share,ᶜ
in case such incidents be described as due to over-
hasty action : but your expulsion of people who by
their personal care provided relief for poverty among
old men and women and fatherless children,ᵈ the majority of them suffering from severe physical handi-
caps—is not this murder ? Isn't it execution ? Isn't
this sentencing them to death, and to a death worse
than ever, by starvation ? For when their means of
support have gone, this is surely the fate in store for
them. Then in massacring their protectors, you have
been massacring these innocents, but you wouldn't
dream of doing so if they had broken the law ! This
by-passing of the courts of law is proof that their victims did not offer sacrifice. This killing without trial

ᶜ As had happened in A.D. 361 (the lynching of George of
Cappadocia) and was to occur in A.D. 391 at the overthrow of
the Serapeum, *cf.* Sozom. *H.E.* vii. 14. Julian had described
the Christians in their religious quarrels as being worse than
wild beasts.

ᵈ On social welfare in the pagan church *cf. Or.* 2. 30 n.

οὕτως οὓς ἔκτειναν[1] οὐ κρίναντες τὸ μηδ' ἀφορμῆς
εἰς τὸ κρίνειν εὐπορεῖν ὡμολογήκασιν.

21. Εἰ δέ μοι γράμματα λέγουσιν ἀπὸ βίβλων
αἷς φασιν ἐμμένειν, ἐγὼ τὰ πράγματα ἀντιθήσω
τὰ παρὰ φαῦλον ἐκείνοις[2] πεποιημένα. εἰ δὲ μὴ
τοῦτο τοιοῦτον ἦν, οὐδ' ἂν ἐτρύφων. νῦν δ' ἴσμεν
αὐτοὺς καὶ ὅπως χρῶνται μὲν ταῖς ἡμέραις, χρῶνται δὲ ταῖς νυξίν. οὔκουν ἦν εἰκὸς τοὺς οὐκ ὀκ-
νοῦντας ἐκεῖνα τοῦτο | φυλάξασθαι; ἀλλ' ἐξῄρηται F 99
τοσαῦτα τοσούτων ἀγρῶν ἱερὰ ὕβρει καὶ παροινίᾳ[3]
καὶ κέρδει καὶ τῷ μὴ βούλεσθαι κατέχειν αὐτούς.
22. τεκμήριον δέ, ἦν ἄγαλμα ἐν Βεροίᾳ τῇ πόλει
χαλκοῦν, Ἀσκληπιὸς ἐν εἴδει τοῦ Κλεινίου παιδὸς
τοῦ καλοῦ καὶ ἡ τέχνη τὴν φύσιν ἐμιμεῖτο, τοσοῦτον δὲ ἦν τὸ τῆς ὥρας ὥστε καὶ οἷς ὑπῆρχεν
αὐτὸν καθ' ἡμέραν ὁρᾶν, εἶναι τῆς θέας ὅμως
ἐπιθυμίαν. τούτῳ θύεσθαι θυσίας οὐδεὶς οὕτως
ἀναιδὴς ὡς εἰπεῖν ἂν τολμῆσαι. τοῦτο τοίνυν, ὦ
βασιλεῦ, τὸ τοιοῦτον πολλῷ μέν, ὡς εἰκός, πόνῳ,
λαμπρᾷ δὲ ἠκριβωμένον ψυχῇ κατακέκοπται καὶ
οἴχεται, καὶ τὰ Φειδίου χεῖρες πολλαὶ[4] διενείμαντο.
διὰ ποῖον αἷμα; διὰ ποίαν μάχαιραν; διὰ ποίαν
ἔξω τῶν νόμων θεραπείαν; 23. ὥσπερ οὖν ἐνταῦθα
καίτοι θυσίαν οὐδεμίαν εἰπεῖν ἔχοντες ὅμως πολλὰ
μέρη τὸν Ἀλκιβιάδην, μᾶλλον δὲ τὸν Ἀσκληπιὸν
ἔτεμνον ἀποκοσμοῦντες τὴν πόλιν τοῖς περὶ τὸ
ἄγαλμα, οὕτω χρὴ νομίζειν αὐτοῖς καὶ τὰ περὶ τοὺς
ἀγροὺς ἐσχηκέναι. τέθυκε μὲν ἱερεῖον οὐδείς, ἐν

---

[1] ἔκτειναν F.: ἔκριναν mss.
[2] ἐκείνοις F. (M marg.): ἐκεῖνα mss.
[3] παροινίᾳ F. (IMV): παρανοίᾳ other mss.
[4] τὰ Φειδίου χεῖρες conj. Monnier: τὰς Φειδίου χεῖρας πολλαὶ F. (mss.): πολλοὶ prop. F.

120

is a confession that there are no good grounds to try them.

21. And if they prate to me of the teachings of the scriptures that they profess to obey, I will counter them with the despicable acts they have committed. If this were not so, they would not be living on the fat of the land. As it is, we know how they spend their days—and their nights. How improbable it is for those who have no qualms about that to be so punctilious about this ! In estate after estate shrine after shrine has been wiped out by their insolence, violence, greed and deliberate lack of self-control. 22. For instance, in the city of Beroea there was a bronze statue of Asclepius, in the likeness of the handsome son of Cleinias. In it art matched nature ; such was its perfection that even those who could see it every day still wanted to look at it. No one was such a scoundrel as to dare say that sacrifice was performed to it. Yet this statue, Sire, so carefully made no doubt with much toil and brilliant genius, has been broken up and exists no more. The mob's handiwork has been to tear apart the masterwork of Pheidias.[a] For what offering of blood ? For what use of the sacrificial knife ? For what illegal act of worship ? 23. At Beroea, though they could not allege any sacrifice, they yet smashed to smithereens the likeness of Alcibiades, or rather of Asclepius, and desecrated the city by the outrage committed against the statue : similarly, we must believe their outrages in the countryside to fall into the same pattern. No one has sacrificed any victim, yet the temples, great

[a] On such artistic attributions cf. R.E. i. 1531. The attribution of this statue to Pheidias is highly unlikely, the language being that of rhetorical exaggeration.

οἷς δὲ κάμνοντες[1] αὑτοὺς ἀνέπαυον ἱεροῖς, ταῦτα ἀνῄρηται μείζω τε ὁμοίως καὶ ἐλάττω. καὶ νεναυαγηκόσιν οἱ ταῦτα παθόντες ἐοίκασιν ἀνθρώποις ἐκπεσοῦσι τῶν νεῶν ἐφ' ὧν ἔπλεον. |

24. Πότεροι τοίνυν τῶν δίκην ὀφειλόντων εἰσίν, F 1 οἱ τετηρηκότες τοὺς νόμους ἢ οἱ τὴν αὑτῶν βούλησιν ἀντ' ἐκείνων πεποιημένοι; εἰ γὰρ δεινὸν μέν, ὦ βασιλεῦ, τὸ τοῖς ὑπὸ σοῦ γραφεῖσιν ἀπειθεῖν, φαίνονται δὲ πεισθέντες μὲν οἱ μὴ τεθυκότες, ἐναντία δὲ πεποιηκότες οἱ διαφθείραντες ἃ μένειν τοῖς ἔχουσιν ἐδέδοκτό σοι, οἱ δίκην εἰληφότες ἐν αὐτῷ τῷ λαβεῖν ὀφείλουσιν· ἣν γὰρ οὐ προσῆκεν ἔλαβον ζῆν μὲν ἐάσαντες οἷς ἐνεκάλουν, ἃ δ' οὐκ ἦν αἰτιάσασθαι τῶν γε ἀψύχων ὄντα κατεσκαφότες.

25. Καὶ μὴν εἰ καὶ σφόδρα τοῦτο ἦν ἀδίκημα, τὸ μὲν ἀξίους δεῖξαι δίκης ἐκείνους τούτων ἦν, τὸ δὲ ἐπιθεῖναι τὴν δίκην τοῦ δικαστοῦ. δικαστοῦ δὲ οὐκ ἦν ἀπορῆσαι τῶν ἐθνῶν ὑπ' αὐτοῖς ὄντων ἁπάντων. οὕτω καὶ τοὺς φονέας οἱ τῶν ἀπεσφαγμένων οἰκεῖοι τιμωροῦνται λόγοις μὲν τοῖς παρ' ἑαυτῶν, ψήφῳ δὲ τῇ τῶν δικαζόντων. οὐδεὶς δὲ ἁρπάσας ἐπὶ τὸν ἀνδροφόνον ξίφος προστίθησιν αὐτὸ τῷ 'κείνου ⟨τραχήλῳ⟩[2] χρησάμενος ἀντὶ τοῦ δικαστηρίου τῇ χειρί, οὐδὲ γὰρ ἐπὶ[3] τυμβωρύχον οὐδὲ προδότην οὐδὲ τῶν τὰ ἄλλα ἀδικούντων οὐδένα οὔτε πρότερον οὔθ' ὕστερον, ἀλλ' ἀντὶ τῶν ξιφῶν εἰσαγγελίαι καὶ γραφαὶ καὶ δίκαι. 26. καὶ τὸ δι' ὧν ὁ νόμος βούλεται γενέσθαι τὴν τιμωρίαν |

---

[1] κάμνοντες mss. : καμόντες F.
[2] τραχήλῳ inserted F. (cf. schol. V : αὐτὸ τὸ ξίφος τῷ 'κείνου τραχήλῳ) : om. mss.
[3] ἐπὶ F. (U, P corr.) : om. other mss.

and small alike, in which the weary used to find repose, have all been demolished, and those who have suffered this loss are like ship-wrecked mariners, swept from the ships in which they sailed.

24. Which party, then, deserves to be punished ? Those who have kept the law or those who have replaced it by their own inclinations ? If it be a crime, Sire, to disobey your edicts, and if those who have refrained from sacrifice have obviously obeyed them, and if these despoilers of things which you have decreed shall remain in their owners' possession have disobeyed them, then the exactors of punishment, by the very fact of exacting it, deserve to suffer it. Their punishment has been misdirected, for they have allowed the persons they accused to live, and have demolished objects which, being inanimate, lay beyond the reach of accusation.

25. Moreover, if this really and truly was a crime, it was their job to show that the accused deserved to be punished, but it was the magistrates' job to impose the penalty. And a magistrate [a] was not far to seek, for all the provinces are under such. This is how the kinsfolk of any murdered man get the murderers punished—by their presentation of the case and by the sentence of the magistrates. Nobody draws his sword against the murderer and puts it to his throat, employing force in place of the forms of law, nor does he do so against the desecrators of tombs, or traitors or any other criminal offender, either past or future, but the place of swords is taken by impeachments and processes, civil and criminal. 26. The magistrate, too, I believe, is satisfied for the

---

[a] δικαστής = *iudex* = provincial governor.

ἀρκοῦν οἶμαι τῷ δικάζοντι. ἀλλ' οὗτοι μόνοι τῶν F 1
ἁπάντων περὶ ὧν κατηγόρουν ἐδίκαζον καὶ δικά-
σαντες αὐτοὶ τὰ τῶν δημίων ἐποίουν. τί δὴ ζητοῦντες; εἰργομένους ἐντεῦθεν τοὺς τὰ τῶν θεῶν
τιμῶντας ἐπὶ τἀκείνων ἐνεχθῆναι. τουτὶ δ' ἐστὶ
πάντων εὐηθέστατον. τίς γὰρ οὐκ οἶδεν ὡς αὐτοῖς οἷς ἔπαθον μᾶλλον ἢ πρὶν ἐν οἷς ἦσαν ταῦτα
τεθαυμάκασιν; ὥσπερ οἱ τῶν σωμάτων ἐρῶντες
ἐκ τοῦ κωλύεσθαι μὴ τοῦτο ποιεῖν μᾶλλον τοῦτο
ποιοῦσι καὶ γίγνονται τῶν αὐτῶν ἐρασταὶ σφο-
δρότεροι. 27. εἰ δὲ ταῖς κατασκαφαῖς ἐγίγνοντο
τῆς γνώμης αἱ περὶ ταῦτα μεταβολαί, πάλαι ἂν
σῇ ψήφῳ τὰ ἱερὰ κατέσκαπτο· πάλαι γὰρ ἂν
ἡδέως ταύτην εἶδες τὴν μεταβολήν. ἀλλ' ᾔδεις οὐ
δυνησόμενος. διὰ τοῦτ' ἀπέσχου τῶν ἱερῶν τούτων. τούτους δ', εἰ καί τι τοιοῦτον προσεδόκων,
μετὰ σοῦ προσῆκεν ἐλθεῖν ἐπ' αὐτὸ καὶ μεταδοῦναι τῷ κρατοῦντι τῆς φιλοτιμίας. ἦν δέ, οἶμαι,
μηδὲν ἁμαρτάνοντας κατορθοῦν ἅπερ ἤθελον κάλλιον ἢ μετὰ τοῦ πλημμελεῖν.

28. Εἰ δέ σοι[1] φήσουσί τινας ἑτέρους ὑπὸ τούτων γεγενῆσθαι τῶν ἔργων καὶ μετ' αὐτῶν εἶναι
τῇ περὶ τοῦ θείου δόξῃ, μή σε λανθανέτωσαν δοκοῦντας οὐ γεγενημένους λέγοντες. ἀφεστᾶσι μὲν

---

[1] δέ σοι : A resumes : similarly Re.

---

[a] On the inefficacy of forced conversion cf. Or. 18. 121 ff.
(Vol. I, pp. 357 ff.) where Libanius commends Julian's
refusal to have recourse to it ; Athanasius (*Ep. ad solitariam
vitam agentes*), quoted by Gothofred and Reiske : οὐ γὰρ
ξίφεσιν ἢ βέλεσιν οὐδὲ διὰ στρατιωτῶν ἡ ἀλήθεια καταγγέλλεται
ἀλλὰ πειθοῖ καὶ συμβουλίᾳ.

penalty to be exacted by agents defined by law. But these people here were the only ones ever to judge the cases of those whom they accuse and, having passed judgement, themselves to play the hangman's part. And with what object ? For the worshippers of the gods thenceforth to be barred from their own rites and be converted to theirs ? But this is utter nonsense. Everybody knows that, as a result of their very sufferings, people have become more confirmed than ever in their faith,[a] just as in physical desire the lover has only to be barred from the act and he does it all the more and becomes more ardent towards the same object of his affections. 27. If such conversion could be effected simply by the destruction of temples, they would have been long ago destroyed by your decree, for you would long since have been glad to see this conversion. But you knew that you could not, and so you never laid a finger on these shrines. These people, even if they looked forward to some such result, ought to have advanced towards it in step with you and should have let the emperor share in their ambition. It would have been better, surely, to succeed in their objective by staying on the right side of the law rather than by abusing it.[b]

28. And if they tell you that some other people have been converted by such measures and now share their religious beliefs, do not overlook the fact that they speak of conversions apparent, not real.[c] Their

[b] Libanius here regretfully accepts Theodosius' christianizing policy, but insists that he, unlike these monks, promotes it by due force of laws.

[c] Theodosius grew increasingly severe upon apostasy during the course of his reign, cf. C. Th. 16. 7. 1-5.

R ii. 177 γὰρ οὐδὲν μᾶλλον | αὐτῶν, φασὶ δέ. τοῦτο δέ F ·
ἔστιν οὐκ ἐκείνους ἕτερα τιμᾶν ἀνθ' ἑτέρων, ἀλλὰ
τούτους πεφενακίσθαι. ἔρχονται μὲν γὰρ ἐπὶ τὰ
φαινόμενα ⟨καὶ⟩[1] τὸν τούτων ὄχλον καὶ διὰ τῶν
ἄλλων ὧν οὗτοι πορεύονται, καταστάντες δὲ εἰς
σχῆμα τὸ τῶν εὐχομένων ἢ οὐδένα καλοῦσιν ἢ τοὺς
θεούς, οὐ καλῶς μὲν ἐκ τοῦ τοιούτου χωρίου, καλοῦσι δ' οὖν. ὥσπερ οὖν ἐν ταῖς τραγῳδίαις ὁ τὸν
τύραννον εἰσιὼν οὐκ ἔστι τύραννος ἀλλ' ὅπερ ἦν
πρὸ τοῦ προσωπείου, οὕτω καὶ ἐκείνων ἕκαστος
τηρεῖ μὲν αὐτὸν ἀκίνητον, δοκεῖ δὲ τούτοις κεκινῆσθαι. 29. καίτοι τί τὸ πρᾶγμα αὐτοῖς γεγένη-
R ii. 178 ται | βέλτιον, ὅταν λόγος μὲν ᾖ τὰ 'κείνων, τὸ δὲ
ἔργον ἀπῇ; δεῖ γὰρ δὴ τά γε τοιαῦτα πείθειν, οὐ
προσαναγκάζειν. εἰ δ' ὁ μὴ τοῦτο δυνάμενος ἐκεί-
R ii. 179 νῳ χρήσεται, εἴργασται | μὲν οὐδέν, οἴεται δέ.[2]
λόγος δὲ μηδ' ἐν τοῖς τούτων αὐτῶν τοῦτο ἐνεῖναι
νόμοις, ἀλλ' εὐδοκιμεῖν μὲν τὸ πείθειν, κακῶς δὲ
ἀκούειν τὴν ἀνάγκην. τί οὖν μαίνεσθε κατὰ τῶν |
ἱερῶν, εἰ τὸ πείθειν μὲν οὐκ ἔστι, βιάζεσθαι δὲ F
⟨δεῖ⟩[3]; σαφῶς γὰρ οὕτως καὶ τοὺς ὑμετέρους ἂν
αὐτῶν παραβαίνοιτε νόμους.
30. Ἀλλὰ τὸ μηδ' εἶναί φασιν ἱερὰ χρήσιμον
εἶναι τῇ γῇ καὶ τοῖς ἐπ' αὐτῆς ἀνθρώποις. ἐνταῦθα
τοίνυν δεῖ μέν μοι πολλῆς, ὦ βασιλεῦ, τῆς παρρησίας, δέδοικα δὲ μή τινα λυπήσω τῶν ἐμαυτοῦ
κρειττόνων. χωρείτω δ' οὖν ὅμως ὁ λόγος ἐν
τοῦτο ἀπαιτούμενος, τὴν ἀλήθειαν.

---

[1] ⟨καὶ⟩ ins. F.
[2] After δέ, τουτὶ ἀσθενές inserted in mss. Re. (edition)
and F. bracket as gloss. Re. (Animadv.) had conjectured
τουτὶ δὴ τὸ ἀσθενές.

converts have not really been changed—they only
say they have. This does not mean that they have
exchanged one faith for another—only that this
crew have been bamboozled. They go to their
ceremonies, join their crowds, go everywhere where
these do, but when they adopt an attitude of prayer,
they either invoke no god at all or else they invoke
the gods. It is no proper invocation from such a
place, but it is an invocation for all that. In plays,
the actor who takes the part of a tyrant is not a
tyrant, but just the same as he was before putting
on the mask *a* : so here, everyone keeps himself un-
changed, but he lets them think he has been changed.
29. Now what advantage have they won when adherence to their doctrine is a matter of words and the
reality is absent ? Persuasion is required in such
matters, not constraint. If persuasion fails and constraint is employed, nothing has been accomplished,
though you think it has. It is said that in their very
own rules it does not appear, but that persuasion
meets with approval and compulsion is deplored.
Then why these frantic attacks on the temples, if
you cannot persuade and must needs resort to force ?
In this way you would obviously be breaking your
own rules.

30. But, they assert, the very absence of temples
is a blessing to the world and the people in it. Well,
here, Sire, I must speak fully and frankly, though I
fear that I shall upset some in higher station than
myself. However, let my argument proceed, according to the demands of truth alone.

a Cf. Or. 64. 74.

---

[3] βιάζεσθαι F., conj. Monnier (PBU): -εσθε Re. (other
mss.). | δεῖ inserted F., conj. Re.

R ii. 180   31. Εἰπάτω γάρ μοί | τις τῶν τὰς μὲν πυράγρας
καὶ σφύρας καὶ ἄκμονας ἀφέντων, περὶ δὲ οὐρανοῦ
καὶ τῶν τὸν οὐρανὸν ἐχόντων ἀξιούντων διαλέγεσθαι, ποτέροις ἀκολουθοῦντες οἱ τὰ μέγιστα ἀπὸ
μικρῶν καὶ φαύλων τῶν πρώτων ἀφορμῶν Ῥωμαῖοι δυνηθέντες ἐδυνήθησαν, τῷ[1] τούτων ἢ οἷς
ἱερὰ καὶ βωμοί, παρ' ὧν ὅ τι χρὴ ποιεῖν ἢ μὴ
ποιεῖν διὰ τῶν μάντεων; Ἀγαμέμνονα δὲ τὸ πανταχοῦ τεθυκέναι πλέοντα ἐπ' Ἴλιον αἰσχρῶς ἐπαν-
ήγαγεν ἢ νενικηκότα τῆς Ἀθηνᾶς αὐτῷ τὸ τέλος |
εὑρούσης; Ἡρακλέα δὲ τὸν πρὸ τούτου τὴν αὐτὴν F
καθελόντα πόλιν οὐ θυσίαις ἴσμεν τῶν θεῶν προσ-
λαβόντα τὴν ῥοπήν; 32. ἔτι τοίνυν λαμπρὸς μὲν ὁ
Μαραθὼν οὐ διὰ τοὺς μυρίους μᾶλλον Ἀθηναίων
ἢ διὰ τὸν Ἡρακλέα καὶ Πᾶνα, θεία δὲ ἡ Σαλαμὶς
οὐ διὰ τὰς[2] τῶν Ἑλλήνων μᾶλλον ναῦς ἢ τοὺς ἐξ
Ἐλευσῖνος συμμάχους οἳ μετ' ᾠδῆς τῆς αὑτῶν ἐπὶ
τὴν ναυμαχίαν ἧκον. μυρίους ἄν[3] τις ἔχοι λέγειν
πολέμους τῇ τῶν θεῶν εὐνοίᾳ κυβερνηθέντας καί,
νὴ Δία γε, καὶ εἰρήνης καὶ ἡσυχίας χρόνους.

33. Τὸ δὲ μέγιστον, οἱ μάλιστα τοῦτο τὸ μέρος
ἀτιμάσαι δοκοῦντες καὶ ἄκοντες τετιμήκασι. τίνες
οὗτοι; οἱ τὴν Ῥώμην τοῦ θύειν οὐ τολμήσαντες
R ii. 181 ἀφελέσθαι. καίτοι | εἰ μὲν μάταιον ἅπαν τοῦτο

---

[1] After τῷ F. inserted θεῷ, following gloss (θεῷ δηλ.) in
V.   [2] τριακοσίας (i.e. τ′) inserted F., before τῶν.
[3] <δ'> ἄν F.

---

[a] A sourly classical reference to Homer, Od. 3. 434.
Libanius' criticism of the monks is the more bitter, in that
ignorant and untaught, they aspire to be interpreters of
divine philosophy, the most select and exclusive of the higher
professions of paganism.
[b] The arguments of Symmachus also, Rel. 3.

128

31. These people who have cast aside tongs, hammers and anvils [a] and now claim to discourse upon heaven and its occupants—let any of them tell me which it was the Romans followed, when from such small and humble beginnings they attained supreme power.[b] Was it the god of these people? or was it the gods with temples and altars, from whom they heard, by means of seers, what they should or should not do? Did Agamemnon's far-flung sacrifices on his expedition to Troy ensure his return in disgrace or in triumph, once Athena had devised the means to the end? [c] Heracles before him sacked this same city, and do we not know that he gained the support of the gods by sacrifice? [d] 32. Moreover, the glory[e] of Marathon is due not so much to the 10,000 Athenians as to Heracles and Pan, and the crowning mercy of Salamis not to the Greek fleet so much as to the helpers from Eleusis,[f] who came to the battle to the accompaniment of their own sacred hymn. You could cite wars without number that have been directed by the favour of the gods,—yes, by Zeus, and times of peace and quiet, too.

33. And the most crucial point of all—those who appear to have been our chief opponents in this particular have honoured the gods even against their will. And who might these be? Why, those who have not dared rob Rome of its sacrifices.[g] Yet, if

[c] *Cf.* Homer, *Od.* 1. 327, 3. 144.   [d] *Cf.* Pausan. 5. 14. 2.

[e] *Cf.* Herod. 6. 105, Polemo, *Decl.* 1. 35, 2. 41.   Lib. *Or.* 18. 66.

[f] For " divine Salamis " *cf.* the oracle quoted by Herod. 8. 65 ; *cf. Or.* 15. 40 ; for the supernatural aid from Eleusis *cf.* the mystic procession, Plut. *Them.* 15, Herod. *ibid.*

[g] Sacrifices in Rome were not banned until Feb. A.D. 391 (*C. Th.* 16. 10. 10), an indication of the *terminus ante quem.*

τὸ περὶ τὰς θυσίας, τί μὴ τὸ μάταιον ἐκωλύθη;
εἰ δὲ καὶ βλαβερόν, πῶς οὐ ταύτῃ γε μᾶλλον; εἰ
δ' ἐν ταῖς ἐκεῖ θυσίαις κεῖται τὸ βέβαιον τῆς ἀρχῆς,
ἀπανταχοῦ δεῖ νομίζειν λυσιτελεῖν τὸ θύειν καὶ
διδόναι τοὺς μὲν | ἐν Ῥώμῃ δαίμονας τὰ μείζω, F
τοὺς δ' ἐν τοῖς ἀγροῖς ἢ καὶ τοῖς ἄλλοις ἄστεσιν
ἐλάττω, δέξαιτο δ' ἄν τις εὖ φρονῶν καὶ τὰ τηλικαῦτα. 34. καὶ γὰρ ἐν τοῖς στρατεύμασιν οὐκ
ἴσον μὲν τὸ παρ' ἑκάστου, φέρει δέ τι τῇ μάχῃ τὸ
παρ' ἑκάστου. οἷον δή τι κἂν ταῖς εἰρεσίαις· οὐκ
ἴσοι μὲν ἅπαντες οἱ βραχίονες, συντελεῖ δέ τι καὶ ὁ
τοῦ πρώτου λειπόμενος. ὁ μέν τις τῷ σκήπτρῳ
τῷ τῆς Ῥώμης συναγωνίζεται, ὁ δὲ[1] ταύτῃ σώζει
πόλιν ὑπήκοον, ὁ δέ τις ἀγρὸν ἀνέχει παρέχων εὖ
πράττειν. ἔστω τοίνυν ἱερὰ πανταχοῦ ἢ ὁμολο-
γούντων οὗτοι δυσμενῶς ὑμᾶς πρὸς τὴν Ῥώμην
ἔχειν δόντας αὐτῇ ποιεῖν ἀφ' ὧν ζημιώσεται.[2]
      35. Οὐ τοίνυν τῇ Ῥώμῃ μόνον ἐφυλάχθη τὸ θύ-
R ii. 182 ειν, ἀλλὰ καὶ τῇ τοῦ Σαράπιδος | τῇ πολλῇ τε καὶ
μεγάλῃ καὶ πλῆθος κεκτημένῃ νεῶν, δι' ὧν κοινὴν ἁπάντων ἀνθρώπων ποιεῖ τὴν τῆς Αἰγύπτου
φοράν. αὐτὴ δὲ ἔργον τοῦ Νείλου, τὸν Νεῖλον δὲ
ἑστιᾷ[3] | ἀναβαίνειν ἐπὶ τὰς ἀρούρας πείθουσα,[4] ὧν οὐ F
ποιουμένων ὅτε τε χρὴ καὶ παρ' ὧν, οὐδ' ἂν αὐτὸς
ἐθελήσειεν. ἅ μοι δοκοῦσιν εἰδότες οἱ καὶ ταῦτα
ἂν ἡδέως ἀνελόντες οὐκ ἀνελεῖν ἀλλ' ἀφεῖναι τὸν

---

[1] δέ <τις> F.   [2] ζημιώσεται F., Re. : -ετε mss.
[3] ἑστιᾷ Re. (A) : ἔστια other mss. (ἐστιν ἃ οἴδαμεν C marg.) :
ἑστιάματά ἐστιν F. : ἱερά ἐστι τὰ Cobet.
[4] πείθουσα Re. : πείθοντα F. (mss.).

---

[a] Alexandria, where sacrifices were banned in June A.D.
391 (*ibid.* 10. 11). This was soon afterwards followed by the
sack of the Serapeum by Theophilus and his monks.

all this business of sacrifice is nonsense, then why
has not the nonsense been stopped ? If it is harmful, then isn't this all the more reason ? But if the
stability of empire depends on the sacrifices performed there, we must consider that sacrifice is
everywhere to our advantage ; the gods in Rome
grant greater blessings, those in the countryside and
the other cities, lesser ones, but any sensible man
would welcome even such as these. 34. In an army,
a man's individual contribution may not be com-
parable with another's, but it all counts towards
winning the battle. Similarly, among ships' rowers,
also : their arms do not all pull alike, but even the
less capable does his bit. So with the gods : one
supports the might of Rome, another protects for
her a city under her sway, another protects an estate
and grants it prosperity. Let temples everywhere
remain in being, then, or else let these people agree
that you emperors are ill-disposed to Rome since
you allow her to act in a manner that will cause her
harm.

35. And it is not only in Rome that sacrifice has
been maintained. They are also performed in the
great and mighty city of Serapis,[a] with its fleet of
ships whereby it makes the produce of Egypt common
to all mankind. Egypt is the work of the Nile, and
offers feasts to the Nile inducing him to flood the
fields, and if these are not performed in due season
and by due persons, he too would refuse.[b] I feel
that, in awareness of this, the eager supporters of
abolition have refrained from abolishment of them,

[b] Constantine had already withdrawn the " Nile cubit,"
the ceremonial unit of measurement for the Nile flood, from
its traditional place in the Serapeum.

131

ποταμὸν εὐωχεῖσθαι τοῖς παλαιοῖς νομίμοις ἐπὶ
μισθῷ τῷ εἰωθότι. 36. τί οὖν; ἐπεὶ μὴ ποταμός
ἐστι καθ' ἕκαστον ἀγρὸν τὰ τοῦ Νείλου τῇ γῇ
παρέχων, οὐδ' εἶναι τὰν τούτοις ἱερὰ δεῖ, ἀλλ' ὅ
τι δόξειε τοῖς γενναίοις τουτοισὶ πάσχειν; οὓς
ἡδέως ἐκεῖνο ἂν ἐροίμην εἰ τολμήσουσι παρελθόντες
R ii. 183 γνώμην εἰπεῖν πεπαῦσθαι | μὲν τὰ γιγνόμενα τῷ
Νείλῳ, μὴ μετέχειν δὲ αὐτοῦ τὴν γῆν μηδὲ σπεί-
ρεσθαι μηδὲ ἀμᾶσθαι μηδὲ διδόναι πυροὺς μηδ'
ὅσα δίδωσι μηδ' ἀνάγεσθαι γῆν ἐπὶ πᾶσαν ἃ νῦν.
εἰ δ' οὐκ ἂν ἐπὶ τούτοις διάραιεν τὸ στόμα, οἷς οὐ
λέγουσι διελέγχουσιν ἃ λέγουσιν. οἱ γὰρ οὐκ ἂν
εἰπόντες δεῖν τῶν τιμῶν ἀποστερεῖσθαι τὸν Νεῖλον
ὁμολογοῦσι τοῖς ἀνθρώποις συμφέρειν τὰς τῶν ἱε-
ρῶν τιμάς. |

37. Ὅταν τοίνυν καὶ τοῦ σεσυληκότος μνημο- F
νεύωσι, τὸ μὲν ὡς οὐκ ἐπὶ τὰς θυσίας προῆλθε,
R ii. 184 παρείσθω, ἀλλὰ τίς | οὕτω μεγάλην τῶν περὶ τὰ
ἱερὰ χρήματα δέδωκε δίκην τὰ μὲν αὐτὸς αὑτὸν
μετιών, τὰ δ' ἤδη καὶ τεθνεὼς πάσχων ἐπ' ἀλλήλους τε ἰόντων τῶν ἐκ τοῦ γένους καὶ λελειμμένου
μηδενός; καίτοι πολὺ βέλτιον ἦν αὐτῷ τῶν ἀπ'
ἐκείνου τινὰς ἄρχειν ἢ τὴν ἐπώνυμον αὐτῷ τοῖς
οἰκοδομήμασιν αὔξεσθαι πόλιν δι' ἣν καὶ αὐτὴν
πλὴν τῶν ἐκεῖ κακῶς τρυφώντων ἅπαντας ἀνθρώ-

---

a Constantine's self-inflicted punishment was the murder
of his son Crispus for an alleged amour with his wife Fausta ;

but have allowed the river to be feasted in the time-honoured ritual for the customary reward. 36. What, then? Since there is not a river on every estate bestowing the blessings of the Nile upon the land, must the temples in them cease to exist and be misused in whatever way these fine fellows may decide? I would like to put this question to them. Will they dare come forward and propose the abolition of the Nile feast, and with it the banning of the land from partaking of it, and from the sowing and reaping and production of corn and all its products and their transportation to all the world as now? If they would not utter a word under these conditions, then by their silence they refute what they do say, for by denying that the Nile should be deprived of his honours, they agree that the honouring of the temples is to the benefit of mankind.

37. And when they mention their desecrator, leaving aside the fact that he did not proceed against the sacrifices,—who paid more dearly for his policy concerning temple property, by punishment whether self-inflicted or suffered even after death,[a] when the members of his family attacked each other and not a single one was left? For him it would have been far better to have descendants of his own upon the throne than for the city that bears his name to sprout a crop of buildings, when simply because of it he has all men, save those who wallow there in base extravagance, calling down curses upon him

after his death, the family suffered from family feuds—his half-brothers were murdered in the bloodbath of A.D. 337, Constantine II by Constans in A.D. 340, Constans himself by the usurper Magnentius in A.D. 350, and Constantius died without male issue in A.D. 361.

R ii. 185 πους ἔχει καταρωμένους | τῇ σφῶν αὐτῶν ἀπορίᾳ
τὴν εὐπορίαν ἐκείνῃ παρέχοντας.

38. Καὶ ὅταν τοίνυν μετ' ἐκεῖνον τὸν ἐκείνου
λέγωσι καὶ ὡς καθεῖλε νεὼς οὐκ ἐλάττω περὶ τοῦτο
πονησάντων τῶν καθαιρούντων ἢ τῶν οἰκοδομη-
σάντων,—οὕτως οὐκ ἦν ῥᾴδιον ἀλλήλων διαζεῦξαι
τοὺς λίθους δεσμοῖς ἰσχυροτάτοις εἰσενηνεγμένους,
—ὅταν οὖν ταῦτα λέγωσιν, ἐγὼ μεῖζόν τι προσ-
τίθημι, ὅτι | ἐκεῖνός γε καὶ δῶρα ναοὺς τοῖς ἀμφ' F 1
R ii. 186 αὐτὸν ἐδίδου καθάπερ ἵππον ἢ ἀνδράποδον | ἢ κύνα
ἢ φιάλην χρυσῆν, κακὰ δὲ ἀμφοῖν τὰ δῶρα τοῖς τε
δοῦσι τοῖς τε λαβοῦσιν. ὁ μὲν γὰρ ἐν τῷ τρέμειν
καὶ δεδιέναι Πέρσας ἅπαντα τὸν βίον ἐβίω φοβούμενος ἔαρ[1] ἕκαστον ἔξοδον ἔχον,[2] ὥσπερ τὰ παιδία
τὰς Μορμόνας, τῶν δὲ οἱ μὲν ἄπαιδες καὶ πρὸ
διαθηκῶν ἀπῆλθον οἱ δυστυχεῖς, τοῖς δ' ἦν ἄμεινον
μὴ παιδοποιήσασθαι. 39. τοιαύταις μὲν ἀδοξίαις,
τοσούτῳ δὲ πολέμῳ τῷ πρὸς ἀλλήλους συζῶσιν οἱ
R ii. 187 ἀπὸ τούτων ἐν μέσῳ τῶν ἀπὸ τῶν | ἱερῶν κιόνων
στρεφόμενοι, δι' οὕς, οἶμαι, ταῦτα. τοιαύτας τοῖς
τέκνοις εἰς εὐδαιμονίαν ἀφορμὰς οἱ πλουτεῖν εἰδότες ἐκεῖνοι παρέδωκαν. καὶ νῦν οὓς ἄγει μὲν
εἰς Κιλικίαν νοσήματα τῆς τοῦ Ἀσκληπιοῦ χρή-

---

[1] φοβούμενος ἔαρ F., conj. Re. : φοβούμενος. ἀρ' MSS.
[2] ἔχον F., conj. Re. : ἔχων MSS.

---

[a] Pagans tended to criticize Constantinople for its luxury
and parasitical rôle in the empire, cf. Or. 1. 279, Zos. 2. 30.
Libanius was always critical of the vulgarity of the high life
in the Christian court, e.g. Or. 1. 75 f.

[b] Cf. Or. 17. 7. The furore caused by Julian's decree to

for the prosperity with which they endow it by beggaring themselves.[a]

38. And if, after him, they tell of his son and his destruction of temples, when the demolition was as laborious as their erection,—such were the difficulties of tearing apart stones that had been bound together by strongest of ties,—when they prate of this, I add a rider of more importance, that he presented his courtiers with gifts of temples, as though it were a present of a horse, a slave, a dog or a golden goblet,[b] but these gifts were fatal both to the givers and to the takers. He spent all his life in fear and trembling of the Persians : just as children are scared of the bogey-man, he was scared of every spring-time and the invasion it brought.[c] They either died in misery without issue and without testament, or else they would have done better to have had no children at all. 39. In such infamy, in such mutual strife do their children pass their lives wandering amidst the columns of temples, the reason for their plight, I am sure. Such is the source of the prosperity bequeathed by those money-grubbers to their children. And now the people whom their illnesses, that require the hand of Asclepius,[d] attract to Cilicia are

restore temples and temple property reveals the extent to which this process had gone : v. Liebeschuetz, p. 152.

[c] A condensed adaptation of Or. 18. 206 ff. For Μόρμονες cf. Xen. Hell. 4. 4. 12, Lib. Or. 33. 42.

[d] The temple of Asclepius at Aegae, a noted pilgrim shrine, with miraculous cures produced by incubation, Philostr. V. Apol. 1. 1. 6 ff. Christian writers (e.g. Euseb. V. Const. 3. 56, Sozom. 2. 5) attribute its demolition to Constantine. Under Julian it was restored to its former status (Ep. 695), and Libanius had recourse to it during his illness of A.D. 367 (Or. 1. 143).

ζοντα χειρός, αἱ δὲ περὶ τὸν τόπον ὕβρεις ἀπρά-
R ii. 188 κτους ἀποπέμπουσι, πῶς ἔνεστι | μὴ κακῶς τὸν
τούτων αἴτιον λέγοντας ἀναστρέφειν;

40. Βασιλεῖ δὲ τοιαῦτα ἔστω τὰ βεβιωμένα, ὥστε
τοῖς ἐπαίνοις ζῆν καὶ τετελευτηκότα, οἷον γενό-
μενον | ἴσμεν τὸν¹ τὴν μὲν ἀρχὴν ἐκδεξάμενον τὴν F 1
ἐκείνου, τὴν Περσῶν δὲ καθελόντα ἄν, εἰ μὴ προδοσία τὸ πέρας ἐκώλυσε. μέγας δέ ἐστιν ὅμως
καὶ τεθνεώς. δόλῳ μὲν γὰρ ἀπέθανεν, ὥσπερ
Ἀχιλλεύς, ἐκ δὲ τῶν πρὸ τοῦ θανάτου πεπραγμένων, ὡς ἐκεῖνος, ᾄδεται. 41. καὶ ταῦτα τούτῳ
παρὰ τῶν θεῶν οἷς ἀπέδωκεν ἱερὰ καὶ τιμὰς καὶ
τεμένη καὶ βωμοὺς καὶ αἷμα. παρ᾽ ὧν ἀκούσας
ὡς τὸ τῶν Περσῶν αὔχημα ταπεινώσας εἶτα ἀπο-
θανεῖται, τῆς ψυχῆς ἐπρίατο τὸ κλέος πολλὰς μὲν
πόλεις ἑλών, πολλὴν δὲ γῆν δῃώσας, παιδεύσας δὲ
τοὺς διώκοντας φεύγειν, μέλλων δέ, ὡς ἅπαντες
ἴσασι, δέξεσθαι πρεσβείαν κομίζουσαν τῶν πολε-
R ii. 189 μίων δουλείαν. τοιγαροῦν ἠσπάζετό τε τὸ | τραῦ-
μα καὶ βλέπων ἠγάλλετο καὶ μὴ δακρύων αὐτὸς
τοῖς τοῦτο δρῶσιν ἐπετίμα εἰ μὴ νομίζοιεν αὐτῷ
παντὸς ἀμείνω γήρως εἶναι τὴν πληγήν. καὶ αἱ
πρεσβεῖαι τοίνυν αἱ πολλαὶ αἱ μετ᾽ ἐκεῖνον ἐκεί-
νου πᾶσαι καὶ τὸ λόγοις | ἀνθ᾽ ὅπλων χρῆσθαι τοὺς F 1
Ἀχαιμενίδας ἐκείνου τοῦ δέους αὐτῶν ἐγκατα-
τεθειμένου ταῖς ψυχαῖς. τοιοῦτος ἡμῖν ὁ τὰ ἱερὰ
¹ <περὶ> τὸν F.

ᵃ Resumes arguments already presented in *Or.* 24. For
allegations of treachery made against the Christians and the
murder of Julian *cf. Or.* 18. 268 ff., 24. 6 ff. (Vol. I, p. 494 n.).
ᵇ *Cf.* Philostr. *Her.* 19. 11.

sent empty away because of the outrages the place has suffered. They cannot help returning with curses for the author of it.

40. An emperor's conduct in life should be such that even after death he lives on in the praise that he has won. Such a one, we well know, was his successor on the throne, who would have broken the power of Persia had not treason prevented his design : yet great he is, even in death.[a] For he died by treachery, as did Achilles, but, like him, his praises are sung in consequence of the deeds he did before he died.[b] 41. And this is his reward from the gods, to whom he restored temples, honours, precincts, altars and offerings of blood.[c] From them he heard that he was destined to die after humbling the pride of Persia,[d] and he paid for his glory with his life, after taking many a town, ravaging many a land and teaching the pursuer to turn tail, just as he was going to receive, as everybody knows, an embassy that brought the enemy's complete surrender. So he welcomed his wound, gazed upon it and was glad, and, tearless himself, he reproved his tearful friends that they did not believe his wound better than a ripe old age.[e] And all the many embassies since his time are due to him, and the Achaemenids'[f] preference for negotiation rather than war is due to the fear that he inspired in their souls. Such then was he that restored the temples

[c] By his edict of toleration in A.D. 361, *E.L.F.* No. 42 (with refs.) ; *cf. Or.* 18. 121 ff.

[d] *Cf.* the oracle cited in Suidas, *s.v.* " Julianus."

[e] For accounts of the death of Julian *cf. Or.* 18. 272 f., 24. 7. Amm. Marc. 25. 3. 15 ff.

[f] For this classicizing reference to the Persian royal house *cf. Or.* 17. 32 (Vol. I, p. 270 n.).

LIBANIUS

τοῖς θεοῖς ἀνιστάς, κρείττω μὲν ἔργα λήθης ἐργα-
σάμενος, κρείττων δὲ λήθης γεγενημένος.

42. Ἐγὼ δὲ ἠξίουν τὸν πρὸ τοῦδε τὰ μὲν τῶν
ἐναντίων καθαιρεῖν καὶ κατασκάπτειν καὶ κατα-
κάειν, ἐπειδήπερ ἐγνώκει τῶν θεῶν καταφρονεῖν,
εἰ καὶ[1] ἱερῶν γε καὶ ὁ τῶν ὄντων τοῖς πολεμίοις
φειδόμενος ἀμείνων, οἰκείων μέντοι ναῶν πόνῳ καὶ
χρόνῳ καὶ πολυχειρίᾳ καὶ πολλοῖς ταλάντοις κατε-
σκευασμένων καὶ προκινδυνεύειν ἄξιον. | εἰ γὰρ
πανταχόθεν μὲν σωστέον τὰς πόλεις, λάμπουσι δὲ
τούτοις μᾶλλον ἢ τοῖς ἄλλοις αἱ πόλεις καὶ οὗτοι
τῶν ἐν αὐταῖς μετά γε τὰ κάλλη τῶν βασιλείων
κεφάλαιον, πῶς οὐ καὶ τούτοις μεταδοτέον προνοίας καὶ ὅπως ἐν τῷ σώματι τῶν πόλεων εἶεν
σπουδαστέον; πάντως δέ εἰσιν οἰκοδομήματα κἂν
εἰ μὴ νεῴ γε. δεῖ δέ, οἶμαι, τῷ φόρῳ τῶν δεξομένων. δεχέσθω τοίνυν ἑστώς, ἀλλὰ μὴ καταφε-
ρέσθω. μηδὲ τὸ χεῖρα μὲν ἀποκόπτειν ἀνθρώπου
δεινὸν ἡγώμεθα, πόλεων δὲ ὀφθαλμοὺς ἐξορύττειν
μέτριον μηδ᾽ ἐν μὲν | τοῖς σεισμοῖς τὸ πίπτον ὀδυ-
ρώμεθα, σεισμῶν δὲ οὐκ ὄντων οὐδὲ βλαπτόντων
αὐτοὶ τὸ ᾽κείνων ποιῶμεν. | 43. οὐκοῦν τῶν μὲν
βασιλέων οἱ νεῴ κτήματα, καθάπερ καὶ τὰ ἄλλα,
τὸ δὲ τὰ αὐτῶν καταποντίζειν ὅρα εἰ σωφρονούν-
των. ἀλλ᾽ ὁ μὲν βαλάντιον ῥίπτων εἰς τὴν θάλατταν οὐχ ὑγιαίνει οὐδ᾽ εἴ τις κυβερνήτης τέμνοι
κάλων οὗ δεῖ τῷ πλοίῳ, καὶ ναύτην δὲ εἰ κελεύσειε[2] τῇ θαλάττῃ τὴν κώπην ἀφεῖναι, δεινὰ ἂν

R ii. 190

F

R ii. 191

[1] εἰ καὶ F., conj. Monnier : ἐπεὶ Re. (mss.).
[2] κελεύσειε F., Re. (Par. gr. 853) : κελεύεις other mss.

[a] As pagans had claimed, and had been conceded by Constantius and Theodosius himself (C. Th. 16. 10. 3, 8 of A.D.

138

to the gods, the author of deeds unforgettable, himself unforgettable.

42. As for his predecessor, once he had made up
his mind to spurn the gods, even though he would
have done better to spare the temples and property
of the enemy, I would have expected him to demolish,
overthrow and burn the temples of the enemy, but
to be a proper champion of our own shrines that have
been erected with so much toil and time, labour and
expense. If we must protect our cities everywhere,
if our cities owe their fame to the temples in particular, and if these temples are, after the glories of
the palace, their chief pride, we must surely give
them some consideration and be zealous for their
maintenance as part of the fabric of the cities. They
are at least buildings, even though not used as
temples.[a] Taxation, presumably, requires offices of
collection [b] : so let the temple stand and be the
collecting office, and keep it from demolition. Do
not let us think it a crime to cut off a man's hand
and a credit to gouge out the eyes of cities. Let
us not lament the destruction caused by earthquakes
while we ourselves create the havoc of earthquakes
when none occur to cause damage. 43. Temples, like
other things, are imperial property. Look! when
anyone causes what is his own to founder, is he behaving properly ? Any man who hurls his purse
into the sea is out of his mind : if the pilot cuts
the cable on which the safety of his ship depends,
or bids the sailor jettison his oar, he would be

346 and 380). This was to be reiterated by *C. Th.* 16. 10.
19 of A.D. 408.

[b] For the collection of produce in kind, under the ἀποδε-
κταί.

δοκοῖ ποιεῖν· πόλιν δὲ εἴ τις ἄρχων ποιοῖ μέρει
τηλικούτῳ χείρονα, τὰ μέγιστα ὤνησε; τί γὰρ δεῖ
διαφθείρειν, οὗ τὴν χρείαν ἔνι μεταποιῆσαι; πῶς
R ii. 192 δὲ οὐκ αἰσχρὸν στρατόπεδον πολεμεῖν λίθοις | οἰ-
κείοις καὶ στρατηγὸν ἐφεστηκότα παρακαλεῖν κατὰ
τῶν πάλαι πολλῇ σπουδῇ πρὸς ὕψος ἀναβάντων,
ὧν τὸ πέρας ἑορτὴν τοῖς τότε βασιλεῦσιν ἔθηκε;

44. Καὶ μηδεὶς οἰέσθω σὴν ταῦτ' εἶναι κατηγο-
ρίαν, ὦ βασιλεῦ. κεῖται μὲν γὰρ πρὸς τοῖς ὁρίοις
R ii. 193 Περσῶν νεὼς ᾧ παραπλήσιον | οὐδέν, ὡς ἔστιν
ἁπάντων | τῶν τεθεαμένων ἀκούειν. οὕτω μέγι- F
στος μεγίστοις ἐγεγόνει τοῖς λίθοις, τοσοῦτον ἐπ-
έχων τῆς γῆς ὁπόσον καὶ ἡ πόλις. ἤρκει γοῦν ἐν
τοῖς ἐκ τῶν πολέμων φόβοις τοῖς οἰκοῦσι [τὴν
πόλιν][1] μηδὲν εἶναι πλέον τοῖς ἑλοῦσι τὴν πόλιν οὐκ
ἔχουσι κἀκεῖνον προσεξελεῖν τῆς ἰσχύος τοῦ περι-
βόλου πᾶν ἐλεγχούσης μηχάνημα. ἦν δὲ δὴ καὶ
ἐπὶ τὸ τέγος ἀναβᾶσι πλεῖστον ὅσον τῆς πολεμίας
ὁρᾶν, οὐ μικρὸν πολεμουμένοις πλεονέκτημα ἀνθρώποις. ἤκουσα δὲ καὶ ἐριζόντων τινῶν ἐν ὁπο-
R ii. 194 τέρῳ τὸ θαῦμα μεῖζον | ἱερῷ, τῷ μηκέτ' ὄντι τού-
τῳ ἢ ὃ μήποτε πάθοι ταὐτόν, ἐν ᾧπερ ὁ Σάραπις.
45. ἀλλὰ τοῦτο μὲν τὸ τοιοῦτο καὶ τοσοῦτον ἱερόν,
ἵν' ὑπερβῶ τὰ τῆς ὀροφῆς ἀπόρρητα καὶ ὅσα ἀγάλματα σιδήρου πεποιημένα κέκρυπται[2] τῷ σκότῳ
διαφεύγοντα τὸν ἥλιον, οἴχεται καὶ ἀπόλωλε, θρή-

---

[1] τὴν πόλιν mss., edd. Here bracketed as gloss.
[2] κέκρυπται V : κέκρυπτο Re., F. (other mss.).

---

[a] e.g. Theodoret (H.E. 5. 21) recounts the destruction of
the temple at Apamea by the bishop Marcellus. He was
"the first of all to use the law [i.e. C. Th. 16. 10. 9] as a
weapon," by calling in the Comes Orientis and troops to

thought a lunatic. If a magistrate diminishes a city by however little, is he its great benefactor ? What need to destroy what can be applied to another use ? It is surely disgraceful for an army [a] to wage war upon stones of its own, and for the general in charge to direct it against towering structures, erected long ago with great zeal, whose completion was the occasion for a festival for monarchs of yester-year.

44. And let none believe that this is an accusation against you, Sire. On our frontier with Persia there lies in ruins a temple that, to judge from the report of all that have seen it, was without peer, so massive was it, built with mighty stones, covering as much ground as the city itself.[b] At any rate, in the alarms of war it sufficed the inhabitants that if the enemy captured the city, they would get nothing more, since they would be unable to capture the temple because the strength of its wall defied all the engines of war. Moreover, if they mounted to its roof, they could observe a vast area of enemy country, which is a considerable advantage to people at war. I have even heard it argued which temple held the greater marvel, this that is now no more or that of Serapis, which I pray may never suffer the same fate.[c] 45. But this magnificent temple, leaving aside the concealed splendours of its ceiling and all the statues wrought in iron that were hidden in its shadow far from the sunlight,—it is vanished and gone, to the

destroy it. In A.D. 391 Theophilus is to do the same and call up troops for the destruction of the Serapeum.

[b] Edessa, as suggested by Gothofredus : cf. Or. 20. 27 f. In C. Th. 16. 10. 8 (A.D. 382) Theodosius had refused to have the temple closed.

[c] Terminus ante quem for this speech. For the Serapeum cf. Amm. Marc. 22. 16. 12 ff., and Eunap. V.S. 472.

νος μὲν τοῖς ἰδοῦσιν, ἡδονὴ δὲ τοῖς οὐχ ἑωρακόσιν,
οὐ γὰρ ἴσον ἐν τοῖς τοιούτοις ὀφθαλμοί τε καὶ ὦτα,
μᾶλλον δὲ τοῖς οὐκ ἰδοῦσιν ἄμφω, καὶ λύπη καὶ
ἡδονή, τὸ μὲν ἐκ τοῦ πτώματος, τὸ δ' ὅτιπερ οὐ
τεθέανται. 46. ἀλλ' ὅμως εἴ τις ἀκριβῶς σκοπή-
σειεν, οὐ σὸν τοῦτο, τοῦ δὲ ἡπατηκότος ἀνθρώπου
μιαροῦ καὶ θεοῖς ἐχθροῦ καὶ δειλοῦ καὶ φιλοχρη-
R ii. 195 μάτου | καὶ τῇ τικτόμενον αὐτὸν | δεξαμένῃ γῇ F
δυσμενεστάτου, ἀλογίας μὲν ἀπολελαυκότος τύχης,
κακῶς δὲ χρωμένου τῇ τύχῃ δουλεύοντος τῇ γυναικί, πάντα ἐκείνῃ χαριζομένου, πάντα ἐκείνην
ἡγουμένου. τῇ δ' ἀνάγκῃ πάνθ' ὑπηρετεῖν τοῖς
ταῦτα ἐπιτάττουσιν ὧν τῆς ἀρετῆς ἀπόδειξις τὸ ζῆν
ἐν ἱματίοις πενθούντων καὶ μείζων[1] γε ταύτης τὸ
ἐν ἐκείνοις ὧν οἱ καὶ τῶν σάκκων ὑφάνται. | 47.
R ii. 196 τοιοῦτον ἐργαστήριον ἠπάτησέ σε,[2] ἐφενάκισεν, ὑπ-
ηγάγετο, παρεκρούσατο, πολλοὺς δὲ καὶ θεοὺς παρὰ
⟨τῶν παίδων⟩[3] τῶν θεῶν μαθόντες ἴσμεν ἀπατη-
θέντας. ὡς γὰρ δὴ καὶ θυόντων ἱερεῖα καὶ οὕτως
ἐγγύς, ὡς ἐπὶ τὰς ἐκείνων ῥῖνας τὸν καπνὸν εἰστρέ-
R ii. 197 χειν, καὶ ὡς ἀπειλούντων[4] | καὶ μείζω μικροῖς
ἐπαγόντων καὶ κομπούντων καὶ πεπιστευκότων
μηδὲν ἂν αὐτῶν ποτε φανῆναι δυνατώτερον, τοιούτοις πλάσμασι καὶ τέχναις καὶ ῥήμασι μεμη-
χανημένοις δεινοῖς ἐμβαλεῖν ὀργὴν τὸν πρᾳότατον |
R ii. 198 βασιλέων ἐξήγαγόν πως αὐτοῦ, ἐπεὶ τά | γε ὄντως F

[1] μείζων F., conj. Re.: μεῖζον mss.
[2] ἠπάτησέ σε F., conj. Re., Cobet: ἠπάτησεν mss., except
I, which omits.
[3] παίδων τῶν inserted F. (cf. Plat. Resp. 366 b).
[4] ἀπειλούντων M corrected (Schol. M (marg.): εἶχεν
ἀπλούντων, οἶμαι δὲ ἢ ἀπολούντων ἢ ἀπειλούντων θέλει), F., Re.:
ἀπλούντων other mss.

grief of those who had seen it and the comfort of those who had not, for in such cases seeing and hearing do not have the same effect. In fact, these who had not seen it experience the twin emotions, of grief at its fall and of comfort at not having witnessed it. 46. However, on a careful consideration of the matter, this is none of your doing, but of the person that misled you, a scoundrel hated of the gods, cowardly and avaricious, and a plague to the earth that welcomed him at his birth. He profited by fortune's folly and abused his fortune foully, a slave to his wife's whims, obliging her in all and regarding her as his all.[a] And she must in all things needs obey the givers of orders such as this, whose profession of virtue [b] is to live in mourning garb, and an even greater than this, to live in clothing made by weavers of sack cloth. 47. Such is the cabal that has deceived and hoodwinked you, led you on and bamboozled you, but from the sons of gods [c] we know that many even of the gods have been deceived. Alleging against them the sacrifice of victims, so close that the smoke of it wafts to their nostrils, and the bandying of threats, provocations great and small, boastings and a confidence in their everlasting invincibility,—with such fictions, such devices and such contrived accounts calculated to arouse his wrath, they have induced the gentlest of emperors to behave unlike his true self, for his character is one

---

[a] Petit, " Sur la date du *Pro Templis*," *Byzantion*, xxi, pp. 295 ff., convincingly shows that this official must be Cynegius, ppO A.D. 384–388. His wife was Achantia (*M.H.G.* (*A.A.*) 9. 245).

[b] *Cf. Or.* 2. 32.

[c] The poets : *cf.* Plat. *Resp.* 366 B.

αὐτοῦ φιλανθρωπία, ἔλεος, οἶκτος, ἡμερότης, ἐπι-
είκεια, τὸ σώζειν μᾶλλον ἢ ἀπολλύναι. ἀλλ' ὄντων
R ii. 199 τῶν τὰ δικαιότερα | λεγόντων ὅτι, εἴπερ τι τοι-
οῦτον εἴη, δίκην μὲν δεῖ τοῦ τολμήματος λαβεῖν,
τούτῳ δὲ αὐτῷ προνοηθῆναι τοῦ μέλλοντος ὁ τὴν
Καδμείαν νικῆσαι νίκην οἰόμενος δεῖν πανταχόθεν
ἐνίκησεν.

48. Ἔδει δὲ αὐτὸν ⟨μὴ⟩[1] μετὰ τὰς οἰκείας ἡδονὰς
τὰ[2] σαυτοῦ θεραπεύειν μηδ' ⟨ὁρᾶν⟩[3] ὅπως μέγας
εἶναι δόξῃ τοῖς τὴν μὲν γεωργίαν ἀποδρᾶσιν, ὁμι-
λεῖν δὲ ἐν τοῖς ὄρεσι λέγουσι τῷ τῶν ὅλων ποιητῇ,
ἀλλ' ὡς τὰ σὰ καὶ[4] καλὰ καὶ ἐπαίνων ἄξια παρὰ
πᾶσιν ἀνθρώποις δοκεῖ. νῦν δὲ μέχρι μὲν τοῦ λαβεῖν καὶ κενῶσαί σοι τοὺς θησαυροὺς πολλοὶ φίλοι
καὶ ἐπιτήδειοι καὶ πρὸ τῶν ψυχῶν αὐτοῖς ἡ σὴ
βασιλεία, καιροῦ δὲ ἥκοντος καὶ βουλῆς παρούσης
R ii. 200 εὔνοιαν ἀπαιτούσης ταυτὶ μὲν ἠμέληται, | τὰ δὲ
ἴδιά σφισιν[5] ἐσπούδασται. 49. κἂν προσελθών τις
αὐτοῖς τί ταῦτα; ἔρηται, τὸ μὲν αὐτῶν ἔξω τῆς
αἰτίας ποιοῦσι, καὶ ὅτι πεποιήκασιν ἀποκρίνονται
ἅ γε[6] τῷ βασιλεῖ ἔδοξε καὶ ἐκεῖνον τὴν ἀπολογίαν
ὀφείλειν καὶ τοιαῦτα λέγουσιν. οἱ δ' ὀφείλοντες |
ἦσαν οὗτοι οἱ οὐδέποτε λόγον ἕξοντες οὐδένα ὑπὲρ

---

[1] μὴ inserted F., conj. Monnier.
[2] τὰ F. : τὰς Re. (mss.). | ἑαυτοῦ V.
[3] ὁρᾶν inserted F., following similar suggestion by Re.
[4] καὶ bracketed F.   [5] σφισιν F. : τισὶν Re. (mss.).
[6] ἀποκρίνονται F., conj. Re. : ἀποκρύπτονται Monnier
(mss.). | γε F. : δὲ VU, inserted in PM : om. Re. (other
mss.).

---

[a] Theodosius himself : Gothofredus suggested Valens,
but the humane characteristics are highly inapplicable.
[b] Cf. Or. 28. 18 ; Paroem. Gr. Zenob. 4. 45 ; Apost. 9.

of genuine humanity, compassion, pity, kindliness and moderation, and an eagerness to protect rather than to destroy.[a] But despite the protests of those who urged the juster course, that if any such crime occurred, it should be punished and its recurrence thereby prevented, this fellow, convinced of the need to win at all costs,[b] has won all along the line.

48. He ought not to have put his private pleasures before your interests, nor sought influence with the renegades from the farms who claim to commune among the mountains with the creator of the universe [c] : rather should he have taken care that your reign should appear noble and praiseworthy in the eyes of all people. As it is, while ever it is a matter of money making and emptying your treasuries, you have plenty of friends and intimates, and your majesty means more to them than their own lives, but when it comes to the point and a council is assembled where consideration is required, these pious sentiments are forgotten and they ride their own hobby-horses. 49. And if we approach them and ask them to explain what they are up to, they disclaim any responsibility : their reply is that they have done as the emperor decreed [d] and that he is the one to provide an explanation, and so on. But they should provide it, they who can never justify

30 (Leutsch-Schneidewin, vol. i, p. 97 ; ii, p. 470). Equivalent to the Latin " Pyrrhic victory."

[c] *Cf.* on § 31 above. The monks set up their cells in the mountains around Antioch, *cf.* Theodoret, *H.E.* 5. 20, and Festugière, *Antioche.* Libanius' prejudice is indicated by his assertion that they are runaway peasants, and so, by implication, Greekless. The bitter tone is heightened by the reference to Plat. *Tim.* 28 c.

[d] *C. Th.* 16. 10. 9 (May A.D. 385).

τῶν πεπραγμένων· τίς γὰρ ἂν ὑπὲρ τοιούτων κακῶν
γίνοιτο λόγος; οἱ δὲ πρὸς μὲν τοὺς ἄλλους ἀρνοῦν-
ται μὴ σφῶν εἶναι τοῦτο τὸ ἔργον, ἐντυγχάνοντες
δὲ σοὶ καταμόνας δι' οὐδενὸς ἄλλου τὸν σὸν οἶκον
οὕτως εὖ πεποιηκέναι φασίν. ὧν τὸν σὸν ἀπαλ-
λάξειαν οἶκον οἱ γῇ τε καὶ θαλάττῃ τὴν σὴν ἐπι-
στήσαντες κεφαλήν· ὡς οὐκ ἔσθ' ὅ τι μεῖζον ἂν
παρ' αὐτῶν λάβοις. οἱ γὰρ ἐν φίλων ὀνόματι καὶ
κηδεμόνων ἀφ' ὧν ἂν βλάψαιεν λέγοντες τῷ πι-
στεύεσθαι πρὸς τὴν βλάβην ἀφορμῇ χρώμενοι ῥα-
δίως ἐζημίωσαν.

50. Ἀλλ' ἐπὶ τούσδε μέτειμι τῆς ἀδικίας αὐτῶν
τὴν ἀπόδειξιν ἐκ τῶν νῦν εἰρημένων ποιησόμενος. |
R ii. 201 φέρε γάρ, διὰ τί φατε κατασκαφῆναι τὸ μέγα τουθ'
ἱερόν; οὐ διὰ τὸ δόξαι τῷ βασιλεῖ; καλῶς. οὐκοῦν οἱ καθαιροῦντες οὐκ ἠδίκουν τῷ τὰ δοκοῦντα
τῷ βασιλεῖ ποιεῖν. ὅστις οὖν τὰ μὴ δοκοῦντα τῷ
βασιλεῖ πεποίηκεν, ἀδικεῖ; οὐκοῦν ὑμεῖς οὗτοί γέ
ἐστε οἷς οὐδὲν ἔνι τοιοῦτον εἰπεῖν ὑπὲρ ὧν δεδρά-
κατε. | 51. εἰπέ μοι, διὰ τί τὸ τῆς Τύχης τοῦτο F
σῶν ἐστιν ἱερὸν καὶ τὸ τοῦ Διὸς καὶ τὸ τῆς Ἀθηνᾶς
καὶ τὸ τοῦ Διονύσου; ἆρ' ὅτι βούλοισθ' ἂν αὐτὰ
μένειν; οὔ, ἀλλ' ὅτι μηδεὶς τὴν ἐπ' αὐτὰ δέδωκεν
ὑμῖν ἐξουσίαν. εἰλήφατε δὲ τὴν κατ' ἐκείνων ἃ
διεφθάρκατε; οὔ.[1] πῶς οὖν οὐκ ὀφείλετε δίκην; ἢ
R ii. 202 πῶς ἃ δεδράκατε | καλεῖτε δίκην τῶν πεπονθότων
οὐδὲν ἐν οὐδενὶ πεποιηκότων ὃ δέχοιτ' ἂν αἰτίαν;

---

[1] οὔ. F., conj. Re. : om. mss.

---

[a] The temple of Fortune in Antioch is that of Calliope, the
tutelary deity of the city, cf. Or. 15. 79. Secular uses of
temples noted by Libanius are of the Museum, used as a
school A.D. 354–362 (Or. 1. 102), of that of Dionysus, used as a

their behaviour. Indeed, what justification could there be for such misdeeds ? In public they disclaim such responsibility, but in private conclave with you they claim that none of their other actions has served your house so well. May the powers that have placed your person in authority over land and sea deliver your house from such service ! You could receive no greater gift from them, for these self-styled friends and protectors, by their hurtful counsel and by employing your confidence to occasion hurt, have had no difficulty in harming you.

50. But I will cross-examine them, to demonstrate their guilt from the account I have just given. " Tell me : What is your reason for demolishing this great temple ? That it was the emperor's decree ? All right ! Then those who destroyed it did nothing criminal because they did as the emperor decreed. So if anyone has done what the emperor has not decreed, he is a criminal, then ? Well, you fall precisely into this category, for you have no such excuse to offer for your actions. 51. And tell me ! Why is the temple of Fortune here still intact and that of Zeus, Athena and Dionysus ? [a] Because you wanted them to remain so ? No, but because no one has given you the authority to move against them. But have you received any authority against those that you have destroyed ? No ! Then why should you not be punished ? How can you describe your action as the imposition of a punishment when the victims in no single particular have done anything that could be described as a crime ? "

courtroom by the *consularis* Tisamenus in A.D. 386 (*Or.* 45. 26) and of Athena, used as a lawyer's meeting place in A.D. 388 (*Ep.* 847).

52. Ἦν σοι, βασιλεῦ, κηρύξαι· μηδεὶς τῶν ὑπ'
ἐμοὶ νομιζέτω θεοὺς μηδὲ τιμάτω μηδὲ αἰτείτω τι
παρ' αὐτῶν μήθ' ἑαυτῷ μήτε παισὶν ἀγαθὸν πλὴν εἰ
σιγῇ τε καὶ λανθάνων, ἅπας δὲ ἔστω τοῦ παρ' ἐμοὶ
τιμίου καὶ βαδιζέτω μεθέξων τῶν ἐκείνῳ δρωμέ-
νων καὶ τάς τε εὐχὰς ᾗπερ ἐκείνῳ ποιείσθω καὶ
τὴν αὑτοῦ κεφαλὴν ὑπαγέτω τῇ τοῦ τὸν λεὼν ἁρ-
μοττομένου χειρί. τὸν δ' ἀπειθοῦντα πᾶσα ἀνάγκη
τεθνάναι. 53. ταῦτ' ἦν μέν σοι κηρύξαι ῥᾴδιον,
οὐ μὴν ἠξίωσάς | γε οὐδ' ἐπέθηκας[1] ζυγὸν ἐνταῦθα F 1
ταῖς τῶν ἀνθρώπων ψυχαῖς, ἀλλ' οἴει μὲν τοῦτ'
ἐκείνου βέλτιον εἶναι, οὐ μὴν ἀσέβημά γε ἐκεῖνο
οὐδ' ἐφ' ᾧ τις ἂν δικαίως καὶ[2] κολασθείη. ἀλλ'
οὐδὲ τῶν τιμῶν τούς γε τοιούτους ἀπέκλεισας, |
R ii. 203 ἀλλὰ καὶ ἀρχὰς ἔδωκας[3] καὶ συσσίτους ἐποιήσω
καὶ τοῦτό γε πολλάκις καὶ προὔπιες καὶ νῦν πρὸς
ἄλλοις τισὶ παρέζευξας σεαυτῷ συμφέρειν τῇ βασιλείᾳ νομίσας ἄνδρα ὀμνύντα θεοὺς πρός τε τοὺς
ἄλλους καὶ σὲ καὶ οὐκ ἀγανακτεῖς οὐδ' ἀδικεῖσθαι
τοῖς τοιούτοις ὑπολαμβάνεις ὅρκοις οὐδ' εἶναι πάντως κακὸν τὸν ἐν τοῖς θεοῖς ἔχοντα τὰς βελτίους ἐλπίδας.

54. Σοῦ τοίνυν οὐκ ἐλαύνοντος ἡμᾶς, ὥσπερ οὐδ'
ὁ τοὺς Πέρσας ἐκεῖνος μεθ' ὅπλων ἐληλακὼς τοὺς
ἐναντίως ταύτῃ τῶν ὑπηκόων πρὸς ἑαυτὸν ἔχον-

---

[1] ἐπέθηκας F. : ἐπέστησας Re. (mss.).
[2] καὶ om. V : F. brackets.
[3] ἔδωκας F. : δέδωκας Re. (mss.).

---

[a] i.e. the bishop.
[b] A mark of high favour, reserved for a select company of

52. You could have issued an edict, Sire : " Let none of my subjects revere or honour the gods, or invoke them for any blessing either for himself or for his children, save in silence and in secret. Let everyone worship the one that I adore, go share in his rites, pray as he did, and bow his head under the hand of the director of the people.[a] And any who disobeys must die." 53. It would have been easy for for you to promulgate such an edict, yet you have refused to do so, nor have you imposed this yoke upon the conscience of men. You regard your religion as better than the other, but that is no act of impiety nor yet just cause for punishment either. Nor have you excluded its adherents from advancement, but you have given them office and made them your companions at table,[b] and often too, you have drunk their health, and even now, in addition to other individuals, you have linked to yourself, in the belief that it is to the benefit of the crown, a man who takes his oath by the gods in the presence of others and yourself.[c] Nor do you take it amiss and conceive such oaths to be an offence against yourself, nor do you regard one who places his higher hopes in the gods as being necessarily evil.

54. You do not persecute us any more than he who harried the Persians by force of arms persecuted those of his subjects whose religious beliefs differed

comites, praepositi, and tribuni scholarum (C. Th. 6. 13. 1), together with some honorary officials (e.g. Prohaeresius, Eunap. V.S. 492).

[c] παρέζευξας implies tenure of the consulship (as ὁμόζυξ described Sallustius as Julian's colleague, Or. 17. 22). Foerster identified this pagan with Richomer (cos. A.D. 384), Seeck and Van Loy with Tatianus, ppO ; Petit with Eutropius, cos. A.D. 387, and therefore cos. des. in 386.

τας, πῶς ἐλαύνουσιν οὗτοι; κατὰ τί δὲ δίκαιον
ποιοῦνται τὰς ἐφόδους; πῶς δ' ἀλλοτρίων ἅπτονται μετ' ὀργῆς ἀγρῶν; πῶς δὲ τὰ μὲν καταφέ-
ρουσι, τὰ δὲ ἀράμενοι φέρουσιν ὕβρει τῇ τοῦ τὰ
τοιαῦτα ποιεῖν προστιθέντες ὕβριν τὴν ἐκ τοῦ καλ-
λύνεσθαι τοῖς πεπραγμένοις;

55. Ἡμεῖς, ὦ βασιλεῦ, σοῦ μὲν ταῦτα καὶ ἐπαι-
νοῦντος καὶ ἐπιτρέποντος οἴσομεν οὐκ ἄνευ μὲν λύ-
F 118 πης, | δείξομεν δ' ὡς | ἄρχεσθαι μεμαθήκαμεν. εἰ δ' R
οὐχὶ καὶ σοῦ διδόντος οἶδε ἥξουσιν ἢ ἐπὶ τὸ δια-
πεφευγὸς αὐτοὺς ἢ διὰ τάχους ἀναστάν, ἴσθι τοὺς
τῶν ἀγρῶν δεσπότας καὶ αὐτοῖς καὶ τῷ νόμῳ βο-
ηθήσοντας.

from his own.*a* Then why do these people persecute us ? By what right do they launch their attacks ? How is it that they extend their furious grasp to the estates of others, and wreak destruction, or pillage and loot, and add insult to injury by boasting of their exploits ?

55. If, Sire, you commend and command such actions, we will put up with them, not without sorrow, but we will demonstrate that we have been schooled to obedience. But if these people without your permission proceed to attack anything that has escaped them or has been hastily restored, you may be sure that the landowners will defend both themselves and the law.

a Julian, as above, §§ 26, 40 ff., *Or.* 18. 121 ff.

ON PRISON CONDITIONS

ORATION 45
TO THE EMPEROR,
ON THE PRISONERS

ORATION 33
TO THE
EMPEROR THEODOSIUS,
AGAINST TISAMENUS

INTRODUCTION

THE orations *On the Prisoners* and *Against Tisamenus* are an example of Libanius' practice of composing orations as "doublets." They are supplementary to each other, both ostensibly destined for the emperor's consideration and drawing his attention to the same situation from two different starting points. The problem at issue is that of administrative abuses in the management of the prisons, but, despite the similarity of content and argument, there is a crucial difference of approach.[a] The *De Vinctis* is a model of Libanius' " reform " speeches : it is marked by a genuine and generous humanity, and presents a wide-ranging and sensible argumentation upon the need for reform in prison conditions. As such, it was obviously designed to have some effect in court circles, especially in view of Theodosius' repeated protestations of humane and liberal administration. The oration *Against Tisamenus*, however, uses the same situation to launch a bitter personal tirade against the current *consularis* for his brutality and incompetence, not least in his administration of the

---

[a] Thus Paul Petit (*Historia*, v (1956), pp. 479 ff.) describes them as a " false doublet," similar to those of *Or.* 15 and 16, 27 and 28, 48 and 49. They do, however, by presenting the emperor as the addressee in both cases, provide a much closer parallel with the genuine doublet, *Or.* 51 and 52.

LIBANIUS

prisons, but the address to the emperor is almost immediately vitiated by the *caveat* (§ 2) of the hostility to be anticipated from some high official at court. The oration is much more controversial, and its circulation likely to be more selective. Publication was intended to be restricted to a small circle of friends in Antioch or, at best, transmitted to an equally select coterie at court to provide propaganda, possibly against the Christian prefect Cynegius, by attacking his creature Tisamenus, if Pack's suggestion (p. 96) be accepted. In the *Autobiography*,[a] Tisamenus appears in a context that may certainly be dated to A.D. 386, *i.e.* after the episode of the chameleon (*cf. Or.* 36) and before the riots of the statues. The internal evidence of the orations gives more precision to this. The legislation limiting the amounts to be expended on public festivals (*C. Th.* 15. 9. 1 of A.D. 384) is described as passed two years previously (*Or.* 33. 15: προπέρυσιν),[b] and from the reference of *Or.* 33. 19 (μὴν μὲν γὰρ οὑτοσὶ τῷ ἔτει τέ-

---

[a] *Or.* 1. 251: ἧκεν ἐπὶ τούτοις ἄρχων ἥκιστα τὸν αὑτοῦ πάππον ἐν τοῖς πρὸς ἐμὲ μιμούμενος. ὁ μὲν γὰρ οὐκ ἐπαύσατο τιμῶν, οἷα ἀνὴρ ἐπιστάμενος λέγειν, ὁ δὲ οὐκ ἐβουλήθη με εἰδέναι, ἐν αἰτήσει τε χάριτος δικαίας τε καὶ οὐ μεγάλης ἐξελεγχθεὶς ἀνόητός τε εἶναι δοκῶν. καὶ τῶν μὲν ματαίων ἐπιμελῶς, τῶν δὲ ἀναγκαίων ἀμελῶς ἤρχετο, διαμένων ἡμετέρων ἄγευστος λόγων. οὐ γάρ μοι τοῦδε τοῦ γέρως ἄξιος ἐφαίνετο. μία μὲν ἤδε δίκη, ἑτέρα δὲ πρὸς τὰ τέρματα τῆς ἀρχῆς, ὑπάρχου πέμποντος, ἥκων ἐν ἐρημίᾳ τε καθῆστο καὶ ἡλίῳ φλέγοντι διψῶν τε ἀεὶ καὶ πίνων.

[b] More debatable is the identification of *C. Th.* 15. 5. 2, attributed to 20 May A.D. 386, with the situation of *Or.* 45. 21. Gothofredus believed that the speech inspired the law, Foerster that it referred to it. Seeck redated the edict to A.D. 394 (since it is addressed " Rufino ppO " ; *cf. Regesten* 94 ; 284). Pack (p. 93) evades the issue, but the coincidence is remarkable enough to allow the presumption that the error lies not in the date but in the address.

ταρτος, τὸ τρίτον τοῦ ἐνιαυτοῦ μέρος), Pack dates the speech precisely to December, since ἐνιαυτός is the calendar year, ἔτος the year of the indiction, beginning in September. The composition of the *De Vinctis* is therefore almost contemporary with that of the *Pro Templis*, and both orations reveal the attitudes characteristic of the current propaganda of paganism —respect for law, the necessity of its impartial enforcement, the claims of the social virtue of *philanthropia*, and the need for stability in the social order. Such emphasis, by implication, is a protest against the remissness of the ruling class of officialdom, with its increasingly Christian bias ; and the *Contra Tisamenum* provides the detailed evidence for such protest.

Roman legal theory, from the earliest days of the Republic, had viewed imprisonment not as a type of punishment after conviction but as the exercise of the magisterial power of *coercitio* designed to secure the person accused and to make him available for trial. As such it was always regarded as a temporary expedient, and this view had remained valid, in theory at least, throughout the principate.[a] By the fourth century, however, authoritarianism and laxity combined had brought about a change in practice and in outlook. By A.D. 320 Constantine, even while seeking to ameliorate prison conditions, can speak of the abuses of commitment as " poenae carceris "

[a] So Ulpian, *Dig.* 48. 19. 8. 9 : " Solent praesides in carcere continendos damnare aut ut in vinculis contineantur : sed id eos facere non oportet. Nam huiusmodi poenae interdictae sunt : carcer enim ad continendos homines, non ad puniendos haberi debet. " The abuses of commitment had evidently been of long standing. Almost all of those here described by Libanius had been anticipated by Lucian (*Toxaris*, 29).

LIBANIUS

(*C. Th.* 9. 3. 1). In A.D. 326 (*ibid.* 9. 3. 2) commitment itself is more specifically stated to be " poena carceris." The growing ambiguity of the terms and the laxity of administration produced half a dozen imperial enactments between A.D. 320 and 380, all designed, in the best humanitarian tradition, to remedy the abuse of imprisonment, and all evidently failing to achieve this end. The law of A.D. 380 (*ibid.* 9. 3. 6) repeats in general terms the provisions of Constantine's legislation, and is itself reinforced in A.D. 409 (*ibid.* 9. 3. 7) by an edict of Honorius in which the corruption of prison officers is admitted.

The social problem is presented in the context of the fiscal pressures exercised by and upon the governor. Complaints against the brutality of prison conditions, for which he is responsible and where he acts only too often with irresponsible potentates against the lower classes of both town and country, are combined with complaints against his excessive zeal in the collection of fiscal dues, where he tyrannizes the decurions who are responsible for this task. The increased demands of the central government in preparation for the ultimate clash with Maximus were working their way downwards through the system, and the combination of bad government and excessive government was becoming intolerable, even for the highest stratum of the municipal administration. The activities of Tisamenus set the scene for the riots of A.D. 387.

MANUSCRIPTS AND BIBLIOGRAPHY

For *Oration 33* (*Contra Tisamenum*) eight manuscripts only survive, consisting of the major codices

CAPIBV with the addition of Neapolitanus II E 17 (N) and Vaticanus gr. 81 (Va), both of which are closely allied with B. V alone represents a variant manuscript tradition as compared with the rest. The form of the title supplied by Foerster is, however, derived from none of these, but from the excerptor Macarius (fol. 90 πρὸς βασιλέα κατὰ Τισαμένου). The first edition was that of Morel in vol. II of his edition of Libanius' works, based upon Va but lacking the final sections from πεπραγμένον (§ 37). This deficiency was remedied in the editions of Reiske and Foerster.

Oration 45 (*De Vinctis*) survives in the same eight manuscripts as above, plus Patmius 471 (Pa) of the 14th century and Urbinas gr. 126 (U) dated A.D. 1316. As before, V alone provides a variant tradition, but the lacuna in § 24 is common to all. Macarius here agrees with them as regards the title. The *editio princeps* was that of Gothofredus (Geneva, 1631 : *cf*. Introduction to *Or*. 50, p. 59 above), with Latin version, reprinted in his *Opera Iuridica Minora*, Leiden, 1733, later editors being Reiske and Foerster. The speech is translated, with notes, and with detailed social commentary by R. A. Pack in *Studies in Libanius and Antiochene Society under Theodosius*, Ann Arbor, 1935. Further discussion appears in P. Petit, *Vie municipale*, and W. Liebeschuetz, *Antioch*.

XLV

ΠΡΟΣ ΤΟΝ ΒΑΣΙΛΕΑ
ΠΕΡΙ ΤΩΝ ΔΕΣΜΩΤΩΝ

R ii. 439 1. Εἰ μὲν ἅπαν ὃ προσῆκον ἦν περὶ τοὺς δε- F i
σμώτας παρὰ τῶν τὰς ἀρχὰς ἐχόντων ἐφυλάττετο,
ὦ βασιλεῦ, τοῖς μὲν ἂν συνέχαιρον, σοὶ δὲ οὐκ ἂν
ἠνώχλουν· ἐπεὶ δὲ οἱ μὲν κακοὶ περὶ τουτὶ γεγένηνται τὸ μέρος, λέγει δὲ οὐδὲν πρὸς σὲ περὶ τούτων οὐδεὶς τῶν εἴτε ἀγνοοῦσιν ἀδικούντων εἴτε εἰδότες σιωπῶσιν, ὅ τι τε ἂν περὶ ταῦτα γίγνηται
δυσσεβές, οὐκ ἔστι μὴ συνδιαβάλλεσθαι τὴν βασιλείαν, ὁ τὴν σὴν πρᾳότητα θαυμάζων ἐγὼ καὶ ἅμα
χάριν τὴν μεγίστην | εἰληφὼς δίκαιος ἂν εἴην τῇ F 2
σῇ ψήφῳ θεραπεῦσαι τὸ ἁμαρτανόμενον.

2. Οἶσθα μὲν οὖν, ὦ βασιλεῦ, τοῦτό γε δίκαιον
ὂν τὸ τοὺς μὲν ἀξίους θανάτου θνήσκειν, τοὺς δὲ
μὴ ζῆν τε καὶ περιεῖναι, καίτοι γε δι᾽ ὑπερβολὴν
φιλανθρωπίας ἤδη τινὶ καὶ τούτων ζῆν ἔδωκας,
ἀλλ᾽ ἔστω κύρια τὰ παρὰ τῶν παλαιῶν νόμων.

---

[a] Cf. Or. 33. 8.

[b] Cf. Introduction to the Pro Templis, above, and the discussion by Petit (op. cit.).

[c] The most sensational example occurred in winter A.D. 385/6, when an ex-pupil of Libanius, of Senatorial rank, was charged with magic. Libanius' secretary was alleged to have been implicated. No death penalty was inflicted, unusually in such cases: cf. Or. 1. 239 ff., Themist. Or. 19. 229 d.

ORATION 45

TO THE EMPEROR,
ON THE PRISONERS

1. If care were taken,[a] Sire, by the holders of governmental office to maintain in full the proper procedure in dealing with persons held in custody, I would be congratulating them and not worrying you. However, although the officials have been at fault in this matter, no one informs you of these malpractices by them, whether done in ignorance or deliberately veiled in silence, and the commission of any impiety here necessarily involves the imperial authority in the odium incurred. So, because of my admiration for your clemency and because I am in receipt of your greatest honour, it would be right for me by your decree to correct the error.[b]

2. Well, Sire, as you know, justice involves death for those who deserve to die, and life and survival for those who do not. Admittedly, in your remarkable generosity you have in the past granted reprieve to some miscreants even,[c] but let the provisions of old-established legislation [d] be regarded as the norm.

---

[d] παλαιοί is a fairly elastic term. The last legislation was that of *C. Th.* 9. 3. 6 of A.D. 380. Similarly, *C. Th.* 12. 1. 80 (of A.D. 380 and 381) are described as παλαιοί in A.D. 385 (*Or.* 27. 13).

LIBANIUS

ταῦτα δέ ἐστιν ἀποθνήσκειν μὲν ᾧ τι τοιοῦτο τε-
τόλμηται, ζῆν δὲ ὃς οὐδὲν τηλικοῦτον ἠδίκηκε. τὸ
δὲ τετολμηκέναι καὶ τὸ ἠδικηκέναι τί ποτέ ἐστι;
R ii. 440 τὸ ἐξεληλέγχθαι. | ὡς τό γε πρὸ ἐλέγχων ἀπο-
θανεῖν οὐδὲν ἕτερόν ἐστιν ἢ ἠδικῆσθαι. καὶ γὰρ εἴ
τῳ πέπρακται μὲν ἄξιον θανάτου, τουτὶ δὲ συγ-
κέκρυπται, τοῦτον ὁ κτείνας ἀδικεῖ τὴν τιμωρίαν
πρὸ τῆς πίστεως λαβών. 3. ἴσθι τοίνυν σοι φονέας
ὄντας τοὺς ἐπὶ τὰ ἔθνη πεμπομένους ἄρχοντας, ὦ
βασιλεῦ. τίνα τρόπον; πολλαὶ μὲν ὀργαὶ πολλὰς
ποιοῦσι μέμψεις, κἂν θυμωθῇ τις, εὐθὺς παρὰ τὸν
ἄρχοντα τρέχει καί φησιν ὑβρίσθαι καὶ πεπονθέναι
κακῶς, ὁ δὲ ἑαυτὸν μὲν οὔ, τὴν γυναῖκα δέ, ὁ δὲ
τούτων μὲν οὐδέτερον, τοὺς παῖδας δέ, καὶ ῥήματα
πλάττουσι καὶ πληγὰς καὶ καταρρήξαντές τι τῆς
ἐσθῆτος ἐκείνῳ καὶ τοῦτο προσέθεσαν. ὁ δὲ ἀρ-
νούμενός τε καὶ σεσυκοφαντῆσθαι λέγων καὶ μεμνημένος γραφῆς καὶ νόμων πέμπεται δεθησόμενος
καὶ ταῦτα ⟨ἐν⟩ ἐγγυητῶν ἀφθονίᾳ.[1] 4. πάσχουσι
R ii. 441 δὲ τοῦτ᾽ ἐπιεικῶς | οἱ | ἀσθενέστεροι παρὰ τῶν F
δυνατωτέρων, καὶ οἷς οὐκ ἔνι χρήματα παρὰ τῶν
εὐπορούντων, καὶ οἱ πολλοὶ παρὰ τῶν ὀλίγων οἳ
τὰς αἰτίας τὰς παρὰ σφῶν πλέον ἔχειν ἀξιοῦσιν
ἀποδείξεων. ταῦτα παρὰ τῶν ἐν τῷ μεγίστῳ συνεδρίῳ, ταῦτα παρὰ τῶν ἄλλων βουλῶν, ταῦτα παρὰ
τῶν τὰς εὐφημίας ὑμῶν ἐγκεχειρισμένων κατὰ τῶν

---

[1] ἐν ἐγγυητῶν ἀφθονίᾳ Re., F : ἐγγυητῶν ἀφθονία mss.

[a] The expression is intended to shock : it is the exact
opposite of the normal commendations of governors which
were posted to Court. So Florentius, though he did not
execute, is described as a murderer in Or. 46. 9. The term
ἄρχων τῶν ἐθνῶν usually describes the *Comes Orientis* : the

162

These are death for the perpetrators of any such crime and life for those innocent of such misdemeanours. And the definition of a crime and misdemeanour is what ?—the proof of it in a court of law. For a man to be executed before trial is downright illegality, and even if he commits an act that involves the death penalty and it remains undiscovered, anyone who kills him is at fault in exacting the penalty before the proof. 3. Now, Sire, you must realize that the governors sent out to the provinces are murderers.[a] The manner of it is as follows. Lost tempers often involve numerous complaints. Someone takes umbrage : straightaway he scurries off to the governor alleging that he has been the victim of insult and abuse,[b] or, if not he, his wife has been, or, if neither of them, his children. They invent insults and injuries, make a tear or two in their clothes, and use this as a complaint additional to the first. The other party, despite denials, claims of wrongful accusation and appeals to law and statute, is packed off to jail, even though he has plenty to go bail for him.[c] 4. This is the normal treatment of the weaker at the hands of the influential, of the penniless at the hands of the wealthy, of the masses at the hands of the élite who expect any charge they make to count for more than proof. This is their experience at the hands of Senators [d] and decurions : this the treatment accorded to the manufacturing class

slight difference of wording here indicates provincial governors generally.

[b] As was foreseen in *C. Th.* 9. 1. 5 of A.D. 326.

[c] *e.g. Or.* 46. 3.

[d] τὸ μέγιστον συνέδριον =the Senate of Constantinople or (less often for Libanius) of Rome.

163

R ii. 442 ἐν ταῖς χειροτεχνίαις, | ταῦτα παρὰ τῶν [ἐν]¹ ταῖς
ἀρχαῖς ὑπηρετούντων κατὰ τῶν οὐ πάντα αὐτοῖς
χαριζομένων. 5. δεσποτῶν δὲ ὠμότης πλείστῳ
χρῆται ⟨τούτῳ⟩² καθ᾽ ἑκάστην ἡμέραν, ἐπεὶ καὶ
δέον³ δῆσαι τὸν ἠναγκασμένον ὑπὸ τοῦ νόμου κἂν
ἀδικῆται σιγᾶν. ἐνταῦθά που θετέον καὶ τοὺς περὶ
τὴν γῆν πονοῦντας τοῖς κεκτημένοις τὴν γῆν, ἐπεὶ
καὶ τούτοις τινὲς ἴσα καὶ οἰκέταις κέχρηνται, κἂν
μὴ τὰς πλεονεξίας ἐπαινῶσιν ἐκείνων τὰς καθ᾽
ἑαυτῶν, ὀλίγαι συλλαβαί, καὶ στρατιώτης ἅμα ἀλύ-
R ii. 443 σεσιν ἐπὶ τὸν | ἀγρόν, καὶ δεδεμένους τὸ οἴκημα
δέχεται. 6. βούλει με μνησθῆναι καὶ τῶν αἰτίαν
λαμβανόντων φονεύειν τοὺς ὁδοιπόρους; οὐκοῦν
οὗτοι μὲν δύ᾽ ἢ τρεῖς, δῶμεν δὲ καὶ τρὶς τοσούτους
εἶναι καὶ δέκα καὶ πλείους· παρ᾽ οἷς δὲ ἢ | ἔπιον ἢ F 3
ἔφαγον ἢ ἐκοιμήθησαν, ἕλκονται τριπλάσιοι πολλάκις τῶν ἐν ταῖς αἰτίαις ὄντων οὐδὲν εἰδότες τῶν
ἐγκεκλημένων ἢ τὸ⁴ μηδὲν εἰργάσθαι δεινὸν ἐκείνοις ἢ τῶν πεπραγμένων οὐ μετεσχηκότες.

7. Οὗτοι πάντες ὧν ἐμνήσθην, ὦ βασιλεῦ, καί
τινες ἔξω τούτων καθ᾽ ἑτέρους ἥκοντες ἐκεῖσε τρό-
πους ζῶσι τὸν ἐν δεσμοῖς βίον. οἱ δ᾽ αὐτοὺς παρα-
δεδωκότες ἐν εὐωχίαις εἰσί, μᾶλλον δὲ ἐν ἅπασιν
ἡδονῶν εἴδεσιν, εἰς τὴν Δάφνην ἀναβαίνοντες, εἰς
ἀγροὺς ἐλαύνοντες, ἐπ᾽ ἄλλας ἰόντες πόλεις ὑπὸ
νυμφίων καλούμενοι γῆν ὠνησόμενοι, θάλατταν
R ii. 444 ὀψόμενοι. | τῶν δὲ δι᾽ αὐτοὺς δεθέντων τῶν μὲν

¹ ἐν mss. : brackets F., as suggested by Re.
² ⟨τούτῳ⟩ conj. Re., F.
³ καὶ δέον Re. text (mss.) : ῥάδιον conj. Re., Cobet, F.
⁴ τὸ F. (CPUB, AI corrected) : τῷ Re. (PaV, AI before
correction).

ᵃ Cf. Or. 33. 34.   ᵇ i.e. an officialis.

164

by organizers of loyal addresses to you and by the lackeys of the governors to such as do not gratify their every whim. 5. Brutal masters make full use of this technique every single day, for one who is compelled by law to remain silent, however wronged he may be, must needs be arrested also. Into this category are also to be put the peasants who work for the landlords, for some treat them just as though they were slaves, and if they do not acquiesce in the extortions that are practised upon them, just a word or two *a* is needed, and a soldier *b* goes down to the farm, complete with fetters, they are arrested, and the jail takes them in. 6. Would you like me to mention also those accused of murder on the high roads? There are two or three of these, but let us concede that they are three times as many—ten or more. But the persons with whom they drank, ate or slept, often three times the number of the accused, are arrested too, even if they know nothing of the offence other than that the accused are not guilty of it, and even if they had no part in the deed.

7. All these I have mentioned, Sire, and others besides who get there by other ways, live their lives in chains. And those who have sent them there enjoy the high life and indeed live in the lap of luxury. They go up to Daphne, they drive to their estates, they visit other towns, invited by the bridegroom to a wedding, to buy land, to visit the seaside.*c* As for those whose arrest they have secured, they

c For examples of these social activities of the Antiochene upper class at various dates: holidaying in Daphne in summer, *Ep.* 419; their estates, *Or.* 11. 171; weddings, *Or.* 33. 14 ff.; purchase of estates, *Or.* 47. 9, 48. 37; but Libanius is concerned with the immediate troubles of the year A.D. 386.

ἐπελάθοντο, τῶν δὲ οὐ φροντίζουσιν. οἱ δικασταὶ
δὲ οἱ βέλτιστοι οἱ τὸν δεσμὸν αὐτοῖς ὃν ἐβούλοντο
δεδωκότες καὶ περὶ πλείονος τὴν πρὸς ἐκείνους
χάριν τῆς τοῦ δικαίου μοίρας πεποιημένοι οὔτε
ἀγανακτοῦσιν οὔτε καλοῦσιν οὔτε ἐπιτιμῶσιν οὔτε
τί ταῦτα; ἐρωτῶσιν οὐδ' ὡς περὶ ἀσεβοῦς τοῦ
πράγματος διαλέγονται οὐδ' ὡς οὐκ ἂν ἐπὶ πλέον
δύναιντο τὰ τοιαῦτα ἀνέχεσθαι λέγουσιν. 8. εἶτα
μεστὸν μὲν[1] σωμάτων τὸ δεσμωτήριον ἐξιόντος μὲν
οὐδενὸς ἢ κομιδῇ γε ὀλίγων, εἰσιόντων δὲ πολλῶν.
καὶ γίγνεται διπλοῦν τὸ κακὸν αὐτῷ τε τῷ δεδέσθαι καὶ τῷ[2] οὕτως. οὐδὲ γὰρ [οὔθ'][3] ὕπνου λαχεῖν
F 363 ἔστιν | ἀκριβῶς, οὐδὲ γὰρ | κεῖσθαι κατακλιθέν- R
τας,[4] ἀλλ' ὅσον ἑστῶσιν[5] αὐτοῦ μεταλαβεῖν, τοσοῦτον ἔχουσι.

9. Πόθεν τοίνυν τούτοις ἡ τροφή; τὴν μὲν γὰρ
ἐν τοῖς λέβησι φακῆν καὶ τὰ ὀλίγα λάχανα καὶ εἴ
τι τούτοις πρόσεστιν, ἐλάττω ταῦτα πολὺ τοῦ δέοντος εἶναί φασιν. ἀνάγκη δὴ γυναῖκας καὶ ἀδελφὰς
καὶ θυγατέρας, αἷς ἦν ἡ τροφὴ παρὰ τῶν οὔπω
καθειργμένων, αὐτὰς εἶναι τὰς ἐκείνους τρεφούσας.
πόθεν, ὦ βασιλεῦ; τῷ δεσμῷ μὲν γὰρ ἐκείνων οὐκ
ἔστιν αὐτὰς εὐπορωτέρας γεγονέναι. λείπεται δὴ
τὰς μὲν ἀμόρφους ἢ γήρᾳ κατεχομένας προσαι-
τεῖν, ἐν αἷς δέ τι καὶ ὥρας, πάντα ἀνέχεσθαι. ταῦτ'

[1] [μὲν] F.
[2] αὐτῷ τε τῷ . . . τῷ conj. Re., F. (V): αὐτό τε τὸ . . .
τὸ Re. text (other mss.).
[3] οὔθ' mss.: brackets F., as suggested by Re.
[4] κατακλιθέντας F.: -κλιθέντα IB: -κλιθέντ' Gothofred.
(CAPUV): -κλιθέντι Re.: -κλινέντας Pa.
[5] ἑστῶσιν ⟨ἔστιν⟩ F.

either forget all about them or don't bother about them. And our fine governors who have secured the desired arrest for them, and are more interested in ingratiating themselves with them than in the claims of justice,—they don't become angry, or demand their presence, reprove them and ask what is the meaning of this, nor do they talk to them about the heinous character of the affair, or tell them that they cannot tolerate such conduct any longer. 8. In consequence, the prison is packed with bodies.[a] No one comes out—or precious few, at least—though many go in. They are doubly afflicted, by the actual imprisonment and by the manner of it. They cannot get any proper sleep, for they cannot even lie down to rest.[b] Their repose is just what they can get standing.

9. Where does the food come from for all these ? The soup in their pots, their few greens, and anything else besides,—all this, they say, is much below their needs. Their wives, sisters, daughters, who were supported by them before their imprisonment, must needs be the ones to support them now.[c] And how, Sire ? The women cannot possibly be better off as a result of the imprisonment of their menfolk. The consequence is that the ugly and the aged go begging, while those who have any looks at all endure

[a] Tisamenus is criticized for this : *Or.* 33. 41.

[b] On such prison conditions *cf.* Plut. *Mor.* 165 E, Lucian, *Toxaris*, 29 ; *infra*, § 31.

[c] Although prison rations were to be officially organized by provincial governors at a later date (*C. Th.* 9. 3. 7 of A.D. 409), allocations of prison fare had been regular throughout the Principate, *e.g.* Sen. *Ep.* 2. 6. 11. Visiting and maintaining the prisoners, however, remained the responsibility of relatives and friends, *e.g. Or.* 20. 7, 26. 32, 28. 15.

οὖν τοῖς δεδεμένοις τοῦ δεσμοῦ πικρότερα· δεῖ γὰρ
αὐτοὺς δήπου καὶ ἐρωτᾶν καὶ διδάσκεσθαι πόθεν
αὐτοῖς ταῦτα ἔρχεται.

10. Καὶ οὐ ταῦτά γε μόνον, ἀλλὰ καὶ ὅσα δεῖ
παρ' ἑκάστου γενέσθαι τῷ τῆς θύρας κυρίῳ τῷ
R ii. 446 λύχνον μὲν ἕνα πᾶσι παρεχομένῳ, | τοῦ μικροῦ δὲ
ἐλαίου τούτου μέγαν ἀπαιτοῦντι μισθόν. ὁ δὲ οὐ
θεὶς δι' ἀπορίαν εὐθύς ἐστιν ἐν πληγαῖς, κἂν λέγῃ
τυπτόμενος· ἐμοί, ὦ ἄρχων τοῦ τε δεσμωτηρίου
τούτου καὶ τῶν ἐν αὐτῷ κειμένων, πλὴν τοῦδε τοῦ
σώματος ἔστιν οὐδέν, οὐ γονεῖς, οὐ τέκνα, οὐ φί-
λοι · | πόθεν ἂν οὖν ἀμειψαίμην τὸν λύχνον, εἰ μήτ' F ?
ἀπὸ τῆς γῆς ἀργύριον ἔχοιμ' ἂν ἀνασπάσαι μήτ'
ἔστιν ὁ εἰσοίσων; ταῦτα εἰπὼν ἀκούει· διὰ τί οὐ
καλεῖς διὰ τῶνδε τῶν ἐξιόντων γυναῖκα δεῦρο τῶν
ἐπὶ φιλανθρωπίᾳ φιλοτιμουμένων, εἶτ' αὐτῆς πρὸς
τὰ γόνατα προσπεσὼν πείθεις προσαιτοῦσαν ἄγειν[1]
R ii. 447 τί σοι; τουτὶ δὲ ὁ μέν τις ἐδυνήθη, ὁ | δ' οὔ. παρ'
ὅτου δὲ οὐκ ἔνι λαβεῖν, ἀρκεῖ μαστιγῶσαι.

11. Δακρύεις, ὦ βασιλεῦ. πολλὰ ἀγαθά σοι γένοιτο διὰ τὴν ἄγαν χρηστότητα. καὶ ἔγωγε, νὴ τὸν
Δία καὶ πάντας τοὺς θεούς, τοῦτ' ὄψεσθαι προσεδόκων. ἀλλ' ὄντων δεινῶν τῶν εἰρημένων ἔνι τι
μεῖζον, εἰ μεῖζον ὧν ἔφην τὸ τεθνάναι. θνήσκουσι
γάρ, ὦ βασιλεῦ, θνήσκουσι τοῖς τε ἄλλοις κακοῖς καὶ
μεγίστῳ δή, στενοχωρίᾳ, μυρίοι. καὶ ὁ μὲν φύλαξ

---

[1] ἄγειν Re. (mss.) : ἀγείρειν F.

[a] Cf. Or. 33. 30. This abuse had been explicitly forbidden

168

every kind of outrage. For the prisoners then this is a more bitter pill than their imprisonment, for they are bound to ask the source from which they get this support and to be told it.

10. Not only this. There are also the payments [a] each one must make to the jailor [b] who provides a single lamp for them all and who demands a fancy price for this little drop of oil. Anyone who, through lack of means, fails to pay is immediately in for a flogging, and even if he cries when under the lash, " Sir, keeper of this jail and its inmates, I have nothing save this my body—no parents, no children, no friends. How then can I pay for the lamp ? I cannot wrest money from the earth and there is none to bring me any," he receives the answer pat, " Make use of these who are due for release and fetch in one of those women who have a name for good works.[c] Fall at her knees and get her to go begging and bring something for you." Some manage to do this, others don't. When nothing can be got from a man, a flogging makes up for it.

11. You are weeping, Sire ! Bless you for your great goodness ! Heavens above ! this is just what I expected to see ! But grim though my tale has been, there is yet worse to come, if death is worse than the sufferings I have recounted. Yes, people are dying, Sire, and dying as a result of their afflictions, of close confinement in particular, and dying

[a] by *C. Th.* 9. 3. 1 of A.D. 320, but evidently remained a favourite form of extortion.

[b] The *commentariensis* (as in *C. Th.* 9. 3. 7, where his conduct is subjected to close scrutiny) : *cf. Or.* 26. 32, Lucian, *loc. cit.*, Amm. Marc. 28. 6. 24.

[c] Deaconesses, *cf.* Pliny, *Ep.* 10. 96. Lucian, *de morte Peregrini*, 12.

ἐμήνυσεν, ὁ δ' ἄρχων οὐδὲν τῇ ψυχῇ παθὼν θάπτειν
ἐπέτρεψε. τῷ δ' ᾐτιαμένῳ τὴν ἀρχὴν οὐδεὶς φόβος,
ἀλλ' οὐδὲ εἰ τέθνηκεν οἶδεν. ἀποθνήσκουσι δὲ ἐν
τούτοις δοῦλοί τε ἐν ἴσῳ καὶ ἐλεύθεροι, οἱ μὲν
οὐδὲν ἠδικηκότες, οἱ δ' οὐκ ἄξια θανάτου. οἱ θεοὶ
δὲ ταῦτα ἴσασιν οἵ τε ἄλλοι καὶ ὁ πάντα ἐφορῶν
Ἥλιος. οἷς οὐκ ἂν φαίης τὰ τοιαῦτα ἀρέσκειν. ἀντὶ
δὲ τῶν ἀπιόντων ἔστι[1] τὸ πρὸς τὸν δεσμὸν ἀγόμενον
ἢ οὐκ ἔλαττον ἢ καὶ πλέον. |

12. Οὐκοῦν δεινὸν εἰ μέν τις ἐν ἀγορᾷ μαχό- F
μενος ἢ ἄρχων χειρῶν ἢ καὶ ἀμυνόμενος κτεῖναι
τινά, πάντας ἀγανακτεῖν καὶ βοᾶν καὶ ταὐτὰ ποι-
R ii. 448 εῖν τοῖς | τοῦ τεθνεῶτος οἰκείοις καὶ τοὺς οὐ προσ-
ήκοντας, ὑπὸ δὲ τῶν ἀρχόντων διὰ τῶν δεσμω-
τηρίων τοσούτων ἀπολλυμένων πράως ἔχειν σε
δοκεῖν; οὐδὲ γὰρ ἐκεῖνό γ' εἰπών τις εὖ λέγειν ἂν
δόξειεν ὡς οὐδὲν τούτων εἰδείης. ἀπαιτῇ γὰρ ὑπὸ
τῆς βασιλείας, ὦ βασιλεῦ, τὸ πάντα ἐπίστασθαι.
καὶ τοὺς φονέας τούτους πάλαι χρῆν τούτων τῶν
θανάτων ὑπεσχηκέναι δίκην, ἀλλ' εἰ καὶ μὴ πρότερον, νῦν γέ τις ἐπιστροφὴ γενέσθω.

13. Καὶ τί δεινόν, φησί τις, εἴ τις ἀνδροφόνος ὢν
καὶ ἀπὸ ταύτης ἐμπεσὼν εἰς τὸ οἴκημα τῆς αἰτίας
εἶτα οὕτω τέθνηκεν; ἐγὼ δὲ τὸν τοῦτο λέγοντα
ἐροίμην ἂν ἡδέως εἰ ὅσοι τοῦτον τεθνᾶσι τὸν τρόπον
τῶν ἀνθρώπους ἀπεκτονότων εἰσίν. εἰ δὲ καὶ ψευ-
δεῖς αἰτίαι καὶ ῥῆμά τι καὶ μικρὸν ἤδη τινὰς ἀργύριον ἔδησε, προὔβη δὲ ὁ δεσμὸς εἰς θάνατον, τί δεῖ

___

[1] ἔστι F. (V) : ἐστὶ Gothofred. (other mss.) : ἐπὶ Re.

___

[a] Cf. Or. 33. 41: a long standing criticism of prison conditions, which still prevailed, despite the edict (C. Th. 9. 3. 1)
which allowed light and air to prevent prisoners dying.

in thousands.[a] The jailor makes his report [b]; the governor doesn't turn a hair, but merely orders the funeral. The original accuser has no qualms : he doesn't even know whether the fellow is dead or not. And among them slave and free die alike, some guilty of no offence at all, others of offences that do not deserve death. The gods, and especially the all-seeing Helios,[c] know this, and such goings-on cannot be described as pleasing to them : but the influx into the prison that replaces the departed is just as large or even larger.

12. So isn't it a disgrace that, if someone kills a man in a street brawl, either as an aggressor or in self-defence, everyone—even though unrelated to him—is outraged, sets up an outcry and behaves exactly like the dead man's kinsfolk, yet when so many people are killed by the governors by imprisonment, you should be thought unconcerned ? Even if it be asserted that you know nothing of all this, the argument would not be valid, for you are required by your imperial position, Sire, to know all. These butchers should long ago have been punished for these killings, but now at least, if never before, let some attention be paid to them.

13. " Well," it may be said, " what is wrong if some homicide is clapped into jail on this count, and then dies so ? " I would like to ask the proposer of this question whether all who die in this way are homicides. A false charge, an odd word or two, a bit of money have secured someone's arrest before now, and if this imprisonment results in death, what

---

[b] Monthly returns were required of the *commentariensis*, *C. Th.* 9. 3. 6 of A.D. 380.

[c] *Cf. Or.* 13. 35, 42. 41. Homer, *Il.* 3. 277, *Od.* 11. 109.

LIBANIUS

λέγειν τοὺς τὰ μέγιστα ἠδικηκότας κατὰ τῶν ἢ οὐδὲν ἢ μικρά· εἰ γὰρ δὴ καὶ σφόδρα τοῖς ἐκεῖνα
δεδρακόσι προσήκων ἦν θάνατος,[1] ἀλλὰ τούτοις γε
οὐκ ἐχρῆν οὕτω μακρὸν ποιεῖν τὸν δεσμὸν ὥστε αὐτοῖς τὸ κακὸν εἰς θάνατον τελευτᾶν. 14. εἴποι δ᾽ ἄν
τις καὶ ὑπὲρ αὐτῶν ἐκείνων λόγον, οἶμαι, δίκαιον |
ὅτι εἰ μὲν ἀνεξέταστοι τεθνᾶσιν, ἠδίκηνται κρίσεως F
οὐ τετυχηκότες, εἰ δὲ ἐξεληλεγμένοι, πάλιν ἠδίκηνται τοῦ περὶ τὸν θάνατον ἀπεστερημένοι τάχους.
τί γάρ με κατατήκεις, εἴποι ἄν, οὐ τοῦτο τοῦ νόμου
R ii. 449 λέγοντος; τί δὲ κατ᾽ ὀλίγον ἀναλίσκεις ὥστε | ἀπὸ
μόνων τῶν ὀστῶν καὶ τοῦ δέρματος ἀπελθεῖν τὴν
ψυχήν, οὐ τοιαύτης ἐκ τῶν γραμμάτων ἐπικει-
μένης τῆς δίκης; 15. τί δ᾽ ἂν ἀποκριναίμεθα ταῖς
τῶν ἐπὶ μαρτυρίᾳ δεθέντων γυναιξὶ πρὸ τῆς κρίσεως αὐταῖς τῶν ἀνδρῶν οἰχομένων, οὓς ἐχρῆν
ἡμερῶν ⟨ὀλίγων⟩[2] οἴκοι πάλιν εἶναι φράσαντας ὅ
τι εἶχον; ἔτι τοίνυν τῶν οὕτως ἀπιόντων δεσμω-
τῶν τοῖς ἔτι ζῶσι συμβαίνει καὶ λυπεῖσθαι καὶ χαίρειν, λυπεῖσθαι μὲν τεθνεῶτος συνήθους, χαίρειν δὲ
κληρονομοῦσι τοῦ τόπου. ἔπειτ᾽ οὐ πολὺ ὕστερον
ἧκεν ἕτερος ὁ τὸν ἐκείνου καθέξων.

16. Καὶ πῶς ταῦτα σὺ περιεώρας, ἐρήσῃ, δέον
R ii. 450 ἐπιτιμᾶν τε τοῖς ἄρχουσι καὶ | ταῦτα ἃ νυνὶ λέγεις
λέγειν καὶ μηδὲ βουλομένοις ῥᾳθυμεῖν ἐπιτρέπειν;
καὶ τίς οὐκ οἶδεν ὅσα καὶ ὁσάκις εἴρηταί μοι πρὸς

---

[1] ⟨ὁ⟩ θάνατος Re., F.   [2] ⟨ὀλίγων⟩ F.

---

[a] As they failed to do from Tisamenus, *Or.* 33. 9 f.
[b] *C. Th.* 9. 3. 1 (= *C.J.* 9. 4. 1). The governor is liable to
punishment if this happens. This provision is reinforced by
C. Th. 9. 3. 6, where both jailor and governor are held liable.
Further prohibitions were to be enacted in the future, *C. Th.*
9. 1. 18 (A.D. 396), 9. 36. 2 (A.D. 409).

need is there to cite major criminals against those whose offence has been little or none? However fitting a punishment death may be for those guilty of serious crimes, certainly for such as these the term of imprisonment should never be so prolonged that their suffering should end in death. 14. And even for serious criminals a case could be made, and properly so, in my opinion, that if they die without trial, then they are the victims of injustice in having failed to secure a hearing,[a] and if they die after their guilt has been proved, they are again victimized by being robbed of a speedy death. " Yes! why do you leave me to rot? " they could protest. " The law gives no warrant for this. Why make me die a lingering death, so that my life spirit departs from bare skin and bone? Such is not the punishment enjoined by statute." [b] 15. And what answer can we make to the wives of men detained as witnesses,[c] when their husbands are dead before ever the case is heard, though they ought to have been back home again in a day or two after telling all that they had to tell? And what is more, when prisoners depart in this way, the survivors experience both sorrow and joy, sorrow at the death of a companion, and joy at inheriting the place he occupied. But not long afterwards someone else arrives to occupy it.

16. " How comes it, then," you will ask, " that you have neglected this, when you should reprove the governors and tell them the story you are telling me now, and not allow them to be so slack, even if they want to be? " Everybody knows what I have

[c] An abuse to be remedied in part by the elaborate precautions of *C. Th.* 9. 37. 4 (A.D. 409).

αὐτοὺς περὶ τῶν ἐν τῷ δεσμῷ φθειρομένων, ὡς
ἀσεβοῖέν τε ταύτῃ καὶ τοῖς τῆς πολιτείας οὐκ ἐμ-
μένοιεν ὅροις οὐδὲ μᾶλλον ἂν ἑτέρους δικαίως κο-
λάζοιεν ἢ διδοῖεν αὐτοὶ δίκας ἐπὶ τοῖς ἐκ τῶν |
δεσμωτηρίων ἐκφερομένοις νεκροῖς; οἱ δ' ἔλεγον F
μὲν ἔσεσθαι βελτίους, ἦσαν δὲ αὐτοὶ τοσοῦτον τοῖς
δεσμώταις εἰς ἀναπνοὴν διδόντες, ὅσον ἦγον αὐτοὺς
εἰς τὸ πρὸ δικαστηρίου χωρίον. ὡς τὴν αὐτήν
γε ἤγοντο πάλιν ἐλπίσαντες μέν τι κάλλιον, ἐσχη-
κότες δὲ οὐδέν.

17. Νὴ Δία, τὸ γὰρ τῶν πραγμάτων πλῆθος
κρεῖττον τῆς αὐτῶν βουλήσεως, καὶ αὐτοὶ μὲν
ἡδέως ἂν ἐπὶ τοῦθ' ἧκον, τὰ κωλύοντα δὲ ἦν ἰσχυ-
ρότερα. τίνα ταῦτα; εἰπάτωσαν. αἱ εἰσφοραὶ καὶ
τὸ πολλὰ πολλοὺς ὀφείλειν καὶ εἶναι ταῦτα ἐκείνων ἀναγκαιότερα· δεῖσθαι γὰρ τὸν καιρὸν χρημάτων. ἐγὼ δ' εἰ μὲν ἑώρων περὶ ταῦτα τὸν ἅπαντα
ἀναλισκόμενον χρόνον, ἴσως μὲν οὐδ' ἂν τότε λόγων ἠπόρησα τῶν τῇ σῇ βασιλείᾳ πρεπόντων, ἦν
δ' ἄν τι καὶ τούτοις εἰπεῖν, εἰ καὶ μὴ πάνυ καλόν·
νῦν δὲ τίς οὕτως ἀγνοεῖ τὰ τῶν ἀρχόντων, ὡς οὐκ
εἰδέναι πόσον τι τῆς ἡμέρας εἰσπράξεσι νέμοντες
ὁπόσον ἄγουσιν ἐπὶ τὰς δίκας; 18. δίκαι δὲ ὑπὲρ
μικρῶν πολλαί, ὑπὲρ δὲ μεγάλων ὀλίγαι. πολ-

---

[a] Both as sophist and as *honoratus*, Libanius saw this as his duty, and he had certainly fulfilled it with Icarius, *Or.* 26. 32.

[b] Decurions, in particular, who were responsible for the collection of tribute and unable to collect it from the recalcitrant peasants, *cf. Or.* 47 *passim.* Tisamenus was most insistent upon the collection of tribute, *Or.* 33. 13 ff., 32. *Cf.* also *Or.* 62. 43.

told them, and how often I have done so,[a] about the people who are dying in jail,—how abominably they are behaving in this, how they are overstepping the provisions of the constitution, and how they deserve no more to punish others than themselves to be punished for the dead that are carried out to burial from prison. And though they promised to mend their ways, they persisted in their attitude and gave the prisoners just so much respite as to take them to the courthouse yard, for back the inmates would go by the road they had come, hoping for better things and gaining nothing.

17. " Ah, yes ! but pressure of business overrode their wishes. They would have been glad to deal with the matter, the business that stopped them was more urgent." What business ? Let them describe it. Matters of taxation, of course : large numbers of people [b] were owing large sums, and this was a far more pressing matter, for the state of the empire demands ready money ! [c] If I saw them spending their whole time on this, even so I probably would have been at no loss for arguments consonant with your imperial dignity, but they might have presented some plausible, even though not particularly creditable explanation. As it is, no one is so ignorant of the governors' behaviour as to be unaware of what portion of the day they allocate to the collection of taxes and what to court hearings. 18. And court hearings there are in plenty for matters of little moment, for matters of importance, few.

[c] Theodosius was already making preparations against the usurper Maximus. The final breach was to come in a few months. His excessive fiscal demands sparked off the Riots of the Statues early in A.D. 387.

λάκις γοῦν ἤκουσα παρακαθήμενος τριάκοντα στα-
τῆρας καὶ εἴκοσι καὶ πλέθρον καὶ δένδρα τινὰ καὶ
ἀνδράποδον καὶ κάμηλον καὶ ὄνον καὶ χλαμύδα καὶ
χιτωνίσκον καὶ πολὺ τούτων ἐλάττω καὶ πολλοὺς
R ii. 451 μεθ' ἑκατέρων ῥήτορας καὶ μακροὺς | παρ' ἀμφοτέ-
ρων λόγους. καθίζει δὲ αὐτοὺς καὶ ἑσπέρα δικα-
στὰς οὐκ ὀλιγάκις, καὶ τὸ δεῖπνον αὐτοὺς ἡ κρίσις |
ἀφελομένη τὸν ἀγῶνα οὐδὲν μᾶλλον ἔπαυσε. πῶς F
οὖν, ὦ βέλτιστοι, τούτοις μὲν ἔνι χώρα μετὰ τῶν
εἰσπράξεων, τοῖς δεσμώταις δὲ δι' ἐκείνας κέ-
κλειται τὰ δικαστήρια; ἢ καὶ τούτων, ὥσπερ τῶν
εἰσπράξεων, ταῦτα ὕστερα, τῶν χρημάτων αἱ ψυ-
χαί; 19. καὶ μὴν τοῖς μὲν ταῖς ἀναβολαῖς οὐκ
ἀπώλλυτ' ἂν[1] τὰ παρὰ[2] τοῦ πράγματος δίκαια. ἃ
γὰρ τήμερον ἐνῆν εἰπεῖν, ταῦτα ἂν ὑπῆρχε καὶ δύο
μησὶ καὶ πλείοσιν ὕστερον· περὶ δ' αὖ τοὺς θανάτους τοῦτ' οὐκ ἔστιν, οὐδ' ἂν κατάσχοι τις τὴν ψυχὴν εἰπὼν πρὸς αὐτήν· μένε, ἀλλ' ἀπειπόντος τοῦ
σώματος ἀνάγκη φεύγειν ἐκείνην. οἱ δὲ μεταξὺ
περὶ ἀργυρίου δικάζοντες ἢ ἐπὶ τῇ γνώσει γε αὐτῇ
τοὺς τοιούτους ἀκούοντες θανάτους οὐκ εἶναι κατὰ
τῆς ἀρχῆς τοῦτο νομίζουσι. καταφρονοῦσι γάρ,
οἶμαι, τῶν μὲν ὡς οὐκέτ' ὄντων, τῶν δὲ ἐκείνοις
συγγενῶν ὡς ἀσθενῶν.

20. Εἰ δὲ καὶ χρήματα δεῖ συγχωρῆσαι τῶν ψυχῶν εἶναι τιμιώτερα, ἀλλ' οὐ δήπου γε ὀρχηστὰς

---

[1] ἀπώλλυτ' ἂν F. (PaV): ἀπώλλυτο Re. (other mss.).
[2] παρὰ conj. Re., F.: περὶ Re. text (mss.).: om. Gothofred.

---

[a] As was required of him as *honoratus*.

Anyway, I have often sat in attendance [a] and listened to cases dealing with thirty staters, or twenty, an acre of land, a few trees, a slave, a camel, an ass, a cloak or a jacket, and things far less important still,[b] with a galaxy of legal talent on each side and longwinded speeches from both. Even nightfall often finds the judges in session [c]: the verdict robs them of their supper, but it does not put an end to the case, for all that. My dear fellows, how is it that there is room for all this along with your collecting duties, when because of those duties the courts are closed to men under arrest? Is it that here too, as in fiscal matters, one thing must give way to another—men's lives to money? 19. " Yes ! but those caught in the law's delays would not have an intrinsically sound claim lost to them. What they can say today, they could say just as well in two or three months' time ! " But if they are dead, they cannot. Nobody can retain the vital spark by telling it to stay : when the body succumbs, it too must needs depart. But those who hear of such deaths while they are engaged on financial cases or at the very beginning of the investigation, do not regard it as at all damaging to their position. The victims they disregard, so it seems to me, as dead, their kinsfolk as men of little import.

20. And even if I must grant money to be more precious than men's lives, dancers, mimes, horses

---

[b] Tisamenus (*Or.* 33. 13 f.) was guilty of such excess of zeal. Later (*C. Th.* 2. 1. 8 of A.D. 395) such petty cases were to be adjudged improper for the governor's personal attention. He was to concentrate on criminal matters. Here, as often, stater = solidus.

[c] But not so Tisamenus, *Or.* 33. 10.

LIBANIUS

R ii. 452 καὶ μίμους καὶ ἵππους καὶ τοὺς τούτοις | ἐφεστη-
κότας. τί οὖν οὗτοι ποιοῦσιν οἱ σωτῆρες ἀξιοῦντες ὀνομάζεσθαι; τρέχουσιν ὀψόμενοι μὲν ταῦτα,
ὀψόμενοι δὲ ἐκεῖνα, νῦν μὲν καλούμενοι, νῦν δὲ καὶ
οὐ καλούμενοι καὶ τῶν κλήσεων δὲ ἐνίας[1] αὐτοὶ
σφᾶς αὐτοὺς καλοῦσι. | πῶς γὰρ οὐχ αὑτούς, ὅταν F
αὐτοὶ διαπράττωνται φοιτᾶν ἐπὶ θύρας[2] τοὺς καλέ-
σοντας; 21. τὴν ἀνάγκην δὲ ἂν λέγωσι καὶ τὸν
φόβον τὸν ἀπὸ τῆς ζημίας, ἐξαπατῶσιν. ἥ τε γὰρ
R ii. 453 δείλη καθαρὰ τοῦδε τοῦ φόβου ἥ | τε ἀνάγκη τῆς
θέας ἡμερῶν τινῶν ἐστιν, ἀλλ᾿ οὐχ ἁπάσης. οἱ δὲ
ἐπὶ πάσης ἔρχονται καθ᾿ ἑκατέραν[3] τῆς ἡμέρας
μερίδα καὶ τὰ τῶν εἰσπράξεων οὐ χείρω ταύτῃ
καθίσταται. καίτοι πόσῳ βέλτιον καὶ ἀνθρωπινώ-
τερον τοῖς ἠτυχηκόσι τῶν ἀνθρώπων βοηθεῖν εἰς
ὅσον ἔξεστι ἢ ἐν περιττοῖς θεάμασιν ἀναμένειν τὰς
R ii. 454 νύκτας, καὶ δειπνοῦντα | ποιεῖσθαι λόγους ὑπὲρ
τῶν καλῶς ἀφειμένων ἢ ὅσα τοῖς ἡνιόχοις ἐπ᾿
ἀλλήλους εὕρηται. 22. πόθεν δὴ τούτων τὰ μὲν
ἠμέληται, τὰ δὲ ἐν σπουδῇ μεγάλῃ; δόξα τις πονηρὰ τοὺς ἄρχοντας κατέσχεν ὅτι τὰ μὲν ἄλλα
πάντα φαῦλα καὶ οὐδέν, μόνον δὲ ἀγαθὸν αἱ παρὰ
τῶν πολλῶν εἰς αὑτοὺς μετ᾿ εὐφημιῶν βοαὶ καὶ τὸ

[1] ἐνίας conj. Sintenis, F.: ἐν ἐνίαις Re. (mss., ἐν om. B).
[2] θύρας conj. Re., F. (V): θύραις Re. text (other mss.).
[3] καθ᾿ ἑκατέραν om. Re. (A, I in margin).

[a] Like Julian and the intellectuals generally, Libanius disliked the races and theatre, and everything connected with them: e.g. Or. 35. 13 f., 42. 8. Cf. Pack, Studies, pp. 61 ff.
[b] Tisamenus expected to be invited to shows, Or. 33. 26.
[c] Discrimination on the part of the governor was required

and drivers certainly are not.[a] So what do our governors do—these aspirants to the title of " savi-
ours " ? They hurry to see first this show, then
that, sometimes by invitation,[b] sometimes not, sometimes actually self-invited, for obviously they are
self-invited when they personally ensure that the
future hosts flock to their doors.[c] 21. And if they
talk of the need to attend and the fear of unfortunate consequences if they do not, that is mere
deception. The afternoons are free from such fear,
and the need to attend applies to some days,[d] not to
every day. But off they go, every day alike, both
morning and afternoon, without any disruption of
their fiscal duties. Yet how much better and more
humane to assist unfortunate persons to the best
of one's ability than to hang around until nightfall
in extravagant shows, and over dinner to discourse
upon the clean starts or the tactics devised by the
drivers against each other ![e] 22. How is it then
that some of these duties are so neglected and others
performed so enthusiastically ? The governors are
possessed of a pernicious notion that everything else
is cheap and of no account, and that their sum of
happiness consists in the cheers and acclamations[f]

in the acceptance of private invitations, *Or.* 26. 15, 27. 17.
For the problems raised by εἴσοδοι cf. *Or.* 51-52.
   [d] By the terms of *C. Th.* 15. 5. 2 (of May A.D. 386), which
Libanius clearly has in mind here, governors are not to
attend games, etc. except on imperial anniversaries, and then
in the mornings only : cf. *Or.* 52. 38.
   [e] Including magic spells, as Amm. Marc. 26. 3. 3, 28. 1. 27.
   [f] The attitude is not unreasonable (cf. οἱ σωτῆρες ἀξιοῦντες
ὀνομάζεσθαι, § 20). *C. Th.* 1. 16. 6 (cf. A.D. 331) had ordained that acclamations received by a governor be reported
to the emperor, and despatched by public post, as evidence

εἰδέναι χάριν ἐκείνους αὐτοῖς ἀντὶ τῶν ἡδονῶν ἃς
πορίζουσι τῷ πλήθει. ἀφέντες οὖν τὸ διὰ τοῦ τὰ
προσήκοντα ποιεῖν παρὰ τοῖς εὖ φρονοῦσιν εὐδοκιμεῖν, ἀφ᾽ ὧν ἡγοῦνται τοὺς ἀργοὺς τουτουσὶ καὶ
κηφῆνας ἐπισπᾶσθαι, ταῦτα χαρίζονται, οἱ μὲν ἐκ-
δεχόμενοι τὰ τῶν ἔμπροσθεν, οἱ δὲ καὶ προστιθέντες, κἂν τύχωσι τῆς κλαγγῆς τῶν γεράνων,
F 370 εὐδαι|μονίζουσιν | ἑαυτούς. εἶθ᾽ οἱ μὲν μεγάλοι, R
ταπεινοὶ δὲ οἱ βουλεύοντες καὶ τῇ παρ᾽ ἐκείνων
βοηθείᾳ πολλάκις τὰς παρὰ τῶν ἀρχόντων ὀργὰς
διαφεύγοντες. τοῦτο ἄλλα τε πολλὰ καὶ τοὺς δεσμώτας ἀπόλλυσιν.

23. Οἱ δὲ περικλύζεσθαί φασιν ὑπὸ πλήθους[1] τῶν
πραγμάτων. ἃ δίδωσιν ὑμῖν τοσαύτας ἡμέρας
ἑκάστου μηνὸς τηνάλλως ἀναλίσκειν, ἃ δίδωσιν ἐν
Δάφνῃ καθημένοις τέρπειν τε καὶ τέρπεσθαι κακῶς.
ἢ καὶ τότε φήσετε τοὺς ὀφείλοντας εἰσπράττειν;
R ii. 456 ἀλλ᾽ αὐτῷ τούτῳ πρώτῳ τιμᾶτε | τὴν εἰς ἅπαντα
ἐκείνην ἐξουσίαν τὴν ἐν τῇ Δάφνῃ, τοῦτο γάρ ἐστιν
ἡ ἑορτὴ τὸ μηδενὸς ἀπέχεσθαι τῶν αἰσχρῶν. καὶ
τοῦτο τοίνυν αὐτῇ χαρίζονται, βασιλεῦ, τὸ μὴ πάνυ
τότε μεμνῆσθαί τινα τῶν τοῖς σοῖς θησαυροῖς ὀφειλομένων χρημάτων. 24. πάντων δὲ ἀλογώτατον εἰσπράξεων εἰς ἀπολογίαν μεμνῆσθαι τὸν ἄρχοντα τὸν
οὐκ αὐτὸν περιόντα καὶ τῶν ὀφειλόντων λαμβα-

---

[1] τοῦ πλήθους F. (Pa).

of his administrative capabilities. Tisamenus acknowledged
the importance of acclamation, Or. 33. 11 f., as did other
officials in the 380s : e.g. Or. 26. 18 f., 27. 13, 41 passim,
46. 39.

they receive from the commons and the gratitude evinced towards them in return for the pleasure they provide the masses. So they reject the fair fame to be won from men of sense by the performance of their duty, and they distribute these favours, whereby they think to attach to themselves these idlers, these drones.[a] Some inherit the practices of their predecessors,[b] others even make additions of their own and, if they meet with the clamour of cranes,[c] they are full of self-congratulation. Then those fellows rise to greatness, and humbled are the city councillors,[d] who often escape the governors' wrath by means of the assistance they provide. This creates havoc, not least for those in jail.

23. But, their claim is, they are overwhelmed by a mass of business. This business allows you to idle away so many days every month, and it allows you to recline in Daphne and to have and to give enjoyment of a vicious kind.[e] Or will you tell me that you are dunning the debtors at that time too ? But this is the first and foremost factor in the respect you show towards that carnival of misrule in Daphne, where the essence of the festival is to hold aloof from none of its vices.[f] And this is how they favour it, Sire, by utterly and completely forgetting the moneys owed to your treasuries. 24. And it is quite ridiculous for a governor, who does not make a personal tour and arrest of debtors, to make mention

[a] Used to describe the theatrical claque, who arranged the acclamation, *Or.* 46. 17.
[b] Thus Icarius was urged not to adopt the pattern of Proclus, *Or.* 26. 22.   [c] Homer, *Il.* 3. 3.   [d] *Cf. Or.* 2. 35.
[e] On the licence in Daphne *cf.* Sozom. 5. 19.
[f] The Maiuma, *Or.* 10. 14, 50. 11 ; *C. Th.* 15. 6. 1-2.

νόμενον.[1] ἴσμεν γὰρ δι᾽ ὧν σοι τὰ τοιαῦτα πράττε-
ται, τοῦ δὲ ἄρχοντός ἐστιν εἰπεῖν τε ὃ δεῖ ποιῆσαι
καὶ τὸν ποιήσαντα ἐπαινέσαι καὶ τὸν μὴ ποιήσαντα πλῆξαι. σὺ δὲ πρὸς μὲν τοὺς λαμπροὺς
ἑστιάτορας τὴν ἀσχολίαν ταύτην οὐ λέγεις οὐδ᾽ ὡς
οὐκ ἂν δύναιο πίνειν κατακείμενος τοσαῦτα | μέρη F 3
τῆς ἡμέρας, καὶ ἴσως οὐκ ἀδικεῖς ὑπακούων τοιαῦτα τοῖς φίλοις· ἂν δέ τι τῶν μειζόνων τὴν σὴν
ἀπαιτῇ γνώμην, οὐκ ἄγεις σχολήν, ἀλλὰ βαπτίζῃ
καί σε ὁ τῶν πραγμάτων τῶν ἄλλων ὄχλος ὑφ᾽
αὑτῷ πεποίηται, ὥσπερ τῶν πραγμάτων ἐκείνων
ἃ λέγεις τοῖς μὲν ἐκπώμασιν εἰκόντων, σωτηρίας
δέ τισι φθονούντων.

25. Βούλομαι δέ τί σοι διηγήσασθαι τῆς τούτων
R ii. 457 περὶ τὰ | τοιαῦτα ἀργίας. ἀποθνήσκει μέν τις ἐν
ἀγρῷ ξίφει νυκτός, τοῖς ἀπεκτονόσι δὲ ὑπῆρξε διαφυγεῖν τῶν οἰκετῶν πρὸς τὴν ἐπίθεσιν ὑπὸ τὴν
κλίνην ὑποδύντων, νομιζόντων ἀρκεῖν εἰ διασω-
θεῖεν. ἐτεθνήκει μὲν οὖν ἄπαις, οὓς δὲ ἐπεποιήκει
τῶν ἑαυτοῦ δεσπότας διαθήκη τούτους ἔδει κατὰ
τὸν νόμον μηδὲν παραλιπεῖν ἐξ ὧν ἦν[2] ἐλπὶς ἔσεσθαί τινα δίκην. ἄνθρωποι τοίνυν ἐξάγονται τῆς
κώμης σαφὲς μὲν οὐδὲν ἔχειν λεγούσης, ὑποπτεύ-
ειν δὲ τούτων εἶναι τὸ ἔργον. 26. οἱ μὲν οὖν κλη-
ρονόμοι προσιόντες[3] πολλάκις ἐδέοντο τὸν ἐνόντα
ποιήσασθαι περὶ τῆς σφαγῆς ἐξετασμόν, οἱ δὲ
ληρεῖν αὐτοὺς ἔφασκον οὐ παραχωροῦντας τοῦ δι-

---

[1] λαμβανόμενον F.: ἐπιλαβόμενον conj. Re.: λαμένον Re.
text (CAPUI): om. Gothofred. (PaBV).
[2] ἦν conj. Re., F. (mss.): ᾖ Re. text: ἡ Gothofred.
[3] προσιόντες Re., F. (V): om. B: προσίοντο other mss.:
-ίονται Gothofred.

182

of revenue collection to excuse himself. We all know the agents by whom such jobs are done. The governor's task is to tell what needs doing, to commend the one who does it and to flog the one who doesn't. You don't mention this pressing business to your excellent hosts [a] : you don't tell them that you could not possibly lie there drinking for such a large part of the day, and perhaps you are not at fault in so obliging your friends. However, if some matter of major importance requires your attention, you simply haven't the time, you are up to the ears in work, and the weight of other business has bowled you over, just as this business you mention gives way to drinking parties but begrudges men their salvation.

25. I would like to tell you something of their idleness on such matters. A man was murdered on his farm, stabbed to death at night : the murderers managed to get away when the slaves faced the attack by ducking under the bed and thinking it quite enough if they came out alive.[b] Now he died without issue, and those whom he had made masters of his property by testament had the duty according to law of neglecting no means of securing a conviction.[c] So some fellows were arrested, the villagers saying that, though they had no certain proof, they suspected that it was some of their work. 26. So the heirs presented themselves time and again, begging the resident magistrate to hold an investigation of the murder, only to be told that they were stupid in not yielding the court to those who were dealing

[a] Such as the *principalis* Callippus was to Icarius, *Or.* 27. 29.   [b] *e.g.* Amm. Marc. 28. 2. 13.
[c] *Cf. Or.* 30. 25.

LIBANIUS

καστηρίου τοῖς ὑπὲρ τῶν χρημάτων ἄγουσι. μη-
νῶν δὲ ἑπτὰ διελθόντων καὶ οἷς ἦν ἀνάγκη τοῦ
κειμένου φροντίζειν ἐγκειμένων τῷ τὴν ἀρχὴν ἔχον-
τι ποιεῖται μὲν τὴν πρὸ τοῦ Διονυσίου στοὰν ἀνὴρ |
R ii. 458 δικαστήριον.   μελλούσης δὲ εἰσιέναι τῆς δίκης
ἀκούει μὲν | ᾀδόντων τὰ αὑτῶν ᾄσματα τῶν ἐν F :
τοῖς σπηλαίοις οἰκούντων δεῦρο τότε ἡκόντων, ὃ
ποιεῖν τοῦ θέρους εἰώθασιν, ἀναπηδήσας δὲ ἐκ τοῦ
θρόνου τὴν ταχίστην ἀπῆλθεν, ὡς οὐκ ὂν δίκαιον
ἐκείνων φανέντων τῶν δικαίων τι ποιεῖν· ἀπελθὼν
δὲ οὐκέτι προσεῖχε τὸν νοῦν τοῖς ἐπεξιοῦσιν, ἀλλὰ
τοῖς μὲν ἀποστερηθῆναι τῆς οὐσίας αἴτιος ἐγένετο
προαχθεῖσιν, ὡς ἐν μήκει χρόνου, μικροῦ του προσ-
R ii. 459 άψασθαι τῶν ἐκ τῆς γῆς, | πέντε δὲ ἐκείνων ἀπο-
θανεῖν ὑποπτευθεῖσιν, οὐκ ἐλεγχθεῖσιν, ὧν ἂν εἷς
ἐσώθη τις καὶ μάτην νομισθείς, τάχα δ' ἂν καὶ
ἅπαντες. πολλὰ τοιαῦτα νόμιζε καθ' ἕκαστον ἔτος
ἁμαρτάνεσθαι, βασιλεῦ.

27. Εἰσὶ δέ τινες οἳ πάσῃ μὲν τέχνῃ κτῶνται τὸ
παρελθεῖν εἰς ἀρχήν, παρελθόντες[1] δὲ οὐ τῆς αὐτῶν
εἶναι φύσεώς φασιν οὔτε βασανίζειν ἄνθρωπον τὴν
διὰ τῶν πλευρῶν βάσανον οὔτε ξίφος παραδιδόναι
τῷ δημίῳ. πρὸς οὓς εἴποιμ' ἂν ὅτι χρῆν αὐτοὺς

[1] παρελθόντες Re., F. : ἐλθόντες mss.

---

[a] For the temple of Dionysus cf. Or. 30. 51, Malalas 10,
p. 234. Downey, pp. 179 f.

[b] Since the governor is almost certainly the Christian
Tisamenus, it is uncertain why he should decamp at the
advent of the monks (τῶν ἐν τοῖς σπηλαίοις οἰκούντων, cf.
Or. 2. 32, 30. 8).   Their mass interventions before the
governors were certainly influential, as after the riots of
A.D. 387, but Pack's notion (p. 117) of his superstitious
confusion of their appearance with a mourning procession
is appropriate only to a pagan who dreaded the pollution

with a financial case. Seven months passed by, and those who were in duty bound to have regard for the deceased put pressure on the governor, and so his worship turned the colonnade in front of the temple of Dionysus [a] into his courtroom. Just as the case was due to begin, he heard the chanting of hymns from the cave-dwellers, who had then come to town, as they usually do in summer.[b] Up he jumped from his seat and made off hot-foot, giving out that it was improper to observe any of the proprieties of law, once they had put in an appearance. And after his departure, he paid no further attention to the plaintiffs, and so he was responsible for them losing their property, since they were induced, as you might expect considering the delay, to take possession of some small portion of the produce of the estate, and also for the deaths of five of the defendants whose guilt was suspected, not proved. Any one of these could have been suspected without reason and been saved, and perhaps all of them. You may be assured, Sire, that many such crimes are committed year after year.

27. Some people use every possible means to achieve office, and when they achieve it, they say that it is not in their nature to submit a man to examination by flogging or to hand him over to the executioner for beheading.[c] My reply to them is that they should recognize their own limitations [d]

of contact with the dead. More likely is that he was evading the unpopularity which would accrue from a confrontation with the monks. For their interference in secular matters, *C. Th.* 9. 40. 16, 16. 3. 2.

[c] A criticism directed against Christian officials in particular, *e.g.* Eutropius, *Or.* 4. 36. On their dilemma *cf.* Jones, *LRE* 983. [d] The Delphic γνῶθι σεαυτόν.

ἑαυτοὺς ἐγνωκότας ἰδιωτεύειν, ἀλλ' οὐκ ἐθέλειν
ἄρχειν ἀδυνατοῦντας ἄρχειν. ἄρχοντος μὲν γὰρ
ἐστι τὸ καὶ ταῦτα δύνασθαι, οἱ δὲ[1] τὸ μηδὲ[2] ἄρχειν
δύνασθαι σαφῶς | ὡμολογήκασιν. εἰ γὰρ δὴ τὰ F
μὲν πράγματα τούτων ἀμφοτέρων δεῖται, καὶ βα-
σάνων καὶ θανάτων, ὁ δὲ καὶ ταῦτα κἀκεῖνα φεύ-
ξεται, πῶς ἂν ἄρχων εἴη μὴ τὸ τῆς ἀρχῆς ἅπαν
ποιῶν; βασάνῳ γὰρ τἀληθὲς ἐν πολλοῖς εὑρί-
σκοιτ' ἂν μόνῃ τῷ τε τῶν ἐξελεγχομένων θανάτῳ
τάχ' ἄν τις τῶν πονηρῶν γένοιτο μετριώτερος.
28. τουτὶ δὲ ἄρχοντος ἔργον τὸν μὲν οὐκ ὄντα |
R ii. 460 ζῆν ἄξιον πέμπειν ἀποθανούμενον, τοὺς δ' ἄλλους
τῷ φόβῳ τῶν ἴσων κατέχειν. παντὶ γὰρ τῷ τοῖς
νόμοις ἐναντία ποιοῦντι πολεμεῖν τὸν ἐπὶ τῆς ἀρχῆς
προσήκει τὸν βοηθεῖν τεταγμένον τοῖς νόμοις. σὺ
δὲ βραδὺς μὲν ὢν τοὺς πόδας οὐκ ἂν ἧκες περὶ
τάχους ἀγωνιούμενος εἰδὼς ὡς[3] οὐ τῶν σῶν ποδῶν
τὸ ἔργον, ἄρχεις δὲ οὔτ' εἰς φῶς ἄγειν ἀδικήματα
δυνάμενος οὔθ' ὑπηρετοῦσαν τοῖς τοῦ νόμου προστάγμασι[4] τὴν φωνὴν παρέχειν; εἶτα δεινὸν νομίζων εἰ σοῦ φθεγξαμένου τις ἀποθάνοι δικαίως, οὐχ
ἡγῇ δεινὸν εἰ σοῦ σιγῶντος[5] πολλοί τινες ἀποθά-
νοιεν οὐ δικαίως;
29. Ἀλλὰ δῶμεν, ὦ βασιλεῦ, τοῖς οὐκ ἀρχικοῖς
μὲν τούτοις, δεδιόσι δὲ τὰ τοιαῦτα τῶν εἰκότων τι
πεπονθέναι. ὅταν δὲ ἄνθρωποι ῥύακας μὲν αἵ-

---

[1] οἱ δὲ F. (UB, PI corrected) : om. Re. (other mss.).
[2] μηδὲ Re. (mss.). : μὴ F.
[3] ὡς F. (I marg.) : om. Re. (other mss.).
[4] προστάγμασι Cobet, F. : πράγμασι Re. (mss.).
[5] σιγῶντος F. (mss. except AI) : σιωπῶντος Re. (AI).

---

[a] Thus, despite his aversion to corporal punishment, Li-

186

and stay in private life, without aspiring to office when they are incapable of discharging it. A governor's job is to be able to discharge these duties too, but they have made an open admission that they are not even able to govern. In fact, if his duties require him to undertake both examination and execution, and he is going to evade both, how can he be a governor if he does not discharge his duties to the full? [a] In many cases truth can be discovered by examination alone, and by the execution of the guilty some criminal may perhaps be reformed.[b] 28. This is the governor's task, to send to execution the man who does not deserve to live, and to restrain the rest by fear of a similar fate. It is the duty of the official who has been stationed to defend the laws to make war on every man who contravenes them. If you are slow of foot, you would never turn up to take part in a race, for you know that this is not within the capacity of your feet: yet do you take office, though you are incapable of bringing injustice to light or of raising your voice in support of the ordinances of law? And, finally, if you think it shocking for a man to be deservedly executed at your bidding, do you not think it shocking for many persons to be unjustly put to death, because of your silence?

29. Very well, Sire. Let us concede to these incapables who entertain such qualms that theirs is a normal reaction. But when people make streams of

banius requires his governors to be just and humane, but firm in administering it. They should not evade their duty.

[b] Libanius' theory of punishment rarely touches upon the reformative aspect. Primarily, the objective is retribution and deterrence.

ματος | ἐν τοῖς δικαστηρίοις διὰ τῶν μαστίγων F
ποιῶσι, τύπτωσι δὲ καὶ τὴν ψυχὴν ἀφέντας κωφὴν
αἰκιζόμενοι γῆν καὶ τοὺς μὲν εἰς ποταμούς, τοὺς
δὲ εἰς βρόχους ὠθῶσι διὰ τὸν φόβον, ὅταν οὖν οὗτοι
πέμπωσιν ἐπὶ τὰ δεσμωτήρια φάλαγγας, ἐρρῶσθαι
δὲ φράσαντες τοῖς περὶ ἐκεῖνα νόμοις ἐπ' ἄλλοις
διατρίβωσιν ὡς δὴ φιλάνθρωποι δόξοντες εἶναι, τίς
οὐκ ἂν ἀποπνιγείη; 30. ἐγὼ δὲ ἠξίουν αὐτοὺς
εἰδέναι τε τὸ τοῦ Φοίνικος ἐκείνου καὶ μιμεῖσθαι,
μᾶλλον δὲ ἐπίστανται μέν, μιμεῖσθαι δὲ οὐκ ἐθέλουσι. τί οὖν ἦν τὸ 'κείνου; τῶν ἐν Παλαιστίνῃ
δεδεμένων τοὺς μὲν ἐτιμωρήσατο, τοὺς δὲ ἔλυσε
τῷ δικαίῳ καθ' ἑκάτερον ἀκολουθῶν. ἔπειτα κά-
πηλοί τε ἦσαν ἐν ἑκάστῳ[1] καὶ πίθοι καὶ ἐκπώματα
R ii. 461 καὶ σὺν ᾠδαῖς ἡ | πόσις. οὕτω δὲ τῶν ἐπιρρεόντων
πραγμάτων ἑκάστῳ ταχεῖαν εὕρισκε τὴν τελευτὴν
ὥστε μηδὲν ἔτ' αὐτῷ δεῆσαι δεσμωτηρίων. 31.
παρελθὼν τοίνυν εἷς τις ἐρεῖ τῶν νῦν δὴ τούτων
ταὐτὸ καὶ αὑτῷ πεπρᾶχθαι καὶ αὐλοὺς εἰσελθεῖν
ἐκεῖσε. αὐλοὶ μὲν οὖν εἰσῆλθον, οὕτω δὲ κατα-
γέλαστον ἐποιήσατο τὴν μίμησιν ὥστε ἐν πολὺ
χαλεπωτέροις τοὺς δεσμώτας γενέσθαι. οὐ γὰρ
ἀπαλλαγὴν αὐτοῖς παρέσχε τοῦ πράγματος, ἀλλ'
ἤμειψε τὸν τόπον | τοῦ δεδέσθαι μένοντος. ἐπὶ γὰρ F
τὸ τῆς δευτέρας ἀρχῆς οἴκημα πέμπει τὰ σώματα
πολλοῖς πολλὰ προστιθείς, ὥστε ἀλλήλους κατα-

[1] ἑκάστῳ ⟨δεσμωτηρίῳ⟩ F.

---

[a] Homer, *Iliad*, 24. 54.
[b] Libanius was himself threatened with this fate by a
courtier in A.D. 362, *Or.* 1. 126. The bodies of those lynched
in A.D. 354 were thrown into the river, Amm. Marc. 14. 7. 16.
[c] His identity is uncertain. Pack (p. 119) suggested
Andronicus, for whom *cf. Or.* 62. 56 ff.

blood flow in the courts by their floggings, and when they lash lifeless bodies, outraging senseless clay,[a] and force some in panic to their deaths in the river,[b] others in the noose, when, I say, such as these clap into prison whole battalions, let the prison regulations go hang, and waste their time on other business —all this indeed to get a name for humanity—it is enough to take one's breath away. 30. I begged them to get to know the practice of that well-known Phoenician [c] and to follow it ; the fact is, though, that they know it well enough, but refuse to follow it. His method was, in Palestine, to punish some of those under arrest and to release the rest, but in either case he followed the dictates of justice. Then there were stalls set up in every prison, jars and cups of wine, and they drank to the accompaniment of song. And he found such a speedy ending to every problem that beset him that he had no more need of prisons. 31. One of our present-day governors [d] will come and say that he too has done the same, and has let music into the jail. True enough, music did go in, but his following of the pattern was so ludicrous that the prisoners were in a far worse condition. He gave them no release from their affliction : he merely changed their location, and their confinement continued. He packed off the bodies to the jail of his subordinate governor, herding their masses in with the masses there, so that they trampled one

---

[d] The *Comes Orientis*, Deinias (*Or.* 33. 7, described as ὕπαρχος in *Or.* 1. 251, a term usually applied to the ppO). He occupies the μείζων θρόνος or μείζων ἀρχή (*Or.* 1. 210, 27. 6, 33. 27), the *consularis Syriae*, Tisamenus, holding the ἐλάττων ἀρχή (*Or.* 27. 6, see also *Ep.* 21. 7, where however τὸν κρείττω is the ppO).

πατοῦντες ἀπώλλυντο. τοιαῦτα τῶν καλῶν τούτων αὐλῶν ἀπέλαυσαν οἱ ταλαίπωροι. εἶτ᾽ ἐν οὐ
πολλαῖς ἡμέραις αὖθις εἶχε πλείους ἢ πρόσθεν τὸ
οἴκημα. καὶ ταῦτα οὐκ ἠγνοεῖτο μέν, ἐκείνῳ δὲ
ἐδόκει.

32. Φανήτω δὴ κἀνταῦθα τὸ τῆς σῆς φιλανθρωπίας, ὦ βασιλεῦ. καὶ ὡς μὲν ἔθηκας νόμον βοηθοῦντα τοῖς δεθεῖσι περὶ τὸν χρόνον, τοῦτο δέ ἐστιν
εἰς τὴν σωτηρίαν αὐτῶν,[1] οἶδα. οἶδα μέντοι κἀκεῖνο, ὅτι ἅπερ ἂν οὐ κειμένου τοῦ νόμου, ταῦτα
καὶ γεγραμμένου πέπρακται. οὐ γὰρ ὄντων τῶν
βεβαιοῦν αὐτοὺς ἐθελόντων δικαστῶν γράμματά
R ii. 462 εἰσι | μόνον, τοῖς ἀδικουμένοις δὲ οὐ παρέπονται[2]
ποιοῦντες αὐτοὺς τοῖς παρ᾽ ἑαυτῶν ἔργοις τῶν ἠδικηκότων κρείττονας. 33. ἀλλ᾽ ὅταν σὺ μέν, ὦ
γενναῖε, νομοθετῇς ἃ προσήκει, βραχὺς δὲ τούτων
ᾖ λόγος τοῖς ἐπὶ τοῦ δικάζειν καὶ τὴν αὐτῶν γνώμην ἀντὶ τῶν σοὶ δοκούντων ποιῶσι κυρίαν, οὔτε
οὐκ εἰδέναι ταῦτα ὑμᾶς καλὸν οὔτε εἰδότας φέρειν
ῥᾳδίως, ἀλλ᾽ ἐν τῇ τῶν ἐπανισταμένων ὑμῖν μερίδι
τοὺς τοιούτους θετέον καὶ μισητέον ὥσπερ ἐκεί-
νους. καὶ γὰρ οὗτοι τὰ ὑμέτερα ὑμᾶς, καθ᾽ ὅσον |
οἷοί τε εἰσίν, ἀφαιροῦνται τά γε τῶν πονούντων F
ὑπὲρ τῶν ἐθνῶν καὶ ζώντων ἀτιμάζοντες καὶ οἷς
ποιοῦσι λύοντες. εἰ δὲ εἷς ὁ πρῶτος τοῦτο τολ-
μήσας ἐδεδώκει τῷ νομοθέτῃ δίκην, ἴσχυον ἂν οἱ
νόμοι. 34. καὶ μὴν κἀκεῖνό γε ἠξίουν, κάλλη

---

[1] αὐτῶν conj. Re., F. : αὐτὴν Re. text (mss.).
[2] παρέπονται F. (V) : παρέσονται Re. (other mss.).

[a] On crowding in prisons cf. Or. 33. 41.
[b] C. Th. 9. 3. 6. (Dec. A.D. 380): " de his quos tenet carcer

another to death.[a] Such was the advantage the poor devils got from this fine piping. Then, not so many days afterwards, his jail once more was fuller than it had ever been before. And this did not pass unnoticed, for all that he thought it did.

32. Then, Sire, let your humanity reveal itself here too. That you have enacted a law to help people under arrest as regards the length of detention, and that this does serve to protect them, I know.[b] But I also know that the same sort of practices have been current after the passing of the law as would have occurred if it was not in force. When magistrates willing to enforce them are non-existent, laws are mere scraps of paper[c] and do not provide assistance to the victims by allowing them to get the better of their oppressors through their results. 33. But when you, Your Majesty, propose proper legislation and when the appointed magistrates take little notice of it and give validity to their own decisions instead of to your decrees, it is not right either for you to be unaware of this or, if you are aware of it, to be complacent about it. You must class such persons as rebels against your authority and loathe them, just as you do rebels. In fact, these people rob you of your own, as far as in them lies, for they bring into disrepute the work of those who live and labour for the provinces, and by their actions they undo it. If the first who had dared behave so had been punished by the legislator, the laws would now prevail. 34. Moreover, I presented a further

id aperta definitione sancimus ut aut convictum velox poena subducat aut liberandum custodia diuturna non maceret."

[c] Cf. Or. 33. 18. The same complaint was made against Icarius, Or. 29. 29.

προστιθέναι ταῖς πόλεσι φάσκοντας ἔχειν τινὰ δεῖξαι καὶ δεσμωτηρίων πρόνοιαν. οὗ μεγάλα ἂν ἦν
ἀπὸ μικρῶν ὀνῆσαι¹ χρημάτων. ἐπειδὴ γὰρ τοῦ
δεῖν ὡς πλείστους ἀνθρώπους ἐπιθυμοῦσιν, ἐχρῆν
αὐτοὺς δήπου μηδὲ τῶν δεξομένων αὐτοὺς ἠμεληκέναι τόπων· ὡς οὐχ οὕτω δεῖ τοῖς ἀδέτοις τῆς ἀπὸ
τῶν τοίχων φαιδρότητος, ὡς τοῖς δεδεμένοις τοῦ
μετ' εὐρυχωρίας διαφέρειν τὰ κακά.

¹ οὗ . . ὀνῆσαι Re., F. (V): οὐ . . ὠνῆσαι Gothofred.
(other mss.).

argument also, that people^a who claim to beautify
our cities should be capable of showing some concern for the jails, too. Here it should be possible to
do much good at little cost, for since their desire is
to keep as many people as they can in durance vile,
they surely ought not to neglect the places to receive
them. Persons at liberty do not need the splendid
façade so much as the prison-inmates need to endure
their troubles with room to move.

^a As the governors claimed to do by their building pro-
grammes, *cf. Or.* 10 *passim*, 11. 193 ff., 46. 44. Tisamenus'
efforts here in building cages for animals, not for prisoners
were criticized, *Or.* 33. 14.

XXXIII

ΠΡΟΣ ΘΕΟΔΟΣΙΟΝ ΤΟΝ
ΒΑΣΙΛΕΑ ΚΑΤΑ ΤΙΣΑΜΕΝΟΥ

1. Ἔδει μὲν οὕτως ἅπαντας ἀγαθοὺς εἶναι τοὺς F ii
ἐπὶ τὰς τῶν ἐθνῶν ἀρχὰς ἐκπεμπομένους, ὦ βασιλεῦ, ὥστ' ἐμοὶ νῦν ἐξεῖναι λέγειν τι περὶ Τισαμενοῦ
βέλτιον, καὶ γὰρ οὐδὲ κακῶς λέγειν ἥδιόν ἐστί μοι
μᾶλλον ἢ τοὐναντίον· ἐπεὶ δέ εἰσί τινες οἳ τοῦ χεί-
ρονος παρέχουσιν ἀφορμάς, ὧν εἷς οὗτος Τισαμενός, ἀναγκαῖον ἡγησάμην ποιῆσαί σοι φανερὸν
ὅτι παραδέδονται πολλαὶ πόλεις ἀνθρώπῳ πλεῖστον
ἀπέχοντι | τοῦ δύνασθαι δι' ἀρχῆς εὖ ποιεῖν πόλεις.
ἐρῶ δὲ | πρὸς σὲ περὶ τούτων, οὐχ ὅπως λάβοις F 1
τῶν πεπραγμένων δίκην ἀλλ' ὅπως μὴ πλείω κακὰ
δράσειεν ἐπὶ τῆς ἀρχῆς μένων. 2. ὁ μὲν οὖν, ἵν'
οὗτος ἄρξειεν ἡμῶν, πολλὰ μὲν εἰπών, πολλὰ δὲ
ποιήσας, χαλεπός τε ἐπὶ τοῖς λεγομένοις ἔσται καὶ
ζητήσει τὸν λελυπηκότα ποιῆσαι κακῶς οὔσης αὐτῷ δυνάμεως ὁπόσης ἐθέλει· ἐμοὶ δὲ ἴσως μὲν
ὑπάρξει σωτηρία τε καὶ τὸ διαφυγεῖν παρὰ τῆς σῆς
εὐνοίας τε καὶ βοηθείας, ὦ βασιλεῦ. εἰ δ' οὖν

---

[a] Pack (p. 96) suggests that this patron may have been
Cynegius, ppO. Certainly Libanius moves gingerly here and
makes no request for the punishment of Tisamenus, who is
also exculpated from any charge of bribery (§ 38). But (§ 27)
while both Cynegius and Deinias, the *Comes*, were absent in

ORATION 33

TO THE EMPEROR THEODOSIUS, AGAINST TISAMENUS

1. IDEALLY, Sire, everyone sent out to the government of the provinces should be so good that I should be able to tell a better tale about Tisamenus. Indeed my preference is not so much to level abuse as the reverse. However, there are persons, of whom Tisamenus here is one, who occasion ill report, and so I have thought it necessary to demonstrate to you that many cities have been entrusted to a man who is very far from having the ability to benefit cities by his rule, but I shall tell you of these matters, not for you to punish him for what he has done, but to ensure that he may do no more harm by remaining in office. 2. Now, the person,[a] whose many words and actions have secured him as our governor, will be annoyed at my remarks and will seek to do harm to the one who has provoked him, for his influence is all that he could wish it to be. My means of escape and my salvation will perhaps come from your good will and support, Sire. But, anyway, if justice should

Egypt in A.D. 386, Tisamenus' supporters at court got an imperial order passed countermanding the instructions of these two. This order could not be enforced, presumably owing to the persistence of their opposition, and the identity of this patron must therefore remain uncertain.

ἡττηθείη τὸ δίκαιον τῆς ἑνός τινος ἰσχύος, ἀρκέσει
γε εἰς παραμυθίαν ἐμοὶ τὸ μὴ φόβῳ σεσιγῆσθαι
τὰ ῥηθέντα ἂν πρὸς σὲ δικαίως.

3. Οὑτοσὶ τοίνυν Τισαμενὸς γένει μέν ἐστι λαμ-
πρός, καὶ ὅ γε τῆς μητρὸς αὐτῷ πατὴρ ἐν πολλαῖς
γεγένηται διατριβαῖς, αὐτὸς δὲ ἀνάγκῃ μὲν ὅσον
ἅψασθαι μετέσχε λόγων, ἀποκλίνας δὲ ταχέως εἰς
ὀρχηστὰς καὶ μακαρίσας αὐτούς τε καὶ ὅσοι περὶ
αὐτούς, ἥδιστα μὲν ἂν ἡγεμὼν ἐγένετο τοῦ χοροῦ,
τούτου δὲ πολλοῖς εἰργόμενος αἰτιάμασι, δι᾽ ᾀσμάτων ἃ ποιῶν παρεῖχεν αὐτοῖς ἦν ἐπὶ τῆς σκηνῆς
χάριν τε διδοὺς αὐτοῖς καὶ παρ᾽ αὐτῶν λαμβάνων.
τοῖς μὲν γὰρ ᾀσμάτων ἔδει, τῷ δὲ τοῦ ταῦτα εἰς
ὄρχησιν ἄγεσθαι. 4. ἔπειτα ἦν ἐξαίφνης ἡγεμὼν
ἔθνους, ἐν ᾧ τῶν ὑπτίων εἶναι δοξάντων οὐδενὸς
διενεγκὼν ἀπῆλθεν οὐδὲν ἔχων διηγήσασθαι περὶ
αὐτοῦ καλόν. καὶ πά|λιν οὐ πολλοῖς ἔτεσιν ὕστερον
παρεδρεύει στρατηγῷ οὐ διὰ τὴν περὶ τὸ πρᾶγμα F
ἐμπειρίαν, οὐδὲ γὰρ ἐν συνδίκων τάξει πώποτε
ἐγεγόνει, ἀλλ᾽ οὐδέν, οἶμαι, δεῖ[1] τοιαύτης ἐμπει-
ρίας ἐνταῦθα, καθῆσθαι γὰρ οὐκ ἐπ᾽ ἐξετάσει δικῶν
ἀλλ᾽ ἐπὶ πληγαῖς τὸν στρατηγόν, ὥστ᾽ ἔργον εἶναι

---

[1] οἶμαι Re. (conj. οἰόμενος in *Animadv.*) (mss.) : οἴεται F. |
δεῖ Re. (mss.) : δεῖν Morel, F.

---

[a] The theatre was always a dishonourable profession and
subjected to vicious legislation, *cf. C. Th.* 15. 7, 1-8. Hence
Libanius' contempt.

[b] Liebeschuetz (p. 145) interprets ἔθνος as " profession "—
a common enough use—and refers to Tisamenus' continuing
connection with the theatrical profession. His first provincial
tenure thus was that of Syria itself. However, the post of

not prevail against the influence of a single individual, it will be comfort enough for me not to have kept silence through fear upon matters of which you should have properly been informed.

3. Well, Tisamenus yonder is of distinguished parentage : anyway, his maternal grandfather was a member of many learned gatherings. He personally participated in eloquence perforce, just so far as to get a nodding acquaintance, but he quickly bade it and its professors a tender fond farewell, and took himself off to dancers.[a] His dearest ambition would have been to become the leader of the band, but he was prevented by many complaints. Still, because of the lyrics he composed and provided for them, he attached himself to the stage and offered them his services, while they provided him with theirs. They needed his lyrics : he needed them for them to be produced. 4. Then he suddenly appeared as the governor of a province,[b] where there was no difference between him and any who had a name for dilatoriness. So he left office without having anything creditable to be said about him. And again, a few years afterwards, he became assessor to a military commander, not because of his experience in the job —he had never even been a member of the legal profession ; there is no need of experience in this sphere, I suppose, for the military commander has to sit, not for judicial enquiries, but for corporal punish-

assessor follows on a provincial command, perhaps praesidial, in the case of the anonymous of *Or.* 62. 65, and Syria ranks high in the consular provinces, its governors quite commonly having had prior experience (*e.g.* Eustathius, *PLRE* 311 (6), Florentius, *ib.* 364 (9)). ἐξαίφνης would seem to indicate a sudden change of situation from stage to office, contrasted with the slowness of his later public career.

197

R ii. 241 τῷ τοιούτῳ παρέδρῳ κοινωνίαν | τρυφῆς καὶ μάλιστα δὴ ποτοῦ. 5. καὶ σπέρμα γε πρὸς ἀρχὴν τοῦτο πολλάκις, ὃ δὴ καὶ νῦν γεγένηται τῆς τοῦ ῥήματος εὐφημίας τοῦτο πεποιηκυίας. προσήκειν[1] γὰρ δὴ τῷ παρηδρευκότι τὸ καὶ ἐπιστῆναι πόλεσιν. ἐνταῦθα ἦν ἀκούειν λεγόντων τῶν τὸν ἄνθρωπον εἰδότων ὡς ἀπολεῖται τὰ πράγματα τῇ Τισαμενοῦ μωρίᾳ καὶ ἀτεχνίᾳ. καὶ ταχέως ἠκολούθησεν ἡ πίστις, ἥκων αὐτὸς καὶ δεικνύμενος. ὁ μὲν γὰρ θρόνος καὶ οἱ κήρυκες καὶ οἱ ῥαβδοῦχοι καὶ ὁ τῶν ὑπηρετῶν ἀριθμὸς τῆς ἀρχῆς, τὰς ἡμέρας δὲ ἦν ἰδεῖν ἀναλουμένας μάτην οὔθ' ὁρῶντος τούτου τὸ δέον οὔτ' ἄλλοις ὁρῶσιν ἑπομένου. 6. καὶ ὁ δὴ κελεύσας αὐτὸν περὶ τὸν Εὐφράτην ἐπ' ὠνῇ σίτου διατρίβειν μισοῦντος μὲν ἐδόκει, φιλοῦντος δὲ ἔργον ἐποίει παρ' ἀνθρώποις ἧττον δεξιοῖς ἀναγκάζων αὐτοῦ τὴν ἄνοιαν διάγειν οὗ τῆς ἀνοίας ἔμελλεν ἕξειν ἥττονα τὸν ἔλεγχον. καίτοι μέγα φρονεῖν ἀξιοῖ τὸ καῦμα τὸ παρ' ἐκείνοις τραγῳδῶν. ἐγὼ | δὲ F 1
τῶν ἐπὶ τούτοις αὐτὸν ἐπαίνων οὐκ ἀποστερῶ, πάνυ γὰρ δὴ γενναίως ἐνεγκεῖν τήν τε φλόγα λέγε-

[1] προσήκειν F. (MSS.) : προσήκει Re.

---

[a] Association with the stage is even more contemptible to Libanius when compounded by association with the military—whom he usually (but not always, *e.g. Or.* 1. 165, 47. 28) suspects and dislikes : *cf.* Zos. 4. 27.

[b] ὁ δὴ—his superior, the Christian *Comes* of *Or.* 1. 251, 254, named § 7, below. See *Or.* 45. 31 n.

[c] In times of emergency, the *consulares* of Syria could be allocated special duties in Euphratensis, a sensitive supply area in any Eastern campaign. Thus (*Ep.* 21) Nicentius in A.D. 358 was broken for failure to provision the Euphrates

ment,[a] and the consequence is that such an assessor's job is to share in his excesses, and especially in his drinking. 5. This has time and again been the seed for office, as indeed it has been in the present instance too, for the éclat appertaining to the title has ensured this result. The idea is that anyone who has been an assessor is also qualified to be put in charge of cities. Here you would hear people who knew the fellow say that things would go to rack and ruin because of Tisamenus' stupidity and lack of skill. Confirmation followed soon enough, once he had come and showed his qualities, for the governor's seat, the heralds, the lictors, and members of his staff symbolized his office, but you could see the days wasted, since this fellow neither saw where his duty lay nor followed the lead of others who did. 6. Indeed, though his superior,[b] in ordering him to the Euphrates for the purchase of corn,[c] appeared to be motivated by dislike, his action in fact was that of a friend, when he forced him in his oafishness to stay among less cultured people, where he would be less likely to have his oafishness revealed. For all that, he claims great credit for this, in his dramatic relation of the heatwave that he endured there. I wouldn't dream of depriving him of the praises he claims for this—for, as a matter of fact, he is said to have endured the blazing sun [d] and certain other dis-

garrisons. Tisamenus' duty in A.D. 386 appears to be the reverse of this : the crisis was the continuance of famine in Syria (continuing since A.D. 382), necessitating the procurement of supplies from Euphratensis, then at peace. Icarius had also interested himself in corn supplies in Euphratensis, *Or.* 28. 16. The supply demands were for the preparations against Maximus (for which *cf. Or.* 54. 47).

[d] *Cf. Or.* 1. 251 (cited Introduction, p. 156).

LIBANIUS

ται καί τινας ἑτέρας ταλαιπωρίας, οἶδα δ' ὅτι καὶ
πάντες οἱ περὶ αὐτὸν καὶ οἱ τούτων οἰκέται καὶ
ὀνηλάται τὸν αὐτὸν ἤνεγκαν ἥλιον, ὥστ' εἰ τούτῳ
R ii. 242 σεμνύνεσθαι δώσομεν, κἀκείνοις | καὶ πολλῷ γε
πλέον ἐκείνοις ὅσῳ τῆς θεραπείας ἧς οὗτος ἀπή-
λαυεν, οὐκ ἦν ἐκείνοις. ὅ γε μὴν ἔπραττε, τί ποτ'
ἦν τοῦτο; ὃ καὶ τῶν ὑπηρετῶν ὁστισοῦν ῥᾳδίως
ἄν, ὥσπερ αὖ καὶ τὸν ἔμπροσθεν χρόνον ἐν ᾧ
τῇδε τοῖς ἄρχουσι καθημένοις τὰ τοιαῦτα ὀξέως
ἐπράττετο. 7. ὁ δ' ὠδύρετο μὲν ὡς ἐν ἀγρίοις καθήμενος χωρίοις καὶ τέρψεων τῶν αὐτῷ κεχαρισ-
μένων ἀμοίροις καὶ παρὰ τῶν ἐν τοῖς βασιλείοις
δυναμένων ᾔτει τούτων τὴν ἀπαλλαγήν, τιμᾶσθαι
δὲ ὡς ἐπ' ἔργοις ἑκουσίοις[1] ἀξιοῖ. καίτοι εἴ τι καὶ
χρηστὸν ἐν τούτοις ἐστί, Δεινίου[2] τοῦτο ἔστι τοῦ
κατακεκλεικότος αὐτὸν ἐν ἐκείνοις τοῖς τόποις.
ἐφ' οὓς ἧκον μὲν οἱ ῥήτορες, ὡς μᾶλλον αὐτοῖς
αὐτόθι χρησόμενοι σχολὴν ἄγοντος τοῦ τὴν ἀρχὴν
F 169 ἔχοντος, | ὁρῶντες | δὲ αὐτὸν τῷ σίτῳ μόνον[3] R
προσκείμενον τἆλλα ἐῶντα χαίρειν, οὕτω μεγαλή-
τωρ ἦν κατὰ τοὺς ποιητὰς εἰπεῖν, ἀναβάντες ἐπὶ
τοὺς ἵππους δεῦρ' ἥκοντες συνῇσαν ἀλλήλοις οὐ
πείσαντες, εἶτ' ἀπελθόντες, ἀλλὰ σιγῇ τοῦτο δράσαντες εὖ εἰδότες ὡς ἐδίδοσαν χάριν. τοσοῦτ' ἀπεῖχον τοῦ τι δεινὸν ἐντεῦθεν γενήσεσθαι νομίζειν. 8. ὁ
δ' ἦν αὐτὸς δεῦρ' ἀφιγμένος· φυγῇ μὲν ἀπὸ τῶν δι-

---

[1] ἐπ' ἔργοις F. (CAPV): ἐπὶ τοῖς ἔργοις Re. (BNVa): ἐπὶ
τοῖς ἑκουσίοις I. | τοῖς ins. Re. before ἑκουσίοις, om. F.
[2] δεινοῦ Morel: τοῦ δεῖνος conj. Re. (*Animadv.*): Κυνηγίου
Monnier.   [3] μόνον F. (APIBVa): μόνῳ Re. (CNV).

200

comforts most heroically—but I know that all his staff, and their attendants and donkey drivers, endured this same sun, so that, if we allow him to put on airs on this score, we must allow them the same, and much more so, since they could not enjoy the comforts that he did. Furthermore, just what was this duty that he was trying to perform? Any single one of his subordinates could easily do it, as indeed was the case even in times past, when here in Antioch[a] such duties were quickly performed for the governors in residence. 7. He began to complain that he had been put in charge of a wilderness without any of the delights dear to his heart, and to demand of persons with influence at court relief from these duties, but he still claims the credit due to his voluntary performance of them. However if anybody comes out of this with any credit, it is Deinias, for having him confined in those places. The orators went there, under the impression that they would find more employment for their talents there now that the governor had time to spare; but they saw him concentrating only upon the corn supply and not caring two pence about anything else,—so " stout-hearted " was he, to use a poetic term [b]— and so they mounted their horses and came back here, keeping each other for company. They took their leave, not after deploying their arguments, but in silence, well aware that they were obliging him; unpleasant consequences were the last thing they could expect from it. 8. And when he arrived here he was his old self: he shunned the courts; he

[a] The decurions of Antioch had been responsible for such emergency duties in the 350s, to their cost; cf. Or. 49. 2.

[b] Homeric (Il. 9. 629 etc.) and Pindaric (Isthm. 5. 44).

LIBANIUS

R ii. 244 κῶν, | ἐν εὐχῇ δὲ αἱ κλήσεις ἃς καλεῖ μὲν ἱππό-
δρομος, καλεῖ δὲ θέατρα, ἃς ὁ μὲν ἐπιστάμενος
δικάζειν ζημίαν τε ἡγεῖται καὶ δυσχεραίνει, οἱ δὲ
τούτῳ προσόμοιοι δέχονται μεθ' ἡδονῆς μᾶλλον ἢ
τῶν παίδων οἱ τὰ γράμματα μανθάνοντες. τηρεῖ
δὲ οὐδὲ ἐν τούτοις ὁ Τισαμενὸς τὸ προσῆκον ἀλλ'
ἐν τῷ μάλιστα βούλεσθαι ταῦτα εἰδέναι δοκεῖν
ἀηδίαν ὅτι πλείστην ἐπεισάγει τοῖς γιγνομένοις νῦν
μὲν τῶν δοθέντων ἂν δικαίως ἀποστερῶν, νῦν δὲ
πλήθει πληγῶν τῶν κατὰ γυμνοῦ τοῦ σώματος.
οἱ δ' ἐπαινούμενοι τῶν ἀρχόντων παρόντες ἀπoῦσιν
ἐῴκεσαν τὴν μὲν βασιλείαν τῇ παρουσίᾳ τιμῶντες,
αὐτοὺς δὲ τῷ τὰ τοιαῦτα ἐξετάζειν ἀκριβῶς.

9. Ἀλλ' ἐκεῖσε ἐπάνειμι, ὅτι μεγίστη ταῖς δίκαις
| ἄνθρωπος οὑτοσὶ βλάβη. ἢ γὰρ ἐπ' ἄλλα ἄττα F
καταφεύγει ταύτας ἀφεὶς ἢ δικάσαι καταναγκα-
σθεὶς ἐν τῷ φλυαρεῖν ἀνάλωσε τὸν χρόνον αὐτοῦ
μὲν οὐ τολμῶν ἅψασθαι τοῦ πράγματος, κύκλῳ δὲ
περιερχόμενος καὶ οὔτε οὗ τὸ δίκαιόν ἐστιν ἰδεῖν
ἔχων οὔτε σιωπᾶν αἱρούμενος ἀλλὰ ῥέων ἀχρήστῳ
R ii. 245 ῥεύματι οἵῳ τά τε ὦτα ἀνιᾶσαι | καὶ κόψαι τοῖς
συνδίκοις τοὺς πόδας. ἀντὶ δὲ τοῦ τέλος ζητεῖν
καὶ γνώσει στῆσαι τὴν δίκην ἀποπέμπει πάλιν εἰσ-
όδου δεησομένους ταὐτὸ καὶ αὐτῆς πεισομένης οὐ
τευξομένης τέλους. 10. τίνας οὖν οἴει γίγνεσθαι
τοὺς δικαζομένους ἐν τοιούτοις κακοῖς; τίνα ψυχὴν
ἔχειν; τί μὲν πρὸς αὐτοὺς λέγειν, τί δὲ πρός τε τὴν

ᵃ Cf. Or. 45. 20.
ᵇ Cf. Or. 18. 170 f., 26. 25 f., 41. 7 ff. Julian, *Misop.*
343 d ff.   ᶜ Cf. Or. 45. 1 ; Liebeschuetz, pp. 144 ff.
ᵈ Or. 45. 14.

hankered after invitations to the hippodrome [a] and the theatre, invitations which anyone with any knowledge of administration regards as a disaster and resents,[b] though people like this fellow receive them with more pleasure than do schoolboys learning their ABC. Yet even here Tisamenus [c] failed to maintain a sense of propriety : in his especial desire to be regarded as an expert on this, he imported the utmost possible unpleasantness into the proceedings, first, by withholding presentations that might properly have been made, secondly, by the number of floggings administered to naked bodies. But governors who are well thought of used to look as though they were not there, even when they were : they would show respect for the emperor by their attendance, and for themselves by not poking their noses too far into such matters.

9. But I revert to the point that this fellow is the greatest stumbling block to the administration of justice.[d] Either he turns his back on it and seeks refuge in other business, or if he is compelled to hold court, he wastes his time on drivel, not daring to handle the actual case, but skirting all round it, incapable of seeing where justice lies and refusing to keep his mouth shut. He burbles in a pointless flood of words so as to distress the ears and weary the feet of the lawyers. And instead of seeking a conclusion and bringing the case to an end by reaching a decision, he sends them off so that they need another audience, which in its turn will be treated in the same way and reach no conclusion. 10. So what do you think becomes of the litigants in such a plight ? What do they feel like ? What remarks do they address to themselves, to earth and to

γῆν καὶ τὸν ἥλιον; οἱ δ᾽ ἐπειδὰν παύσωνται θρηνοῦντες, οἱ μὲν ἐπὶ πολλοῖς ἀπῆλθον οἷς δεδαπά-
νηνται ψυχὴν[1] ἄρχοντος ἀναμενοῦντες, οἱ δ᾽ ἀντὶ
πλειόνων ἐλάττω λαβόντες ἠγάπησαν. τοῖς δ᾽ ἐκ
τοῦ συνδικεῖν τὸν βίον ποιουμένοις τὸ τηνάλλως
καθῆσθαι περίεστιν, οἱ κήρυκες δέ τινας ἐπ᾽ οὐδενὶ
καλοῦντες καλοῦσιν ὅμως ὑπὲρ τοῦ δοκεῖν εἶναί τι
τὸ πραττόμενον, ἐπεὶ τό γε ἀληθὲς ὕπνος πολύς.
τὰς δὲ μέχρι τῆς ἑσπέρας καθέδρας οὐκ ἔργων ἐπι-
θυμία ποιεῖ, συμ|βουλαὶ δὲ ἰατρικῆς καὶ τὰ τῇ F
γαστρὶ συμφέροντα, ὥστ᾽ εἶναι γέλωτα τοῖς ὁρῶσι
τὰς πρὸ τοῦ ζεύγους λαμπάδας.

11. Ἔτι τοίνυν, ὦ βασιλεῦ, παραλαβὼν τὸν δῆμον
ἑαυτὸν ἐγνωκότα εἰς τὸ μὴ γιγνώσκειν ἑαυτὸν προ-
ήγαγε διδάξας αὐτὸν ὡς μέγα τι τῷ ἄρχοντι τὸ
λεχθῆναί τι παρ᾽ ἐκείνων εἰς αὐτὸν εὔφημον. δῆ-
μος δὲ πεισθεὶς ὡς ἄρχει[2] τοῦ ἄρχοντος καὶ ὑφ᾽ ᾧ
R ii. 246 τέτακται τῷ νόμῳ τοῦτον | ἐξ ὕβρεως ὑφ᾽ αὑτῷ
πεποίηται, πολλὰ κινῶν τῶν καθεστηκότων ἄρχεται.[3]

12. Ὡς δὲ τοῦτο τοιοῦτόν ἐστι μάθοις ἄν, ὦ
βασιλεῦ, ῥᾳδίως. ἐν τῷ θεάτρῳ ποτὲ συμβὰν οἶ-
μαί τι τὸν δῆμον ἄφωνον ἐκάθισε. τοῦθ᾽ οὗτος
ἡγήσατο συμφορὰν ἄλλοις τε πολλοῖς τοῦτο δηλῶν
καὶ τῇ χρόᾳ. ἔδει δὲ αὐτόν, ὡς ἔοικεν, ὁμολογῆσαι
καὶ τῇ φωνῇ τὸ πάθος, καί, προὔπεμπον γὰρ αὐτὸν
τινες οὐ πλείους ἀνθρώπων εἴκοσιν, ἐφ᾽ ὅσοις ἄν
τις ᾐσχύνθη, λεγόντων οὖν τινα τῶν εἰωθότων ἃ

---

[1] ψῆφον conj. Re.
[2] ἄρχει F. (V): ἄρχοι Re. (other mss., Macarius).
[3] ἄρχεται Cobet, F.: ἔρχεται Re. (mss., Macarius).

---

[a] Cf. Or. 45. 22 n. On the claque cf. Liebeschuetz,
Appendix iv, pp. 278 ff.

204

heaven ? After they cease their laments, they either depart after all their great expenditure to wait for the governor to collect his wits, or are satisfied if they get a reduced amount instead of their full claim. For those who make their living by advocacy, the result is that they sit there idly : the heralds summon some of them to no purpose, but they still summon them, so as to make it appear that the business means something, though in fact it is the sleep of the dead ! It is not his eagerness to get business done that makes his sessions last until evening, but medical advice and his attention to his belly, and so the sight of torches preceding his carriage is a laughing-stock for the spectators.

11. And there is this point, too, Sire. He inherited from his predecessors a populace that knew its place and induced it not to know its place, for he taught it how important it was to the governor for them to address some acclamation to him.[a] The populace is convinced that it governs its governor and that, in consequence of its arrogance, it has under its thumb the person under whom it has been set by law, and is beginning to upset many of the established institutions.

12. That this is the case, Sire, is easy for you to recognize. On one occasion in the theatre something or other occurred and kept the populace seated and silent. This fellow regarded that as a disaster, and showed his feelings in various ways, especially by his change of complexion. But he also had to acknowledge his discomfiture verbally, so it seemed. As he was being escorted home by a group of people, not more than twenty at most—a number small enough to make anyone ashamed—and as they began to

τῶν ἀρχόντων οἱ βελτίους ἔπαυον, καταβαίνων ὁ
θαυμάσιος ἀπὸ τοῦ ζεύγους Τισαμενός, τίς ὑμῖν,
ἔφη, τὰς γλώττας ἀπέδωκεν; ὡς οὐκ ἦσάν γε
ὑμῖν ἐν τῷ θεάτρῳ. τοιούτοις αὐτὸν ῥήμασιν
ἐποίησε ταπεινὸν μηνύσας ὡς τὸ μὲν ζημίαν, τὸ δὲ
ἡγοῖτο κέρδος. |

13. Ἀλλὰ τὰ πρὸς τὴν βουλὴν αὐτῷ καλά τε καὶ F
τὸν ἄρχοντα δεικνύοντα; ἀλλ' ἔπραττε μὲν οὐδὲ
πρότερον εὖ, προσκατεπόντισε δὲ αὐτὴν ὁ κακὸς
ἄνθρωπος οὗτος ἃ παρῶπτο τοῖς ὑπάρχοις δι' ἀσθένειαν τῆς βουλῆς αὐτὸς ἀναζητῶν, διερευνώμενος,
οὐκ ἐῶν κεῖσθαι, μέχρι δραχμῆς καὶ ὀβολοῦ καὶ
τῶν οὕτω μικρῶν ἀκριβολογούμενος, ἄλλοις μὲν
ἐγκαλῶν, ἑτέρους δὲ εἰσπράττων. ἑτέρους δὲ ὅταν
εἴπω, τοὺς βουλεύοντας λέγω τοὺς ἐκ πολλῶν |
R ii. 247 ὀλίγους τεθνεώτων μὲν τῶν ὀφειλόντων, προσαι-
τούντων δὲ τῶν ἐκείνων υἱέων οὐ διὰ κακίαν τῶν
πατέρων, ἀλλὰ διὰ τοὺς τὰ τοιαῦτα ἀξιοῦντας ἐσθίειν, τοὺς δεινοὺς ὑπηρέτας οἳ καὶ λαμβάνουσι καὶ
σιγῶνται τῷ παρ' ἑαυτῶν φόβῳ. 14. ὁ τοίνυν καὶ
στατῆρα καὶ στατῆρος ἥμισυ καὶ τρίτον εἰς μέσον ἕλκων οὗτος ἦν, ἃ τῷ πλήθει τῶν ἐτῶν ἐκάθ-
ευδε, καὶ ταῦτα ἔπραττεν ὅπως εἰς τὴν ποίησιν αὐτῷ τῶν οἰκημάτων εἴη χρήματα, ὧν οὐδεὶς οὐδὲν
οὐδεπώποτε εἶδεν ἀχρηστότερον. ὁ δὲ λίθοις μὲν
ἠξίου μείζω τὴν πόλιν ποιεῖν, τὰ δ' εἰς τὴν βουλὴν
ἐλάττω πάντων μὲν γελώντων, πάντων δὲ[1] ἐλεγ-
χόντων τῆς περὶ τοῦτο σπουδῆς τὴν ἀχρηστίαν τῷ

---

[1] μὲν γελώντων, πάντων Monnier, F. : μὲν ἐλάττω, πάντων
mss. (om. V) : [μὲν ἐλάττω, πάντων δὲ] Re.

---

[a] Cf. Or. 45. 17 n.   [b] Cf. Or. 45. 34 n.

utter some of the usual compliments which the better sort of governors used to stop, our fine fellow
Tisamenus got down from his carriage and exclaimed,
" Who has given you your tongues back then ? You
hadn't got them in the theatre." Such were the
remarks with which he debased himself and showed
that he regarded their earlier attitude as a dead loss,
and this as a clear gain.

13. " But," it may be claimed, " aren't his relations with the town council a credit to him ? Don't
they show him as a real governor ? " Well, it may
have been in distress before this, but this rascal has
torpedoed it, with personal investigations, inquiries
and refusal to let things rest, though the prefects
had turned a blind eye to them because of the decline of the council.[a] He finicks and fusses about
shillings and pence and the last brass farthing, with
charges against some and demands upon others.
And when I say others, I mean the councillors, those
few left of many, for people die in debt and their
sons are reduced to beggary, not through any fault
of their fathers, but because of those persons who
expect to gobble up all of this sort, those dreaded
menials who grab and are never mentioned because
of the fear they inspire. 14. Well, he was the one
who brought forward matters involving a stater, or
half or a third of it, matters that had remained dormant under the lapse of years, and his motive in so
doing was to get money for his building constructions, and nobody has ever seen anything more useless than they are. He claimed that he was enlarging
the city with his masonry,[b] but he reduced the
status of the council, for everyone mocked and condemned the pointlessness of his enthusiasm on this

μηδὲ διὰ τῶν θηρίων τὸν λειτουργήσοντα εἶναι.
15. ὁ | δ' ἐπειδή τις μῖμος τὰ μὲν θάλαμον, τὸν δ'
R ii. 248 ἐπωνόμασε[1] νυμφίον καὶ τὰ μὲν ἔφη πέρας | ἔχειν,
τὸν δ' οὐ φαίνεσθαι, ἀνάπτεται μὲν τουτὶ τὸ κάθ-
αρμα, τὸ δὲ τῶν ἀνοήτων παθῶν πάντως ἔφη δεῖν
φανῆναι τὸν καινὸν τοῦτον νυμφίον, τῶν κωλυόν-
των δὲ οὐδὲν ὁρᾶν ἠξίου, ἀλλὰ τῇ τῶν ἐν τῷ βουλεύειν ἀδυναμίᾳ μεμιγμένας ὕβρεσιν ἀπειλὰς ἀντ-
εξῆγεν οὖσαν μὲν αὐτοῖς δύναμιν οὐκ ἔχων ἐπιδεῖ-
ξαι, τὴν λειτουργίαν δὲ τοὺς ἀθλίους ὑπομεῖναι
κελεύων, σὸν ἐν τῷ τοῦτο τολμᾶν, ὦ βασιλεῦ,
περιυβρίζων νόμον.   σὺ γὰρ ἡμῖν τοῦτον προπέ-
R ii. 249 ρυσιν ἔθηκας τὴν μὲν ἀνάγκην τῆς τοιαύτης | δα-
πάνης ἀναιρῶν, γνώμης δὲ τὸ πρᾶγμα ποιῶν. λέγει γοῦν ὁ νόμος· βούλει καὶ τοῦτο ποιεῖν; οὐδεὶς
ὁ κωλύσων. ἀλλ' οὐκ ἐθέλεις; οὐδεὶς ὁ καταν-
αγκάσων. ἀλλ' οὗτος ἀναγινωσκομένου τοῦ νόμου
προσῆγε τὰς ἀνάγκας, ὥσπερ ἐν τῷ γραμματείῳ
τυραννίδα παρὰ σοῦ λαβὼν ἀλλ' οὐκ ἀρχὴν ἔννομον. 16. καίτοι καὶ εἰ Μίδαι πάντες ἦσαν τὰ εἰς
χρήματα καὶ πολὺς ὁ χρυσὸς παρ' ἑκάστῳ, θηρία
δὲ οὐκ ἐβούλοντο τρέφειν οὐδὲ τοὺς ταῦτα ὑπο-
μενοῦντας ἀνθρώπους, κατ' ἐξουσίαν ἔφευγον ἂν
τὸ | ἀνάλωμα. νῦν δὲ πάντες θεραπεύουσι δανει-
στὰς καὶ λυπηροὶ λήγοντες αὐτοῖς εἰσιν οἱ μῆνες.
εἰσὶ δὲ οἷς οὐδ' ἂν πρόοιντό τινες ὡς οὐ κομιού-

---

[1] ἐπωνόμασε F. (V) : ὠνόμασε Re. (other mss.).

---

[a] Cf. Or. 45. 7. The point of this sally is that Tisamenus
was engaged in marrying off his daughters (cf. §§ 28 f.).

[b] Critical for dating, C. Th. 15. 9. 1 (July A.D. 384) had
made editiones voluntary. Similarly, the Syriarchate had
been made voluntary in July A.D. 383 (C. Th. 12. 1. 103).

issue because of the non-existence of any to sponsor the beast shows. 15. And when an actor dubbed his buildings the bridal-chamber and the sponsor the bridegroom,[a] remarking upon the completion of the one and the absence of the other, this scoundrel flared up in rage and with irrational obstinacy insisted that this new-fangled bridegroom must put in his appearance, and refused to acknowledge any impediment. Against the inability of the councillors he paraded threats and insults combined, and though he could not demonstrate that they had the ability, he ordered the poor wretches to undertake the duty, and in daring to do so he infringed a law of yours, Sire. A couple of years ago you passed this law,[b] and removed compulsion from expenditure of this sort, making the performance voluntary. Anyway, the law states that if you want to perform this duty, there is no one to stop you, but if you refuse, there is no one to compel you. But during the recital of the law this fellow began to apply compulsion, just as though he got from you in his credentials a despotic position, not a constitutional office.[c] 16. Yet, even if they were all as rich as Midas,[d] and each one had lots of money, and still did not want to maintain beasts or the men to fight them, they would have the right to avoid the expense. As things are, they all look to their creditors, and the end of the month is a troublesome time for them.[e] There are some to whom no one would lend money, for they wouldn't

[c] A stock antithesis in Libanius (cf. Or. 12. 8): implicitly contradicts Themistius' assertion of the emperor as νόμος ἔμψυχος.　　　　[d] Cf. Or. 18. 124.

[e] Loans were made on a monthly basis, repayment being due at the beginning of the month.

μενοι. 17. τῶν δὴ τοιούτων λεγόντων τὴν ἀπορίαν, ὀμνύντων, ἃ ὀφείλοιεν ἀριθμούντων, δεομέ-
νων, ἱκετευόντων μὴ σφᾶς ἐμβάλλειν εἰς αἰσχύνην
τὴν ἐκ τοῦ τῆς ἀπορίας ἐλέγχου μηδέ γε εἰς κινδύ-
R ii. 250 νους | τοὺς ἀπὸ τῶν θεωμένων οὐδὲν Τισαμενὸς
ἐγίνετο βελτίων, ἀλλὰ τῶν αὐτῶν εἴχετο ῥημάτων
οὐκ ἐῶν μεμνῆσθαι τοῦ νόμου. καίτοι τούτου τίνα
οὐκ ἂν δικαίως δοίη δίκην; ἢ εἰ μὲν εἰκόνος σῆς
ἀντειλημμένους ἀπέσπα, δεινὸν ἂν ἦν, καταπεφευ-
γότας δὲ ἐπὶ τὸν σὸν νόμον ἀφέλκων οὐκ ἴσον τι
ποιεῖν εἰκότως ἂν δοκοίη; ἀντὶ γὰρ τοῦ χαλκοῦ τὰ
γράμματα ἦν αὐτοῖς. 18. ὁ δὲ μάτην ἐδείκνυ τὸν
νόμον κείμενον, εἶθ'[1] ὥσπερ παραβαίνοντας νόμον
ἀλλ' οὐ νόμῳ χρωμένους πᾶσι κακοῖς περιέβαλλεν
ὑβρίζων, παροινῶν, ἀσελγαίνων, φοβῶν, ταράτ-
των, ἔχθρᾳ τὴν βουλὴν δεχόμενος, ἀνευρίσκων ὅθεν
ἀπολοῦνται, τούς τι τοιοῦτο μηνύοντας αὐτῷ νομί-
ζων | εὐεργέτας. ἐν δὲ ταῖς ἀπροσδοκήτοις βλάβαις F
μεῖζον τὸ διὰ τοῦ τάχους ἐπῆν κακόν. μάλιστα
R ii. 251 μὲν γὰρ | πρὶν ἐξελθεῖν ἠξίου καταβάλλειν, ἡ φιλ-
ανθρωπία δὲ μίαν εἶχεν ἡμέραν, μεθ' ἣν οὐδεμία
συγγνώμη.

19. Καὶ τοῦτο τὸ δίκαιον ἔν τε τοῖς ἄλλοις κἂν
τῷ φόρῳ. μὴν μὲν γὰρ οὑτοσὶ τῷ ἔτει τέταρτος,
τὸ τρίτον τοῦ ἐνιαυτοῦ μέρος, ἠδικῆσθαι δὲ τὸν

---

[1] εἶθ' F.: εἰ δ' C, A marg.: ὁ δ' AVa: ὅδ' PIBNV: οὐδὲ
Morel: καὶ Re.

---

[a] Regulations concerning sanctuary at the Imperial
statues had been very recently enacted: C. Th. 9. 44. 1 of
July A.D. 386.   [b] Cf. Or. 45. 32.

[c] Pack notes, for the dating of the speeches, that ἔτος is
the year of the indiction, the financial year beginning in

210

get it back. 17. Well, when such people talked of
their poverty, gave their word for it, totted up their
debts, begged and prayed him not to inflict upon
them the disgrace of revealing their poverty nor yet
the risks of facing the spectators, Tisamenus behaved
no better, but he stuck to the same story and refused
to allow any mention of the law. Yet what punishment did he not deserve for this ! If he tried to
tear them away when they embraced your statue,[a]
it would be a dreadful business, but if he dragged
them away when they sought the protection of your
law, would it not appear that he was doing something
similar ? For them the letters of the law took the
place of the bronze statue. 18. He began to demonstrate that the law had been passed in vain, and then,
as though they were breaking a law, not using it, he
gave them all sorts of trouble, with his insults, outrages and assaults,[b] setting them into panic and confusion, receiving the council with distaste and seeking
means to ruin them, and regarding those who gave
him such information as might achieve this as his
benefactors. And in these unlooked-for troubles,
the speed with which things were conducted was a
greater disaster still. Mostly, he required money
down before they left ; in his generosity he went as
far as a single day : after that, there was no pardon.

19. And this is his standpoint, especially with regard to tax collection. It is the fourth month of the
year now—the third part of the calendar year [c]—
but he states that it is an offence against the em-

September, while ἐνιαυτός is the calendar year, "the third
part" being September to December. Thus a precise date
(December A.D. 386) may be established. Note that the tribute collected by the decurions is in kind.

βασιλέα φησὶν οὐ τοῦ παντὸς εἰσενηνεγμένου. πῶς,
ὦ καταγέλαστε; καὶ γὰρ ἐν ἀγροῖς κείμενον
ἔκειτ' ἂν ὁμοίως τῷ βασιλεῖ καὶ οὐκ ἂν ἔλαττον.
οὐδὲ γὰρ ἐνταῦθα κείμενον πλέον, τῷ φέροντι δὲ
οὐκ ἴσον ἢ τήμερον ἅπαν ἢ μεμερισμένον εἰς μῆνας
εἰσενεγκεῖν. οὐ δὴ κέρδος ἐκείνῳ, ζημίαν δὲ ἡμῖν
προξενῶν[1] τὸ ταχὺ τοῦτο ζητεῖ. 20. καὶ διὰ τοῦτο
στρατιῶται στρατιώτας μαστιγοῦσι γυμνοὺς οὗ
πολλοὶ τοῦτο μέλλουσιν ὁρᾶν, οἱ αὐτοῦ στρατιῶται
R ii. 252 τοὺς θατέρου, οἱ δὲ ἐπὶ τοὺς βουλευτὰς | χωροῦσι
καὶ δρῶσιν ὃ πεπόνθασιν, ἀρχόμενοι μὲν ἀπὸ τῶν
οἰκετῶν, προϊόντες δὲ ἐπὶ τὰ νῶτα τῶν δεσποτῶν,
καὶ ῥάβδοι ῥάβδων διάδοχοι, πρόγονοι δὲ καὶ χορ-
ηγίαι καὶ δόξα καὶ τὰ ἄλλα δὴ τὰ τῶν πολιτευομένων μικρά τε καὶ ἀσθενῆ καὶ οὐδενὸς ἄξια.
ταύτην δὴ τὴν ἀτιμίαν τί ποιεῖ; τὸ μὴ πλουτεῖν
ἡμῖν τοὺς πολιτευομένους μηδ' ἔχειν τὰ τηλικαῦτα
λειτουργεῖν. εἰ δὲ μὴ μόνοι ταῦτα πεπόν|θασιν, F
ἀλλὰ διὰ τούτους γε καὶ εἴ τις ἄλλος, ὅπως τὸ
τούτων συσκιάζηται καὶ μὴ λίαν ἔκδηλον ᾖ.

21. Ἆρ' οὖν ἐν ταῖς ἐπὶ τῶν δικαστηρίων ὕβρεσι
τὴν παροινίαν ἔστησεν; ἐξεῦρε μὲν οὖν ἃ μηδεὶς
ἂν ἕτερος ἐνεθυμήθη, τὸν ἐν Βεροίᾳ ταύτῃ δεῦρο
καλέσας μετά τε τῶν ὑπ' αὐτοῦ τρεφομένων θηρίων καὶ τῶν ἐπ' αὐτὰ μεμισθωμένων ἀνδρῶν. καὶ
ἧκεν ἄγων ἄρκτους τε καὶ παρδάλεις καὶ τοὺς

---

[1] οὐ before προξενῶν Morel (mss. except V): del. F. (om.
V): ὁ Re.

---

[a] i.e. the curial tax-collectors. The violence used is contrary to C. Th. 12. 1. 85.

[b] Tisamenus failed to cajole or force any decurion of
Antioch to hold the Syriarchate, a position theoretically
voluntary, where the presentation of beast shows was an

peror if all the contributions are not in. How do
you work this out, you ridiculous fool? The produce
on the farms would be just as productive for the
emperor, and it would not be any the less. When
deposited here, it doesn't increase any the more :
nor is it the same thing for the contributor for him to
pay up the sum total on the nail today as it is for
him to divide his payments into monthly instalments.
It is not out of concern for the taxpayer's interest,
but out of a desire to ruin us that he requires such
haste as this. 20. And this is the reason why one set
of agents, his own, strip and flog another set, the
agents of the other fellow, in a place where there
are likely to be plenty to observe it, and why these
advance against the councillors [a] and do as they have
been done to, beginning with the slaves and proceeding to the backs of their owners, with lashing
following upon lashing, and consideration of their
ancestors, civic services and standing and all the
other marks of curial distinction being petty, weak
and worthless. And what is the reason for this disgrace? Just the impoverishment of our decurions
and their inability to fulfil such demands. And if
they are not the only ones to suffer so, everybody else
suffers because of them, so that their sufferings may
be obscured and not become too obvious.

21. So did he confine his insolence to judicial misconduct, then? Not he! He thought up an idea that
nobody else would ever have dreamed of. He invited here that fellow from Beroea,[b] along with the
beasts he maintains and the men hired to fight them.
And along he came, with bears and panthers and

important part of the duties, and then disgraced the metropolis by calling upon this outsider from Beroea (mod. Aleppo).

R ii. 253 τούτων ποτὲ μὲν ἡττημένους, | ποτὲ δὲ κεκρατη-
κότας καὶ ἦν μέγας τῇ βραχυτέρᾳ τὴν μείζω νικῶν
πόλιν· καὶ γὰρ εἰ τίμιον ἐν τῇ Βεροίᾳ τὸ χρῆμα
τῶν λόγων, ἀλλ᾽ οὐκ ἴσον ἥδε κἀκείνη. ἐβούλετ᾽
οὖν ἐκείνην ἐνταῦθα κατὰ τῆσδε κωμάζειν καὶ τὴν
βουλὴν τῆς βουλῆς εἶναι βελτίω δοκεῖν καὶ τῇ μὲν
εἶναι μέγα φρονεῖν, τὴν δὲ τεταπεινῶσθαι καὶ γεγονέναι μικρὰν καὶ ἐξεληλέγχθαι καὶ μηδὲ ἐλεύθερον ἔχειν βλέπειν. 22. ὅστις οὖν τὴν μὲν πρώτην
καθαιρεῖ, τὴν δὲ οὐδὲ δευτέραν ἐπαίρει καὶ παρέχει
προπηλακίζειν τὴν ἑαυτῆς βελτίω, τὸν σὸν οὐδὲν
οὗτος οἶκον ἀδικεῖ; τὰ μέγιστα μὲν οὖν, εἴ τις
ἀκριβῶς λογίζοιτο. ἐπέμφθη γὰρ οὐ συνταράξων,
ὦ | βασιλεῦ, τὸν περὶ τὰς πόλεις κόσμον οὐδὲ ταῖς F 1
μὲν τὸ ὂν σφισιν ἀξίωμα λυμανούμενος, τὰς δὲ
ἐλάττους ἐπάξων ταῖς μείζοσιν, ἀλλὰ τὰ μὲν ὡς
εἶχε διατηρήσων, ἑκάστης δὲ ᾗ προσῆκεν ἐπιμελη-
σόμενος καὶ ποιήσων εὐδαιμονεστέραν προνοίᾳ.
23. ὁ δ᾽ ἐν τῷ δεῦρο τὸν ἐκ Βεροίας ἐφ᾽ οἷσπερ
ἤγαγεν ἄγειν ἐβόα πρὸς ἅπαντας ὅτι τήνδε τὴν πόλιν ὑπ᾽ ἐκείνῃ κεῖσθαι δεῖ καὶ τοῦ τῆς μητροπό-
λεως ὀνόματος ἀποστατέον αὐτῇ καὶ τῇ βουλῇ τὴν
βουλὴν ὑπεικτέον καὶ ἄνδρα ἀνδρὶ καὶ γνωστέον
R ii. 254 τοὺς ἀμείνονας. γνοίης | δ᾽ ἂν ὅτι ταῦθ᾽ ὕβρις ἦν
ἔκ τε ἡδονῆς καὶ λύπης, ὧν ἡ μὲν ἦν τῶν πρὸς ἡμᾶς
εὐνοϊκῶς ἐχόντων, ἡ δὲ ἡδονὴ τῶν οὐχ οὕτως.
ὑβρίζεσθαι δὲ οὐκ ἂν βούλοιο τὰς πόλεις. ἀλλ᾽

ᵃ Cf. Or. 11. 192, 31. 7. Antioch had prided itself,
according to Libanius, upon its pre-eminence as a cultural
centre.

ᵇ For an example of the importance attached to this order
of precedence cf. Or. 18. 187 f.

the fellows who had at times lost to them and at times beaten them, and he was cock-a-hoop at overcoming the greater city with the less. You see, even if the profession of letters [a] carries any weight in Beroea, there is no comparison between there and here. He wanted her to rule the roost over us here, for her council to be regarded as superior to ours, for hers to be able to put on airs and ours to be reduced and diminished, to be proved incapable and to be unable to take an independent line. 22. So if anyone brings the foremost city to ruin and exalts one which isn't even second-rate and allows it to insult its better, does he do no injury to your household ? No ! The injury is of the greatest, if the case is carefully considered. He was not sent, Sire, to disturb the order of precedence among the cities, nor yet to debase the prestige [b] which some possessed and to set the lesser upon the greater : he was sent to maintain the existing order, and to supervise each in a fitting manner and by his administration to increase their prosperity. 23. Tisamenus, however, in bringing here that fellow from Beroea for the purpose he did, proclaimed it aloud to all and sundry that our city must be subordinated to that other, that it must renounce its title of metropolis,[c] that our council must yield precedence to theirs, our citizens to theirs, and that we must recognize our betters. You could see the insult in this from the pain felt by our well-wishers and the pleasure felt by those who are not. Though you might not wish your cities to be subjected to insult,

[c] This threat was actually put into effect for a time after the Riots of the Statues, by Theodosius himself. For a similar threat by Julian cf. Or. 16. 5 n. (Vol. I, p. 214).

οὗτος ὑβρίζειν βούλοιτ' ἄν. πῶς ἂν οὖν ὁ τοιοῦτος
εἰκότως ἄρχοι;

24. 'Αλλὰ σὺ μὲν ὁ τῶν ὅλων κύριος καὶ παρ'
ὅτου καὶ παθεῖν τι τοιοῦτον οὐ λίαν ἀφόρητον,
τιμᾷς ἡμῖν τὴν πόλιν ἐν τοῖς εἰς τοὺς πρέσβεις καὶ
πραττομένοις καὶ λεγομένοις, καὶ γίγνεται καθ'
ἑκάστην πρεσβείαν ἡ πόλις ἡμῖν λαμπροτέρα, Τισαμενὸς δὲ κάθηται σκοπῶν καὶ ζητῶν ἐξ ὅτου
γένοιτ' ἂν ἀδοξοτέρα. εἶτα πονηροὺς μὲν ποιμένας
ἀπελαύνουσι τῶν ποιμνίων οἱ τούτων κύριοι καὶ
παύσαντες ἐκείνους ἑτέροις παρ|έδωκαν τοῖς λυσι- F
τελεστέροις, σὺ δ' ἐκείνους ἐπὶ πόλεως τοιαύτης
οὐ μιμήσῃ; ᾗ τοιαῦτα μὲν τἀρχαῖα, τοιαῦτα δὲ τὰ
μετ' ἐκεῖνα, τοιαῦτα δὲ τὰ νῦν, ᾗ πλὴν δυοῖν πόλεων[1] ἔνι τι πρὸς ἁπάσας εἰπεῖν περὶ αὐτῆς. 25.
νόμιζε δὲ καὶ τὰς ἄλλας ἀπὸ τῶν αὐτῶν διασώσειν,
R ii. 255 αἷς χείρω τὰ πράγματα διὰ | τὴν τοῦδε κακίαν·
ἐπεὶ καὶ αὐτὴν ταύτην ᾗ κεχαρίσθαι φησὶν ἐν αὐτοῖς τούτοις κατέβλαψε μετενεγκὼν εἰς τὴν ἡμετέραν δαπάνην ἐκείνοις ὀφειλομένην, ὥστ' ἢ πέ-
νητα αὐτῇ ποιήσει τὸν πολιτευόμενον τῇ κατ'
ἄμφω δαπάνῃ ἢ τῇ παρ' ἡμῖν ἐκείνην ὧν εἶχεν ἂν
ἀποστερήσει.

26. 'Ηδικῆσθαι γάρ φησιν οὐ κληθεὶς ἐπὶ τὴν
τοιαύτην θέαν ὑπὸ τοῦ τὴν θέαν παρέχοντος. εἰ
δὲ οὐ κληθεὶς ἠδίκηται, παρ' αὐτοῦ ζητείτω τὴν

---

[1] πόλεων F. (P) : πόλέων CI : πολέοιν ABVaV : πόλεοιν
Re.

---

[a] Embassies to court were composed of *principales* mainly :
cf. the list in Petit, *Vie municipale*, App. v, pp. 415 ff.

[b] Cf. *Or.* 25. 55, where the governor is ποιμὴν λαῶν.

[c] Rome and Constantinople. Antioch was held to be on a

his wish would be to inflict insult. So how could a person of this sort be a decent governor ?

24. You are our supreme ruler and to experience some such treatment from you would not be absolutely intolerable. Yet you honour our city in both the words and the deeds you employ towards our envoys,[a] and with each delegation our city's fame grows the greater. Tisamenus, however, sits here scheming and seeking the means whereby its reputation may decline. In the case of shepherds,[b] the owners of the flocks dismiss bad ones from their job and entrust the sheep to more honest ones. So won't you take your cue from them in the case of a city as great as ours, whose glories in early times, in times thereafter and at the present are so great and which boasts of claims to fame against all other cities, with the exception of two.[c] 25. You must believe that, by this same action, you will preserve the other cities also, whose fortunes are declining because of his incapacity. By this very same action he has harmed that very city to which he claims to have been a benefactor,—by his transference to us here of an expenditure which is due there ; thus, he will either impoverish their councillors for them by this expenditure in two places or, by concentrating it upon us, he will deprive Beroea of what she would have had.

26. He complains of having been insulted by not being invited [d] to a show of this kind by the man who promoted it. But if he has been insulted by this lack of invitation, then let him take it out on the level with Alexandria in third place, cf. Or. 15. 59 n. (Vol. I, p. 187).

[d] For the governor's expectations on this v. Or. 45. 20 n.

δίκην τοῦ δόντος τῷ λειτουργοῦντι τὴν τούτου
ἐξουσίαν, ὅτ᾽ αὐτοῦ μνησθέντος κλήσεως ἡνίκα ἐπ᾽
Εὐφράτην οὗτος ᾔει, πράττε, ἀπεκρίνατο, τὸ σόν,
ἐμοὶ δὲ ἐφ᾽ ᾧπερ ἐτάχθην μελήσει, τοὺς πυρούς[1]
λέγων. εἰ μὲν οὖν ἐψεύδου ταῦτα λέγων, οὐ λαμβάνειν δίκην, ἀλλὰ διδόναι δίκαιος εἶ, διὰ τί γὰρ
δὴ καὶ ἐξηπάτας; εἰ | δ᾽ ἀληθεύοντος ἦν ἐκεῖνα, F
R ii. 256 τὸ μὴ καὶ δεύτερον | κληθῆναι παρὰ σοῦ γεγένηται.
εἰ δὲ δὴ καὶ τὸ δίκαιον ἦν ἐν ταῖς αἰτίαις, ἐπὶ τὸν
ἡμαρτηκότα χωρεῖν ἔδει τὴν ὀργήν, οὐ μὰ Δία τὴν
βουλὴν ὅλην. οὐδὲ γὰρ ἐλειτουργοῦμεν, εἴποιεν
ἄν, ἅπαντες οὐδ᾽ ἦν ἔδει ποιεῖσθαι κλῆσιν ἐξελίπο-
μεν. 27. πιστὸν δὲ αὐτὸν ἀρνούμενον ταύτην
ἐποίει τὴν κοινωνίαν καὶ τὸ παρὰ τῆς μείζονος ἀρχῆς προειρῆσθαι τῷδε μένειν τε αὐτοῦ καὶ μὴ
κινεῖσθαι πρὶν ἂν αὐτὸς ἀπ᾽ Αἰγύπτου τε καὶ τῶν
Νείλου ῥευμάτων ἐπανέλθη. καὶ τοῦτο οὕτως
ἐστὶν ἰσχυρὸν ὥστε καὶ λυθὲν σοῖς, ὦ βασιλεῦ,
γράμμασι δόντος τοῖς Τισαμενῷ βοηθοῦσι τὴν χάριν ὅμως ἐτετήρητο. ὁ δὲ τοῦ μὴ καλέσαντος
ὀρθῶς οὐ κεκληκότος μισεῖ μὲν ἐκεῖνον, μισεῖ δὲ
τοὺς ἄλλους, λῆξαι δὲ οὐδὲ ἐν μακρῷ δεδύνηται τῷ
χρόνῳ.
28. Ἀλλὰ τούτους μὲν, εἰ καὶ μὴ δικαίως, ὅμως
ἐγκαλῶν τι ζημιοῖ, τοὺς δὲ δικαζομένους, ἐρῶ γὰρ
ὅ με διέφυγε πρότερον, τί λαβὼν αὐτὸν ἠδικηκότας

_____

[1] μελήσει τοῦ πυρὸς Morel (Va).

_____

[a] §§ 6 f. Or. 1. 251.
[b] Cf. § 1 and note ; Petit, Byzantion, xxi, pp. 302 f.

actual person who gave the sponsor the authority to act so, when he did discuss an invitation at the time when Tisamenus was due to go off to the Euphrates. Tisamenus' reply was, " You get on with your job and I'll get on with mine "—the corn collection,[a] that is. If you were trying to deceive by this statement, you deserve not to punish but to be punished, for what earthly reason was there for you to mislead ? If your statement was made in good faith, then it was your own fault that you got no second invitation. In any case, even if there were any justice in your complaints, you should direct your anger against the person at fault, not, in heaven's name, against the whole council, for, as they could say, " It was not all of us who provided the show or who defaulted upon the issue of an invitation that should have been made." 27. And confirmation that he declined this association came from the strict instructions of his superior [b] that he was to stay where he was and not budge until he himself had returned from Egypt and the streams of Nile. And these instructions were so strict that, even though they were countermanded by a letter of your own, Sire, when you acceded to the request of Tisamenus' supporters, he was still retained there. But, although the councillor who failed to invite him was correct not to do so, he loathes him and he loathes the others, and hasn't been able to stop doing so, however long the time since then.

28. But he might have some cause for complaint, however unjustified, for him to punish these people. Yet, with regard to litigants—for I go on to mention a point that previously escaped me—how did he find them at fault towards him, for him to ruin

ἀπόλλυσι, καὶ ταῦτα διὰ γάμων; τὰς γὰρ αὑτοῦ
θυγατέρας ἐκδιδοὺς πολὺ πρὸ τῆς τῶν γάμων ἡμέ-
R ii. 257 ρας εἰσκαλέσας τῶν ῥητόρων τὸν χορὸν | σιγᾶτε,
ἔφη, τῆς σιγῆς ἀρξάμενοι τήμερον, μέχρις ἂν αἱ
κόραι τῶν νυμφίων γένωνται, τὸ πρᾶγμα ἑορτὴν
ὀνο|μάσας. τὸ δὲ ἦν ἀποφράς, βλάβη μὲν τοῖς F
οὐ λέγουσι, βλάβη δὲ τοῖς τῆς ἐκείνων δεομένοις
φωνῆς. 29. καίτοι θυγατέρας ἄρχων οὐ πρῶτος
τῇδε ἐξέδωκεν, ἀλλ᾽ ἐπὶ πολλοῖς ἑτέροις, οἱ δέ τινες
καὶ αὐτοὶ γυναῖκας ἠγάγοντο. ἀλλ᾽ ὅμως οὐδε-
τέρους οἱ γάμοι τῶν δικῶν ἀπήγαγον ἀλλὰ τὰ μὲν
εἰς τοὺς γάμους φέροντα διὰ τῶν φίλων αὐτοῖς
ἐπράττετο, τὸν ἄρχοντα δὲ ἦν ὁρᾶν ἐν τοῖς ἑαυτοῦ.
ὁδὶ δὲ παρειστήκει μὲν τοῖς ὃ τὴν νύμφην δέξεται
ῥάπτουσιν, ἐν δὲ τοῖς πρὸς τοὺς μαγείρους λόγοις
διέτριβεν. οἷς[1] δ᾽ ἦσαν αἱ δίκαι, πολλοὶ δὲ ἐν αὐτοῖς πένητες, ἐχθροί τε ἦσαν τοῖς γάμοις καὶ κατ-
ηρῶντο τοῖς ἐστεφανωμένοις.

30. Εἶτ᾽ ἀπὸ ταυτησὶ τῆς ἀργίας τῆς πολλῆς |
R ii. 258 πολὺς ἦν ἐν πληγαῖς. τοῦτο γὰρ ἡ τοῦδε ἀρχὴ
συκοφάντην ἡδέως ἰδεῖν, ἀπ᾽ αἰτίας ἐπὶ τὴν δίκην
δραμεῖν, τοῖς διὰ πληγῶν κακοῖς προσθεῖναι δε-
σμόν. ὁ δεσμὸς οὗτος ἑτέραν, ὦ βασιλεῦ, δίκην
ἔχει τὴν ἐν χρήμασι· δεῖ γὰρ ὑπερβαίνοντα τὸν
οὐδὸν τὸν κύριον τῆς θύρας θεραπεῦσαι χρυσίῳ,
χρυσίου δὲ οὐκ ὄντος τὸν μὲν δεῖ καθῆσθαι γυμνόν,
εἶναι δὲ τὴν ἐσθῆτα τοῦ φύλακος, μητέρα δὲ γραῦν,

---

[1] οἷς Re., F.: οἶ mss.

a Arguments resumed in *Or.* 45. 10.

them—and ruin them, what's more, because of a wedding? When he was getting his daughters married, long before the wedding day he summoned all the members of the bar to him and told them, " Starting from today, you will stay silent, until the girls are wedded and bedded," and he called all this a holiday. In fact, it really was a ban, harmful to the advocates who could not plead and to the clients who needed their eloquence. 29. Yet it is not the first time a governor here has had his daughter married : it has happened in plenty of other instances. Some have even got married themselves. But for all that, in neither case did marriage deflect them from the administration of justice : the preparations for the ceremony were performed by his friends, while the governor could be seen fulfilling his proper duties. But this fellow stands over the bride's dress-makers, and spends his time debating with the cooks, but people involved in court actions —and many poor people among them—were bitter against the marriage and cursed the wedding party and all its finery.

30. Then, after this prolonged inaction, he busily engaged himself with floggings. This was the characteristic of his administration—a kindly eye for accusers, haste in moving from accusation to punishment, and, above and beyond the evils of corporal punishment, the imposition of imprisonment. And this imprisonment, Sire, involves another punishment too, a financial one.[a] Anyone who crosses the threshold must cosset the turnkey with a piece of gold, and if he hasn't got one, then he must sit there stripped naked, his clothes taken by the jailor, and his old mother, if the prisoner has one, has to wander

εἴπερ εἴη τῷ δεδεμένῳ, πλανωμένην ἀγείρειν ὅσον ἂν προσαιτοῦσα δύνηται. 31. οἱ μὲν οὖν ἄλλοι μετὰ τὰς πληγὰς τοῖς οἰκείοις ἀφεῖσαν τὸν τοῦτο πεπονθότα καὶ ἰατροῖς δὴ καὶ ἰατρῶν φαρμάκοις, ὁ δὲ πέμπει τοὺς ἀθλίους ἀπολουμένους τοῖς ἐν τῷ δεσμωτηρίῳ κακοῖς. καὶ εἰ μὲν | ἢ αὐτὸν ἀναμι- F μνήσκων ἔλυεν ἢ τοῖς ὑπηρέταις ἦν ἀναμιμνήσκειν ἐξουσία, μετριώτερον ἂν ἦλθε, νῦν δ' ἀνάγκη πρὸς πολλῶν γόνατα προσπεσεῖν οὐ πάντων τὰ τοιαῦτα αἰδουμένων, τῶν δ' αὖ ἐπιεικεστέρων οἱ μὲν ἀσχολίαν, οἱ δ' ἄλλο τι φήσαντες δώσειν μὲν εἶπον τὴν χάριν, εὐθὺς δὲ οὐ δύνασθαι. τῷ δὲ μακρότερον R ii. 259 τὸ | κακόν.

32. Εἶτ' ἂν μὴ φιλάνθρωπος ἀκούσῃ, δεινὰ πεπονθέναι φησὶ καὶ τῇ φύσει τῇ αὐτοῦ προσήκοντος ὀνόματος στέρεσθαι οὐκ αἰσχυνόμενος πληγὰς ἑτέρας τὰς κατὰ τῶν οὐ δυναμένων εἰσπρᾶξαι τοὺς οὐ δυναμένους ἐκτίσαι. καίτοι τί μιαρώτερον τοῦ μὴ δύνασθαι μὲν λέγειν ὡς [οὐχ]¹ οὕτω τοῦτ' ἐχρῆν, τῆς δὲ τῶν εἰσπραττομένων ἀπορίας ἀπαιτεῖν δίκας τοὺς τεταγμένους εἰσπράττειν; ὅμοιον γὰρ τοῦτό γε τῷ παρὰ τῶν ἰατρῶν ἀπαιτεῖν ζῶντας τοὺς τεθνηκότας. οὔτε γὰρ ἐκεῖνο τῶν ἐχόντων ἐστὶ φύσιν τοῦτό τε τῶν ἀδυνάτων. κἂν δείρῃ τις τὸν ὀφείλοντα, τὸ δέρμα μὲν ἀφέλοιτ' ἄν, χρήματα δὲ τὸν οὐκ ἔχοντα ἔχειν οὐκ ἔσθ' ὅπως ἂν ποιήσειεν. ὁ R ii. 260 δὲ τοὺς μὲν πράκτορας, | εἰ μὴ δύναιντ' [ἂν]² εἰσ-

---

¹ οὐχ mss. : "deletum mallem," Re.
² F. suggests deletion of ἂν.

ᵃ He contravened the provisions of C. Th. 9. 3. 6, among others.

222

around getting whatever she can get by begging. 31. Well, other governors, after imposing a flogging, used to release the victim to his relatives, to doctors and their potions, but this fellow sends the wretches to their death through ill-treatment in prison. And if he recollected them and released them, or if his underlings had the power to make him recollect them,[a] his progress would be a more reasonable one. As it is, one must go on one's knees before many people, not all of whom respect such attitudes ; again, more decent folk adduce as an excuse either lack of time or something else, and say that, though they will grant them this, it cannot be done straightaway. So for the victim, the agony is prolonged.

32. And then, if he is not called generous, he says that he is badly treated and is not given the title that befits his character, though he has no qualms about inflicting fresh floggings upon people who cannot extract the sums due from those who cannot pay them.[b] Yet what could be more disgusting than not to be able to say that this course of action should be undertaken, and yet to punish the appointed collectors of taxes for the impoverishment of those who cannot pay them ? It is just like asking of doctors that they should bring the dead to life. That is unnatural, but this is impossible. If you flay a debtor, you may take the hide off him, but you can't make a man of property out of someone who doesn't have it. But he says that it is right for the tax collectors, if unable to gather the due

[b] The decurions had been made responsible, both in their persons and in their property, for the collection of tribute, and were beaten if they did not collect the sum assigned, *cf. Or.* 45. 24, 47. 8, 28. 16.

πρᾶξαι, δίκαιον εἶναί φησιν | οἴκοθεν θεῖναι, οὕτως F
ἐστὶν ἡμῖν Αἰακός, ὁ δ᾽ οὐδὲ τοῦτο δυνάμενος τύπ-
τεται.

33. Τοῦτον οὖν ἐάσεις ἄρχειν, δι᾽ ὃν πολλοὶ μὲν
ὀδυρμοί, πολλοὶ δὲ θρῆνοι, πολλὰ δὲ δάκρυα, πολλὰ
δὲ κατὰ τῶν θεῶν ῥήματα; ναί, τὰ γὰρ ⟨τῶν⟩[1] ἐν
τοῖς ἐργαστηρίοις καὶ πρὸς ταύταις ταῖς τέχναις
ἄμεινον ἔσχεν. ἀλλ᾽ ἄρτι βαρεῖαν αὐτοὺς ὑπο-
μείναντας φορὰν ὁ τῶν πενήτων οὑτοσὶ κηδεμὼν
γράφειν ἠνάγκαζε τὰ περὶ τὰς θύρας οὐσῶν ἐν αὐτοῖς γραφῶν ἃς ἀφ᾽ ὁμοίας ἀδικίας τῶν πρίν τινες[2]
ἀρχόντων ἔδειξαν τὴν μὲν πενίαν ἐπιτείναντες τοῖς
ἀθλίοις, ποιοῦντες δὲ οὐ καλλίω τὴν πόλιν, τῶν
R ii. 261 γὰρ ἐν τοῖς γραφεῦσι [τῶν] φαυλοτάτων | ἔργα
ταῦτα. ὡς δ᾽ ὄντων τούτων[3] ἐκ τῶν ἔμπροσθεν
χρόνων ἐπιβάλλειν ἐκέλευεν ἕτερα τοῖς οὐ διεφθαρ-
μένοις. 34. τί δὴ τὸ τούτων αἴτιον; τοῖς γρα-
φεῦσιν εἴς τινας στοὰς χρησάμενος δοῦναι τῆς
γραφῆς τὸν μισθόν, ᾗ δίκαιον ἦν οὐκ ἐθέλων, δι-
έλυσεν αὐτὸν ἐκ τῶν οὐκ ἀναγκαίων γραφῶν. καὶ
οἱ μὲν ἔγραφον, οἱ δὲ ἐδάκρυον ἐκ τοῦ πεινῆν μέλ-
λοντες τὰ δίκαια πρὸς ἐκείνους ποιήσειν. | ὁρᾷς,

---

[1] ⟨τῶν⟩ F., conj. Re.   [2] τινες Re., F. : τινος Morel (mss.).
[3] [τῶν] φαυλοτάτων ἔργα ταῦτα. ὡς δ᾽ ὄντων F. : τῶν
φαυλοτάτων ἔργα ταύτας (ταῦτα V, conj. Re.) δόντων Morel
(mss.) : τῷ φαυλοτάτῳ ἔργα ταύτας δόντων Re. : τῶν φαυλοτάτων
ἔργα ταῦτα. οὗτος δ᾽ ὄντων Monnier. For ὡς δ᾽ read οὐδ᾽ ?

---

[a] Cf. Or. 16. 19 (Vol. I, p. 222 n.), 37. 7. Aeacus, because
of his piety on earth, was appointed judge in the underworld.
[b] The collatio lustralis or chrysargyron, levied on tradesmen once every five years, cf. Or. 16. 19, 46. 22 f. This
exaction, demanded in A.D. 386 (cf. C. Th. 13. 1. 15) was
merely part of the financial pressures of this year, to be

amount, to contribute it from their personal property
—such a Grand Just Judge is he ! [a]—but anyone who
can't even do this gets a flogging.

33. So will you let this fellow remain as governor,
when because of him there is many a moan and
groan and tear, and many a cry rising up to heaven ?
" Yes, but," says he, " I have brought about an improvement in the conditions of workers in the factories
in the practice of these trades." But this protector
of the poor, for all that they have only recently
suffered a severe tax demand,[b] has forced them to
have their doorways painted,[c] although there were
already in existence there the signs that some
previous governors had had done, with similar injustice,[d] increasing still further the penury of the
poor wretches and yet by no means improving the
appearance of the city, for the job was done by the
most cheap-jack of the painters. On the pretext
that this decoration was old-fashioned he ordered a
fresh coating to be put over even what had not been
spoiled. 34. And what do you think his reason for
all this ? Why ! he had employed the painters on
some colonnades, refused to pay them for their work
in the proper way, and so got out of it by this un-
necessary painting work. The painters began to
paint, and the householders to complain, since they
were going to pay them their due and go hungry in

followed by a *supraindictio* of the tribute inside the next
two months.

[c] An example of the consistent interference which the
tradespeople suffered at the hands of the governors in the
period following Icarius' interventions : *e.g. Or. 4.* 27,
54. 42, 46. 7 ff.

[d] The last recorded example being little more than a year
before, under Icarius, *Or.* 27. 31.

ὦ βασιλεῦ, τοῦ ἄρχοντος τὸν πόνον; ἐπέταξεν ἐν
ὀλίγαις συλλαβαῖς. οὐκ ἦν ἀντειπεῖν τοῖς ἐπιταττο-
μένοις. ἀφῄρουν τῆς ἑαυτῶν τροφῆς. 35. ὁ δ᾽
ἀφορμὴν ὀδυρμῶν παρασχὼν τῇ[1] πόλει πῶς ἂν
R ii. 262 εἴη καλλίω τήνδε πεποιηκὼς | τὴν πόλιν; ἐγὼ μὲν
γὰρ τὸ τοὺς ἀπόρους εὐπορωτέρους ποιεῖν ὥραν
ἡγοῦμαι πόλεως, ὁδὶ[2] δ᾽ αὖ τῶν ἐναντίων αἴτιος
ἡμῖν οἷς τε εἶπον τούτοις τοῖς περιττοῖς καὶ οἷς
ἐρῶ. τοὺς γὰρ αὐτοὺς δὴ τούτους τοὺς ἐν τοῖς
ἐργαστηρίοις κελεύει τριπλάσιον ἐν τῇ νυκτὶ παρέχειν τὸ πῦρ. πόθεν οὖν ἔλαιον τοσοῦτον πρίωμαι
τὸ διὰ τὸ πολὺ πῦρ τοῦτο πλείονος ἢ πρόσθεν πω-
λούμενον; πόσον μοι τὸ παρὰ τῶν χειρῶν ἀργύριον; πόσα δι᾽ αὐτοῦ μοι γένηται; τί πρὸς τοῦτ᾽
ἐρεῖ Τισαμενός; 36. ἐν τοίνυν τῷ καιρῷ τῆς ἀνα-
παύλης, τοιοῦτον γὰρ ἀρχομένη νύξ, ἐκταράττει
τοὺς ταλαιπώρους ταῖς κατὰ τῶν θυρῶν πληγαῖς
ἃς πλήττουσιν οἱ τῶν φυλῶν ἐπιμεληταὶ τῷ περὶ
ταύτας φόβῳ μὴ διαφθαρεῖεν ποιοῦντες τὴν ἀνάγ-
R ii. 263 κην τοῦ πυρός. | οὗ γιγνομένου οἶδα βοήσασαν
γυναῖκα χήραν ἄνωθεν, ὅτι πῶς ἂν ἅψαι δυναίμην;
πόθεν ἂν ἔλαιόν μοι | γένοιτο τῇ[3] πολὺν ἤδη χρόνον F
ἐλαίου μὴ γεγευμένῃ; 37. ἀλλὰ τούτῳ τοῦτ᾽ εἶναι
νεανικὸν δοκεῖ τὸ κελεῦσαι καὶ τὸ πεπραγμένον
ἰδεῖν, εἰ δὲ δίκαιον ἢ μή, εἰ[4] συμφέρον ἢ τοὐναντίον, οὐδεὶς λόγος. κἂν εἰσελθών τις ὡς αὐτὸν
τῶν εἶναι δοκούντων φίλων εἴπῃ τἀληθῆ περὶ τοῦ

---

[1] τῇ om. Re. (mss. except V).
[2] ὁδὶ F. : σὺ Re. (mss.).
[3] τῇ Re. (mss. except V) : τὸν F. (V).
[4] εἰ F. : ἢ Re. (mss.).

---

[a] Cf. Or. 45. 5.

the process. Observe the energy displayed by our governor, Sire. He issued his orders in a few short syllables,[a] and there was no arguing about it. So they had to deduct the sum from what they had to live on. 35. If he has given the city cause for lamentation, how could he possibly have improved the appearance of this city ? In my opinion, to increase the resources of the destitute is to make a city boom : this fellow, however, has been responsible for the exact reverse, both by the excesses already mentioned and by those I now proceed to relate. These very same people in the factories, for instance, he orders to triple the street lighting at night.[b] " And where can I buy so much oil, now that it costs so much more than before because of this huge lighting programme ? How much is the money I earn from my trade ? And how much do I actually get because of it ? " What has Tisamenus to say to that ? 36. Anyway, at the time of rest, that is at nightfall, he scares the poor wretches out of their wits in case their doors should be knocked in, by reason of the watch committee [c] battering on them and demanding the lamps to be lit. I know that, one time when this happened, a widow woman started crying upstairs, " How can I light them ? Where can I get the oil from ? For long enough now I've never had taste of a drop of it." 37. This fellow thinks it a grand thing to issue his order and to see it put into effect. He doesn't care twopence whether it is right or not or whether it is of any use or not. Even if some of his so-called friends come and tell him the

[b] *Cf. Or.* 16. 41 (Vol. I, p. 237 n.). Tisamenus evidently attempts to improve this street lighting system.

[c] For *epimeletae cf. Or.* 24. 26 (Vol. I, p. 508 n.).

πράγματος καὶ παραινέσῃ πεπαῦσθαι ληρεῖν ἔδοξε.
καίτοι τίς ἡ περὶ τοῦτο σπουδή, πῦρ[1] εἶναι τοσοῦτον ἐν καθευδούσῃ τῇ πόλει; οὐ γὰρ ἂν τοῖς
καθεύδουσιν εἴη ἄν τι παρ' αὐτοῦ τοῖς τε φύλαξιν
ἀπόχρη τὸ ἀρχαῖον· κακούργους γε οὐκ ἔστιν εἰπεῖν ἥττους μὲν γεγονέναι νῦν, εἶναι δὲ πρὸ τοῦ
πλείους. ἀλλ' ἔστιν ἅπαν τοῦτο μέθης καὶ ἀσελγείας καὶ τοῦ μηδὲν φροντίζειν τῶν ἐν πενίᾳ ζώντων.

38. Εἶτά με ἐρήσεταί τις, εἰ δεδωροδόκηκεν ὁ
ἄνθρωπος. εἰ δὲ τοῦτο μὲν οὔ, διέθηκε δὲ οὕτω
τοὺς ἀρχομένους, ὡς ἤκουσάς μου διδάσκοντος,
ἀγαθός ἐστι κακὸς ὤν, ἐπεὶ μὴ χρημάτων ⟨εἵ-
νεκά⟩[2] ἐστι κακός; ἐγὼ δὲ αὐτὸν μὲν οὔ φημι λαβεῖν, λαβεῖν δὲ ἑτέρους διὰ τοῦτον τῶν μὲν ἀδικεῖν
προαιρουμένων ἐπί τε τοὺς κηδεστὰς καταφευ-
γόντων καὶ τὸν τούτου ἀδελφὸν καὶ τὴν τούτων
R ii. 264 μητέρα καὶ τὸν οὐδεπώποτε ταύτην | λυπήσαντα F
τὸν βέλτιστον ἰατρόν, ὧν ἕκαστος ὅτου μνησθείη,
τοῦτ' εὐθὺς ἔδει πεπρᾶχθαι, ἢν δὲ οὐχ οἷόν τε ὁμοῦ
καὶ τοὺς νόμους κρατεῖν καὶ τούτους κερδαίνειν.
οἱ δὲ ἐκέρδαινον καθ' ἑκάστην ἡμέραν. οὐκ ἄρα
τοῖς νόμοις ὑπῆρχε κρατεῖν. ὁ δὲ τὸ δύνασθαι τοὺς
νόμους ἀφαιρούμενος σῴζειν ἂν αὐτοὺς οὗτος δοκοῖ; τί γάρ; εἰ τὸ χρυσίον εἰς μὲν τὰς τοῦδε χεῖρας
οὐκ ἔρχοιτο, εἰς δὲ τὰς ἑτέρων[3] τούτου πέμποντος,
ἧττον τὸ δίκαιον ἐκ δωροδοκίας ἀπόλωλεν; 39. διὰ

---

[1] ⟨τὸ⟩ πῦρ ins. F.
[2] ⟨εἵνεκά⟩ ins. F. Possibly ⟨χάριν⟩.
[3] τὰς τῶν ἑτέρων A, Re. (conj. τὰς τῶν ἑταίρων).

---

[a] Cf. note on § 1 above. Libanius walks warily here,
drawing a delicate distinction between personal responsibility

228

truth about what is going on and advise him to stop, they are held to be talking nonsense. Yet why all the eagerness on this point, for so much lighting in the city while it sleeps ? No good results from it for the sleeping populace, and the lighting that existed before was good enough for the police. You can't tell me that there has been any decrease in the number of criminals now, or that there were more of them previously. All this business reeks of drunken insolence and disregard of the folk who live in poverty.

38. Then someone will ask me whether the fellow has gone in for bribery. If he has not, but has yet brought his subjects to the state of which you have heard me tell, is he a good man, for all that he is a rascal, just because his rascality is not for money ? I will not go so far as to say that he has taken bribes himself, but others have done so because of him [a] : some, who deliberately choose to act unlawfully, have recourse to his sons-in-law, his brother, his mother and that excellent physician who has never done anything to distress her. When any of these mentions something, it must needs be done on the spot, for it was not possible for the laws to prevail and, simultaneously, for this lot to make their pickings. And make their pickings they did, every single day, and so the laws could not prevail. If he deprives the laws of their power, how can he be regarded as their protector ? Why ! if your gold piece greases not his palms, but those of other people at his direction, is it any the less true that justice is subverted by bribery ? 39. Thus whenever a man

for bribery and the improper exercise of family influence that encourages it. Eutropius (*Or.* 4. 30 ff.) is more directly attacked on this issue.

LIBANIUS

τοῦτο ὅταν τις μέγα ἐργάσηται κακὸν καὶ φόβοι
παρὰ τῶν νόμων ὦσι γελᾷ· δρόμον γὰρ αὐτῷ μὲν
ἔσεσθαι παρὰ τὸν κηδεστὴν μετὰ χρημάτων, ἐκείνῳ δὲ παρὰ τὸν πατέρα τῆς γυναικός, ἐκ δὲ τῶν
καλῶν τούτων εἰσόδων καὶ λόγων οἰχήσεσθαι τὸ
δίκαιον καταπατηθέν. οὗτος μὲν οὖν οὐκ ἔσχε
πόρον τοιοῦτον, ἑτέροις δὲ παρέσχε, καὶ τὰ αὐτοῦ
μὲν ἐντεῦθεν οὐκ ηὔξησεν, οἶκον δὲ ἀνθρώπου πο-
νηροῦ. 40. πολλοὶ δὴ τῶν πανδοκέων τοῖς λῃσταῖς
συμπράττουσι μὲν εἰς τὴν ἀπὸ τῶν φόνων πρόσοδον, λαμβάνουσι δὲ οὐδέν, ἀλλ᾽ ἀρκοῦν αὐτοῖς κέρδος τὸ τοῖς κακούργοις κεχαρίσθαι. καὶ κάθηται
Τισαμενὸς ψήφους περὶ[1] τοιούτων φέρων. οἶδα δέ
τινας τούτων μὲν οὐδέτερον πεποιηκότας οὔτ᾽ αὐ-
τοὺς λαβόντας οὔθ᾽ ἑτέρους πεποιηκότας | λαβεῖν, F 1
τῇ δὲ ἄλλῃ κακίᾳ λυμηναμένους τὰς πόλεις καὶ
μισουμένους ὅμως ἐκ τῶν ἄλλων συμφορῶν καὶ οὐ
δόξαντας εἶναι χρηστοὺς διὰ τὸ πεπρακέναι μηδέν.
R ii. 265 41. ὥστ᾽ εἰ καὶ πᾶν τοῦτο | ἦν ὑπὲρ αὐτοῦ τὸ μέρος,
ἔκ γε τῶν ἄλλων κατεκλύζετ᾽ ἄν, ὃς τοῖς δεσμώ-
ταις διετέλεσε προστιθείς, ἐξάγων δὲ οὐδένα οὔτ᾽
ἀπολογησόμενον οὔτ᾽ ἀποθανούμενον, ὡς[2] πολλῷ
τοῖς δεσμώταις κουφότερον ἀφεῖναι τὴν ψυχὴν ἢ
τὰ σφῶν αὐτῶν ὁρᾶν ὀστᾶ διὰ τοῦ δέρματος. ὁ δ᾽
ἐμπλήσας τὸ οἴκημα σωμάτων ἀπὸ πάσης αἰτίας
αὐτῷ κτείνει τῷ πλήθει τοὺς δεθέντας. 42. ὧν
οὐ ταύτην οἱ πλείους ὤφειλον δίκην, ἀλλ᾽ οὐδ᾽ οἱ
θάνατον ὀφείλοντες τὴν δίκην τὸν οὕτω. τέμνει

---

[1] περὶ F.: ὑπὲρ Re. (mss.).   [2] ὡς F.: ὃ Re. (mss.).

---

[a] Cf. Or. 45. 6. Innkeepers were always suspect on this
account.   [b] Or. 45. 8, 31 f.

230

commits a serious crime and legal deterrents exist, he just laughs at them, for he knows that all he has to do is to scurry to the son-in-law, cash in hand ; the son-in-law goes to his wife's father, and as a result of these fine interviews and discourses, justice is bamboozled and done for. He never had anything to do with income of such a sort—Oh no !, but he allowed it to others, and though he did not increase his property from that source, he has increased the household of a wicked man. 40. Many innkeepers assist brigands to make money from murders, without touching a penny themselves [a] : it is gain enough for them to have obliged the criminals. And Tisamenus sits there in judgement on people like them ! Yet I know of people who have been innocent both of taking bribes themselves and of causing others to take them, who have yet harmed the cities by their other deficiencies and are particularly disliked because of the other troubles they have caused : they are not held to be good simply because they have never indulged in corrupt practices. 41. So, even if in this aspect of the matter everything was in his favour, he would still be in difficulties from other considerations. He has continued to add to the number of prisoners : he never lets one out either for trial or execution,[b] and the consequence is that it is a much easier matter for the prisoners to give up the ghost than to see their bones sticking out through their hides. He packs the jail full of bodies for every possible reason and murders those under arrest by their very numbers. 42. The majority of them never deserved this punishment : not even those who deserve to be punished by death, deserve it by a death like this. The law has their heads

γὰρ ὁ νόμος τὴν κεφαλήν, οὐκ ἀποπνίγει τῇ στενοχωρίᾳ. καὶ τὴν ἐνταῦθα ὀξύτητα κέρδος εἶναι
συμβαίνει τῷ τεμνομένῳ, ὁ δ' ἐν μὲν τῷ δῆσαι
ταχύς, ἐν δὲ τῷ κρῖναι βραδύς, μᾶλλον δὲ φεύγει
τὰς κρίσεις μᾶλλον ἢ παιδία τὰς Μορμόνας καὶ τὸν
ἄρχοντα τοῦτ' εἶναι νομίζει τὸ διὰ λήρων ἐπ' ἄριστον προελθεῖν.

43. Ἀπάλλαξον δὴ τὰς σαυτοῦ πόλεις τοιούτων
κακῶν καὶ πέμψον ἄνδρα νοῦν τε ἔχοντα καὶ πόνων
ἐπιθυμητὴν καὶ πλείω πράξοντα ἢ λαλήσοντα καὶ |
πείσοντα μᾶλλον ἢ ἀναγκάσοντα καὶ βοηθήσοντα F 1
πένησιν, οὐκ ἐπιτρίψοντα, καὶ διαγνωσόμενον, τί
μὲν δυνατόν, τί δὲ οὔ, καὶ καιρὸν μὲν πληγῶν, καιρὸν δὲ εἰσόμενον ἀπειλῆς, ὅλως οὐδὲν ἐοικότα τῷ
λοιμῷ τούτῳ.

ᵃ Cf. Or. 30. 38 n. Xen. Hell. 4. 4. 17.

chopped off : it doesn't suffocate them with over-
crowding. In this case, the quickness of the act is
to the victim's good. But this fellow here is so quick
to arrest and so slow to come to a decision. In fact,
he is more frightened of court hearings than children
are of the bogey-man,[a] and he thinks that being a
governor is to proceed to lunch through a mass of
drivel.

43. So free your cities of such ills and send us a
man of sense who is eager to work, a doer rather
than a talker, and one who will use persuasion rather
than compulsion, a helper of the poor rather than
their oppressor, who will distinguish what is and
what is not possible, and recognize a time for flogging
and a time for threatening—in short, a man who is
nothing at all like this plague here.

THE RIOTS OF THE STATUES

ORATION 23
AGAINST THE REFUGEES

ORATION 19
TO THE
EMPEROR THEODOSIUS,
ABOUT THE RIOTS

ORATION 20
TO THE
EMPEROR THEODOSIUS,
AFTER THE
RECONCILIATION

ORATION 21
TO CAESARIUS,
MASTER OF OFFICES

ORATION 22
TO ELLEBICHUS

INTRODUCTION

The Orations upon the Riots of a.d. 387

The narrative of the *Autobiography* shows Tisamenus leaving office and the sudden outbreak of the riots following almost immediately. Here, says Libanius, through the intervention of evil spirits, imperial portraits were stoned and statues demolished in a furious outbreak of popular violence. There followed a panic exodus from the city, for it was feared that the soldiers would be let loose upon it, but it was saved from such a fate largely by his own intercessions with the newly-arrived commissioners of investigation. Such a crisis called for many speeches on his part, and these were uniformly successful.[a] However, he adds (*Or.* 1. 254) that the numbers of his audience declined thereafter in consequence of governmental opposition.

[a] *Or.* 1. 252 : ἕτερος ἄρχων, ἐφ᾽ οὗ τὰ δεινότατα πολέμῳ πονηρῶν δαιμόνων δόξαντα κεκινῆσθαι, λίθοι τε ἐπὶ τοὺς ἐν ταῖς γραφαῖς βασιλέας ἐκ χειρῶν ἐρχόμενοι, καὶ ἦν πολὺς ὁ ψόφος, χαλκαί τε εἰκόνες διὰ γῆς ἑλκόμενοι ῥήματά τε ἐπὶ τοὺς τῶν ὅλων κυρίους πικρότερα παντὸς ἀφιέμενα λίθου δι᾽ ἃ πολλαὶ δὴ μεταναστάσεις, ὡς οὐκ ὂν μένοντι σωθῆναι, καὶ ὁ φεύγων τὸν οὐ φεύγοντα ἐθρήνει. ἐν μὲν οὖν ταῖς ἐλπίσι κατασκαφαί, τὸ δὲ ἐλπίδος ἔξω σωτηρία. (253) τούτου δὲ καὶ αὐτὸς αἴτιος εἶναι ἐδόκουν· λόγοις τε ἡμερώσας καὶ δάκρυσι τοὺς ἐπὶ τὴν κρίσιν ἥκοντας γραμμάτων ἐρᾶν ἔπειθον . . . καὶ τοῦτο ἔργον ἡγώμεθα τῆς Τύχης καὶ προσέτι γε τοὺς πολλοὺς λόγους περὶ μὲν τὴν αὐτὴν πεποιημένους ὑπόθεσιν, . . . δόξαντας δὲ εὖ ἔχειν.

LIBANIUS

There is no doubt that Libanius prides himself
consistently upon the positive rôle which he played
as sophist in this crisis. His various references to it
all contain the characteristic note of self-congratulation or of depreciation of his opponents,[a] but the
evidence for the whole series of events is full of un-
certainties. Thus Zosimus, deceived by Libanius'
posture in *Orations* 19 and 20, talks of Libanius,
chosen as Antiochene envoy, successfully pleading [b]
before the emperor in person. Sozomen [c] makes an
error of chronology in sandwiching his story of the
incident into the account of the usurpation of
Eugenius. From Libanius himself little can be deduced about the details of time ; from the other eye-
witness, Chrysostom, equally little about details of
the events themselves ; from neither can any certain
conclusion be drawn about the financial demand
which caused this explosion of feeling.

The relationship between Libanius and Chrysostom
has indeed been a point of controversy, mostly interpreted to the disadvantage of Libanius. Chrysostom's *Homilies*, delivered during the course of the
investigation and the weeks thereafter and exactly
contemporary with the events, give some precise
indications of chronology (*e.g.* for the outbreak of
the riots, the departure of Bishop Flavianus to Constantinople, his return on Easter Day, a week after

---

[a] *e.g. Or.* 32, 34. 12 ff., 63. 9.
[b] Zos. 4. 41 : αἱροῦνται τοίνυν Λιβάνιόν τε τὸν σοφιστὴν . . .
καὶ Ἱλάριον. καὶ ὁ μὲν σοφιστὴς τὸν περὶ τῆς στάσεως αὐτῷ τε
βασιλεῖ καὶ τῇ γερουσίᾳ λόγον εἰπὼν ἴσχυσε τὸν βασιλέα μεταστῆσαι
τῆς κατὰ Ἀντιοχέων ὀργῆς· ὥστε ἀμέλει τούτῳ καὶ τὸν περὶ τῶν
διαλλαγῶν ἐπιθεῖναι, τελέως τοῦ βασιλέως τὸ πρὸς τὴν πόλιν ἔχθος
ἀποθεμένου.   [c] Sozom. *H.E.* 7. 23.

the receipt of the news of the imperial pardon), as well as some insight into the course of events in the intervals. Libanius, however, certainly composed these orations after a settlement had been reached. His narrative shows so many coincidences of detail and of language with Chrysostom that Goebel, followed by Baur, conjectured that at the time of composition he had before him and deliberately imitated the *Homilies* already current in Antioch.[a] The paradox of such a view is heightened by the fact that the Christian and the pagan each seem deliberately to have ignored the other in this flood of oratory. Apart from a casual sneer at Flavianus by Libanius and an equally casual reference to classical rhetoric which is probably a sneer at Libanius,[b] there is no indication of any religious confrontation or co-operation at this time. Libanius insists, in fact, that pagan and Christian are to be treated alike. The coincidences of content and form are to be explained by the common subject-matter and the common rhetorical store of topic and rule, which made any account with pretensions to accuracy and to plausibility inescapably similar to another. Plagiarism on this issue by Libanius would be the more unlikely since it would almost certainly have been noted immediately.

The *Orations to the Emperor* (*Or.* 19 and 20) may perhaps be regarded somewhat differently. If coincidence was unavoidable, why should Libanius compose these orations when he did and in the way

[a] Goebel, pp. 19 ff. compares *Hom.* 21 (the oration of Flavianus) with *Or.* 19, to reach this surprising conclusion.

[b] Flavianus, "not at home," *Or.* 19. 28. Demosthenes' self-cure, *cf.* Jo. Chr. *Hom.* 1. 9 (*cf.* Lib. *Dem. Hypoth.* 10 f., vol. viii, p. 603 F.).

he did ? There is no such question about Chrysostom. His *Homilies* are strictly contemporary with the events and are designed to sustain and improve the morale of his flock. Composition, delivery and publication of these addresses are immediately linked with the circumstances. In the case of Libanius, however, this immediacy is lost. All the orations except *Oration* 23 were composed after the conclusion of the whole affair. In the case of *Orations* 21 and 22, miniature panegyrics upon the two commissioners, this is natural enough, since they are personal thanksgiving for services rendered during the emergency even though publication was delayed by the perfectionism of the author. *Orations* 19 and 20, although purporting to be pleas presented to the emperor at the time, were manifestly composed after the event. In this they are no less fictitious than his self-claimed status of ambassador. They could not have exerted any influence upon the course of events, nor were they intended to do.[a] Yet, as the *Autobiography* indicates, they were published—unless Libanius is there guilty of the grossest deception—and they had purpose. This was, at least in part, to do with the maintenance of his professional prestige. As fictions they are on a par with Chrysostom's *Twenty-first Homily*—expressions of the speaker's views and of what might actually have been said in the situation, and like it, they are designed to instruct and comfort their audience, whether at first- or second-hand, in civic or in court circles. Significantly enough, Chrysostom speaks of Christian

[a] *Cf.* P. Petit, "Recherches sur la publication et la diffusion des discours de Libanius," *Historia*, v (1956), pp. 493 ff.

converts gained by the activities of Bishop Flavianus and the monks during this crisis.[a] Libanius in *Oration* 23 concentrates upon the immediate task of rallying the backsliders to their Hellenic duty, but it was no less important that the social virtues of Hellenism and of classical culture should after the event not be regarded as having gone by default before a Christian emperor whose government, for all his good professions, had shown increasing indecisiveness in everything except religious partiality and fiscal repressiveness. It was no accident that the keyword was " reconciliation," just as it had been under Julian. The pagans had to be assured that they too were to be included in this settlement not merely for the present but also for the future. At the same time, Libanius was, as sophist of his city, acting as the mouthpiece of the curial class, who were willy-nilly held responsible for civic order, by imputing responsibility to the more unstable sections of the community, the claque, the mob, and the wealthy non-curial classes. The arguments of class and culture combine in these pleas for a restoration of good order, as they had done in the *Pro Templis* and the *De Vinctis* for its maintenance.

As for the fiscal demand which caused the disturbance, there is much vagueness. The church historians speak of it as intolerable, a term used by Libanius (*Or.* 46. 22) to describe the *chrysargyron*, and as new, which the *chrysargyron* was not, since it had been levied only the year before (*Or.* 33. 33). Libanius connects it with demands for Theodosius' *decennalia* and Arcadius' *quinquennalia*, that is *aurum coronarium*, due in A.D. 388. The pressure, however, is much

[a] *De Anna*, 1. 1 ; Migne, *P.G.* liv 634.

more immediate, and the classes subjected to it wider than the usual decurions. This extraordinary tax, in view of the vagueness and contradictions in the sources, seems to be most probably a supra-indiction of the tribute.[a] At any rate, it was the propertied classes who initiated a peaceful protest. Their lead was followed by the mob, who rapidly turned protest into riot, looting and arson, and attacked the imperial statues, under the leadership of expert rabble-rousers. The governor remained momentarily inactive, taken by surprise, and a panic flight of the horrified populace immediately took place, decurions leading, and there was a mass evacuation of the city, in fear of military reprisals. Libanius remained at his post, deserted by all but a few of his pupils and of his associates from the upper classes, of whom Olympius was the most notable. Martial law was instituted immediately, and a commission of investigation, composed of the *magister militum* Ellebichus and the *magister officiorum* Caesarius, pagan and Christian respectively, despatched from Constantinople. Bishop Flavianus had already set off to court to plead for the city, and the monks came down from the hills to intercede with the commission. Along with the imposition of martial law, the decurions had been arrested, Antioch deprived of its metropolitan and urban status, all public amenities—circus, baths, theatre—closed, and these disabilities remained while the commission continued its work, until Caesarius was sent in haste to recommend leniency to the emperor, while Ellebichus

[a] *Cf.* Petit, *Vie municipale*, p. 146 ; Browning, *J.R.S.* (1952), pp. 14 f.

remained in charge in Antioch. By Palm Sunday the news had been rushed to Antioch that Theodosius had graciously consented to pardon the city for its late misdemeanours, and it regained its status and privileges.

The consistency and efficacy of Libanius' support of his city cannot be denied, but the enmities which he made in doing so then and afterwards, as for instance with Thrasydaeus, were to affect him adversely. The supporter of the decurions in A.D. 387 becomes the most vocal critic of the curia in the next year, while his feud with the *honorati* and various governors continued unabated. His oratory throve upon the opposition which caused his influence and position to decline.

MANUSCRIPTS

There is great variation in both manuscript density and editorial tradition in these orations. At the one extreme, *Oration* 23 survives in six manuscripts only, its single excerpt in Macarius appears under a false title, and it received no publication until A.D. 1754. At the other, the two *Orations to the Emperor* can boast a density of twenty-six manuscripts each, and *Oration* 19, in particular, can boast an *editio princeps* in A.D. 1517, along with at least five other editions and two translations antecedent to Foerster's work, the relationship with John Chrysostom's " Homilies on the Statues " being chiefly responsible for such a concentration of editorial interest. In contrast, *Orations* 21 and 22, while fairly heavily represented in the manuscript tradition with seventeen MSS. each (which is fair testimony to the interest aroused by both form and content), were treated by two editors only before Foerster. The excerptors also are oddly divided, Planudes drawing his citations from *Orations* 19-21, Macarius from *Orations* 21-23.

The manuscripts common to the five speeches are CAPIMV. Four others (B, L (=Laur. LVII 20), La (=Laur. XXXII 13) and Mo (=Monacensis gr. 113)) give the text of *Orations* 19-22. The majority of the others deal with *Orations* 19 and 20 only, and of the manuscripts no more than five appear as singletons. These, however, have an importance in the editorial tradition disproportionate to their number, since Bad. (=Laurentianus Conv. Suppr. Bad. 9, *cf.* Foerster, vol. ii, pp. 380-381) forms the basis for the Florentine *editio princeps* of *Oration* 19, and Par. 3014 performs the same service for Morel in his first edition of that speech. Of the variant traditions, CAP universally represent the first, V the second.

BIBLIOGRAPHY

Oration 19 was first published as part of the Florentine edition of the orations of Aelius Aristides (A.D. 1517). It was twice edited by Morel, (*a*) in A.D. 1610 as part of the separate edition of the two speeches to Theodosius upon the Statues, (*b*) in A.D. 1627 in the second volume of the works of Libanius. Savile's edition of the works of John Chrysostom (Eton, A.D. 1612) included this and *Oration* 20 as part of his eighth volume. Reiske's edition of A.D. 1791 was followed by that of de Sinner (*Novus Ss. Patrum Graecorum saec. iv Delectus*, Paris, 1842), and by a translation by I. L. Genin (*Discours*

244

de Flavien et de Libanius à l'empereur Théodose . . ., Paris, 1826). *Oration* 20 also appeared in the two editions of Morel mentioned above and in those of Savile, Reiske and Foerster, *Orations* 21 and 22 in the general editions only of Libanius' works by Morel (A.D. 1627), Reiske, and Foerster. Foerster's *Oration* 23 (in Reiske numbered *Or.* 34) was first published in Bongiovanni's Venice edition (A.D. 1754) of the sixteen unedited orations of Libanius.

Subsidiary sources are Zosimus, 4. 41 ; Sozomen, *H.E.* 7. 23 ; Theodoret, *H.E.* 5. 19-20 ; the other primary source is the collection of twenty-one *Homilies on the Statues* of John Chrysostom (Migne, *P.G.* xlix : translated into English by E. Budge, in the Library of Fathers of the Catholic Church, Oxford, 1854). Discussion upon the incident is to be found in A. Hug, *Antiochia und der Aufstand des Jahres 387*, Winterthur, 1863 ; Sievers, *Das Leben des Libanius*, pp. 172 ff. ; R. Goebel, *De Jo. Chrys. et Lib. orationibus quae sunt de seditione Antiochensium*, Göttingen, 1910 ; C. Baur, *Johannes Chrysostomus und seine Zeit*, Munich, 1929, I, pp. 212 ff. ; R. Browning, " The Riot of A.D. 387 in Antioch," *J.R.S.* xlii (1942), pp. 13 ff. ; P. Petit, *Libanius et la vie municipale*, pp. 235 ff. ; G. Downey, *History of Antioch in Syria* (1961), pp. 426 ff.

XXIII

ΚΑΤΑ ΤΩΝ ΠΕΦΕΥΓΟΤΩΝ

1. Τὰ μὲν ἀγγελλόμενα πάντες ἀκούομεν, ἅπαντα [a]
εἶναι μεστὰ νεκρῶν, τάς τε ἀρούρας τάς τε ὁδοὺς
τά τε ὄρη τούς τε λόφους τά τε σπήλαια καὶ τὰς
κορυφὰς τῶν ὀρῶν καὶ τὰ ἄλση καὶ τὰς φάραγγας,
τῶν τε νεκρῶν τοὺς μὲν ἑστιᾶν ὄρνιθας καὶ θηρία,
τοὺς δὲ ὑπὸ τοῦ ποταμοῦ πρὸς θάλατταν φέρεσθαι.
2. πρὸς τοίνυν τὰς ἀγγελίας ποτὲ μὲν πλήττομαι,
ποτὲ δὲ τοῖς παθοῦσιν ἐγκαλῶ καί φημι δίκαια
πεπονθέναι τοὺς τῆς φυγῆς ταῦτα ἀπολαύσαντας.
οὓς φαίη τις ἂν αὐτοὺς ἐπισπάσασθαι τὰ τῶν κακούργων ξίφη. ἃ γὰρ οὐκ ἂν ἐπεπόνθεσαν οἴκοι
μένοντες, τούτοις περιέπεσον πλανώμενοι θοίνην
μὲν αὐτοὺς προθέντες τοῖς πάλαι λῃστεύουσι, ποιή-|
σαντες δὲ λῃστὰς ἑτέρους τῷ ποιῆσαι πολὺ τὸ [b]
πεισόμενον. ἑκόντας οὖν ἀπολωλότας τίς ἂν ἐλεή-
σειε;

3. Φόβος γὰρ ἦν ἐπὶ τοῖς τετολμημένοις, φήσει
τις. πάνυ γε τοῖς τετολμηκόσιν αὐτοῖς, οἷς ἦν
αὐτὸ τοῦτο πρὸς φυγὴν ἀνάγκη τὸ τοιαῦτα ἑαυτοῖς
συνειδέναι. εἰ δέ τις μήτε τῶν ῥημάτων μήτε τῶν

---

[a] Or. 23 ed. F. Or. 34 ed. Re.
[b] On brigandage cf. Or. 33. 40 etc.; endemic in certain

ORATION 23 [a]

AGAINST THE REFUGEES

1. We all hear the news that everywhere is full of the bodies of the dead—fields, roads, hills, ridges, caves, hilltops, groves and gullies,—some a feast for birds and beasts, others borne by the river down to the sea. 2. At such tidings, I am at times shocked, at other times am full of reproof for the sufferers and feel that they have just got what they deserve in these consequences of their flight. You could say that they drew upon themselves the swords of the assassins. If they had stayed at home, they would not have suffered such a fate ; but now they have encountered it in their wanderings, and they have offered themselves as a feast to those who have long made a pursuit of banditry, and moreover, by multiplying the number of potential victims, they have induced others to take up banditry.[b] Who then could pity those who voluntarily made away with themselves ?

3. "Ah, yes," it will be asserted, " but there was a panic after these late outrages." Of course there was—among those who had actually committed them : consciousness of them was the very thing that compelled their flight. But for anyone who had no part

rural areas, Amm. Marc. 28. 2. 13. For brigandage after these riots *cf.* § 18 below, *Or.* 19. 58, 34. 7.

ἔργων ἐκοινώνησεν, ἐν οἷς ἀμφοτέροις ὕβρις, τί
τοῦτον ἔδει θορυβεῖσθαι καὶ τρέμειν οὐκ ὄντος τοῦ
R ii. 297 φοβοῦντος; | 4. οἱ τοίνυν καταμείναντες οὐκ ἔσθ' ὃ
πεπόνθασιν εἰπεῖν. τί οὖν μὴ τῶν μεινάντων ἦσαν
οἱ πεφευγότες, ἀλλ' ὥσπερ θεῶν του κηρύξαντος
ὡς οὐκ ἔνι σωθῆναι μένουσιν, ἀλλ' ἐν τῇ φυγῇ
μόνῃ πᾶσιν ἡ σωτηρία, οὕτω κενὰ μὲν ἐργαστήρια,
κενὰς δὲ¹ οἰκίας τε καὶ συνοικίας ἀφέντες ᾔεσαν
οὐκ εἰδότες τὸ δεξόμενον; κἀνταῦθα οἷς ἦσαν ὄνοι
καὶ ἡμίονοι καὶ κάμηλοι, σεμνοί τε καὶ τὰς ὀφρῦς
ἐν τῷ μισθοῦν ἀνέσπων, ὡς ἂν συχνοῦ τοῦ μι-
σθουμένου περιρρέοντος. 5. καὶ ἦν ἰδεῖν γυναῖκας
ἅμα τέκνοις κομιζομένας δεησομένας τῶν ἐν τοῖς
ἀγροῖς οὓς οὐκ ᾔδεσαν, μεταδοῦναι σφίσι τῆς γῆς.
οὐ γὰρ οἰκημάτων γε. πόσα γὰρ δὴ ταῦτά γε;
ἢ τίς ἄν τινας ἀγνοουμένους² ῥᾳδίως ἀνέμιξεν ἑαυτῷ; θάνατος δὲ παιδίοις τοῖς μὲν ἐκ τοῦ χαμαὶ
κεῖσθαι, τοῖς δὲ καὶ καταπεσοῦσιν ἀπὸ τῶν κομι-
ζόντων, ὁ δ' ἐκ λιμοῦ καὶ πᾶσιν. ἀλλ' ὅμως ἐπὶ |
τοσοῦτον πλῆθος ἠπείγοντο τῶν κακῶν. 6. καὶ οἱ
πρῶτοι διὰ τούτων ἀπολωλότες τοὺς ἄλλους οὐκ
ἐπαίδευον, ἀλλ' ἑτέρους ἕτεροι κατελάμβανον ἐπ'
ἴσοις, καὶ τὰ παραδείγματα σωφρονεῖν οὐκ ἔπειθεν, ἀλλὰ σκιὰς φοβούμενοι συμφορῶν εἰς τὰς με-
γίστας ἑαυτοὺς ἐνέβαλλον. οἱ δὲ ἀνοητότατοι ταῖς
γυναιξὶ παρηκολούθουν. ὧν ἀμφότερα καταγνοίη
τις ἄν, εἶτ' αὐτοὶ τὰς γυναῖκας ἐφόβουν εἴτε μάτην
φοβουμένας οὐκ ἐθάρρυνον.

---

¹ ⟨τὰ⟩ ἐργαστήρια, κενὰς δὲ ⟨τὰς⟩ Re.
² ἀγνοουμένους Re. (mss. except P): -μένας F. (P).

either in the words or in the acts which both involved such indiscipline, what need was there to fly into a panic of fear and trembling when there was no cause for alarm ? 4. Well, one cannot name any injury suffered by those who stayed here, so why did the refugees not join those who stayed ? It was as if one of the gods had told them that they had no hope of safety if they stayed, but that salvation for all lay in flight alone. So they left their workshops, their houses and tenements empty, and decamped without knowing who would welcome them. Here the owners of asses and mules and camels put on airs and supercilious frowns at their hiring, since they had customers in plenty milling around them. 5. You could see women, with children, riding to beg the country folk, whom they did not know from Adam, to let them stay on their land—not in their houses, that's certain. There weren't buildings enough, and besides, no one would readily consort with any person not of his acquaintance. So death came upon the children, some from exposure on the bare ground, some even falling from the arms of those who carried them, and death from starvation afflicted them all. But still they hurried on to meet such a multitude of evils. 6. And those who were the first to die provided no lesson for the rest. These came upon the others in the same plight, and the example did not persuade them to control themselves. Fearing imaginary disasters, they rushed headlong into the worst possible disaster. The most foolish of them accompanied their womenfolk, and deserve the most severe condemnation on both counts, whether because they put their wives into a panic, or because they gave them no encouragement to counteract their idle fears.

7. Ζήτησις γὰρ ἦν, φησί, καὶ τοὺς ἡμαρτηκότας
ἦσαν οἱ θηρεύοντες. οὐκοῦν τοὺς ἡμαρτηκότας,
ἀλλ᾽ οὐ τὰς ἁμαρτούσας. οὔτε γὰρ ἠδικήκεσαν
γυναῖκες οὔτε ἐδόκουν οὐδ᾽ εἶπέ τις οὐδὲ ἤκουσε
καὶ γυναῖκας συνεφῆφθαι τῶν ἐπὶ τῆς χαλεπῆς
ἡμέρας ἐκείνης ἢ εἰρημένων ἢ πεπραγμένων. 8. τί
R ii. 298 οὖν ἔδει καὶ γυναικῶν ἐρημοῦσθαι | τὴν πόλιν, ὧν
οὐκ ὀλίγας ἦν ὁρᾶν ἐγκύμονας; εἰ γὰρ δὴ καὶ τοὺς
ἄνδρας ἔδει τι κακὸν λαβεῖν καὶ νοῦν αὐτοῖς εἶχεν
ἡ φυγή, ταῖς γε δὴ γυναιξὶν οὐδαμόθεν ἦν λόγος.
ἀλλ᾽ ὅμως νῦν μὲν οὐκ ἐλάττους, νῦν δὲ καὶ πλείους
τῶν ἀνδρῶν ἐξῄεσαν οὐ δήπου γε μέλλουσαι παρα-
δοθήσεσθαι δικαστηρίῳ καὶ μάστιγας καὶ δεσμὸν
ὑπομενεῖν.[1] 9. τοιγαροῦν διὰ τὸν μάταιον τουτονὶ
φόβον ὃ εἶχον ἀργύριον, μικρὸν δὲ ἄρα τοῦτ᾽ ἦν,
ἀνηλωκυῖαι παιδίοις ἄρτον αἰτοῦσιν οὐχ οἷαί τε
οὖσαι δοῦναι δακρύουσαι πεινῶντα κατέθαπτον,
εἶτα ἐκ τῶν αὐτῶν ἐπαπέθνησκον. οὐδὲ γὰρ προσ-
αιτούσαις ἦν εὐπορῆσαι τροφῆς. | οὐ γὰρ ἦν παρ᾽ ὅτου
πάντων ὄντων ἐν τῷ δεῖσθαι λαβεῖν, πλὴν εἴ τις
ἀπεχώρησεν εἰς ἀγροὺς τοὺς ἑαυτῆς, τοῦτο δὲ οὐ πολύ.
10. Ταῖς μὲν δὴ γυναιξὶν οὐδεμία συγγνώμη,
ταὐτὸ δ᾽ ἂν ἰσχύοι καὶ κατὰ τῶν ἀνδρῶν τῶν ἐν
τοῖς ἐγκλήμασιν οὐκ ὄντων. οὓς γὰρ οὐκ ἤλαυνε
τὸ συνειδός, τί τούτοις ἔδει φυγῆς καὶ ταῦτα Κέλσου τοῦ πανταχοῦ δικαίου κἂν τοῖς πράγμασι τούτοις τοιούτου πεφηνότος; ὁρμήσας γὰρ ἐπὶ τὴν

---

[1] ὑπομενεῖν Cobet, F. : ὑπομένειν Re. (mss.).

---

[a] Identified by Liebeschuetz and Foerster (*Or.* 19. 36, 55)
with the *Comes* ; by Seeck (*BLZG* 107) with the *consularis*.
The unflattering description of the *Comes* in *Or.* 1. 254 f.
makes identification with the *consularis* more likely here.

7. "Well," I hear it said, "there was an inquiry, and the hunt was up for the wrongdoers." Yes, for the male wrongdoers, not for women culprits. Women had done no harm, nor were they thought to have done. No one even said, or heard it said, that our womenfolk had taken any part in anything said or done on that dreadful day. 8. So what reason was there for our city to be bereft of its womenfolk too, many of whom you could see advanced in pregnancy? If indeed the men had to experience any trouble, there was some sense in their exodus, but for the women there was not the scrap of an excuse. Yet, for all that, they started to leave, in numbers, sometimes no less, sometimes even more than those of their menfolk, however unlikely it was that they would be committed to court or would endure flogging and imprisonment. 9. Anyway, because of this idle fear, after spending what money they had, and precious little it was, they were unable to give their children bread when they asked for it, and tearfully buried their starving brats, and then themselves died, of the same cause, for even women who went a-begging couldn't get much food. Everyone was in need and, except for those who had retired to their own estates, and there were not many of these, there was no source from which they could come by it.

10. No pardon, then, can be extended to the womenfolk. The same would also hold good of those men who were not implicated in the crime. What need had they to take flight when it was not the consciousness of guilt that harried them, especially when Celsus, that paragon of justice,[a] displayed his qualities in this business too ? When he set

τιμωρίαν οὐχ ὅπως ὡς πλείστους ἀποκτείνειε τῶν
τῆδε ἀνθρώπων ἐσκόπησεν, ἀλλ᾽ ὅπως οἱ δίκην
ὄντως ὀφείλοντες οὗτοι μόνοι καὶ δῶσιν. 11. ἔδειξε
γὰρ τοῖς τῶν φυλῶν ἐπιμεληταῖς ὡς ἐν ταῖς συκο-
φαντίαις αὐτοὶ μᾶλλον ἢ οὓς ὡς ἠδικηκότας παρα-
R ii. 299 δώσουσιν ἀπολοῦνται. καί τινες τὰς τῶν¹ | αὐτῶν
πλευρὰς ἐπεῖδον τεμνομένας ἐπὶ τοιαύταις ὑπ-
οψίαις οἵ τ᾽² εἰκότως τὰς αἰτίας λαβόντες μετὰ τῆς
ἐσχάτης ἀκριβείας ἁλόντες παρεδόθησαν τῷ δημίῳ.
οὐκοῦν καὶ τῇ τοῦ δικαστοῦ δικαιοσύνῃ φόβος ἅπας
ἄδικος ἀνῄρητο.

12. Λόγος γὰρ ἐγεγόνει, φήσει τις, ἐπιχυθήσε-
σθαι στρατιώτας δόρασι καὶ ξίφεσι τὸ ἐνοικοῦν
ἀναλώσοντας. τουτὶ δὲ ἐν ἁμαρτίαις πόλεων οὐδεὶς οἶδε πώποτε γεγενημένον. καὶ γὰρ ἂν ἦν
ἄτο|πον δίκην ἐθέλειν λαμβάνειν ἐπιζήμιον τῷ λη- F 5
ψομένῳ. ζημία δὲ οὐ μικρὰ δήπου βασιλεῖ πόλις
ἀπολλυμένη. τοῦ γὰρ ἐκεῖνο θυμῷ ποιοῦντος ἦν
δήπου τὸ μηδὲ τῶν ἀψύχων φείδεσθαι. τίς οὖν
βασιλεὺς τοιαύτην ἂν ἔλαβε παρὰ πόλεως δίκην, ἢ
τὴν ἀρχὴν ἔμελλεν αὐτῷ ποιήσειν ἐλάττονα; 13.
καίτοι καὶ εἴ τι τοιοῦτον ὑπ᾽ ἄλλων ἐπέπρακτο,
τοῦτόν γε οὐκ ἐχρῆν ἀκολουθήσειν οἴεσθαι τὸν τῷ
R ii. 300 μὴ κολάζειν μᾶλλον | ἢ τῷ κολάζειν ἡδόμενον.
μάρτυς δὲ ὁ τῆς βασιλείας χρόνος πολλὴν αὐτῷ
συνειδὼς πολλαχοῦ τὴν συγγνώμην. ὅς γε καὶ

¹ τὰς τῶν F.: τὰς Re. (MV, A marg., correction in C):
τῶν API, C before correction.
² οἵ τ᾽ F. (mss. except M): οἱ δ᾽ Re. (M).

ᵃ Cf. Or. 24. 26 (Vol. I, p. 508 n.).   Or. 33. 36.
ᵇ In A.D. 390, however, this did happen in Thessalonika.

himself to the matter of punishment, he was at pains not to execute all the males here that he could, but to inflict punishment only on those deserving of it. 11. He made it clear to the watch committee [a] that, if there were any trumped-up charges, they, rather than the persons they committed as malefactors, would be executed. In fact, some beheld the flanks of their own people lacerated for such suspicions, and those who were involved by circumstantial evidence were brought to justice with most scrupulous care, and handed over to the executioner. Thus, by reason of the uprightness of the judge, all unjustified fears had been removed.

12. "Ah, yes," it will be said, "but the story had gone about that the military would be let loose on us in a flood, to destroy the inhabitants with spear and sword." But nobody knows of this ever having happened when cities have put themselves in the wrong.[b] Indeed it would be absurd to want to inflict a punishment which would be detrimental to the exactor of it, and the destruction of a city is obviously no small loss to an emperor : for surely a refusal to spare even inanimate objects is in keeping with the angry execution of this act. So what emperor would ever have punished a city in such a way as to diminish his own realm ? 13. Yet even if any such action by others formed a precedent, this emperor, at least, should not be thought of as ready to follow it, since his delight is to forgo rather than to inflict punishment.[c] The proof of this is to be found in the period of his reign, and in it the widespread awareness of pardon in plenty. Why, he has even saved those

[c] The customary eulogy of Theodosius' *philanthropia, cf. Or.* 20. 15 etc.

τοὺς τῆς βασιλείας αὐτῆς ἐπιτεθυμηκότας ὠθου-
μένους τῇ ψήφῳ πρὸς θάνατον ἐρρύσατό τε καὶ ζῆν
ἀφῆκεν. οὕτως οὐδ' ὁστισοῦν τοῦτ' ἔδεισεν ὀρθῶς
φαίνεται δείσας. 14. οὐ τοίνυν οὐδ' ὅστις ἐξουσίαν ἔδεισεν εἰς ἁρπαγὴν τῶν ἐν τῇ πόλει χρημάτων, ὃ πεποιήκασιν ἤδη τινὲς βασιλεῖς ἐφέντες[1]
στρατιώταις ἁρπάζειν προειπόντες ἐν ὅσῳ δεῖ τοῦτο
μέρει τῆς ἡμέρας γενέσθαι, οὐδ' οὗτοί μοι κακῶς
δεῖσαι δοκοῦσιν. ἐν γὰρ ἀπουσίαις βασιλέων ἥκιστα τὸ τοιοῦτον γίγνεσθαι, παρὼν δὲ εἰ βουληθείη
καὶ ταύτῃ δίκην λαβεῖν, οὐ κωλύειν φασὶ τὸν νόμον.
15. καὶ τοῦτο ἦν ἀκούειν παρὰ τῶν ἀκριβῶς τὸ
πρᾶγμα ἐπισταμένων ἀνδρῶν πολλὰ δή[2] βασιλεῦσιν
ἐστρατηγηκότων. παρ' | ὧν ἡμεῖς μαθόντες ἐβοῶ- F 5
μεν ἐπερχόμενοι τὴν πόλιν· τί τετάραχθε; τί
πεφόβησθε; τί πλάττετε τὰ δοκοῦντα δείματα;
ἀλλ' ἐδοκοῦμεν φλυαρεῖν. οἱ δὲ ἀπῄεσαν καὶ ταῦτα
τοὺς ταῦτα λέγοντας ὁρῶντες οὐκ ἀπιόντας. τοῦτο
γὰρ δή, τοῦτο μέγιστον εἰς πίστιν, ἔργα λόγοις
ἀκολουθοῦντα καὶ μονὴ βεβαιοῦσα ῥήματα. 16. εἰ
μὲν γὰρ θαρρεῖν ἑτέροις παρακελευόμενος ἃ τῶν
φοβουμένων ἦν ἐποίουν καὶ μετανιστάμην, εἰκότως
ἂν ἡγοῦντο πιστοτέραν συμβουλὴν τὴν ἀπὸ τῶν
πραγμάτων· εἰ δ' οὐδὲν τῶν πρὸ τῆς ταραχῆς ἐν
οὐδενὶ τῶν ἐμῶν ἐκίνουν, ἠδίκουν οἱ μὴ μιμού-
μενοι, πλὴν εἰ τοῦτο λέγοιεν ὡς ἐθανάτων καὶ τῆς

[1] ἐφέντες Cobet, F. (V): ἀφέντες Re. (other mss.).
[2] δὴ F. (V): δὲ Re. (other mss.).

who, after aspiring to the throne itself, were being
hustled out to the death to which they had been
sentenced, and let them live. So, obviously, anyone
who feared this had no real grounds for his fear.
14. Nor yet, I feel, was there any justification for
the fears of all who were afraid that he would allow
free rein for plundering property in the city, though
some emperors have acted so in days gone by, giving
their soldiers licence to plunder but stipulating the
precise period of the day for this to be done. Such
a course, I am told, is most unlikely to be taken in
the emperor's absence, though, if he is present in
person and decides to impose punishment in this
way, there is no law to prevent it. 15. This you
could have heard from men who had held many high
imperial commands and had accurate knowledge of
the matter. I got this information from them and
went all around the city protesting, " Why are you
in such confusion and alarm ? Why are you invent-
ing unreal fears ? ", but I was held to be talking
nonsense. The exodus continued, even though they
saw that I, who told them this, was not going to
leave, for this, this was indeed the greatest assurance
of reliability, that what I did was in line with what
I said and that my remaining here confirmed my
statements. 16. If I, while encouraging others to
be of good cheer, behaved like one in a panic and
decamped, they would naturally regard the lesson
to be learnt from the circumstances to be more
reliable. If, however, in all that I did I did not
deviate from the way I conducted myself previous
to the riots, then anyone who did not follow my
example behaved improperly, unless he would assert
that I was bent upon dying and was eager for death

ἀπὸ τῶν ξιφῶν ἐπεθύμουν τελευτῆς. ἀλλ᾽ οὐδεὶς
R ii. 301 οὕτως | ἄθλιος οὐδ᾽ εἰ σφόδρα δυσχεραίνοι τὸ γῆρας.
17. Πονηρᾶς τοίνυν οὔσης τῆς τῶν πολλῶν ἐξ-
όδου μείζων ἐν τοῖς ὑπὲρ τοὺς πολλοὺς ἡ κατηγορία, οἳ πόλεων ἄρξαντες καὶ ἔθνη διῳκηκότες
καὶ τιμῶν τετυχηκότες καὶ δικαίως ἂν ἀμειβό-
μενοι τήν τε πόλιν ἐν ᾗ κατοικοῦσι καὶ τὴν βασιλείαν δι᾽ ἣν αὐτοῖς καὶ δόξα καὶ γάμοι καὶ χρήματα, ταῦτα πάντα ἀτιμάσαντες ἀπώλλυσαν τὸ
καθ᾽ αὑτοὺς τῷ βασιλεῖ τὴν πόλιν. 18. εἰ γὰρ δὴ
τῆς ὀλιγανθρωπίας τῆς ἐν αὐτῇ καταφρονήσαντες
οἱ κατὰ τὴν χώραν λῃσταὶ διεσπαρμένοι στῖφος ἐν
ποιήσαντες ἑαυτοὺς εἰσπεσόντες ἐληίζοντο τὸ ἄστυ,
τὰ μικρὰ τὰ καταλελειμμένα, καὶ τελευτῶν|τες F 5
ἐνεπίμπρασαν ἄνθρωποι τῷ κακῶς ποιεῖν χαίροντες
καὶ πολὺν ἐν τούτῳ βεβιωκότες χρόνον, ποῦ ποτ᾽
ἂν ἦν ἡ πόλις, ἧς ἔχων πολλὴν πρόνοιαν ὁ βασιλεὺς
ὁρᾶται; ἀλλ᾽ ὅμως οἱ σεμνοὶ καὶ τῇ τῶν ἄλλων
πενίᾳ πεπλουτηκότες καὶ δεινὸν εἰ μὴ τὰ τῶν
θεῶν ἕξουσιν ἡγούμενοι, τὰ μὲν ἐν νυξί, τὰ δὲ πάντων ὁρώντων μεθίστασαν οὕτω δή τι πολὺν ἄρ-
γυρον, ὡς συχνῶν τε δεῖν ὀχημάτων ἑκάστῳ καὶ
πολλῶν ὀρέων καθ᾽ ἕκαστον, οὓς ἠνάγκαζε τὰ ἑλ-
κόμενα στένειν. 19. τίνος οὖν τούτους ἀξίους εἶναι
φήσαι τις ἄν, οἳ προδόντες τὴν πόλιν καὶ τὸ σφῶν
αὐτῶν μόνον ἰδόντες τὸν πλοῦτον ἑτέρωσε κατα-
R ii. 302 θέμενοι | γυμνοὶ πρὸς τὸν ἔξω δρόμον ἦσαν ἕτοιμοι;
καίτοι χρῆν αὐτοὺς καὶ τοὺς ἐν πενίᾳ κωλύειν καὶ
κατέχειν, τὰ μὲν πειθοῖ, τὰ δὲ καὶ ἀπειλαῖς. οἱ δ᾽

---

a The *honorati* are again the chief target for criticism, the
worst of them being, *ex hypothesi*, the Christians (§ 18).

by the sword. Yet nobody is as wretched as all that, however much he might resent his old age.

17. Well, if the departure of the commons was disgraceful, the accusation to be levelled at the classes elevated above the commons is more serious still. These have been magistrates of cities, governors of provinces and have won distinction,[a] and they might properly be grateful to the city in which they live and to the empire through which they have attained fame, marriages and wealth. Yet they have dishonoured all this and have done their level best to ruin the city for the emperor. 18. Then, if the brigands scattered about the countryside had gathered into one body and, despising the small numbers left in the city, had plundered it, if these men, who delight in evil doing and have spent a long time engaged upon it, had finally set fire to it and its paltry remnants, what on earth would have been the position of our state, for which the emperor is seen to show so much consideration? But for all that, this high and mighty crew, who have grown rich on the poverty of the rest and who think it a scandal if they do not get their hands on the property of the gods, began to remove, some by night, some in full view of everyone, such quantities of silver that each one required a train of carts and a string of mules which groaned perforce under their burdens. 19. What then would you say these people deserve? They betrayed the city; they looked solely to their own interests; they deposited their wealth elsewhere, and then, unencumbered, were ready for the hurried exodus. Yet they are the people who should, by cajolery or even by threats, have prevented and restrained the poor. But they commended such con-

ἐπῄνουν τε τοὺς ἐκεῖνο ποιοῦντας καὶ ἀνθρώπους
ἔλεγον εἶναι σῴζεσθαι βουλομένους, ὥσπερ ὧν εὖ
ἔπραξαν ἐν τῇ πόλει δίκης παρὰ τῆς πόλεως αὐτοῖς
ὀφειλομένης. οἳ τοῦθ' ἓν μόνον εὖ πεποιήκασιν, ὅτι
τὸν ἄλλον χρόνον ἀρνούμενοι μὴ πλουτεῖν νῦν αὐτοὺς
ἐξήλεγξαν ὡς πλεῖστα κεκτημένοι πόνῳ πολλῷ καὶ
πραγματείᾳ μεταθέντες ἄλλοσε τὰ συνειλεγμένα.

20. Περὶ δὲ τῶν νέων τί φήσομεν ἢ τῶν τούτων γονέων; τί δ' ἕτερον ἢ ὡς οἱ μὲν ἥρπασαν τὸν
καιρὸν | εἰς ἀργίαν, γονεῖς δὲ ταῖς τούτων ἐπιστο- F 5
λαῖς ἐξαπατηθέντες καλεῖν ταῖς παρ' αὐτῶν ἀν-
επείσθησαν τοὺς νέους. οἱ δ' οὐ τοσοῦτο μόνον
ἠδίκουν, ἀλλ' εἰσὶν οἳ γράμμα οὐδὲν οὔτε πέμψαν-
τες οὔτε λαβόντες αὐτοὺς τοῦ δρᾶν ὃ βούλοιντο
καταστήσαντες κυρίους δήσαντες τὰς διφθέρας
ἀναβάντες ἐφ' ἵππους οἱ μὲν ἀγροὺς σφῶν αὐτῶν
ἐνέπλησαν ἀλλοτρίους, οἱ δὲ πατρῴους, οἱ δὲ καὶ
τροφοῖς καὶ τροφεῦσιν ἧκον εἰς χεῖρας καὶ μητρὸς
ἕτερος καὶ πατρὸς ἄλλος, τρέμοντες δὴ καὶ τοὺς
ὀδόντας κροτοῦντες καὶ μεταστρεφόμενοι, καθάπερ
διωκόμενοι διώκοντος μὲν οὐδενὸς οὐδὲ σπεύδοντος
ἑλεῖν, αὐτοὶ δὲ τῆς περὶ λόγους σπουδῆς διώκοντες
τὴν ἀπαλλαγήν. καὶ ὁ χρόνος τοῖς ἀθλίοις ἐν ἐδω-
δῇ καὶ οἴνῳ καὶ ὕβρει καὶ ὕπνῳ πᾶς οὗτος ἀνα-
λοῦτο, προσθείην δ' ἂν καὶ εὐχαῖς,[1] ἐν αἷς ᾔτουν
ἐκταθῆναι τὴν τῆς ῥᾳθυμίας ἀφορμὴν ἐπὶ μήκιστον
χρόνον. ἐφ' ᾧ δ' ἄν τις μάλιστα ἀγανακτήσειεν,

---

[1] ἐν before εὐχαῖς Re. (M) : bracketed F.

[a] This desertion by his students forms the real ground of
complaint in this speech. The numbers attending his school
during the crisis and after fell to twelve at first, and later to
seven ; Or. 34. 14.

duct : they said that it was only human to wish for safety, as though the city owes them liability for the prosperity they enjoyed in it. This is the only benefit they have conferred on us, that, for all their previous protestations that they were not wealthy, they have now proved themselves to be possessors of vast fortunes by the considerable toil and trouble they have in depositing their hoards elsewhere.

20. And what shall I say of the students or their parents ? [a] What else than that the students seized upon the event as an excuse for idleness and the parents, hoodwinked by their letters, were induced to call their sons home by letters of their own ? And that was not the sum of their misconduct : there are some who, without having sent or received a single line, took it upon themselves to behave as they liked. They tied up their books,[b] mounted their horses, and crammed themselves into estates belonging, in some cases, to other persons, in others, to their own families. Others went into the keeping of foster mothers and fathers either of their mother or their father, all of a tremble, with teeth chattering and turning to look behind them, as though they were being chased, though there was no one chasing them nor yet eager to seize them. They themselves were chasing a riddance to the pursuit of oratory, and all this time was spent by the wretches in dining and wining, in misbehaving and sleeping, and, I would go as far as to say, in praying too, when they prayed that this excuse for idleness should be stretched to the furthest limit possible. And this is

---

[b] διφθέρα for Libanius is usually the covering of the papyrus book-roll (πήρα).

LIBANIUS

R ii. 303 οὐδὲ γὰρ αὐτὸ τοῦτο πρὸς ἡμᾶς | εἰπόντες ὡς ἀπιέναι καιρός, ἀπῆλθον, ἀλλ᾽ ἔδοξεν, ἐσίγησαν, ἔπραξαν. ὁ δ᾽ ἐξιὼν ἤδη τὸν διαβουλευόμενον ἐνῆγε τραγῳδίας καὶ Ἰλιάδα κακῶν ἐπισείων ταῖς μελλήσεσι.

21. Καίτοι τίς οὐκ ἂν εἰκότως μισήσειε τούτους τοὺς μισοῦντας κτῆμα οὕτω καλόν, τοὺς λόγους, οὓς | ἔδωκε μὲν Ἑρμῆς, ἠγάπησε δὲ τῶν Ἀθηναίων ἡ πόλις καὶ θρέψασα καὶ αὐξήσασα καὶ κοσμήσασα πανταχῇ[1] διέπεμψεν. οὗτοι συγκρύπτουσι μὲν δυσγένειαν, κρύπτουσι δὲ ἀμορφίαν, πλοῦτον δὲ φυλάττουσι, λύουσι δὲ πενίαν, ἀρκοῦσι δὲ πόλεσιν εἰς σωτηρίαν πάντων ὄντες ὅπλων ἐν πολέμοις χρησιμώτεροι καὶ πάσης πολυχειρίας ἐν μάχαις ἰσχυρότεροι.[2] οἱ τούτους ἔχοντες πρὸς τὰ μαντεῖα πολλάκις ἁμιλλῶνται τῷ τὸ μέλλον δύνασθαι προορᾶν· ὃ γὰρ ἐκείνοις τὰ πνεύματα, τοῦτο τούτοις ἡ γνώμη. μόνους δὲ τοὺς παιδείᾳ διενεγκόντας φαίη τις ἂν καὶ ἀθανάτους εἶναι φύσει μὲν τελευτῶντας, δόξῃ δὲ ζῶντας.

22. Ἀλλ᾽ ὅμως οἵδε οἱ νέοι πεφεύγασι μὲν τὴν τοσοῦτα ἀγαθὰ προξενοῦσαν, ἐπὶ δὲ τὴν μυρίων μητέρα κακῶν, νωθείαν καὶ μαλακίαν, κεχωρήκασιν ἕρμαιον αὐτῶν τὴν τῆς πόλεως ἀτυχίαν ἡγησάμενοι, δεδιότες μὲν οὐδέν, προσποιούμενοι δὲ πολλά. τίς γὰρ ἧκεν ἂν ἐπ᾽ αὐτοὺς ἄρχων, τίς
R ii. 304 ὑπηρέτης, | τίς γείτων, τίς πολίτης, τίς ξένος πόρρω μὲν ὄντας τῶν βλασφημιῶν, πόρρω δὲ τῶν ἐπ᾽

[1] πανταχῇ F. (CIMV) : πανταχοῖ Re. (AP).
[2] πολέμοις ἰσχυρότεροι . . . μάχαις χρησιμώτεροι Re. (M).

---

[a] Borrowed from Demosth. *Fals. Leg.* 148 : *cf. Or.* 59. 136, 61. 19.

the chief reason to be annoyed with them, for they left without breathing a word to me on this very matter, that it was time to leave ; they made up their minds, kept mum and acted. And those who were on their way out egged on the waverers by parading before them dismal dramas and chronicles of woe *a* as the consequences of their dilly-dallying.

21. Yet who would not be justified in loathing those who loathe so noble an acquisition as eloquence, which is the gift of Hermes and which the Athenian state lovingly received, and nurturing, increasing and adorning it, has despatched over the whole world ? *b* Eloquence helps to conceal lowly origin : it hides ugliness, protects wealth, relieves penury and suffices cities for their protection, since in war it is more useful than any equipment and in battle is more potent than any superiority of numbers. The possessors of it often vie with the oracles in their ability to foresee the future. What inspiration is to the prophet, their intellect is to them. Only those who excel in education can be described as immortal too, for though they die in the course of nature, they live on in their fame.

22. Despite all that, these students have fled the art that confers such great blessings. They have betaken themselves to the mother of countless evils, sloth and idleness, regarding our city's evil plight as a godsend for themselves, fearing nothing though pretending to be much afraid. What governor, which of his subordinates, would have attacked them, or what neighbour, what citizen, what stranger ? They steered clear of the insults and of their conse-

b Hermes, god of eloquence : *cf. Or.* 24. 37 ; also 18. 75 (Vol. I, p. 326 n.), of which this passage is a reminiscence.

ἐκείναις; καὶ γὰρ ὅτε ταῦτα ἐτολμᾶτο καὶ ἦν ἔτι
ἐν προοιμίοις ἡ μανία, οἱ μὲν ἀπῆλθον οἴκαδε
θέοντες, οἱ δ᾽ ἦσαν οὗπερ ἐγώ, τοῖς τῶν ἑωρα-
κότων λόγοις, οὐ τοῖς αὑτῶν ὀφθαλμοῖς μανθάνοντες τὰ τοῦ τότε χειμῶνος. πῶς οὖν ἐσυκοφαν-
τοῦντο ἄν; 23. τῆς δ᾽ ἐκείνων κακίας καὶ τόδε |
τεκμήριον. εἰσὶ μὲν γὰρ οὓς ὁ περὶ τοὺς λόγους
ἔρως ἔπεισε μένειν ὀλίγους δή τινας κομιδῇ. τούτων δὲ οὐδεὶς οὔτε ἐφήψατο οὔτε ἐμέλλησεν οὔτε
αὐτῶν οὔτε παιδαγωγῶν οὔτ᾽ οἰκετῶν. ἐπὶ τῆς
αὐτῆς τοίνυν ἦσαν ἂν ἀδείας οἱ μὴ μείναντες ἧσπερ
οἱ μεμενηκότες ταὐτοῦ δικαίου κἀκείνοις καὶ τούτοις ὑπάρχοντος, τοῦ μηδὲ κατὰ μικρὸν μετεσχηκέναι τῶν ὕβρεων.

24. Ἔτι τοίνυν εἰ μὲν ἐμίσουν ἐμὲ διὰ τὰς ἐπὶ
τοὺς πόνους παρακλήσεις, τίς αὐτῶν ἀδικώτερος;
καὶ γὰρ ἀθλητὴς ἄδικος, ὅστις οὕτως ἔχει[1] πρὸς
τὸν γυμναστὴν τὸν ὅτι δεῖ πάντα πόνον ἀνέχεσθαι
λέγοντα. εἰ δ᾽ ἐφίλουν τε καὶ ζῆν ἐβούλοντό με καὶ
τὸ μένειν οὐκ ἀσφαλὲς ἡγοῦντο, τί μὴ προσιόντες
ἐδέοντό μου σῴζειν αὑτοῖς ἐμαυτόν; πάντως δὲ
οὐδὲν καινὸν νέον γέροντος ἰδεῖν που τὸ συμφέρον
ἄμεινον. δόξαν δ᾽ ἂν αὐτοῖς ἤνεγκε καὶ τὸ μέμψασθαι καὶ τὸ καταβοῆσαι καὶ τὸ πάντα καὶ εἰπεῖν
καὶ ποιῆσαι πειρωμένοις ἐξάγειν, νῦν δὲ διὰ σιωπῆς
ἐξεπήδησαν τήμερον συγγενόμενοι, νυκτὸς δὲ ἀπο-
R ii. 305 δράντες, | θάνατόν μου κατεψηφισμένοι καὶ οὐ δε-
δοικότες μὴ αὖθις ἀλλήλους ἴδωμεν.

---

[1] ἔχει F. (MV) : ἔχοι Re. (CAPI).

quences. In fact, when this outrage occurred and the frenzy was still in its initial stages, some left hot-foot for home, while others stayed with me, and learned of the disaster that then occurred from the accounts of eye-witnesses, not by their own eyes.[a] How then could a charge be trumped up against them? 23. And of their wickedness there is also this as testimony. Some their love of eloquence induced to stay—precious few, admittedly. No one laid a hand on them, or had any intention of doing so, either on their persons, or their attendants or slaves. Any who did not stay would, then, have enjoyed the same immunity as those who did, for the same justification applied to both in that they had not taken the slightest part in the outrages.

24. Moreover, if they hated me because of my exhortations to study, who is more wicked than they? Indeed an athlete is wicked in adopting this attitude towards the trainer who tells him that he must sustain every effort. If they loved me and wanted me to live and thought it was dangerous to stay, why did they not approach me and beg me to save myself for them? In any case, it is nothing out of the ordinary for a youth to see the advantageous course better than an old man. It would have redounded to their credit for them to have reproached me, cried me down, and to have left nothing unsaid or undone in their efforts to get me away. As it was, they scuttled away in silence, attending my lectures during the day and decamping at night, having condemned me to death and with no fear of us seeing one another again.

[a] As Libanius himself had learned of the riots in A.D. 354, *Or.* 1. 103.

LIBANIUS

25. Γνοίη δ' ἄν τις κἀκεῖθεν τουτουσί· τῆς γὰρ τοῦ βασιλέως ὀργῆς τῇ βουλῇ μὲν ἐγκαλούσης καί τισι τῶν συνδίκων, τῶν δ' ὑπὲρ παιδείας ἐνταυθοῖ | διατριβόντων οὐδαμοῦ μεμνημένης καὶ τούτων τῶν γραμμάτων ἐκκειμένων καὶ τοῦ περὶ αὐτῶν λόγου πανταχοῦ πεφοιτηκότος, ὥστ' εἶναι καὶ τοῖς πεφευγόσιν εἰδέναι, οὐδεὶς τὸ τῶν χαιρόντων ἐποίησεν οὐδὲ ἀνέπνευσεν οὐδὲ προσεκύνησε τὴν Τύχην οὐδ' ἔδραμεν ἐπὶ τὴν ὧν ἀπεστέρητο μετουσίαν. 26. καὶ τί θαυμαστόν; οὐδὲ γὰρ μετὰ δικαστήρια καὶ κρίσιν καὶ δεσμὸν ἀποκρίνοντα τοὺς ἄλλους καὶ δημηγορίαν τοῦ στρατηγοῦ τε καὶ δικαστοῦ καὶ ὅρκους ἐξαιροῦντας τὸν φόβον οὐδ' οὕτως ἐπὶ τοὺς λόγους ἐπανῆκον οὐδ' ἡδέως εἶδον τοὺς τῶν βελτιόνων ἀγγέλους, ἀλλ' οἱ ταχεῖς ἐνθένδε ἀπελθεῖν βραδεῖς εἰς τὰ δεύτερα κατεχόμενοι τῇ τῆς ἀργίας ἡδονῇ μᾶλλον ἢ ζήλῳ τῳ[1] μεμφόμενοι τῷ τῶν παρὰ τοῦ βασιλέως ἀπεσταλμένων τάχει λόγων οὐκ ἀποροῦντες ἀναισχύντων, ὅτι ἀλλὰ περιῄρηται τὸ τῆς πόλεως ἀξίωμα καὶ μετείληφε σχῆμα φρουρίου καὶ οὔθ' ὁ ἱππόδρομος οὔτε τὸ R ii. 306 θέατρον ἔχει τὰ αὑτοῦ. 27. καὶ τί | τοῦτο, ὦ Μουσῶν ὑμεῖς ἐχθροί; πολὺ γὰρ δὴ βελτίων ἡ πόλις εἰς λόγους ἐν οἷς δίκην ἔδωκε γεγένηται, καὶ τὰ μὲν βλαβερὰ περιῄρηται, τῶν δ' ὄντων ἀγαθῶν οὐδὲν τῇ μεταβολῇ τῆς προσηγορίας βέβλαπται.

[1] τῳ Re., F. : τῷ CAPIV : τῶν M.

---

[a] Cf. Or. 22 passim.
[b] Cf. Or. 20. 6. The penalties immediately imposed on Antioch included the loss of metropolitan status and a ban on civic amenities. These had not been restored at the time of composition of this oration—hence the importance of this
264

25. You might recognize these fellows for what they are from this consideration too. The emperor in his wrath accused the city council and some of the lawyers, but never made any mention of those who were resident here to be educated. This imperial despatch was published and the talk of it had been noised abroad everywhere, so that even the evacuees knew about it, but none of them behaved as though he was glad, drew a breath of relief, thanked his lucky stars or hurried back to enjoy the pursuits of which he had been deprived. 26. Nor is there anything surprising in this ! Even after the trials and the verdict and the arrests, which sorted the sheep from the goats, after the public address of Ellebichus, the military commander and investigator,[a] and the oaths that removed all cause for alarm,—not even then did they return to their studies or look with favour on the bearers of good tidings. Those who were so quick to leave here were slow in what followed, for they were gripped by the pleasures of idleness rather than by any feeling of enthusiasm. They resented the speed of the emperor's emissaries, and were at no loss for arguments of barefaced impudence. " The reputation of the city is ruined," they said. " It has taken on the appearance of a garrison. Neither the race-course nor the theatre is as it should be." 27. And what does this matter, you enemies of the Muses ? The city has indeed been much improved, as regards eloquence, by the punishment she has undergone ; and the harmful elements have been removed. None of its true blessings has suffered harm by its change of title.[b]

passage for the sequence of the orations. The remaining speeches were obviously written after the remission of the ban.

LIBANIUS

αὐτός γέ τοι χείρων οὐδὲν ἐντεῦθεν εἰς τοὺς | εἰω- Ι
θότας γέγονα πόνους. οὐδ᾽ ὅσοι τῶν νέων ἔμειναν,
[οὐκ]¹ ᾐτιάσαντο τὴν μονήν, οὓς οὐδὲν τὸ μὴ λοῦσθαι κωλύει καρποῦσθαι τὰ βιβλία.

28. Οἶμαι δέ, καὶ λούσονται κἂν τοῖς ἔμπροσθεν
ἅπασιν αὖθις ὄψονται τὴν πόλιν βελτίους ὑμῶν
αὐτῷ τούτῳ φανέντες τῷ καὶ τὰ δυσκολώτερα τῇ
πόλει συνδιενεγκεῖν. ὑμεῖς δὲ αἰσχύνεσθε μὲν τοὔ-
δαφος, αἰσχύνεσθε δὲ τὰς πύλας, αἰσχύνεσθε δὲ
τὸ τῶν λόγων χωρίον, αἰσχύνεσθε δὲ καὶ² ἡμᾶς,
εἰ μὴ καὶ τοῦτο ὑμῖν ἀπόλωλεν.

¹ [οὐκ] bracketed F., conj. Sintenis.
² [καὶ] bracketed F. (deleted in A).

Chrysostom (*Hom.* 17, *P.G.* xlix. 176) expresses sentiments similar to those of Libanius here.
 ᵃ Since settling in Antioch in A.D. 354, he had taught in a

266

I personally have experienced no ill-effects as regards my usual task in consequence of it, nor yet have those of the students who stayed any cause to blame themselves for staying : their lack of bathing facilities doesn't stop them from reaping the fruits of their books.

28. My belief is that they will use the baths again, and will see the city once more in all its former state, and they will have proved themselves better than you by the very fact that they have shared in enduring the city's inconveniences. But you, you will feel shame at the sight of the city, its gates, its place of learning,[a] and of me also, unless you are even thus far lost to any sense of shame.

room attached to the City Hall. The City Hall itself was used by the commissioners at this time as a place of confinement for the arrested decurions, which may well have been a deterrent to his scholars.

ΠΡΟΣ ΘΕΟΔΟΣΙΟΝ ΤΟΝ
ΒΑΣΙΛΕΑ ΠΕΡΙ ΤΗΣ ΣΤΑΣΕΩΣ

R 626   1. Ἠτύχηκε μὲν ἡμῖν ἡ πόλις, ὦ βασιλεῦ, τοι- F ii
ούτων ἐν αὐτῇ πρὸς τὸν ἐραστὴν τὸν ἑαυτῆς γεγενημένων, αἰσχύνεται δὲ ὡς ἠδικηκυῖα καὶ τούτῳ
κεκώλυται πέμψαι πρὸς σὲ πρεσβείαν τὴν ὑπὲρ
τῶν συμβάντων καὶ λόγῳ χρησομένην καὶ ἔργῳ
δεησομένην.   2. ἐγὼ | δὲ ἐμαυτὸν χειροτονήσας F 3
ἥκω μέγα μὲν ποιούμενος εἰ ὁπόσον εὔχομαι δυ-
νηθείην, οὐ μικρὸν δὲ καὶ αὐτὸν τὸν ὑπὲρ τῆς οἰ-
R 627 κείας πόνον, κἂν ἀτυχῆσαι | τοῦ τέλους γένηται.
κριθήσεσθαι γὰρ ἡγοῦμαι τῇ γνώμῃ μᾶλλον ἢ τοῖς
οὐχ ὑπάρξασι τοῦ δοῦναι κυρίοις.   3. τὸ μὲν οὖν
γῆρας οἴκοι μοι παρῄνει καθῆσθαι καὶ πολλοὶ τῶν
τε οἰκείων καὶ τῶν ἐπιτηδείων, ὧν ἦν ἀκούειν ὡς
οὐκ ἀσφαλὲς εἴη λέγειν ὑπὲρ τοιούτων πρὸς ὠργι-
σμένον βασιλέα, ἐγὼ δὲ τὸ μὲν μηδὲν ἐκ τῶν λεγομένων ἔσεσθαί μοι δυσχερὲς ἀπὸ τῆς σῆς φύσεως
εἶχον καὶ τρόπου, γῆρας δὲ θεῶν βουλομένων καὶ
πρὸς δὶς τοσαύτης ὁδοῦ μῆκος ἀρκέσειν ἐπεπεί-
σμην, καὶ ὡς ὀρθῶς, αὐτὸ τὸ πρᾶγμα δηλοῖ.   4. ὁ
γὰρ οὐκ ἂν τὸν πρῶτον σταθμὸν ἐλπισθεὶς δια-
268

ORATION 19

TO THE EMPEROR THEODOSIUS, ABOUT THE RIOTS

1. Our city, Sire, has met with misfortune, in that it has been the scene of such behaviour towards its ardent admirer, and is ashamed at its misconduct and thus has been prevented from sending you an embassy to present our explanation of what occurred, and to make our real pleas about it. 2. I have come self-elected, and though I regard it of great consequence to be able to achieve all I could wish, my actual efforts for my native city are, I feel, of no little moment, even though I should not succeed in attaining my end. I shall be judged, I believe, by my intention rather than by the lack of the means to grant me its fulfilment. 3. So, though my advanced years bid me stay at home, as do many of my friends and relations, who could be heard telling me that it was not safe to plead such a case before an emperor in his wrath, I have deduced from your character and conduct that there will be no untoward consequences for me from my remarks. I was convinced that, if the gods so will, my old age would suffice for a journey even twice as long—and how correctly, the event itself reveals. 4. For I, who by no stretch of imagination could have been expected

269

βῆναι διά τε πολλῶν οὕτως ἀφῖγμαι καὶ διέβην
Βόσπορον ἔν τε τοῖς βασιλείοις εἰμὶ καὶ τοῖς περὶ
τῆς πόλεως λόγοις. ὧν οὖν συλλαμβανόντων ἐνή-
νοχα τὴν ὁδὸν καὶ οὐκ ἀπεῖπον, τούτους καὶ πρὸς
τὴν ὅλην σπουδὴν ἕξειν ἡγοῦμαι συμμάχους. |

5. Ἤδη μὲν οὖν τινος ἤκουσα ζηλοῦντος τὴν F 3
ἡμετέραν πόλιν ὑδάτων τε εἵνεκα καὶ πνευμάτων
καὶ μεγέθους καὶ κάλλους ⟨καὶ⟩[1] τῶν ἐνοικούντων
R 628 καὶ τοῦ λόγους ἐν αὐτῇ καὶ δίδοσθαι καὶ | λαμ-
βάνεσθαι καὶ εἶναι τούς τε παιδεύεσθαι βουλομένους
τούς τε παιδεύειν δυναμένους. 6. ἐγὼ δὲ οὐκ εἰς
εὐδαίμονας αὐτὴν μᾶλλον ἂν θείην ἢ τοὐναντίον
λογιζόμενος σεισμούς τε καὶ τὰ ἀπ' αὐτῶν πτώ-
ματα καὶ Περσῶν ἐπιστρατείας καὶ πορθήσεις καὶ
κατασκαφὰς καὶ πῦρ καὶ τά, ὡς ἐγὼ φαίην ἄν,
δυστυχίας μείζονος,[2] θυμόν τε κατ' ἀρχόντων ἄδικον καὶ ἐν ἕλξεσι ταῖς ἀπὸ τῶν ποδῶν θανάτους,
ἃ παρ' ἄλλων ἐν ὀνείδεσιν ἀκηκόαμεν πολλάκις·
ἃ γὰρ ἠτύχηκε, καὶ ἐγκέκληται. 7. καίτοι ποῦ
δίκαιον τοῦτό γε; τοῦ αὐτοῦ δὴ καὶ τὸ νῦν εἶναι
χρὴ νομίζειν δαίμονος προσλαβόντος καὶ τὴν ὑβρι-
σμένην Νέμεσιν. ἡ δ' ὕβρις μηκέτ' εἶναι τὸ ἕδος.

---

[1] ⟨καὶ⟩ P corrected, F.
[2] μείζονος mss. except Bad., F. : ἁπάσης μείζονα Bad., Re.

---

[a] This is the fiction which deceived Zosimus (4. 41) into
stating that Libanius delivered this oration before the emperor and Senate of Constantinople, and succeeded in his
plea.
[b] Cf. Or. 1. 2, 11 passim. The praises of the locality by
tradition occupy the first place in a set oration.
[c] Especially the sack of Antioch by the Persians in the
250s. Cf. Vol. I, p. 520 n., Downey, pp. 252 ff.
[d] The riots of A.D. 354, with the lynchings of Theophilus,

to cover the first day's journey, have covered many, and so have made my way here. I have crossed the Bosporus; I am in the palace and participate in the debate about our city.[a] So from the people with whose assistance I undertook the journey without flinching, I believe that I shall have support also in my whole enterprise.

5. Now, in the past I have heard people expressing envy for our city, because of its streams, its breezes, its size and beauty, its inhabitants, the instruction in oratory that is both given and received here, and because of its willing students and able teachers.[b] 6. However, I would not consider her fortunate so much as the contrary, when I consider earthquakes and the ruin they have caused, invasions of the Persians, with their pillaging, demolition and arson,[c] and the elements of a still greater disaster, to my mind,—the unprovoked rage against the governors, and their lynchings, as they have been dragged along by their tied feet,[d]—all of which we have heard in reproving comment from other people, for our misfortune is also the ground for complaint against us. 7. Yet where is the justification for this? The present situation surely must be regarded as the responsibility of the same spirit [e] which has gained the aid of an outraged Nemesis also,—the outrage being the disappearance of her temple.[f] This has

Montius and Domitianus, Amm. Marc. 14. 7, *Or.* 1. 103; *infra*, § 47.

[e] The intervention of πονηροὶ δαίμονες is a feature of the accounts of the riots in Libanius (*Or.* 1. 252; *infra*, § 29 (with manifestations)) and in Chrysostom, *Hom.* 15 (*P.G.* xlix. 154) and 21 (*ibid.* 214 f.).

[f] The temple of Nemesis, in Diocletian's reconstruction, was located in the stadium at Daphne, and was occupied by

καὶ | τοῦτ' ἀπεδείχθη τοῖς ἐξ ἱεροῦ Νεμέσεως ἑτέ- F
ρου γεγενημένοις.

8. Καὶ ὡς μὲν οὐ δεινὰ τὰ περὶ τὰς ὑμετέρας
εἰκόνας, τίς ἂν ἀντείποι; τίς δ' οὐκ ἂν σκοτεινὴν
ἐκείνην προσείποι τὴν ἡμέραν; ἦν δέ, ὦ βασιλεῦ,
μαινομένης πόλεως, τὸ δ' ἐκβάλλον τοῦ φρονεῖν ἦν
τι ἰσχυρότερον, ὥστ' εἰ καὶ συγχωρῆσαι δεῖ τῆς
πόλεως ἁπάσης εἶναι τὸ ἀδίκημα, τὴν ἀπολογίαν
ἐκ τοῦ κινοῦντος ἔχει. ἃ γὰρ οὐκ ἂν ἔδρασε φρο-
νοῦσα, ταῦτα ἐτόλμα παραφρονοῦσα. 9. τὸν δὲ
τοῦτο πεπονθότα ἄνθρωπον οὐ κολάζειν νόμος, ἀλλ'
R 629 ἐλεεῖν καὶ πειρᾶσθαι τέχνῃ τῇ τῶν ἰατρῶν | ἐπανορ-
θοῦν. οὐδεὶς δὲ τύπτει τὸν μαινόμενον οὐδὲ ἔγ-
κλημα νόσου ποιούμενος τὴν νόσον κατηγορεῖ.[1]
νοσοῦσι καὶ πόλεις, ὦ βασιλεῦ, τὰ δὲ νοσήματα
τούτων ταραχαί, θόρυβος, ὀργῆς ἡττηθῆναι, τὰ τῶν
ἡττημένων ἁμαρτεῖν, τὰ νόμῳ κεκωλυμένα πρᾶξαι.
10. τουτὶ γὰρ αἱ στάσεις, ἐν αἷς ἄλλα τε πολλὰ
δεινὰ καὶ σφαγαὶ οὐ πολιτῶν μόνον ἀλλ' ἤδη καὶ
συγγενῶν, τῆς ἐκ τοῦ θυμοῦ βίας νικώσης τὰ παρὰ
τῆς φύσεως. καὶ τουτὶ τὸ κακὸν | ἔλθοι μὲν ἄν F
ποτε καὶ ἐπὶ σμικρὰν πόλιν, αἷς δέ ἐστι μεγέθη,
πολὺ τοῦτο ἐν ταύταις. 11. κἂν ἐξετάζῃς τῆς
Ῥωμαίων βασιλείας τὸν χρόνον, καὶ στάσεις ἐν
ταῖς τηλικαύταις εὑρήσεις· ἃς οἱ μὲν ἄμεινον τῶν
βασιλέων φρονοῦντες συγγνώμης ἠξίωσαν, παρ'

---

[1] κατηγορεῖ Re. text (mss.) : κακηγορεῖ Re. conj., F.

---

the judges and officials of the Olympic games. Thus,
symbolically, the conduct of games and officials is under the
protection of Justice, *qua* Nemesis. The temple had been
demolished by A.D. 387, and for that reason was a source of
divine vengeance. The "other temple of Nemesis" is the

been proved by the proceedings which have emerged from another temple of Nemesis.

8. It cannot be denied that the treatment of your statues was shocking. That day must be called a black day. It was, Sire, the behaviour of a city gone mad, but the force which robbed it of its senses was something too potent, so that, even if we must admit that the misconduct belongs to the city as a whole, it has its excuse in what inspired it. Out of her senses she dared to behave in a way she never would have done in her right senses. 9. With regard to any human being in this plight, it is normal not to punish, but to pity him, and to try to correct him by the art of medicine.[a] No one gives a flogging to a madman, nor, in bringing a case of disability to court, does he make that disability the charge. Cities too suffer from disabilities, Sire,—disturbances, riots, fits of temper, misconduct in consequence of them, and activities forbidden by law. 10. Such are the outbreaks of violence in which, to cap the many other outrages, murders are committed, not just of fellow citizens but, at times, even of relations, when the violence of temper overcomes natural affection. Even a small town may sometimes be visited with this evil, but it becomes serious in cities of any size. 11. And if you examine the history of the Roman empire, you will find outbreaks in such cities. The more sensible of emperors thought fit to pardon

emperor, and his commission, sitting in judgement on Antioch.

[a] The analogy of the ailments of the city, as a collective body, with those of the individual is a commonplace (*e.g. Or.* 12. 50, 20. 40, 22. 9), and harks back to Plato and beyond (*e.g.* Xen. *Mem.* 3. 5. 18, Plat. *Menex.* 243 E).

ἐνίων δὲ οὐκ εὖ βεβουλευμένων ἦλθον ἐπ' αὐτὰς
ζημίαι ζημιοῦσαι καὶ αὐτοὺς τοὺς ζημιοῦντας.
πρὸς γὰρ τῷ τὰ αὐτῶν ἀσθενέστερα ποιεῖν οὐδ' εἰδέναι θεοῖς ἀκολουθεῖν ὡμολόγουν. 12. τίνα γὰρ
δὴ τὰ τῶν θεῶν; συγγνώμη τοῖς καθ' ἡμέραν ῥή-
R 630 ματα ἐπ' αὐτοὺς ἀφιεῖσιν ὅταν | τι παρὰ τῶν πραγ-
μάτων λυπῶνται. καίτοι πολλάκις αὐτοὶ σφᾶς
αὐτοὺς ἀπολλύουσιν, ἀλλ' ὅμως[1] συκοφαντοῦσιν, οἱ
δὲ ἀνέχονται. καὶ διὰ τοῦτο πολὺ τὸ τῶν ἀνθρώπων γένος, εἰ δ' εἵποντο πᾶσιν ἁμαρτήμασι δίκαι,
σφόδρα ἂν ὀλίγον ἦν τὸ σωζόμενον. ὅστις οὖν
ἐοικέναι βούλεται θεοῖς, ἀφιεὶς τιμωρίας χαιρέτω
μᾶλλον ἢ λαμβάνων. 13. ᾧ μεγίστῳ καὶ τοὺς
Ἕλληνας εὑρίσκω τῶν βαρβάρων διαφέροντας. οἱ
μέν γε ἐγγύς εἰσι τῶν θηρίων ἀτιμάζοντες ἔλεον,
οἱ δὲ ὀξεῖς τε | ἐλεεῖν καὶ ὀργῆς περιόντες. οὕτω F
Λακεδαιμόνιοι μὲν ἐξὸν Ἀθήνας ἀνελεῖν ἐφείσαντο,
οἱ δὲ πρὸς τὸν Μῆδον τῶν Ἑλλήνων πολεμήσαντες
τῶν μετ' ἐκείνου στάντων καὶ ταῦτα ἀνάγκην οὐ
μικρὰν εἰς τὴν δίκην ἔχοντες τὰ δεδογμένα περὶ
αὐτῶν. ἦν δ' ἂν καὶ Ἀλέξανδρος ὁ Μακεδὼν
βελτίων οὐ κατασκάψας Θήβας. οὐ γὰρ ἂν ἀπήντα
R 631 τοῦτο τοῖς ὑπὲρ αὐτοῦ λόγοις, ἀλλ' ἦν | ἂν πρῶτον
ἐν τοῖς ὑπὲρ αὐτοῦ λόγοις.

[1] After ὅμως, ⟨οἱ μὲν⟩ Morel, Re. : del. F.

---

[a] Hints at the emperor as being θεοείκελος (as he had
described Julian, *Or.* 15. 34, 16. 18). This is expanded in
Or. 20. 12 ff. to the notion of the emperor as διοτρεφής, in a
classical Hellenic and current pagan sense. As, before
Julian (*Or.* 15. 24 ff.), forgiveness had been paraded as an

them, but by some less well advised, punishments were inflicted on them, which harmed those who imposed them too, for not only did they make themselves weaker, but they were self-confessedly incapable of following the ways of the gods. 12. By the ways of the gods, I mean pardoning those who every day disparage them whenever they are at all upset by circumstances. Why, they often call down destruction on themselves, but for all that they go on slandering the gods, and the gods turn a blind eye. So the human race abounds, but if punishment inevitably followed the crime, there would be precious few surviving. Anyone, then, who wants to be like the gods should have more joy in remitting punishment than in inflicting it.[a] 13. In this respect in particular I find the Greeks also to be superior to barbarians. These approximate to brutes in despising pity, while the Greeks are quick to pity and get over their wrath. So the Spartans spared Athens when they had it in their power to destroy her[b]; those of the Greeks who fought against the Medes spared those who sided with them, even though they had no small urge to vengeance in the shape of the decrees passed about them.[c] Alexander of Macedon, too, would have been the better for not razing Thebes to the ground,[d] for this would not then have countered the eloquence expended on his behalf, but would have held pride of place among it.

Hellenic virtue, so here before Theodosius, but the religious implications are now more contentious.

[b] After the Peloponnesian War, 404 B.C., Xen. *Hell.* 2. 2.

[c] The oath of revenge against the Greeks collaborating with Xerxes, Hdt. 7. 132. Thebes spared, Hdt. 9. 86-88.

[d] In 336 B.C., *Or.* 14. 34, 20. 22, Dio Chrys. *Or.* 2, p. 83 R.

14. Δεινὰ τὰ γενόμενα.[1] τὰ δ' ἐν Ἀλεξανδρείᾳ
μέτρια τὰ πολλὰ καὶ πυκνά; οἷς τὸ θέατρον τοῦ
πρὸς τοὺς ἄρχοντας αὐτῶν πολέμου χωρίον. ἐν δ'
αὖ τοῖς πρὸς ἐκείνους πολέμοις καὶ ὑμῖν τοῖς τὰ
σκῆπτρα ἔχουσι πολεμοῦσι ῥῆμα οὐδὲν ὀκνοῦντες,
οἳ καὶ τοὺς τῶν βασιλέων τῶν περὶ τὴν ἑσπέραν
φονέας καὶ τὰ ἐκείνων ἔχοντας πάντων ἀκουόν-
των ἐκάλουν ἐπὶ τὴν Αἴγυπτον. ἀλλ' ὅμως ἔστι
τε ἡ πόλις καὶ μένει. καὶ | δέδοται τῇ φύσει τῶν
πόλεων τὰ τοιαῦτα πλημμελεῖν καὶ οὐ τὸ ἁμαρτάνειν θαυμάζομεν, ἀλλὰ τὸ μή. οὕτως εἰ καὶ μὴ
γράμμασιν ἀλλ' ἔργῳ τοῦτον τεθείκατε τὸν νόμον,
R 632 συγγνώμην ἔχειν πόλεων ἀνοίᾳ. | 15. τοῦτο δὲ ἄρα
εἶδε καλῶς καὶ τοῖν ἀδελφοῖν τοῖν Παίονοιν ὁ νεώτερος. τὴν γὰρ αὖ μεγάλην πόλιν ἡδέως ὑποδεξαμέ-
νην τυράννου θράσος καὶ τὰ μὲν εἰποῦσαν, τὰ δὲ καὶ
πράξασαν, ἐν οἷς ἀμφοτέροις ταῖς εἰς ἐκεῖνον ὕβρεσιν ἐχαρίζετο τῷ τυράννῳ, τοῦτον τοίνυν ἐκεῖνος
καθελὼν ἥξειν τε ἐλπιζόμενος ἐπί τε τὸ σῶμα καὶ
τὸ πλήρωμα τῆς πόλεως τοῦτο μὲν οὐδὲ ἐνενόησεν,
ἐκάθητο δὲ ἀναμένων ὅστις αὐτὴν ἐξαιτήσεται, καὶ
φανέντος τὸν μὲν ἐπήνεσε, τὴν δὲ οὐκ ἐκόλασε.

[1] Before δεινὰ, Morel, Re. ins. δεινὰ τὰ λεγόμενα: after
γενόμενα ins. καὶ (Bad.) : om. F.

---

[a] e.g. the murder of Georgius, Dec. A.D. 361; Amm. Marc.
22. 11. Julian, E.L.F. No. 60 (=Socr. H.E. 3. 3).
[b] Maximus, usurper A.D. 383–388, responsible for the
murder of Gratian and the expulsion of Valentinian II.
A concordat between Maximus and Theodosius remained
until A.D. 386, with Maximus recognized as Augustus and
his statues erected throughout the East. Cynegius, ppO,
had been sent to Alexandria early in that year to set
these statues up and to institute curial reforms, but had
then proceeded to attack pagan institutions there. As in

14. " What happened was dreadful," it may be said. Then are the many frequent occurrences in Alexandria commendable ? There the theatre is their battleground against their governors.^{a} Moreover in the warfare they wage against them, they wage war also against you, their emperors, with no mincing of words, since they invited to Egypt, in the hearing of all, the murderers of the Western emperors and the usurpers of their kingdom.^{b} But for all that the city still exists and remains. Such misguidedness is conceded as natural to cities ; we are not astonished at their misconduct, but at the lack of it. So, if not by ordinance, certainly by practice you have set this rule, to pardon cities for their stupidity. 15. The younger of the Pannonian brothers realized this well enough.^{c} When the capital gladly welcomed a bold usurper with words and deeds, and in both sought to ingratiate itself with the pretender by insulting the emperor, after putting down the usurper, he was expected to descend upon the body and the complement of the city, but he never even entertained the idea ; instead he sat waiting for someone to come and plead for it and, when he turned up, he praised him and refrained from punishing the city. 16. Then

A.D. 361, such interference produced pagan rioting, this time in favour of Maximus. By this time Theodosius was ready to break with the usurper ; cf. Petit, Byzantion, xxi, pp. 303-304.
^{c} Valentinian and Valens, born at Cibalis in Pannonia (Grecized into Paeonia). For Valens and his reactions to the supporters of Procopius in Constantinople and elsewhere (A.D. 365-366) cf. Zos. 4. 5, Amm. Marc. 26. 6. 14. Themistius (Or. 7, περὶ τῶν ἠτυχηκότων) dilates on Valens' " clemency." In actual fact, there followed a bloody repression which included not only the rebels but pagans generally.

16. λεγέσθω δή τι καὶ περί σοῦ τοιοῦτον, ἄλλως θ'
ὅτε σοι καὶ δόξα πλείων ἐντεῦθεν ἢ παρὰ τῶν
[ἐν]¹ ὅπλοις κατωρθωμένων ἅ σε δεσπότην καὶ Σκυ-
θῶν ἐποίησε | δούλων εὔνων. τὸ δὲ ἐκείνους οὕτως
ἔχειν ἐκ τῶν σῶν εἰς ἐκείνους. ἀντὶ γὰρ τοῦ κακοῦν, ῥάδιον δέ, οἶμαι, παντί, τοὺς ἀρχομένους²
R 633 ὅπως ἀδεεῖς³ ἔσονται ποιεῖς. ἐντεῦθεν | ἔστιν
ἀκούειν ὁριζόντων τῶν μὲν ὡς πολεμικώτερος εἴης
μᾶλλον ἢ φιλανθρωπότερος, τῶν δὲ ὡς φιλανθρωπότερος μᾶλλον ἢ πολεμικώτερος. 17. ὁ δὲ ἔπαινος πολλῷ λαμπρότερος ὁ τὴν φιλανθρωπίαν ἔχων,
αὐτοῦ γάρ τινός ἐστι καθαρῶς, βασιλέως δὲ πολεμίων κεκρατηκότος τὸ μέν τι γίγνεται τοῦ στρατηγοῦ, τὸ δὲ τῶν στρατιωτῶν, τὸ δὲ τῶν ὅπλων,
τὸ δὲ τῶν ἵππων, τὸ δὲ τῶν ἱππέων, τὸ δὲ τῶν
νεῶν, εἰ δὴ διὰ τούτων μάχοιντο.

18. Μὴ τοίνυν, ὦ βασιλεῦ, δόξαν οὕτω καλὴν ἀν-
έλῃς, ἀλλ' ἐνθυμοῦ μὲν ὡς ἐοικέναι δεῖ πατρὶ τὸν
βασιλέα, πατέρων δ' ἐστὶ τὸ πράως φέρειν προ-
πετείας | υἱέων. πολλὰ μὲν οὖν ἔστιν ἐγκώμια
κατὰ σοῦ λέγειν, πλεῖστον δ' ἀληθείας ἐν τῷ τῆς
ἡμερότητος ἔνεστιν. ὥστ' εἰ καὶ πάντες ἦσαν
ἀπηνεῖς καὶ χαλεποί, σὲ τοῦτο φυλάττειν ἐχρῆν.
19. νῦν δ' ὁρᾶν ἔξεστι καὶ τὸν Ἰουλιανὸν ἐντεῦθεν
εὐδοκιμεῖν ἐσπουδακότα τόν τε ἀντιθέντα τῇ Ῥω-
R 634 μαίων πόλει⁴ τὴν νέαν | ὁμώνυμον⁵ ἔστιν οὗ τοῦτο

---

¹ ἐν F. (CA Bad.) : om. other mss. : bracketed Re.
² ἀρχομένους conj. Re., F. (Par. 3014 Bad.) : ἐχομένους
Re. text (other mss.).
³ ὅπως ἀδεεῖς F. (M marg., P corrected) : οἷς ἀδεεῖς Savile
(Bad.) : οἷς ἐνδεεῖς Morel (Par. 3017) : ἐνδεεῖς Re. (other
mss.). ⁴ πόλει F. : βουλῇ Re. (mss.) : πόλιν Cobet.
⁵ ὁμώνυμον Cobet, F. : ὅμως Re. (mss.).

let some such thing be said of you too, especially when more renown will accrue to you from it than from all the successes in arms which have made you master of the Scyths and them your loyal slaves.[a] That they are so results from your treatment of them, for instead of doing them harm, which I feel any man might easily do, you ensure that your subjects shall be free from fear. Hence we can hear their attempts at definition, some saying that you are more of a warrior than a humanitarian, others that you are more of humanitarian than a warrior. 17. The praise which embraces humanity is much the more glorious, for it belongs to the individual personally, whereas some of the praise received by the emperor who has overcome his enemies belongs to the appropriate general, his soldiers, his equipment, horses, horsemen and ships, if indeed they fight by means of them.

18. Then, Sire, do not ruin such a noble fame. Consider that an emperor must be like a father, and a father's duty is to handle the waywardness of his sons gently. So, though we can sing your praises on many counts, the greatest truth lies in the account of your clemency,[b] and thus even if all men were stubborn and difficult, you must protect this. 19. Indeed, we can see both that Julian sought to achieve fame from this source, and that the founder of the new capital, which he built to rival the city of Rome and which bears his name,[c] displayed this

---

[a] The Goths under Athanaric, Amm. Marc. 27. 11, Zos. 4. 34, Socr. *H.E.* 5. 10.　　[b] *Cf. Or.* 20. 16.

[c] Of the commentators, Reiske and Cobet (misled by the omission of τε after τόν in I and Bad.) confuse the issue here by supposing a textual error to underlie τὸν Ἰουλιανόν, so

ἐπιδεδειγμένον. τοῦ 'Ρωμαίων γάρ ποτε δήμου
βοαῖς αὐτὸν ἀσελγεστέραις βεβληκότος, τί χρὴ
ποιεῖν ἐρόμενος τοὺς ἀδελφοὺς καὶ τοῦ μὲν εἰπόντος
δεῖν πέμπειν ἐπ' αὐτοὺς δύναμιν καὶ κατακόπτειν,
ἡγήσεσθαι δὲ αὐτός, τοῦ δὲ ὅτι βασιλικὸν εἴη τὸ
μηδὲ εἰδέναι τά γε τοιαῦτα, τὸν μὲν ἃ δεῖ παρ|αι- F
νεῖν, τὸν δὲ πικρὸν ἐκεῖνον ἥκιστα βασιλεῖ συμφέρειν εἰπών, τοὺς δὲ κρατοῦντας πρέπειν ἀνέχεσθαι τῶν τοιούτων σκιρτημάτων, τὸν μὲν ἐποίησε
μέγαν τῇ δόξῃ, τὸν δὲ συστείλας ἀπέπεμψεν, εὔ-
νουν δ' ἑαυτῷ τὴν 'Ρώμην ἐποίησε νομοθετήσας
γέλωτος ἀφορμὴν τοὺς βασιλέας τὰ τοιαῦτα ποιεῖσθαι.

20. 'Αλλ' ὅμως σοί γε οὐκ ἴσος ἐκεῖνος[1] εἰς
φιλανθρωπίας λόγον,[2] <ὃς>[3] πρὸς μὲν τὰ τοιαῦτα
R 635 πράως εἶχε, χαλεπώτατος δὲ ἦν | τοῖς ὀρεγομένοις
βασιλείας καὶ τὰ τοιαῦτα ἐπιβουλεύουσι καὶ οὐ
τούτοις δὲ μόνοις, ἀλλὰ καὶ ὅσοι μάντεσιν ὑπὲρ
τοῦ ποῖ χωρήσει τὰ ἐκείνων[4] διελέγοντο, καὶ οὐδεμία τέχνη τόν γε τοιοῦτον ἐξεῖλετ' ἂν τοῦ πυρός.
21. σὺ δέ γε ποῖός τις ἐν τοιούτοις, τίς μὲν 'Ρω-
μαίων, τίς δὲ βαρβάρων οὐκ | οἶδεν; ὑπὸ μὲν γὰρ F
ὁμοίων ἐγκλημάτων ἤεσάν τινες ἀποθανούμενοι καὶ
ἡ ψῆφος εἶχε θάνατον, ἡ δὲ λύουσα φωνὴ τὴν ψῆφον

---

[1] ἐκεῖνος conj. Re., Cobet, F. : ἐκείνοις mss., Re. text.
[2] φιλανθρωπίας λόγον conj. Re., Cobet, F. (I corrected) :
φιλανθρωπίαν ὁ λόγος Savile, Re. (M Bad.) : φιλανθρωπίαν λόγος
Morel (other mss.).   [3] <ὃς> F. (P corrected).
[4] τὰ ἐκείνων Re. (mss.) : τὰ ἐκείνου F. (τἀκείνου P corrected).

---

referring the whole sentence to Constantine, Sievers by refer-
ing τόν τε ἀντιθέντα to Julian. For Julian's clemency cf.
Or. 12. 85, 18. 200 ff., et al. and for Constantine's foundation

quality at times. For instance, once when the Roman populace assailed him with catcalls,[a] he asked his brothers what he ought to do. One of them answered that he should let loose an armed force upon them and cut them down, and offered to take charge of the operation himself. The other replied that it became his majesty to take not the slightest notice of such behaviour. Constantine told them that this advice was the correct one and that of that harsh brother was of little use to an emperor : it was proper for rulers to put up with such skittishness. So he made the one great in renown and dismissed the other crest-fallen, and he put himself on good terms with Rome by ordaining that emperors might have fun poked at them in this way.

20. But yet, in any count of humanity, there is no comparison between him and you. He was clement enough on such occasions as these, but he was most severe on aspirants to the throne and members of such conspiracies,—and not just on them, but on any who associated with soothsayers to find out the course their fortunes would take.[b] There was no device that could have saved such a man from being burnt at the stake. 21. But everyone, both Roman and barbarian, knows your habit in such matters. On some such charge as this some persons were going out to meet their doom, and the verdict involved was

of Constantinople as a " rival " to Rome *cf. Or.* 20. 24, Sozom. 2. 3, Zos. 2. 30.

[a] For this anecdote *cf. Or.* 20. 24. The two brothers were Hannibalianus and Julius Constantius, the hawk and the dove respectively.

[b] *e.g.* his murder of Licinius, justified by Socr. *H.E.* 1. 4, described as treacherous by Zos. 2. 28 ; his attitude to soothsaying, Zos. 2. 29.

LIBANIUS

λαβοῦσα τὴν ἀρχὴν ἐκ τῶν βασιλείων ἐχώρει διὰ
τῆς πόλεως ἀπάγουσα τῶν αὐχένων τὰ ξίφη, καὶ
νῦν ζῶσιν ἐν χωρίοις παρέχουσιν ἡδονὰς ἐπ᾽ ἐλέγ-
χοις ἀπαιτοῦσι θάνατον.[1] 22. ἀπολέλαυκέ σου τῆς
φιλανθρωπίας, ὦ βασιλεῦ, καὶ ἡ πολλαῖς καθ᾽
ἑκάστην ἡμέραν τιμωμένη δαπάναις, δι᾽ ὧν ἀεὶ
μείζων τε καὶ καλλίων γίγνεται. οἱ τοίνυν Σκύθην
τινὰ στρατιώτην αἰτιαθέντα τι ἐπὶ μὲν δικαστήριον
οὐκ ἀγαγόντες, ἐπὶ δὲ τὴν θάλατταν μετὰ τὴν ἐν
τῇ γῇ σφαγὴν προσαποστεροῦντες καὶ ταφῆς ἐλύ-
πησαν μὲν οἷς ἐτόλμησαν κινοῦντες τὸ Σκυθικόν,
R 636 ἔδεισαν | δὲ τὴν ὀργὴν καὶ οὐδὲ ὅλην ἡμέραν, ἀλλ᾽
ἐλπίσαντες πεινήσειν ἦσαν ἐν ἄρτῳ πάλιν παρὰ
τῶν διαλλαγῶν.

23. Ἦ οὖν ἕτερόν σε δεῖ γενέσθαι σήμερον καὶ
ἄνω ποταμῶν πορευθῆναι τὸ πρᾶγμα ἢ ἕως ἂν
ἐκεῖνος | ᾖς, μηδὲ νῦν ἐπὶ δίκην ἐλθεῖν. τί γὰρ δὴ
καὶ νεανικὸν πόλιν ὑπήκοον ποιῆσαι κακῶς; οὐδὲ
γὰρ τοῖς ποιμέσι θύειν ὁπόσα βούλοιντο τῶν προβάτων, οὐδὲ τοῖς βουκόλοις τῶν βοῶν οὐδὲ τοῖς
αἰπόλοις τῶν αἰγῶν, ἀλλὰ τὸ μὲν ὑπὲρ αὐτῶν μάχεσθαι τοῖς ἐπιοῦσι τῶν θηρίων καὶ κρατεῖν καὶ
ἀπωθεῖν καὶ[2] μέγα καὶ λαμπρόν, τὸ δὲ κατεσθίειν
ἅ τις νέμει, θαυμαστὸν οὐδέν.

24. Οὕτω μέν, ὦ βασιλεῦ, καὶ κοινῇ τῆς πόλεως

[1] ἀπαιτοῦσι θάνατον F. (V): ἀποῦσι θανάτου Re. (other mss.):
⟨μικρὸν⟩ ἀποῦσι θανάτου conj. Re.
[2] καὶ om. Savile (Bad.) : bracketed F.

---

[a] e.g. the incident in Or. 1. 239 ff., Themist. Or. 19. 229
d ff., figures prominently in the recitals of the clemency of
Theodosius, Or. 20. 15, 23. 13.
[b] Constantinople, usually referred to with dislike, e.g. Or.
1. 74 ff., ibid. 279. For this incident, Or. 20. 14.

death, when news of their reprieve,[a] issuing first
from the palace and proceeding through the city,
removed the sword-blades from their throats, and
now they live in places that give them pleasure, after
the charges that demanded their death. 22. That
city also has enjoyed your humanity, Sire, which is
honoured with great expenditure every day, whereby
it now becomes the greater and the more handsome.[b]
Anyway, they did not bring to court a Scythian
soldier who had been accused of some offence, but
they murdered him on land and then cast him into
the sea, robbing him of burial besides. Although by
this outrage they distressed you by the provocation
offered to the Scyths, they did not spend even one
whole day in fear of your wrath, but, for all that
they expected to starve, they were supplied with
bread once again in consequence of the reconciliation.

23. You must then either today become a quite
different person and things go all topsy-turvy,[c] or
else, while ever you remain as you are, you must not
now have recourse to punishment. Anyway, where
lies the valour in injuring a subject city ? There is
none either for shepherds, or cowherds, or goatherds,
in slaughtering as many as they like of their sheep
or cows or goats. What matters and what is of note
is for them to fight on their behalf against any attacking predator, and to overcome them and repel
them. There is no admiration to be won by feeding
upon one's charges.

24. So, Sire, by your natural qualities you would

[c] Proverbial—the rivers run up-hill. *Paroem. Gr.* (ed.
Leutsch-Schneidewin), pp. 47, 185 (Zenob. 2. 56, Diogen.
1. 27), Eurip. *Med.* 410.

ἡμαρτηκυίας τῇ γε σῇ φύσει προνοητέον ἂν ἦν,
νῦν δ' ἄκουσον ἕκαστα διηγουμένου· γένοιο γὰρ ἂν
οὕτω δικαιότερος κριτὴς καὶ διαιτήσαις[1] ἀπ' αὐτῶν
τῶν πεπραγμένων τοὺς οἰκοῦντας τὴν πόλιν.

25. Ἧκε τὰ περὶ τοῦ χρυσίου γράμματα, πρᾶγμα
πάλαι φοβερόν. πιστευομένου δὲ τοῦ τέως ἀπι-
στουμένου καὶ τῆς γῆς οὐ φερούσης τὸ ἄχθος κατ-
ηνέχθησαν οἱ τῆς ἐπιστολῆς ἀκηκοότες εἰς γῆν ἐξ-
ετάζοντες οἱ πολλοὶ τὴν πολλὴν αὐτῶν ἀδυναμίαν
καὶ ὡς εἰ ἃ μὴ δύνανται μέν, οὐδ' εἰ πάνυ βού-
R 637 λοιντο δυνήσονται, | τὰ σώματα δέ σφισιν ἐν ταῖς F 8
ἐσχάταις ἀνάγκαις ἔσται. καταφεύγουσι τοίνυν
ἐπὶ τὴν παρὰ τοῦ θεοῦ συμμαχίαν αὐτὸν ἐκεῖνον
καλοῦντες οἷόν τε ὄντα πεῖσαί σε τοῦ πλήθους
ἀφελεῖν. 26. μεστοῦ δὲ ὄντος ἀνδρῶν τοῦ δικαστηρίου ὧν οἱ μὲν ἐν ἀρχαῖς ἐγεγόνεσαν, οἱ δὲ
ἐπολιτεύοντο, οἱ δὲ τὴν ἀπὸ τοῦ συνδικεῖν εἶχον
πρόσοδον, τοῖς δ' ὁ χρόνος λελύκει τοὺς στρατιω-
τικοὺς πόνους, τούτων τοίνυν τῶν ἠριθμημένων οἱ
μέν, ὅπερ ἔφην, ἱκέτευον δάκρυσιν, οἱ δ' ἄνευ φωνῆς
ἐδάκρυον, οὓς καὶ αὐτοὺς ἐν τοῖς ἱκετεύουσι δήπου
θετέον. ὁ δ' ἄρχων οὐκ εἶχεν ἐπιτιμᾶν· τίνα γὰρ
ἂν καὶ μέμψιν ἱκετεία δέχοιτο; 27. οὐκοῦν μέχρι
μὲν τούτων οὐδὲν ὑπ' οὐδενὸς ἠδίκησαι, βασιλεῦ·
ποῖον γὰρ ἀδίκημα παρ' οὗ καὶ αὐτὸς αἰτεῖς τὰ
ἀγαθὰ καθ' ἑκάστην ἡμέραν, τοῦτόν τινα ἀνθρώπων
βοηθὸν αὐτῷ γενέσθαι βούλεσθαι; ἤδη δὲ ὄντων
ἔξω καὶ ληγόντων τῶν τοιούτων ῥημάτων ἄνθρω-

---

[1] διαιτήσαις F. (V) : -σοις Savile (Bad.) : -σεις Re. (other
mss.).

---

[a] Cf. Introduction pp. 241-242, for discussion on the nature
of this demand.

have had to take official measures to deal with our miscreant city. As things are, listen to my narration of the particulars, for in this way you would be more just in your judgement and would treat the inhabitants of the city in the light of the actual occurrences.

25. There arrived the decree concerning the gold, something long dreaded.[a] What up to then seemed incredible was only too credible ; the land could not bear the burden, and so those who had heard the directive cast themselves to the ground, the majority revealing their utter incapacity : however much they might wish it, they would be incapable of doing what they could not, and their persons would be in the direst straits. They had recourse, then, to the support of the god, invoking his name,[b] for he could persuade you to remit some of the burden. 26. The court-room was crammed with people—ex-governors, city-councillors, professional lawyers, retired military men. Of these that I have listed, some, as I have said, began to make tearful supplication, others wept without speaking, though they too must obviously be classed as suppliants. The governor [c] could not reprove them—for what reproof, indeed, is applicable to supplication ? 27. So up to that point, Sire, you had been wronged by none, for what wrong is there in any man wanting to have to aid him the one for whose blessing you personally pray every day ? But now, when they had come outside and were bringing their entreaties to an end, some fellows began to

[b] The protesters are thus mainly Christians—a word he cannot bring himself to use : they form a πονηρὰ συμμορία, *Or.* 20. 3.

[c] On the identity of the *consularis*, successor to Tisamenus, *cf. Or.* 23. 10 n. (p. 250 above).

ποί τινες σεσιγηκότων ἐκείνων | εἰσῆγον τὴν ταρα- F 3
χήν. 28. καὶ προελθόντες οὗ Φλαβιανὸν εὑρή-
σειν ἔμελλον, οὐχ εὑρόντες εἶτα ἀνέστρεφον ὅθεν
πρῶτον ἐκινήθησαν, ἁπτόμενοι μὲν ῥημάτων οὐ
καλῶν, μέλλοντες δὲ καὶ ἔργων, τουτὶ δὲ οὐκ
ᾤοντο οἵ γε ἐπιεικέστεροι. τίνες οὖν ἦσαν ἐκεῖ-
R 638 νοι; οἱ | καὶ ἡλίου καὶ σελήνης καὶ νεφῶν αὐτῶν
τοὺς ὀρχουμένους προτιθέντες. ὧν ἤδη τις καὶ
τῶν ἐν Βηρυτῷ συμφορῶν αἴτιος ἐγεγόνει· τουτὶ
γὰρ ὕστερον ἔγνωμεν. 29. τοιούτοις οὖν ὑπηρέ-
ταις ὁ κακὸς χρώμενος δαίμων ἔπραξεν ἃ σιωπᾶν
μὲν ἐβουλόμην, ὁ παιδείας δὲ νόμος οὐκ ἐᾷ μὴ
λέγειν.[1] ἃς γὰρ μετ' αἰδοῦς ἑωρῶμεν ὑμετέρας
εἰκόνας, ταύτας οὐχ οὕτως εἶδον οἱ τολμηρότατοι.
τοῦ δὲ σὺν δαίμονι πονηρῷ τὰ τοιαῦτα ποιεῖν τεκμήριον ἐναργὲς τὸ ῥᾳδίως ἅπαν τοῦτο πεπρᾶχθαι
παιδαρίων πολὺ πρὸ ἥβης ἐπὶ πάντα πετομένων,
ὀξέως ἀναβαινόντων, καταβαινόντων, ἀπ' ἄλλων
ἐπ' ἄλλα διαπηδώντων μετὰ ἰσχύος πλείονος τῆς
ἐν ἀκμάζουσιν | ἐνούσης. 30. λέγεται δὲ καὶ γέ- F
ροντα μείζονα ἢ κατὰ γέροντα δυνηθέντα περὶ τὸν
ἵππον, εὖ γε, ὦ γέρον ἀκούσαντα ἀμεῖψαι πολλῶν
ὁρώντων πρότερον μὲν εἰς νεανίσκον ἑαυτόν, ἔπειτα
δὲ εἰς παῖδα, εἶτα ἀφανισθῆναι καὶ φρίκην οὐ μι-
R 639 κρὰν ἐπελθεῖν αὐτοὺς ταύτας ἰδόντας τὰς | μετα-
βολάς.

[1] ὁ παιδείας δὲ νόμος οὐκ ἐᾷ μὴ λέγειν I, correction in marg. :
ὁ παιδί· C, corrected by later hand to λέξαι δ' ὅμως ἀνάγκη : ὁ
π..δί A, followed by erasure : εἴπω δέ Re. (Par. 3017 Bad.) :
om. other mss. | παιδείας] ἀληθείας F.

cause a disturbance, and they kept quiet. 28. They proceeded to the place where they were likely to find Flavianus,[a] but they didn't find him there and began to make their way back to the place from which they had first started. They began to employ shocking language, and soon were to translate it into action, which was something the more respectable elements did not expect. Who were these fellows,[b] then ? Why, those who think more of the dancers of pantomime than of sun and moon and darkness itself ! One of their kidney had already been responsible for the sad occurrences in Berytus, as we afterwards discovered. 29. Using such instruments, then, the evil spirit performed such acts as I would prefer not to mention, but which my regard for the code of my upbringing forbids me to leave unspoken. We used to gaze with reverence upon your statues ; not so those blackguards then. Clear evidence for their performance of such outrages under the direction of some evil spirit is to be found in the fact that it was all performed so easily. Urchins, mere boys, darted upon them all, quickly clambered up and down, jumped from one to another with more vigour than that of men in their prime. 30. It is even said that an old man whose activities against the equestrian statue [c] surpassed those of any ordinary old men was greeted with the cry, " Well done, old fellow," and in full view of lots of eye-witnesses changed, first, into a youth, then into a child, and finally vanished ; and they felt no small alarm upon seeing these transformations.

[a] Bishop of Antioch, *Or.* 30. 15 n., 19. Jo. Chrys. *Hom.* 21.
[b] For the rôle of the claque in the riots *cf.* Browning, *J.R.S.* xlii, pp. 16 ff. [c] *Cf. Or.* 20. 10.

31. †Ἐγὼ μὲν οὖν ἦν ἐν ταῖς βοαῖς χρυσὸς πολλῶν ἦν ὅτε δρόμος αἰτεῖ, ὑπὲρ τούτων φωναί.†¹
τοῦ πράγματος δ᾽ ἐπὶ τὰς εἰκόνας προελθόντος οἱ
μὲν ἠδίκουν, οἱ δὲ ἐθεώρουν ὄντες πολλῷ πλείους
τῶν τὰ δεινὰ ταῦτα ποιούντων. πῶς οὖν οὐκ ἐκώ-
λυον; τὸν αὐτὸν ἐρῶ πάλιν λόγον, ὅτι τὸ κωλύον
ἦν ἰσχυρότερον. †ἦν γάρ τι δαιμόνιον ἐνταῦθα, ἦν
ἔνδον, ὃ τοῦθ᾽ ἕκαστον | κατηνάγκαζεν εἰσβλέ- F 4◍
πειν,†² αὐτὸν δὲ οὐκ εἴα ῥῆξαι φωνήν. 32. ἀρχῆς
δὲ μὴ φαινομένης ἠρεμεῖν ἦν ἀνάγκη καὶ πλῆθος
ὄντας. οἱ πολιτευόμενοι δὲ πόρρω τοῦ ταῦτα ἦσαν
καὶ πράττειν καὶ ὁρᾶν καὶ καταδύντες ὅπῃ τύ-
R 640 χοιεν ἑαυτοὺς | διέσῳζον δεδιότες μὴ φανέντες ἕλ-
κοιντο. πολὺ δὲ δεινοτέρων ὄντων τῶν πεπραγμένων ἐκεῖθεν εἶχον εὔλογον τὸν ἐπὶ τοῖς ἐλάττοσι
φόβον. τοὺς γὰρ ἐκείνων οὐκ ἀπεσχημένους τίνας
ἔδει νομίζειν ἐν τοῖς ἄλλοις ἔσεσθαι καὶ ταῦτα ἤδη
πυρὸς εἴς τινος τῶν λαμπροτέρων οἰκίαν ἐμβεβλη-
μένου; ἦν δὲ αὐτοῖς πολὺ πλείων τῶν ψυχῶν ἢ τῶν
οἰκιῶν λόγος. 33. διεσπαρμένοι τοίνυν κατὰ τὸν
ἐμπεπτωκότα φόβον καὶ οὐκ ἔχοντες ἰδεῖν ἀλλή-

---

¹ Corrupt reading of majority of mss. Variants : ἦν ἐν]
ᾤμην ἐν ταῖς βοαῖς δραμεῖν τὸ πλῆθος ὅπου χρυσὸς πολλῶν B, C
corr. ἤκουον καὶ ἐν ταῖς βοαῖς χρυσὸς πολύς Bad., Re. (ἦν ὅτε . . .
φωναί om. Bad.). F. conj.: ἐγὼ μὲν ἤκουον καὶ ἐν ταῖς βοαῖς
πολλῶν χρυσὸς ἦν (ἅ γε δρόμος αἰτεῖ, ὑπὲρ τούτων φωναί).
² Corrupt. ἦν repeated before τι Re. (Bad.): om. F. |
ἐνταῦθα ἦν ἔνδον ὃ Re., F. (Bad.): ᾧ ταῦτα ἦν ἔνδον ἢ other
mss. | τοῦθ᾽ ἕκαστον mss. except CV: τὸ (τοῦ CV) καθ᾽ ἕκα-
στον Re., F. (CV). | κατηνάγκαζεν εἰσβλέπειν Norman : εἰς (ἧς
U: εἴσω Par. 3017) κατηνάγκαζε (-ον Bad.) βλέπειν mss.:
εἰς del. F. : ἠνάγκαζε Re.

ᵃ Textually corrupt. The translation is that of Foerster's
conjecture, cf. app. crit.

288

31. So I began to listen, and in the shouts of many of them there was the word " gold "—the shouting naturally having to do with the object of the crush.[a] When things reached the stage of meddling with the statues, there were some offenders, but the spectators far outnumbered the performers of this outrage. Then how was it that they did not try to stop them ? I repeat what I have said before—that a stronger power prevailed to stop them. There was some superhuman agency here and within them, which forced each man to look upon this and prevented him from uttering a word. 32. No magistrate put in his appearance, and so, numerous though they were, they were forced to be still.[b] The city councillors, so far from participating in or witnessing such behaviour, went to ground wherever they could and tried to save their own skins, for they were afraid that if they appeared on the scene, they would be lynched. Upon the commission of even more shocking outrages, the fear they entertained because of the lesser deeds appeared justified in consequence, for after the commission of such excesses, how were they to expect them to behave in other matters, especially when the house of one of the notables had already been set on fire ?[c] They were much more concerned, though, for their lives than for their homes. 33. Anyway, they scattered because of the panic that affected them. They could not see one

[b] Although the *curia* is, through the *epimeletae*, theoretically responsible for public order, the initiative must come from the provincial governor.

[c] Arson as a sign of class grievance? It was used by the mob against the upper class in A.D. 354 (*Or.* 1. 103, Amm. Marc. 14. 7) ; and the example was only too fresh in their minds.

λους οὐδ' εἰπεῖν οὐδ' ἀκοῦσαι περὶ τῶν παρόντων
καὶ ἅμα τῶν ἀγγελλομένων πλείους ποιούντων τοὺς
ταῖς εἰκόσιν ἐπιθεμένους ἔκειντο εὐχόμενοι μὲν
λαβεῖν τὰ παρόντα λύσιν, προβῆναι δὲ εἰς ἔργον
οὐκ ἔχοντες. |

34. Ἴδοι δ' ἄν τις κἀκεῖθεν ὡς οὐκ ἄνευ δαιμο- F 40
νίας ἦν τινος ταῦτα ἀνάγκης. ὃν γὰρ καὶ ἄκλητον
ἔδει τὰ τοιαῦτα κωλύειν τοξόταις ἐνταῦθα ἐφεστηκότα τρεφομένοις ὑπὲρ καιρῶν ἀπαιτούντων βέλη,
καλούμενος οὗτος μυρίαις φωναῖς ματαίους λέγων
προφάσεις ἐκάθητο. 35. καίτοι καὶ μηδενὸς κα-
R 641 λοῦντος εἰκότως ἂν[1] καὶ ἀναστὰς | καὶ δραμὼν ὅδ'
ἔμπειρος ὢν πολέμου καὶ τἄλλ' οὐ κακὸς καὶ εἰδὼς
ὡς οὐδὲ τὴν ὄψιν οἱ θορυβοῦντες οἴσουσι τῶν τόξων, ἐν μὲν τοῖς ὑπὲρ ὑμῶν οὐκ ἐκινεῖτο ἀλλ' ἦν
εὐλαβὴς καὶ ἔμελλεν, οἰκίᾳ δὲ ἐβοήθει προθύμως
καὶ πολλὴν ἐλπιζομένην φλόγα δύο βέλεσιν ἐν προοιμίοις ἔσβεσεν, ὥστ' αὐτὸν αὐτοῦ κατηγορεῖν οὐκ
ἐπὶ τῶν σεμνοτέρων ταὐτὸν πεποιηκότος. 36. ὁ δὲ
ἄρχων τῶν ἐθνῶν ὡς ἤκουσε τοξότας ἥκοντας ἐπὶ
τοὺς τὸ πῦρ προσάγοντας, ἧκέ τε αὐτὸς καὶ τὰ ἀπὸ
τῶν λόχων[2] εἰσήνεγκε δῆλον τούτῳ ποιήσας ὡς
μετὰ τῆς αὐτῆς χειρὸς αὐτὸς ἂν ἦν κἂν τοῖς προ-
τέροις. τοὺς μὲν οὖν κάοντας παρέδωκε τῷ δικα- |
στηρίῳ τὰ διὰ τῶν κεραμίδων τραύματα, τοὺς δὲ F 4
ἠσεβηκότας πολλαὶ πρὸς τὴν θήραν ὁδοί, κατή-

---

[1] ἄν conj. Re., F. (V): om. Re. text (other mss.).
[2] λόχων Morel, Re., F. (Par. 3014): λόγων Savile (other
mss.).

---

a Liebeschuetz (pp. 124 f.) identifies this official with the
νυκτέπαρχος—commander of the watch. His archers are
clearly distinguished from army units. There was, in fact,

another, or tell or hear the news about the situation, and at the same time rumour exaggerated the numbers of those who attacked the statues, and so they lay low, praying for the end of the business, but incapable of venturing to act.

34. One might infer that this did not occur save under divine compulsion from the following fact also. The commander who should have put a stop to such activities even without being summoned to do so, since he was in charge of archers maintained here against emergencies that require armed intervention, was summoned time and again but remained inactive, putting out idle excuses.[a] 35. Yet even if he had not been summoned at all, it would have been reasonable to expect him to up and run to the scene. He was an experienced soldier, and quite good otherwise, and he knew that the rioters would not stand even the sight of his bowmen. Yet in these matters that affected you, he would not move but dilly-dallied cautiously, though he was keen to assist one household and with a couple of bowshots extinguished all the incendiarism that was expected as soon as it began, so that he stands self-condemned for not having done the same for more important matters. 36. However, when the Count of the East heard that archers had engaged the incendiaries, he visited the scene in person, and brought in troop reinforcements, and so made it abundantly clear that with the same force he could have done the same in the previous stages too. Wounds sustained by the incendiaries from roof-tiles caused them to be handed over to trial, and the many ways of search did the same with

no settled garrison in Antioch at this time. He also acts independently of both *curia* and the governors.

γοροι δὲ ἀλλήλων οἱ συνασεβήσαντες ἀλλήλους τε
καὶ τὰ ἀλλήλων εἰδότες. καὶ ταχύς τε καὶ σαφὴς
καὶ ῥᾷστος ὁ ἔλεγχος. 37. ἔδει δὴ χωρίζειν τοὺς
εἰλημμένους κατὰ τὸ τῶν ἀδικημάτων μέτρον. |
R 642 τοῦτ᾽ οὖν ἐγίγνετο. ἔδει χωρεῖν εὐθὺς ἐπὶ τὴν
τῶν πονηροτέρων τιμωρίαν. καὶ τοῦτο τοίνυν
ἐπράττετο τῶν μὲν ξίφει πεσόντων, τῶν δὲ πυρὶ τὰς
ψυχὰς ἀφιέντων, τῶν δὲ στόμασι θηρίων δαπανη-
θέντων, ἔσωζε δὲ οὐδὲ τοὺς κομιδῇ παῖδας τοῦτο
αὐτό, ἀλλ᾽ ἦν αὐτοῖς ἀνωφελής, ὡς ἐν τηλικούτοις,
ὁ τῶν ἐτῶν ἀριθμός. ὁ δὲ μὴ δοὺς δίκην οὐδὲ ἠδικήκει πανταχοῦ τοῦ δικάζοντος ἰόντος τοῖς λογι-
σμοῖς τὴν ἀκρίβειαν ἑκάστῳ προσάγοντος, ὡς μη-
δαμοῦ τἀληθὲς ἡττηθῆναι μηδενός.

38. Σκέψαι δή, βασιλεῦ, τί ποιῶν ἐπὶ τούτοις
τοὺς ἐπαινοῦντας ἕξεις. ἐμοὶ μὲν γὰρ δοκεῖς ἀρκεῖν ἡγούμενος τὸ μηκέτ᾽ εἶναι μηδένα τῶν ταῦτ᾽
ἠδικηκότων. | εἰ μὲν γὰρ ἦν πολλοὺς θανάτους
ἀποθανεῖν ἄνθρωπον, τοῦθ᾽ ἡμᾶς ἔδει ποιεῖν· τούτου
δὲ οὐκέτ᾽ ὄντος ὥρα παύσασθαι τῆς ὀργῆς. 39.
μὴ γὰρ δὴ τῶν θρυλουμένων μηδὲν εἰς ἔργον ἔλθοι.
τίνα δὴ ταῦτ᾽ ἔστιν; οἱ μὲν εἰς ἁρπαγὴν τῶν ὄντων
ἑκάστοις χρημάτων φασὶν ἐπαφήσειν σε στρατιώτας, οἱ δ᾽ ἐπὶ σφαγὰς τῶν ἐχόντων τὴν πόλιν,
οἱ δὲ διὰ μεγέθους καταδίκης ἀμυνεῖσθαι[1] τὴν ὕβριν,
οἱ δὲ αἵματι τῶν ἐν τῇ βουλῇ γνωριμωτέρων.[2] 40.

---

[1] ἀμυνεῖσθαι F. (VIBM) : ἀμύνεσθαι Morel (Bad.) : ἀμύνα-
σθαι Re. (other mss.).   [2] γνωριμωτάτων Morel, Re.

---

[a] By their attack on the imperial statues.
[b] For the proceedings of the courts martial cf. Jo. Chrys.
Hom. 3 (P.G. xlix. 56).

those guilty of sacrilege.[a] Their accomplices, who knew the identity and the actions of their fellows, turned state's evidence, and conviction was quick, clear and easy. 37. The prisoners had to be classified according to the seriousness of their crimes. So this was done. Then proceedings had to be instituted immediately for the punishment of the worst offenders. This too was done : some fell by the sword, or lost their lives at the stake, or met their deaths at the jaws of beasts. Nor could mere boys be saved by the very fact of their youth—their tender years, in fact, were a disadvantage to them in their involvement in such misdeeds. Those who escaped punishment were simply the innocent, for the investigator everywhere applied such rigorous examination to everyone that no one at all could evade the truth.[b]

38. Well, consider, Sire, the means by which after this you may have people to praise you. You will, I think, succeed if you regard it as sufficient that none of these malefactors should remain alive. If it were possible for a man to die the death many times over, we ought to have died so. But since this is impossible, it is time to put an end to yourwrath. 39. I can only trust that none of the rumoured courses of action is put into effect. Well, what are these? Rumour has it that you will unleash the military to pillage the property of us all, or to massacre the inhabitants of the city, or that you will avenge the insult by a huge fine or by shedding the blood of the leading lights of the city council.[c] 40. I tried to combat these

[c] As had been done by Diocletian after Eugenius' revolt in A.D. 303, *cf.* on § 45 below.

ἐγὼ δὲ πρὸς ταύτας ἐμαχόμην τὰς δόξας οὐκ εἰδέναι σε λέγων τοὺς τὰ τοιαῦτα οἰομένους. ὅτι
μὲν γὰρ οὐχ ἁπάσης τὸ ἔργον τῆς πόλεως, ἤκουσας
διηγουμένου. πάντας οὖν ἀποθνήσκειν ποῦ δίκαιον
τούς τε ὅτε ταῦτα ἡμαρτάνετο μηδὲ ἐπιδημοῦντας,
τούς τε νόσῳ πεπεδημένους, τούς τε εἰ μή τις αὐ-
R 643 τοὺς ἀποκτείνοι τοῖς | θεοῖς εἰδότας χάριν;

41. Ἀλλὰ μὴν καὶ γυναιξὶν ἔστιν ἔπιπλα. γυναῖκας δ' οὐδ' ἂν εἷς φαίη μετεσχηκέναι τοῦ τολ-
|μήματος. αἵ γε σιδηρᾶς ἂν αὐταῖς ηὔξαντο εἶναι
τὰς θύρας. οὕτω περὶ αὐταῖς ἔδεισαν. οὐκοῦν καὶ
τὰ τούτων τῶν γυναικῶν αἷς οὔτε ἀνὴρ οὔτε παῖδες οὔτε ἀδελφοί, τῶν εἰς ἁρπαγὴν ἐξουσίαν λαβόντων ἔσται; 42. ἐὰν οὖν εἴπωσι προσελθοῦσαι ὅτι,
ὦ βασιλεῦ, ἀλλ' ἡμεῖς γε ταῦτα οὔτε ἐβουλήθημεν
οὔτε ἐζητήσαμεν οὔθ' ὅπως ἔσται προὐτρέψαμεν οὔτε
τολμηθέντων ᾔσθημεν οὔτε ἐν δίκῃ νῦν προσαι-
τεῖν ἠναγκάσμεθα καὶ ταῦτα οὐκ ὄντος τοῦ διδόντος τῷ κοινὴν ἐν τῇ πόλει γενέσθαι τὴν πενίαν, τί
πρὸς ταῦτα ἐρεῖς, ὦ βασιλεῦ; τί δαί,[1] εἰ πρὸς σὲ
μὲν οὐδὲν τοιοῦτον, πρὸς δὲ τὸν Ἥλιον λέγοιτο;
ἢ καὶ τοῦ θρήνου ληψόμεθα παρὰ τῶν ὀδυρομένων
R 644 δίκην; 43. οὐ τοίνυν οὐδὲ τῇ καταδίκῃ | χώραν
ἐνοῦσαν ὁρῶ. πῶς γὰρ οὓς οὐκ ἔστιν ἐλέγξαι πε-
πονηρευμένους, τούτους ἔνι ζημιῶσαι χρήμασι;
καὶ μὴν εἰ μὲν κατὰ πάντων τοῦθ' ἥξει, καὶ οὓς ὡς
φίλους τῷ θεῷ τιμᾶν ἀξιοῖς, ζημιῶν ὀφθήσῃ· εἰ δ'
ἔσται τὸ χωρὶς κεισόμενον καὶ οὐ πεπληξόμενον τῇ
καταδίκῃ, δεινὰ φήσουσι πάσχειν οἱ καθαροὶ μὲν

---

[1] δαί F. (CAPU) : δὲ Re. (other mss.).

opinions, asserting that people with such ideas as these are quite unacquainted with you. You have heard my explanation that the action was not that of the city as a whole, so how can it be just for everyone to be put to death, for instance, those who at the time of this offence were not even resident here, or who were fettered by illness, or who thanked their lucky stars that they had not been murdered by someone?

41. Besides, women also have belongings. And no one would say that women had any part in the outrage. Why, they would have offered up a prayer for their doors to be of steel, so frightened were they for their persons. So will the property of these women too, who are without husband, sons or brothers, lie at the mercy of those who are given a free hand to loot? 42. If they come and address you thus, " Sire, it was certainly not by our wish or seeking or encouragement that these occurrences took place. We didn't enjoy such misconduct, nor is it right that now we are reduced to beggary, especially when there is no one to relieve us, owing to universal poverty in the city," what will be your reply to this, Sire? Well, then? What if such remarks were made not to you but to Helios? Shall we punish the grief-stricken for their lamentations, too? 43. No, and I see no room for any fine either. How can you impose a monetary fine upon those who cannot be proved to have gone wrong? What is more, if this is applied to us all, you will be seen to punish those whom you say you respect for their devotion to God. If there are to be exceptions and persons not to suffer the fine, then anyone like them, innocent of blame, will complain of victimization if

LIBANIUS

αἰτίας, ὥσπερ ἐκεῖνοι, μὴ τῶν ἴσων δὲ ἐκείνοις τετυχηκότες. 44. καὶ μὴν εἰ μὲν τῶν τὰς εἰκόνας
κεκινη|κότων εἰσὶν οἱ τοῦτο πεισόμενοι, θάνατον F
ὀφείλουσι τὴν δίκην, ἀλλ' οὐ τὴν εἰς χρήματα· εἰ δ'
οὐδεὶς ἂν τοῦτο φήσαι, τίνος ἀπαιτοῦνται δίκην;
λείπεται δὴ τὸ τῶν πολιτευομένων καὶ τῶν ἐκείνων
κεφαλῶν. οὓς εἴ τις ἀποκτείνοι[1] μηδενὸς ἔχων
αἰτιάσασθαι χεῖρας, πολιτείας ἀντ' ἀδικήματος εἰ-
ληφὼς ἔσται τιμωρίαν, καὶ τὸ πρᾶγμα φυγῆς ἄξιον
καὶ νῦν εἶναι δοκοῦν ἔτ' ἔσται φοβερώτερον.

45. Τί οὖν ἐξ ἁπάντων δείκνυται τούτων; ὅτι σοι
τῆς ὀργῆς παυστέον. ὁ δὲ Διοκλέα λέγων σοι καὶ
τὸν ἠναγκασμένον Εὐγένιον καὶ τὴν ἐκ Σελευκείας
δεῦρο μετὰ μέθης εἴσοδον καὶ τὸν ἐμὸν πάππον καὶ
R 645 τὸν | Βρασίδαν καὶ ὡς ἀπέθανον οὗτοί τε καί τινες
ἕτεροι κρίσεως μὲν οὐ τυχόντες οὐδὲ ἀπολογίας,
κατ' αὐτὸ δὲ τὸ πολιτεύεσθαι μόνον, οἱ ταῦτά σοι
λέγοντες οὐχ ἃ μιμεῖσθαι προσήκει λέγουσιν. 46.
οὐ γὰρ ἴσον, οὐκ ἴσον Θεοδόσιος καὶ Διοκλῆς.
ἐλυσιτέλει δέ, οἶμαι, | κἀκείνῳ μὴ τὸ ξίφος ἀκονᾶν, F
νῦν δὲ πολλῷ τούτῳ χρησάμενος ὢν οὐκ ἐν ὀλίγοις
θαυμαστὸς διέβαλε τὰ καλὰ τοῖς χείροσιν, ὥστε καὶ
τοὔνομα συνάγειν τοῖς ἀκούουσιν ἀηδίαν καὶ ποιεῖν
ἀποπηδᾶν. 47. μᾶλλον οὖν μεμνήσθω τις Κων-
σταντίου τοῦ πρὸς τὰς τῶν πόλεων ἁμαρτίας ἡμέρου. ὃς ὕπαρχον ἐνταῦθα πέμπων Στρατήγιον ἐπὶ

---

[1] ἀποκτείνοι F. (VM Par. 3017): ἀποκτείνει U Bad., P
corrected : ἀποκτείνῃ Re. (other mss.) : ἀποκτενεῖ Cobet.

---

[a] Cf. Or. 2. 10 n. Members of Libanius' family, as above,

296

he does not receive the same treatment as they. 44. Moreover, if the future victims really are some of those who destroyed the statues, the punishment they deserve is death, not just financial. And if no one can say that this is the case, what are they being punished for? Obviously, only for their curial station and their lives. And if one should resort to execution even if he can complain of no one's personal responsibility, this will be a punishment for their social status, not for their crime, and the duty which even now is regarded as one to evade will become even more terrifying.

45. The indication of all this is that you must cease from your anger. If anyone mentions to you Diocletian, Eugenius, the usurper willy-nilly, the drunken march upon Antioch from Seleuceia, and my grandfather and Brasidas, and how they and some others were executed without trial or hearing simply because they were some of the leading members of the city, then he is mentioning to you behaviour which you ought not to copy.[a] 46. You cannot, I repeat, cannot compare a Theodosius with a Diocletian. It was to his advantage, too, not to whet the sword, but in fact after such a blood bath, despite his exceptional ability, he ruined his great achievements by his faults, and the result is that the very mention of his name excites dislike in the hearers and induces them to shy away. 47. Rather you should be reminded of the clemency employed by Constantius towards the misconduct of the cities. After the death of Theophilus which that fine

were executed and part of their property confiscated in Diocletian's punishment, cf. Or. 1. 3, 125 ; Or. 51. 30 ; Ep. 1154.

τῷ Θεοφίλου θανάτῳ, ὃν οὐκ ἄξιον ἐκεῖνος τῶν τρό-
πων ἐδέξατο χρηστὸς ἄρχων ὑπὸ χαλκέων πέντε
κατενεχθεὶς ἐν ἁμίλλαις ἁρμάτων, τότ' οὖν ἤλ-
γησε μὲν τὴν καρδίαν ὁ Κωνστάντιος, τιμωρίας δὲ
πρὸς αὐτὸν μνημονεύων, ὅπως μετριώτατα χρήσε-
ται τῷ πράγματι πολλάκις εἶπε, κἀκεῖνος οὐκ ἠτί-
μασε τὰς ἐντολάς, οὐδὲ πλείους ἢ προσῆκε μητέρες |
R 646 ἐθρήνησαν.

48. Ἀλλὰ Θεόφιλος ἔθνησκεν, ἐρεῖ τις, τότε, τὸ
δὲ νῦν ὕβρις εἰς βασιλέων[1] εἰκόνας. ἐγὼ δέ, ὡς
κἀκεῖνο μὲν ὕβρις εἰς βασιλέα παρήσω νῦν, ἐπι-
|δείξω δὲ ὡς ἐν ὁμοίοις αὐτὸς ἐκεῖνος ἐγένετο.
Ἔδεσσα[2] γὰρ ἡ πόλις, μεμψάμενοί τι τῶν πρὸς αὐτοὺς χαλκῆν εἰκόνα αὐτοῦ καθελόντες, εἶτα ἄραντες
πρηνῆ κατὰ τὸν ἐπὶ τοὺς παῖδας τοὺς ἐν τοῖς διδα-
σκαλείοις νόμον ἔτυπτον ἱμάντι τά τε νῶτα καὶ τὰ
μετὰ τοῦτο κάτω, προστιθέντες ὡς ὅτῳ πληγαὶ
τοιαῦται προσήκουσι, πλεῖστον ἀπέχοι βασιλείας.
49. ταῦτα μαθὼν ὁ Κωνστάντιος οὐκ ἔπεσεν εἰς
ὀργήν, οὐκ ἐζήτησε δίκην, οὐδενὶ χείρω κατέστησε
τὴν πόλιν, ἀλλ' ὥσπερ οὐκ ἂν ἐκόλασε γεράνους
διὰ τὴν κλαγγήν, οὕτως οὐδὲ ἐκείνους. ταῦτα καὶ
τὰ τοιαῦτα οὕτως εἶναι ἐδόκει καλά τε καὶ ἐπαίνων
ἄξια ὥστε τοῖς ἐκ τῆς ἐπιεικείας ἡ κατὰ τοὺς πολέ-

---

[1] βασιλέων F. (V) : βασιλέως Re. (other mss.).
[2] Ἔδεσσα Par. 3014, Morel, F. : Ἔμεσα other mss. :
Ἔμεσσα Re.

---

[a] Consularis Syriae, lynched A.D. 354, cf. Or. 1. 103,
Amm. Marc. 14. 7. 6 ff. Liebeschuetz (p. 58) suggests that
these χαλκεῖς were smiths from the arms factories.
[b] Cf. Or. 1. 106 ff., Amm. Marc. 15. 13. Seeck 282 (i),
PLRE (s.v. Musonianus) 611.

governor suffered at the hands of five copper-smiths [a]
at the chariot races quite contrary to his deserts,
Constantius sent here Strategius as prefect,[b] and,
though sore at heart, when he spoke to him of
punishment, he repeatedly insisted that he should
go about the business with the utmost moderation.
Nor did Strategius disregard these instructions, nor
yet did any more matrons than was proper go into
mourning.

48. " Ah, but what took place then," it will be
objected, " was the murder of Theophilus. Now we
are concerned with an outrage against the imperial
statues." Now I will ignore the fact that that
incident also was an outrage against an emperor,
and will demonstrate that, in precisely similar circumstances to these, Constantius remained true to
himself. In the city of Edessa,[c] the inhabitants,
resenting some treatment they had received, cast
down his bronze statue, turned it face down, lifted
it up, as they do with children in school, and administered a thrashing to the back and back-side,
commenting also that anyone visited with such a
whipping was far removed from imperial dignity.[d]
49. When Constantius heard of this, he did not fly
into a temper, he sought no punishment, nor did he
humble the city in any way. He refused to punish
them, any more than he would have punished cranes
for their clatter. This and such-like behaviour
seemed so noble and praiseworthy, that by his
moderation his slackness in military matters was dis-

[c] Cf. Or. 20. 27, where the phrase ἐν τοῖς ὁμόροις τῇ Συρίᾳ
confirms the reading of Par. 3014 here.

[d] The traditional method of punishing schoolboys, as
shown in Greek and Roman art.

LIBANIUS

R 647 μους ἐκρύπτετο ῥαθυμία, καὶ | Περσῶν καθ᾿ ἕκα-
στον ἔτος ἀεί τι παρασπωμένων καὶ τὰ αὐτῶν
μείζω ποιούντων τοῖς ἡμετέροις χωρίοις ὅμως εἶχε
τοὺς συνευχομένους αὐτῷ καὶ ζῆν βουλομένους ὑπὸ
τῇ ἐκείνου περὶ τὰς πόλεις πραότητι. 50. ἅπαντα
μὲν γὰρ ἄνθρωπον τοῦτο κοσμεῖν δύναται, δια-
φερόντως | δὲ τοὺς ἐν ταῖς ἐξουσίαις. τὸ γὰρ πάντα F 4
ποιεῖν ἐπιτρεπούσης τῆς τύχης εἶναι τὸ ἐπισχῆσον
καὶ διακωλύσον μέγα μέρος εἰς εὐφημίαν τε καὶ
δόξαν. εἶτ᾿ ἀκούειν περὶ ἑτέρου ταῦτα μᾶλλον
ἐθελήσεις ἢ παρέχειν τοῖς ἀνθρώποις περὶ σεαυτοῦ
λέγειν; μηδαμῶς, ὦ γενναῖε, μηδενὶ τῆς ἐνταῦθα
παραχώρει νίκης.

51. Ἀλλὰ πρὸς τοῖς εἰρημένοις καὶ περὶ ποίας
πόλεως ὁ λόγος ἐστί, σκόπει. μάλιστα μὲν γὰρ
οὐδεμίαν περιοπτέον οὐδὲ τὴν σμικροτάτην οὐδὲ
τὴν ἐν σκοπέλῳ κειμένην. ἁπάσης γὰρ δὴ μέλει
θεοῖς καί εἰσιν ἐκείνων κτήματα. εἴποι[1] δ᾿ ἂν ἴσως
τις ὡς οὐ μεγάλη τὰ τοιαῦτα ζημία, ὥσπερ ἐν χορῷ
τοῦ φαυλοτάτου χορευτοῦ σιωπῶντος. 52. ἀλλ᾿
οὐ περὶ τῆς ἡμετέρας ἔνι γέ τι τοιοῦτον εἰπεῖν οὔτε
ἐνθυμηθῆναι ἢ πρὸς τοσοῦτον μὲν ἐκτέταται μῆκος
ὡς μὴ εἶναι ῥᾴδιον ἐκ πυλῶν εἰς πύλας ἐλθεῖν, τοι-
αύτην δὲ καὶ οὕτω πολλὴν περίκειται γῆν ὥστε |
R 648 πάντα μὲν φέρειν, αὐτῇ δὲ ἀποχρῆν. πηγαὶ δὲ οὐ
μικραὶ μὲν αἱ εἴσω τειχῶν | οὐδὲ ὀλίγαι, ταῖς δὲ F 4
ἀπὸ τῆς Δάφνης ἐπὶ τὸ ἄστυ θεούσαις οὐ πολλὰς
ἀντιθήσεις. 53. καὶ μὴν χειμών τε πρᾶος καὶ θέρος
ἀνέμοις ἥδιστον ἀγορά τε ἡ καθ᾿ ἡμέραν ἀνθεῖ
παρέχουσα τοῖς ὁρῶσιν ὠνῆς ἐπιθυμίαν, πολὺ δὲ τὸ

---

[1] εἴποι F. : εἶπε Re. (mss.).

[a] Cf. Or. 18. 206.

guised. Every year the Persians nibbled away bits of our territories and increased theirs at our expense,[a] but he still had his devotees to wish him long life because of his clemency towards the cities. 50. This can be a credit to any man, but especially to those in authority. When fortune allows omnipotence, it redounds greatly to a man's praise and renown that there should be some restraint and some moderating influence. Then will you want this said of another rather than let mankind say it of you ? Never, noble Sire, withdraw your claim to victory in this sphere in favour of any man.

51. But, in addition to these remarks, consider the kind of city it is of which I speak. In the first place, no city should be overlooked, not even the smallest, nor one perched on a cliff-top.[b] The gods' concern is for every one, and they are their possessions. It might be said that in such cases it would be no great loss as, for instance, in a chorus when the worst member stays quiet. 52. But of our city you can neither say nor think any such thing, for it extends over such a great area that it is hard to travel from one gate to another, and it has such an extent of fertile land surrounding it that it produces everything and is self-sufficient. The fountains inside the city walls are no small ones, nor are they few in number, and there are not many that you can compare with those flowing from Daphne to the city. 53. Besides, the winter is mild, the summer most pleasantly tempered by the breezes. Our daily market flourishes and induces in the beholders a wish to purchase. The produce imported from every

[b] *Cf.* Phocyl. *fr.* 4 (quoted by Dio Chrysostom, *Or.* 36. 13).

πανταχόθεν εἰς αὐτὴν μετοικιζόμενον, ἡ δὲ δέχεταί
τε ἀσμένη καὶ θεραπεύει καὶ οὐκ ἐᾷ μέμψασθαι τὰ
βεβουλευμένα. 54. τὴν ἰσχὺν δὲ τὴν διὰ πάντων
τῆς πόλεως πολλοὶ μὲν πόλεμοι πρὸς τὴν Περσῶν
ἀρχὴν πολεμηθέντες ἐπέδειξαν, οὐχ ἥκιστα δὲ ᾧ
πέρας Ἰουλιανὸς ἐκεῖνος ἐπέθηκε διδάξας διώκειν
τοὺς φεύγειν μεμαθηκότας διὰ χρόνου Ῥωμαίοις
ἔργον αὐτῶν ἀποδούς. 55. μὴ οὖν ἄλλο τι νομίσῃς
νῦν ἢ περὶ τῶν ὅλων εἶναι τὴν βουλήν, εἴπερ ὑπὲρ
πόλεώς ἐστιν ἣν ὁ Μῆδος ἢ μὴ εἶναι βούλοιτ' ἂν ἢ
πράττειν κακῶς, ὡς τὰ αὑτοῦ βέλτιον παρὰ τοῦτο
ἕξοντα. μὴ τοίνυν συναγωνίσῃ ταῖς τῶν βαρβάρων
ἐπιθυμίαις. μηδὲ τὴν ἀρετὴν τὴν Κέλσου περι-
F 410 υβρίσῃς. εἰ γὰρ | σὺ | ζητήσεις τι πλέον, ἐκείνῳ τὸ R
μέτρον ἠμέληται, καὶ¹ τιμῶν ἀνὴρ ἄξιος.
56. Ἀλλὰ μικρὸν οἱ τεθνηκότες πρὸς τὴν σὴν
ἀθυμίαν. σὺ δὲ μηδὲ τὴν ἐπὶ τούτῳ τιμωρίαν
ἀγνόει, τὴν φυγήν, ὦ βασιλεῦ, τὴν πολλὴν ἀνδρῶν,
γυναικῶν, παίδων, γεγηρακότων, ὧν ἀφ' ἑκάστου
πολλὰ δάκρυα κατὰ τῶν ὄνων, κατὰ τῶν ὀρέων,
κατὰ τῶν καμήλων. ὧν ὁ μισθὸς διπλάσιος τῇ
χρείᾳ τῶν μισθουμένων, ὁ δὲ τήμερον ἐγκαλῶν τῷ
μεμισθωμένῳ τῶν ταὐτὸ ποιούντων τῆς ἐπιούσης
ἐστίν. 57. ἐπείγονται δὲ οἱ μὲν εἰς ἑτέρας πόλεις,
οἱ δὲ εἰς ἀγρούς, καὶ κενὴ μὲν ὡς εἰπεῖν ἡ πόλις,
αἱ δὲ πρὶν τὰ ἀπὸ τῶν ἀγρῶν δεῦρο ἄγουσι καθ'
ἑκάστην πύλην ὁδοὶ τἀκ τῆς πόλεως πολλαχῇ μερί-

¹ καίτοι conj. Re. ("probabiliter, nisi ἀνάξιος scribendum
est," F.).

ᵃ A summary of the praises of Antioch described in *Or.* 11,

side is plentiful : it receives it gladly and looks after it and allows no complaint against its regulations.[a] 54. Of the over-all strength of the city many wars against the Persian empire have given us proof,[b]— and not least, that which the late Emperor Julian completed, when he taught those trained to flight to become pursuers, and at long last he gave back to the Romans their proper function.[c] 55. So do not think your deliberations now to be concerned with anything else than the well-being of the empire, since they deal with a city which the Persians would want either out of existence or in distress, since their own ends would then be furthered. Do not then further the desires of the barbarians, nor yet slight the abilities of Celsus, for if you go to excess, then his moderation is ignored ; and yet he is a man deserving of honour.

56. " Those who have been put to death are a small matter as compared with your discomfiture." But, Sire, do not ignore the damage to follow—the mass exodus of men, women, children and old people, from each of whom come tears over their asses, mules and camels. And the price of hiring these is doubled because of the need of the hirers, and if a man today reproaches another for hiring them, to-morrow he will be one of those doing the same thing. 57. They hurry off, either to other towns, or to their estates, and the city is practically empty. The roads, which used to bring here the produce of the countryside through every gate, now disperse the city-dwellers far and wide. They believe that, if

frequently recurring in Libanius, especially in arguments *ad misericordiam* (*e.g. Or.* 1. 2).
   [b] *Cf. Or.* 11. 177 ff.   [c] *Cf. Or.* 18. 208 ff., 24. 39.

ζουσιν. οἴονται γὰρ μένοντες μὲν ἀπολεῖσθαι ξιφῶν ἐπελθόντων, διασπαρέντες δὲ ᾗ δύναιτο ἕκαστος τυχεῖν ἂν ἴσως ἀσφαλείας. 58. καιρὸς δὲ τοῖς
λῃσταῖς οἷος οὐχ ἕτερος, χρημάτων μὲν κομιζο-
μένων, ῥᾳστώνης δὲ οὔσης εἰς σφαγήν. φέρει δὲ
R 650 ὁ ποταμὸς | νεκροὺς ἐς τὴν θάλασσαν οὓς ἐμβαλ-
λόντων τῶν πεφονευκότων δέχεται. καὶ στενο-
χωρία μὲν ἐν ἀγροῖς, ὀλιγανθρωπία δὲ ἐν τῇ πόλει,
ὥστ' εἶναι βραχὺ τοῖς σιτοποιοῖς τὸ ἔργον. 59.
δακρύουσι δὲ οἱ μὲν οὔπω τὴν πόλιν ἀφέντες τῷ
μήπω, | οἱ δ' ἀπελθόντες τῷ πόθῳ. νοσήματα δὲ F 4
ἰατρῶν σπάνει[1] νικᾷ. ὁ δ' ἀποθανὼν πατρῴων
ἐστέρηται μνημάτων. λιμὸς δὲ ἐν οὐ λιμῷ διὰ τὸ
πλῆθος τῶν ἑκασταχοῦ καθημένων. ἄρχοντες δὲ
ἄχθονται μὲν ταῖς μεταναστάσεσι, κωλῦσαι δὲ οὐκ
ἔχουσι τῇ τοῦ μέλλοντος ἀγνοίᾳ· πρὸς γὰρ τὸν τρέ-
μοντα τὸ μηδὲν ἔσεσθαι λυπηρὸν οὐκ ἂν ἐγγυήσα-
σθαι δύναιντο. ἔστι δ' οὖν οὐδέτερος ἔξω φόβου,
οὔτε ὁ μένων οὔτε ὁ πορευόμενος. καὶ γὰρ οὗτος
τὸ μεμενηκέναι δέδοικε. τὸ οὖν χρόνον τοσοῦτον
τοσούτῳ συνεζηκέναι φόβῳ πόσην ἔχει τὴν δίκην;
ἐλπὶς γὰρ θανάτου καὶ τοῦ μὴ γενησομένου τῆς
ἄνευ προσδοκίας πληγῆς ἀλγεινότερον. 60. πολλοῖς ἀπόλωλε χρήματα, βασιλεῦ, πολλοῖς θεράπαι-
ναι ἐν οὐ φορητοῖς καμάτοις, πολλαῖς μητράσιν ἐκ
τῶν γονάτων ἐξέπεσε τὰ παιδία, πολλοὺς ἄνδρας
ἥρπασε λῃστῶν κύματα, πολλοὶ ταῖς ψυχαῖς καὶ
ταφὴν προσαφῃρέθησαν. ἑτέρα γέγονεν ἡμῖν ἡ

[1] σπάνει conj. Re., F. (U, correction in P): σπάνιν Re.
text (other mss.): σπάνις Morel, Savile.

---

[a] Cf. Or. 1. 252 (cited Introduction, p. 237 n.).
[b] This exodus is the contrary of conditions prevailing in

they stay, they will die at the thrust of the sword, but, if they scatter wherever they can, they perhaps stand a chance of safety. 58. For highwaymen there never was such a heaven-sent opportunity ; they get the money, and have a free hand to murder. The river carries the bodies of their victims down to the sea, receiving them when the murderers throw them in. On the country estates there is hardly room to move, while there are so few people left in town that the bakers are on short time. 59. Those who have not yet left town weep that they have not done so ; those who have, weep in their longing for it.[a] Epidemics are rife because of the lack of doctors. The dying are robbed of the family tomb. There is famine in the midst of plenty because of the crowds of squatters everywhere.[b] The governors resent the migrations, but in the uncertainty about the future, they cannot stop them. They cannot guarantee the panic-stricken citizens that no harm will come to them. So in neither case, whether he stays or goes, is anyone free from fear. Indeed, in the latter case, he is already afraid to stay. So what a punishment is involved in having lived so long wedded to such fear ! The expectation of death, even if it never comes about, is more painful than the unexpected blow. 60. Many persons, Sire, have lost their money or their maid-servants in their intolerable distress : many a mother has had her child fall from her lap ; many a man has been stripped by the hordes of bandits, and has been robbed of life and burial too. Our city has changed entirely—to

Antioch since A.D. 382 ; the city had then been a place of refuge for squatters, the hungry peasantry. Hence the unusual feature of the bakers on short time now.

R 651 πόλις ἢ τό γε ἀληθέστερον, οὐδὲ πόλις. | κέκλει-
ται[1] μὲν | θέατρον ἐκεῖνο, κέκλειται[1] δὲ ἱππόδρομος. F 4
οὐ κόρην ἄγεται νυμφίος, οὐ δᾷδες ἅπτονται γάμοις, οὐχ ὑμέναιος ᾄδεται. ἐξῆλθον αὐλοὶ πάντες,
ἐξῆλθον σύριγγες, ἐξῆλθον ᾄσματα. οὐ σκῶμμα,
οὐκ ἀστεῖον, οὐ συμπόσιον. οὐδὲν ἁπλῶς τῶν
ἡδονὴν φερόντων καὶ χάριν ἴδοι τις ἂν[2] ἐν αὐτῇ.
61. καταλέλυνται μὲν αἱ περὶ τοὺς λόγους διατρι-
βαί, καταλέλυνται δὲ αἱ περὶ τὰ γράμματα διδα-
σκαλίαι. διδάσκει δὲ οὐδεὶς οὐδὲ μανθάνει. νο-
σούντων μὲν ἡ χρόα, οὐκ ἐρρωμένων δὲ ἡ φωνή,
πεπλανημένων δὲ ἡ γνώμη, καί τις ἐπ' ἄλλον ὁρμήσας λόγον ἐπ' ἄλλον ἀπηνέχθη.
62. Οἶμαι δὲ καὶ τὸν θεὸν βοηθοῦντά μου τοῖς
λόγοις ἄγειν ἐπὶ τὴν Ῥωμαίων γῆν Περσικὴν
πρεσβείαν. οὐ γὰρ ἂν ἔχοι καλῶς ἰδεῖν ἐκείνους
πόλιν τὴν ⟨τῶν⟩[3] πρὸς ἕω μεγίστην ἐν μίσει τε τῷ
παρὰ σοῦ καὶ κολάσεσιν αἰσχύνην ἐχούσαις τῷ
τρόπῳ τῆς πόλεως. νομίσας οὖν μηδὲ ταῦτα ἀθεεὶ
γεγενῆσθαι γίγνου πρᾷος καὶ μὴ στερήσῃς τὴν ἡμετέραν ὧν Παφλαγόνων τισὶ μεταδέδωκας ὀλίγοις
ὀλίγην οἰκοῦσι πόλιν ἢ καὶ φυλῆς μιᾶς τῶν ὀκτω-
καίδεκα τῶν παρ' ἡμῖν λείπεται.
63. Καλόν, καλόν, ὦ βασιλεῦ, καὶ σὲ τούτοις
σεμνύνεσθαι καὶ παῖδας σοὺς καὶ ταῦτα φιλοτιμίαν

---

[1] κέκλεισται Re. (IM Bad., correction in C).
[2] ἂν F. (V, ins. I) : om. Re. (other mss.).
[3] τὴν mss., om. Re. : τὴν before μεγίστην Re. (Bad., ins.
I), om. F. : ⟨τῶν⟩ ins. Re., F.

---

[a] Cf. Or. 23. 20, 34. 14.   [b] Cf. Or. 20. 47.
[c] Including the withdrawal of civic amenities, as in § 60 ;

be more accurate, it is not a city at all. The theatre there is shut : so is the race course. No bridegroom takes his bride back home, no torch is lit for the marriage, no marriage song is sung. All the flutes and pipes and songs have left us. There is no jest, no witticism, no drinking party. Absolutely nothing can be seen here that is conducive to pleasure and enjoyment. 61. The classes of rhetoric have melted away [a] ; so have the elementary classes. There is no one to teach and no one to learn. There is the pallor of illness, the voice of invalids, the mind of bewilderment. If they start on one topic, they fly off at a tangent to another.

62. I believe that heaven also assists my pleas, and has brought into Roman territory an embassy from Persia.[b] It would not be right for them to see the greatest city of the East visited with your displeasure and with punishments that bring shame upon the life of the city.[c] So consider that this too has not been brought about without gods' aid, and be lenient. Do not deprive our city of the privilege which you granted a few Paphlagonians who inhabit a wretched little town [d] that cannot match any one of the eighteen wards that make up our city.[e]

63. It is a fine thing, Sire, a very fine thing for you to pride yourself on this, and your sons too,[f] and

and the transfer of metropolitan status to Laodicea, Theodoret. *H.E.* 5. 20.

[d] Jones, *LRE* iii. 348, identifies this with the formation of the province of Honorias from areas of Bithynia and Paphlagonia. This was founded and named in honour of Honorius (born Sept. A.D. 382) : *v. R.E.* viii. 2277.

[e] Cf. *Or.* 24. 26 n. (Vol. I, pp. 508 f.).

[f] Arcadius was already Augustus, the infant Honorius not yet so.

τε | καὶ διδαχὴν αὐτοῖς εἶναι τοῦ πῶς δεῖ καιροῖς F
ὁμοίοις προσφέρεσθαι. φέρων μὲν γὰρ δυσκολίας
ὁ χρόνος οὐ παύσεται, μέγα δὲ ἐκείνοις οἶμαι μὴ
τὸν συμβουλεύσοντα ζητεῖν οἴκοθεν καὶ παρὰ τοῦ
R 652 φύσαντος | ἔχουσι τὴν παραίνεσιν.

64. Λύε δὴ τὴν πολλὴν συμφοράν, ὦ βασιλεῦ, καὶ
ταῖς φυγαῖς καὶ τοῖς ὀδυρμοῖς ἐξίσωσον τὴν τῆς
καθόδου φαιδρότητα. κομισάσθω τις τὸν παρ-
θενῶνα, κομισάσθω τὸ δωμάτιον, φιλησάτω τὰς
πρώτας θύρας, τὰς δευτέρας, τὰς ἐπ’ ἐκείναις, ἀπο-
λαυσάτω τῆς νυκτὸς εἰς ὕπνον ἐν τοῖς αὐτοῦ κατα-
κείμενος. 65. πολλῶν μὲν ἀκήκοας ἐγκωμίων[1] τῶν
μὲν σθένει ῥητόρων, τῶν δὲ καὶ μανίᾳ ποιητῶν
εἰργασμένων ἐν οἷς πατρῷαί τε ἀρεταὶ καὶ σαὶ
καὶ ὅπλα καὶ στρατηγίαι καὶ μάχαι καὶ νῖκαι καὶ
τὸ παρὸν δὲ σχῆμα τοῦτο, καθ’ ὃ τοῖς ἄλλοις ἐφ-
έστηκας ἑκόντων ὑπὸ σὲ τῶν βαρβάρων ἰόντων.
ποίησον δὴ καλλίους τοὺς μετὰ ταῦτα λόγους τῷ
καλλίω τοῖς παροῦσι δὴ τούτοις ποιῆσαι τὴν
ὑπόθεσιν. ὄντων γὰρ ἐκείνων μεγάλων ἔνι τι πλέον
ἐν τούτοις ὑπὲρ ὧν ὁ νυνὶ λόγος. |

66. Νεῦσον τοίνυν, ὦ θεία κεφαλή, καὶ ποιήσας
μοι τὸ γῆρας εὔδαιμον τῷ περὶ ὧν ἀφῖγμαι κατωρ-
θωκέναι χρηστὴν ἀγγελίαν φέροντα τοῖς ἐμαυτοῦ
πολίταις ἀπόπεμψον.

---

[1] ἐγκωμίων Morel, F. (Par. 3014): ἐγκωμία Re. (other mss.).

for this to be a stimulus and object-lesson to them as to how to deal with similar situations. Time will not cease to bring its disillusionments, but, I feel, it will be of great importance not to have to seek out counsellors, since they have their inspiration in the family and in their father.

64. Relieve us, then, Sire, of our grave distress, and equate with our exile and our lamentation the gloriousness of our restoration. Let us recover our boudoirs and our bedrooms. Let us kiss our front doors, the inner doors, and those thereafter, and let us enjoy our sleep of nights as we lie down in our own beds. 65. You have heard many panegyrics composed by the strength of oratory and the inspiration of poetry. In them your father's virtues [a] and your own loom large, as do your wars and campaigns, your battles and victories, and this your present state, whereby you are set over all others, now that the barbarians of their own free will acknowledge your sway.[b] Ennoble the orations which will follow hereafter by ennobling the theme of this address of mine. Great though those achievements may be, there is something higher still in the subject of my present discourse.

66. Consent then, most hallowed majesty, and bless my old age with the successful attainment of the object of my coming, and dismiss me as the bearer of good tidings to my fellow citizens.

[a] Count Theodosius, *PLRE* (3), 902 ff. *Cf. Pan. Lat.* 12. 5. 2.   [b] Athanaric ; *cf.* § 16 n.

XX

ΠΡΟΣ ΘΕΟΔΟΣΙΟΝ ΤΟΝ ΒΑΣΙΛΕΑ
ΕΠΙ ΤΑΙΣ ΔΙΑΛΛΑΓΑΙΣ

R 653 1. Ὃ μὲν πολλάκις προεῖπον, ὡς οὔτ᾽ ἔσται τῇ F
πόλει δεινὸν οὐδὲν ἕτερον ἅ τε ἦν ἐν τῇ τιμωρίᾳ
πεπαύσεται, δέδεικται πᾶσιν ἀνθρώποις, ὅπου γε
καὶ πόλιν ὑπῆρξέ μοι προσειπεῖν ἣν οὐκ ἐξῆν πρότε-
ρον· ἐπεὶ δὲ δίκαιον τοῖς εὖ πεποιηκόσιν ἀποδοῦναι
χάριν, δι᾽ ἐμοῦ τοῦτο ποιεῖ τῶν Ἀντιοχέων ἡ πόλις
τῆς μὲν δι᾽ ἔργων ἀμοιβῆς ἀπολελειμμένη, τῇ δὲ
διὰ λόγων, αὕτη¹ γὰρ ἂν εἴη μόνη, χρωμένη. δοκεῖ
δέ μοι καὶ | τοῖς θεοῖς ὕμνος ἅπας εὖ ἔχων ἅπαντος F
ἀναθήματος εἶναι τιμιώτερος, ὡς δηλοῖ Πίνδαρος ὁ
Θηβαῖος μειζόνων παρὰ τοῦ Πυθίου τετυχηκὼς ἢ
οἱ πλεῖστον χρυσίον ἐκεῖσε κεκομικότες.ᵃ 2. αἰσχύ-
νομαι μὲν οὖν τοῖς κατὰ τῆς ἐμαυτοῦ ῥηθησομένοις
R 654 λόγοις, ἐπεὶ δὲ οὐκ ἔνι τοῦτο | φυγόντα σῶσαι τὸ
προσῆκον τῷ περὶ τῆς χάριτος λόγῳ, φράσω τὰ
ἀπὸ τῆς ἀληθείας βουλόμενος μὲν ἂν ἔχειν εἰπεῖν
τι περὶ αὐτῆς ἄμεινον, τῆς ἀνάγκης δὲ ταύτῃ ἀγού-
σης ἐρῶ.

---

¹ αὕτη Re., F. : αὐτὴ mss.

ᵃ Cf. Pausan. 9. 23. 3 ; Eustathius (Biographi Graeci,

310

ORATION 20

TO THE EMPEROR THEODOSIUS, AFTER THE RECONCILIATION

1. I OFTEN foretold that the city would suffer no further harm and that there would be an end put to the business of punishment. This has been demonstrated to all mankind, not least by the fact that I have been able to speak of her as a city, which I could not do before. However, since it is right to to return thanks to one's benefactors, the city of Antioch does so through me and, finding it impossible to make due exchange by deeds, she uses the method of words—the only one left to her. Every hymn well done is, I feel, more precious to the gods than any offering, as is proved by Pindar the Theban,[a] who received a greater reward from the Pythian than any who had bestowed there vast treasures of gold. 2. Ashamed as I am of the tale I have to tell against my native city, it is impossible for me, if I seek to evade the issue, to preserve the elements appropriate to a speech of thanks. Hence I shall speak the plain truth. For all my desire to be able to tell a pleasanter tale about her, I shall say my say in the way that necessity dictates.

ed. Westermann, pp. 92 ff.). Special privileges for Pindar's descendants at Delphi, Plut. *De sera num. vind.* 13.

3. Ἐγένετο φαύλη περὶ βασιλέα χρηστὸν ἡ ἡμε-
τέρα πόλις μετὰ μὲν τὴν τῆς ἐπιστολῆς ἀνάγνωσιν
ἀποσειομένη τὴν ἀρχὴν ἐν τῷ δοκεῖν ἐπὶ τὸν θεὸν
καταφεύγειν, τῶν γὰρ ἀδικουμένων ἀφαιρεῖν οὐκ
ἐνῆν δήπου ταυτὶ τὰ ῥήματα. λαβοῦσα δὲ ταύτην τὴν ἀρχὴν ἐν τῷ δικαστηρίῳ πονηρὰ συμμορία
πλείους ἔξω τῶν θυρῶν προσλαβοῦσα καὶ μετ᾽
ἐκείνους ἔτι πλείους καὶ πάλιν ἄλλους συνέχεαν μὲν
τὰν τῷ κοινῷ βαλανείῳ νόμῳ διατεταγμένα, κινη-
θέντες δὲ ὑπ᾽ αὐτῶν ὧν ἔδρασαν ἐπὶ μείζω καὶ
παρανομώτερα προσπίπτουσι μὲν οὕτω σφοδρῶς
τῇ τοῦ ἄρχοντος κιγκλίδι καὶ ταῖς μετ᾽ ἐκείνην
θύραις, ὥστε δεῖσαι τοὺς ὑπηρέτας μὴ καὶ | ῥή- F
ξαντες αὐτὰς ἀποκτείνωσιν αὐτόν, οἷα τοιοῦτοι και-
ροὶ πεποιήκασι πολλαχοῦ, τοῦτο δὲ οὐ δυνηθέντες
κατέχεαν μὲν τῶν ἑαυτῶν κεφαλῶν ὕβρεις, οὕτω
γὰρ ἄμεινον εἰπεῖν, ἃς οὐδ᾽ ἐν καπηλείῳ τῶν τις
R 655 ἀγοραίων | ἐφ᾽ ἕτερον τῶν ἴσων. 4. τούτῳ δὲ ὄντι
τοσούτῳ τὰ διὰ τῶν ἔργων ἐπέθηκαν δραμόντες ἐπὶ
σέ τε καὶ τὴν γυναῖκα τὴν σὴν καὶ τέκνα,[1] χερσί τε
καὶ κάλοις ταῦτα δείξαντες χαμαί. καὶ οὐκ ἀπέχρη
ταῦτα, ἀλλ᾽ εἷλκον οἱ μὲν ὅλους, οἱ δὲ διεσπασμέ-
νους. καὶ οἱ μὲν τοιαῦτα ἠδίκουν, οἱ δὲ τῷ βασιλεῖ
ταῦτα ἀγγελοῦντες ᾖσαν πεφρικότες οἷα σφᾶς δεή-

[1] τέκνα ⟨καὶ⟩ χερσί F.

---

[a] Cf. Or. 19. 25 ff. Again the responsibility for protest is
placed on Christians (τὸν θεὸν).

[b] The claque, as shown by Browning, J.R.S. 1952. The
δικαστήριον is the headquarters of the consularis (δικαστής),
cf. Or. 19. 28.

[c] For the activities of the mob outside the baths cf. Or.

3. Our city let herself down towards a good emperor when, after the recital of the imperial rescript, it tried to shake off the bonds of discipline by having recourse ostensibly to the god,[a] for obviously such words could not remove any of its grievances. An unscrupulous gang found the start for this in the courtroom,[b] and gained more support outside its doors, and yet more and more again. The official regulations for the public baths [c] they turned upside down, and spurred on by their own actions to worse excesses still, they attacked the railings of the governor's house, and then its doors, so violently that the servants were scared that they would break them down and murder him, as has often occurred elsewhere on such occasions. However, failing in this, they heaped upon their heads [d] insults—to employ a euphemism—insults which none of the market people would apply to one of their own kidney even at their stalls. 4. That was bad enough, but they set the seal upon it by their actions, rushing to the attack against the statues of yourself, your wife and children,[e] and revealing them cast down to the ground by hands and ropes. Even that was not enough ; they dragged them along, either whole or smashed to bits. Such were their crimes, and messengers went to inform the emperor of it, in fear and trembling for the news

22. 6. For the narrative of the sequence of events cf. Downey, *Antioch*, pp. 426 ff.

[d] A play on language, as noted by Scholiast on V : κεφαλὰς ἐνταῦθα τοὺς βασιλεῖς αὐτοὺς λέγει, emphasized by ἑαυτῶν. Thus the pun is (a) their sovereign heads, (b) their own persons.

[e] Cf. Sozom. *H.E.* 7. 23, Theodoret, *H.E.* 5. 20. Libanius rarely mentions the princes by name, their mother (Flaccilla) never.

313

σει μηνύειν. ἡ πόλις δὲ ἐθρηνεῖτο παρὰ τῶν τὰ
τοιαῦτα τεθεαμένων. 5. αἱ δὲ ἐλπίδες, ἡ[1] μὲν ἥξειν
λόχον[2] ἐπὶ τῷ τῶν παραπιπτόντων φόνῳ, ἡ δὲ οὐ
κτενεῖν μέν, δι᾽ ἁρπαγῆς δὲ τὰ πάντων ἕξειν,[3]
ἑτέρα δὲ[4] ψῆφος ἐπῆγε δημίων δεξιαῖς ἀπολέσθαι
μὲν τὸ βουλεῦον, ἀπολέσθαι δὲ μοῖραν οὐ μικρὰν
τῶν ἐν τῷ δήμῳ. |

6. Πῶς οὖν οὗτος; παιδεύει μὲν τιμωρίᾳ τινὶ τὴν F
ἴασιν ἐχούσῃ δυναμένην[5] τὸ πεπαυμένον τῇ λύπῃ πάλιν ἐλεύθερον τῶν λυπούντων ποιῆσαι καὶ μὴ ἁμιλ-
λάσθων ἵπποι, μηδ᾽[6] εἰς θέατρον ἴτω μήτε ὁ τέρπων
μήτε ὁ τερπόμενος καὶ μικρᾶς ὀνόματι πόλεως ἡ
μεγάλη κεκλήσθω καὶ τῆς ἐκ βαλανείων ἀπεχέσθω
τρυφῆς, ὧν οὐδὲν ἄλυπον, ἐπὶ δὲ τὴν ἐνίων κρίσιν
πέμπει μὲν οἷς συνῄδει δικαιοσύνην, ἐλέγχου δὲ
ποιήσας κυρίους ὅμως[7] αὐτῷ τὸ λοιπὸν ἐφύλαξεν
R 656 | ὅπως ὁπόσον ἀφήσει ἅπασιν εἴη καταφανές. 7.
καὶ οἱ μὲν ἀποροῦντες ἀρνήσεως ἔκειντο ἐν τῷ οἰκήματι καὶ παρῆσαν οἱ τούτων οἰκεῖοι διὰ τῶν πρὸ
τοῦ θανάτου φιλημάτων τὴν μετ᾽ ὀδυρμῶν χαρι-
ζόμενοι χάριν. ἔπειθ᾽, ὅπερ ἥλιος ἐργάζεται νικῶν
ἀκτῖσι νέφη, φῶς ἧκεν ἐπιστολῆς ἀπελαῦνον τὸ
σκότος, καὶ πᾶν μὲν στυγνὸν ἐξεκεχωρήκει, πᾶν δὲ
εἰς εὐφροσύνην ἄγον εἰσεληλύθει καὶ προσηγορίαν
τε τὴν πρὶν αὖθις εἴχομεν καὶ θεαμάτων εἴδη καὶ
λούσασθαι δὴ καὶ τὴν αὑτῆς γῆν ἡ πόλις καὶ τὴν

---

[1] ἡ Cobet, F. (T) : αἱ Re. (other MSS.).
[2] λόχον Re., F. : λόγον MSS. [3] ἥξειν Cobet.
[4] δὲ F. (V) : om. Re. (other MSS.). | ψῆφον M.
[5] δυναμένην Re. (PU) : -μένη F. (other MSS.).
[6] μηδ᾽ F. (conj. Sintenis) : μήτ᾽ Re. (MSS.).
[7] ὅμως Re., F. : ὡς MSS. (om. V).

[a] Cf. Or. 19. 62, Jo. Chrys. Hom. 17 (P.G. xlix. 176).

they had to tell, and the city was filled with the lamentations of those who had seen such enormities. 5. It was expected either that a regiment would come to massacre all in its path, or else, even though bloodshed were avoided, that it would loot and take possession of all private property. Yet another opinion had it that the council would be put to death at the hands of the executioners, along with no small number of the populace.

6. How, then, does our emperor behave ? He schools us by a punishment which involves the ability to cure ; and this cure, by its discomfort, can once again rid the lately afflicted portion of the sources of discomfiture. So he proclaimed, " There are to be no horse races : no one is to go to the theatre, either to give or to partake of enjoyment. The great city is to have the title of a petty town, and it is to keep away from the luxury of the baths." [a] None of this is without discomfort. He also sent to try individual cases men [b] whom he knew to be people of integrity, and while giving them full judicial powers, he yet reserved for himself the possible means of allowing all to see the extent of his leniency. 7. The prisoners could make no denial : they lay in jail and their relatives went to see them for the last embrace before their execution, doing them this mournful service. Then, just as the sun's rays dispel the gloom, a despatch arrived with a light that banished the darkness. All our miseries had vanished, and everything conducive to our happiness returned. Once more we had our former title and our various entertainments and our baths, and our city had its own lands restored,

[b] Caesarius, *mag. off.*, and Ellebichus, *mag. mil.*, cf. *Or.* 21-22.

αὐτοῦ τροφὴν ὁ πένης. 8. ὁ μὲν γὰρ ᾿Ασκληπιὸς
ἑνί τινι λέγεται | λῦσαι θάνατον καὶ ῾Ηρακλῆς μιᾷ F 4
τινι γυναικί, σοὶ δὲ περὶ ὅλην τοῦτο πέπρακται
πόλιν· ἢν ὅστις ἀναβεβιωκέναι λέγοι, καλῶς ἂν
λέγοι. τοσοῦτον εἴργαστο δρασμὸν ὁ φόβος οὐ σοῦ
φεύγειν ἀναγκάσαντος, τῆς δὲ προσηκούσης τιμωρίας τοῦ δέους.[1] ὃ παύσας, ὦ βασιλεῦ, μεστὴν
αὖθις σωμάτων ἀπέφηνας τὴν πόλιν.

9. Γνοίη δ᾿ ἄν τις, ἡλίκα δέδωκεν, εἰ λογίσαιτο
πόσος ἂν ἦν αὐτῷ λόγος ἐπιθέντι τὴν ὀφειλομένην
δίκην, ἣν εἴ τις ᾐτιάσατο λαβόντα συκοφάντης ἂν
ἦν. ἦν δ᾿ ἂν ἡ προσήκουσα δίκη πολὺ μὲν αἷμα,
πολλοὶ δὲ νεκροί, δήμευσις τῶν ὄντων, ἐκβεβλῆ-
σθαι τῆς οἰκείας[2] καὶ μηδ᾿ ἀποθανόντι μετεῖναι
πατρῴων μνημάτων. 10. εἰ δή τις ἐπελαμβάνετο
R 657 τούτων, τὸ στόμα ἂν ἐνεφράττετο | τοῦτο μὲν ταῖς
βλασφημίαις, τοῦτο δὲ ταῖς εἰκόσιν οὕτω πολλαῖς.
πρὸς γὰρ δὴ τὸν ἄτοπον ἐκεῖνον ἦν ἂν τῷ βασιλεῖ
λέγειν· ἄνθρωπε, τῶν ῥημάτων οὐκ ἀκήκοας; τοὺς
ἑλκομένους οὐκ εἶδες; εἰ γὰρ περὶ μόνον τὸν νεώ-
τερον τῶν παίδων ταῦτ᾿ ἦν ἠσελγημένα, φέρειν
ἔδει· εἰ δὲ πρόσκειται μὲν ὁ πρεσβύτερος, τούτῳ
δὲ ἡ τεκοῦσα, τῇ τεκούσῃ δὲ ἐγώ, καὶ τὸ δὴ τούτων ἀφορητότερον ἐμοί, τὸν ἱππέα τὸν πατέρα τὸν
ἐμὸν αὐτῷ ἵππῳ κατενεγκόντες, ὥσπερ ἐν ἱπ|πο- F

---

[1] τοῦ δέους Re., F. (V, C corrected) : τὸ δέος Morel (other
mss.).   [2] οἰκείας Re., F. : οἰκίας Morel (mss.).

---

[a] For organized poor relief cf. § 38 below. The Christian
church daily maintained 3000 poor in Antioch, Jo. Chrys.
Hom. in Matth. 66 (*P.G.* lvii. 658). See also Liebeschuetz,
p. 129.

and the poor,[a] their food.   8. Asclepius, so it is said,
freed a single individual from death : Hercules did
the same for a single woman,[b] but you have done
that for a whole city, for people would be quite right
to speak of her restoration to life.   Panic had caused
such an exodus, not under any compulsion from you
to do so, but from fear of condign punishment.   In
putting a stop to that, Sire, you revealed the city
once more with its full quota of inhabitants.

9. You may recognize the extent of his generosity
if you consider how much reason he would have had
for imposing the penalty due, and if anyone had
criticized him for imposing it, that would have been
sheer humbug.   The proper punishment would be
mass executions and killing, confiscation of property,
exile from one's own land, and a ban even on the
dead having anything to do with the family tombs.
10. Indeed, if anyone complained of this, his mouth
would be stopped by the thought of those insults,
and the treatment meted out to all those statues.
In fact, to such an idiot the emperor could rejoin,
" Sir, did you not hear those words ? did you not see
them pulling down the statues ?   If such outrages
as this had been committed against my younger son
only, I would have had to bear it.   But if, besides
him, my elder son was the victim, and besides him,
his mother, and besides her, myself, and—most
intolerable of all for me—if they have demolished
the equestrian statue of my father,[c] horse and all,
hacking it as though they were in a cavalry charge,

[b] Asclepius and Hippolytus, cf. Or. 13. 42 (Vol. I, p. 26 n.).
Heracles and Alcestis, v. Eurip. Alc.

[c] Honorius, Arcadius, Flaccilla and Count Theodosius.
For the demolition of the equestrian statue cf. Or. 19. 30.

μαχίᾳ τρώσαντες, ἀμφοτέρους ἐγέλων ὡς οὐκ ὄντος τοῦ χαλεπανοῦντος ὑπὲρ τοιούτων κακῶν οὐδὲ καταλελειμμένου τοῦ ληψομένου δίκην, πόσους δέοι καθ᾽ ἕκαστον τῶν ὑβρισμένων ἀποθανεῖν;

11. Οὐκοῦν τὸ μὲν θανάτῳ λαβεῖν ὑπὲρ τοιούτων τιμωρίαν ἄμεμπτον διότιπερ ἔννομον, τὸ δὲ μὴ τοιαύτης δεηθῆναι δίκης ἥμερον καὶ τὸ μὲν ὅλως τινὰ λαβεῖν νουθετοῦντος, τὸ δὲ μηδὲ τηλικαύτην πράου τε καὶ πειρωμένου τοῖς θεοῖς εἰς ὅσον οἷόν τε ἀφομοιοῦν ἑαυτόν. τί γὰρ δὴ τὸ 'κείνων; 12. ἄνωθεν μὲν ἅπαντα καθορῶσι καὶ ἀκούουσιν, ἐν δ᾽ αὖ
R 658 τοῖς ἐπὶ | γῆς καὶ λεγομένοις καὶ πραττομένοις ἀδικήματα πολλά τε ἄλλα καὶ δὴ καὶ ὅταν δι᾽ αὐτοὺς ἄνθρωποι πράττωσι κακῶς, ἀδικεῖσθαί τε λέγουσι παρ᾽ ἐκείνων καὶ βλέποντες εἰς τὸν οὐρανὸν οὐδενὸς ἀπέχονται ῥήματος. εἶδον ἐγώ τινας καὶ λίθους ἐπ᾽ αὐτὸν ἀφιέντας. οἱ δ᾽ ἐν τοσαύτῃ[1] δυνάμει τοῦ λαβεῖν δίκην εἰ βουληθεῖεν ὄντες, οὐ βούλονται. εἰ δ᾽ ἅπασιν εἵποντο τοῖς τοιούτοις αἱ δίκαι, πάντα ἂν ἦν καθ᾽ ἡμέραν τῶν ἀπολλυμένων πλέα καὶ οὐδ᾽ ἂν ἐξήρκουν οἱ ζῶντες πρὸς τὰς ταφάς. νῦν δὲ καὶ ἐν αὐτῷ τούτῳ τὸ κρείτ|τους F 4 εἶναι δεικνύουσι τῷ μηδὲ δικαίῳ χρῆσθαι θυμῷ πολλάκις. 13. οὕτως οὖν ἡγεῖτο θεοῖς ἴσος ὄντως ὁ βασιλεὺς φανεῖσθαι καὶ διοτρεφὴς ὡς ἀληθῶς, εἰ μὴ τιμωρίαις ἥδοιτο ταῖς κατὰ τὴν ἀξίαν. καὶ τοῦτ᾽ εἶναι νομίζει βασιλικώτερον καὶ ᾧ μᾶλλον ἂν ἀρχὴ διασώζοιτο. οὐ γὰρ οὕτως ἀγαπᾶται τὸ κρατοῦν οὔτε ἀπὸ τροπαίων οὔτε ἀπὸ πόλεων ἢ λαμβανομένων ὅπλοις ἢ ποιουμένων σπονδὰς οὔτε

_____
[1] τοσαύτη F. (mss.) : τοιαύτη Re.

[a] Or. 19. 11 n.

and made fun of them both, just as though there was no one to resent such wickedness and none left to punish it, how many should be put to death for each one of their outrages ? "

11. So there could be no complaint against the imposition of the death penalty for such misconduct, for it is quite legal. But to have no recourse to such a penalty denotes clemency. The application of some general punishment would be a corrective ; to omit even that signifies a gentleness which attempts to equate itself with the gods to the very utmost.[a] For how do the gods go on ? 12. They observe everything from on high, and listen to it, but in what is said and done on earth, many crimes are committed, especially when men get into a mess through their own fault and say that the gods have wronged them. They glare up at the heaven and abstain from absolutely no kind of abuse. Why ! I have even seen people hurl stones to heaven ! Though the gods have such power to punish if they see fit, they still refrain. If punishment automatically followed on such misdeeds, the whole world would be full of men dying every day, and those left alive would not be enough to bury them. As things are, they reveal their divine attributes by the simple fact of their repeated refusal to exercise their wrath, even when it is justified. 13. In this way, then, the emperor believed that he would reveal himself as a peer of the gods, truly nurtured of the divine, if he did not delight in merited punishments. He thinks this more imperial, and the means by which an empire may be more safely preserved. For the ruling power gets its popularity not so much from its trophies, from cities either taken in war or received into alliance,

ἀπὸ πλήθους στρατιωτῶν οὔτε ἀπὸ νόμων θέσεως
οὔτε ἀπὸ σοφίας οὔτε ἀπὸ τῆς ἐν τῷ δικάζειν ἀκριβείας, ὡς ἀπὸ τοῦ συγγνώμην ἐν ἁμαρτίαις νέμειν.

14. Ἃ μοι δοκεῖ καλῶς οὗτος ἐπιστάμενος οἷς
εἶχεν ἐγκαλεῖν τὰ μέγιστα πρὸ τῶν τῆς ταραχῆς[1]
χρόνων, τούτων[2] ἐξὸν κτεῖναι φείσασθαι †ἀπὸ τῆς
αὐτῆς ἀρετῆς. τοῖς μὲν†[3] καὶ πλήξασι καὶ ἑλκύσασι
R 659 τὸν Σκύθην καὶ καταποντίσασι | τὸν νεκρόν, ὧν καθ᾽
ἕκαστον ἠδικεῖτο βασιλεύς, τῆς μέμψεως ⟨δ᾽⟩ ἐπὶ
τὸ τῆς πόλεως κοινὸν εἰκότως ἐρχομένης τὸ μὲν
τῆς ἡμέρας ἥμισυ τὴν ὀργὴν ἐδέξατο τὴν μέχρι
τῶν οὐ δεδομένων ἄρτων, ἔπειτ᾽ ἦν, ὃ πρότερον,
καὶ ἡ λῆψις καὶ ἡ δόσις, καὶ σὺν ἐκείνοις ἕκαστος
οἴκαδε ἤρχετο, οἱ ἀπεκτονότες τε καὶ τὰ ἄλλα
προστεθεικότες. 15. ἕτερον τοίνυν πολὺ θαυ|μα- F
στότερον. τοὺς γὰρ ἐπ᾽ αὐτῇ τῇ βασιλείᾳ πολλάκις συνελθόντας καὶ ἐν τοιαύταις βουλαῖς δια-
τρίψαντας καὶ οἷα περὶ τοιούτων εἰκός, τὰ μὲν εἰ-
ρηκότας, τὰ δὲ ἀκηκοότας καὶ δὴ καὶ μαντείοις
ἠνωχληκότας λαβὼν ὁμολογοῦντας ἀκούσας ψήφῳ
πρὸς θάνατον ἀγομένους ἀφῆκεν ἕως ἔξεστι βιω-
σομένους τιμήσας τὸν ταῦτα εἰς μέσον ἀγαγόντα
θεὸν τῷ τὸ ξίφος οὕτως ἐγγὺς ὂν ἐπισχεῖν.

16. Διὰ τοιαύτης τοίνυν φιλανθρωπίας ἥκων καὶ

---

[1] ταραχῆς F. : ἀρχῆς Re. (MSS.).   [2] τούτους VM.
[3] Corrupt. ἀπὸ τῆς αὐτῆς ἀρετῆς. τοῖς μὲν . . . MSS., editors. ἀπὸ . . . ἀρετῆς seems to be a gloss derived from § 13 which has usurped the true reading. Read : φείσασθαι. ἐπετίμησε γὰρ τοῖς καὶ πλήξασι . . . τῆς μέμψεως ⟨δ᾽⟩.

---

[a] Reading corrupt in MSS. The translation is that of the suggestion in the critical note.   [b] Cf. Or. 19. 22.
[c] The canon of corn supply for Constantinople was estab-
lished by Constantine himself (cf. C. Th. 14. 16. 2 of A.D. 416).

from the multitudes of its soldiery, or from its legislation, wisdom and scrupulous administration of
justice, as from its grants of pardon in their misdeeds.

14. It seems to me that our emperor was fully
aware of this ; though he could have executed those
against whom he could have brought the most serious
charges in the period before the present distrubances,
he spared them.[a] When the Scyth was attacked and
lynched,[b] and his body thrown into the sea—every
single one of these actions being a crime against
his majesty—he reproved those responsible for them ;
and though his reproof naturally applied to the whole
civic community, for just half a day it experienced
his wrath, which was confined to the stopping of the
bread distribution. Thereafter things were as they
had been before [c] : the distribution took place, and
the bread was received, and everyone made his way
home with it, those who had committed the murder
and the other outrages too. 15. There is yet a more
remarkable instance. He arrested the seditious gang
who had often assembled to conspire against the
imperial house and spent their time in such plots,
uttering or listening to the statements usually made
on such occasions,[d] and who had even resorted to
sorcery, and they confessed. However, having heard
their confessions, just as they were being led to the
execution to which they had been sentenced, he released them, to live their normal span of life. By
withholding the sword which loomed so close he
honoured the god who had brought all this to light.

16. After pursuing such a course of humanity and

His regulations on *annonae civicae* referred to, *ibid.* 17. 9,
10, 12.   [d] *Cf. Or.* 19. 21 n.

πολλῇ τῇ περὶ αὐτὴν μελέτῃ κεχρημένος καὶ προσ-
R 660 ηγορίαν | ἐντεῦθεν κτησάμενος οὐκ ἔμελλες οὔτε
ἐκείνην καταλύσειν οὔτε ταύτην ἐξελέγξειν ἀλλὰ
συμφωνοῦντα σαυτῷ παρέξεσθαι τὸν χρόνον καὶ
τῶν προτέρων οὐ χείρω δείξειν τὰ δεύτερα. ἐπαι-
νῶν δήπου σὺ καὶ Λακεδαιμονίων καὶ Ἀθηναίων
τὸ σεσωκέναι πόλεις ἐμέμψω πολλάκις ἑκατέρων
τὸ διεφθαρκέναι πόλεις καὶ ᾤου δὴ βελτίους ἀμφοτέρους εἶναι μὴ προσθέντας τὰ σκυθρωπότερα.
καίτοι πῶς οὐκ ἐγγὺς θεῶν βασιλεὺς τοιαῦτα μὲν
θαυμάζων, τοιαῦτα δὲ αἰτιώμενος;

17. Ἔδει καὶ τὸν τειχίσαντα στρατιώταις τε καὶ
ὅπλοις τὴν Ῥωμαίων ἀρχὴν καὶ τοῦτ᾽ ἔχειν ἐν τῇ
ψυχῇ τἀγαθὸν τὸ μὴ ῥᾳδίως ἐπὶ τοὺς τῶν ὑπηκόων
| χωρεῖν αὐχένας. οὕτω γὰρ οὐκ ἄν[1] οὑμὸς πατὴρ F 4
τὸ τοῦ πατρὸς ἑαυτοῦ ποτε σῶμα ὑπεδέξατο καὶ
R 661 τῇ τετμημένῃ κεφαλῇ | συγκατέθαψεν[2] οὐκ ὀφει-
λούσῃ δίκην. 18. σκόπει δέ· πεντακοσίων τις ἦρ-
χεν ἐν Σελευκείᾳ ταύτῃ στρατιωτῶν οἷς ἔργον ἦν
βαθὺ ποιεῖν τοῖς αὐτῶν πόνοις τῷ λιμένι τὸ στόμα.
τούτους ἔδει καὶ περὶ ἄρτον ᾧ θρέψονται τῆς νυκτὸς
ταλαιπωρεῖν, ὡς μὴ εἶναι καθεύδειν. ταῦθ᾽ οἱ
πεντακόσιοι μὴ δυνάμενοι φέρειν ὠθοῦσιν εἰς βασιλέως προσηγορίαν τὸν ἐφεστηκότα κτείνειν ἀπει-
λοῦντες οὐκ ἀνασχόμενον. ὁ δὲ τὸν ἐγγυτέρω δια-
κρουόμενος θάνατον ἤγετο στένων πινόντων ἐκ τῶν
ἀγρῶν ἄχρι μέθης τῶν περὶ τὸν λιμένα κεκακω-

---

[1] οὐκ ἄν F. (U, insertions in Pl.) : before ποτε, conj. Re. :
οὐ γὰρ ἂν conj. Cobet : om. Re. text. (other mss.).
[2] συγκατέθαψεν conj. Re., Cobet, F. : συγκατέσκαψεν Re.
text (mss.).

concerning himself so much with the practice of it, and winning a name therefrom, you were not likely to do away with the habit or prove your title false. Rather you set the times in harmony with yourself, and show your later actions to be not inferior to your previous ones.   Indeed, while singing the praises of the Spartans and of the Athenians for saving cities,[a] you often blamed them both for destroying cities, and you certainly thought both would have been better without the addition of their atrocities.   Then, an emperor who expresses such admiration and disapproval is obviously close to the divine.

17. That emperor [b] who set a wall of armed soldiery to defend the Roman empire ought to have been endowed also with the virtue of an unwillingness wantonly to attack the persons of his subjects. For then my father would never have had to recover his father's body and bury it with the severed head that never deserved the punishment.   18. Just imagine it ! There was a commander of a battalion of 500 soldiers stationed in Seleuceia here.   Their duty was to work on deepening the harbour mouth, and they had to do night fatigues to bake the bread for their rations, and so they could get no sleep. The battalion found this intolerable, and forced their commander to adopt the imperial title, threatening to murder him if he refused.   He evaded the death which loomed the nearer and was led on lamenting, while his men, after their privations at the harbour, went on a drinking bout and got thoroughly drunk with the stuff from the farms.

[a] Cf. Or. 19. 13.
[b] Diocletian, and the revolt of Eugenius, Or. 19. 45 n.

LIBANIUS

μένων. 19. εἰσπεσόντων δὲ δεῦρο περὶ ἡλίου δύσιν
τῶν οὐδὲ οὗ[1] γῆς ἦσαν διὰ τὸν οἶνον εἰδότων μοχ-
λοὺς τοῖς δόρασιν ἀντιτάξαντες οἱ τότε τὴν πόλιν
ἔχοντες, ἐκοινώνουν δὲ ἄρα καὶ γυναῖκες τοῦ ἔργου,
περὶ πρῶτον ὕπνον τὸ τέλος ἐπέθηκαν καὶ ἦν οὐ-
δεὶς ὃς οὐκ ἔκειτο. τούτους τοίνυν τοὺς | τῆς μὲν F
ταραχῆς[2] οὐ κεκοινωνηκότας, τοὺς δ' ἁμαρτόντας |
R 662 κατενεγκόντας καὶ τὸ πραχθὲν οὐ βουλομένους μὲν
γεγενῆσθαι, γεγονὸς δὲ σβέσαντας ἀπεστέρησε τῶν
ἐν τῇ βουλῇ πρώτων, ὥσπερ αὖ καὶ τὴν Σελεύ-
κειαν. ἠδικήκει δὲ οὐδετέρα οὔθ' ὅθεν ὡρμήθησαν
οὔθ' οὗ διεφθάρησαν. ἀλλ' ὅμως ἐδόκει δεῖν τοὺς ἐξ
ἑκατέρας πόλεως[3] ἀπολωλέναι. 20. καὶ πλείστων
δὴ τὸν ἐμὸν πάππον λέγεται δακρύων τετυχηκέναι
κάλλους τε καὶ μεγέθους τοῦτο πεποιηκότων. εἰ δ'
ἐῴκει σοὶ καὶ κατὰ μικρόν, ὦ βασιλεῦ, τῇ μὲν οὐκ
ἂν ἐνεκάλεσε καθαρευούσῃ τῆς αἰτίας, τὴν δ' ἡμετέραν κἂν ἐστεφάνωσεν ἐφ' οὕτω ταχείᾳ νίκῃ.

21. Ὥσπερ οὖν ἐκεῖνα μένει τε καὶ μνημονεύεται
καὶ μνημονευθήσεται καὶ λήθην οὐδεὶς ἂν αὐτοῖς
ἐμποιήσειε χρόνος, οὕτω καὶ τὰ σὰ δὴ ταῦτα
μνήμης ἀθανάτου τε τεύξεται[4] καὶ οὔτε τῆς ἡμετέρας ἀνοίας ἀνήκοος οὐδεὶς ἀνθρώπων ἔσται, οἷός
R 663 τε | ἡμῖν ἐφ' οἷος γεγένησαι πᾶν τὸ ἐπιγιγνόμε-
νον εἴσεται.

22. Νικᾷς δὲ οὐ τοῦτον μόνον, ἀλλὰ καὶ τὸν τοῦ
Διὸς παῖδα δόξαντα εἶναι τὸν Ἀλέξανδρον εἴς γε

---

[1] οὗ F. (Par. 3017) : ᾗ V : οἱ Re. (other mss.).
[2] ταραχῆς conj. Re., F. : ἀρχῆς Re. text (mss.).
[3] πόλεως ⟨πρώτους⟩ conj. Re., F.
[4] τε τεύξεται F. : τετεύξεται CAPVTU : τεύξεται Re. (other mss.).

324

19. About sunset they made their entry into the city here, without the slightest idea of where on earth they were because of the drink taken, and the citizens of that time opposed their spears with crowbars. Why, even the women joined in, and early in the night they had the job finished, and not a man of them was left alive. Well, these people who had had no part in the uprising and who had crushed the rebels, who never wanted such an incident to occur and had quelled it when it did—these people he robbed of the foremost members of their council, as, for that matter, he did in Seleuceia also. Neither city, not the one from which they had marched out nor the one where they were slain, had committed any crime, but for all that it was decreed that the civic heads of each should be put to death. 20. The story goes that my grandfather in particular was much lamented, for both his handsome features and physique. If that emperor had been only a little like you, Sire, he would have brought no accusation against Seleuceia, since it was free from guilt, and our own city he would even have crowned after such a quick victory.

21. Those events linger on. They are remembered and will continue to be remembered, and no lapse of time can cause them to be forgotten. Similarly, these actions of yours also will achieve immortal fame, and there will be no man unacquainted with our stupidity, and all posterity will know of your generosity to us who so little deserve it.

22. You excel not just him, but also Alexander, the reputed son of Zeus,[a] as regards clemency, at

---

[a] Cf. Or. 18. 297 (Vol. I, p. 479 n.).

ἡμερότητα· | ὁ μέν γε Θήβας, ἐπειδήπερ ἐλευθε- F
ρίας ἥν ποτ᾽ εἶχεν ἐπεθύμησεν ἡ πόλις, ἀνέσπασε
πόλιν ψευδέσιν ἀγγελίαις ἀπατηθεῖσαν, ὃ κἂν εἷς
ἀνὴρ πάθοι σύνεσιν ἔχειν δοκῶν· σὺ δ᾽ οὐδ᾽ ὅσον
εἰς οἰκίδιον τοῦτο ἔδρασας ἡμέτερον. ὁ δὲ πλὴν
μιᾶς οἰκίας τῆς Πινδάρου τὴν ἄλλην καθελὼν πόλιν
καὶ τούτῳ τιμήσας τὸν ποιητὴν καλλίων ἂν ἦν ὅλῃ
τῇ πόλει τιμήσας τὸν ποιητήν. ἐκείνῳ τε γὰρ
ἔπρεπε δοῦναι τοσοῦτον καὶ τῷ Πινδάρῳ λαβεῖν.
μιᾶς δὲ οἰκίας ἑστώσης ἐν πόλει κειμένῃ τί τὸ
κέρδος ἢ τῇ πόλει παρ᾽ ἐκείνης ἢ αὐτῇ γε ἐκείνῃ,
ἣν οὐδ᾽ ἂν οἰκεῖν ὁ δεσπότης ἐν τοιούτοις τοῖς περὶ
αὐτὴν ἔχοι;

23. Ἀλλὰ μὴν πρός γε τὴν δοκοῦσαν Φιλίππου
φιλανθρωπίαν περὶ τοὺς ἁλόντας Ἀθηναίων ὅτ᾽
Ἀργαῖον κατῆγον, οὐ χαλεπὸν ἀντειπεῖν ὡς οὐκ
εἴη τοῦτο φιλανθρωπία. τοῦ θεραπεύειν γὰρ Ἀθη-
R 664 ναίους ἀνάγκην ἔχων τὴν ἀσθένειαν | αὐτοῦ οὓς
ἡδέως ἂν | ἐκόλασεν ἄκων ἀφῆκε τὸ μηδὲν παρ᾽ F
Ἀθηναίων ὕστερον παθεῖν ὠνούμενος. οὐκοῦν οὐκ
ἦν αἰχμαλώτους ἐλεοῦντος τὸ γιγνόμενον ἀλλὰ τὴν
αὐτοῦ χώραν πειρωμένου ῥύεσθαι, πολὺ δέ, οἶμαι,
τὸ μέσον φιλανθρωπίας καὶ φόβου. σὺ δὲ ποίους
μὲν Ἀθηναίους, ποίους δὲ Ἀθηναίων στρατηγούς,
ποίας δὲ ναῦς, ποίας δὲ ἱππαγωγοὺς τριήρεις δεί-
σειν ἔμελλες; οὕτως εἰλικρινὲς ἐνταῦθα τὸ τῆς
φιλανθρωπίας, καὶ οὐδεὶς ἂν οὐδαμόθεν αἰτίαν φαυ-
λοτέραν περιάψειε τῷ πράγματι.

24. Λείπεται κἀκεῖνος τῶν σῶν δὴ τοῦτο ὁ τῇ

___

<a> In 335 b.c. Rumours of Alexander's death caused this

least. He razed to the ground the city of Thebes, when, misled by false news, it tried to recover the liberty it once possessed [a]; but any seemingly sensible individual might be similarly misled. But you have not done this even to any shanty of ours. When he destroyed the whole town except for Pindar's house alone, and so did honour to the poet, he would have done better to honour the poet by sparing the whole city, for it would have been to his credit to grant so much and to Pindar's to receive it. But what is the profit for one house to stand in a ruined city, either for the city or for the house, when the owner cannot occupy it because of the desolation all round ?

23. Moreover, with regard to the reputed generosity of Philip towards his Athenian prisoners when they tried to restore Argaeus, it was not difficult to retort that this was not generosity at all.[b] His own insecurity forced him to court Athenians, and he reluctantly released them when he would gladly have punished them, so purchasing from Athens his immunity for the future. So the incident was due not to pity for the prisoners, but to an attempt to protect his own territory ; and there is any amount of difference, in my opinion, between generosity and fear. But in your case, Sire, what sort of Athenians, or their commanders, ships or horse-transports had you to fear ? Here then is the quintessence of generosity, and nobody at all could affix any lesser title to the business.

24. Constantine, too, who built up a city with the

abortive revolt by Thebes : cf. Or. 15. 42 (Vol. I, p. 175 n.), 19. 13 ; Diod. Sic. 17. 15, Dio Chrys. Or. 2, p. 83 R.

[b] Cf. Or. 15. 42 (Vol. I, p. 174 n.), Diod. Sic. 16. 3.

Ῥώμῃ μὲν ὁμώνυμον ἐγείρας πόλιν, τὸ σχῆμα δὲ
τὸ 'κείνης ἅπαν εἰς ταύτην εἰσαγαγών, εὐδοκιμῶν
δὲ τῷ τὸν Ῥωμαίων δῆμον ἐνεγκεῖν ἀγροικισά-
μενόν τι. ῥήματα[1] μὲν γὰρ εὖ ποιῶν ἤνεγκεν,
ἔργον δὲ οὐδὲν προσῆν οὐδὲ κατ' εἰκόνος[2] ὕβρις.
καίτοι πολλαί γε εἰστήκεσαν ἐκείνῳ, αἷς οὐχ ὅπως
χεῖρα ἐπήνεγκαν, ἀλλ' οὐδ' ὅσον εἰς βλέμμα παροινίας ἔρχεται φαίνονται λελυπηκότες. οὐκοῦν ἐν-
R 665 ταῦθα | μὲν καὶ ῥήματα καὶ ἔργα, ἐκεῖ δὲ τοὐλαττον
μόνον, τὰ ῥήματα. οὕτω τοῦ βραχυτέρου μὲν
ἐκείνῳ κοινωνεῖς, κοινωνὸν δὲ ἐκεῖνον τοῦ μείζονος
οὐκ ἔχεις. |

25. Ἐξεταζέσθω δὴ καὶ τοῖν ἀδελφοῖν οἷς πόλις F
ἡ Κίβαλις ὁ νεώτερος, ὃς ὑβρισμένος ἐν γράμμασιν
ἐν τῇ μεγάλῃ πόλει καθῃρημένης ἤδη τῆς τυραν-
νίδος οὐκ ἐμνησικάκησεν. ὁ μὲν οὖν μὴ καλὸν
τοῦτο νομίζων κακὸς ἂν εἴη. ἀλλὰ πρῶτον μὲν
γράμματα ἔνι κἀνταῦθα, δεινότερον μὲν ἀγράφου
ῥήματος, ἧττον δὲ ἔργου πάλιν. 26. καίτοι καὶ
εἰκόνες ἑωρῶντο τοῦ ταῦτα ἀκηκοότος. ἀλλ' ὅμως
αὐτὰς παρῇεσαν οὔτε τιμῶντες οὔτε ἀτιμάζοντες.
τὸ δὲ μέγιστον, οἱ μὲν τυραννούμενοι τὰ τοιαῦτα
ἔγραφον καὶ οὐκ ἦν αὐτῶν μᾶλλον ἢ τῆς ἀνάγκης
τῆς παρὰ τοῦ δεσπότου ἤτοι φανερῶς κελεύοντος
ἢ καὶ παραδηλοῦντος ὅτι βούλοιτ' ἂν αὐτῷ τὰ τοιαῦτα δίδοσθαι. οὐ δὴ δίκαιον ἐνόμιζε λαμβάνειν

---

[1] τι.   ῥήματα Re., F. : τι ῥῆμα.   τὰ (τα V) MSS.
[2] εἰκόνος MSS. : εἰκόνων Re., F.

---

[a] Cf. Or. 19. 19 n.
[b] Valens (born at Cibalis, Zos. 3. 36) and the revolt of
Procopius, cf. Or. 19. 15 n.

name of a second Rome and introduced into it all
the pomp of Rome,—he falls short of you in this
matter, for all that he is famed for having borne
with some rudeness from the Roman populace.[a]
For though he had the goodness to put up with their
utterance, there was no action committed beyond
that, nor yet any outrage against his statue. Yet
though there were plenty of them erected in his
honour, not only did they refrain from manhandling
them, but they obviously refrained from abusing them
even by any insolence of glance. Here, then, was a
combination of words and deeds, there, the lesser
offence only, that of the words. So you are on a par
with him over the minor issue, but, as regards the
major, you don't have him on a par with you.

25. And again, suppose a comparison is made
with the younger of the imperial brothers who were
born in Cibalis.[b] He was lampooned in the capital,
but, once the rebellion had been put down, he nursed
no grievance. If anyone fails to regard this as a
noble attitude, he would be a rogue. But, in the
first place, even there it was a matter of the written
word, and this, though more serious than the unwritten word, is again not so serious as actual deeds.
26. Moreover, his statues were to be seen, even
though he heard those remarks, and yet they passed
them by, treating them neither with respect nor
with disrespect. The crux of the matter is that
they wrote such stuff while they were under the
control of a usurper, and the responsibility was not
so much theirs as that of the compulsion exercised
by their master who, either by direct order or by
hints, indicated that he would like such treatment
to be accorded him. So Valens did not think it

329

δίκην ὧν τινες ἐβιάσθησαν ἡνίκα ἐδούλευον. τὰ δ'
R 666 εἰς σὲ κρατοῦντά τε αὐτῶν καὶ | ἄρχοντα καὶ βασι-
λεύοντα πεπραγμένα ἀφορμὴν μὲν ἐξ ἑαυτῶν εἰς
συγγνώμην οὐκ εἶχον, μίαν δὲ καταφυγὴν τὸ σὲ
πρὸς φιλανθρωπίαν πανταχοῦ καθέλκεσθαι.

27. Πρὸς τίνα δή σε λοιπὸν ἐξεταστέον ἢ πρὸς
τὸν ἐν τοῖς ὁμόροις τῇ Συρίᾳ δι' εἰκόνος καὶ αὐτὸν
| ὑβρισμένον; ἀλλ' εἴ τις Ἔδεσσαν[1] καὶ τὰς ἐκεί- F
νης ἑορτὰς καὶ τοὺς περὶ τὰς ἑορτὰς ἐνθυμηθείη
νόμους καὶ ὡς παλαιόν τι τοῦτο διὰ πάντων βασιλέων ἧκον καὶ δι' ἀρχαιότητα μᾶλλον ἡδονὴν φέρον
ἢ λύπην, πολὺ τὸ οὐκ ἴσον τῶν περὶ τὰς εἰκόνας
ἀμφοτέρων εὑρήσει καὶ τοσοῦτον ὅσον ὕβρεως καὶ
παιδιᾶς τὸ μέσον. 28. λέγεται δὲ καὶ σοφῶν ἀνδρῶν ἐπιστήμῃ τοῦτο καταδεδεῖχθαι χαριζομένων
τισὶ τὰ τοιαῦτα δαίμοσι καὶ ταῖς μετὰ παιδιᾶς
λοιδορίαις ἑστιώντων ἐκείνους ὅπως ταύτῃ κεκο-
ρεσμένοι μηδὲν πλέον παρὰ τῶν ἀνθρώπων ζητῶσι,
R 667 καὶ ἀπιστεῖν γε οὐκ ἄξιον ὁρῶντα καὶ | σφᾶς αὐτοὺς
κωμῳδοῦντας ἐκείνους καὶ τούς γε ἐν δόξῃ παρ'
αὐτοῖς ὄντας ἀφορμὴν γιγνομένους τοῖς μετὰ δρό-
μου σκώμμασι. καθ' ἕκαστον τοίνυν ἔτος τοιαῦτα
θέοντες ἔχουσι τὴν ἀπὸ τοῦ καιροῦ καὶ τοῦ πλήθους αὐτῶν ἀσφάλειαν, οὐ τὴν ἐπὶ ῥήμασι μόνον
ἀλλ' ὅλως[2] ἐφ' ἅπασιν ἃ ποιεῖν ἡδίω δύναται τὴν
ἑορτήν. κἂν ἄρχων οὐκ ὀρθῶς ἀνιαθεὶς ἐπὶ τὴν
τιμωρίαν ἴῃ, μικρόψυχός τε εὐθὺς καὶ σκαιὸς ἐνο-

[1] Ἔδεσσαν F. : Ἔμεσαν Re. (MSS.).
[2] ὅλως conj. Re., F. (UP) : ὄντως V : ὅμως other MSS. :
ὁμοίως Re. text.

proper to punish individuals for what they had been forced to do under duress. Our citizens, however, in their behaviour towards you, their lord and ruler and emperor, had no reason of themselves to expect pardon : their sole recourse lies in your general tendency towards humanity.

27. The only one left with whom comparison can be made is Constantius, who also suffered personal insult through his statue in the area bordering upon Syria.[a] Yet if one bears in mind Edessa, the festivals there, the customs of the festivals, and the fact that this is an old-established procedure, applied to all emperors alike, and because of its antiquity more productive of pleasure than of pain, one will find that there is a great difference between the two incidents that concern the statues, all the difference in fact between insolence and fun. 28. They say that this practice was evolved by the understanding of wise men, even when they sought to satisfy some of the gods in this way and feasted them with jocular abuse, for them to be satisfied with that and to make no further demands of the people. Indeed this cannot be disbelieved, when you see them poking fun at themselves and the notables among them providing occasion for a comic race and horse-play. They run this race every year, and have the immunity of the occasion and of the numbers of the participants, not just for what they say, but for absolutely everything that can make the festival more enjoyable. And if a governor becomes unjustifiably angry and engages on a campaign of punishment, then straight-

---

[a] *Cf. Or.* 19. 48. For the temple of Zeus at Edessa, recently destroyed, *cf. Or.* 30. 22, 44 f.

μίσθη καὶ νόμων ἱερῶν ἀλλότριος. 29. ἀλλ' οὐχ
ἡμῖν γε ἦν ἀπο|στροφή τις οὐδαμόθεν οὐδ' αὖ τὸ F
παραιτησόμενον, ἀλλ' ἐν τῇ σιγῇ τῶν δεδρακότων
ἡ κατηγορία τῶν πεπραγμένων ἐστίν. ὥστε σὺ
μὲν ἐκείνη πάντως ἂν συνέγνως τῇ πόλει, τῇ δὲ οὐ
πάντως ἂν ἐκεῖνος. οὕτω καὶ τὸν ἥμερον εἶναι
δόξαντα τῇ γαλήνῃ παρελήλυθας.

30. Οἱ δὲ δὴ τὸν πατέρα τὸν Τίτου μηδέν σου
ταύτῃ λείπεσθαι λέγοντες τὸν ἐν μὲν ταῖς εἰκόσιν
ὅμοια πεπονθότα, κτείναντα δὲ οὐδένα τῇ παρ'
ἑαυτοῦ ψήφῳ, τά τε περὶ τὸν σῖτον οὐκ ἐθέλουσιν
ὁρᾶν τά τε περὶ τοὺς ἐκ Παλαιστίνης ἱκέτας, ὧν τὸ
R 668 μὲν | αὐτοῖς ἐποίει λιμόν, τὸ δὲ ἀσεβείας ἀνάγκην.
ὃ δὲ δὴ διὰ ταῦθ' ἡμάρτανον οὐκ αὐτῶν ἦν μᾶλλον
ἢ τῶν ἐπὶ ταῦτα ἀγόντων, ὥστ' ἐκεῖνοι δίκην ὡς
ἀληθῶς ὤφειλον ὧν 'Αλεξανδρέας ᾤοντο. 31. καὶ
γὰρ ὅστις χαλεπὸν ἀποδιδράσκει δεσπότην, ἠδίκηται μᾶλλον ἢ τοῦτο πεποίηκεν· ἃ γὰρ οὐκ ἐβούλετο
βιασθείς, ταῦτ' ἄγειν ἐπ' ἐκεῖνον δύναιτ' ἄν. ἐν
αὐτοῖς οὖν οἷς ἐκόλαζε, τοῖς ἐλάττοσιν ἡμάρτανε·
πῶς οὖν τοῦ μὴ κἂν[1] μείζοσιν ἐπαινοῖτ' ἂν εἰκότως;
ἐνταῦθα δὲ ποῖα σιτο|δεία; τίς λιμός; τίς ὠμότης F
ὑπακοῦσαι καιρῷ δεομένῳ χρημάτων καὶ ποιῆσαι
μείζω τὴν 'Ρωμαίων δύναμιν καὶ τὸ μὴ περὶ τοῖς
ὅλοις δεδοικέναι διὰ τούτου κερδᾶναι; 32. τὸ δὲ
μέγιστον, οἱ μὲν ἀπεσφάγησαν 'Αλεξανδρεῖς ὑπὸ
τῶν ἐγκαθημένων τῇ πόλει στρατιωτῶν οὕτω δὴ
πολλοί τινες, ὥστε καμεῖν τοῖς τύπτουσι τὰ ξίφη. |

[1] κἂν Re., F. (U): καὶ other mss.

[a] For the blockade of Rome by the Flavians, Tac. *Hist.*
3. 48 ; the suppliants at Taricheae, Josephus, *B.J.* 3. 10. 10.

away he is thought to be a petty-minded dunce, unacquainted with religious customs. 29. But for us there was no excuse at all, nor yet any palliation. In the silence of the offenders lies the condemnation of the offence. Thus, you would have pardoned that city in any case, but he would certainly not have pardoned ours. Thus in your calmness you have surpassed him, for all his reputed clemency.

30. Moreover, if people say that Titus' father was not inferior to you on this issue, since he suffered similar treatment with regard to his statues and executed no one by his own decree, they refuse to observe his actions concerning the corn supply and concerning the suppliants from Palestine.[a] The first of these imposed famine upon them, the second the necessity to commit impiety. Their misconduct in consequence was not so much due to them as to those who drove them to it, so that these were really guilty of what the Alexandrines were thought to have committed. 31. Indeed, any runaway from a harsh master has suffered rather than committed injustice, for, if compelled to do what he did not wish, he could lay the responsibility for it on him. So in the actual punishments administered, Vespasian was at fault in minor matters. How could he reasonably meet with approval for not having adopted them in major ones ? But here what shortage of food occurred ? What famine ? What brutality is there in complying with the critical need for money and in increasing the power of Rome and in profiting from the general security of the empire ? 32. Last but not least, the Alexandrines were butchered by the soldiers billeted in the city, in such numbers that the swords became weary in

R 669 τί οὖν ἔδει ζητεῖν, ὃ πρὶν ἢ πυθέσθαι περὶ τῆς στάσεως εἶχε; τούτῳ δὲ οὐδὲν τοιοῦτον παρὰ τῶν τῇδε τόξων ἐγεγόνει. δυοῖν γὰρ δὴ σωμάτων ἥψατο δύο βέλη βοηθοῦντα τῶν γνωρίμων τινὸς οἰκίᾳ θορυβουμένῃ. οὐκοῦν ὁ μὲν διὰ τῶν στρατιωτῶν ἀπεκτόνει, σὺ δὲ οὐκ ἂν αἰτιαθείης, ὅς[1] οὐδὲ ἐν φόβῳ ζῆν ἐᾷς, τοὺς ἐνίους δὲ οὐδὲ λέγειν ἄξιον. οὕτω δὴ καὶ οὗτος ἥττηται.

33. Τῶν τοίνυν εἰρημένων μοι τὰ πολλὰ καὶ μάντιν ἐποίει με, οὐχ ὁ Λητοῦς καὶ Διὸς οὐδ᾽ ἄλλος τις θεῶν, ἀλλ᾽ ὡς μετὰ τὴν ἀτυχίαν ἐκείνην ἡ πόλις ἦν ἐν φόβῳ τῷ τῆς δίκης καὶ πολὺς ἦν ὁ τῶν ὀλέθρων κατάλογος, ἐγὼ δὴ[2] διὰ πάσης ἐρχόμενος θαρρεῖν τε ἐκέλευον καὶ τρέμοντας ἔπαυον καὶ πᾶν ἀκριβῶς ἔλεγον τὸ μέλλον προορῶν, ὥστε τοῖς κακοηθεστέροις ἐπῄει πρὸς ἀλλήλους λέγειν ὅτι ἀνὴρ ἐξ ὀρνίθων | ἡμῖν ἀφῖκται καὶ ποιεῖ νῦν ὃ F 4 πάλαι παρὰ τοῖς Ἀχαιοῖς ὁ Κάλχας ὁ Θέστορος. |

R 670 34. τότε οὖν εἶναι μάντις οὐκ ἀπηρνούμην, θορυβούντων δὲ παρὰ σοῦ τε μάντις ἔλεγον γεγενῆσθαι καὶ βλέπειν ἐμαυτὸν εἰς ἀετὸν ἕνα σὲ καὶ τὸ μὴ φαινόμενον ἐκ τῶν ἤδη γεγενημένων ὁρᾶν.[3] ἐπεὶ καὶ τὸν Ἡρακλέα πορευόμενον ἐπ᾽ ἔργον ἑκόντα ἢ καὶ πεμπόμενον ὅστις ᾔδει καλῶς τὴν Ἡρακλέους φύσιν, λέγων ὅτι καὶ κατορθώσει, μάντις ἂν ἦν ἐκ τῶν Ἡρακλεῖ κατειργασμένων εἰς τὸ

---

[1] αἰτιαθείης F. (Par. 3017) : αἰτιαθεὶς V : αἰτιαθῇς Re. (other mss.). | ὅς F. (UP) : om. Re. (other mss.).
[2] δὴ conj. Sintenis, F. : δὲ Re. (mss.).
[3] ὁρᾶν F. (UP, I corrected) : ἐρεῖν Re. (other mss., Planudes).

---

[a] Cf. Or. 19. 35.   [b] Apollo.   [c] Homer, Il. 1. 69.

the smiters' hands. So what need for an inquiry into the situation prevailing before the news of the revolt ? For our emperor, however, nothing like that happened through the archers stationed here. An arrow or two certainly caused one or two casualties in defence of the house of one of our notables, which was the scene of disturbance.[a] Thus, though Vespasian was responsible for a massacre by the agency of his troops, no one could lay that charge against you, for you refuse even to let us be terrorized, and the odd one or two are hardly worth mentioning. So Vespasian too falls far short of you.

33. Well, many of the things I have said have begun to make me something of a prophet, not by the doing of the son of Leto and Zeus [b] or any other of the gods, but because after that disastrous occurrence, the city went in fear of punishment, and a long list of executions was expected, while I went through the whole town and told them to cheer up. I began to check their panic, and in my foreknowledge to tell the whole future accurately, so that my denigrators were moved to remark to one another, "Here is a fellow come to us from birds, who now behaves as Calchas, Thestor's son,[c] did long ago among the Achaeans." 34. At the time, then, I did not deny that I was a prophet, but as they kept up their clamour, I asserted that I had got my gift of prophecy from you, that I gazed upon one single eagle, yourself, and that I saw from past events what was not yet revealed. In Heracles' case, too, when he set out upon some labour, either of his own free will or even at another's volition, anyone with a thorough knowledge of his character would, in predicting his success, be a prophet moved to foretell the future as a

προειπεῖν κινούμενος. 35. μαντεύεται δὲ καὶ
Ἀγαμέμνων κακὸν ἔσεσθαι Τρωσὶ τὰς Ἀχιλλέως
διαλλαγὰς εἰδὼς τὰς πρὸ τῆς ὀργῆς τῆς ἐκείνου
πεπορθημένας πόλεις, μαντεύεται δὲ καὶ αὐτὸς
Ἀχιλλεὺς περί τε τῆς Ἕκτορος ἀριστείας καὶ ὅπως
αὐτὸν ζητήσει τὰ πράγματα. καὶ περὶ Ἀριστείδου
δὲ τοῦ Λυσιμάχου μετὰ τοὺς φόρους ἀργυρολόγου
πλέοντος ἦν ἄν μοι τὸ τῶν μάντεων ποιεῖν, προ-
R 671 λέγειν ὡς | μεθ᾽ ὁμοίας ἐπάνεισι πενίας. 36. καὶ
νῦν τοίνυν ἐβόων, ὅτι ταῦτα βασιλεὺς εἴσεται μὲν
οὕτως ἀκριβῶς ὡς μηδὲν εἶναι πλέον τοῖς αὐτ-
όπταις γεγενημένοις ἡμῖν, αὐχένα δὲ οὐδένα ὑποθήσει
σιδήρῳ. | καὶ εἴπετο δὴ τούτοις ἐξέτασίς τε πονη- F
ρῶν ἔργων, δεῖ γὰρ τό γε ἀληθὲς ὁμολογεῖν, καὶ
δικασταὶ τοῦτ᾽ ὄντες ὃ δὴ καὶ ἐκέκληντο, καὶ
γράμματα λύσιν ἔχοντα τῶν προτέρων. ἐν οἷς
ἔνεστιν ὁρᾶν λάμπουσαν τῷ βασιλεῖ τὴν φύσιν,
ὅταν ἀπολογῆται μὲν ἐκ τῆς τῶν ἠδικηκότων κα-
κίας, φάσκῃ δὲ αὐτοῦ τὴν ὀργὴν ἀλλοτρίαν τε εἶναι
καὶ διὰ τοῦτο ταχέως μεταπηδᾶν ἐπὶ τὰ πραότερα καὶ
τούτου πλείω λόγον ἔχειν ἢ τοῦ τιμωρίαν λαμβάνειν.
37. Χρηστὸς δὲ ὢν καὶ φιλόδωρος χαρίζεται καὶ
τῷ μεγάλῳ συνεδρίῳ καὶ τῷ μεγάλῳ δήμῳ τὸ καὶ
ταῖς ἐκείνων ἱκετείαις πεπρᾶχθαί τι τῶν ἐπιεικε-
στέρων. ἐπεὶ ἔγωγε πέπεισμαι ταὐτὰ[1] ἂν γενέσθαι τἀναντία βουλομένων οὐκ ἐκείνων μόνον,
ἀλλὰ καὶ πάντων ἀνθρώπων. νῦν δὲ πλείω μὲν
ἀγαθὰ γένοιτο τῇ καὶ νῦν πολλὰ καρπουμένῃ πόλει
R 672 δακρύων τε εἵνεκα καὶ | τῶν ἄλλων ἃ τὴν βοήθειαν

---

[1] ταὐτὰ Cobet, F. (mss. except BM) : ταῦτα Re. (BM).

result of Heracles' past exploits. 35. Agamemnon[a] also foretells that his reconciliation with Achilles will be a black day for Troy, for he knows the cities Achilles had sacked before he fell out with him. Achilles,[b] too, personally foretells of Hector's prowess, and says that the turn of events will demand his presence. Also, about Aristeides son of Lysimachus, when he sailed as collector for the tribute, I could play the seer and foretell that he would return as poor a man as he left.[c] 36. Now, indeed, I began to exclaim, "The emperor will have such exact knowledge of all this that we, the actual eyewitnesses, could not better him, and he will set the steel to no man's throat." And there followed upon this the investigation into acts of treason,—yes, we must admit to the truth. Judges, who really lived up to their title, were appointed, and instructions sent, rescinding the earlier ones. And in them we can see our emperor's character illumined when he speaks in self-defence, in consequence of the misconduct of the guilty, and asserts that wrath is foreign to his nature, and so he quickly reverts to a policy of clemency, setting more store by this than he does by punishment.

37. In his goodness and generosity he obliges both the Senate and People of the capital with the performance of acts of clemency in response to their entreaties, for I am convinced that the result would have been the same, had not only they but the whole of mankind opposed it. For all that, I pray that blessings in greater abundance light upon that city which now enjoys so many blessings, both for its tears

a Homer, *Il.* 9. 115 ff.   b *Ibid.* 1. 240 ff.
c Plutarch, *Aristid.* 24.

εἶχεν, ἴστωσαν μέντοι χάριν ᾐτηκότες ἣν ἔδωκεν ἂν τῇ γῇ καὶ μηδενὸς ἐπαγγέλλοντος. οἱ δ' αὐτοὺς μὲν ἔδειξαν καλῶς καὶ ὡς | εἰσιν εὖ πράττειν ἄξιοι, F 4 βασιλέα δὲ παρεκάλουν ἐφ' ἃ καὶ πρὸ ἐκείνων αὐτὸς αὑτόν.

38. Δηλοῖ δ' οἷός ἐστιν ἐκεῖνος ἐν τῇ τῶν[1] φιλανθρώπων διατριβῇ. διελὼν γὰρ ἃ δίδωσι, χωρὶς ἕκαστον ἀπαριθμεῖ, τὰς οὐσίας, τὰ θεάματα, τὰ λουτρά, τοὺς ἐξεληλαμένους, οἷς περὶ τὴν ψυχὴν ὁ λόγος, τὴν τὰ αὐτῆς ἀπειληφυῖαν ἀρχήν, ἔχων ἐν δυοῖν, εἴπερ ἐβούλετο, ῥήμασι περιλαβεῖν τὴν δόσιν. ὁ δέ, ὥσπερ οἱ τῶν ἀνθέων βραδέως ἀπαλλαττόμενοι, μακρηγορεῖ καὶ μόλις ἐξέρχεται καὶ δέδοικεν ὑπὲρ τῶν πενομένων, ὡς ἴσον ὂν ἀπορεῖν καὶ τεθνάναι. 39. διὰ τοῦτο τῷ ζῆν προσέθηκε τὸ καὶ ἐν οἷς εἶχον ζῆν. εἰσὶ δὲ οἳ δι' ἀδίκων θανάτων ἐπὶ τάς τινων ἧκον οὐσίας, ἡ δὲ ἐντεῦθεν ὠφέλεια R 673 νῦν τε καὶ | ἐς ἀεὶ τῶν ἀεὶ τὸ κράτος ἐχόντων διδασκομένων μὴ τῶν ὄντων ἐκβάλλειν τοὺς κεκτημένους μηδὲ κέρδη τὰ τοιαῦτα νομίζειν.

40. Τῶν μὲν οὖν ἴσων ἔτυχεν ἂν καὶ οὐ τοσαύτη πόλις ἐν τοιούτοις ἁμαρτήμασιν εἰδότος ὅτι καθάπερ ἐν σώματι κἂν τὸ μικρότατον ἀφέλῃς τὸ πᾶν ἐζημίω|κας, οὕτω κἂν τῇ μορφῇ τῇ διὰ τῶν F

---

[1] ⟨περὶ⟩ τῶν conj. Re. and F.

[a] μέγα συνέδριον is also used to describe the Senate of Constantinople in Libanius' narrative of Julian's humanity, *Or.* 18. 154 f. Here he is unusually complimentary in his references to the institutions of the capital,—reasonably enough, considering the recent crisis.

[b] *Cf. Or.* 21. 21 ff. According to Jo. Chrys. *Hom.* 21

and other efforts to assist us,[a] but they should realize
that they have asked a favour he would have granted
the world even without any asking. They showed
up nobly and proved that they deserve to prosper, but
they commended to the emperor a course of action
which he had decided for himself, before even they
suggested it.

38. He shows his mettle in the recital of his acts
of generosity. Categorizing his gifts, he lists each
one separately [b]—property, shows, baths, refugees,
those whose life is in hazard, the restoration of the
city authorities to their position—though he could,
if he so wished, have embraced the whole grant in a
couple of sentences. However, like people who
reluctantly turn their backs on a flower garden, he
dwells on this theme and is reluctant to leave it,
expressing his fear for the poor, for whom depriva-
tion and death, he feels, come to the same thing.[c]
39. Hence he has dealt with not just their lives, but
with the circumstances of their lives. Some persons,
by illegal executions, have gained possession of
people's property ; but the assurance we have from
this both now and for the future is that the powers
that be should learn not to expel the rightful owners
or to regard such conduct as a source of gain.

40. A city of less importance also might have been
treated equally well after such misconduct, for he
realizes that, as in the human body, if the smallest
portion is removed, harm is done to the whole, the

(*P.G.* xlix. 220), Theodosius entrusted Bishop Flavianus
with the task of delivering the news of the amnesty. He
sent an official message ahead of him.

[c] Thus the municipally organized poor relief was restored
(*cf.* § 7 above). *Cf.* Liebeschuetz, pp. 127 ff.

LIBANIUS

πόλεων ποθουμένου τοῦ τέως μένοντος,[1] εἶτα ἀπολωλότος. νῦν δὲ δυοῖν μὲν ἥδε δευτέρα, τρισὶ δὲ
ἴση, τῶν δ' ἄλλων περίεστι. 41. καὶ γέγονας οἰ-
κιστὴς διὰ τῆς σωτηρίας οὐ λίθους ἐπὶ λίθους διὰ
τεκτόνων τιθεὶς οὐδ' ἐναρμόττων ξύλα οὐδ' ἐπάγων
κέραμον οὐδ' εἰς πόνον καὶ τὸ καθῆσθαι μερίζων
τὸν ἐνιαυτὸν οὐδὲ πολλῶν ἐτῶν εἰς τὸ πᾶν δεόμενος, ἀλλ' ἀπὸ γνώμης τε ἡμέρου καὶ γραμμάτων
ὀλίγων καὶ τοῦ κρείττων θυμοῦ γενέσθαι. 42. καὶ
νῦν ἅπαντ' ἐκεῖνα τὰ τῶν πρὸ τῆς Ἰοῦς, τὰ τῶν
ἐκείνην ζητούντων, τὰ Ἀλεξάνδρου, τὰ Σελεύκου,
τὰ τῶν μετ' ἐκεῖνον ἀρξάντων σὰ γίγνεται, τὸ
μῆκος, τὸ πλάτος, τὰ ἱερά, τὰ ἴδια, τὰ δημόσια,
στοῶν κάλλος, ἀγορῶν φαιδρότης, βουλευτήρια,
R 674 θέατρα, | λουτρά. τὰ μὲν γὰρ ἐκείνων οἴχεται τῇ
στάσει, τὴν δ' οὖσαν σὴν ἡ συγγνώμη πεποίηκεν.
43. ὁ γὰρ εἰκότως ἂν ἀνελὼν φεισάμενος εἰς τὴν
τοῦ κτίσαντος χώραν ἐξ ὧν οὐκ ἀνήρηκεν εἰσάγε-
ται, ἐπεὶ καὶ ὅστις ἄνθρωπον ποταμοῦ ῥύμης ἐξ-
ήρπασε, πατὴρ ἂν εἰκότως εἶναι τοῦ σεσωσμένου
δοκοίη. ὅταν οὖν τις ἐπαινῇ βασιλέας | ἐξ ὧν ἔδο- F
σαν τῇ γῇ πόλεων, ἔξεστιν ἑτέρῳ τήνδε παρὰ σοῦ
δεδόσθαι λέγειν. καὶ γὰρ τὸν Ἕκτορα τῇ Τροίᾳ
τὸν ἐν τῇ μονομαχίᾳ πεσόντα παρ' Ἀπόλλωνος
δεδόσθαι τοῦ γε ἀναστήσαντος· ὥστε σὲ μηδ' ἂν

---

[1] μένοντος Re. text (mss., Planudes): μὲν ὄντος conj. Re., F.

---

[a] Comparisons with others loom large in the praises of
Antioch, cf. Or. 11. 270, 15. 59. The two cities are Rome
and Constantinople, the other three, Alexandria, Trèves,
Milan, cf. Auson. Ord. Nob. Urb. 2-5.
[b] Commonplace, cf. Jo. Chrys. Hom. 21 (P.G. xlix. 217).

same happens in the organization by cities, that what has existed for a time and has then been destroyed is always missed. As it is, our city is inferior to two only, is on a par with three others, and is superior to the rest.[a] 41. By preserving it, you have become its founder,[b] not by having builders lay stone upon stone, fitting timbers together or roofing it with tiles, nor yet by dividing up the year into work and leisure, nor by requiring many years to finish the whole job, but simply in consequence of your gentle disposition, a few decrees and your control over your temper. 42. Now, all that was achieved by the inhabitants who preceded the time of Io, or by those who searched for her, by Alexander, Seleucus or succeeding rulers, becomes your own— the length and breadth of the city, its temples, its buildings private and public, its fine colonnades and handsome markets, its council chambers, theatres and baths. What they had achieved has vanished in the riots ; your forgiveness has made the existing city yours. 43. For anyone who might reasonably have destroyed it and yet spares it, steps into the position of its founder simply because of the destruction he has not wrought, just as the rescuer of a man from a flowing river could properly be regarded as a father to the man he has saved. So whenever emperors are praised for the cities they have given the world, somebody else can retort that our city has been a gift from you. Indeed, when Hector fell in single combat he was given to Troy by Apollo who raised him up.[c] Thus no one could blame you

The reigning monarch is compared with the legendary and historical founders of Antioch, for whom *cf. Or.* 11. 44 ff. (Io), 72 ff. (Alexander and Seleucus).   [c] Homer, *Il.* 7. 272.

ὄνομα τῇ πόλει μεταθέντα[1] ἐκ τῆς σῆς οἰκίας μηδένα ἂν αἰτιάσασθαι.

44. Καὶ δὴ τοῦτό γε ἐν πολλοῖς οἷς ἡμαρτήκαμεν ὀρθῶς εἴδομεν τὸ τοιαῦτα περὶ δευτέρας προσηγορίας, οἷάπερ ἀκήκοας, εἰπεῖν. δεῖ τοίνυν σε τοῖς πεπραγμένοις οἰκιστὴν πεφηνότα σαυτοῦ τε ἔργον τὴν χειμασθεῖσαν νομίσαι καὶ τῷ μὴ διαφθεῖραι προσθεῖναι προσθήκας τῆς σῆς τύχης ἀξίας, οἵαις δὴ καὶ τὴν Δάφνην καλλίω κατέστησας βασίλεια παλαιὰ τοῖς νέοις ἀποκρύψας. δεχέσθω δή τι καὶ τὸ ἄστυ παραπλήσιον, εἴτ' ἐν τῇ νήσῳ βούλει τῇ πέραν τοῦ ποταμοῦ εἴτ' ἐν τῷ πρὸ ταύτης ᾠκι-
R 675 σμένῳ χωρίῳ. παρακαλῶ δέ σε[2] | ἐπὶ ταῦτα, ὦ βασιλεῦ, οὐ μόνον ὑπὲρ μεγέθους καὶ κάλλους, ἀλλ' ὅπως καὶ μαθεῖν ἡμῖν ἐγγένοιτο εἴτε ἔτι ἐραστὴν ἐκεῖνον ἔχομεν εἴτε ἤδη πέπαυται. |

45. Σὺ δὲ κρείττων μὲν γένοιο τῆς παροινίας, F φυλάττοις δὲ τὸ γενόμενον ἀπὸ τῆς τοῦ θεοῦ λαμπάδος, δι' ἣν ὡς ἥδιστα μὲν ἑώρας τὰς ἐνθένδε πρεσβείας ὁρᾶν ἐν τοῖς παροῦσι τρόπον τὴν ἀφεστηκυῖαν δοκῶν, εὐφραίνου δὲ τῷ τε πυνθάνεσθαι τῷ τε ἀκούειν τι περὶ ἡμῶν. μέγα μὲν δὴ καὶ τὸ λῆξαι τὴν ὀργήν, πολλῷ δ' ἔτι μεῖζον τὸ μὴ τὸν ἔρωτα λῆξαι. τῷ προτέρῳ τοίνυν τιμήσας τίμησον, ὦ βασιλεῦ, καὶ τῷ δευτέρῳ. 46. θεοῦ δ' ἂν εἴη καὶ τὸ τρίτον παρασχεῖν, τὸ τῆσδέ σ' ἐπιβῆναι καὶ χώρας καὶ πόλεως· πάλιν δ' αὖ τοῦδε μεῖζον

---

[1] μεταθέντα conj. Re., F. (P corrected): μεταθεῖναι Re. text (MSS.).   [2] σε conj. Re., F.: ἔτ' Re. text (MSS.).

---

even if you changed the city's name and gave it one from your own family.

44. Indeed, in all our many errors, we were right in this much at least, in conceiving an address to you upon the renaming of the city in the terms you have heard. You, who by your conduct have shown yourself to be our founder, must regard our storm-tossed city as your creation, and besides not destroying it, you must make additions to it worthy of your station, such as those with which you have beautified Daphne,[a] by the eclipse of the old palace with a new one. So let the city also obtain some similar edifice, whether you wish it to be in the island beyond the river[b] or in the built-up district facing it. I invite you to this task, Sire, not just for the sake of its size and beauty, but also that we may learn whether we still have our erstwhile admirer, or whether he has ceased to be such.

45. I trust that you will rise superior to our disorderliness, and cherish the outcome of that bright and heavenly day when you beheld with the utmost pleasure the embassies from here, thinking to behold, in a manner of speaking, in those there present your rebellious city, and were pleased to ask questions and to hear something about us. Important as it may be that you should abate your anger, it is far more important that you should not abate your affection. Thus, having honoured us with the first, honour us, Sire, with this second also. 46. It would be a divine revelation if you were to provide us with yet a third,—to set foot in our land and our city,—and even more so, if you would do so with

projects in Antioch at the time *cf.* Downey, *Antioch*, p. 434.　　　　　[b] *Cf. Or.* 11. 203 ff.

τὸ σὺν τῷ νέῳ βασιλεῖ. τότε ἡμῖν, τότε καὶ πρὸς
βίαν δώσεις τὴν ἀπὸ τοῦ παιδὸς ἐπωνυμίαν. λέγω
δὲ βίαν, ὅση δὴ γένοιτ᾽ ἂν παρ᾽ ὑπηκόων σωφρο-
νούντων· ὡς καλὸν τά γε τοιαῦτα βασιλέα καὶ
R 676 προσαναγκάζειν. 47. ἡμᾶς | μὲν οὖν ἐκ τούτων
προσερεῖ τις εὐδαίμονας ἔνδον τε σοῦ καθημένου
καὶ βουλὰς βουλεύοντος σωτηρίους κἂν τῷ πεδίῳ
τὰ πολέμια μελετῶντός τε αὐτοῦ καὶ τὴν στρατιὰν
παιδεύοντος καὶ γιγνομένου τε καὶ ποιοῦντος βελτίους Πέρσαις τε σφᾶς αὐτοὺς ἐπαινεῖν παρέχοντος
ἐπὶ τὴν ἐκ τῆς εἰρήνης ἀσφάλειαν δραμοῦσιν. εἰ δ᾽
οὖν καὶ πολέμου δεήσειεν, ἕξεις καὶ τοὺς ἀόπλους
ἡμᾶς συναγωνιστάς, ἄνδρας τε καὶ γυναῖκας καὶ
παῖδας, | ὅσοι τὴν πόλιν οἰκοῦσι καὶ ὅσοι τὴν γῆν F
ἐργάζονται καὶ ὅσοι δεσπόταις ὑπηρετοῦσι. 48.
τίς οὖν ἡ παρὰ τῶνδε τῶν γυμνῶν συντέλεια; τοὺς
θεοὺς ἕκαστοι τούτων καλέσουσιν ἀπ᾽ εὐνοίας
ἀκριβοῦς, τὸν Ἄρη, τὴν Ἀθηνᾶν, τοὺς ἄλλους ὧν
ταῖς γνώμαις ἐκβαίνει τὰ τῶν πολέμων τέλη, μεμνημένοι τῶν τε λελυμένων κινδύνων τῆς τε ἀνελπί-
στου ταύτης σωτηρίας, αἰτοῦντες τοὺς ἐναντίους,
εἴ τινες ἄρα φανεῖεν, εἰς δέος τε πίπτειν καὶ τρόμον
καὶ μᾶλλον ἢ διώξεως ἐρᾶν. ὅσην δὲ ἐν πολέμου
πράγμασιν ἔχουσιν εὐχαὶ ῥοπήν, ὁρῶμεν ἐν ταῖς
ποιήσεσι.

49. Καὶ μήτοι νομίσῃς παρὰ τῆσδε μόνης τοῦτο
ἕξειν τἀγαθόν, ἀλλ᾽ ὅσον ἐστὶ τὸ βασιλευόμενον,
τοσοῦτον τὸ συνευξόμενον. τὸ γὰρ τῶν ἀδελφῶν
δίκαιον ἔστι δήπου κἂν ταῖς πόλεσι καὶ συνάχθον-
ταί τε πληττομέναις καὶ συγχαίρουσιν ἐν τοῖς ἀμεί-

the young prince. Then, then indeed, you will be forced to grant us the renaming of our city after your son[a]; and by force, I mean that which would be applied by loyal subjects, for the application of this kind of compulsion, at least, upon an emperor is a good thing. 47. So we shall be called happy as a result of this, if you are settled among us, exercising your thoughts for our preservation, participating in the battle manoeuvres on the plain and schooling your army, improving both yourself and it, and letting the Persians thank their lucky stars as they scurry to the security afforded by peace.[b] Anyway, should there be need for war, you will have us to support you, unarmed though we may be, men, women, children, all the inhabitants of the city, all the workers of the soil, and all subservient to their masters. 48. The contribution to be made by these unarmed folk will be that they will all, from the bottom of their hearts, invoke Ares, Athena and the rest of the gods by whose counsels the issues of war are decided. They will remember the dangers from which they have been preserved and this their unhoped-for salvation, praying that the enemy, should they dare to put in an appearance, may be cast into fear and trembling, and be more desirous of flight than of pursuit. And the influence that prayers can have on the fortunes of war, we can observe in poetry.

49. And do not think that you will have this blessing from our city alone : all the empire you rule will be united in prayer on your behalf. The bond of brotherhood, to be sure, exists in cities too, and they sympathize with one another in their afflictions

[a] Arcadius Augustus.   [b] Cf. Or. 19. 62.

LIBANIUS

R 677 νοσι. | καὶ ὥσπερ ὁ μέρει πόλεως λυμηνάμενος καὶ τὸ μηδὲν πεπονθὸς ἠνίακεν, οὕτως ὁ μιᾷ πόλει λελύπηκεν ἁπάσας. οὐκοῦν καὶ ὅτῳ τι χρηστὸν εἰς μίαν γεγένηται, πάσας οὗτος ἀνηρτήσατο. ἀπὸ τοσούτων οὖν στομάτων εὐχὴν πόσον τι χρὴ νομίζειν δυνήσεσθαι; |

50. Οὕτως οὐ φιλάνθρωπά σοι μόνον, ἀλλὰ καὶ F λυσιτελοῦντα πέπρακται. καὶ φύσει γε τὸ πρᾶγμα τοιοῦτόν ἐστιν. ἡ μὲν ἀρετὴ συμφέρον· καίτοι καὶ εἰ μηδὲν κέρδος ἔμελλεν ἐντεῦθεν ἀκολουθήσειν, αὐτό γε σὺ δήπουθεν τὸ καλὸν τιμήσειν ἔμελλες, τὸ καλὸν δέ, οἶμαι, τὸ μὴ πικρῶς ἔχειν τοῖς ἁμαρτάνουσιν οὖσιν ἀνθρώποις. εἰς μὲν γὰρ τὸν οὐρανὸν τοῦτο οὐκ εἰσέρχεται, τῶν δὲ ἀπὸ τῆς Ἄτης[a] οὐκ ἔνι καθαρεῦσαι τὴν γῆν. θεῖος δέ τις εἶναι δοκεῖ καὶ πολλῶν ἐπαίνων ἄξιος, ὃς ἐν ταῖς παρ' ἐκείνης ἐπηρείαις τοῖς παραπεσοῦσιν οὐκ ἐπέθετο.

51. Καὶ νῦν οὗτος πανταχοῦ πολὺς ὁ λόγος, οἷα μὲν τὰ παρ' ἐμοῦ, οἷα δὲ τὰ παρὰ σοῦ. οἶμαι δὲ καὶ ἐν θεῶν συλλόγοις μνήμην ἀμφοτέρων εἶναι καὶ παρὰ μὲν τῶν ἐγκώμια λέγεσθαι, Μουσῶν τε καὶ Ἑρμοῦ καὶ Ἀπόλλωνος,[c] τοὺς δ' ὑπὲρ δωρεῶν ἃς δεῖ σοι παρ' ἐκείνων ἐλθεῖν γνώμην ἀποφαίνεσθαι. Καλλιόπη δὲ τὸ μὲν δράσει μετὰ τῶν ἀδελφῶν, ὑπὲρ δὲ R 678 τῆς | ἑαυτῆς πόλεως ἀποδώσει καὶ δευτέραν ἀμοιβὴν ἔρωτα τοῖς σοῖς υἱέσι παιδείας ἐνθεῖσα καὶ μουσικῆς.

---

[a] Cf. Or. 2. 47. This passage is perhaps the source of the proverb ascribed to Libanius (Apostol. 15. 81d =Paroem. Gr. ii, p. 648 : συγχαίρειν χρὴ τοῖς φίλοις καλῶς πράττουσιν).

[b] Homer, Il. 19. 91.

[c] The patrons of eloquence and poetry : linked with Calliope, the tutelary deity of Antioch, Or. 31. 40, cf. Or. 1. 102 f. The pagan terminology of the whole peroration culminates in this emphatic assertion of the virtues of

and rejoice with them in their prosperity.[a] He who injures one part of a city, afflicts also the portion which has not been touched : similarly, whoever injures one city injures them all. So, too, anyone responsible for any benefit towards one city binds all to himself, and when prayers rise from so many lips, what must we think their effect will be ?

50. Hence your actions have been not just humane, but also advantageous to yourself. The fact of the matter is bound to be something like this. Virtue is profitable ; but even if no advantage were likely to accrue from it, you would certainly respect goodness for itself, and goodness, I feel, involves bearing no resentment against those who err, since they are but human. Though this does not enter into the kingdom of heaven, it is impossible to purge the earth of the consequences of infatuation.[b] A man is held to be divine and deserving of high praise, if he does not attack those who have fallen by the wayside in the mischief which it causes.

51. And now the tale is told everywhere and at length, both of what I and of what you have done. Even in the councils of the gods, I believe, there is mention of us both, and some of them—the Muses, Hermes and Apollo [c]—utter words of praise, while others express their opinions upon the gifts which you should receive from them. Calliope, in company with her sisters, will bring them to pass, and on behalf of her own city she will make a double repayment by instilling into your sons the love of learning and of music.

the Hellenic παιδεία, as a counterblast to the Christian propaganda current following the reconciliation ; cf. Or. 1. 253 (cited Introduction, p. 237).

XXI

ΠΡΟΣ ΚΑΙΣΑΡΙΟΝ ΜΑΓΙΣΤΡΟΝ[1]

R 678   1. Ἐπειδὴ ταῖς ὑποσχέσεσι ταῖς παρὰ σοῦ τὸ F
ἔργον ἠκολούθησεν, ὦ γενναῖε Καισάριε, καλῶς ἂν
ἔχοι καὶ ταῖς ἐμαῖς παρ' ἐμοῦ προστεθῆναι τὸ
ἔργον. ἦν δὲ ἐν μὲν ταῖς σαῖς πάσῃ[2] προθυμίᾳ τῇ
πόλει βοηθήσειν ὅσηπερ ἂν τῶν πολιτῶν ἕκαστος,
ἐν δὲ ταῖς | ἐμαῖς τὸ λόγον ἔσεσθαι παρ' ἐμοῦ τοῖς F
πράγμασι πειρώμενον καὶ τοὺς ἐσομένους διδά-
σκειν οἷος ἡμῖν ἐν οἵῳ καιρῷ γεγένησαι. βουλοίμην δ' ἂν εἰπεῖν τι τῶν τετελεσμένων ἄξιον καὶ
δύναμιν τοσαύτην εἰς τὸν λόγον παρὰ τῶν Μουσῶν
R 679 λαβεῖν ὅσηνπερ αὐτὸς ἔσχηκας | εἰς τὸ περισῶσαι
τὴν πόλιν.   2. ὁ μὲν οὖν ὄχλος, ἐν ᾧ πολλοὶ μὲν
ἄνδρες, πολλαὶ δὲ γυναῖκες, πολλὴ δὲ νεότης, πολὺ
δὲ γῆρας, ἀφ' οὗπερ πρότερον ἐποιοῦντο χωρίου
τὰς ἱκετείας, ἀπὸ τούτου νῦν καὶ τὰς ἐπὶ τοῖς δε-
δομένοις εὐφημίας. ἃς ἦν μέν σε κάλλιον παρόντα
δέχεσθαι μετὰ τῆς φωνῆς ὁρῶντα καὶ τὴν τῶν σωμάτων κίνησιν, φοιτᾷ δὲ ἴσως οὐ μικρόν τί σοι καὶ
διὰ τῶν ἀγγέλων.   3. ἐγὼ δὲ κεκοινώνηκα μὲν
ἐκείνοις τῶν ἡδίστων ἡμῖν βοῶν πρᾶγμα νῦν πρῶτον πεποιηκὼς τῆς δωρεᾶς τοῦτο πειθούσης, ὃ δ'

---

[1] πρὸς PIBM, Macarius : εἰς F. (other mss.).   μάγιστρον om.
B., Macarius.   [2] ⟨τὸ⟩ πάσῃ F.

348

ORATION 21

TO CAESARIUS,
MASTER OF OFFICES [a]

1. Since your promises have been translated into action, noble Caesarius, it would be but right for action to follow upon those promises that I too have made. In your promises there was a readiness to assist our city with all the enthusiasm to be expected of any of her own citizens : in mine there was the rendering of a factual account to try to inform posterity of your services to us in our hour of need. I could wish to make my narrative worthy of your accomplishments, and to get from the Muses such inspiration for my oration as you showed in saving the city. 2. The thronging crowd of men, women, children and the aged now utter praises for the gifts bestowed upon them from the very same place where they had previously uttered prayers. It would be nicer for you to receive them in person, and to see the physical movements that accompany their voices, but perhaps no small part of this reaches you even through messengers. 3. I have joined them in the cries which gladden our hearts, and have been induced by your generosity now for the first time to perform an action which, though impossible

[a] *PLRE* 171 (6).

LIBANIUS

οὐκ ἔνι μὲν γενέσθαι παρὰ τῶν πολλῶν γένοιτο δ᾽ ἂν παρ᾽ ἐμοῦ, τοῦτ᾽ ᾠήθην δεῖν προσθεῖναι χάριν εἰδὼς τοῖς θεοῖς τοῦ δόξης σοι μέλειν ἀντὶ χρημάτων. ἐκείνως μὲν γὰρ οὐκ ἂν εἶχον ἀμείβεσθαι, νῦν δέ, εἰ καὶ μὴ ὅσον ἄξιον, ἀλλ᾽ ἀποδοίην ἄν τι.

4. Εἰ μὲν οὖν ἁπάντων τῶν παρὰ πάντα τὸν χρόνον αὐτῷ πεπραγμένων βούλοιτό τις, ὦ παρόντες, | μεμνῆσθαι καὶ τῆς [τε][1] ἐν παισὶ σωφρο- F συνης, εἶτ᾽ ἐπειδήπερ ἐκ παίδων ἐξῆλθεν, ἀνδρίας τε ἐν οἷς ταύτης ἔδει καὶ γνώμης καὶ τῶν εἰς παρρησίαν ἁπασῶν ἀφορμῶν καὶ ὡς ἑτέρους ἔχων φοβεῖν αὐτὸς ἄληπτος ἦν | ἅπασι καὶ ὡς τῆς βασιλείας ἄλλοτε ἄλλων οὔσης δι᾽ ἴσων αὐτὸς ἐπαίνων διηκόνει τοῦ ἀεὶ κρατοῦντος ἐν κέρδει ποιουμένου τὴν Καισαρίου φύσιν—εἰ μὲν οὖν ἁπάντων ἁπτοίμεθα νῦν, κατεγνωκέναι τῶν παρόντων δόξομεν ὡς οὐκ ἀποχρώντων εἰς λόγον· εἰ δὲ ἐπὶ τούτῳ,[2] δόξομεν τιμᾶν τὴν βοήθειαν[3] τῷ μηδὲν ἐπεισάγειν. οἵων τοίνυν ἀπολελαύκαμεν ἐν ζέοντι τῷ κλύδωνι λέγωμεν.

5. Τοῦ κακοῦ ἀρξαμένου μὲν ἀπὸ φωνῆς ὀλίγης, προβάντος δὲ εἰς πολλοὺς τοῦ κεκινημένου τὸ μήπω πρὸς ὁμοίαν ταραχὴν ἐπισπωμένου καὶ ῥημάτων μὲν ἐκδραμόντων δίκην ἐχόντων θάνατον, ἔργων δὲ προστεθέντων οὕτω δεινῶν ὡς μικρὸν εἶναι τὰν τοῖς ῥήμασιν, εἰκόνων χαλκῶν καθελκομένων ὕβρει

---

[1] [τε] suggested by Re. and F.

[2] τούτων ⟨ἐστήξομεν⟩ conj. F.

[3] τιμᾶν τὴν βοήθειαν F. (mss., except CMo.) : δικαίως (δικαίων Re.) τιμᾶν ἐξ ὧν νῦν εὐηργετήμεθα (εὐηργετούμεθα Re.) παρ᾽ αὐτοῦ καὶ μὴ δεῖσθαί τινος εἰς βοήθειαν Re. (C marg., Mo.).

---

[a] For the sequence of events cf. Or. 19. 25 ff., Downey, pp. 426-433.

350

for the majority of people, could perhaps come from me. I felt that I should add this contribution, for I am grateful to the gods that you are more interested in fame than in material things. Otherwise I could not make any repayment but, as it is, even though it is not as much as you deserve, I would at least be making some return.

4. So, gentlemen, if we wish to give an account of all that he has done throughout his life—of his good behaviour as a child, and then, childhood left behind him, of his courage, whenever courage was needed, and of his resolution, his general affability, the manner in which, despite his capacity to inspire fear in others, he personally remained beyond the reach of criticism, and of the way in which, with different emperors on the throne at different times, he continued in his administrative duties, praised by all alike, since each successive emperor valued his abilities so highly—if we deal with all this now, we shall give the impression of disparaging our present theme as being insufficient for our narration. If, however, we confine ourselves to this alone, we shall be regarded as honouring his assistance without the intrusion of any additional matter. So let me recount the benefits we have enjoyed in this seething tide of disaster.

5. The trouble began with a few outcries, but the disturbance extended to a larger number of people and incited to like disorder that section of them which was as yet unaffected. Words were blurted out, for which death was the penalty, and were capped by actions so dreadful that the implications of the words were of minor importance.[a] The bronze statues were forcibly torn down and were dragged

351

καὶ τῶν | μὲν ὅλων ἑλκομένων διὰ παντὸς ὁμοίως F
τόπου, τῶν δὲ καὶ κατατετμημένων εἰς μέλη, τοιούτων τοίνυν ἠσεβημένων καὶ τῶν τετολμημένων
R 681 τῆς πόλεως | ἀπάσης κοινῶν γεγενημένων τῷ τοὺς
μὲν δρᾶσαι, τοὺς δὲ μὴ κωλῦσαι, τὴν γὰρ δὴ γνώμην ὑπὸ τὴν αὐτὴν ταῖς χερσὶν αἰτίαν ἦγον, δρα-
μόντων τοίνυν τῶν ταῦτα μηνυσόντων βασιλεῖ καὶ
τῆς πόλεως φόβῳ κεκενωμένης ὡς τῶν μενόντων
πάντων ἀπολουμένων πέμπεται μετὰ τοῦ ταῖς δυ-
νάμεσιν ἐφεστηκότος οὗτος ἐπὶ βασάνῳ τε καὶ
κρίσει τῶν πεπραγμένων. 6. οἱ μὲν οὖν τὸν ἄνδρα
οὐκ εἰδότες οἰχήσεσθαι τούς τε οὐκ ἀποδράντας
τούς τε τοῦτο πεποιηκότας, ἁλώσεσθαι γάρ, ἔλεγον, καὶ οἱ μὲν ἧττον, οἱ δὲ μᾶλλον, ἀμφότεροι δὲ
σφᾶς αὐτοὺς ἐθρήνουν, ἐγὼ δέ, οὐ γὰρ ἠγνόουν
αὐτόν, τοὺς μὲν ταῦτά μοι φρονοῦντας καὶ τὸ βέλτιστον[1] προσδοκῶντας ἐπῄνουν, τοὺς δὲ θορυβου-
μένους ἔπαυον ὅστις εἴη διδάσκων. 7. νὺξ μὲν οὖν
ἐκείνη πολλὰς μὲν φροντίδας, ὀλίγον δὲ εἶχε τὸν
ὕπνον. οὐδὲ γὰρ εἰ πάντες | μάντεις ἐνηγγυῶντο F
τὸ τέλος λέγοντες εἰς ὅπερ ἧκεν ἥξειν, ἦν οἷόν τε
μὴ πλήττειν ἑαυτοὺς καὶ κυκᾶν τούς τε δεῦρο μετ-
οικοῦντας ὅσοι τε ἐν τῷ τῆς πόλεως ὀνόματι, γε-
R 682 νομένης δὲ ἡμέρας τῶν μὲν | ἄλλων οὐ πολὺς εὐθὺς
ὁ λόγος, τὴν βουλὴν δὲ ἡ αἰτία περιίστατο. καὶ
τοὺς ὑπὲρ τούτων λόγους ἐδέχετο[2] μὲν ἡ τοῦ στρατηγοῦ καταγωγή, πικρὸν δὲ οὐδὲν ἀπὸ τοῖν δικα-

---

[1] βέλτιστον Re. (CAI La) : βέλτιον F. (other mss.).
[2] λόγους ἐδέχετο F. (correction in I) (λ. ἐδέξατο conj. Sievers):
λόγους. ἠλέγχετο mss., Re. (who punctuates περιίστατο καί) :
λόγοις ἠλέγχετο Morel.

along in their entirety through every place alike, or else were hacked to pieces. In such acts of sacrilege and outrage the whole city bore some responsibility ; though one section perpetrated the deed, the rest had not prevented it, and their attitude laid them open to the same charge as the actual malefactors. Couriers were sent in haste to inform the emperor, and the city suffered a panic evacuation, since it was believed that all who stayed would be executed.[a] Then Caesarius here was sent, in company with the master of the soldiery,[b] to conduct an inquiry and examination into what had taken place. 6. Well, people unacquainted with him began to say that that would be the finish for those who had not decamped and for those who had,— for they would certainly be arrested. Some less, others more loudly, together they began to lament their fate. I, however, being not unacquainted with him, commended those who felt the same as myself and were optimistic in outlook, and I tried to check the more clamorous by explaining the kind of person he was. 7. That night, then, gave us plenty of food for thought but precious little sleep. Not even if all the prophets in creation had backed me up with declarations that things would turn out as they actually have done, could they possibly have stopped upsetting themselves and setting both our non-citizen residents and the members of our citizen body into a turmoil, and when day dawned, there was not much immediate concern with the rest : it was the city council around which the blame was centred. The general's headquarters was the scene of pleas on their behalf, but no harsh measures were

---

[a] Cf. Or. 23.   [b] Ellebichus, cf. Or. 22.

ζόντοιν, ὃ τὴν νύκτα τῆς ἡμέρας[1] ἐποίει πραοτέραν.
ἡμέρα δευτέρα καὶ δικαστήριον καὶ δεσμὰ καὶ τοῖς
δεθεῖσιν ὁ δήσας τά γε εἰς λύπην προσόμοιος.

R 683 8. δύσεσθαι δὲ | μέλλοντος ἡλίου καὶ τῷ μὲν ἀσχο-
λίας οὔσης ἄνω,[2] κάτω δὲ ὄχλου περὶ τὰς θύρας
ἔρχομαι μέν, ὡς δ' ἂν μὴ ἐνοχλοίην, ἀπεχώρουν.
ὁ δὲ αἰσθόμενος τὸ τοῦ Πινδάρου ποιεῖ καὶ δι' ἀνα-
βολῆς τῶν | ἐπειγόντων συγγίνεταί μοι παρακαθ- F 4
ισάμενος ἁπτόμενός τε τοῦ καρποῦ καὶ θαρρεῖν ἐν
τῷ τοῦτο ποιεῖν παρέχων ὡς οὐδεὶς τῶν ἐν δεσμοῖς
στεροῖτο τῆς ψυχῆς, ὃ δὴ καὶ ἡμῖν ἀπέχρη. δεινὸν
δὲ οὐδὲν τῶν ἄλλων, οὐ τὸ τῆς οἰκείας[3] ἐκπεσεῖν,
οὐ τὸ τῶν ὄντων, οὐκ αὐτὸς ὁ δεσμὸς οὐδ' εἰς γῆρας
καὶ τελευτὴν αὐτόματον προϊών. 9. πολλῶν δέ
μοι ῥεόντων δακρύων οὐκ ὀλίγα τῆς βελτίονος ἦν
ἐλπίδος. ἐπῄνει τε ἅμα ταῦτα καὶ προσετίθει τὰ
ἑαυτοῦ, οὐ τὸ γῆρας, ἐμοὶ δοκεῖν, ταύτῃ τιμῶν,
πολλοὺς γὰρ ἂν ἐτίμα πρὸ ἐμοῦ, οὐδ' αὖ ἀποδιδοὺς
ἃς ὤφειλε χάριτας, οὐ γὰρ ὤφειλεν οὐδ' ἦν ὅ τι
προεισενήνεκτο παρ' ἐμοῦ, ἀλλ', οἶμαι, βέλτιστος
ὢν καὶ τὰ καλὰ μὲν ἀξιῶν αἰδεῖσθαι, τῶν καλῶν
δ' ἡγούμενος τοὺς λόγους ἀνεπήδα τε φαινομένου
R 684 καὶ τοῖς ἄλλοις | ἅπασιν ἐκόσμει καὶ δι' ὧν αὐτός
τε ἔσομαι ῥᾴων καὶ ποιήσω τοὺς δεδεμένους παρ-
εῖχε. 10. παρ' οὓς ἐλθὼν ἐγὼ παρ' αὐτοῦ καταβὰς
ἀπειρηκότας καὶ κειμένους ἀφώνους σκοποῦντας

---

[1] ἡμέρας F. (BM) : νυκτὸς Re. (other mss.).
[2] Two pages missing in A : resumes § 26 τὴν ἡμε]τέραν.
[3] οἰκείας Re., F. (I) : οἰκίας Morel (other mss.).

---

[a] Cf. Ep. 868. Chrysostom also gives a similar account
of the scene at the inquiry, Hom. 13 (P.G. xlix. 135 ff.).
[b] Fr. 279.

taken by the two inquisitors, and in consequence
the night was less troubled than the day had been.
The second day dawned, and the judicial examination began. Arrests were made, and the arresting
officers looked just as dejected as the prisoners.[a]
8. Just before sunset, he was busy upstairs, with a
large crowd gathered below at his doors. I made
my way there, but started to retire, not wishing to
be a nuisance. However, he saw me and, in Pindar's
words,[b] set aside his pressing duties and gave me an
interview. He sat me down at his side, clasped my
arm, and by so doing gave me encouragement to
believe that none of those arrested would lose his
life, and that indeed was enough for me. No other
punishment held such terrors—not exile, confiscation
of property, or imprisonment itself, even though it
should last until old age and natural death.[c] 9. I
shed many a tear, but there were plenty of grounds
for hope. He commended my tears, and added his
own. In this, I feel, he was not showing respect for
my years—he might have honoured many before
me—nor again was he repaying some kindness he
owed me, for he owed me none, and I had not done
anything for him before this either. It was, I believe,
a case of an excellent man who wanted to reverence
goodness and believed that eloquence was part of it.
Thus, on my appearance he jumped to his feet, and
showed me every mark of esteem, and in particular
inspired in me a feeling of confidence for me to trans-
mit to the prisoners. 10. On leaving him, I went
down to see them, and found them in despair, lying

[c] On imprisonment in the penal system cf. Or. 45 (Introduction).

ὅπως ἂν αὐτοὺς ἀπενέγκαιεν ἔσχον τε καὶ παρε-
μυθησάμην | λέγων τε τὰ τοῦδε καὶ διδάσκων ὡς F
ἔνι καὶ βιῶναι. ὥστ' εἰ φαίην τὸ¹ τοὺς τοσούτους
ἐξειλκύσθαι τελευτῆς ὑπὸ τοῦδε, τὰ ὄντα ἂν εἴην
εἰρηκώς. εὔφραινε δὲ καὶ τῷ λέγειν πρὸς ἡμᾶς ἃ
πρὸς τὸν ἠδικημένον ἔμελλεν ὑπὲρ ἡμῶν. τὰ δὲ
ἦν ὅτι τῷ βασιλεῖ κάλλιον μὴ λαβεῖν ἢ λαβεῖν
δίκην, εἴ γε τὸ μὲν ἡδονὴν ἔχει ταχέως παυομένην,
τὸ δὲ δόξαν οὐ δυναμένην λῆξαι. 11. τοῖς μὲν οὖν
ἐκ τούτων ὁ δεσμὸς ἐλαφρὸς οὐ δεχομένων τῶν
ὑποσχέσεων ἀλαζονείας ὑποψίαν, οὐδαμοῦ γὰρ ἀνὴρ
ὃ μὴ πράξων ᾔδει κατεπηγγελμένος ἐλέγχεται,
ποιῶν δὲ τῇ πόλει ταχεῖαν τῆς συμφορᾶς τὴν
ἀπαλλαγήν, εἰ μὲν οἷόν τε ἦν δεηθέντα τῶν θεῶν
πτερῶσαι τὰ ζεύγη, τοῦτ' ἂν ἐποίησεν, ἢ εἰ τὸ
τῶν Βορέου παίδων αὐτόν² ποθεν λαβεῖν, τοῦτ' ἂν
R 685 ἐκείνου μᾶλλον, | ἢ εἰ παραπλήσιον ἵππον τῷ³ παιδὶ
τῆς Γοργόνος, τοῦτ' ἂν ἐδέξατο. 12. ἐπεὶ δὲ οὐκ
ἦν παρ' | ὅτου ταῦτα ἐγένετ' ἄν, πόνου συνέχειαν F
φύσει πτερῶν ᾠήθη δεῖν ἐξισῶσαι καὶ τὰ παρέχοντα δὴ τὴν⁴ ἐν ταῖς ὁδοῖς τρυφὴν πάντα ῥίψας
καὶ χαίρειν ἀφεὶς καὶ κουφότατον ἀπεργασάμενος
ὡς οἷόν τε τὸ φέρον ἀναβὰς παντὶ τῷ τάχει τῶν
ὀρέων ἐχρῆτο προσόντος τοῦ παρὰ τῆς μάστιγος.
13. καὶ τὸ μὲν προπέμψον τοσοῦτον ἦν, ἦν δὲ ἄρα
τοῦδε τὸ πλέον γυναῖκες, αἳ δὴ καὶ τὴν πόλιν εἶχον,

---

¹ τὸ om. F. (BM Vat. 64).
² αὐτὸν F. (V): αὐτὸς Re. (other mss.).
³ τῷ F. (corrections in PI): τῇ Re. (other mss.).
⁴ τὴν Re., F.: τῶν mss.

ᵃ A double-edged remark : Caesarius was a Christian.
ᵇ So Pindar, Ol. 1. 124 ff. (the wooing of Hippodameia).

silent and wondering how to do away with themselves.
I kept them from this and encouraged them by
telling them what he had said and explaining that
their lives could still be saved. So if I were to say
that all these men were snatched from death by him,
I would be speaking the simple truth. He cheered
us also by telling us of the report he was going to
send on our behalf to the emperor we had wronged—
namely, that it was more creditable for the emperor
to forgo punishment than to exact it, since punishment brings a mere transitory pleasure, forgoing
it brings a renown that can never fade. 11. As a
result their imprisonment was lightened, for no
suspicion of vainglory attached itself to his promises,
and he stands revealed as never a man to promise
something he knew he could not fulfil. In his
efforts to ensure a speedy end to our city's troubles,
could he, by his pleas to the gods,[a] have got wings
for his chariot, he would have done so[b]; could he
have somehow got the offspring of Boreas for his
steeds,[c] then he would have preferred this course;
or if he could have had a horse like the Gorgon's
offspring,[d] he would have taken that. 12. But, as
there were no means of bringing this about, he
thought that his continued efforts must attain the
speed of flight, and so he jettisoned all means of
easy living while travelling, and bade them farewell:
he stripped the carriage that bore him and made it
as light as he could, mounted it, and got the utmost
speed out of his mules by instant application of the
whip. 13. A great crowd was there to see him off,
mostly composed of women. These women, indeed,

[c] Homer, *Il.* 20. 223 ff.
[d] Pegasus: Hesiod, *Theog.* 280.

357

τριάκοντα δὴ σταδίους τοῖς αὐτῶν αὐταὶ καλύ-
ψασαι σώμασιν ἔξω τὸ πρὸς ἑσπέραν ἔμενον, ὁ δέ,
ἔστι γὰρ σώφρων καὶ εἰδὼς ἃ διωθεῖσθαι κάλλιον,
καὶ τὰς τιμὰς ἐν τοῖς ὑπ' αὐτοῦ πραττομένοις ἀξιῶν
ἔχειν πέμψας μὲν οὐκ ἀπήλασε[1] τὸν ὄχλον οὐδὲ
R 686 ἐλύπησε, διὰ δὲ τῆς ἑσπέρας αὐτῆς | τοῦτο ποιή-
σας, ἐπειδὴ καιρὸς ἦν, εἰς γίγνομαι δὴ τῶν ἀνα-
στρεψάντων καὶ αὐτός. 14. καὶ ὡς ἐκαθήμην πρὸς
ταῖς ἐμαυτοῦ θύραις, βοῆς ἀκούομεν ἱκετείαν
ἐχούσης. εἰκάσας οὖν, ὅπερ ἦν, ἐξιέναι τὸν ἄνδρα,
πάλιν ἐπὶ τὸν ἵππον ἀναβὰς ἀσθενὴς ὁ γέρων τὰ
πρῶτα μὲν εἱπόμην, εἶτα παρήλαυνον, ἔπειτα πολὺ
τὸ μέσον ἐμαυτοῦ πρὸς ἐκεῖνον ποιήσας ἀνέμενον,
δακρύσας δὲ ἥκοντος, τοῦτο | δὴ τὸ πολλάκις μοι F
πεπραγμένον, πολλὰ διεκωλύθην εἰπεῖν τοῖς παρὰ
τοῦδε λόγοις ἔχουσι μάλισθ' ἅ γ' ἂν ἐβουλόμην.
15. ἐντεῦθεν ἡμεῖς μὲν ἐκαθεύδομεν, ὁ δ' ἠπείγετο
καὶ τῆς δευτέρας ἑσπέρας ἥπτετο Καππαδοκίας
ὁρίων, εἶτα τῶν μετ' ἐκεῖνα, καὶ τῆς ἕκτης ἡμέρας
μετὰ μέσην ἔδειξεν αὐτὸν τῷ βασιλεῖ λανθάνοντα
τοὺς ἁπάντων ὀφθαλμοὺς τῷ τὸ μὲν ἡγούμενον μὴ
R 687 εἶναι, τὸ δ' ἑπόμενον ἐν | δυοῖν καὶ μάλιστα δὴ τῇ
τοῦ σώματος διὰ τῶν πόνων δαπάνῃ. 16. πόνοι
γὰρ δὴ πόνοις συνήπτοντο καὶ τὸ διιστὰν εἰς ἀνά-
παυλαν ἦν οὐδέν, οὐ σῖτος, οὐκ ὄψον, οὐ ποτόν,
οὐχ ὕπνος, οὐκ ἐπιθυμία κλίνης. ὃς οὕτως εἴχετο
τοῦ πρόσω ὥστε καὶ ταῖς διαδοχαῖς τῶν ὀρέων
ἄχθεσθαι τοῖς τε περὶ ταῦτα τάχεσιν ὡς βραδυτῆ-
σιν ἐπιτιμᾶν· ἐπεὶ οὐδὲ ὑπόδημα ἔλυσεν οὐδ' ἀνα-

occupied the city also, and for thirty stades beyond it they waited until evening, packing the road so that it could not be seen. He, being a man of prudence and well aware of the sort of situation not to get involved in, preferred his honours to come from his actions, and he did not send anyone to disperse the crowd and so hurt their feelings. He let the coming of evening disperse them, and when the time came, I myself was one of those who sent them back home. 14. And as I sat at my door, I heard a cry of entreaty. Thus I guessed, correctly, that he was about to leave, and once more, old and ailing though I may be, I mounted my horse and followed him at first, then rode past him, and finally, putting a good distance between him and me, I waited for him. I wept as he came up—a thing I had done often enough before—but was prevented from making a long address by the message he gave, which contained all I could wish for. 15. Thereafter, while we retired to rest, he hurried on his way. The second evening, he reached the borders of Cappadocia, and then of the next province and so on, until by the afternoon of the sixth day he presented himself before the emperor. He escaped the gaze of everyone, for he had no one to ride ahead, and his suite consisted of two persons only, in a state of complete physical exhaustion. 16. For toil followed toil with no interval for rest, with no bread to eat, no dessert, no drink, no sleep and no desire for bed. He was so eager to proceed that he fidgeted at the changes of mules, and however speedily this was managed, he still complained of delay. He did not undo his

---

[1] ἀπήλασε F. (mss. except ILa Vat. 64): ἀπήλαυνε Re. (ILa): ἠπείλησε Vat. 64.

ξυρίδα ἀφείλκυσεν οὐδ᾽ ἐγυμνώθη τῆς ἐνθένδε ἐσθῆτος πρὶν ἐν τοῖς πρὸς βασιλέα λόγοις τῆς ἡμέρας τὸ λοιπὸν ἀναλώσας ἧκεν ἐπὶ λουτρόν. ὡς τά γε διὰ πάσης τῆς ὁδοῦ παραθέων | ἠρίθμει, καὶ κά- F ματος οὐδεὶς αὐτὸν ἐπὶ τοῦτο[1] κατεβίβασεν, ὅν γε οὐδὲ αἱ πόλεις. τί ποτ᾽ οὖν ἦν τὸ τοῦτο ποιοῦν; σφοδρά τις ἐπιθυμία λῦσαι μὲν τῇ βουλῇ τὸν δε-
R 688 σμόν, λῦσαι δὲ τῇ πόλει τὴν | ἀτιμίαν. ἐῴκει γὰρ οὐχ ἑτέροις ἐπικουροῦντι μᾶλλον ἢ αὐτὸν ῥυομένῳ.

17. Καὶ τὰ μὲν τῆς γνώμης τοιαῦτα, μάταιον δὲ ὁρμὴ πᾶσα μὴ προσλαβοῦσα τὴν Τύχην. τὸ μὲν γὰρ ἂν κινοίη, τὸ δ᾽ ἀποστερεῖ[2] τοῦ τέλους· μὴ γὰρ δὴ συμπνέοντος τοῦ δαίμονος πόσον ἄν τι εἴη παρ᾽ αὐτοῦ τοῦ βουλεύεσθαι; ὡς δήτοι καὶ κυβερνήτης ἅπας σῴζειν μὲν ἂν θέλοι τὴν ναῦν, σῴζει δὲ οὐχ ἅπας, ἀλλ᾽ οἷς συμπράττει τὰ πνεύματα. τοῦτο δ᾽ ἂν εἴη τῆς Τύχης. 18. καὶ νῦν τοίνυν τῷ βουλομένῳ ταχέως διαδραμεῖν παρ᾽ ἐκείνης[3] καὶ τὸ δεδυνῆσθαι μηδενὸς τῶν ὑποσκελίζειν εἰωθότων παρηνωχληκότος, οἷα πολλὰ ἂν ἐξ ὀχήματος συμπέσοι, ἀλλ᾽ ὥσπερ ἐξ ἀδάμαντος ὄντων μὲν τῶν τροχῶν, ὄντων δὲ τῶν ἐπ᾽ αὐτοῖς, οὕτω πάντα κρείττω τοῦ τι παθεῖν ἤρχετο πληττόμενα | μὲν F
R 689 τοῖς πεφυκόσι λυμαίνεσθαι, | κρατούμενα δὲ ὑπ᾽ οὐδενός. 19. καίτοι τὸν ἀπερισκέπτως τῇ τοῦ

---

[1] τοῦτο F. (CPV) : τούτῳ other mss., Re. text (conj. τούτων ἔν τι).

[2] ἀποστερεῖ F. (La, Macarius) : ἀποστεροίη Re. (I) : ἀποστεροῖ other mss.

[3] ἐκείνης Re., F. : ἐκείνοις I : ἐκείνου La : ἐκείνῳ Morel (other mss.).

360

shoes, or take off his breeches, or change from the garments he wore on leaving here, until, after spending the rest of the day in making his report to the emperor, he finally retired to his bath. As he ticked off the stages in passing throughout his whole journey, no fatigue caused him to dismount for that purpose, nor did the cities he passed through. What then caused him to behave so ? Simply his urgent desire to relieve the council of its arrest and the city of its disgrace. It was not so much as if he was helping other people as rescuing himself.

17. Such then was his resolve, but all his energy would have been in vain had it not had the backing of Fortune.[a] She may set some things moving, but others she robs of their objective. Without this divine connivance, what would the plans of men be worth ? Every helmsman, to be sure, wants to save his ship, but not all do—only those who have the winds to help them. That is where Fortune comes in. 18. So now, he wanted a speedy journey and Fortune provided the means. He experienced no trouble from the usual kind of set-back and the many accidents which can occur when travelling by carriage. [b] Its wheels were as though composed of adamant, and the body that rested on them too, and so everything went on beyond the reach of accidents, experiencing the usual alarms and excursions but overcome by none. 19. Yet when anyone

[a] For Fortune in the religion of Libanius *cf.* Misson, *Le paganisme de Libanius* (Louvain, 1914), *passim.*
[b] A not inconsiderable risk for travellers : *e.g.* Obodianus, envoy of Antioch in A.D. 361/2, fell and broke an arm, and could not complete his mission, *Ep.* 698 ; in A.D. 391 Cimon, Libanius' son, was to die in consequence of a similar fall, *Or.* 1. 278 ff.

LIBANIUS

τάχους ἐπιθυμίᾳ χρώμενον πολλὴν ἐφέλκεσθαι καὶ
τὴν βλάβην ἀνάγκη. ἀλλ' ὅμως ἐνίκα τὰ νικώμενα,
καθάπερ δι' ἀέρος οὐδὲν ἐφαπτόμενα τῆς γῆς πο-
ρευόμενα. οὐκοῦν συμμαχία μὲν τῆς Τύχης διὰ
τούτων δηλοῦται, τοῦτο δὲ οὐκ ἂν ὑπῆρχε μὴ τῶν
ἄλλων συμβουλομένων[1] θεῶν. ὁμόνοια μὲν γὰρ ἐν
αὐτοῖς καὶ τὸ τὰ αὐτὰ φρονεῖν, στάσις δὲ καὶ τὸ
διαφέρεσθαι πόρρω μὲν οὐρανοῦ, πόρρω δὲ τοῦ τὸν
οὐρανὸν οἰκοῦντος χοροῦ. οὕτως ἔτρεχες δρόμον
ὑπὸ θεῶν ἐπαινούμενον καὶ ἦν ἐβούλοντο πόλιν
συνδιέσωζες, καὶ ἧς ἐκήδοντο κηδόμενος ἐφαίνου.

20. Ὡς γὰρ δὴ κατέθηκε πρὸ τῶν ποδῶν βασιλεῖ τὰ τὸν ἔλεγχον ἔχοντα γράμματα καὶ κελεύοντος ἀνεγίνωσκε καὶ τοῖς μανεῖσιν οὐδαμόθεν ἦν
σωθῆναι, γονάτων τε εὐθὺς ἥπτετο καὶ περὶ δόξης
ἐποιεῖτο τοὺς λόγους καὶ οἷα ἂν ἐξ ἑκατέρου συμ-
βαίη, τοῦ τε κολάσαι καὶ τοῦ μή. ἔλεγε δ' ἄρα
καὶ κεκολάσθαι τὴν πόλιν διδάσκων ὡς αὐτοὶ σφᾶς
αὐτοὺς ἀπώλλυσαν τῇ φυγῇ πάσχοντες ἃ ὅπως μὴ
πάθοιεν ἔφευγον, ἀποροῦντες στέγης, ἀποροῦντες
τροφῆς, οὐκ ἔχοντες | ἰατρὸν ἀντιθεῖναι τοῖς ἐκ τῆς F 4
ταλαιπωρίας. καὶ ἐδείκνυ δὴ λέγων αὐτοῖς οἷς
R 690 εὐπόρουν θνήσκοντας τοὺς | εὐπόρους καλοῦντας
ἐφ' ἑαυτοὺς τὰ τῶν κακούργων ξίφη ⟨καὶ⟩[2] τῶν

[1] συμβουλευομένων Re. (B).
[2] ⟨καὶ⟩ F.

---

[a] Christians constantly criticized the pagan myths which
depicted the gods at war. Rationalizing pagans sought to
rebut them by allegorical interpretations of the stories in
Homer and Hesiod. Libanius' use of this sentiment here is
the more appropriate since Caesarius was Christian.

[b] Libanius naturally refrains from mentioning the initiative of Bishop Flavianus, who had left Antioch to intercede

362

recklessly indulges his desire for speed, much harm
must of necessity result. Nevertheless such vulner-
ability triumphed : it was as if his progress was
through the air, with no foot set on the ground. So
the support of Fortune is here demonstrated, and
it would not have been provided without the consent
of the other gods. There is harmony among them
and a unanimity of purpose : faction and quarrels
are far removed from heaven, and from the company
of its inhabitants. Thus you ran a course that had
the approval of the gods [a] ; you assisted them in the
preservation of the city they wanted to save, and
you were seen to care for her which was the object of their care.

20. For as he placed before the emperor's feet the
report containing the charge, and began to read it
at his bidding, and we, in our criminal lunacy, had
no possible means of salvation, he embraced the
emperor's knees with no more ado and took up the
theme of his reputation and the consequences of
either course of action, of imposing or refraining
from punishment.[b] He told him, in fact, that the
city had been punished already, and explained how
the citizens had themselves done away with themselves, by suffering in their flight all that they had
fled to avoid, without shelter, without food, with no
doctor to combat the consequences of their misery.
In this account he showed how the wealthy were
dying because of their wealth, since they brought
upon themselves the knives of brigands and had the

with the emperor immediately after the riots (Jo. Chrys.
Hom. 3 ; *P.G.* xlix. 47 ff.), and had been in Constantinople
for some days before Caesarius reported (*Hom.* 21 ; *P.G.*
xlix. 211 ff.).

ἰχθύων τὰς γαστέρας ἀντὶ ταφῆς ἔχοντας. ὁ δ᾽ ἀπὸ τοιαύτης ἀκοῆς ἐπὶ τὸν θρῆνον ὁρμήσας τὰς παρὰ τῶν ἄλλων δεήσεις ἔφθασε τοῖς παρ᾽ ἑαυτοῦ δάκρυσιν, ἐν οἷς ἦν τῶν λυπηρῶν ἡ λύσις.

21. Πολλὰ μὲν οὖν τὰ¹ σὲ περιφανῆ ποιοῦντα, Καίσαριε, μάλιστα δὲ τοῦτ᾽ αὐτὸ τὸ νῦν. σεσώσμεθα γὰρ τῇ βασιλέως ψήφῳ, ἔρχεται δέ τι σωτηρίας καὶ ἐπὶ τὴν σὴν γνώμην. ἄλλου μὲν γὰρ ἴσως ἦν τοῦ μὴ κατὰ σὲ τὸν τρόπον χαρίσασθαι θυμῷ μεγάλῳ λόγοις προσερεθίζουσι καὶ νὴ Δία γε οὐκ ὄντα μέγαν ποιῆσαι τηλικοῦτον πικραῖς τε κατηγορίαις καὶ τὸ πρᾶγμα αἴρουσιν ὀνόμασι φόβῳ τε τῶν ὁμοίων, εἰ μὴ τὸ σπέρμα τις ἀνέλοι· σοῦ δ᾽ ἦν ἀκούειν πρᾳότητος ἐπαίνους καὶ σοφίαν ὁρᾶν ἀφαιροῦσάν τι τοῦ μεγέθους καὶ λογισμοὺς ἐκ τῆς τῶν ἡμαρτηκότων φειδοῦς τὴν τῶν ἄλλων ἐγγυωμένους σωφροσύνην. 22. φιλῶ μὲν οὖν καὶ τὸν Ἀθηναίων ῥήτορα τῇ Μιτυλήνῃ βοη|θοῦντα, ἀλλ᾽ οὔτε² τοσ- F οῦτον ἦν τὸ κινδυνευόμενον, ποῦ γὰρ ἴσον ἡμεῖς καὶ Μιτυληναῖοι; τό τε πᾶν ἐκεῖνος οὐκ ἔστησεν, R 691 ἀλλ᾽ ἴσμεν ἐφ᾽ ὁπόσον ἧκεν ἡ δίκη. | νῦν δὲ διὰ τοῦ παντὸς ἀφῖκται τὸ φάρμακον.

23. Σκοπῶμεν δὴ κἂν τῷ κεκομικότι τὰς διαλλαγὰς τῇ πόλει ἀνθρώπῳ τὸν ἐπίκουρον αὐτόν. ὃς γὰρ ἐγένετ᾽ ἂν τῇ πόλει λυσιτελέστερος ἑτέρου, τοῦτον ὅπως οἴσει τὴν φιλτάτην ἡμῖν ἐπιστολὴν ἔπραξεν, ὃς ἄνευ τε βαρύτητος ἔμελλε τῇ βουλῇ

---

¹ τὰ σὲ Re. : σὲ τὰ F. (mss.).   ² οὔτε F. : οὔ τι Re. (mss.).

ᵃ Cf. Or. 23. 1 ff.
ᵇ Cf. Jo. Chrys. Hom. 21. 4 (P.G. xlix. 219).

bellies of fish for their tombs.[a]   At such a recital, the emperor began to lament and by his own tears, which involved relief from our troubles, he anticipated requests from the rest.[b]

21. There is much that makes you a man of mark, Caesarius,—our present situation in particular.   We have been saved by the emperor's decision, but some part of our salvation can be referred to your resolve.   Another man perhaps, unlike you in character, would have heaped fresh fuel on the fire of his wrath or even, by heaven, have fanned it from a tiny flame with bitter accusations and with exaggerated terminology and fear of a recurrence if the seed were not destroyed.   From you, however, there could be heard the praises of clemency, and your wisdom could be seen to reduce the extent of our offence somewhat, and your reasoning to guarantee the good conduct of the majority by sparing the offenders.   22. I fully approve of the Athenian orator who aided Mitylene,[c] but the issues at stake were not nearly so great.   How can Mitylene be set on a par with us ?   Besides, he did not bring the whole matter to an end ;   we know the extent of the punishment exacted.   But in the present instance the cure has been applied to the whole citizen body.

23. Let us observe, then, our supporter himself in the person of the man who brought the news of the reconciliation to the city, for he ensured that the bearer of the despatch which blessed us all should be one of the utmost possible assistance to her—a man who was likely to conduct himself before our city

[c] Diodotus in 427 B.C. (Thuc. 3. 41 ff.) opposed Cleon's proposal for the mass extermination of the Mitylenaeans after their revolt, but even so one thousand were executed.

συνέσεσθαι καὶ τοὺς ἐκείνης λόγους ἀνέξεσθαι πρὸς
τῷ καὶ λαμπρὸν τὸ δίκαιον ἐνεῖναι τῷ πράγματι.
τίς γὰρ μᾶλλον ἂν εἰκότως ἐκαρπώσατο τὰ γράμματα τοῦ μόνου τῶν ἵππους[1] ἐλαυνόντων μιμησα-
R 692 μένου τὰ Καισαρίου | πτερά;

24. Ἔδει μὲν οὖν ὄρος τε ἡμῖν εἶναι καὶ ποταμὸν
χρυσίον, ὥσπερ Λυδοῖς, φέροντα, ὥσθ' ἡμᾶς μὴ
μείζω βούλεσθαι τοῦ δύνασθαι, νῦν δ' οὐκ ἦν
ἐφικέσθαι τοῦ μέτρου τοὺς ἐν τοιαύτῃ μεταβολῇ.
σὲ δὲ μακα|ρίζω μὲν τῆς τοῦ βασιλέως εὐνοίας, F 4
μακαρίζω δὲ τοῦ πρὸς ἐκεῖνον φίλτρου, μακαρίζω δὲ τῆς φρονήσεως, μακαρίζω δὲ τοῦ τὰ[2] τοιαῦτα μὲν εἰργάσθαι, τοιαῦτα δὲ σεαυτῷ συνειδέναι.
καὶ γὰρ ἔτι βελτίονος ἐλπίδος ὑπάρχει τοῖς τοιούτοις εἶναι καὶ ζῶσι καὶ ἀπιοῦσι, κἄν τί ποθεν
προσβάλλῃ δυσχερές, ὧν πεποίηκεν ἡ μνήμη τὴν
λύσιν ἐπαγγέλλεται. 25. καλὸν μὲν οὖν καὶ ἀνδρὶ
συνειπόντα κινδύνου σαφοῦς ἐξαρπάσαι καὶ τὸ νηὶ
ναῦν ἐπαμύνασαν ἀποκρούσασθαι λῃστάς, σοὶ δὲ
οὐκ ἀφ' ἑνὸς σώματος ἢ δέκα ἢ εἴκοσιν ἢ δὶς τοσούτων ἡ φιλοτιμία, ἀλλ' ὅσων οὐδ' ἀριθμῆσαι ῥᾴδιον. ὅτῳ δὲ εἰπεῖν ἔνι καὶ σεσωκέναι πόλιν, ἀλλ'
οὔ τι γε τοσαύτην οὐδ' οὕτως ἀρχαίαν οὐδ' οὕτω
πολλοῖς ἀνθοῦσαν τοῖς ἀγαθοῖς. μάρτυρες δὲ τοῦ
γέμειν αὐτὴν ἀγαθῶν οἱ προστιθέντες τῷ πλήθει
καθ' ἡμέραν ταῖς μεταναστάσεσι. 26. καὶ ὅταν δή

---

[1] τοὺς before ἵππους Re. (B), bracketed F.
[2] τὰ Re.: τε Morel (mss.), bracketed F.

---

[a] Chrysostom (*Hom.* 21 ; *P.G.* xlix. 220) asserts that this
courier was sent by Theodosius to save Bishop Flavianus
from the excessive rigours of his enforced return. The
messenger arrived on Palm Sunday. Despite all Libanius'
eloquence, the whole context of the incident is Christian.

council without heavy-handedness and endure what
it had to say, as well as having the best qualifications
for the mission. For who could more properly have
gained profit from the message than the one courier
who had emulated Caesarius in his winged course ? [a]
24. Well, we ought to have a mountain and a river
of gold, as the Lydians had,[b] for our desire not to
exceed our capacity. As it was, those who had experienced such vicissitudes were unable to attain
the happy mean. You I congratulate upon the emperor's favour, upon your affection for him, upon
your good sense, upon the performance of all you
have done, and upon your consciousness of such performance. Men such as you may have high hopes
both in this life and beyond ; and should any dis-
cordant element arise, memory promises the disappearance of anything this causes. 25. It is indeed a
fine thing for one to be a man's advocate and to
rescue him from certain danger, or for one ship to
help another in repelling pirates, but your claim to
fame comes not from one person, or ten, or twenty,
or twice as many, but from a number that almost
defies accounting. Should anyone boast even of
saving a city, yet it certainly was not a city of our
size and antiquity, or one with such abundance of
good things. And witnesses to its fullness of good
things are to be found in those people who are daily
added to its numbers by leaving their home town to
come and live here.[c] 26. And whenever men in

[b] Mount Tmolus and river Pactolus : for the gold produced there and exploited by the Lydian kings *cf*. Hdt. 5.
101, *Or*. 11. 263.
[c] The immigration into Antioch, commended here and
in *Or*. 11. 164 ff., is usually deplored by Libanius (*cf. Or*. 10).

τινες ἐν συνουσίᾳ σεμνύνωσιν ἑαυτοὺς μνήμῃ καλῶν
πράξεων, σοὶ τὸ νικᾶν ὑπάρξει λέγοντι τὴν ἡμετέραν.
R 693 ἢ σὺ μὲν ἴσως οὐκ | ἐρεῖς ἔργον ὑπερήφανον σιωπῇ
κοσμῶν, ἡμᾶς | δὲ οὐκ ἔστιν ὅ τι παύσει λέγοντας F
τὸ μέγεθος τῆς εὐεργεσίας, τὸν περὶ αὐτῆς ποιοῦντας λόγον ἀθάνατον παισὶ πατέρων παραδιδόντων
ἅ τε ἐπλημμελήσαμεν ἅ τε ἐδείσαμεν ὧν τε ἀπε-
λαύσαμεν. 27. καὶ εἰ μέν τις ὀρθώσειέ τί ποτε τῶν
ἡμετέρων ἀνδρὸς ἀρετῆς δεόμενον, τὰ σὰ τοῦτον
ἐζηλωκέναι ἐροῦμεν, εἰ δὲ ἀμελείᾳ πρόοιτο κακόν
τι, εἰς μίμησιν τῶν ⟨σῶν⟩[1] καλῶν τοῦτον ἡγησό-
μεθα. καὶ τῶν πεπραγμένων ἡ διήγησις εἰς μέσον
ἥξει νῦν μὲν ταῦτα πολλῶν λεγόντων, νῦν δὲ τοῦ
μᾶλλον μεμνημένου τὸν ἧττον ἐπανορθοῦντος. 28.
πολλαὶ μὲν ἡμῖν, ὦ χρηστέ, πανηγύρεις ἅτε καὶ
παλαιοτάτοις οὖσι καὶ πρεσβυτέροις τοῦ τὴν Ἰὼ
βοῦν ποιήσαντος ἔρωτος. καὶ γὰρ τοὺς ἐκείνην
ζητοῦντας οἱ τὸ ὄρος οἰκοῦντες πόλιν τινὰ ἐπ' αὐτοῦ κεκτημένοι φαίνονται ξενίσαντες. ἐν οὖν ταύταις δὴ ταῖς ἑορταῖς ᾀσόμεθα μὲν τὸν ἐν ἑκάστῃ
R 694 τιμώμενον θεόν, ᾀσόμεθα δὲ καὶ μεθ' ἑκάστους | σέ
τε καὶ τὰ παρὰ σοῦ. 29. δοκεῖ δέ μοι καὶ βασιλεὺς
φροντίζειν ὅ τι ἄν σοι δοὺς δόξειε πᾶν ὅσον ἦν
ἄξιον δεδωκέναι. καί μοι | δοκεῖς διὰ πολλῶν F
σχημάτων ἀφιγμένος ἐπὶ τὸ καὶ βασιλεῦσι τετιμη-
μένον προϊὼν ἥξειν, τὸν ὕπατον. καθ' ἕκαστον οὖν

[1] τῶν ⟨σῶν⟩ conj. Re., F.

---

[a] Notably the Olympia, as in *Or.* 11. 268.

[b] For the legend of the founding of a city, Ione, near
the site of the future Antioch by Triptolemus in his search
for the wandering Io, *cf. Or.* 11. 44-53. It is used as commendation of the city both to Julian in A.D. 363 (*Or.* 15. 79)
and to Theodosius himself after these riots (*Or.* 20. 42).

company put on airs at the recollection of their
noble deeds, you will be able to outdo them all by
mentioning our city. Or else, perhaps, you will
say nothing and enhance your peerless action with
modest silence ; yet there is nothing which will stop
us recounting the extent of your kindness and making
the story of it eternal. Fathers will pass down to
their children the story of our misdeeds, our fears and
our joys. 27. And if ever anyone directs aright any
of our actions when it requires a man of merit, we
will say that he has emulated you, and if, by lack of
consideration, he proposes something wrong, we will
direct him to imitate your noble deeds. The narration of what you have done will come to the fore,
either when many speak of it, or when anyone with
a good memory corrects his more forgetful fellow.
28. We have many festivals,[a] my good friend, for
we have a very long history that goes back beyond
the passion that transformed Io into a cow.[b] Indeed,
the dwellers on the mountain, who had a city of a
sort upon it, are known to have given hospitality to
those who came in search of her. In these festivals,
then, we shall sing the praises of the god honoured
in each of them, and after them recite the praises
of yourself and what you have done. 29. The
emperor, I believe, is considering what gift he can
bestow upon us so as to be thought to have given
you your full due. You, I believe, will crown your
varied career of service by advancing to the attainment of that office which emperors too honour by
their acceptance—the consulship.[c] In every stage

[c] This prophecy was fulfilled in A.D. 397. For the
prestige of such a nomination cf. Or. 12. 12.

τῶν σχημάτων ἕξεις δήπου καὶ σοφιστῶν ἐπαίνους
μεγάλων ὄντως ἐν οἷς περὶ σοῦ λέγουσι γιγνομένων.
αὐτῶν δέ γε τῶν λεγομένων κεφάλαιον ἃ τήνδε
μέλλοντα τὴν πόλιν ἐπικλύσειν ἔστησας.

30. Ἡμεῖς μὲν οὖν χαλκῶν ἐμνημονεύομεν εἰκόνων οὐκ ὂν ἐπαγγείλαί τι παρὰ τοῦ βασιλέως
σεμνότερον, ἀλλ' αἱ μὲν οἷός τις ἀνὴρ τὸ σῶμα
δεικνύουσι, ψυχῆς δὲ εἶδος τοῖς ἔργοις μηνύεται.
ὅστις οὖν αὐτὸν ἐπέδειξεν ἄριστον, ἐν τῷ καλλίονι
καὶ τοῖς ὕστερον ἐσομένοις φαίνεται καὶ τὸ μὲν
πολλαῖς κινεῖται τύχαις, τὸ δ' ἐστὶ κρεῖττον ἤ τι
τοιοῦτον παθεῖν ἐν βεβαίῳ κείμενον. 31. τά τε οὖν
ἄλλα πάντα εἰρήσεται τὸν χρόνον καὶ οἷα πρὸς τὸν
τῶν ἀμεινόνων ἄγγελον τουτονὶ διελέχθης, ὅτι ὦ
σὺ δείξας σεαυτὸν ἐν οὐκ ὀλίγαις ὁδοῖς, φάνηθί μοι
νῦν, εἰ μὲν οἷόν τε, θάττων, εἰ δὲ μή, μήτι γε βρα-
δύτερος. ὡς ἔγωγε κάμνω τοῖς τῆς Ἀντιοχείας
R 695 κακοῖς, ἢ γυναικὸς | νόσῳ πιεζομένης οὐδὲν δια-
φέρει. | ἐν δὴ τῷ σῷ τάχει κἀκείνοις τὰ¹ τῆς τῶν F
ἀνιαρῶν λύσεως. 32. εἰ δὴ τοῖς ὀφείλουσι χάριν
ἔξεστι πρὶν ἐκτῖσαι τὴν χάριν ἑτέραν αἰτῆσαι, τῶν
παρ' ἡμῖν οἰκοδομουμένων καὶ αὐτὸς ἡμῖν, ὦ θαυ-
μάσιε, γενοῦ καὶ δὴ καὶ τῶν γεωργούντων καὶ
ποίησον ἀμφοτέροις λαμπροτέραν τὴν πόλιν καὶ
μηδέτερον τῶν ἀναλωμάτων φύγῃς, ὅπως ἡμῖν μὲν
ὡς περὶ πολίτου διαλέγεσθαι πρός τε ἀλλήλους καὶ

¹ τὰ F. (V) : om. Re. (other mss.).

ᵃ A conventional symbol of reconciliation or of recognition of favours received, presented (e.g.) to Datianus (Ep.
1184. 8) and Ellebichus (Or. 22. 41). Offended emperors

of that career, then, you will certainly receive the praises of sophists, who really attain greatness in the orations which they deliver about you. And in these very orations, pride of place is taken by your achievement in halting the disastrous flood that nearly overwhelmed our city.

30. So we made suggestions for the erection of bronze statues, for no higher mark of esteem can be solicited from the emperor, but these only show what a man is like in his physical appearance. The bent of his character is indicated by his actions. So anyone who shows himself a man of excellence is revealed in the better part of him to future generations too : statues can be upset by many mishaps, but this, based upon sure foundation, is above experiencing any such accident. 31. So the story will be related for all time, as will the instructions you gave to this bearer of good tidings. " You, who have proved your mettle on many a long road, now, if you please, show yourself more speedy still, if possible, but, failing that, no slower than before. I am sorely grieved by the evils of Antioch, which is exactly like a woman afflicted by illness. In your speed, then, lies the relief of their discomfort." 32. If those who owe a debt of gratitude may ask a second favour before repaying the first, then do you, admirable sir, yourself become one of those to build a residence in our midst, and become one of the land-owners too.[a] By both means increase our city's fame, and do not evade the expenditure on either project. Thus in our conversations among ourselves, and with others too, we may speak of you are similarly asked to visit the city, *Or.* 15. 86 (Julian), 20. 46 (Theodosius).

LIBANIUS

πρὸς τοὺς ἄλλους ἐξείη, σοὶ δ' ὁπότε εἴης ἐνθάδε, πολλάκις δὲ τοῦτο γένοιτο, διαιτᾶσθαί τε ἐν οἰκείοις καὶ τῇ παρὰ τῶν ἀγρῶν φορᾷ τοὺς ἐπιτηδείους ἑστιᾶν.

33. Ἐμοὶ δὲ ἐγγὺς μὲν ἴσως ἡ τελευτὴ δηλουμένη τῷ τῶν ἐτῶν ἀριθμῷ, τάχα δ' ἂν τύχοιμι τότε λόγου παρὰ τῶν δυναμένων λέγειν, οἷς ἀφορμὴ καὶ τῶν φίλων ἡ κτῆσις ἣν ἐκτησάμην μάλα δὴ φίλων σαφῶν. ἐν τούτῳ δὴ καὶ πλέον τι περὶ σοῦ λέγειν
F 466 ἕξουσι μέ|γιστον τοῦτο τῶν | ἐμῶν τιθέμενοι καὶ R (τήν γε ἀπόδειξιν ἐξ ὧν εἴληφα ποιούμενοι. σὺ δέ, ὦ μεγάλων ἔργων δημιουργέ, πατήρ τε ἡμῖν γένοιο καὶ τοιούτων υἱέων, ὡς ἐξισοῦσθαι τὰς ἐκείνων ἀρετὰς τῇ τοῦ γεγεννηκότος.

as our own citizen ; and whenever you are in residence here, which I trust will be often, you will be able to spend your time among your own folk and feast your friends on the produce of your farms.

33. For me, perhaps, because of my tale of years, death reveals itself close at hand, but, when I am gone, I may perhaps be spoken of by those who have ability in speaking. For them their theme will be the friendships, the very firm friendships, I have possessed. Here too they will have yet more to say of you, asserting your friendship to be the most important of my possessions, and proving their case by the favours I have received. And may you, who have wrought mighty deeds, become the father of a family among us, and of such a family that their virtues may equal those of their sire.

XXII

ΠΡΟΣ[1] ΕΛΛΕΒΙΧΟΝ

R ii. 1   1. Εἰσί τινες, οἳ τοῦθ᾽ ἓν μέγιστον ἀγαθὸν ἀν- F
θρώπῳ νομίζουσι χρήματα καὶ τὸ πλουτεῖν καὶ διὰ
τοῦτο κἂν δι᾽ ἐπιορκίας τουτὶ λαβεῖν οὐκ ἀποκνοῦ-
σιν, ἀλλ᾽ εἰ καὶ πείσονταί τι κακὸν ἐντεῦθεν ὕστερον, οὐκ ἀποτρέπονται. ἕτεροι δέ γε βούλοιντ᾽ ἂν
ἐπαινεθῆναι μᾶλλον ἢ πάνθ᾽ ὅσα ἐν ἀνθρώποις ἔνι
χρήματα κεκτῆσθαι καὶ τοῦθ᾽ ὁμολογοῦντες οὐκ
αἰσχύνονται. οἱ δὲ | τοῦ μὲν αὐτοῦ τὴν ἴσην ἔχου- F
σιν ἐπιθυμίαν, προσποιοῦνται δὲ μηδὲν ἐπαίνων
δεῖσθαι. 2. κακοὺς τοίνυν ἀμφοτέρους ἡγούμενος
ὅσοι τε τὸ πλουτεῖν πρὸ ἐπαίνων ποιοῦνται καὶ
ὅσοι μεῖζον ἡγούμενοι τοὺς ἐπαίνους οὔ φασιν οὕτως ἔχειν, ἄνδρας ἀρίστους ἡγοῦμαι τοὺς μήτ᾽
ἀγνοοῦντας ὅσον ἐστὶν ἔπαινος χαίρειν τε τῷ πράγματι λέγοντας, ὥστε καὶ ἐπαγγέλλειν παρὰ τῶν
δυναμένων λέγειν. ὧν ἕνα τοῦτον[2] εἰδὼς τὸν θαυ-
R ii. 2 μαστὸν Ἐλλέβιχον | νῦν οὐκ αἰτοῦντι τοῦτο παρέξω
πρότερον ᾐτηκότι δεδωκώς. οἶμαι γὰρ αὐτὸν καὶ

---

[1] πρὸς Re. (mss. except BPaV, Macarius): εἰς F. (BPaV).
[2] τοῦτον F. (C, Pl corrected): τούτων Re. (other mss.):
τουτονὶ Cobet.

---

[a] Libanius had been on friendly terms with Ellebichus at
374

ORATION 22

TO ELLEBICHUS

1. Some people think that the greatest single blessing for man lies in money and wealth, and so they do not shrink from its acquisition, even by perjury, but even if they have to suffer some evil in consequence, they are not deterred. Others, though, would prefer to be praised rather than to get all the money in the world, and they are not ashamed to confess it. Others, again, are possessed of an equal desire for the same object, but profess that they have no need of praise. 2. Well, I think that both those who think more of wealth than of praise and those who think praise to be of greater importance and yet deny that it is, are wrong. The best men, I feel, are those who, though not unaware of the value of praise, do not bother about it, so that they actually invite it from those qualified to utter it. Of these I know that our admirable Ellebichus is one, and now I will provide him with it unsolicited, though previously I had conferred it upon him at his request.[a] In my opinion, he has remained silent through his convic-

least from A.D. 383, when he was appointed *magister militum* (*Ep.* 2). The panegyric here mentioned was delivered in A.D. 385 (*Or.* 1. 232: ἐποίησα λόγον αἰτήσαντι στρατηγῷ). He was, unlike Caesarius, a pagan. *Cf.* Seeck 167 ; *PLRE* 277.

LIBANIUS

διὰ τὸ πεπεῖσθαί με τὰ παρόντα ἐπαινέσαι σεσιγη-
κέναι τε καὶ μὴ τὸ πρότερον πρὸς ἐμὲ πεποιηκέναι.
3. ἀηδὲς μὲν οὖν παρελθόντων μεμνῆσθαι κακῶν·
ἃ γὰρ μηδὲ συμβῆναι τὴν ἀρχὴν ἔδει, σιγᾶσθαι,
φαίη τις ἄν, προσῆκεν. ἀλλ' ἐπειδήπερ οὐκ ἄν τις
ἴδοι τὴν βοήθειαν καλῶς μὴ τῶν δεινῶν ἃ τῆς βοηθείας ἔχρῃζε πρὸ αὐτῆς εἰρημένων, τῆς ἀνάγκης
ἡ μνήμη δήπου γίγνεται. |

4. Χρημάτων ἐδέησε βασιλεῖ πρὸς τὴν τῶν ὅλων F 4
σωτηρίαν καὶ μάλιστα δὴ τῷ μὲν εἰς ἔτος δέκατον,
τῷ παιδὶ δὲ πέμπτον τῆς βασιλείας προϊούσης.
νόμος δὲ ἐν τοῖς τοιούτοις χρόνοις χρυσὸν ἰέναι
παρὰ τῶν κρατούντων εἰς χεῖρας τοῖς στρατιώταις.
τῶν τοίνυν περὶ τῶν χρημάτων γραμμάτων ἀν-
R ii. 3 εγνωσμένων ἔδει | μὲν ἡδεῖαν τότε¹ ἀνθρώποις γε-
νέσθαι τὴν ἀκοὴν καὶ προθυμίαν περὶ τὴν εἰσφορὰν
τοσαύτην, ὥστ' εὐθυμίαν ἐνεγκεῖν τῷ βασιλεῖ τὴν
ἐνταῦθα ἑτοιμότητα, οἱ δὲ πρὸς τοῦθ' ἧκον ἀτοπίας
ὥστ' ἐξέπεσόν τε αὐτῶν καὶ φρονεῖν οὐκέτ' εἶχον,
ἃ μὲν ἔδει δοῦναι καθορῶντες, ἃ δ' ἀντὶ τούτων
ἦν ἔχειν οὐδὲ λογιζόμενοι. 5. καὶ πρῶτον μὲν
ἐγγὺς τοῦ θρόνου καὶ τῶν τοῦ ἄρχοντος ὀμμάτων
φωνὴν ἔρρηξαν στασιαστικήν, σχῆμα μὲν ἔχουσαν
ἱκετείας, ἔργον δὲ ἀπειθείας. ὥσπερ γὰρ ἐν τοῖς

¹ τότε] τοῖς conj. Cobet.

ᵃ Sources which mention this demand are Jo. Chrys. *Hom.*
3. 7, 5. 3, 8. 4 (*P.G.* xlix. 58, 73, 102), Sozom. *H.E.* 7. 23,
Zos. 4. 41, Theodoret, *H.E.* 5. 20 (who calls it a new tax).
Libanius alone connects it with imperial anniversaries (which
fell in A.D. 388, in fact). This should imply *aurum coronarium*. However, his comment that it was ear-marked for
military donatives implies no less that the levy would be
collatio lustralis. Neither tax was new. Browning (*op. cit.*
376

tion that I commended his present attitude and has not made overtures to me. 3. The recital of troubles past is an unpleasant business. It could be said that it is proper to leave unmentioned events which ought never to have happened at all. Yet since none could see in its true light the support we have received without a preliminary account of the troubles that made it necessary, obviously a recital of our dire situation is called for.

4. The emperor needed money for the maintenance of the empire, especially since his reign was approaching its tenth anniversary and his son's its fifth. Normally on such occasions a donative is handed by the rulers to their soldiery.[a] So when the decrees about this money were published, people should then have been pleased to hear them, and should have shown such eagerness to contribute that their readiness in the matter brought good cheer to the emperor. Instead their attitude was so wrongheaded that they lost control of themselves and behaved like lunatics. They concentrated on the payment they had to make and never gave a thought to what they could get in return for it. 5. First of all, near the throne and the gaze of the governor [b] they broke out into disorderly cries. Ostensibly it was a cry of supplication, but, in reality, one of disobedience.

pp. 14 f.) suggested that it was an extraordinary demand for both (so Downey, p. 427, also). Since veterans and other classes not normally liable to either impost are among the protesters, Petit, Ste-Croix (followed by Liebeschuetz, p. 164) identify it with a superindiction of tribute. Libanius, composing this oration in or after A.D. 388, the year of imperial anniversaries (*cf.* § 42 below), confused the issue with these references, deliberately or not.

[b] *i.e.* the *consularis*, at the *dikasterion*.

μεγίστοις κακοῖς τοὺς θεοὺς εἰώθαμεν καλεῖν δεό-
μενοι βοηθεῖν, οὕτω τότε τὸν θεὸν οἱ βοῶντες σφᾶς
ἐλεεῖν, ὡς εἰς τὸ πράττειν ἀξίως ἐλέου | παρὰ τῶν F 4
γραμμάτων ἀφιγμένοι. 6. ὄντος δὲ οὐδὲ τούτου
φορητοῦ πολὺ δεινότερον τὸ ἐπὶ τούτῳ. μετὰ γὰρ
δὴ τῶν ῥημάτων ἐκείνων ἐπὶ τὴν πρὸ τοῦ δικαστηρίου στοὰν ποιησάμενοι τὴν ἔξοδον καὶ τὴν βοὴν
ἐπιτείναντες καὶ γυμνωθέντες τῶν χλαμύδων καὶ τὸ
οὔπω κεκινημένον ταῖς δεξιαῖς κινοῦντες παρακα-
λοῦντες εἰς κοινωνίαν ὧν ἐτόλμων, ἐλθόντες ἐπὶ
R ii. 4 τὸ πλησιάζον¹ βαλανεῖον κάλους ὧν ἐξήρτηντο | τὰ
τὸ φῶς ἐν νυκτὶ παρέχοντα μαχαίραις ἐξέκοπτον²
δεικνύντες ὅτι δεῖ τὸν ἐν τῇ πόλει κόσμον ταῖς
αὐτῶν βουλήσεσιν ὑποχωρεῖν καὶ ὡς ὁ μὲν νόμος
οὐδέν, τὸ δὲ ἐκείνοις δοκοῦν μέγα. 7. τοιούτου
τοίνυν ᾀσθέντος προοιμίου μετὰ ῥημάτων ἑτέρων
ἃ κέρδος ἂν ἦν μοι μὴ ἀκηκοέναι, τὸ μὲν τὰ εἰω-
θότα ταῦτα ποιεῖν καὶ ταράττειν καὶ συγχεῖν τὰν
τοῖς ἐργαστηρίοις μικρόν τε καὶ ἀνάξιον τῆς αὐτῶν
ἀνδρίας³ ἡγήσαντο, βλέψαντες δὲ εἰς τὰς πολλὰς
τὰς ἐν ταῖς σανίσιν εἰκόνας βλασφημίας πρὸ λίθων
ἐπ' αὐτὰς ἀφέντες ἐπὶ μὲν ταῖς ῥηγνυμέναις ἐγέλων,
πρὸς δὲ τὰς ἀντεχούσας ἠγανάκτουν. 8. ἔπειθ'
ἡγούμενοι τὰς ἐν τῷ χαλκῷ | τιμιωτέρας καὶ τὴν F

---

¹ πλησιάζον] πλησίον conj. Cobet.
² ἐξέκοπτον F. (CAPIV): ἀπέκοπτον Re. (other mss.).
³ ἀνδρίας F. (mss.): ἀνδρείας Re.

ᵃ In addressing a pagan official here Libanius makes no
bones about imputing blame to Christians. The parallel
passage in *Or.* 21. 5 is much more muted.
ᵇ The *chlamys*, although part of official dress (*Or.* 30. 15,
C. Th. 14. 10. 1), is also a civilian garment (*Or.* 45. 18).
ᶜ Cf. *Or.* 16. 41 (Vol. I, p. 237 n.).

In our times of dire trouble we usually call upon the gods and beg them to help us. In the same way on that occasion the rowdies called upon their god to pity them for reaching such a pitiable plight because of these decrees.[a] 6. This was intolerable enough, but there was much worse to follow. With remarks like these they trooped out to the colonnade in front of the courtroom, raised their clamour anew and stripped off their jackets.[b] That section of the populace which was as yet unaffected they began to stir into action by their gesticulations, and they egged them on to participate in their own misconduct. They proceeded to the bath near by, and used their knives to cut the ropes, from which were suspended the lamps that give us our light of a night-time,[c] and they made it plain that good order in the city must give place to their own whims, that law meant nothing and that their decisions were the ones to count. 7. This, then, was the sort of prelude that was performed, along with other expressions which it would have done me good not to have heard. The adoption of their usual techniques, rioting and disturbances in the factories,[d] they considered paltry and unworthy of their manliness. Instead, they cast their eyes on the many portraits on the panels, and hurled at them first insults and then stones. They roared with laughter at those they shattered and lost their temper with those that stood up to this. 8. Then they took it into their heads that bronze statues were of more account, and that mis-

[d] As with the murder of Theophilus in A.D. 354, *Or.* 19. 47. Here the scene moves from the old town area to the environs of the palace where the portraits and statues would normally be placed.

εἰς ἐκείνας παροινίαν ἀφορητοτέραν δραμόντες ἐπ᾽
αὐτὰς ἅμα σχοινίοις περιθέντες τοῖς αὐχέσι κατα-
βαλόντες εἷλκον, οἱ μὲν οὐ διατεμόντες, οἱ δὲ καὶ
R ii. 5 τοῦτο ποιήσαντες. | καίτοι περὶ μὲν τοῦ πατρὸς
ἴσως ἂν εἴποιεν τὸ χρυσίον, Ἀρκαδίῳ δὲ τί ἄν τις[1]
ἐγκαλέσειε; τῷ δὲ μετ᾽ ἐκεῖνον τί; τῇ δὲ τούτων
μητρί; τῷ δὲ τοῦ βασιλέως πατρί; περὶ ὧν οὐκ
ἔστιν εἰπεῖν ὡς μετεῖχον τῶν περὶ τὴν φοράν. 9.
παραδόντες τοίνυν τοῖς παιδαρίοις ἐν τοῖς οὕτως
αἰδεσίμοις παίζειν ἐχώρουν αὐτοὶ μετὰ πυρὸς ἐπ᾽
οἰκίαν ἀνδρὸς ἀδικοῦντος μὲν οὐδέν, δοκοῦντος δὲ
τοῖς οὐ βουλομένοις ἀκούειν τῶν γραμμάτων, καὶ
τὰ μὲν ἔκαον, τὰ δὲ διενοοῦντο, ὧν ἦν τὰ βασίλεια.
καὶ εἰ μὴ τόξα τε καὶ τοξότας ἰδόντες ἔδεισαν,
κρεῖττον ἂν ἦν ἢ κωλυθῆναι τὸ πῦρ ὡς ἐπὶ πλεῖστον ῥέον. περὶ τοίνυν τὸ μέσον τῆς ἡμέρας μετά-
μελός τε εἰσῄει τοὺς μανέντας καὶ κοινὸς ἦν ὁ
φόβος τῶν τε ἠδικηκότων τῶν τε οὐχ ἁμαρτόντων,
| ὡς ἐν τοῖς τοιούτοις κακοῖς κοιναὶ τῶν πόλεων αἱ F
δίκαι καὶ τὸ τῆς ὀργῆς ἀμφοτέρους ὁμοίως ἐπέρ-
χεται τούς τε ἐν ταῖς αἰτίαις τούς τε πόρρω τῶν
ἐγκλημάτων. 10. ἤδη δὲ τῶν ἀγγέλων ἐξεληλυ-
R ii. 6 θότων καὶ τῶν πραγμάτων | δηλούντων ἃ δεῖ προσ-
δοκᾶν, καὶ τῶν μὲν δαίμονας αἰτιωμένων, τῶν δὲ
ἀλλήλους, πάντων δ᾽ ἑαυτοὺς θρηνούντων καὶ γυναῖκας καὶ τέκνα καὶ στέγας ἐν ἐδόκει μόνον ἔχειν
τὴν σωτηρίαν, ἡ φυγὴ καὶ τὸ ζητεῖν ἄλλην γῆν.
11. τοῦ μὲν οὖν λεὼ τὸ πλεῖον μετανίστατο, τὴν

---

[1] τί ἄν τις Cobet, F. (V): τί τις IMPa: τί τίς Re. (other
mss.).

---

[a] Cf. Or. 19. 34 f.

conduct towards them was more intolerable, and so they rushed upon them. They slung ropes around their necks, hauled them down and began to drag them along, some without chopping them up, others doing just that. Yet though they might perhaps talk of the gold in connection with his father, what accusation could anyone make against Arcadius? or against his younger brother? or their mother? or the emperor's father? It cannot be said of them that they had any part in this tax demand. 9. However, they left the urchins to make sport with such revered objects, and themselves went with fire to attack the house of one who was guilty of no wrong-doing but yet was held to be so by these people who refused to listen to the decrees. They started to set fire to some places, and had designs on others, the palace among them, and had they not seen the bowmen and their bows [a] and got into a panic, the fire would have extended far and wide, and would have been too great to stop. Well, about mid-day a change of mind came over the lunatics, and guilty and innocent alike experienced a common fear, for in such troubles the punishment inflicted on cities is universal, and wrath is visited without distinction on both the ringleaders and the utterly blameless. 10. The couriers had already left and the march of events showed the shape of things to come. Some began to put the blame on the supernatural,[b] others on one another : all began to bewail themselves, their wives, children and homes, and it seemed that there was but one means of salvation, to flee and seek another land. 11. So the greater part of the populace began to depart, but the administration

[b] *Cf. Or.* 19. 29, Jo. Chrys. *Hom.* 21. 3 (*P.G.* xlix. 214 f.).

βουλὴν δὲ τὸ ἄρχον ἀπειλαῖς ἐπειρᾶτο κατέχειν. νέοι δὲ οἱ περὶ ἡμᾶς τε καὶ τοὺς λόγους οὐδὲν πρὸς οὐδένα εἰπόντες ἐκποδὼν εὐθὺς ἦσαν. οἰομένων δὲ ἡμῶν ἥξειν ἐκεῖθεν λόγον ἔχοντα τὴν τιμωρίαν, τὴν δὲ ἄλλην ἄλλος ἔφασκε, δειναὶ δὲ πᾶσαι, καὶ περὶ τάφους[1] τοῖς πολλοῖς ἡ φροντίς, εἰσὶ δὲ οἳ καὶ τοῦτ' ἀπέγνωσαν ὡς ἐμπρησμοῦ τά τε ἄψυχα καὶ ἡμᾶς ἀναλώσοντος. |

12. Οὕτω δὲ ἡμῶν ἐπτηχότων καθάπερ ἐν προσ- F 4 δοκίᾳ βροντῆς ἢ σεισμῷ πάντα κινοῦντι ἔρχεται Φήμη, ἡ θεὸς ἧς πόρρω τὸ ψεῦδος, τὸν ἄνδρα τοῦ- τον ἀγγέλλουσα δικαστὴν ἡμῖν ἀφίξεσθαι. καὶ τοῦτ' εὐθὺς τὴν τῶν χαλεπῶν ἐλπίδα τῇ παρ- εχούσῃ τι βέλτιον εἰς | ἔλαττόν τε ἦγε καὶ τὰν ταῖς ψυχαῖς ἐποίει κουφότερα καί τις ἐσθίων τε ἐμει- δίασε καὶ μετέλαβεν ὕπνου καθαρεύοντος πηδη- μάτων, καὶ περὶ ἀγρῶν τις ἤρετο τῶν ἑαυτοῦ τολ- μήσας εἰπεῖν ἑαυτοῦ πρότερον τῷ φόβῳ τοῦτο κεκωλυμένος, καὶ ὁ μὲν οἷς ἤκουσε πιστεύων μεθ' ἡδονῆς ἕτερον ἐδίδασκεν, ὁ δὲ ὑπὸ τοῦ μεγέθους τῶν ἀγαθῶν ἀπιστῶν παρὰ τοὺς εἰδέναι τι δοκοῦν- τας ἤρχετο. καὶ πολὺς πανταχοῦ τε καὶ παρὰ πᾶσιν Ἑλλέβιχος ἐν οἰκίαις, ἐν ἀγοραῖς, ἐν στοαῖς, ἐν στενωποῖς, ἐν βαδίζουσιν, ἐν καθημένοις, ἐν νέοις, ἐν πρεσβυτέροις, ἐν ἀνδράσιν, ἐν γυναιξίν, ἐν ἐλευθέροις, ἐν δούλοις, ἐφ' οὓς καὶ αὐτοὺς ἤρ- χετό τι τῆς τῶν δεσποτῶν τύχης. 13. ἐμπεπλη- κὼς δ' ἑαυτοῦ τὴν | πόλιν οὗτος ὁ λόγος ἧκε μὲν F 4 ἐπὶ τὰ προάστεια ταχέως, ἧκε δὲ ἐπὶ τὰ πεδία, προὔβη δὲ ἐπὶ τοὺς λόφους ἅπασι ποιῶν ἐλαφρό-

R ii. 7

____
[1] τάφου Cobet.

[a] Cf. Or. 23.　　　[b] Hesiod, Op. 763 f.

382

with threats tried to restrain the councillors. The students who attended me for their lessons removed themselves forthwith, with never a word to anybody.[a] I thought that some account of our punishment would come from the capital, but various people told various stories of what it would be—all of them gruesome—, and most of us began to concern ourselves about our funerals. Some, however, even despaired of that, for they believed that both our persons and the lifeless fabric of the city would be consumed in flames.

12. While we cowered thus, as though in dread of a thunderbolt or an earthquake that would lay all in ruins, there came Rumour, that goddess from whom falsehood is far removed,[b] to tell us that Ellebichus here would come to be our judge. This immediately, by the hope of some alleviation, caused our expectation of trouble to diminish and lightened our spirits. Men raised a smile at their meals and enjoyed a sleep free from nightmares; they began to inquire about their estates, even daring to speak of them as their own, though fear had prevented them doing so before. One, confident in what he had heard, gladly began to inform another, while yet another, incredulous because of the magnitude of the good news, would make his way to those he thought did know something. Everywhere the name of Ellebichus was on everyone's lips, in their homes, the markets, the colonnades, the back streets, whether they were walking or seated, young or old, men or women, free men or slaves, for slaves too were personally involved in what befell their masters. 13. This tale filled the city and quickly spread to the suburbs and to the plains beyond; it advanced to the hill-tops, and

383

τερα τὰ παρόντα καὶ ὅσοι κινδύνων μὲν ἦσαν
ἐκτός, τοῖς δὲ τῶν κινδυνευόντων ἐβαρύνοντο κακοῖς. ἑωρᾶτο τοίνυν ἡ γνώμη τοῦ τὸν δικαστὴν
ἀπεσταλκότος ἐν τῇ γνώμῃ τοῦ τὴν ψῆφον ἐγκε-
R ii. 8 χειρισμένου, | καὶ ἐδόκει μήποτ᾽ ἂν ἐπὶ τῇ θανα-
τούσῃ χρήσασθαι τῇ τοῦδε κεφαλῇ, ἣν ᾔδει πρὸς
οὐ τὰ τοιαῦτα πεφυκυῖαν. 14. ἦν οὖν ἀκούειν
πολλῶν οὐ βοώντων μέν, οὑτωσὶ δὲ λεγόντων σωτηρίας γε εἶναι ταῦτα σημεῖα καὶ τοῦ μὴ διὰ τρα-
χήλων διαδραμεῖσθαι ξίφη τὸ τὸν δεῖνα ἥξειν ἐπὶ
τὴν κρίσιν, τὸν ἥδιστα μέν, εἴ τι σώζοι τὸν κινδυ-
νεύοντα, τοῦτο ἀκουσόμενον, ἀλγήσοντα δὲ ἐν ταῖς
τῶν ἡμαρτηκότων ἀπωλείαις, δείξοντα δὲ ὡς βού-
λοιτ᾽ ἂν εἰς ἐπιεικές τι τελευτῆσαι τοῦ καιροῦ τὴν
χαλεπότητα.

15. Τί δὴ τούτων αἴτιον τῶν ἐλπίδων; καὶ πόθεν
αὐταῖς ἡ γένεσις; τὰ μέχρι τῆς ἡμέρας ἐκείνης
αὐτῷ βεβιωμένα καὶ τούτων γε μάλιστα τἀν τῷ
τῆς δυνά|μεως χρόνῳ, ὃν ἡμερότητι κοσμήσας, ὃ F 4
δὴ καὶ τὸν τῶν ὅλων κύριον ἑώρα πεποιηκότα, δι-
R ii. 9 καιοσύνης δόξαν ἐν | ἐξουσίᾳ τοῦ κακῶς ποιεῖν
ἠνέγκατο, δεινὸν εἶναι νομίζων εἰ ταῖς μὲν παρ᾽
ἑτέρων βλάβαις χαλεπανοῦμεν, αὐτοὶ δὲ εἰς ἑτέρους
τοῦτο ποιεῖν ἀξιώσομεν. 16. εὖ ποιῶν τοίνυν δια-
τελῶν πολλοὺς μὲν ἄνδρας, οὐκ ὀλίγας δὲ πόλεις
καὶ τῶν ἐν τοῖς ὅπλοις τοὺς ἠτυχηκότας ποιῶν
ἀμείνους ταῖς τιμωρίαις μᾶλλον ἢ διαφθείρων ἀν-
έσχεν ἡμᾶς τότε βαπτιζομένους. ⟨τοὺς⟩[1] μήπω

---

[1] ⟨τοὺς⟩ conj. Re., F.

---

[a] Cf. Jo. Chrys. Hom. 17 (P.G. xlix. 171), who, with
more precision than Libanius here, records the arrival of

lightened the present misery of all, even of those who, though beyond the reach of danger, were grieved at the troubles of those who were not.[a] Indeed, the attitude of him who had sent the inquisitor was deduced from that of his commissioner. It was felt that he would never have employed the person of Ellebichus upon a bloody assize, since he knew that it was uncharacteristic of him. 14. So you could hear many persons, not shouting it aloud, yet simply saying that it was a sign of our preservation and for us not to have the sword slicing through our throats, that there should come to judgement such and such a man who would be most pleased to hear it said that he could save the life of one in peril, who would grieve at the death of sinners, and who would show that he wanted to bring to some reasonable conclusion the rigours of the times.

15. What then was responsible for these hopes, and whence did they originate? Why! it was the manner of his life up to that day, and especially during his period of command which he adorned by his clemency—as indeed he saw that our supreme emperor had done—, and which had won him a reputation for just dealing when he had it in his power to behave very differently. He thought it shameful for us to resent ill-treatment at the hands of others and yet want to inflict the same upon them. 16. So he continually bestowed benefits on many persons and no few cities and, rather than destroying those who had suffered reverses under arms, he improved them by correction. So he sustained us as we were then fast sinking. Those who had not

the monks from their mountain retreats to intercede for Antioch before the commissioners.

μεθεστηκότας κατέσχε καὶ τούς, εἴπερ οὐκ αὐτὸς
ἠλπίζετο, πάντως ἂν αὐτοὺς πλάνοις δόντας ἔπεισεν
ὑπομεῖναι τὴν παρουσίαν. 17. ὅτι δὲ ταῦθ' οὕτως
εἶχεν, ᾤοντο μὲν οἱ τῆς ἀληθείας ἡμαρτηκότες δι'
ἐρήμης μὲν τῆς ὁδοῦ τὸν ἄνδρα τῶν πυλῶν ἅψεσθαι,[1] δι' ἐρήμου δὲ τοῦ πρώτου τῆς πόλεως μέρους
ἥξειν ἄχρι τῆς καταγωγῆς, οἱ δ' ὅσονπερ ἐπὶ τῶν
προτέρων ἀγαθῶν[2] διαδραμόντες, οἱ μεμενηκότες,
| ἦγον αὐτὸν ὑπ' εὐφημιῶν ἐπὶ τὴν πόλιν ἀναμίξαν- F
τες ἱκετείας. ὁ δὲ οὐκ ἀπήλαυνε μὲν φιλανθρωπίᾳ,
R ii. 10 διὰ δὲ τῶν παρὰ τῆς δεξιᾶς | ἐδείκνυ τὸν κατεγνω-
κότα ποιῶν ὅπερ οἱ παιδοτρίβαι πρὸς τοὺς παρὰ τὸ
εἰκὸς ἡττημένους, ὡς δὴ τῆς διδαχῆς προδεδομέ-
νης αὐτοῖς. 18. καὶ οὗτος τοίνυν ὡς ἐπὶ προδεδομέ-
νων αὐτῷ παρ' ἡμῶν τῶν παρ' αὐτοῦ περὶ ἡμῶν
ἐπαίνων οὕτω μὲν εἶχε τὴν γνώμην, οὕτω δὲ ἐχρῆτο τῇ χειρί. ἦν γὰρ δὴ πολὺν ἡμῶν ἐμβεβληκὼς
ἔρωτα τῷ βασιλεῖ πυκνοῖς τε καὶ μακροῖς τοῖς ὑπὲρ
ἡμῶν ἐγκωμίοις ληρεῖν μὲν ἅπαντας λέγων τοὺς ἑτέρας πόλεως μεμνημένους, εἶναι γὰρ ἐν οὐδεμιᾷ
τοσαύτην ἀγαθῶν σύνοδον, ἀλλὰ τὸ μὲν ἔχειν, τοῦ
δὲ ἐπιδεῖσθαι καὶ πολλὰς ἐν μὲν τοῖς ἄλλοις ἔχειν
εὐδοκιμεῖν, τὸν δὲ κοινὸν τῆς πόλεως οὐ καλῶς
αὐταῖς ἔχειν τρόπον, ἀλλὰ τῇ μὲν ἐπιζεῖν θυμόν,
τὴν δὲ ἀναισθήτως διακεῖσθαι, τὴν δ' ἐστερῆσθαι
Χαρίτων, τὴν δὲ ἀργῶς ἔχειν, τὴν δὲ τῇ φωνῇ
λυπεῖν, τὴν δὲ οὐκ εἰδέναι φέρειν βασιλέως καθ-
R ii. 11 έδραν, τῇδε δὲ μόνῃ τά τε | ἀπὸ τῆς Τύχης ὑπάρχειν
ὅσα τε εἰς ἀρετὴν ἔρχεται. ἐκεῖνον δὲ εἰδέναι τε

[1] ἅψεσθαι F. (V, correction in I) : ἅψασθαι Re. (other mss.).
[2] ἀγαθῶν : σταθμῶν conj. Re. (" probabiliter," F.).

yet taken their departure he restrained, and those who, unless he personally were expected, would certainly have given themselves up to flight, he induced to stay and await his presence. 17. Because this was the case, people of faulty judgement believed that the road would be deserted of spectators when he reached the gates, and that the first quarter of the city would be deserted when he passed through it right to his headquarters. Actually, those who had stayed behind went out as far as they used to do in the times of prosperity past, and escorted him into the city with acclamation mingled with entreaty. In his kindliness he did not repulse them, but by the gestures of his hand he showed disapproval of them, in this acting as trainers do towards those who have suffered unexpected defeat, feeling that their training has gone for nothing. 18. He too then adopted such an attitude and employed such gestures, as if the praises he had lavished upon us had gone for nothing because of our actions. He had, in fact, inspired in the emperor a great love for us, by the many long eulogies he had spoken of us. He used to say that all those who mentioned other cities were talking nonsense, for in none of them was there such a concourse of blessings. One they might have, but they lacked another : many might have good claims to fame otherwise, but the general behaviour of the city was by no means perfect. In one, tempers would flare : in another, the attitude was boorish ; or it lacked grace, or was not go-ahead, or it had an irritating accent, or it was incapable of supporting an imperial residence. Here alone, he said, were all the advantages of Fortune and the qualities conducive to virtue. The emperor, while knowing the

387

καὶ οὐκ | εἰδέναι τῶν αὑτοῦ τὸ κάλλιστον, ἀγγελ- F 4
λόντων μὲν γὰρ ἀκούειν, οὐδέπω δὲ αὐτὴν[1] ἰδεῖν,
εἶναι[2] δὲ οὐκ ἴσον ὦτα καὶ ὄμματα. καὶ παρεκάλει
δὴ πρὸς τὴν ὡς ἡμᾶς ὁδὸν προστιθεὶς τῇ πόλει τὴν
Δάφνην, ἣν ἔχειν τε μουσικὸν θεὸν καὶ πέμπειν
ἀφ᾽ ἑαυτῆς ἐπὶ τὴν πόλιν λόγων ἐπιθυμίαν. 19.
διεμέμφετο μὲν οὖν τὴν πολλὰ μὲν ἐπηγγελμένην,
τοιαῦτα δὲ ἐπιδεδειγμένην καὶ λόγους καλοὺς ἔργοις χείροσιν ἀνελοῦσαν, ἔχων δέ, εἴπερ ἐβούλετο,
δίκην ἣν ἐβούλετο λαβεῖν οὐδ᾽ οὕτως ἕτερος γίνεται οὐδὲ ὑπὸ τῶν ποιούντων τὰς αἰτίας ἐξέβαλλε[3]
τὸ φίλτρον, ἀλλ᾽ ἠγάπα τε ὁμοῦ καὶ κατηγόρει.
δειπνοῦντα δὲ αὐτὸν ἀκούομεν οὐ δειπνῆσαι μᾶλλον
ἢ τῇ διανοίᾳ βλέπειν εἰς τὰ σχήματα τῆς πόλεως
παραβάλλοντα τὰ δεύτερα τοῖς ἀμείνοσι.

20. Τίνα δὴ τἀπὶ τούτοις; εἰσεκαλεῖτο μὲν οὖπερ
R ii. 12 ὁ δικαστὴς κατήγετο τῶν τε ἀρξάντων | οὐκ ὀλίγον
τῆς τε βουλῆς ὁπόσον οὐκ ἐπεφεύγει, καὶ ἦν τοῦτο
πραοτέρα τις ἐπὶ τὴν δίκην ἀρχὴ τῷ τε χωρίῳ τοῖς
τε παρακαθημένοις, κελεύοντος δὲ ἕκαστον αὐτὸν
ἀποφαίνειν δίκαιον ἦν μέν τις ἑκάστῳ καὶ λόγος,
τὸ πλέον δὲ τῆς σωτηρίας ἐν δάκρυσι τῶν μὲν
ὀδυρο|μένων νεότητα καὶ τὸ μήπω πατέρας γε- F 4
γενῆσθαι, τῶν δὲ τὸ πατέρας τε εἶναι καὶ παῖδας
γενναίους τρέφειν, τῶν δὲ γήρας γονέων, τῶν δὲ
λειτουργίας ἀρχὴν μὲν δεξαμένας, ποθούσας δὲ τε-

---

[1] αὐτὴν F. (MSS.): αὐτὸν Re. [2] εἶναι Re., F.: εἰδέναι MSS.
[3] ἐξέβαλλε Re., F. (CA, P before correction): ἐξέβαλε
other MSS.: ἐξεβάλετο Morel (om. τὸ).

---

[a] The phrase is repeated from Or. 30. 45.
[b] For Apollo and the legend of Daphne cf. Or. 11. 94 ff.
[c] Cf. Or. 21. 7 for the location of this commission. Libanius,

brightest star in his crown, yet knew it not, for he heard of it from the reports of others, but had never yet seen it himself, and there was no comparison between hearing and seeing.[a] Ellebichus used to invite the emperor to come here, and he spoke not merely of the city itself, but also of Daphne, the possessor of the god of music,[b] from which there emanated into the city the desire for eloquence. 19. So he reproached the city which had shown so much promise and yet given such a poor account of itself, ruining its fine eloquence with unworthy deeds : yet though he had it in his power, if he so wished, to exact any punishment he wished, not even so did he alter, nor yet did he lose his affection for us because of those responsible for the crimes, but even while accusing us he maintained his liking for us. I am told that at dinner he did not so much dine as reflect upon the situation of the city, comparing this outcome with its better days.

20. And the next step was that he summoned to his judge's lodging many of the ex-magistrates and all the councillors who had not fled.[c] This was a rather auspicious beginning to the investigations, both because of the location and because of his assessors. He bade each man prove his innocence, and though each had some argument to adduce, salvation generally lay in their tears, as some bewailed their youth, and the fact that they had no children to their name, and some lamented that they were parents and were bringing up noble sons, others bewailed their aged parents, or the civic duties now begun and needing completion, yet another his

as one of the *honorati*, sits in attendance upon the commissioners (*infra*, § 23).

λευτήν, ἑτέρου γυναικὸς χηρείαν καὶ τὴν ἐσομένην
περὶ τὸ μνῆμα διατριβήν. ὁ δὲ γενναῖος οὑτοσὶ
τοῖς τε ἐκείνων ἐξουσίαν ἐδεδώκει δάκρυσι καὶ τοῖς
ἑκάστου τῶν παρ᾽ ἑαυτοῦ προσέθηκεν οὐκ ἀγνοῶν
ὅσοις δὴ δικασταῖς ἢ πληγαῖς ἢ πληγῶν ἀπειλαῖς
R ii. 13 τὸ τοιοῦτον | εἴργεται τὰ παρόντα ὑβρίζεσθαι διὰ
τῶν ὀδυρμῶν ἡγουμένοις. 21. καὶ ἡ μὲν κρηπὶς
οὕτω καλὴ καὶ φιλάνθρωπος, προϊόντος δὲ τοῦ
πράγματος εἰς ἀκμὴν καὶ δέξεσθαι¹ τὸ δικαστήριον
τῆς ἐπιούσης τὴν κρίσιν εἰρημένον² χαρίζεται μὲν
κἀνταῦθα τὸ³ μήτε ἐν μέσαις νυξὶ μήτε ἐν πρώταις
ἀλεκτρυόνων ᾠδαῖς ἥκειν ἐπὶ τὸν θρόνον, ὡς αὐτῶν
γε ἐν αὑτοῖς τῶν καιρῶν ἐχόντων εἰς ἔκπληξιν
ἀφορμάς, μικρὸν δὲ τὴν ἀκτῖνα φθάσας, ὥστ᾽ αὐτῷ⁴
καὶ λαμπάδας νόμου μᾶλλον ἢ χρείας εἶναι, τὰς
R ii. 14 θύρας ἐξελθὼν ἔργῳ | φιλανθρώπῳ πᾶν ἀπέκρυψε |
τοιοῦτον παράδειγμα. 22. μήτηρ γὰρ δὴ τῶν ἐν F
τοῖς κρινομένοις ἑνὸς νέου τε καὶ καλοῦ καὶ πολλαῖς
μὲν πρεσβείαις, ἁπάσαις δὲ λαμπρυνομένου λειτουργίαις, τοῖς πράγμασι δὲ ἀντὶ τοῦ πατρὸς ἀρ-
κέσαντος γυμνώσασα μὲν τὴν κεφαλήν, λύσασα δὲ
τὴν γεγηρακυῖαν τρίχα, προσδραμοῦσα τῷ στήθει
καὶ περιθεῖσα τούτῳ μετὰ τῶν χειρῶν τοὺς τοιούτους πλοκάμους ᾔτει μὲν τὸν υἱὸν ἐλεεινὸν βοῶσα,
δάκρυα δὲ τὰ μὲν ἐκείνης ἔρρει κατὰ τῶν ποδῶν
τοῦ στρατηγοῦ, τὰ δὲ ἐκείνου κατὰ τῆς ἐκείνης
κεφαλῆς. ἀφείλκυσε δὲ αὐτὴν οὐδείς, ἀλλ᾽ οὐδὲ
αὐτὸς ἀπεώσατο, ἀλλ᾽ οὕτως ἔδωκεν αὐτὸν τῷ
μήκει τῆς ἱκετείας ὥστ᾽ ἐδόκει κρείττων εἶναι

¹ δέξεσθαι Cobet, F. (V) : δέξασθαι Re. (other mss.).
² εἰρημένον Cobet, F. (mss. except Par. 3016): εἰρημένου
Re. (Par. 3016).   ³ τὸ F. (V) : om. Re. (other mss.).

wife's widowhood and her future sojourn at his tomb.
This noble man gave full licence to their tears and
shed tears of his own at those of every one, for he
knew full well how many judges prevent such things
either by blows or by threats of blows, since they
feel that the case is jeopardized by reason of these
laments. 21. Such was the first step, so fine and
humane. As the affair proceeded to a climax, and
once it had been announced that the case would be
heard in court next day, here too he was kind enough
not to take his seat either at midnight or at first
cock-crow—times which in themselves give cause
enough for terror.ᵃ He went from his doors just
before sun-rise, so that the lamps attending him were
conventional rather than necessary, and with an act
of humanity he made every such precedent pale into
insignificance. 22. Among those to be examined
was a fine young man who had won renown in many
embassies and all forms of public service, and had
taken his father's place in fulfilling civic duties.
His mother, then, bared her head and loosed her
aged hair, ran to his bosom, took her hair in her hands
and clasped it about him, pleading for her son with
pitiful cries. Her tears flowed over the general's
feet, his over her head. No one dragged her away,
nor yet did he himself repulse her.ᵇ He so devoted
himself to her long-drawn prayers that he seemed to

ᵃ Nocturnal inquisitions always carried with them the
implication of an official reign of terror, cf. Amm. Marc.
28. 1. 54.
ᵇ Chrysostom gives an account of the same incident, Hom.
17 (P.G. xlix. 173).

⁴ ὥστ' αὐτῷ conj. Re., F. (ὥστ' αὐτῶι correction in C):
ἐν αὐτῷ Morel (Par. 3016): ταὐτῷ Re. text (other mss.).

φύσεως ἀνθρωπείας, καὶ πανταχόθεν εὐχαὶ σώζε-
σθαί οἱ τὴν[1] παῖδα τοιούτῳ τε ὄντι πρὸς ἀτυχοῦντας καὶ πᾶν τραχύ τε καὶ ἀπηνὲς τῆς γνώμης
ἐξεληλακότι. 23. οἱ μὲν δὴ ἐδίκαζον, ἡμεῖς δὲ
προσηδρεύομεν. ὁ δὲ ἐδόκει τισὶν οὐχ αὑτοῦ ποιεῖν εἰς ὁμολογίαν ἕκαστον τοῦ τῆς ἀδικίας σπέρ-
R ii. 15 ματος κατακλείων | ἀπειλῶν ἑτέρους βασανίσειν[2]
τοὺς ταῦτα κατεροῦντας, εἰ μὴ συγχωροῖεν ἐκεῖνοι.
καὶ ἅμα πολλοὺς τῶν πέλας ἐκίνει νεύμασι τὸν
κρινόμενον εἰς ὁμολογίαν ἐνάγειν, ᾧ δὴ | μάλιστα F
ἠγανάκτουν οἱ πεισόμενοι[3] νομίζοντες εἶναι κάλλιον
ἐν ἀρνήσει τι παθεῖν ἢ σφᾶς αὐτοὺς ἐλέγξαντας.
τοῦτο δὲ ἦν οὐκ αὐχένας εἰς τομὴν ἑτοιμάζοντος
τῷ βασιλεῖ, τὴν σωτηρίαν δέ, οἶμαι, λαμπροτέραν
ποιοῦντος. οὐ γὰρ ἴσον εἰς ἔλεγχον φωνὴ μάρ-
τυρος καὶ ἡ τοῦ φεύγοντος αὐτοῦ, ἀλλὰ κατὰ μὲν
ἐκείνης ἴσως ἄν τις εὑρεθείη καὶ λόγος, τὴν δ᾽ οὐκ
ἄν τις αἰτιάσαιτο. 24. ταῦτα [αὐτὰ] αὐτῷ[4] τὸ τοῖς
ἑαυτῶν στόμασιν ὁμολογεῖν ἀδικεῖν τοὺς αἰτια-
θέντας ἐδύνατο, οἳ τὴν μὲν παροῦσαν ἡμέραν ὁριεῖν
αὑτοῖς ἡγοῦντο τὸν βίον, ἠγνοεῖτο γὰρ ἐφ᾽ ὅτῳ
R ii. 16 ταῦτα, τὸ | δὲ ἔμελλε φανεῖσθαι. τοῦ γὰρ ὄχλου
μόνον οὐχ ὁρᾶν ἡγουμένου τὴν δεινὴν ἐκείνην ἔξοδον ὁ μὲν ἀποκτενῶν[5] οὐδείς, δεσμὸς δὲ καὶ δη-
μεύσεις χρημάτων καὶ οὐδὲν ὀξὺ περὶ ταῦτα,[6] καὶ

[1] τὴν F. (P corrected) : τὸν Re. (other mss.).
[2] βασανίσειν conj. Re., F. (V) : βασανίζειν Re. text (other mss.).
[3] πεισόμενοι conj. Boissonade, F. : πυθόμενοι I : πειθόμενοι Re. (other mss.).
[4] [αὐτὰ] F. : om. V : αὐτὰ αὐτῷ om. B : ταῦτα αὐτὰ αὐτῷ om. Morel (Par. 3016) : ταῦτα δ᾽ PI.
[5] ἀποκτενῶν F. (-κτένων AILMo.BM) : ἀποκτείνων Re. (CPVPar.).   [6] ταῦτα F. : ταύτην Re. (mss.).
392

be superhuman. From every side there rose prayers for the preservation of his daughter, since he so conducted himself to people in distress and had expelled all harshness and severity from his mind. 23. So they began the assize and we acted as assessors. Some were of the opinion that he behaved in a manner foreign to his nature in confining every one to an admission about the origin of the crime by threatening to hold an examination of other persons who would give him this information, should they not agree. At the same time he nodded to many of the bystanders to attempt to get the man in the dock to make a confession. At this the prospective victims became most annoyed since they thought it nobler to meet their fate with staunch denial than by convicting themselves out of their own mouths. Yet his action was not that of one who was preparing for the emperor throats to be cut, but rather, I feel, of one who made their preservation the more remarkable, for there is no comparison, as regards proof, between the voice of a witness and that of the defendant himself. Against the first some plea could perhaps be devised, but against this last no one could complain. 24. That was the real point of his insistence upon a confession of guilt out of the defendants' own mouths. They began to think that that day would be their last, for they were unaware of the purpose of this procedure. As it happened, its revelation was imminent. The populace thought that they were almost witnessing that dread outcome, but there was no one to play the executioner. Imprisonment and confiscation of property were the only penalties imposed—and there was nothing very severe in this, either—and the city retained its

εἶχε τὴν βουλὴν ἡ πόλις, ἣν οὐκ ἔχειν ἡγεῖτο. οἳ[1] γὰρ ἤστην, οὗτός τε καὶ ὁ κοινωνός, ἀπο|κτεῖναι F 4 κυρίω, ψήφω[2] βασιλέως ἐφυλαξάτην τὴν τομὴν ⟨τὸ μὲν⟩ αὐτῶν[3] ἐν τῇ κρίσει στήσαντες, τὰ δ᾽ ἐφεξῆς τῇ βασιλείᾳ τηρήσαντες. 25. τοιαῦτα τοίνυν ὑπηρετηκότες τῇ δίκῃ καὶ οὐ ποιήσαντες ἐλάττω τοσούτοις οἴκοις τὴν πόλιν, ταὐτὰ μὲν βουληθέντες, ταὐτὰ δὲ ἐπαινέσαντες πάσης ἔριδος ἀπηλλαγμένην R ii. 17 βοήθειαν βεβοηθηκότες μέσοι | μὲν ἐγενέσθην πλήθους τοῦ πρὸ τοῦ δικαστηρίου τί τῶν ἁπάντων οὐ φθεγγομένου καινὰς ἐπὶ ταῖς εἰωθυίαις δεήσεσιν εὑρίσκοντος. καὶ ὁ μὲν χρόνος τῶν ἱκετειῶν πολὺς καὶ περὶ δύσιν ἥλιος, σιγὴν δὲ οὐδεὶς ἐπέταξεν οὔτε ῥάβδοις οὔτε ψιλαῖς ταῖς χερσίν.

26. Ἀλλὰ τοῦ περὶ τὴν δίκην πόνου διάδοχος ἕτερος ἦν ὁ περὶ τὴν στάσιν. καὶ περιερρεῖτο πολλοῖς μὲν ἀνδράσι, πλείοσι δὲ γυναιξὶ μόνον οὐ προσπιπτούσαις ὑπὸ τῆς ἐνταῦθα ἀδείας, ὁ δ᾽ αὐτὸς τά τε λεγόμενα μετ᾽ εὐμενείας προσίετο καὶ ὧν ᾔδει πολλὴν | ἐσομένην τὴν ἰσχύν, ὑπέβαλλεν ἱκετευό- F 4 μενός τε καὶ μετὰ τῶν τοῦτο ποιούντων ἱκετεύων ποιῶν ἅπαν εἶναι τὸ περὶ ταῦτα τοῦ κρατοῦντος. 27. εἶτα μέντοι καὶ τὸν πορευόμενον, ἐδόκει γὰρ δεῖν τὸν μὲν καθῆσθαι, τὸν δὲ βαδίζειν, ἐκόσμει τῷ[4] τὰς γλώσσας ἐπ᾽ ἐκεῖνον ἀπ᾽ αὐτοῦ μεταφέρειν καὶ ἐδεῖτο μετὰ τῶν ἡμαρτηκότων δικα-

---

[1] οἳ F. (PBMV, A marg.) : οὐ Re. (other mss.).
[2] ψήφω ⟨δὲ⟩ conj. Re., Cobet.
[3] τὴν τομὴν del. Cobet. | ⟨τὸ μὲν⟩ conj. Re., Cobet, F. | αὐτῶν Re., F. (C) : αὑτῶν other mss.
[4] τῷ F. (ILMo.) : τε Re. (Par. 3016) : τὸ other mss.

---

[a] For Chrysostom's account of the activities of the com-

council it thought it had lost.*a* Both he and his colleague had the powers of life and death, but they reserved any death-sentence for the emperor's decision and, confining their activity to the investigation, they awaited the emperor's instructions for the next step.*b* 25. Such then were the services they rendered to justice. They did not diminish the city by so many households, but with the same desire, the same commendations, they provided aid free from all rancour. They were surrounded by the crowd in front of the court-house which uttered cries of every kind and devised fresh pleas, besides their usual ones. The time taken up by these supplications was a long one. The sun was near its setting, but no one ordered silence, either with their staffs or with their bare hands.

26. The business of the trial was succeeded by another, to do with the riot. He was surrounded by many men and more women—women who almost mobbed him in their freedom to do so. He personally attended to their statements with kindliness, and made suggestions which he knew would be very effective. By receiving their pleas and joining his own with theirs he ensured that the emperor's will on the matter was paramount. 27. Then, again, he honoured his colleague who was travelling back,*c* for it had been decided that one should stay and the other should go, by referring their pleas to him, and so a judge joined the wrongdoers by pleading with a

mission *cf. Hom.* 13 (*P.G.* xlix. 136–139). He saw the councillors taken in chains through the market place.

b Chrysostom, *Hom.* 17 (*P.G.* xlix. 174).

c Caesarius' hurried return to Constantinople, *cf. Or.* 21. 11 ff.

R ii. 18 στῆς | δικαστοῦ, τὰ μὲν ἐν μέσῳ ποιῶν, τὰ δὲ καὶ καταμόνας.

28. Καὶ τίς πώποτε ἄνδρα τοιοῦτον ἑώρακεν ἢ ἀκήκοε; πῶς δ' οὐ μακαρίζειν τοὺς τοῦδε τοκέας μᾶλλον ἐπὶ τούτοις ἄξιον ἢ τῇ τε ἀρχῇ καὶ τῷ τοσούτοις ἐφεστηκέναι σώμασιν, ὃ πολλῶν τε γεγένηται πρότερον καὶ πάλιν ἑτέρων ἔσται. δάκρυα δὲ τοιαῦτα στρατηγῶν οὐδενὶ σύνοιδεν οὐδεὶς ἀνθρώπων οὐδ' οὕτω μεθ' ἡδονῆς εἶδεν ἐν ταῖς τῶν ἀρχομένων ψυχαῖς πανταχοῦ τε καὶ ἀεὶ περιφερόμενον στρατηγόν. πρὸς γὰρ αὖ τοῖς ἄλλοις ἔργον αὐτῷ πέπρακται καλὸν μεταξὺ τῶν τε δεδικασμένων καὶ τῆς ἅπαντα λυούσης ψήφου. 29. ἔγνωστο μὲν γὰρ καὶ ἐδόκει δεῖν δεδέσθαι τὴν βουλήν, οὗ δ' ἦσαν, στενόν τε λίαν τοῦτο καὶ οὐκ ἐπῆν ὀροφή. τὰ μὲν οὖν ἀπὸ τῆς στενότητος εὐθὺς ἐλύπει κατα-
R ii. 19 πατεῖν τε ἀλλήλους ἀναγκάζοντα | καὶ καιρὸν ἅπαντα χείρω ποιοῦντα τὸν ὕπνου, τὸν τροφῆς, | τὸν ἔξω τούτων. εἴτε γὰρ οὐδεὶς εἰσίοι[1] τῶν φίλων, ἀνιαρὸν ταῖς τε εἰσόδοις τὸ χωρίον λυπηρότερον, εἴτε ὄμβρος ἐπιγένοιτο, τὸ σῶσον οὐκ ἦν. καὶ ἦν δή τινων ἀκούειν ὡς φθήσεται τοῦ βασιλέως τὸν ἔλεον, εἴ τις ἄρα ἔσται, τὰ ἀπὸ τοῦ δεσμωτηρίου. 30. ἔδει δὴ παρὰ τοῦ ταῦτα ἐψηφισμένου τὸ καὶ τῷ βουλευτηρίῳ χρῆσθαι, τοῖχος δὲ εἷς ἀμφοῖν, εὑρέσθαι ἢ ἀπολωλέναι. πάλιν τοίνυν τὸ[2] τὰ τοιαῦτα τολμᾶν αἰτεῖν τῆς τοῦδε φύσεως μόνης προκαλουμένης, οἶμαι, θαρρεῖν τε καὶ ἐπαγγέλ-

---

[1] εἰσίοι F. (V) : εἰσήει Re. (other mss.).
[2] τὸ conj. Re., F. (CPV, inserted in A) : om. Re. text (other mss.).

judge, in some matters in public, in others also in private.

28. Who has ever seen or heard of such a man? We should surely count his parents blessed more properly because of these actions than because of his office and command over so many persons. That is something that many people before have had, and others in future will have. But no one can testify to such tears in any military commander, nor yet has he beheld a commander everywhere and at all times borne with such pleasure in the hearts of the men he governs. For besides all else, in the interval between the court proceedings and the decree which gave us total release he performed a noble deed. 29. In accordance with an earlier decision, it was decided that the council must be arrested, but the place where they were was very restricted and lacked a roof. Thus hardship immediately resulted from the cramped quarters, forcing them to trample upon each other and interfering with their sleep and their meals, and the rest. If none of their friends came to visit, that was discouraging, and if they did, the place became more uncomfortable because of it, while if it rained, there was no protection. You could hear the remark passed that the conditions of their confinement would do their work before the emperor's pardon arrived, if ever it should. 30. From the person who had made the original decision they had to obtain permission for the use of the city-hall, which was separated by a single party wall, or else they would die. Here again, that we should dare make such a request was due solely to his generous character, for it induced us, I feel, to take our courage in both hands and suggest measures whereby

λειν, ἐν οἷς ἦν τι τῶν λυπηρῶν ἀφελεῖν. ὁ δ᾽ εὐθὺς
βουλευσάμενος εὗρεν ὅπως τοῖς μὲν ἃ βούλοιντο
ἔσται, ῥῆμα δὲ αὐτῷ μηδὲν κατὰ τῶν γεγραμ-
μένων. 31. εἰπὼν οὖν αὐτὸς ἐπὶ τῶν αὐτῶν μέ-
R ii. 20 νειν, | εἰ παρὰ τῶν ταῦτα ὑπηρετούντων ἕτερόν τι
γένοιτο, ἔφη κἂν εἰδῇ, οὐκ εἴσεσθαι.[1] τοῦτ᾽ αὐτοῖς
τοῦ βουλευτηρίου μετέδωκεν, οὗ θέατρον ὑπωρό-
φιον, στοαὶ δὲ τέτταρες αὐλὴν αὐτῶν ἐν μέσῳ ποι-
οῦσαι εἰς κῆπον | βεβιασμένην, ἀμπέλους ⟨ἔχον- F 4
τα⟩,[2] συκᾶς, δένδρα ἕτερα, λαχάνων εἴδη, τέρψιν
τοῖς δυσκόλοις ἀντίπαλον, δι᾽ ἣν καὶ ἐγέλασάν που
καὶ ἔσκωψαν καὶ προὔπιον καὶ ὕμνον ᾖσαν καὶ οὗ
τύχης εἰσὶν ἐπελάθοντο κλινῶν τε ἀπολαύοντες αἷς
πολὺ πρὸς ἀλλήλας τὸ μέσον, καὶ τραπεζῶν οἵων[3]
πρὸ τῆς συμφορᾶς, λόγων τε ἐν βίβλοις παντο-
δαπῶν καὶ τῶν ὑπὲρ τούτων λόγων οὓς αἱ βελτίους
ποιοῦσιν ἔριδες. 32. τοῦ δὴ[4] τὰ δεινὰ μὴ λίαν
εἶναι δεινὰ καὶ τοῦ μηδένα προδιαφθαρῆναι τῆς τοῦ
βασιλέως δωρεᾶς μὴ ἡλίῳ, μὴ ὄμβρῳ, μὴ λύπῃ,
μὴ δάκρυσι καὶ τοῦ δεδέσθαι τε ὁμοῦ καὶ μὴ δεδέ-
R ii. 21 σθαι καὶ | τοῦ τὰ τῶν οὐκ ἐν μεγάλοις ἐγκεκλη-
μένων ἔχειν ἐν τηλικούτοις ἐγκλήμασι, τούτων δὴ
τῶν ὀνειράτων, οὕτω γὰρ ἄμεινον προσειπεῖν, οὗτος
αἴτιος, οὗτος δοτήρ, οὗτος χορηγός. 33. οὗτος μὴ
πανταχοῦ πάντα ἀκριβῶς ἐξετάζων[5] ἐπέδειξεν ἅπα-

---

[1] κἂν εἰδῇ, οὐκ εἴσεσθαι. τοῦτ᾽ Cobet, F.: καὶ ὁ ᾔδει που
κείσεσθαι τοῦτ᾽ BM: καὶ εἰ δεῖ σου κεῖσθαι τοῦτ᾽ Morel (Par.
3016): καὶ ἤδη σ + lacuna + τοῦτ᾽ V: καὶ εἴδη σου κείσεσθαι
τοῦτ᾽ Re. (other mss.).   [2] ⟨ἔχοντα⟩ conj. Re., F.
[3] οἵων ⟨οὔ⟩ F. (V).   [4] δὴ conj. Re., F.: δὲ Re. text (mss.).

some of the distress might be alleviated. He immediately went into conference and devised means for them to get what they wanted, without himself uttering any word against his instructions. 31. So he stated that he stood by these same instructions, but that, if any alteration were made by his subordinates in charge, he would turn a blind eye, even if it were brought to his notice. This allowed them the use of the city-hall where there was a covered theatre, and four colonnades with a central courtyard which had been turned into a garden with vines, figs and other trees, and different kinds of green-stuff. It gave them relaxation to offset their discomfort, and in consequence they raised a laugh or a joke, offered a toast or sang a song, forgetting their plight. They enjoyed beds with plenty of room between them and fare such as they had had before their arrest, books of literature of various kinds and the literary discussions about them which are the product of first-class argumentation. 32. He, then, was the cause, the donor, the sponsor of the fact that the disaster did not become too disastrous, and that none should prevent the emperor's generosity by dying of sun-stroke or exposure, of grief or tears. He was responsible for their simultaneous arrest and freedom from arrest, and that, despite the seriousness of the charges, they were treated like those charged of minor offences, and for all these dream-like happenings, for such it is proper to describe them. 33. Without conducting a rigorous inquisition into every detail, he proved in its entirety his good sense

---

⁵ ἐξετάζων conj. Re. (*Animadv.*), F. (V): ἐξετάζειν Re. text (other mss.).

LIBANIUS

σαν αὐτοῦ[1] τὴν περὶ τὴν κρίσιν σοφίαν οἷς ἔπραξεν
ἐπὶ ταῖς διαλλαγαῖς, ἃς οὐ τῶν ἱκετευσάντων περὶ
R ii. 22 | τὸν Βόσπορον ἡγήσομαι μᾶλλον ἢ τοῦ χώραν ταῖς
ἱκετείαις τούτου[2] δεδωκότος. |

34. Μνήμης δ᾽ ἄρα καὶ τοὐπεισόδιον ἄξιον ἐν F
μεγάλῳ δή τινι τὴν εὐεργεσίαν ἔχον οὐκ εἰς βου-
λεύοντα μὲν πεπραγμένον, γένει δὲ τῇ πόλει προσήκοντα, μυρία μὲν ἐν δίκαις ἠγωνισμένον, πολλῶν
δὲ λόγων εἰς κάλλος συγκειμένων πατέρα, πατρὸς
δὲ ἐν ἀρχαῖς ἀμείνω τοῖς ἀρχομένοις φανέντα τοῖς
πρώτοις, τοῖς δευτέροις, τοῖς τρίτοις. ἐπὶ τοῦτον
βέλος ἀφῆκε συκοφάντης, οἷα δὴ τῆς τοιαύτης τέχνης τὰ βέλη, καὶ ἡ σιγὴ πονηρὸς λόγος ἐκαλεῖτο.
35. ἀλλ᾽ ἐνταῦθα ἀντέστησεν ὁ μισῶν ἀδικίαν οὗτος
τῷ συκοφάντῃ μὲν αὐτόν, τῷ ψεύδει δὲ τὴν ἀλήθειαν, τῇ κακίᾳ δὲ τὴν ἀρετήν, τῇ πικρίᾳ δὲ τὴν
χρηστότητα, καὶ ὅπερ αὖ καὶ δίκαιον ἦν, τοῦτ᾽ εἶχε
τὴν νίκην, τὸ δίκαιον. ὁ δὲ τῷ τε διαφυγόντι συν-
έχαιρε καὶ τῇ πόλει καὶ αὐτῷ, τῷ μὲν τοῦ διαπε-
φευγέναι, τῇ πόλει δὲ τοῦ μὴ δι᾽ ὃν ἔνδοξός ἐστι
τοιούτου στερηθῆναι πολίτου, αὐτῷ δὲ τοῦ κακῶν
R ii. 23 ἄνδρα ἀγαθὸν ἐξαρπάσαι, καθάπερ | Ἀθηνᾶ τῆς
Στυγὸς τὸν Ἡρακλέα.

36. Εἶεν. τουτὶ μὲν τοσοῦτον ἀγαθόν, ποῖος δέ
τις ἦν ἡμῖν ἐν τοῖς ὑπὲρ τῆς πόλεως γράμμασιν;
ὁποῖός περ ἡμῶν ἕκαστος, ὧν οὐδεὶς ἥσθη μᾶλλον
τῆς τοῦδε | ψυχῆς. ὃς μετήνεγκε μὲν αὐτὸν ἀπὸ F

---

[1] αὐτοῦ Re. (mss.) : αὐτοῦ F.
[2] τούτου Re. (mss.) : τούτων F.

---

[a] One of the usual periphrases to describe Constantinople,
a name he increasingly avoids with advancing years. For
400

in the matter of the trial by his acts to ensure the subsequent reconciliation. For this, I shall continue to believe, our advocates up by the Bosporus [a] are not so much responsible as he who gave room for their pleas.

34. A further interlude worthy of narration involved a benefaction on an important matter, not bestowed on an ordinary councillor, but on one who is connected with the city by birth, who had engaged in countless legal battles and had been father of many beautifully composed orations,[b] and in his periods of office had shown himself better than a father to those whom he governed in his first, second and third terms of office. An informer launched an attack upon him—the usual method of attack for such gentry—and his silence was described as a poor defence. 35. But here Ellebichus, this hater of wrong, opposed himself to the informer, truth to falsehood, virtue to vice, goodness to rancour, and, as was but right, right won the day. And he congratulated the man he acquitted, the city and himself—him, upon his acquittal, the city, upon her retention of such a citizen who brought her fame, and himself, upon rescuing a good man from evil, as Athena had rescued Heracles from the Styx.[c]

36. Well! so much for that boon. Now what was his attitude like on the arrival of the messages [d] that relieved the city ? He behaved like any one of us, for none felt more joy within him than he did. He

the advocates of Antioch there *cf. Or.* 20. 37. Libanius, naturally, does not mention Flavianus.

[b] *Cf. Or.* 18. 14 (πατὴρ τῶν λόγων).

[c] When Heracles went to bring up Cerberus, Homer, *Il.* 8. 362 ff., *Od.* 11. 625 f.

[d] For the imperial letter of pardon *cf. Or.* 20. 7, 37 ff., 21. 21.

τῆς θοίνης ἐπὶ τὴν ἀνάγνωσιν ἤδη τείνων, ὥς
φασιν, ἐπὶ τὰ προκείμενα τὴν δεξιάν, εὔξατο δὲ
ταχέως μὲν ἀπελθεῖν[1] τὴν ἑσπέραν, ταχέως δὲ
R ii. 24 ἀναφανῆναι | τὴν ἡμέραν. ᾔει δὲ ἐπὶ τὸ αὐτὸ
δικαστήριον οὐκ ἴσῳ τῷ προσώπῳ, τοσοῦτον ἦν
ἐνταῦθα τὸ ἄνθος, ἐγάννυτο δὲ οὐχ ἧττον τῇ σωτηρίᾳ τῆς πόλεως ἢ εἰ τηλικαύτην ἐτύγχανε δι᾽ ὅπλων
ἑλών. 37. ἐξαληλιμμένων δὴ τοῖς γεγραμμένοις
τῶν χαλεπωτέρων στὰς οὗπερ πρότερον, εὐφημί-
αις ἐστεφανοῦτο παρὰ πολὺ πλειόνων ἢ πρότερον
ἤδη τῶν καταδεδυκότων ἀναδύντων θεόντων εἰς
τὰ πινάκια. δάκρυα δὲ κἀνταῦθα οὐκέτι θρηνούντων, ἀλλ᾽ ἡδομένων. οἶδε γὰρ καὶ ἀπαλλαγὴ κακῶν ἄγειν εἰς ὀδυρμὸν ἄνθρωπον, ὥσπερ αὖ καὶ
τότε. μεστὴ μὲν δαιτυμόνων ἡ πόλις αὐτῶν ἑαυτοὺς ἐν μέσῳ τῶν κιόνων ἑστιώντων, δάκρυα δὲ
ἔρρει κατὰ τῶν ἐκπωμάτων οὐ φόβου τοῦτο ποι-
οῦντος, ἀλλὰ τοῦ μηκέτι | φοβεῖσθαι. ἦν δὲ τοῖς F
μὲν πίνουσιν ἐκ τοῦ πίνειν ἡ τέρψις, τοῖς δὲ ὁρῶσιν
ἐκ τοῦ ταῦτα ὁρᾶν. 38. ὧν εἷς καὶ οὗτος, ὃς μετὰ
τὰς πολλὰς παραινέσεις αἷς ἐπηνώρθου τὴν πόλιν,
ἐνόμισεν εὖ ἔχειν ὡς ἐνῆν κοινωνῆσαι τῆς εὐωχίας
καὶ παριὼν τοὺς κατακειμένους οὐκ ἐξανισταμέ-
R ii. 25 νους, οὐ γὰρ εἴα, τοῖς | καθ᾽ ἑκάστους[2] ῥήμασιν
ἡδίους τὰς φιάλας ἐποίει τὸ μὲν ὕψος τῆς ἀρχῆς
ὑποχωρῆσαι κελεύσας, πρέποντα δὲ τῷ καιρῷ αὐτὸς αὑτὸν καταστήσας, ὥστε καὶ ἰχθύν ποθεν ἐπὶ
γέλωτι τῶν παρακειμένων ἁρπάσας, ἐπεὶ γέλωτα
τοῦτ᾽ ἐποίησεν, ἀπέδωκε. 39. τοιαύτην ἐπορεύθη

---

[1] ἀπελθεῖν conj. Re. (Animadv.), F.: ἐπελθεῖν Re. text
(mss.).
[2] ἑκάστους F. (IV, correction in P): ἑκάστου Re. (other
mss.).

402

betook himself from his meal to read them just when, so I am told, he was stretching out his hand to the food before him. He prayed for the speedy passing of the night and the speedy dawning of the day. Then he went to the same courthouse, but not with the same expression on his face—such was his gaiety now : he rejoiced at the preservation of the city just as much as if he had taken such a one by force of arms. 37. Our disgrace was erased by the decrees, and he stood where he had stood before, and was garlanded with praise by many more people than before, since they who had been plunged into the depths now emerged and hurried to look at the notice-boards. Here again tears flowed, not tears of lamentation, but of joy ; the ending of troubles can cause a man to weep, and that happened on this occasion. The city was filled with revelry [a] ; the inhabitants feasted themselves in the middle of the colonnaded streets, and tears ran down over their tankards, not from fear, but from relief from fear. The drinkers got joy of their drinking, the observers, of what they observed. 38. He too was one of their number, for after many exhortations by which he sought to correct the city he thought it right that he should be able to share in their jollifications. He passed among the diners : they did not rise to him, for he would not let them. With a few words to each of them, he made their cups the sweeter, and he bade his high office take second place and comforted himself in keeping with the occasion. Why ! he even filched a fish from one of the dishes by way of a joke, and having so raised a laugh, handed it back. 39. Such then was the tour

[a] Cf. Chrysostom, Hom. 21 (P.G. xlix. 220).

πορείαν καὶ τοιούτων μετασχὼν ἐλθὼν ἠρίστα πάντων ἀρίστων ἐκεῖνο γλυκύτατον ἄξιον αὐτὸν τῶν
πολλῶν εἰκόνων ἐπιδεικνύς, ἃς διὰ παντὸς ἔξεστιν
ἰδεῖν τοῦ ἄστεος ἑλκούσας ὡς αὐτὰς[1] τοὺς παριόν-
τας καὶ πολιτῶν καὶ ξένων καὶ τριχὶ καὶ ὄμματι
καὶ παρειᾷ καὶ χροιᾷ. 40. κἂν[2] ταύταις ἴδοι τις
ἂν τὸν τρόπον τῆς πόλεως· ἀντὶ γὰρ ὧν εὖ ἔπαθον
τῶν πολλῶν τῶν πρότερον ἔχειν ἐν ἑκάστῃ φυλῇ
καὶ ταύταις[3] τὸν ἄνδρα ἐβούλοντο,[4] | ὅπως ἐν μὲν F 4
R ii. 26 ταῖς παρουσίαις αὐτοῦ τε ἀπολαύοιεν καὶ | τοῦ δευ-
τέρου, ἀπόντος δὲ μὴ τοιούτου παντὸς στέροιντο.

41. Ἡμεῖς μὲν οὖν αὐτὸν ἔχειν τε εὐχόμεθα καὶ
συνεῖναι καὶ διαλέγεσθαι, καλῶν δὲ ἐξαίφνης ὡς
ἑαυτὸν ὁ βασιλεὺς ὃν ἡμῖν ἐδεδώκει, τῷ τιμᾶν μὲν
τὸν ἄνδρα καὶ σὺν αὐτῷ περὶ τῶν μεγίστων ἐθέλειν
σκοπεῖν εὔφρανεν ἡμῖν τὴν πόλιν, ἐρωμένου δὲ ἀποστερῶν ἠνία, παρ᾽ ὃν οἱ μὲν ἦλθον ἰσχυρότατά
σφισι ποιήσοντες τὰ[5] δίκαια, οἱ δὲ ἀρκεῖν ἡγούμενοι
τὸ τὸν ἄνθρωπον ἰδεῖν, πολλοῖς δὲ καὶ οὐχ ὁρῶσιν
ἀπέχρη τὸ ὁπότε βουληθεῖεν εἶναι ἐλθοῦσιν ἰδεῖν.
42. ἀποδότω τοίνυν ἡμῖν ὁ βασιλεὺς τὸν διὰ πολλῶν εὐεργέτην, τὸν τῆς αὐτοῦ γνώμης μιμητήν,
τὸν ὥσπερ ἐκεῖνος[6] τοῖς θεοῖς, οὕτως αὐτὸν ἑπό-
R ii. 27 μενον ἐκείνῳ, τὸν τῆς παιδὸς | παῖδας ὀψόμενον
ἐοικότας αὐτῷ τῆς Ἀρτέμιδος ᾗ τῆσδε μέτεστι τῆς

---

[1] αὐτὰς Re., F. (CBV) : αὑτὰς Morel (other mss.).
[2] κἂν F. : καὶ Re. (mss.).
[3] ταύταις F. : ταυτησὶ mss., Re. (conj. ἑαυτῆς). Read ταύτῃ?
[4] ἐβούλοντο F. (P corrected) : ἐβούλετο Re. (mss.).
[5] τὰ conj. Re., F. (BM) : om. Re. text (other mss.).
[6] ἐκεῖνος F. (V) : ἐκεῖνον Re. (other mss.).

he made, and such the revelry in which he shared. Then he went and dined, and that was the most enjoyable dinner he ever had had. He proved himself worthy of the many statues, which can be seen throughout the whole city, attracting to themselves the gaze of passers-by, citizen and stranger alike, by their hair, their eyes, their cheeks and colouring. 40. In them, too, you may see the city's reactions. In return for the many past benefits received, they wanted to keep the man in each ward of the city [a] by these means also, so that when he is present they may enjoy the company both of him and of his duplicate, and in his absence that they may not be entirely deprived of such a personage.

41. So we pray to retain his person, his company and his conversation, but the emperor has suddenly summoned to his presence the man he had bestowed on us. By honouring him and wishing to confer with him upon high matters of state, he has pleased our city, but he has distressed us by depriving us of the object of our affections. Some of us have visited him to strengthen their legal claims, some have thought it enough simply to see him, many too, who have not seen him, find it sufficient to be able to go and do so whenever they like. 42. Then let the emperor restore to us our constant benefactor,[b] who imitates his imperial resolve, and follows him as he himself follows the gods. Let him be restored to us to see his daughter's children like himself, by

---

[a] Cf. Or. 11. 231, 19. 62, 24. 26 (Vol. I, p. 509 n.).
[b] This peroration indicates a date of composition in A.D. 388 or later, since Ellebichus' recall (which occurred in that year) is not in the immediate past. His daughter was evidently married and settled in Antioch.

LIBANIUS

πόλεως, ἐν τοῖς τόκοις προθυμότερον καὶ παρούσης καὶ βοηθούσης μεμνη|μένης, οἷον ἐν οἵῳ καιρῷ περὶ F τὸ κτῆμα τὸ ἐκείνης Ἑλλέβιχος ἑαυτὸν ἀπέδειξεν.

---

[a] Artemis, associated with Eileithyia of childbirth, *cf.* *Or.* 5. 27. She is associated with Antioch by a festival in

the more eager presence and help in childbirth of
Artemis,[a] who shares in the life of this city, when
she remembers the kind of man Ellebichus proved
himself to be in such a crisis in defence of her own
possession.

Meroe, a suburb of the city, held in the month Artemisios
(May), *ibid.* 42 ff.

ON THE CITY COUNCILS

ORATION 48
TO THE CITY COUNCIL

ORATION 49
TO THE EMPEROR,
FOR THE CITY COUNCILS

INTRODUCTION

In these orations, Libanius again speaks in support of his city council, but in very different tones from those used hitherto. In almost all of his earlier orations, whether of the reign of Theodosius or before, his councillors had been presented as innocent victims of pressures from without. Now, however, in a significant shift of attitude he defends the council as an institution while bitterly criticizing its members who, far from being innocent victims, are themselves responsible for the drastic and, as he clearly implies, sudden deterioration in the status and membership of the order. The arguments previously deployed in their interest, as in *Oration* 2, are here used against them, indicative of the sharp change which had occurred in the relationship between the council and its sophist.

Libanius had a generation previously painted a glowing picture of the urban society of Antioch, and had then given a brief account of the composition of the city council.[a] It appears as an harmonious body administering the affairs of an harmonious civic society, and comprises three sections, each directed by " generals " appointed by the order as

---

[a] *Or.* 11. 144 : τρία γὰρ (ἡ βουλὴ) αὐτὴν διελοῦσα τέλη τὴν μὲν ἡγεμονίαν καθ' ἕκαστον τοῖς ἀρίστοις ἀνατέθεικε, τὸ λοιπὸν δὲ ἕπεται στρατηγοῖς ἐπισταμένοις ὑπὲρ τοῦ μέρους πονεῖν.

a whole, the rank and file dutifully following such a lead. To judge from this eulogy, this type of organization is something new and unusual for an eastern city, and it bears obvious resemblances to that of the new Senate in Constantinople, a body composed of three or four classes, each of which has duties defined according to the wealth of its members.[a] Hence, when Julian in A.D. 362 directed two hundred new members into the council of Antioch it is tempting to assume that he proposed to add a fourth panel to the nominal roll of six hundred who constituted the three existing panels.[b] It is known that about the same time a fourth panel was *certainly* being enrolled in the council at Tarsus.[c] However, Julian's campaign was a failure from the very start and by A.D. 381, the date of *Or.* 2, so far from any fourth panel surviving, the humbler members in the existing panels were under the severest pressure, and by the time of these two orations their condition had deteriorated further. Moreover, the πρῶτοι in the council are now asserted to be the ruination of the δεύτεροι and the τρίτοι (*Or.* 48. 40)—a rôle which had previously been reserved for officials and *honorati.*

These πρῶτοι among the decurions are to be identified with the *principales* of the Codes, where their emergence to a position of privilege and authority over their fellows is clearly observable in this period. An unofficial convention, long established

---

[a] *Ep.* 252. 5 (A.D. 359), three classes : *Ep.* 1277. 3-4 (A.D. 364), four classes.

[b] Julian, *Misop.* 367 c. He also allocates 3000 κληροί for these, *ibid.* 370 d.

[c] *Ep.* 1393. 5 : ταῦτα διαλέγου τοῖς τὸν τέταρτον χορὸν οὐ καλῶς συντιθεῖσι.

in social practice, is now transformed into an officially recognized and organized part of the system of administration, since the central government, deferring both to its own needs and to the pressures and aspirations of this select group in municipal society, creates a new kind of caste system by the grant of special duties, privileges and status. Whereas, in Libanius' boyhood, he can speak of the *curia* as a unity, in his later years, both to him and to the legislators, a great gap exists between the *principales* and the *curiales.*[a] Admittedly, the central government had, in the first half of the century, attempted to check such separatist tendencies. Under Constantine the *principales* were barred from the allocation of certain duties, a task to which they evidently aspired, and even in the last years of Constantius an attempt is made to counter the growing practice of differentiating between different sections of the order by banning the imposition of physical punishment upon *curiales* in general.[b]

By contrast, by A.D. 373 at the latest, the *principales* are found controlling all allocations of duties [c]; and an edict of A.D. 371 specifically gives them

[a] Compare *C. Th.* 12. 1. 39 (A.D. 349), " primarii *et* curiales " with 12. 1. 85 (A.D. 381), " principales *vel* decuriones."

[b] *Ibid.* 11. 16. 4 (A.D. 328) : " extraordinariorum munerum distributio non est principalibus committenda " ; *ibid.* 12. 1. 47 (A.D. 359 ; *cf.* 12. 1. 39 above) : " Oppidaneis ordinibus consulentes dudum iussimus ab iniuriis corporalibus tutam esse ordinis dignitatem."

[c] *C. Th.* 8. 15. 5 : " officiales atque municipes qui exactiones quascumque susceperint, eos etiam quibus vel discussionis indago vel negotium censuale mandatur, insuper principales, a quibus distributionum omnium forma procedit, curatores etiam lex ista contineat."

413

immunity from corporal punishment, and dangles
before them the prospect of an honorary *comitiva*.[a]
By these means under Valens the *principales* had
been elevated far above the rank and file of their
fellows, and though the accession of Theodosius sees
some reversion to the notion of equality of treatment
for all decurions, especially with regard to immunity
from punishment by the cat-o'-nine-tails, inside a
dozen years this privilege is once more reserved
solely for these municipal magnates,[b] who very soon
are acknowledged by the central administration
as being on a par with the imperially appointed
curator or *defensor*.[c] The gap so quickly established
between decurion and *principalis* can best be judged
by consideration of the monetary fines imposed on
the Donatists in Africa in A.D. 412 [d]—for a senator,
30 pounds of gold, for a *clarissimus* or a *principalis*,
20 pounds, for a decurion or a *negotiator* or a *plebeius*,
5 pounds. Sectional aspirations and social practice
here moved in parallel with administrative conve-
nience and, as so often, were finally embodied in
legal form.

The *principales* had thus assumed the position of
an executive committee responsible for the allocation to the members of the municipal order of duties
required for the maintenance of local society, in the
interest both of the imperial administration and of
the community as a whole. By definition they had
themselves completed the full progression of the

[a] 12. 1. 75 : " liberumque sit corpus eorum ab his iniuriis,
quas honoratos non decet sustinere. honorem etiam eis ex-
comitibus addi censemus . . ."
[b] 12. 1. 80 of A.D. 380 ; *ibid*. 85 of A.D. 381 ; *ibid*. 126 of
A.D. 392.   [c] 8. 5. 59 of A.D. 400.   [d] 16. 5. 52.

liturgies, but the official recognition of their status quickly engendered an attitude more than ever before élitist and exclusive. Their rapacity and arrogance were notorious,[a] the improper use of the powers of recommending nomination to or exemption from the municipal order was obnoxious,[b] and their allocation of the liturgies among its existing members secured for themselves the description of *potentes*, with all the perquisites implied thereby, and was used to depress the status of the lesser decurions still further.[c] Particularly vulnerable was the decurion of the lower grade who was allocated any duty of tax collection at this time of financial stress, since he was made personally responsible for making good any deficiency out of his own property, usually after a flogging by the governor's agents.

In consequence there occurred allegedly enforced sales of curial land, as in *Or.* 47 ; and it follows from the present orations that the *principales*, who made the allocation, were themselves prominent purchasers of such property from the victims. Certainly the recent legislation which had placed some limi-

---

[a] *e.g.* Salvian, *de Gub. Dei*, 5. 4 (Migne, *P.L.* liii. 98) : " quot curiales, tot tyranni." *Cf.* Jo. Chrys. *Hom. in Matt.* 61. 3 (Migne, *P.G.* lviii. 591-592). Theodoret, *H.R.* 14 (Migne, *P.G.* lxxxii. 1413), who tells of Letoïus.

[b] *e.g.* Julian, *Misop.* 369 c ff. ; *C. Th.* 12. 1. 140 ; 148 (A.D. 395).

[c] *C. Th.* 12. 1. 173 (A.D. 410) ; *cf.* Lib. *Or.* 32. 8 : ἐγὼ δὲ τὸ μὲν τὸν Κίμωνα λειτουργῆσαι πολλάκις καὶ ἐβουλήθην καὶ εὐξάμην, καιρὸν δὲ ἀναμένειν ᾤμην δεῖν. οὗτος δὲ ἦν ἀναβιῶναι τὴν βουλὴν καὶ γενέσθαι τὴν προτέραν ἐκείνην. ἐκεῖνο μὲν γὰρ ἦν λειτουργεῖν, τὸ δὲ νῦν ἀπολωλέναι. οὕτω κακῶς τὸ πρᾶγμα ἔχει ἄλλαις τε οὐκ ὀλίγαις αἰτίαις καὶ τῷ τῶν λειπομένων τοὺς ἰσχυροτέρους πορθεῖν τὰ τῶν ἀσθενεστέρων. *Ep.* 1496.

tation upon the decurion's right to sell his land is indicative of the scale upon which this was now taking place under duress, and the experience of the next generation was to make clear that the law was aimed particularly at such acquisitions by the *principales.*[a] It must, however, be admitted that, although almost every method of curial evasion as listed in the Codes may receive confirmation in the writings of Libanius, the orator's viewpoint is far from impartial. The Codes make it clear that the desire of the depressed decurions to get out of the council was no less than that of the *principales* to get them out, and that they were only too often willing victims. The methods of escape comprise both social ascent and descent : immunity from curial obligation is sought not only by obtaining the status of senator, official, government agent, advocate or sophist, but also that of cleric, monk, client to one of the *potentes*, or mere run-away, and a successful escape required a deliberate act of choice on the part of the alleged victim, and no less deliberate persistence in this course of action.

The extent of the decline may be gauged by the numbers cited by Libanius. The distinction is presented with all the exaggeration of formal rhetoric—from six hundred to sixty (*Or.* 48. 4 ; *cf.* 2. 33), from twelve hundred to twelve (*Or.* 49. 8)—a fact which renders the final figure suspect in each case.[b] However, there is no doubt of the suddenness and the seriousness of the decline which had made the curial

---

[a] *C. Th.* 12. 3. 1 ; 2 (A.D. 386 ; 423).

[b] Petit (p. 323) suggests that the councillors numbered 60, including 12 *principales*. This is highly unlikely, *cf.* Liebeschuetz, p. 181.

organization of the *Antiochicus* completely out of date. What remains in doubt is the distinction between the original numbers cited, which must be regarded as a matter of fact. The solution appears in *Or.* 48. 3, where Libanius asserts that in time past the council actually consisted of six hundred councillors who performed their services from their property and were full members, and that a supplementary group of six hundred performed as ordered tasks with their persons. These clearly had never been, however aspiring, full members of the council,[a] and they had apparently vanished completely well before the 380s. Presumably they had not survived the reign of Constantine, and for the first time, there was no obvious source of recruitment to the *curia* from below.

With regard to the composition of these orations, it has been taken as self-evident by commentators other than Sievers and Liebeschuetz that they constitute an example of Libanius' practice of composing " doublets." Seeck, Foerster, Pack and Petit place both speeches after the death of the prefect Cynegius and the appointment of his successor Tatianus in the summer of A.D. 388, as indicated in *Or.* 49. 1 and 31. Liebeschuetz dates this oration more precisely to A.D. 391,[b] but places *Or.* 48 in the year 384/5, following Sievers' identification of the person mentioned in *Or.* 48. 27 as Cynegius, and so placing the date of composition as earlier than his journey as prefect through the East. Textual difficulty in the passage (*cf.* note *ad loc.*) and the

---

[a] *Cf.* Jones, *Greek City*, p. 180, for municipal services performed by persons below the status of decurion.

[b] *Cf.* Liebeschuetz, *Antioch*, Appendix II, pp. 270 ff.

LIBANIUS

complications of chronology render such an interpretation hazardous.

MANUSCRIPTS AND EDITIONS

The manuscript density for these two orations is low, consisting of twelve for *Oration* 48 and seven for *Oration* 49, with no representative of the tradition which is normally provided by V. For the constitution of the text the major manuscripts for *Oration* 48 are CAPIBM, with Mo. (employed by Reiske) as the best representative of a nucleus attached to the same branch as C (*viz.* Laur. LVII 27, Patmius 471, Vat. gr. 939, Mutinensis LXXXI). U appears as a twin of BM. The earliest of these is A (of the tenth century) antedating all the rest by three centuries. For *Oration* 49, the relevant manuscripts are CAPIBM, with the addition of U. Of the excerptors, Macarius draws upon *Oration* 48, Planudes upon *Oration* 49.

Both orations first appeared in full in the Venice edition of 1754 by Bongiovanni ; editions by Reiske and Foerster have followed. *Oration* 48, however, was known a century earlier, even though it remained unpublished, since Valesius cites § 36 in his notes on Ammianus (28. 2), to illustrate the fate of Marathocupreni.

BIBLIOGRAPHY

These orations are important in the general studies of the history of the councils, *e.g.* in A. H. M. Jones, *The Greek City*, and *Later Roman Empire*, and in Declareuil, *Quelques Problèmes d'histoire et des institutions municipales etc.* (1911). Detailed studies

418

of their contents appear in Pack (*op. cit.* pp. 30 ff., 121 ff.), Petit, *Libanius et la vie municipale* (*passim*), Liebeschuetz, *Antioch* (Oxford, 1972), *passim*, but especially pp. 270 ff.

XLVIII

ΠΡΟΣ ΤΗΝ ΒΟΥΛΗΝ

1. Ὅσοις μὲν πρὸς ὅσους ἐχρησάμην ὑπὲρ ὑμῶν
παρὰ πάντα τὸν χρόνον, ὦ βουλή, λόγοις οὐ πρὸς
τοὺς ὑπὸ τοῖς βασιλεῦσιν ἔχοντας τὰς ἀρχὰς μόνον
ἀλλὰ καὶ πρὸς αὐτῶν ἐκείνων τὸν ἄριστον, οὔθ᾽
ὑμᾶς οὔτ᾽ ἄλλων ἀνθρώπων οὐδὲ ἕνα ἀγνοεῖν ἡγοῦμαι. καὶ γὰρ εἰ δύναμιν ἔχοντάς τινας οἷς ἐπαρ-
ρησιαζόμην ἐλύπουν, δεινότερον ὅμως ἐδόκει μοι
τοῦ παθεῖν τι κακὸν εἰπόντα ἃ προσῆκεν ἡ μετὰ
τῆς σιωπῆς ἀσφάλεια· ἐπεὶ δ᾽ ὑμῖν ὑπὲρ ὑμῶν
αὐτῶν διαλεχθῆναι καιρός, | οὐδὲ τοῦτο παρήσω
τῶν ἀτόπων εἶναι νομίζων ἑτέρους μὲν ἀξιοῦν εὖ
ποιεῖν ἡμῖν τὴν βουλήν, αὐτὴν δὲ μὴ πείθειν τῶν
αὑτῆς προνοηθῆναι.

2. Ἐλπίζω μὲν οὖν ὑμᾶς ἔσεσθαί μοι χαλεπούς,
εἰ καὶ τὸ συμφέρον ἔχουσαν κομίζων ἥκω γνώμην.
πεφύκασι γὰρ ἄνθρωποι τῶν σὺν μέμψεσιν ὠφε-
λίμων προκρίνειν τὰς μετὰ βλάβης χάριτας. ἀλλ᾽
οὔτε πρὸς | ἄλλους ἐγὼ τοιοῦτος οὔτε νῦν πρὸς
ὑμᾶς, ὡς τοῦ μὲν μισουμένου καὶ δίκας ἐθέλοντος
λαβεῖν ἐκεῖνο ἂν ἦν, τοῦ δὲ τιμῶν τετυχηκότος καὶ

---

[a] Or. 47. 2, 52. 1 begin with similar sentiments.

ORATION 48

TO THE CITY COUNCIL

1. I BELIEVE, gentlemen, that neither you nor any other person can be unaware of the numerous pleas that throughout my career I have directed on your behalf to so many people, not simply to the holders of office under the emperors but also to this, our most excellent of emperors. And if, by the frank expression of my opinions, I ever distressed persons of influence, it still seemed to me that the safety of silence was more odious than the troubles in store for me for saying what was right.[a] However, circumstances now require me to address you on your own account, and here too I will not be negligent, for I consider it quite absurd to require others to act on behalf of our city council and yet not to induce it to have some regard for itself.

2. Now, I expect you to be annoyed with me, even though I come as the bearer of good counsel. People naturally prefer compliments, though detrimental, to good advice accompanied by reproof.[b] But I have never behaved so towards others, nor will I now do so towards you: such conduct would be that of a curmudgeon and of a rancorous disposition, while

[b] Cited by Macarius, with title τοῦ πρὸς τὴν ἐν Ἀντιοχείᾳ βουλήν.

δικαίως ἂν ἀμοιβὰς ἀποδόντος τοῦτο. καὶ δοῖεν
μὲν οἱ τὴν πόλιν ἡμῖν ἔχοντες θεοὶ τῆς τε παραι-
νέσεως ὄνησίν τινα γενέσθαι καὶ πεισθῆναι τοὺς
ἀκούοντας τῶν ὠλιγωρημένων ποιήσασθαι πρόνοιαν. εἰ δ᾽ οὖν καὶ μάταιόν μοι τὴν συμβουλὴν
ἀποδείξετε, κέρδος ἔμοιγε ἱκανὸν τὸ συμβεβουλευ-
κέναι.

3. Ἦν, ὅτ᾽ ἦν ἡμῖν ἡ βουλὴ πολλή τις, ἄνδρες
ἑξακόσιοι. οὗτοι μὲν ἐλειτούργουν τοῖς οὖσιν, ἕτεροι δὲ τοσοῦτοι τὸ κελευόμενον ἐποίουν τοῖς σώ-
μασι. τοῦτο τὸ καλὸν μέχρι τῆς τοῦ δεῖνος βασιλείας σῶον ὑπῆρχε τῇ πόλει, μετὰ ταῦτα δὲ οὐκέτι
πολλῶν πολλα|χόθεν ὀλέθρων τῇ βουλῇ λυμηνα- F
μένων. ὥστε ἕκαστον ἔτος ἀεί τι τοῦ πληρώματος
ἀφαιρούμενον διήρχετο. καὶ τὰ τούτων ἦν ὁρᾶν
ἑτέρους γεωργοῦντας τό τε καταλειπόμενον ἀσθε-
νέστερον ἐγίγνετο διχόθεν, τῷ μήτ᾽ ἀριθμῷ τοσοῦτον ὅσονπερ πρότερον εἶναι καὶ τῷ τὰς οὐσίας
αὐτοῖς εἰς ἔλαττον ἰέναι. 4. καὶ τί με χρὴ τὰ παρ᾽
ὑμῶν ἐν τοῖς δικαστηρίοις εἰρημένα πολλάκις αὐτὸν διεξιέναι; πολλῶν γὰρ στομάτων οὗτος ὁ

---

[a] Cf. Or. 35. 2 (also addressed to members of the city council).

[b] The reduction from 600 to 60 is resumed from Or. 2. 33, where the rhetorical pattern is emphasized by the addition of οὐδὲ μὲν οὖν ἐξ παρ᾽ ἐνίοις. The reduction from 1200 to 12 appears in Or. 49. 8—this numerical discrepancy leading Sievers to his conclusion that Or. 48 and 49 were of different dates. Petit (pp. 54 ff.) identified the original 600 as the decurions proper, performing munera patrimonii, the additional 600 as curiales performing munera personalia, noting that the distinction between decurion and curialis nowhere appears in C. Th. He further concluded (pp. 322 ff.) that the total membership of the curia in A.D. 388 was 60, 12 being principales. This ignores the rhetorical pattern

mine is that of one who enjoys respect and makes a proper return for it. And may the gods who keep our city[a] grant that there be some profit from my advice and that my hearers be induced to redress their neglectfulness. At all events, even if you prove my counsel to be in vain, it will be profit enough for me to have offered it.

3. Once, when our council was a large one, it consisted of 600 members. These served it with their property, but as many again performed their ordained tasks with their persons.[b] This laudable situation for our city lasted intact until the reign of a certain emperor,[c] but thereafter it was no longer so, for many destructive forces of various origins adversely affected the council. Thus every year part of its personnel was progressively removed, and one could see other people farming their estates, while the remainder became weaker for two reasons, first that its numbers were declining from the previous level, secondly that their property was decreasing.

4. What need is there now for me to relate the arguments you have often put forward in the courts?[d] This lament has been thought suitable for many a man to

of the decline in all three speeches. Liebeschuetz (pp. 220 f., following Jones, *G.C.* p. 180 n.) sees the second now defunct group of 600 as liable to plebeian rather than curial liturgics. Their duties had by the late 4th century been allocated to the *collegia* or *corpora*—the tradesmen's guilds.

[c] Petit (pp. 54 ff.) identified this emperor with Diocletian, but this cautious periphrasis is more often applied to Constantine, who is certainly alluded to in *Or.* 49. 2, where these destructive forces are more precisely described.

[d] *i.e.* before the provincial governor, *Or.* 54. 74. The councillor's job in combating curial evasion is to report any instance to the governor, who only then sets in motion the means to counter it.

θρῆνος ἠξίωται. τὰς μὲν οὖν συμφορὰς οὐ κακῶς
τετραγῳδήκατε, περὶ δὲ τὴν τουτωνὶ τῶν κακῶν
ἐπανόρθωσιν οὐκ ἀκριβεῖ σπουδῇ τε καὶ προθυμίᾳ
R ii. 528 κεχρημένους ὑμᾶς | εὑρίσκω. μετὰ γὰρ δὴ τὸ
εἰπεῖν· οἰχόμεθα, ἀπολώλαμεν, ἦμεν ἑξακόσιοι ἤ,
νὴ Δία γε, δὶς τοσοῦτοι, νῦν δ' οὐδὲ ἑξήκοντα,
μικρὰς συλλαβὰς προσθέντος ἑνός τινος περὶ τοῦ
δεῖν γενέσθαι τινὰς τῆς βουλῆς παρὰ τῆς ἀρχῆς
ἀπήλθετε καὶ δεδώκατε πολλοῖς περὶ ὑμῶν λέγειν
εἰκότως ὡς ἀφοσιοῦνται καὶ φασὶ μὲν δεῖσθαι προσ-
θήκης, ὅπως δὲ μὴ τοῦτο ἔσται ποιοῦσι μένειν τε
αὐτοῖς[1] βουλόμενοι τὴν τῶν ὀδυρμῶν ὑπόθεσιν, ἵν'
εἴη καὶ ἀδικοῦσι συγγνώμη, καὶ ἅμα δεδιότες μὴ
κοινωνοὺς λάβωσι τῶν λημμάτων ἢ καί τινες αὐτῶν
ἱκανώτεροι φανέντες μείζω κατακτήσωνται δυνα-
στείαν. 5. ἐγὼ δὲ τοῦτον μὲν οὐ προσίεμαι τὸν
λόγον, ἐκεῖνο δὲ οἶδα, ὅτι εἰ καὶ μὴ κακία, ῥαθυ-
|μία γε νωθρὰς ἐποίει τὰς βοηθείας. πολλάκις, F
ἐρεῖτε, περὶ τούτων εἰρήκαμεν, τὸν πεισόμενον δὲ
οὐκ εἴχομεν. οὐ γάρ, ὡς ἐχρῆν, περὶ τοιούτου
διείλεχθε πράγματος οὐδὲ ἅπαντι τῷ τόνῳ οὐδὲ
ἁπάσῃ ⟨τῇ⟩[2] ῥώμῃ οὐδὲ ἄραντες τὴν φωνὴν οὐδὲ εἰς
γόνυ πεσόντες οὐδὲ ἀφέντες δάκρυα οὐδ' οἷς[3] ἠμεί-
ψασθε δηλώσαντες ὅτι οὐκ ἀνέξεσθε, ἀλλὰ τὰς ἑτέρων ὁδοὺς ἥξετε. οἷα πολλὰ πεποιηκέναι πολλάκις
Γαλάτας τούτους ἀκούομεν, οἳ ἐπειδὴ λέγοντες οὐκ
εἶχον πείθειν Κωνστάντιον, πρηνεῖς καταπεσόντες
R ii. 529 ἔκλαον[4] καὶ ἅμα | τῶν τε ποδῶν εἵλκοντο καὶ

---

[1] αὐτοῖς Re., F.: αὐτοῖς Bongiovanni (mss.).
[2] ⟨τῇ⟩ Re., F.: om. Bong. (mss.).
[3] οἷς Re., F.: ὡς Bong. (mss.).
[4] [οὐκ εἶχον πείθειν] ἔκλαον conj. Sintenis, F.: οὐκ εἶχον πείθειν ἕλκειν mss.: ὡς εἶχον, ἐπεχείρουν, and ὃν οὐκ εἶχον πείθειν,

utter. Well, though you have made no bad recital of your woes, for the correction of these troubles I find that you have employed no great eagerness or zeal. For after exclaiming, " We're ruined ! We're done for ! We used to be 600,—twice that number, in fact. Now we're not even 60," someone or other adds a few words about the need for the governor to appoint some councillors, off you go, and you allow many people to say of you, with good reason, " They are just going through the motions ! They say they need more members, but their actions are designed to prevent it. They want the excuse for their complaints to continue, so that they can be forgiven even when in the wrong. They are afraid, too, of having some people to share their perquisites, or even of some more suitable than themselves emerging to gain greater influence." 5. I do not agree with this argument, but this much I do know, that slackness, if not malice, has rendered efforts of assistance vain. You will tell me, " We have often spoken about it, but we found no one who would believe us." No, because you did not speak as you should have done on such an issue : you did not do so with full intensity and vehemence : you neither raised your voices nor cast yourselves at their knees, neither did you shed tears nor, in your replies, make it clear that you would not put up with it but would rather proceed on the paths taken by others. This, we are told, was the line of conduct that the Galatians here persisted in : when they could not persuade Constantius by argument, they fell flat on their faces and set up cries of lamentation, and at

τοῦτον ἐπεχείρουν ἕλκειν conj. Re. (*Animadv.* and edit.): καταπεσόντες ⟨οὐκ ἂν ἔφασαν ἀναστῆναι καὶ ἐκέλευον⟩ ἕλκειν conj. Cobet.

LIBANIUS

ἐδέοντο, ἕως αὐτοῖς ὑπῆρξεν ὑπὲρ οὗ ταῦτα ἐποίουν. 6. ὑμεῖς δὲ οὐδ' ὅτε ἔναγχος ἐπέμπετε τὴν
πρεσβείαν, τοῦτο ἐπηγγείλατε, ἀλλ' ὑπὲρ μὲν ἵππων
καὶ χρυσίου καὶ γῆς καὶ σίτου καὶ τοιούτων τινῶν
ἐκόμιζεν ὁ πρεσβεύων γράμματα καὶ ἦν τοῦ φορτίου ταῦτα οὐ μικρὸν μέρος, περὶ δὲ τοῦ κεκενῶ-
σθαι μικροῦ τὸ βουλευτήριον καὶ τῶν δικαίων βου-
λεύειν οὐδὲ γρῦ. καίτοι τίν' εἶχε πόνον | τοῖς πολ- F 4
λοῖς τοῦτο προσθεῖναι; τῷ δ' ἂν ἀδικεῖν ἐδόξατε
χεῖρας ὀρέγοντες τῇ βουλῇ; 7. ἀλλ', οἶμαι, βραχὺ
φροντίζετε τούτων ὧν μάλιστα προσῆκε. διὰ
τοῦτο πᾶσα πρόφασις ἀρκεῖ τοῖς βουλομένοις πρὸς
ἀπαλλαγὴν λειτουργιῶν. οὗτος ὁπλίτης, καὶ σιω-
R ii. 530 πᾶται. ἐκεῖνος φέρει τὰς βασιλέως ἐντολάς, | ἅπ-
τεται δὲ οὐδείς. ἕτερος ἄρχοντι παρήδρευκεν.
ἀφεῖται. διατρίβει τις ἐν τῷ πωλεῖν τὴν αὐτοῦ
τοῖς δικαζομένοις φωνήν. τὴν πατρῴαν τάξιν οὗτος ὑπερεπήδησε. προσκρούειν γὰρ ἀνάγκη τοῖς
τούτων κηδομένοις. 8. καὶ τί δεινὸν ποιοῦντα τὰ
δίκαια πρὸς τὴν ἑαυτοῦ πόλιν ἐχθρόν τινα ἐπισπάσασθαι; πῶς δὲ τὴν μὲν ἐκείνων ὀργὴν φοβῇ, ταύτην δὲ τὴν ἀδικίαν οὐ δέδοικας; ἢ κἂν εἰ τὴν

ᵃ For the embassies of Antioch of this period cf. Petit,
pp. 418 f., Pack, *Studies*, pp. 123 f., Liebeschuetz, pp. 265 ff.
This embassy seems to be that of *Ep.* 850-852, 864-868.

ᵇ *Cf. Or.* 49. 7, where the same complaint is made.

ᶜ For these methods of curial evasion, and measures
taken to prevent it, *cf.* Jones, *LRE* 740 ff. Enlistment is,
for Libanius, the least commendable form of evasion (*cf.*
§ 42, *Or.* 49. 19 : the best known example is, of course,
Ammianus). Under Constantius he had been known to
befriend and support individual *agentes-in-rebus*, but the
expansion of numbers (*Or.* 2. 58) in Theodosian times made
the situation more serious. The demand for the position of

426

the same time clutched his feet and pleaded with him, until they gained their objective. 6. But you, even on the despatch of your recent embassy,[a] made no reference to this matter. Our envoy took a message that dealt with horses, gold, land, corn and such like, and this made up the bulk of the message he bore, but about the almost total emptying of the City Hall and about suitable candidates for the council —never a word! Yet what trouble would it have been to have included this item with all the rest? Who would have thought you wrong in extending a helping hand to the council?[b] 7. The fact is, in my opinion, that you have little interest in subjects that you really should be interested in. Hence any excuse is enough for those who want to rid themselves of civic obligations. This one is a serving soldier, and not a word is said about him. Another is an imperial courier; nobody claims him. Yet another has been a governor's assessor. He is excused.[c] If somebody makes a career of hiring his vocal powers out to litigants, he escapes from his ancestral station.[d] Those who are distressed at this are bound to take offence. 8. And what harm is there in attacking enemies, if one does one's duty towards one's birthplace? How comes it that you are scared of their resentment, but have no fears about this injury? If

assessor also seems to have increased in these years (*cf.* the anonymous of *Or.* 62; also Tisamenus).

[d] As advocate. This method was checked (*e.g.*) by *C. Th.* 12. 1. 46, 87 (of A.D. 358 and 381), but it remained a well-trodden way of escape. Even though not an official post, its close connection with the administration gave it influence. Libanius had often petitioned for his pupils to be registered in the governors' courts, and his own son Cimon unsuccessfully tried this method.

μητέρα τυπτομένην ἑώρας, εἱστήκεις ἂν οὐδένα
ἀμύνων τρόπον, ὅπως εἴης τῷ παίοντι κεχαρισμένος; ταχέως μέντ᾽ ἂν ἔγνως μείζονι σαυτὸν ὑπο-
θεὶς κινδύνῳ, τῷ παρὰ τῶν θεῶν, τὸν ἐλάττω
φυγών, τὸν παρὰ τῶν ἀνθρώπων. 9. ὃν ἐδείξατε
πολλάκις οὐ φοβηθέντες καὶ ταῦτα ἐν πολλῷ τούτου βραχυτέροις. ἵνα γὰρ ἵππος ὑμῖν ἀνθ᾽ ἵππου
καὶ ἡνίοχος ἀνθ᾽ ἡνιόχου γένηται καὶ πλέον ἀργύ-
ριον δοθῇ τοῖς γήρας | θεραπεύουσι τυχὸν καὶ μείνῃ F
παρὰ τοῖς εἰρηνοφύλαξιν ὁ τῶν κορυνηφόρων μι-
σθός, τί μὲν οὐ λέγεται; τί δὲ οὐκ ἀκούεται;[1] δεινὸν
δὲ οὐδέν, κἂν ἐξωσθῆναι δέῃ, κἂν εἰς τὸ οἴκημα
R ii. 531 ἐλθόντα | καθῆσθαι. καὶ πληγὰς δὲ οἶδά που γε-
γενημένας. εἶτ᾽ ἐν μὲν τοῖς ἐλάττοσι κοῦφος οὗτος
ὁ φόβος, ὑπὲρ δὲ τῶν μειζόνων ἀφόρητος; καὶ τίνα
ἂν ἔχοι λόγον;

10. Χωρὶς δὲ τούτων, ὅταν ταῦτα λέγητε, κακίαν
ἀρχόντων λέγετε. τετυχήκαμεν δέ, ὡς ἅπαντες
ἴσασι, καὶ βελτίστων χαιρόντων τῇ τῶν πολιτευομένων ὑπὲρ τῆς βουλῆς προθυμίᾳ. οἳ οὐκ ἔμελλον
δήπου χαλεπῶς ὑμῖν ἕξειν τῇ κρηπῖδι τῶν πραγμάτων βοηθεῖν προαιρουμένοις. ἀλλ᾽ ὑμεῖς οὐκ ἐν

_____

[1] λέγετε Cobet. | ἀκούετε Cobet (B).

_____

[a] *Alimenta* were provided by the *curia* (*Or.* 11. 134).
Those in Antioch were temporarily withdrawn after the Riots
of the Statues, to be restored with the emperor's pardon.
They were subsidized—and evidently could be embezzled.

[b] The only mention of an *eirenophylax* in Antioch. At
Elusa the position was coveted by decurions, and was
therefore probably profitable; *cf. Ep.* 53, 101-102. The
position was abolished in A.D. 409, *C. Th.* 12. 14. 1.

[c] Not surprisingly, since the floggings were becoming increasingly reserved for the lesser decurions.

[d] An odd statement in an oration of A.D. 388/9, con-

you saw your mother being assaulted, would you
stand there without raising a finger to defend her,
just to curry favour with her assailant? In that
case, you would soon have recognized that, in seeking
to avoid the lesser danger that originates from men,
you are laying yourself open to the more serious one
from the gods. 9. And you have often shown that
you have no fear of that, even in matters more
ephemeral than this. For you to get one horse or a
jockey instead of another, for a bigger sum to be
given for old-age relief,[a] for the constables' pay to
stay in the hands of the justices of the peace,[b] every
possible argument, every possible allegation is
bandied about. And it is of little consequence, even
if a councillor has to be demoted, or go to jail and
stay there. There are times, I know, when floggings
have taken place, too. This fear causes you no qualms
in minor issues [c] : is it intolerable, then, in the case
of matters of more importance? What justification
could there be for that?

10. Moreover, in such statements, you are stating
that the governors are at fault. But, as everyone
knows, we have been fortunate in having excellent
governors who welcome the councillors' enthusiastic support for the council.[d] They certainly would
not be likely to be annoyed with your resolve to
support the very basis of society. But, between

sidering his denunciations of Lucianus, Eustathius and
Eutropius (*Or.* 56, 54, 4), as Liebeschuetz (p. 273) implies.
However, as Liebeschuetz himself points out (pp. 184 f.),
the governor rarely takes the initiative in curial recruitment :
this lies with the *principales*, the object of criticism here.
The governors, who at least act when they receive recommendations from the *curia*, are therefore to be commended,
in comparison with these back-sliders.

ὁμοίοις ἄρχουσιν ὑμῖν αὐτοῖς ὅμοιοι, ῥάθυμοι. καὶ
προσγελᾶτε δὴ τοῖς τῆς ἀδείας ταύτης ἀπολαύ-
ουσιν αὐτὸς ἕκαστος βουλόμενος ταύτης ἀπολε-
λαυκέναι δοκεῖν. 11. πρώην τις ἐνεχθεὶς χορηγὸς
ἐγγυητὴν καταστήσας ἀπέδρα. πῶς οὖν ὑμεῖς;
τὸν μὲν ἐγγυητὴν ἀδικοῦντα οὐδέν, ἐξηπάτητο γάρ,
καθείρξαντες εἴχετε, καὶ ὁ θυμὸς πολὺς καὶ αἱ
ἀπειλαὶ δειναὶ καὶ διασπώμεθα τὸν ἄνθρωπον ἦσαν
οἱ λέγοντες, μικρὸν δὲ ὕστερον τὸν ἐξεγγυηθέντα
ἠκούομεν ἀρχὴν πριάμενον τῆς πατρῴας οἰκίας
ἀγρὸν αὐτῇ προστεθεικότα συλλέγειν τὴν τιμὴν
τοῖς ἐπὶ τῆς ἀρχῆς | κακοῖς. 12. τί οὖν οἱ πάντα F 4
R ii. 532 σείοντες ὑμεῖς καὶ θανάτου τὸν | ἐγγυητὴν ἄξιον
εἶναι κρίνοντες; εἰρήνην ἤγετε πρὸς τὸν ἠδικηκότα
καὶ διαπηδήσαντα τοσοῦτον ἀπὸ τῆς βουλῆς ἐπὶ τὸν
θρόνον; καὶ οὔτε βασιλεὺς τούτων ἤκουσεν οὐδὲν
οὔτε ὕπαρχος οὔτε ἄλλος ἀρχόντων οὐδὲ εἷς, ἀλλ᾽
ὡς ἂν ὧν μάλιστ᾽ ἂν εὔξασθε συμβεβηκότων οὕτω
διετέθητε. ἤδη δέ τις αὐτὸν καὶ νοῦν ἔχειν ἔφησε.
13. καὶ πρότερόν γε τούτου δρασμὸς ἕτερος διὰ
θαλάττης, πρᾶγμα καινότατον. ἐκ Σελευκείας ἀν-
ήγετό τις ἐπιστησόμενος Ἴωσιν, οὐκ ἀπορῶν, οἶμαι,
ζεύγους, ἀλλ᾽ ἐδεδίει τὴν γῆν. καὶ οὗτος τοίνυν
δεινὰ ποιεῖν τότε δόξας καὶ τὴν βουλὴν ἀδικεῖν
ἐπανῆκε φίλος οὐδὲν τῶν παρ᾽ ὑμῶν φοβηθείς, οὐδὲ

---

[a] On this passage *cf.* Petit, pp. 59 f. Since the duty is
allocated by the council and the guarantee given to the
council, the procedure is outside the governor's sphere until
he receives formal complaint.

[b] τὴν γῆν has a double meaning : (i) by this desertion he
had betrayed his country ; (ii) he could more easily have
been stopped on an overland journey and restored to his

430

you and the governors, it is not a case of birds of a
feather : you are just like yourselves, idle. You poke
fun at those who enjoy this security, but every one
of you wants to be thought to have enjoyed it.
11. Just recently someone was appointed to manage
the shows, found a guarantor, and decamped. And
what did you do ? You had the guarantor arrested,
though he had done no wrong, for he had been let
down, and you had him kept in prison. Tempers
ran high ; threats were bandied about, and there
were calls to tear him apart. But a little while later
we were told that the bail-jumper had purchased an
office at the cost of his family home, with the estate
thrown in, and was recovering the price by his misconduct as governor.[a] 12. And what did you do—
you, who were moving heaven and earth against the
guarantor and saying that he deserved to be executed? You made peace with the rascal who had taken
such a jump from the city council to the magistrate's chair ! Neither the emperor, nor the prefect,
nor any other magistrate heard a single word about
it. You behaved as though things had turned out
exactly to your liking, and it was even said that
he was a sensible fellow. 13. And even before
this, there was another instance of desertion—by
sea, that time—quite a novelty. The fellow set sail
from Seleuceia to go as governor to Ionia,—not
that he had no carriage, I think, but he was afraid
of the land.[b] Well, he at the time was held to be a
rascal and guilty of misconduct towards the council,
but he came back your friend and had no worries

curial duties before he reached the protection of this governor-
ship. Having thus become an *honoratus*, he could throw his
weight about in the council chamber.

γὰρ ἦν οὐδέν. ἀλλ᾽ ἐπὶ μὲν τῶν ἐργαστηρίων ὁ δρασμὸς ἤκουε κακῶς, δι᾽ ὧν δ᾽ ἄν τις ἐγένετο καὶ δίκη, παρεωρῶντο. ὁ δὲ μάλα σεμνὸς εἰς τὸ συνέδριον εἰσῄει.

14. Τοιαῦτα τὰ παρ᾽ ὑμῶν εἰς τὴν βουλὴν μιμουμένων τὰ τῶν ἀστυγειτόνων. καὶ γὰρ Ἀπαμέων οἱ βουλεύοντες πολλὰ τοιαῦτά εἰσι κεχαρισμένοι, βέλτιον γὰρ οὕτως εἰπεῖν ἢ πεπρακότες. οἳ τὸν μὲν Δία φασὶν αἰδεῖσθαι καὶ προσέτι γε καὶ δεδιέναι πάντα ἐγγύθεν ὁρῶντα, τὴν δὲ τοῦ θεοῦ πόλιν οὐκ αἰσχύνονται ποιοῦντες ἐλάττονα. ἔχω δέ τι τοιοῦτον καὶ περὶ τῶν ἐν Κύπρῳ βουλευόντων εἰπεῖν. καὶ γὰρ οὗτοι πανοῦρ|γον ἄνθρωπον καὶ F 4 δολερὸν καὶ ἀλώπεκα δι᾽ ἀτελείας ἀδίκου Μίδαν ἀπ R ii. 533 έφηναν | αὐτοῖς τοῖς παρὰ τῶν αὐτὸν ἀτελῆ πεποιηκότων τόκοις εἰς περιουσίαν ἐπιδόντα. ἐγὼ δὲ ἠξίουν ὑμᾶς ὄντας Ἀντιοχεῖς ἡγεμόνας εἶναι τοῦ προσήκοντος τοῖς περιοίκοις μᾶλλον ἢ κείνοις ἀκολουθεῖν καὶ ταῦτα ἐν τηλικούτοις.

15. Καὶ μὴν κἀκεῖνό γε ἀκούω πολλάκις ἐνταυθοῖ λεγόμενον ὡς εἴη νόμος βασιλέως ἐνδοξοτάτου πάντας ὧν οἱ πάπποι βουλευταί, δεῖν ἐν τῇ βουλῇ τετάχθαι, κἂν ὦσι θυγατριδοῖ. καὶ ὄμνυτέ γε τοῦτον εἶναι τὸν νόμον καὶ παρ᾽ ὅτῳ κέοιτο προστίθετε, καὶ οὐκ ἀπιστῶ. διὰ τί οὖν μὴ ἧκεν εἰς μέσον; διὰ τί μὴ δέδεικται; διὰ τί μὴ ἀνέγνωσται;

<hr/>

^a For the factories as centres of social gossip cf. Or. 8. 4, 31. 25.
^b For Zeus Olympios in Apamea, and an Olympic festival there, cf. Ep. 663, 668 of A.D. 361. The passage may be adduced in support of Liebeschuetz's dating, since the temple of Zeus, destroyed by Deinias and the monks, is
432

about any reactions from you—for there were none. For all that his desertion was ill spoken of in the factories,[a] the people who might have secured some redress turned a blind eye to it. And he used to strut into the council chamber, as large as life.

14. Such is your attitude towards the council, in this following the lead of our neighbours. For the councillors at Apamea have granted—that is a nicer way of putting it than saying " sold "—many such favours. They claim to reverence Zeus,—indeed, to fear him, since he beholds everything from near by—but they have no shame in diminishing the god's city.[b] I can cite something similar in the case of the councillors in Cyprus, too. They, by an illegal grant of immunity, made a rascally, treacherous, foxy fellow into a millionaire : he came to affluence by the very interest he squeezed out of those who granted him his immunity.[c] I expected you, as Antiochenes, to set an example of duty to our neighbours rather than to follow their lead, especially in important matters like this.

15. What is more, I often hear the statement made here that there is a law of a most renowned emperor,[d] that all those whose grandparents were councillors must take up their position in the council, even if they are in the female line of descent. You take your oath that this law exists, and you go on to say in whose bureau it lies, and I don't disbelieve you. But why has it not been published ? Why not dis-

apparently still in existence (cf. Or. 30, Introduction, p. 97).

[c] For similar condemnation of usury cf. Or. 62. 68 ff.

[d] Julian (C. Th. 12. 1. 51 ; cf. E.L.F. No. 99). Foerster, however, identified the emperor with Theodosius himself.

διὰ τί μὴ τὸ βουλευτήριον σωμάτων ἐνέπλησεν;
εἰ γὰρ ἔστι μὲν ὁ νόμος, εἰσὶ δὲ ὑμῖν γλῶτται, ἔστι
δὲ ὦτα τοῖς ἄρχουσι, τί τὸ κωλῦον τὴν βουλὴν τὰ
αὑτῆς κομίσασθαι; ὅτι, φαίην ἄν, ἡ πενία τῆς βουλῆς τοὺς μὲν ὑμῶν οὐ λυπεῖ, τοὺς δὲ τέρπει, τοῖς
δὲ καὶ λυσιτελεῖ. 16. διὰ τοῦτο νέοι πολλοὶ τήνδε
ἀφέντες παρ' ἄλλοις λειτουργοῦσιν, εἶτα ἀναστρέ-
φουσι τὴν ἀσφάλειαν τὴν περὶ ταῦτα παρὰ τῆς |
μικρᾶς ἐκείνης δαπάνης ἔχοντες, μόνον οὐκ ἐπὶ F
τῶν κεφαλῶν τὸ συνέδριον φέροντες, δεσπόται τῶν
R ii. 534 ὑμετέρων υἱέων οὐδενὶ μὲν δικαίῳ, | πῶς γὰρ τῶν
τὰ δίκαια πεποιηκότων οἱ ἠδικηκότες καὶ τῶν μεγάλα ἀνηλωκότων οἱ μικρά; δεσπόται δ' οὖν[1] διὰ
τὰ κακῶς δοκοῦντα καὶ νενικηκότα κἂν τοῖς δικαστηρίοις ἑστηκότας αὐτοὶ καθήμενοι τοὺς ὑμετέρους ὁρῶσι. τούτων τοίνυν οὐδὲν ἂν ἦν εἴ τις ὑμῶν
ἤθελε χρῆσθαι τῷ νόμῳ, νῦν δ' ὁ μὲν νόμος κεῖται,
οἱ δὲ τρυφῶσιν.

17. Ὑμεῖς δὲ ἔσεσθαί τινά φατε χρόνον ἀποδι-
δόντα ταῖς βουλαῖς τὰ ὀφειλόμενα. καὶ τί τοῦτ'[2]
ἀναμένειν ἔδει παρὸν ἔχειν; καίτοι τινὲς ἀπολο-
γοῦνται τῆς Ἰουλιανοῦ μεμνημένοι βασιλείας ἐν
ᾗ τινας εἰς βουλὴν ἐνέγραφον. καὶ οὐκ ἠλεγχόμεθα,
φασίν, ἐπὶ τῆς ἐξουσίας ἀργοί. ἐγὼ δὲ ὅτι μὲν καὶ
R ii. 535 τότε ἐκράτουν αἱ | ἄδικοι χάριτες καὶ διεκλάπησαν
οὐκ ὀλίγοι τῶν δικαίως ἂν ἐγγραφέντων, ἐάσω.

[1] δ' οὖν Re., F. (P.) : δοῦναι Bong. (other mss.).
[2] τοῦτ' F. (mss. except IM) : τοῦτο Bong. (IM) : τοῦτον Re.

---

[a] Cf. Plato, Resp. 600 D ; Themist. Or. 21. 254 a.
[b] The honorati and the principales (C. Th. 12. 1. 109 of
A.D. 385) had the privilege of attending the governor's court
hearings as παρακαθήμενοι. The ordinary decurions stood
in attendance.

played ? Why not read aloud ? Why has it not filled the city hall with members ? For if the law exists, and you have tongues and the governors have ears, what is stopping the council from claiming its own ? Simply this, I suggest,—that the poverty of the council either does not distress, or it pleases or it even profits some of you. 16. Hence many young men turn their backs on our council and perform their civic duties elsewhere, and then they return with an immunity from such obligations gained at that small expense. They practically rule the roost over the council chamber,[a] and lord it over your children, quite improperly—for how could defaulters and penny-pinchers properly do so with the generous contributors who have done their duty ? But lord it they do, none the less, because of your perverse decisions that have won the day, and in the courts they sit on the bench and see your sons standing there.[b] None of this would occur if any of you were willing to apply the law. As it is the law lies dormant, and they live in the lap of luxury.

17. You say that a time will come when the councils will regain all they should have. But what is the point of waiting for it, when you can have it ? Yet some people recall the reign of Julian when they set about enrolling new members,[c] and they defend themselves by saying, " We were not found idle in the exercise of our powers." Leaving aside the fact that even then illicit influence was rife and many who should properly have been enrolled wriggled out

[c] *Cf. Or.* 18. 146 ff. for the programme ; for the evasions *cf.* Julian, *Misop.* 367 c ff.

ἀλλ' ἐκεῖνό γε τίς οὐκ οἶδεν ὡς οὐδ' εἰ σφόδρα
τινὲς ἐβούλοντο μηδένα ἐγγράφειν, ἐξῆν ἄν. εἰ γὰρ
ὁ μὲν ὡς μεγάλα εὐεργετῶν τοῦτο ἐδίδου, δέχεσθαι δὲ οὐδεὶς ἠξίου, πονηρόν τ' ἂν ἦν καὶ δίκης
ἄξιον, καὶ σαφὴς ἡ προδοσία καὶ κεκολάσθαι χρῆν.
18. μὴ οὖν ἃ τοῦ τῆς | τιμωρίας ἦν φόβου, ταῦτ' F
εἰς τὴν γνώμην ἀνάφερε. τίς γὰρ ἂν ἤνεγκε τὸν
ἐκείνου θυμὸν ἔχοντα τὸ δίκαιον, εἰ ὃ τῆς ἀρετῆς
τῆς Ἰουλιανοῦ κεφάλαιον ἦν ὀρθωθῆναι τὰς βουλάς,
τοῦτό τις ἐνεπόδιζε καὶ κωλυτὴν αὐτὸν ἐποίει τοῦ
μεγίστου πράγματος καὶ ἐφ' ὅτῳ μάλιστα αὐτῷ
φιλοτιμεῖσθαι παρῆν; μὴ οὖν μοι τὴν ἀνάγκην
ἀντὶ τῆς προαιρέσεως λέγε, ἀλλ' εἰ μὴ νῦν, ἡνίκα
ἀδεὲς τὸ ῥαθυμεῖν, τοῦτο ποιεῖται.

19. Καὶ τί τὸ κέρδος, φήσει τις, ἂν ὁ μὲν βασι-
R ii. 536 λεὺς ἐπινεύσῃ, τὸ δὲ ἀντικροῦον | γένηται καὶ
τούτῳ[1] τὸ δόγμα λυθείη; οἶδα ὅθεν ὁ λόγος οὗτος.
τὸν Ἀπρώνιον ἐννοεῖτε τὸν ἀπὸ τῆς Χαλκηδόνος
μέχρι τῶν πρὸς Κιλικίαν ὅρων ἄρχοντα καὶ ὡς
ἠλέησε τὰς βουλὰς καὶ ὡς ἐμήνυσε βασιλεῖ τὴν
περὶ αὐτὰς τύχην καὶ ὡς ᾔτησεν ἴασιν καὶ ὡς εἰπὼν
ἔπεισε καὶ ὡς ἐγένετό τι τὸ μεταπεῖθον. 20. ἀλλὰ
πρῶτον μὲν ἀμφοτέροις κόσμος οὐ μικρός, ταῖς τε
βουλαῖς τῷ τε Ἀπρωνίῳ, τὸ τὰς μὲν μὴ σιωπῆσαι,
τὸν δὲ συναλγῆσαι. ἔπειτα χρὴ νομίζειν τινὰς τῶν
φυγὴν[2] βουλευόντων μεμενηκέναι γνόντας ὡς οὐ

---

[1] τούτῳ conj. Re., F. : τοῦτο Re. text (mss.).
[2] φυγὴν Cobet, F.: φυγεῖν Re. (mss.): φυγεῖν βουλευσαμένων
conj. Re.

---

[a] Cf. PLRE 89. Apronius was vicar of the diocese of
Pontica (cf. § 21). The emperor in question, in the absence

of it, it is common knowledge that, however much people may have wanted to make no new enrolment, such a course was impossible. For if the emperor had made this offer as a great concession, and people refused to accept it, it would have been a criminal act deserving of punishment, and barefaced treason was bound to be penalized. 18. So don't claim what was due to the fear of punishment as an example of your own attitude. Who could have endured the emperor's justifiable wrath if he tried to block the most fundamental item of Julian's legislation, the reform of the councils, or attempted to prevent his finest achievement, for which he could claim the utmost credit? So don't mention compulsion to me instead of intention. The present situation apart, idleness is your practice whenever you can get away with it.

19. " But what is the good," I will be asked, " if the emperor gives his consent and something occurs to hinder it ? ", thus rendering his decree ineffective. I know the origin of this argument. You have in mind Apronius, who governed from Chalcedon to the Cilician frontier,[a] and how he took pity on the councils, informed the emperor of their critical situation and asked for some relief : he convinced him by his arguments but something occurred to cause a change of policy. 20. But, in the first place, considerable credit should be given both to the councils and to Apronius, in that they refused to hold their peace and he shared their concern. Secondly, it is to be believed that some of those who were planning their escape finally stayed when they

of any of the customary laudations of Theodosius, is presumably Valens.

παντάπασιν ἠμέληνται παρὰ τῷ κρατοῦντι τῶν
πόλεων αἱ βουλαί. | εἰ δὲ καὶ μὴ τοῦτο, ἀλλὰ πε- F
φύλακταί γε τῇ σπουδῇ τῇ περὶ ταῦτα ταῖς βουλαῖς τὰ πρὸς αὐτὰς δίκαια, γράμμαθ᾽ ἃ ἧκεν εἰς τὸ
βασίλειον ἀπὸ τῶν ἐκείνων λόγων ζητοῦντα ἐπι-
κουρίαν. 21. εἰσὶ δὲ οἳ λέγουσιν αὐτὸν ἐφ᾽ ὃ μὲν
εὐθὺς ἧκεν ἐᾶσαι, βουλεύεσθαι δὲ τοῖς Βαλεντι-
R ii. 537 νιανῷ | δόξασιν ἀμῦναι ταῖς βουλαῖς. ὃ οὐκ ἂν
ἔτ᾽ ἦν ἐν μετεώρῳ τῶν ἁπανταχοῦ βουλῶν τὰ τινῶν
μιμησαμένων. εἰ γὰρ ἄλλα ἐπ᾽ ἄλλοις ἀφικνεῖτο
γράμματα ταυτὰ[1] δεόμενα καὶ πόλεως ἑκάστης
ἑώρα τὴν ῥίζαν κεκακωμένην καὶ γῆ τε καὶ θά-
λασσα ταυτὰ[2] ὠδύρετο, πᾶν τὸ μαχόμενον ἡττᾶτο
ἂν τοῦ πλήθους τῶν ἱκετευόντων. νῦν δὲ τοῖς οὐ
δεηθεῖσι τὰ τῶν δεηθέντων βέβλαπται. ὥστ᾽ εἰκὸς
ἂν καὶ ἡμῖν ἐγκαλοῖεν οἱ περὶ τὸν Πόντον ὡς παρ᾽
ὑμᾶς[3] ὧν ἔχρῃζον ἀτυχήσαντες, καὶ μᾶλλόν γε
ἡμῖν ἢ ἄλλοις, ὅσῳπερ ἐν μείζονι τάξει τὸ τῆς
Ἀντιοχείας ὄνομα.

22. Πρὸς τοίνυν τούτοις κἀκεῖνο ἄν τις ὑμῖν[4]
ἐπιτιμήσειεν, ὅτι πλέοντας καθ᾽ ἕκαστον ἔαρ ὁρῶντες τῶν ἔτι βουλευόντων ἢ βεβουλευκότων γε παῖδας τοὺς μὲν εἰς Βηρυτόν, τοὺς δὲ εἰς Ῥώμην οὔτε
ἄχθεσθε οὔτε | ἀγανακτεῖτε οὐδ᾽ ὡς τοὺς ἄρχοντας F
εἰσιόντες φθέγγεσθε τὰ εἰκότα. καίτοι τίς οὕτω
βραδὺς τὴν γνώμην ἢ λίαν παῖς ἢ Κρόνος ὡς μὴ

---

[1] ταυτὰ Re., F. : ταῦτα Bong. (mss.).
[2] ταυτὰ Re., F. : ταῦτα Bong. (mss.).
[3] ὑμᾶς Bong. (mss.) : ἡμᾶς Re., F.
[4] ὑμῖν F. (mss.) : ὑμῶν Bong., Re.

---

[a] For the study of law and Latin ; cf. Or. 39. 17, 19 ;
40. 5 ff. The burden of Libanius᾽ complaints against such

realized that the city councils had not been entirely ignored by their emperor. And, even if this possibility is discounted, the councils, in consequence of the enthusiastic support the matter received, yet have had preserved for them a statement of their claims, in the shape of despatches requesting assistance, submitted to Court following their arguments. 21. One suggestion is that he gave up his original idea and intended to aid the councils by means of Valentinian's decrees, but the business would not still be hanging fire if the councils generally had followed the line taken by some of them. If despatch after despatch arrived, all with the same plea, and if the emperor had seen the root of every city damaged, and if land and sea alike had raised the same lament, all opposition would have been crushed by the mass of the suppliants. As it is, those who complain have been let down by those who do not, and so the inhabitants of Pontus could justifiably reproach us also, for failing to receive from you here the support they required, and they could reproach us more than anyone else, since the name of Antioch is the more exalted.

22. And, moreover, you are open to reproof on the following grounds. Every spring you see the sons of present, or past, members of the council sailing off to Berytus or to Rome,[a] and you are not angry or annoyed, nor do you seek audience with the governors and complain as you should. But who is so dull-witted, such a booby or simpleton[b] as to be incap-

competitive studies is not simply educational, but, as here, a combination of educational and political grievances.

[b] Proverbially the reign of Cronos was the golden age of primitive simplicity (cf. Hesiod, Op. 108 ff.), the Saturnia

δύνασθαι μαθεῖν ὅ τι βούλεται τούτοις τὸ πλεῖν;
οὔτε γὰρ ὑπὲρ δικαιοσύνης καὶ τοῦ μὴ λαθεῖν τι
δράσαντες παρὰ τοὺς νόμους εἰς Φοινίκην πλέουσιν
οὔτε εἰς τὴν ἑτέραν, ἵν' ἀφ' ἑκατέρας φωνῆς ἔχοιεν
R ii. 538 τὴν βουλὴν | ὠφελεῖν, ἀλλ' ἵνα ἀφορμὴν εἰς τὸ τὴν
βουλὴν ἐκδῦναι τοὺς νόμους μὲν ἔχοιεν οὗτοι, τὴν
γλῶτταν δὲ ἐκεῖνοι. καὶ οὐκ ἐψεύσθησάν γε ἐλπίδος. ἀλλ' ἴσμεν οὗ δικαίως ἂν ὄντες οὗ καθεστᾶσι[1] νῦν. 23. ἔδει τοίνυν ὑμᾶς, εἰδότας ὡς ἐπὶ
τῇ βουλῇ ταῦτα, βοηθεῖν. καὶ τίς ἂν ἦν λόγος
εὐπρεπὴς τοῖς ἐναντιουμένοις πρὸς τοὺς ἔχοντας
εἰπεῖν· τί μοι νομοθετεῖς, ἄνθρωπε, περὶ παιδείας;
πολλαὶ γὰρ ὁδοὶ ταύτης, καὶ πορεύσομαί γε τούτων
ἣν ἂν ἐθέλω; σοὶ δ' ἐξῆν ἀντειπεῖν ὅτι ὁ ταύτας
ἐρχόμενος τὰς ὁδοὺς μονονουχὶ βοᾷ δρασμὸν αὐτὰς
ἀπὸ τῆς βουλῆς εἶναι. τῷ γὰρ ἐν ταυταισὶ ταῖς
πόλεσι πολιτευομένῳ μάταιον ἐκείνοιν ἑκάτερον ἢ
εἰ μὴ τοῦτο, σμικρόν. ἔδειξαν δὲ οἱ σφόδρα εὐ-
δοκιμήσαντες ἀπ' οὐδετέρου τούτοιν εἰς ὄνομα ἐλ-
F 440 θόντες. | ἀλλ' ἀπὸ τίνων; ἐκείνων[2] ἃ νῦν | ὕβρισταί R
τε καὶ προπεπηλάκισται οὐ χείρω γενόμενα τὴν
φύσιν, πῶς γὰρ ἄν; ἀλλὰ διὰ τοὺς σεμνοὺς τουτουσὶ τοὺς οὐκ ἀξιοῦντας εἰδέναι τὰς ἑαυτῶν.
ὅστις οὖν ἐπὶ τοὺς νόμους ἐπείγεται, ταὐτὰ[3] δ' ἂν

---

[1] καθεστᾶσι Re., F. : καθιστᾶσι Bong. (MSS.).
[2] ἀπὸ τίνων ; ἐκείνων Re., F. : ἀπὸ τινων ἐκείνων Bong.
(MSS.).   [3] ταὐτὰ Re., F. : ταῦτα Bong. (MSS.).

---

regna of Virgil. Simplicity, however, is soon equated with

able of understanding what their trip implies for
them ? It is out of no concern for justice or to avoid
any inadvertent breach of the laws that they set sail
for Phoenicia, nor do they sail to the other place so
as to assist the council by their proficiency in both
languages ; their concern is to have their legal or
linguistic qualifications as a means of getting out of
membership of council. Nor have they been deceived
in their ambition. We know what their status
should rightly be and what it now is. 23. So you,
aware that this is detrimental to the council, should
have rendered assistance. It may be said, " And
what reasonable argument has the opposition to the
proponents of arguments like this ? ' Why, Sir, are
you laying down the law to me about my education ?
There are many ways of approaching it, and I shall
take whichever one I like.' " You could have countered with the argument that the one who proceeds
by such ways practically shouts it aloud that they
are methods of evasion from the council. For a
councillor in these cities either of these courses is
useless or, if not that, unimportant. This is proved
by their most notable citizens who have employed
neither of these methods to achieve renown. Well,
what methods did they employ ? Those that are
now held up to scorn and insult, not because there
has been any actual defect in them, for that would
be impossible,[a] but because of these pompous snobs
who refuse to acknowledge their own home town. So
whoever embarks on the study of law, and I would

stupidity, cf. Aristoph. Clouds, 929, Wasps, 1480 (schol. ad
loc. κρόνους · ἀρχαίους, μωρούς, λήρους, ἀναισθήτους).

[a] i.e. the study of Greek rhetoric, and particularly that of
Libanius himself.

εἴποιμι καὶ περὶ τῶν ἑτέρων, κέκραγεν οὗτος οὐκ
αὐτῶν ἐκείνων ἐρᾶν, τῶν δὲ ἐξ αὐτῶν φυομένων.

24. Οὐκοῦν καὶ σὲ δεῖ σκοπεῖν ὅπως ἢ ἐμφράξεις[1] τὰς ὁδοὺς ἢ πάλιν ἕξεις αὐτοὺς ἐν τῷ βουλευ-
τηρίῳ. πολλὰ δ' ἂν ἐξεύροιεν φροντίδες. τὸ δ'
οὖν προχειρότατον, ὁ πατὴρ εἰσελθὼν εἰς τὸ δικαστήριον ἢ ὁ ἐπίτροπος ἢ ὁ ἔφηβος αὐτὸς[2] ὁμο-
λογησάτω, κἂν ἐπ' ἄκρον[3] ἐκείνοιν ἀφίκηται, μήτοι
τῶν γε ὀφειλομένων ἀποστερήσεσθαι τὴν πόλιν.
τί τοιοῦτον δεδράκατε, μᾶλλον δὲ ἐμελλήσατε;
25. τῶν ἐν Φοινίκῃ τινὰ βουλὴν ᾄδουσιν ἀπὸ
Ῥώμης ἐξ αὐτῶν τῶν τοῦ σοφιστοῦ χειρῶν ἀφελ-
κύσασαν νεανίσκους ἐν λειτουργοῦσιν ἔχειν ὥστε
ἐκείνοις μεταμέλειν τοῦ τε πλοῦ καὶ τῶν περὶ τὸν
Θύμβριν ἀνηλωμένων. τοῦτο πολλαῖς ἂν ὑπῆρξε
πόλεσιν ἐφ' ὅσας ἡ τοῦ ταῦτα συμπράξαντος ἄρ-
R ii. 540 χοντος ἐγίγνετο | πρόνοια. ἀλλ' οὐκ ἐβουλή|θη- F
σαν, ὥσπερ οὖν οὐδὲ ὑμεῖς. αἰδεῖσθε γὰρ τοὺς λόγους.
τὴν πόλιν δὲ οὔ; τὴν βουλὴν δὲ οὔ; τὴν γῆν δὲ ἢ
τικτομένους ἐδέξατο, τὸ βουλευτήριον δὲ τουτὶ τὸ
δι' ὑμᾶς ἄθλιον οὐκ αἰδεῖσθε, ἐν ᾧ ποτε τὰς λειτουργίας ἥρπαζον οἱ ἑξακόσιοι;

26. Νόμοι γὰρ ὑπὲρ τῶν συνηγόρων κεῖνται, κἂν
ἐπ' αὐτοὺς ἔλθῃ τις, γέλως πολύς. ὑμεῖς δὲ κειμένους μὲν μὴ παραβαίνετε, διδάσκετε δὲ τοὺς λῦσαι κυρίους ὡς ἀμείνους αὐτοῖς ἐστι νόμους ἀντὶ

---

[1] ἐμφράξεις conj. Re., Cobet, F. (PB) : ἐμφράξῃς Bong.,
Re. text (other mss.).
[2] αὐτὸς conj. Re., F. : οὗτος Bong., Re. text (mss.).
[3] ἄκρον Re., F. : ἄκρων Bong. (mss.).

---

[a] Cf. § 3 above.

say the same for the others too, proclaims that he is not enamoured of the study itself but of the results that it produces.

24. So you too must consider means either of barring the ways or of reclaiming these persons for the council chamber. Consideration could devise plenty of methods. The handiest, anyway, is for the father, or guardian, or the lad himself to enter the court and guarantee that, even if he reaches the top in both those professions, he will not deprive the city of what is due to it. What such course have you taken, or even thought of taking? 25. They tell the tale of a council in Phoenicia which fetched back youngsters from Rome, snatching them from their teacher's very hands and holding them for the performance of their duties so that they rued their sailing and the money spent by Tiber's side. It would have been open to many cities to do this—to all that enjoyed the consideration and support of a governor in this action. But they refused, just as you do, too. You, of course, have a high regard for education. But none for your city? none for its council? none for the land that welcomed you upon your appearance in the world, or for this city hall which, because of you, has been brought so low, where once upon a time its 600 members [a] used to snatch at the chance to perform duties of state?

26. "Ah!" you say, "but there are laws to protect lawyers.[b] If you tackle any of them, you make a fool of yourself." Then don't break existing laws: just demonstrate to those who have the power to repeal them that they must enact better laws instead

[b] On advocacy as a means of curial evasion cf. Liebeschuetz, pp. 242 ff., and on § 7 above.

LIBANIUS

τούτων θετέον, οἳ βουλήσονται μᾶλλον αὐξηθῆναι πόλεις ἢ τοὺς ἐνίων οἴκους. πολλοὶ δὲ ἤδη νόμοι περὶ τοῦδε τοῦ ἔθνους καὶ ἐτέθησαν καὶ λέλυνται, καὶ δεινὸν οὐδὲν τῶν ὑπὲρ τῶν πόλεων τεθέντων ἀναιρεθέντων τοὺς κατ᾽ ἐκείνων ταὐτὸ παθεῖν. |

27. Ὁ δ᾽ ἀνὴρ ἐρᾷ τε[1] ἡμῶν καὶ τῷ μήπω δεῦρ᾽ ἥκειν ἐζημιῶσθαί φησιν. ἐθελήσει τοίνυν κοσμῆσαι τὴν ἡμετέραν νόμον τιθεὶς σωτῆρα μὲν τῶν βουλῶν, τὸ σπέρμα δὲ παρ᾽ ἡμῶν εἰληφότα. πεμπέσθω τοίνυν πρεσβεία. πάντως δὲ ἐν τοῖς ὀλίγοις ὑμῖν εἰσί τινες τῇ διακονίᾳ πρέποντες. ἀλλ᾽ οὔτε αἱρήσεσθε πρέσβεις οὔτε ἀποστελεῖτε. περιέσται γὰρ τῶν βουλομένων, ἂν ἄρα τινὲς βουληθῶσι, τὸ νοσοῦν. |

28. Ἥκω δὲ ἐπ᾽ αὐτὸν ἤδη τὸν κολοφῶνα τῶν κα- F κῶν. οἱ γὰρ διὰ τὴν γενομένην αὐτοῖς ἐπὶ τὰ βελτίω μεταβολὴν τοὔδαφός τε τῆς πόλεως προσκυνεῖν ὄντες δίκαιοι καὶ πανταχόθεν μείζω τὰ ταύτης ποιεῖν καὶ τὰ μὲν ὄντα μικρὰ διατηρεῖν, πειρᾶσθαι δὲ τὰ ἀπόντα προσκτᾶσθαι καὶ μηδὲ τοῦ Ἐρεχθέως

---

[1] ἐρᾷ τε conj. F., assuming preceding lacuna : αἴρεται MSS., edd. : ἱμείρεται Sievers.

---

[a] A corrupt and disputed passage. The dating of the speech to A.D. 384 relies heavily upon it and the identification of this man. Reiske identified him with Arcadius, Foerster with Theodosius, Sievers and Liebeschuetz with Cynegius (ppO A.D. 384–388). Neither the existence of a lacuna (assumed by Foerster himself) nor the specific reference to the emperor, which Liebeschuetz, objecting to the expression ὁ ἀνήρ, asserts is necessary for Foerster's interpretation, is essential. The whole of § 26 deals implicitly

of these, intended for the increase of the communities rather than that of individual households. There have been plenty of laws about this province made and repealed before now, and if laws that have been passed for the good of the cities have been repealed, there is nothing wrong in those, that are not, suffering the same fate.

27. " But the man is fond of us [a] : he says that it is a blow to him that he has not yet visited us. He will be ready to show his respect for our city by passing a law to protect the city councils, the inspiration for which comes from us." Then send an embassy. Surely in your small number there are some fit to undertake the service. But you will neither choose nor send envoys, for any volunteers, if there really be any, will find their ailments too much for them.

28. And now I come to the worst trouble of all. Those persons who, because of the improvement in their circumstances, should properly worship the very soil of the city and do their very utmost to increase her fortunes, maintain the little that she has, and try to get for her what she has not, and who ought to do no less than Erechtheus in a similar

with the legislator, the emperor. Moreover, even Julian is referred to as ὁ ἄνθρωπος (Or. 16. 18); and the phrase ὁ ἀνήρ is paralleled, with specific reference to Theodosius, in Or. 1. 220 : (Richomer) λέγεται ... ποιῆσαι ἐρῶντά μου τὸν ἄνδρα μᾶλλον ἐρᾶν φάναι τε καὶ τῆς δεῦρο ἐπιθυμεῖν ὁδοῦ ἐμοῦ χάριν. This desire of Theodosius to visit Antioch had been canvassed in the intervening period, and especially in A.D. 387, cf. Or. 20. 44 f., Jo. Chrys. Hom. de Stat. 21 (P.G. xlix. 214). Similarly the reluctance of the *principales* to act as envoys had been well illustrated since then, as Libanius knew to his cost in the case of Thrasydaeus, Or. 32. 2 ff. This passage cannot, therefore, bear the weight of the interpretation placed upon it.

ἐν ὁμοίοις λείπεσθαι καιροῖς αὐτοὶ σύμβουλοι βουλευταῖς γεγένηνται πέμπειν εἰς Ῥώμην τοὺς ἑαυτῶν.
R ii. 542 οἱ δὲ εἰς | τὸν λιμένα κατέβησαν εἰδότων, παρ-
αινούντων, παρακαλούντων, ἐπαινούντων, ἴσως τι
καὶ προστιθέντων ἀργύριον τῷ παρὰ τῶν γονέων.
29. εἶτ᾽ ἐρωτῶσι τοὺς ἐπαναπλέοντας τῶν ἐμπόρων
εἰ τῶν λαμπόντων εἰσίν, εἰ τῶν εὐδοκιμούντων, εἰ
φίλοι γεγόνασί σφισιν οἱ τὴν Ῥώμην ἄγοντες, εἰ
δι᾽ ἐκείνων αὐτοῖς ἀρχαὶ πλησίον. κἂν ἀκούσωσί
τι τοιοῦτον οἷον βούλοιντ᾽ ἄν, εὐθυμία ⟨καὶ⟩[1] κρό-
τος καὶ γεγόνασιν ἡδίους. κἂν ᾖ δῆλον αὐτοῖς, ὡς
οὓς ἔχουσιν ἐν τῇ βουλῇ παῖδας, ὑπ᾽ ἐκείνοις ἔσον-
R ii. 543 ται | καὶ θεραπεύσουσιν υἱεῖς πατέρων τοῖς αὐτῶν
πατράσι δεδουλευκότων, θύουσι τοῖς θεοῖς καὶ συγχαίρουσιν αὐτοῖς τε καὶ τοῖς ἀπεσταλκόσι καὶ τοῖς
ἀπεσταλμένοις καὶ λέγουσι δὴ σαφῶς ὡς ἐπαν-
ήξουσι τῇ βουλῇ φοβεροί. 30. οἷς δὲ καὶ θυγατέρες
εἰσί, συνοικίζουσι[2] μὲν αὐτὰς στρατιώταις,[3] μέμ-
φεται δὲ ὑμῶν οὐδεὶς | τοὺς γάμους, τοῖς βουλεύ-
ουσι δὲ τίκτουσι παῖδας αἱ δοῦλαι. εἶτα ἐξελήλυ-
θεν οὐσία τῆς βουλῆς δι᾽ ὑμεναίων καὶ Ῥώμης.
ὁ δὲ τοιαῦτα εἰργασμένος πατὴρ διά τε τοὺς κηδεστὰς διά τε τὰς ἐλπίδας τίμιος. ὃν ἐχρῆν ἅπασι

---

[1] ⟨καὶ⟩ F.
[2] συνοικίζουσι F. : συνοικοῦσι Bong., Re. (mss.).
[3] αὐτὰς στρατιώταις F. : αὗται στρατιώταις Bong., Re.
(AIM) : αὐταῖς στρατιῶται CMo.PB, A marg.

---

[a] *i.e.* they should be prepared to sacrifice their own
children for the sake of their country. For Erechtheus'
sacrifice of his daughter *cf.* Eurip. *Erechtheus* fragg. (Nauck[2]
464 ff.), and the story in Lycurgus, *c. Leocr.* 98 ff.

[b] *Cf. Or.* 2. 54. The offenders criticized here are pagans
(θύουσι τοῖς θεοῖς).

crisis,[a]—these are the very people who have counselled our councillors to send their sons to Rome.
The lads go down to the harbour, with their connivance, advice, encouragement and approval, and at
times with a present of money above and beyond
that from the parents. 29. Then they enquire of the
merchants who are on the voyage home whether
they have become people of importance and renown.
Are the leading men in Rome their friends ? Have
they any prospect of office with their aid ? And if
they are told something of the sort that tickles their
fancy, there is cheering and applause, and they are
as pleased as Punch. And even if it is clear to them
that their own children in the council will be under
their thumb, and will kow-tow to the children of
parents who were once their fathers' slaves, they
sacrifice to the gods,[b] congratulate themselves, the
senders and the sent, and openly declare that they
will come back somebody to be reckoned with by
the council. 30. Those who have daughters, too,
marry them off to soldiers, and none of you disap-
proves of the marriages : meanwhile slave women
bear children to our city councillors.[c] Then the
property of the council vanishes through the attrac-
tions of marriage and of Rome. And the parent who
has behaved so is respected by reason of his in-laws
and his prospects, though he deserves to be oppressed

---

[c] *Cf. Or.* 2. 36, 28. 21, 49. 2 for the unwritten rule of
curial intermarriage, and its breach. Ironically, Libanius'
aunt had become the wife of a military officer (*Or.* 47. 28),
and his own son Cimon was born of a union with a slave or
freedwoman (*cf. Or.* 1. 145, 195 ; *PLRE* 92 f. (*s.v.* Ara-
bius). For legislation regulating this practice, *C. Th.*
4. 64. 5).

φορτίοις πιέζεσθαι καὶ μηδ' ἀναπνεῖν ἐπιτρέπειν
αὐτῷ τῶν ἠδικημένων μηδένα δίκης τε εἴνεκα¹ καὶ
ὅπως εἴη τοῖς οὔπω τῇ βουλῇ λυμαινομένοις παράδειγμα.

31. Ἤδη τοίνυν τις ὑμῶν καὶ τοιοῦτόν τι πρὸς
ταῦτα εἶπεν ὡς ἀνεπίφθονον εἴ τις ὀρέγοιτο βελτίονος σχήματος. τοῦτο δέ ἐστι τὴν πολιτείαν
καθ' ἣν ζῶμεν κινούντων. εἰ γὰρ ἐν ᾧ μέν τις ὑπὸ
τοῦ νόμου τέτακται, τοῦτο καταλείψει, ζητήσει δέ
τι μεῖζον, ζητῶν δὲ οὐκ ἀδικήσει, ὁ μὲν στρατιώ-
R ii. 544 της | ἕξει τοῦ ταξιάρχου τὴν τάξιν, τὴν τοῦ στρα-
τηγοῦ δὲ ὁ ταξίαρχος. ἔσται δὲ ὁ μὲν ναύτης ἀντὶ
τοῦ κυβερνήτου, ὁ δὲ χορευτὴς ἀντὶ τοῦ διδασκάλου,
ὁ δ' οἰνοχόος τὴν κύλικα ῥίψας κατακλινεὶς πίεται
μετὰ τοῦ δεσπότου. 32. διὰ τί δὲ καὶ τοὺς τὴν
τάξιν λελοιπότας ἀποτυμπανίζουσιν οἱ στρατηγοί;
ῥᾴδιον γὰρ κἀκείνοις εἰπεῖν ὡς τὸ μὴ μάχεσθαι τοῦ
κινδυνεύειν ἄμεινον. ἴσμεν τοὺς ἐπανισταμένους
τοῖς βασιλεῦσι πολεμουμένους καὶ δοκοῦντας θά-
νατον ὀφείλειν τὴν δίκην. | τοῦ χάριν; εἴποι ἂν F
ὁ πηδήσας ἐπὶ τὴν ἀρχήν· τὸ γὰρ κρατεῖν τοῦ
κρατεῖσθαι καὶ τὸ προστάττειν τοῦ τὸ κελευόμενον
ποιεῖν αἱρετώτερον εἶναι. 33. τηροῦντα μὲν οὖν
τὴν τάξιν ἥτις ἂν ᾖ λαμπρὸν ἐπ' αὐτῆς εἶναι καὶ
καλὸν καὶ εὔδαιμον, τὸ δ' ἀφορμὴν ποιεῖσθαι λαμ-
πρότητος τὴν εἰς τοὺς νόμους ἀδικίαν ποῦ καλόν;
τὸ γὰρ δι' ἀδικίας κτηθὲν πῶς ἂν εἴη δίκαιον;
ἀνάγκη γὰρ ἐοικέναι τῇ ῥίζῃ τὸν καρπόν. ὁ δ' ἐν
μὲν τῷ μὴ βουλεύειν ἀδικῶν, ἐκ δὲ τοῦ τοῦτο φεύγειν ἐπ' ἀρχὴν ἥκων ἴστω τὸ καλὸν τοῦτο κακὸν

¹ εἴνεκα conj. Re., F. : εἶναι Bong., Re. text (mss.).
448

by every burden, and none of those whom he has wronged should allow him a moment's respite, both as punishment and as a signal warning to those who so far have not desecrated the council.

31. However, some of you before now have made some such comment on the subject, that no one can cavil at anybody who is ambitious of a better station. This is simply to undo the social order in which we live. If a man deserts the position in which he is lawfully put and seeks something higher, and does no wrong in the seeking, then the private will become the colonel, and the colonel the general. The sailor will take the helmsman's place, the dancer in the chorus that of the director, and the butler throws away his cup, settles himself at table and drinks with his master. 32. Why then do generals have deserters flogged to death ? It is easy enough for deserters to claim that it is better not to fight than to risk their lives. We know that rebels fight against the emperors and are held to deserve the death penalty.[a] " Why, pray ? " would be the question of the fellow who has leapt straight into office : for ruling is much preferable to being ruled, giving orders better than carrying them out. 33. So goodness and happiness consist in a man's maintenance of his station, whatever it may be, and gaining fame in it, but how can it be good to make misconduct towards the laws his pathway to fame ? How can what is unjustly got possibly be just ? Like fruit, like root must ever be the case, and any who behaves unjustly by evading his curial station and comes to office as a result of this evasion may be assured that this good name

[a] Pack (p. 122) saw this as referring to the suppression of the usurpation of Maximus in A.D. 388.

⟨ἔχων⟩[1] τῷ κακῶς ἐσχηκέναι. 34. φέρε, εἴ τις ἀρρωστούσῃ μητρὶ πένητι μίαν ἐχούσῃ καταφυγὴν τὸν υἱὸν παρακαθῆσθαι μὲν οὐκ ἀξιοίη, χωρήσας δὲ ἐπὶ δένδρα καὶ κήπους καὶ ἄνθη τρυφῶν ἐνταῦθα διάγοι κᾆτα ὡς κακὸς περὶ τὴν τεκοῦσαν κρίνοιτο, τοῦτον, εἰπέ μοι, σώσει τὸ τῆς προσεδρείας ἐκείνης ταύτην ἡδίω τὴν διατριβὴν εἶναι; ὦ κάκιστε ἀνδρῶν, ἓν τοῦτο ἑώρας, τὴν τέρψιν, ἃ δὲ ἀδικήσεις οὐκ εἶδες;[2] οὐδ᾽ ὡς ἄμεινον ἦν τοῦ κυλινδεῖσθαι ἐν ἄνθεσι τὸ ἀσθενούσης ἐπιμελεῖσθαι μητρός;

35. Οὐ δὴ τοῦτο δεῖ σκοπεῖν, εἰ τὸ μὴ βουλεύειν | R ii. 545 τοῦ βουλεύειν ἀπονώτερον, ἀλλ᾽ εἰ τὸ βουλεύειν τοῦ μὴ βουλεύειν εὐσεβέστερον. εἰ δ᾽ οὗτοι δόξουσί τι | λέγειν, τί μὴ τοὺς λῃστὰς θαυμάζομεν οἳ ταῖς F σφαγαῖς τὰς ὁδοὺς κεκλείκασιν, ἀφέντες ὃ νῦν ποιοῦμεν, τὸ σκοπεῖν ὅθεν ἂν ἀσφάλεια τοῖς ὁδοιπόροις εἴη; καὶ γὰρ τούτοις δοτέον τὰ αὐτῶν οὕτω μείζω ποιεῖν, ἐπειδὴ ταῦτα αὐτοὺς τὰ ξιφίδια βοῶν τε ἀπαλλάττει καὶ ἀρότρου καὶ σπορᾶς καὶ τῶν ἄλλων τῶν περὶ τὴν γῆν πόνων καὶ ταχέως φέρει τὸ πλουτεῖν. 36. ἀλλ᾽ ἴσμεν δὴ τήν τε κώμην ἐκείνην καὶ τὸ ἐν αὐτῇ γένος ὡς ἐξεκόπη μέχρι τῶν ἐν γάλακτι παιδίων προελθόντος τοῦ πυρός, προνοηθέντος, οἶμαι, τοῦ τότε βασιλέως ὅπως μὴ πάλιν ἀναφύσεται τὸ δεινὸν ἐκεῖνο γένος. διὰ τοῦτο φέρουσαι ταῖς ἀγκάλαις αἱ μητέρες τὰ τέκνα ταῖς τῶν δημίων χερσὶν ἐωθοῦντο μετ᾽ ὀργῆς εἰς τὴν φλόγα.

---

[1] ⟨ἔχων⟩ conj. Re., F. : ὃν conj. Sintenis.
[2] ἀδικήσεις οὐκ εἶδες ; Re. (mss. except BM) : ἠδίκεις οὐκ εἶδες F. (BM).

---

[a] Marathocupreni, punished so by Valens in A.D. 369.

is bad because it has been badly got. 34. Why! if you refuse to sit at the bedside of your poor, ailing mother, whose sole solace lies in her son, and instead make your way to woodlands, gardens and flowers, and have a good time there, and then are judged as basely neglectful of the mother that bore you, tell me, will the fact that these pursuits are more pleasant than such attendance save you? You blackguard, you had eyes for one thing only, your own enjoyment: did you not foresee your baseness? or that care for your ailing mother was better than lolling among flowers?

35. This then should not be our concern, whether the evasion of civic duty is less burdensome than its performance, but whether the performance is more responsible than the evasion. If the arguments of these people hold good, why don't we follow the lead of the bandits who have closed the highways by the murders they commit, and give up our present activities of ensuring protection for wayfarers? Indeed we ought to allow them to increase their possessions in this way, for it is their daggers that rescue them from their oxen, their plough, the seed-time and all the labours of the land and quickly bring them wealth. 36. But we know how that village and its entire population was cut down, right to the babes at the breast, and how it was consumed by fire, since the ruling emperor took pains, I feel, to ensure that that terrible brood should never sprout again.[a] Hence the mothers, with their babies in their arms, were angrily thrust by the hands of executioners into

Valesius was able to cite this passage of Libanius in his explanatory note on the passage of Ammianus (28. 2. 11), a century before the first publication of the speech.

εἰ δὲ τὸ αὐτῶν ἐποίουν οὗτοι καὶ ἐγεώργουν, οὔτ᾽
ἂν ἐπλούτουν κακῶς οὔτ᾽ ἂν ἀπέθνησκον. οὕτω
δὴ καὶ περὶ τοῦ παρόντος. γιγνέσθω τις εὐδαίμων
δίκαιος ὤν, ἀδικῶν δὲ καὶ κατὰ τοῦτο ἰσχύων
ἴστω δίκην ὀφείλων τῆς ἰσχύος. ἦν εἰ κατ᾽ αὐτὸ
τὸ[1] δύνασθαι μὴ διδοίη, μειζόνως κακοδαίμων ἢ εἰ
ὑπεσχήκει τὴν δίκην.

37. Ἄξιον δὲ μηδὲ ἐκεῖνο παρελθεῖν πολλὴν ἔχον
αἰτίαν. | οὐ βοηθεῖτε τοῖς βοηθείας δεομένοις, οἷς F 4
πάρεστι ⟨τὸ⟩[2] δύνασθαι. ἀλλ᾽ οἱ μὲν πωλοῦσι τὰ
σφῶν αὐτῶν ἀπορίᾳ συμμάχων, ὑμεῖς δὲ πράως
φέρετε τὰς τοιαύτας τῶν πράσεων ὡς δὴ οὐδὲν τοῦ
κακοῦ μετέχοντες. καὶ οὐ τοῦτ᾽ ἔστι τὸ χείριστον,
R ii. 546 ἀλλ᾽ ὅτι τῶν μὲν αὐτοὶ καταβάλλετε | τὴν τιμήν, τὰ
δὲ τοῖς ἐν δυνάμει προξενεῖτε καὶ κολακεύετε τὰς
ἐκείνων τραπέζας τοῖς τῶν βουλευόντων κτήμασι.
κἂν ἀγρόν τις αὐτῶν τοῦ βουλεύοντος θαυμάσῃ καὶ
διὰ τοῦ θαυμάζειν εἰς τὸ ἐρᾶν προέλθῃ, ταχὺ τὸ
ἔργον προσετέθη, καὶ ὁ μὲν ἠνάγκασται πωλεῖν,
τῷ δὲ ἕτοιμον ἀγοράζειν. 38. οἱ δὲ τοῦτο κατα-
πράξαντες ἠριστευκέναι τε νομίζουσι καὶ μέγα τεῖ-
χος αὑτοῖς προστεθεικέναι[3] τὴν τῶν ἐωνημένων
χάριν. εἶτ᾽ αὐτοῖς ἐπὶ τὰς θύρας ὁσημέραι φοιτῶσι
καὶ παρακολουθοῦσιν ἐπὶ τὰς τῶν ἵππων φάτνας
κἂν ἃ τῶν οἰκετῶν ἐστι ποιεῖν ἐπιταχθῶσι, γεγή-
θασιν. οἱ μισθοὶ δὲ τούτων φαγεῖν, πιεῖν, μεθυ-

---

[1] ἦν εἰ κατ᾽ αὐτὸ τὸ F. (PB): ἡνίκα τ᾽ (τὲ IM, Bong.) αὐτῷ
τῷ (τε I) Bong., Re. (other mss.).
[2] ⟨τὸ⟩ Macarius, conj. Re., F.   [3] περιτεθεικέναι F.

---

[a] Cf. Or. 32. 8, 49. 8. In C. Th. 12. 3. 1 (of A.D. 386) the
sale of curial land is forbidden, except with the governor's

the flames. But if they did their duty and tilled their land, they would not amass ill-gotten gains, nor would they be executed. So surely in the present instance. Good luck to the man who abides by the law, but if he does not, and gains power thereby, he should realize that he ought to be punished for his power. And if, by reason of his very influence, he remains unpunished, then he is more ill-starred than if he had paid the penalty.

37. Yet another matter, that gives much cause for complaint, should not remain unmentioned. You, who have the ability to do so, provide no assistance to those who need it. Rather, they sell their possessions through lack of supporters, and you view such sales with equanimity, for you, of course, have no part in their troubles. And that is not the worst of it, either [a] : in some cases, you personally put down the money, in others you stand in for persons of influence and curry favour at their tables by means of the property of the councillors. If any of them admires a councillor's estate, and proceeds from admiration to desire, it is no sooner said than done : the councillor is forced to sell, and he is all in readiness to buy. 38. And those who have managed the affair think they have done a fine job, and believe that they have gained for themselves considerable additional protection, in the shape of the purchasers' support. Then they haunt their doors every day, escort them to the stables and are cock-a-hoop, even if bidden to perform any menial service. And their reward for this is to be dined and wined, to get

permission (*ibid.* 2 of A.D. 423 explicitly names the *principales* as the guilty parties in such sales). For the continuance of such sales *cf. Or.* 47. 18, 22, 34 ; 52. 33.

σθῆναι, βιασθῆναι τοὺς καταδεεῖς. κἂν ἡ Τύχη
τινὰ αὐτῶν ἐξάγῃ τῆς πόλεως, πεσόντες εἰς γόνυ
καὶ δεηθέντες μένειν ἀπεστέρησαν τῶν παρὰ τῆς
Τύχης τὴν πόλιν. εἶτ' εὐθὺς παρακαλοῦσιν οἰκο-
δομεῖν. εἶθ' ἡ κύων ἐμι|μήσατο τὴν δέσποιναν[1] F 44
οἰκοδομουμένη καὶ αὐτή. τουτὶ δὲ ἐσμὸς κακῶν
ἁπάσαις τέχναις. αἱ δὲ παρὰ τῶν κήπων τῷ ἄστει
παραμυθίαι διολώλασι, καὶ πανταχοῦ λίθοι καὶ ξύλα
καὶ τέκτονες.

39. Εἶτα θαυμάζετε τῶν ἀρχόντων εἰ ταῦτα εἰ-
R ii. 547 δότες ὑβρίζουσι; τί δαὶ | αὐτοὺς ἐχρῆν ποιεῖν;
αἰδεῖσθαι καὶ τιμᾶν τοὺς σφᾶς αὐτοὺς τεταπεινω-
κότας; ὁρᾶθ' ὡς ὑφ' ὑμῶν αἱ τιμαὶ τῇ βουλῇ διεφθάρησαν. πῶς γὰρ ἂν ὁ δικάζων δύναιτο τὸν τοῦ
δεῖνος αἰδεῖσθαι κόλακα τὸν προπεπωκότα αὐτῷ τὰ
τῶν ὁμοσκήνων δένδρα, τὸν καταπολεμοῦντα τὴν
βουλὴν ἧς καὶ αὐτὸς εἶναι τέτακται; 40. οὐδὲ ταῦ-
ρον ἴδοι τις ἂν ἡδέως πηροῦντα τὰς βοῦς τοῖς κέρα-
σιν οὐδὲ κριὸν ἀναρρηγνύντα τῇ κεφαλῇ τοὺς ἄρνας
οὐδὲ ἀλεκτρυόνα τῇ τῶν νεοττῶν ἐπιτιθέμενον
ἀσθενείᾳ· οὐ τοίνυν οὐδ' ἐν βουλῇ τοὺς πρώτους
ἀπολλύντας τοὺς δευτέρους καὶ τρίτους. ὃ κακὸν
μέν ἐστι τοῖς προδιδομένοις, κακὸν δὲ τοῖς προ-
διδοῦσιν. ἐν γὰρ αὐτοῖς τοῖς δοκοῦσι κέρδεσιν ἡ
βλάβη. ἢ πόθεν οἴεσθε τὸν δῆμον οὕτως ἐπῆρθαι
καὶ ἀσελγαίνειν καὶ παροινεῖν; ἐῶ τὰ ἄλλα. ἀλλὰ
ἔναγχος οἵας ἀφῆκαν ἐν τῷ θεάτρῳ φωνάς, ἐπεὶ |

---

[1] δέσποιναν conj. Re., Cobet, F.: δεσποτείαν Bong., Re.
text (mss.).

---

[a] Proverbial, cf. Or. 18. 133 (Vol. I, p. 366 n.).
[b] e.g. the angariae of Or. 50. For the nuisances attendant
on such redevelopment cf. Or. 2. 54 ff., 50. 31 ; and for the
affront to sentiment, Or. 46. 44.

drunk and to oppress the needy. And should Fortune send any of their patrons from the city, they fall at their knees, beg them to stay and swindle the city of Fortune's gift. And then they straightaway invite them to build ; and—like bitch copying mistress *a*—they go in for building themselves. This involves a swarm of troubles for all the tradesmen,*b* and the amenities enjoyed by the city from its gardens are ruined : everywhere there is masonry, timbers and builders.

39. And then you are surprised that the governors, when they know all this, insult you ! What should they do, then ? Respect and honour people who have abased themselves ? Just see how you have ruined the council's prestige. How could a magistrate have any respect for the lackey of any Tom, Dick or Harry, one who has made him a present of his comrades' orchards and who behaves as an enemy of the council of which he personally has been set as a member. 40. You would not enjoy seeing a bull goring his cows, a ram butting his lambs or a cockerel attacking his poor little chicks. Nor should you in the council enjoy seeing the highest class of members destroying those of the second and third class.*c* This is bad for the betrayed, and for the betrayers, for in the seeming gain itself disaster lies. Or how do you think it is that the commons gives itself such airs and behaves with such outrage and insubordination ? Aside from all else, just consider the abuse they recently uttered in the theatre when

c On the three classes in the *curia cf. Or.* 11. 144, 49. 8 ff., and Introduction, p. 411 f. The subject is discussed by Petit (pp. 85 f.), Liebeschuetz (pp. 170 ff.), and Norman (*J.R.S.* xlviii, pp. 79 ff.).

LIBANIUS

μὴ χρυσίον εὐθέως εἶχε τῆς τραγῳδίας ἀηδὴς ὑπο- F 4⟨
κριτής. ἤλπιζον γὰρ ὑμᾶς σιγῇ καὶ ταῦτα οἴσειν
οὐ κακῶς ἐλπίζοντες. οὔκουν ἐγρύξατε.

41. Γένεσθε τοίνυν ἀμείνους μὲν ὑμῶν αὐτῶν,
ὅμοιοι δὲ τοῖς πατράσιν οἷς τοὺς ἐπὶ τῶν ἀρχῶν καὶ
καταπλήττειν ὑπῆρχε. γένεσθε τοῖς πενεστέροις
τῶν ἐν τῇ βουλῇ λιμένες καὶ μιᾷ γνώμῃ τὰ συμφέροντα καὶ ζητεῖτε καὶ πράττετε. καὶ τὸ ἑνός
τινος ἀγαθὸν κοινὸν κεκρίσθω καὶ τὸ δυσχερὲς ὡσ-
αύτως. ὡς νῦν γε ἐπιχαίρομεν ἀλλήλοις,[1] καὶ οἱ
μὲν πιέζουσιν, οἱ δὲ καταρῶνται. μηδὲν ὑμῖν ἔστω
φοβερώτερον τοῦ τὴν πατρίδα κακοῦν μηδ' αὐτὸς
ὁ θάνατος.

R ii. 548   42. Ἀλλ' ἀγέσθω τις | ἐπὶ τὸ βουλεύειν, κἂν
μέλλῃ τό τινος λυπήσειν βαλλάντιον. οὐχ ὁρᾶτε
τὸν Λητόιον ὡς καλὰ περὶ αὑτοῦ διηγεῖται πολλάκις, τὸν Μακρέντιον, τὸν Μάτερνον, τὸν Ἰουλιανόν, πολλοὺς ἄλλους, τὰς ὑπὲρ τούτων πρὸς τοὺς
στρατηγοὺς μάχας ἃς οὐκ ἀζημίους μέν, καλὰς δὲ
καὶ οὕτως ἐνόμιζεν; τί τοιοῦτον ἔστιν ὑμῖν εἰς
φιλοτιμίαν ἐπαῖρον[2]; περὶ τοῦ τῶν ὑμετέρων[3] ἐν
συνουσίαις διατρίψετε; τίνος μνημονεύοντες ἀμεί-
νους εἶναι δόξετε; νίκας μὲν Ὀλυμ|πικὰς οὐκ F 4⟨
ἐρεῖτε οὐδὲ αἰχμαλώτους καὶ λάφυρα· εἰ δὲ μήτε
ἐκεῖνα μήτε ταῦτα, τῷ ποτε χρήσεσθε;

43. Μὴ ὑμεῖς γε, μὴ μέχρι παντὸς ἐπὶ τῶν ἡμαρ-

---

[1] ἀλλήλοις conj. Re., F. : ἄλλοις Bong., Re. text (mss.).
[2] ἐπαῖρον Re., F. : ἑταῖροι Bong. (mss.).
[3] ὑμετέρων F. (M) : ἡμετέρων Bong., Re. (other mss.).

---

[a] Cf. Or. 49. 19, Ep. 1365. In A.D. 363, during the
campaign of curial recruitment instituted by Julian, he had
been instrumental in recalling to the council the three

some miserable actor did not get a gold piece for his performance on the spot. They expected that you would put up even with this in silence, and their expectation was not ill-founded. You never made a murmur!

41. So reform yourselves : be like your fathers who had it in them even to inspire alarm in the governors. Be for the poorer members of the council havens of refuge, and with unanimity of purpose seek the proper course and act upon it. Let the individual's good fortune be regarded as the good fortune of all alike ; similarly, his ill-fortune. As things are we exult over one another. One section is oppressive : the other curses them for it. Let nothing be more fearsome to you than to harm your native city, not even death itself.

42. Let there be recruitment to the position of councillor, even if it is likely to hurt the pocket of one or two people. Don't you see Letoïus and the fine stories he often tells of himself—of Macrentius, Maternus, Julianus and a host of others, and the battles on their account that he fought against the generals, battles that he regarded as honourable, though he did not emerge unscathed ?[a] What such example can you show to spur you to rival this ? On which of your number will you dilate in your clubs ? What can you call to mind for you to be thought superior ? You will not cite Olympic victories nor yet the prisoners and spoils of war : and failing the one and the other, what on earth can you use ?

43. So don't, don't remain content with your mis-fugitive decurions here named, who had enlisted and were serving as army officers.

τημένων μένετε, ἀλλὰ ἅλις μὲν δρυός, ἀποθέμενοι
δὲ τὴν πολλὴν ταύτην μαλακίαν δείξατε πάλιν τὴν
βουλὴν ἀνθοῦσαν.

---

[a] Proverbial, *cf. Paroem. Gr.* (ed. Leutsch-Schneidewin),

takes for all time. Enough is enough [a] ! Cast off this
excessive slackness and reveal the council in its prime
once again.

i, p. 42 (=Zenob. 2. 40, *et al.*), of the progress of man from
his primitive acorn-eating state.

XLIX

ΠΡΟΣ ΤΟΝ ΒΑΣΙΛΕΑ
ΥΠΕΡ ΤΩΝ ΒΟΥΛΩΝ

1. Τὸ μὲν σόν, ὦ βασιλεῦ, μέρος καὶ τοῦ μετὰ σὲ F ii
τοῖς ἄλλοις ἄρχουσιν ἐφεστηκότος, ἐπανήκουσιν εἰς
τὰ πρόσθεν αἱ βουλαὶ καὶ τὸν αὐτῶν ἀριθμὸν ἔχουσι,
παρὰ δὲ τῶν ἐν αὐτῷ βουλεύειν κεκώλυται τοῦτο
πρὸς ἔργον ἐλθεῖν, ὥστε σὲ μὲν δικαίως ἂν ἅπαντες
ἐπαινοῖμεν καὶ τὸν ὕπαρχον, ἐκείνους δὲ καὶ μι-
σοῖμεν καὶ κακοὺς ἡγοίμεθα καὶ διδόντας δίκην
ἡδέως ἂν ἴδοιμεν. εἰ γὰρ δὴ τοῦτο γένοιτο, τάχ᾽
ἂν ἡ τιμωρία παύσειε τὰ νῦν ἐναντιούμενα τῇ παρὰ
σοῦ ταῖς βου|λαῖς βοηθείᾳ. τούτων οὖν εἵνεκα καὶ F 4
τοῦ μαθεῖν ἅπαντας ὡς τοῖς σοὶ δοκοῦσιν εὐθὺς
ἀκολουθεῖν ἄξιον, ὀργῇ τῇ προσηκούσῃ φαίνου χρώμενος κατὰ τῶν οὐκ ἀξιούντων ἄρχεσθαι. ὡς
δ᾽ ἂν γένοιτό σοι σαφὲς τὸ ᾽κείνων κακούργημα,
μικρὸν ἄνωθεν ἀρξάμενος διηγήσομαι.

2. Ἤνθουν αἱ βουλαὶ πάλαι ταῖς πόλεσιν ἁπάσαις, καὶ ἦν ἥ τε γῆ τῶν βουλευόντων καὶ τῶν γε
οἰκιῶν αἱ βελτίους καὶ χρήματα ἦν ἑκάστῳ καὶ
παρ᾽ ἀλλήλων ἐγάμουν καὶ ἦν εὔδαιμον τὸ βουλῆς

---

^a *Or.* 49 F. *Or.* 50 Re.
^b The praetorian prefect (τὸν νῦν ὕπαρχον, Tatianus, § 31),
sharply distinguished from his Christian predecessor, Cynegius, named in § 3. ^c *Cf. Or.* 2. 35 f., 48. 30 n.

ORATION 49 [a]

TO THE EMPEROR,
FOR THE CITY COUNCILS

1. As far as concerns you, Sire, and the official who, subordinate to yourself, is in charge of all other governors,[b] the city councils have returned to their pristine state and possess their full complement of members ; but this has been prevented from being put into practice by those who actually hold the position of councillor. Thus, while rightly commending the prefect and yourself, we should loathe them, regard them as rascals and gladly see them punished. If this were to happen, the punishment perhaps would put an end to the opposition that your efforts to assist the city councils encounter. So for their sake and so that all may know that your decrees must be followed without delay, use, for all to see, your well-merited anger against those who refuse to be subjects. And that their misconduct may be made clear to you, I will begin my account with a brief recapitulation of recent history.

2. In times past the councils used to flourish in every city. The land and better-class houses used to belong to the councillors, and every one of them had money : they would intermarry, and to be a member of the council was to be well-to-do.[c] That

461

μετασχεῖν. οὕτω τοίνυν ἐχούσας αὐτὰς παραλα-
R ii. 571 βών τις βασιλεὺς χείρους ἐποίησεν | ἄλλοις τε οὐκ
ὀλίγοις καὶ τῇ γε ὑφ' αὑτοῦ πεποιημένῃ πόλει.
τεθνεῶτος τοίνυν αὐτοῦ τὸν πόλεμον ἤδη πεφυ-
τευκότος τὸν Περσικὸν τὰ περὶ τὸν πόλεμον τοῦτον πράγματα ταῖς βουλαῖς ἐλυμήνατο καθ' ἕκαστον αὐτὰς ἔτος ἐπὶ τὸ χεῖρον ἄγοντα τῶν ἐπὶ τὸν
Τίγρητα πεμπομένων βουλευτῶν ταῖς ἐκεῖ βλάβαις
τὰ πατρῷα πωλούντων. οἱ δ' οὐκ οἶδ' ὁπόθεν
ἥκοντες ἐωνοῦντο ῥᾳδίως γεωργοῦντες τὰ βασίλεια. 3. τοῦτ' εὔξατο λῦσαι τὸ κακὸν Ἰουλιανὸς
ὁ βασιλεύς, τοῦτ' ἔλυσε δυνηθείς, οἷς ἦν κτήματα
καθ' ἑκάστην πόλιν ἐγγράφων πλὴν κομιδῇ τινων
ὀλίγων. τῆς οὖν ἐκείνου τελευτῆς ἐπὶ ταὐτὰ[1] πάλιν
τὰς βουλὰς ἀπενεγ|κούσης, μᾶλλον δὲ εἰς πολὺ F 4
φαυλότερα καὶ πολλῆς ἀπὸ τῶν βουλευτηρίων ἐφ'
ἑτέρους βίους γιγνομένης τῆς φυγῆς καὶ τῶν πόλεων τεταπεινωμένων τῷ τῶν βουλῶν σχήματι
τῶν ἄλλων ἀκολουθούντων ἤλγησας μὲν ἀξίως τοῦ
πράγματος, ὦ βασιλεῦ, καὶ τὸν Κυνήγιον ἔτ' ἐπὶ
R ii. 572 τῶν δεήσεων τεταγμένον ᾠήθης | ἐκπέμψαι δεῖν
τοῦτο μόνον ἔργον ἔξοντά τε καὶ ἰασόμενον, πρὶν

---

[1] ταὐτὰ Bong., Re., F. : ταῦτα mss.

---

[a] Constantine.

[b] For the beginning of the Persian war under Constantine
and its continuance under Constantius cf. Or. 18. 206 ff.,
59. 66 ff.

[c] On the distress caused both in Antioch and in Euphratensis by the Persian wars of Constantius' reign cf. Or. 17. 19,
and Liebeschuetz, pp. 162 f. The duty of provisioning the
fortress at Callinicum then (Ep. 21) is matched by the duty

was their situation when a certain emperor took them over, but by various acts of policy, not least by the foundation of his new capital, he brought them low.*a* And after his death, when he had already sown the seeds of the Persian war,*b* the troubles connected with this war wrought havoc with the councils, and every year caused a deterioration in them, since councillors sent to the Tigris were forced,*c* by the losses there incurred, to sell their family property. And purchasers flocked in from heaven knows where, since they were comfortably reaping the harvest of office in the imperial administration. 3. It was the emperor Julian's prayer to remove this evil, and remove it he did when he came to power, for, with very few exceptions, he enrolled men of substance in every city.*d* His death reduced the councils to their previous situation, or rather to one far worse : desertions of the council chamber for other kinds of career became common, and the cities were abased, since the other classes took their cue from the situation to be found in the councils. So you were rightly displeased at the state of affairs, Sire, and thought to send out Cynegius, at the time officer in charge of petitions, with this as his sole duty, to rectify the situation.*e* However, before

of provisioning Barbalissos in more recent years (*cf. Or.* 28. 16).

d Cf. Or. 18. 146 ff., 48. 17. *C. Th.* 12. 1. 52-54 (*E.L.F.* Nos. 119, 120, 127).

e Cynegius (*PLRE* 235 (3)), *Quaestor Sacri Palatii* in A.D. 383 (ἐπὶ τῶν δεήσεων τεταγμένον), was appointed Praetorian Prefect in the next year, engaged on this mission of curial recruitment. For his meeting with Libanius in Antioch *cf. Or.* 1. 231, and for a discussion of the various shifts of policy during this tour of the East *cf.* Petit, *Byzantion*, xxi, pp. 295 ff.

δὲ ἢ τοῦτο πραχθῆναι, γενόμενον ὕπαρχον ἐκέ-
λευες μέχρι τοῦ Νείλου χωρεῖν ἔχοντα καὶ τοῦτο
ἐν προνοίᾳ μηδένα ἀφιέναι παρὰ τὸ ἐν ἀρχῇ γεγενῆσθαι. ὁ δὲ χείρων τῆς προσδοκίας φανεὶς καὶ
μεγάλα μὲν ἀπειλήσας, δείξας δὲ ἃ κἂν αἰσχυν-
θείη τις εἰπεῖν, ἁπτόμενος μὲν ἐν τῇ πορείᾳ τοῦ
πράγματος, ἐν δὲ ματαίοις θορύβοις ἱστάμενος,
οὕτω μὲν εἶδε τὸν Νεῖλον, οὕτω δὲ πάλιν τὸν
Βόσπορον, φρονῶν μὲν ὡς δή τι πεποιηκώς, πεποιηκὼς δὲ οὐδέν.

4. Κἀκείνῳ μὲν ἄν τις ἐγκαλέσειε ῥᾳθυμίαν,
περὶ δὲ τῶν βουλευτῶν τί τις ἂν φήσειε τῶν ὀλίγων
οὐ βουληθέντων γενέσθαι πλειόνων; τί γὰρ ἦν δὴ
τῶν τοῦτο βουλομένων; ἱκετεῦσαι, δακρῦσαι, δεηθῆναι, πεσεῖν εἰς γόνυ, βοῆσαι τὰ τῶν ἀδικουμένων,
R ii. 573 αὐτοῦ μένειν εἰπεῖν εἰ μή τις ἕλκων ἐκβάλοι. | τού-
των | οὐδὲν παρὰ τῶν ὀλίγων, ἀλλ᾽ ἐκλήθη τις, F 4
καὶ ῥήτωρ ἐγγὺς καὶ ῥήματα οὐ πολλά, καὶ ἡ
ἄφεσις εἵπετο καὶ οἶδε ἄφωνοι. 5. ἔτι τοίνυν πολλοὺς μὲν πρὸ τοῦδε τοῦ καιροῦ παρεῖσαν συναγωνι-
ζομένους, πολλοὺς δὲ μετὰ τοῦτον πόσων, ὦ βασιλεῦ, παρ᾽ ὑμῶν ἀφικνουμένων γραμμάτων ἁπάσας
R ii. 574 ἀναιρούντων τοῖς ἀδίκως φεύγουσι | τὰς κατα-
φυγάς. τὰ μέν γέ φησιν· ἦρξας καὶ διὰ τοῦτ᾽ οὐκ
ἀξιοῖς λειτουργεῖν; οὐκοῦν αὐτὸς μὲν κάθευδε,
διὰ δὲ τοῦ παιδὸς τὰ προσήκοντα ποίει. ἀλλ᾽ οὐκ
εἶ πατὴρ ἢ θυγατέρων μόνων; ἄνδρα τινὰ πεί-

---

[a] By his growing concentration upon the suppression of
pagan rituals, which stimulated violent reaction.
[b] e.g. in the cases of Eutropius (Or. 4. 20) and Silvanus
(Or. 38. 20).

any action was instituted, he was appointed Praetorian Prefect and you ordered him to go on circuit
as far as the Nile, one item of his programme being
to excuse no one from curial duty on the grounds of
past service in the administration. He most obviously fell short of what was expected of him and,
for all his bombast, the results he produced were
hardly worth the mention. Although he tackled
the business during his tour, he became the centre
of pointless disturbances,[a] and such was the background of his trip to the Nile and of his return to the
Bosporus. He put on the air of having done something special, whereas he had done nothing.

4. He could be criticized for inefficiency, but what
is one to say of the councillors, that handful who
refused to increase their numbers? What was the
behaviour to be expected of people who really wanted
that to happen? Why! pleading, weeping and
prayer, falling at his knees, crying aloud their protestations of injury, and threatening not to budge
unless forcibly thrown out. Our handful did none
of this, but when a recruit was nominated, up popped
a lawyer, and after the exchange of a word or two, a
notice of release followed—and they stayed dumb
throughout.[b] 5. Besides, both before this opportunity
and after it they have allowed many of their cronies
to get away, despite the many dispatches emanating
from you, Sire, that deprive illegal absconders of
all means of escape. One dispatch states, "Have
you been a governor, and is that the reason for your
refusal to perform civic duties? Then stay in retirement yourself and do your duty by means of your
son. You have no children? or daughters only?
Then get some man to undertake the title and the

465

σας ὑπελθεῖν τοὔνομα καὶ τὸ ἔργον πάλιν αὐτὸς
κάθευδε τοσοῦτον μόνον τῇ πόλει παρέχων, ἀνα-
λίσκων. ταῦτ' ἔστιν ἐν πολλαῖς ἐπιστολαῖς καὶ
τούτων γε ἐν ἑτέραις ἕτερα καλλίω μείζω τὴν
ἀπόδειξιν ἔχοντα τῆς σπουδῆς ᾗ περὶ τὰς βουλὰς
κέχρησαι. 6. ταυτὶ δὲ λέγει τί; εἰ καὶ διὰ πολλῶν ἀρχῶν ἀφῖξαι καὶ κήρυκες ἡγοῦντό σου καὶ
ῥαβδοῦχοι καὶ μαστιγοφόροι καὶ ἡμεροδρόμοι καὶ
στρατιῶταί τινες καί σοι τροφὴ γέγονεν ἐκ τοῦ
βασιλέως οἴκου, ἥξεις ὅμως οἷ σε καθίστησιν ὁ
πατὴρ καὶ ἡ μήτηρ καὶ οἱ τούτων γονεῖς. κἂν
εἴπῃς τὰς ἀρχάς, οὐδὲν ὠφελοῦσαν βοήθειαν κέ-
κληκας. 7. καὶ τὰ μὲν παρ' ὑμῶν τοιαῦτα, τὰ δὲ
τούτων ἀντὶ τοῦ πέμπειν μὲν τοὺς στεφανώσοντας
τὴν οὕτω τῶν βουλῶν ἐπιμελουμένην κεφαλήν, ἔχ-
εσθαι δὲ εὐθὺς τῶν | ἀποδεδομένων, μὴ συγχωρεῖν F 4
δὲ τοῖς ἄρχουσι μέλλειν μηδ' ἀναβολαῖς χαρίζεσθαι
τοῖς ὑπὸ τῶν γραμμάτων τεθηραμένοις, ἀλλ' ἀναγκάζειν ἐμμένειν τοῖς ὑφ' ὑμῶν δικαίως[1] κεκριμέ-
νοις καὶ φόβους ἐφιστάναι τῇ περὶ ταῦτα νωθείᾳ,
ἀντὶ δὴ τοῦ ταῦτα ποιεῖν καὶ ἔτι πλείω τοὺς μὲν
R ii. 575 εἴων ζῆν ἐν οἶσπερ | ἔζων, πρὸς δὲ τοὺς οὐδὲν οὔτε
μεῖζον οὔτε ἔλαττον ἐφθέγξαντο μεγάλας εἰς τὸ
παρρησιάζεσθαι τὰς ἀφορμὰς ἔχοντες. ἀλλ' ὧν οὐ
γιγνομένων παρ' ὑμῶν ἐσχετλίαζον ἄν, ταῦτ' ἔχειν
ἐξὸν οὐκ ἐβουλήθησαν, ἀλλ' οὐ διδόντων μὲν δεινὰ

---

[1] δικαίως F. : δικαίοις Bong., Re. (mss.).

---

[a] The legislation here mentioned is that of C. Th. 12. 1.
106-111, 118, whereby decurions were admitted into the
Senate without being freed from the membership and obligations of their city council. By this shift of policy, sons or
substitutes are no longer acceptable for the performance of

actual performance, and once again retire, and for the service of the city provide just the expenses." This is the gist of many of your rescripts. In others there are more notable statements still, which provide more important indication of your support for the councils. 6. Their contents are as follows : " Even if you have proceeded through a string of offices, and if heralds preceded you, and lictors, attendants, couriers and soldiers, and if you have been paid from the imperial purse, you will still go to the station where your father and mother and their forebears set you. And if you mention your offices, you call upon a source of aid that avails you nothing." [a] 7. Such is the policy you have instituted, but theirs, instead of sending envoys to crown the head [b] that shows such concern for the councils, instead of claiming immediately what has been restored to them and not allowing the governors to dally or to oblige with dilatoriness those persons who are the target of the rescripts, instead of forcing them to abide by your just decisions and causing them alarm for any slackness on this issue—instead of doing all this and yet more, they proceeded to allow some to live in the manner they used to live before, while against others they uttered no word of complaint, whether serious or not, although they had good grounds for frankness. They would complain when the concession was not forthcoming from you, but they refused to keep it when they could. When you did not make them a concession, they

curial duties in their place, and *honorati* remain eligible for the liturgies.

[b] The *aurum coronarium* was required in A.D. 388, on the occasion of the imperial anniversaries.

πάσχειν ἔλεγον, διδόντων δὲ οὐκ ἐχρήσαντο, ἀλλ᾽
ὧν χρῄζειν ἔλεγον, ταῦτ᾽ εἰς χεῖρας ἰόντα ἀπεώθουν.
8. Καὶ παράδοξον μὲν τὸ ῥηθέν, ἔχει δὲ οὐκ ἄλλως ὁ λόγος, ἀλλ᾽ ὅμοιον ποιοῦσιν ὥσπερ ἂν εἴ τις
πένης αἰτήσας παρὰ τοῦ Διὸς θησαυρόν, ἔπειτα
γῆν ὀρύττων εὑρὼν φεύγοι τὸ δῶρον. τί δὴ τὸ
τούτων αἴτιον; ἐν τοῖς ὀλίγοις τούτοις εἰσίν, ὦ
βασιλεῦ, μεγάλαι τινὲς δυνάμεις αἳ τοὺς ἀσθενε-
στέρους ἄγουσι καὶ φέρουσι τούτοις τἀκείνων προσ-
τιθεῖσαι, τά τε ἐκ τοῦ πολιτεύεσθαι κέρδη τὰ τούτων αὔξει. κἂν τοῖς ἀμελουμένοις ἃ δικαίως ἂν
ἐτύγχανε προνοίας, ἐκ τοῦ μὴ πολλοὺς εἶναι τοὺς
βουλεύοντας τοῖς οὖσιν ἡ παραίτησις. καὶ πολὺς
καθ᾽ ἑκάστην ἡμέραν ὁ θρῆνος· | ὁρᾷς τοὺς ἑστη- F
κότας ἡμᾶς τοὺς εὐαριθμήτους τοὺς ἀντὶ τῶν χι-
λίων καὶ διακοσίων δώδεκα; τοῦτ᾽ ἔστιν ἡ βουλή.
ταῦτα μόνα τὰ πρὸς τοιαῦτα¹ πράγματα ἀγόμενα
R ii. 576 σώματα. δι᾽ ἡμῶν τὰν τῇ πόλει, | δι᾽ ἡμῶν τὰν
τοῖς ἀγροῖς, δι᾽ ἡμῶν τὰ μείζω, δι᾽ ἡμῶν τὰ ἐλάττ-
τω, δι᾽ ἡμῶν τὰ κουφότερα, δι᾽ ἡμῶν τὰ βαρύτερα.
διὰ τοῦτο τῶν αὐτῶν ὀνομάτων ἀκούεις. 9. ταύτην
τὴν ὀλόφυρσιν τὰ δικαστήρια δέχεται συγγνώμην
μὲν φέροντα τοῖς ὀλιγωρουμένοις, συγγνώμην δὲ
φέροντα τοῖς κακουργουμένοις. βουλόμενοι δὴ ταύτης τε ἀπολαύειν τῆς ἀποστροφῆς καὶ ἐν μόνοις
σφίσιν ἵστασθαι τὰ λήμματα δεδίασι μή τι τῶν
ἀρχαίων αἱ βουλαὶ κομίσωνται, καὶ τὸ τὰς βουλὰς
ἀναστῆναι παρ᾽ ὑμῶν ζητοῦντες, ὅπως ἀεὶ κεί-
σονται πράττουσι, μᾶλλον δὲ τὸ μὲν προσποιοῦνται

¹ τοιαῦτα Bong., Re. (mss.) : τοσαῦτα F.

ᵃ The *principales*, cf. *Or*. 48. 40.
ᵇ *Cf. Or*. 48. 3, and Introduction, p. 416 f.

claimed to be ill-used : when you did, they would not apply it. What they said they needed came into their hands, and they rejected it.

8. What I have said is barely credible, and the full story is no different. Their behaviour is just like that of a poor man who prays for a treasure from Zeus, and then finds it while he is digging his land and runs away from what has been given him. What then is the reason for this ? In this small number, Sire, are some very influential,[a] who wreak havoc on the weaker members, imposing their own burdens upon them, and the perquisites of curial rank swell their own wealth. One of the sins of omission that deserve to be rectified is the consolation for the existing members derived from the fact that their membership is not large. Every day the lament rises, " You see us standing here ? You can almost count us on the fingers of your hands—twelve instead of twelve hundred.[b] This forms the council. These are the only persons to deal with such important duties. By means of us, and us alone, is conducted the administration in the city and in the country-side, and the management of matters great and small, and the performance of duties light and heavy. That is the reason why you always hear the same names." 9. This is the lament that the courts accept when they bring pardon to the neglected and wronged. In their desire to enjoy this resource and to have the perquisites reserved to themselves alone, the councillors are afraid that the councils may recover any of their former privileges. They ask of you the restoration of the councils, but they act for their permanent humiliation,—or rather they pretend that the first is their objective, but their real

ζητεῖν, τὸ δ᾽ ὄντως ἐθέλουσι. 10. δεῖ τοῖς λουσο-
μένοις πυρός. ἔξεστιν ἐλθεῖν ἐπὶ τὸν δεῖνα καὶ τὸν
δεῖνα, οἱ δὲ οὐκ ἐθέλουσι. δεῖ τοῦ θρέψοντος ἵππους ἡδονὴν παρέξοντας δρόμοις. εἰσὶν ὧν ἄν τις
λαβόμενος ἀναθείη τὴν λειτουργίαν, οἱ δ᾽ αὐτοὺς[1]
γυμνῇ τῇ κεφαλῇ προσεῖπον. εἶτα τοῦ παρόντος
καιροῦ κατηγοροῦσιν ὡς τὰς βουλὰς καταδύσαντος
αὐτοὶ καταδύσαντες καὶ καταποντίσαντες καὶ κε-
κωλυκότες αὐτὰς ἀναβιῶναι. σὺ μὲν γὰρ τοῦτο
ἐβουλήθης, | οὗτοι δὲ τοὐναντίον. 11. τὸν οὖν | F
R ii. 577 πονηρὸν ταῖς βουλαῖς καιρὸν πεποιήκασιν, ὥστ᾽ εἴ
τινα δεῖ δοκεῖν ἐχθρὸν εἶναι τῶν βουλῶν, τοὺς
τοσοῦτον αὐτῶν φυλάττοντας ὅσον αὐτοῖς τηρήσει
τὸ κερδαίνειν νομιστέον. οἳ προδεδώκασι μὲν τὰς
αὐτῶν ἐν τῷ τὰς βουλάς, προδεδώκασι δὲ τὰς ὑφ᾽
ὑμῶν εὑρημένας ταῖς βουλαῖς ὠφελείας. οἱ δὲ
πατρίδας κακοῦντες πῶς οὐκ ἂν καὶ γονέας; οἱ δὲ
ἐκείνους τίνος φείσαιντ᾽ ἄν; τίς γὰρ ἂν εἴη[2] τοῖς
γε τοιούτοις φίλος; οἱ δ᾽ ὑπὲρ χρημάτων τοιοῦτοι
ποίων μὲν ἀπόσχοιντ᾽ ἂν ἀναθημάτων; ποίων δ᾽ ἂν
τάφων; τίνι δ᾽ ἂν συνήθει συνοδοιποροῦντες ἔχοντί
γε χρυσίον οὐκ ἄν, εἴπερ ἐξείη,[3] κτείναντες ἀφέλοιντο;
12. Καὶ τοῦτο, ὦ βασιλεῦ, κοινὸν τὸ κακόν, ἐάν
τε Πάλτον εἴπῃς ἐάν τε ᾽Αλεξάνδρειαν τὴν δεικ-
νῦσαν τὸν ᾽Αλεξάνδρου νεκρὸν ἐάν τε Βαλανέας
ἐάν τε τὴν ἡμετέραν. μέτρῳ μὲν γὰρ διαφέρουσιν,
ἡ δ᾽ αὐτὴ πανταχοῦ νόσος.

---

[1] αὐτοὺς conj. Re.: αὐτοὺς edd. (MSS.).
[2] ἂν εἴη F.: ἄν τι Bong. (MSS.): ἂν ᾖ Re.
[3] ἐξείη F.: ἐξῇ Planudes, Bong., Re. (MSS.).

---

[a] Cf. Or. 2. 34. The heating of the baths and the provision of horses for the races were among the most important
and expensive liturgies of the decurion of this highest class.

intention is the other. 10. Fire is needed for the bathers. They can call upon one person or another for this, but they refuse.[a] Someone is needed for the upkeep of horses to provide entertainment at the races : several people could be claimed and the duty imposed on them, but they nominate themselves, and are bare-faced about it. Then they decry the present state of affairs as being the ruin of the councils, whereas they personally are responsible for their ruin and their wreck and the prevention of their revival. This was what you intended,—but not they. 11. They have caused this disastrous state of affairs for the councils, and so if anybody should be thought to be the enemy of the councils, they must be so regarded—the protectors of just so much of them as will maintain their personal gain. They, in betraying the councils, have betrayed their native cities, and they have betrayed the programme of assistance that you devised for the councils. And if they harmed their cities, they would surely harm their parents too, and if them, whom would they spare ? Who could be the friend of such as these ? When they behave like this for money's sake, would they keep their hands off temple offerings or tombs ? If they were travelling with some companion who had a gold piece, would they not kill him and rob him of it, if they had the chance ?

12. And this evil, Sire, is universal, whether you mention Paltus or Alexandria where the body of Alexander is to be seen, whether Balaneae or our own city.[b] They may differ in size, but the same ailment afflicts them all.

[b] Paltus and Balaneae were two of the smaller cities of Syria.

13. Καίτοι φήσουσι λέγεσθαι τοῖς ἄρχουσι κατά-
λογον τῶν ἀποδράντων καὶ τῶν ἀτελεῖς αὐτοὺς πολλοῖς τρόποις πεποιηκότων. ἔστι δὲ τὸ μὲν οὐκ
ἐκείνων, ἀλλὰ τῶν τε ἀρχόντων καὶ τῶν ἐπὶ τοῖς
R ii. 578 τοιούτοις γράμμασι, τῶν | μὲν ἀπειλαῖς οὐδένα
κρύπτειν ἐώντων, τῶν δὲ φόβῳ πάντα εἰς μέσον
ἀγόντων. οἱ γενναῖοι δὲ οἵδε τοῦ πράγματος εἰς
κρίσιν ἥκοντος | νῦν μὲν σιωπῇ, νῦν δὲ τῷ μηδὲν F
ἰσχυρὸν εἰπεῖν ἐθελῆσαι τοῖς ἀδικοῦσι τὴν βουλὴν
συνέπραξαν μαλακῶς συνηγωνισμένοι, ὡς μηδὲν
ὀνειράτων τὸ πρᾶγμα διαφέρειν. σπείραντες δὲ
τοιαύτας χάριτας ἐν τοῖς δικαστηρίοις ἀπελθόντες
ἀμῶσι τῆς προδοσίας τοὺς μισθοὺς δεχόμενοι γελῶντες[1] πρὸς τοὺς διαφυγόντας ὡς ἄριστα προὔ-
δοσαν. οἱ δ' εἰσὶν ἐν τοῖς πρὸ τοῦ τῇ μὲν αὐτοῦ
γαστρὶ χαριζόμενος ἕκαστος, βεβαιοτέραν δὲ ἔχων
τὴν ἀτέλειαν τῇ κρίσει. 14. γνοίης δ' ἂν ὡς ἀληθῆ
λέγω, διὰ τῶν τριῶν τῶν ἐκ μὲν ἑκατὸν τῇ βουλῇ
δεδομένων, ἐφ' ᾧ τίς τῶν εὖ φρονούντων οὐκ ἠγα-
νάκτησε, τρεῖς ἐκ τοσούτων; τὸ βουλεύειν δὲ καὶ
τούτων διὰ τούτους ἀποσεισαμένων, τῶν τούτοις
R ii. 579 βοηθούντων | ἐν πλούτῳ παῖδας οὐ κεκτημένων
καὶ διὰ τοῦτο χάριτας τοιαύτας δυναμένων λαμβάνειν. εἶτα τίς αὐτοῖς ὁ ἄρχων; καὶ ἦν[2] εὖ ποιῶν
χαλεπὸς τοῖς ἀφεικόσιν, ἐν οἷς ἀφεῖντο[3] τῶν ἀφέντων τὴν ἀδικίαν ἰδών. 15. τὴν γὰρ τῶν ἀμυνούν-
των αὐτοῖς δύναμιν ἄξιον, φησίν, ὑφορᾶσθαι. ἀλλ'

---

[1] γελῶντες Bong., Re. (mss.) : λέγοντες F.
[2] αὐτοῖς ὁ ἄρχων ; καὶ ἦν conj. Re. (*Animadv.*), approved
F. : εἶτα καθήπτετό τις αὐτῶν ἄρχων Re. (edit.) : αὐτῶν ἄρξων καὶ
ἦν mss. [3] ἀφεῖντο conj. Re., F. : ἀφεῖτο Bong., Re. text (mss.).

13. However, they will say that they recite to the governors a list of absconders and of persons who by various manner of means have rendered themselves immune. But this is not attributable to them but to the governors and to the secretarial staff, since the governors, by their fulminations, allow no one any concealment, and the staff in alarm bring every instance to light. But these fine fellows, once the matter comes to judgement, either by their silence or by their refusal to present a forceful case, have, by their feeble support of it, acted in collusion with those who are in default towards the council, so that the business is nothing more than an illusion. After sowing such favours broadcast in the courts they go off and reap the harvest, when they receive the rewards for their treachery and jokingly tell the absconders what a good job they have made of this betrayal. And these stay as they were, every one of them indulging his appetites and with his immunity further confirmed by the verdict. 14. You can recognize the truth of my statements from the fact that three people out of a hundred have been enrolled into the council—and for any sensible person the deplorable fact is that they were but three out of so many. And even those three, assisted by these people, managed to avoid membership, for they were aided and abetted by persons wealthy and childless, and therefore able to obtain such favours. What was the governor's attitude towards them then? He was justifiably angry with those who had granted the remission, since he saw in the circumstances of their release the unscrupulousness of those who had secured it. 15. " Yes ! The influence of their protectors," it is remarked, " is deservedly suspect."

εἰ τοῦτ᾽ ἔστιν ἀληθές, οὐκ ἔστιν αὐτοῖς ἐκεῖνο λέγειν ὡς ὑπ᾽ αὐτῶν τὰ τῶν κλεπτόντων ἑαυτοὺς ὀνόματα τοῖς ἄρχουσι φανερὰ καθίσταται. εἰ γὰρ οὐκ ἀδεές, οἱ κηδόμενοι τούτων οὐδ᾽ ἂν τοῖς ὀνόμασιν ἐλύπουν οὓς[1] ἐφοβοῦντο. οὐ γὰρ μᾶλλον ἐν τοῖς | δευτέροις ἐχαρίζοντο τοῖς συμμάχοις ἢ διὰ F τοῦ | σπέρματος ἐλύπουν. οὕτως ὅταν αὐτῶν τὸ τῶν ὀνομάτων ποιῶσιν ἐξαπατῶσιν. ἀλλὰ μήν, ὅταν ὡς ἔδεισαν λέγωσι τὴν τῶν ταῦτα οὐ βουλομένων ἰσχύν, ὁμολογοῦσιν εἶναι περὶ τὴν αὐτῶν κακοί. οὐ γὰρ τὸ μὴ ἠδικηκέναι ταύτῃ δεικνύουσι, τὴν δ᾽ αἰτίαν ἀφ᾽ ἧς ἠδικήκασι λέγουσιν. 16. ἔνι δὲ καὶ τοῖς δειλοῖς ὧν οἱ μὲν λείπουσι τὰς τάξεις, οἱ δ᾽ οὐδὲ μετέχουσιν αὐτῶν, τοιαῦτα κρινομένοις λέγειν· δειλὸν γάρ με ἡ μήτηρ ἔτεκε καὶ τὰ ὅπλα λαβεῖν οὐκ ἐδυνήθην. ὁ δὲ τοῦτο μὲν πεποιηκέναι φήσει καὶ συμπαρατάξασθαι, τὸ δ᾽ ἔργον καὶ τὰ ἀπὸ τῆς μάχης οὐκ ἐνεγκεῖν. ἀπορήσει[2] δ᾽ οὐδ᾽ ὅστις ἱερῶν χρημάτων οὐδ᾽ ὅστις ἅπτεται τάφων αἰτίας ἀφ᾽ ἧς ἐπὶ ταῦτα ἧκεν, ἀλλ᾽ ὀδυροῦνται τὴν πενίαν, ὥσπερ αὖ καὶ ὁ προδότης. ἀλλ᾽ οὐδεὶς τοῖς τοιούτοις σώζεται, τὴν δίκην δὲ ὑπέχων εἴσεται μόνην οὖσαν σωτηρίαν ἐν τῷ τῆς αἰτίας ἐλέγχῳ.

17. Καὶ νῦν μή τις λεγέτω τὸν φόβον, ἀλλ᾽ εἰ μὴ προεῖτο τὴν βουλὴν μηδὲ κακὸν ἑαυτὸν ἐπέδειξε. καὶ γὰρ εἴ τινα λυπήσειν ἔμελλε καί τινος πειράσεσθαι δυσχεροῦς, τό γε πρὸς τὴν ἐνεγκοῦσαν δίκαιον πρότερον ἔδει πεποιῆσθαι καὶ τῆς ψυχῆς

---

[1] οὓς conj. Re., F. : οἷς Bong., Re. text (mss.).
[2] ἀπορήσει F. : ἀπορήσειε Bong., Re. (mss.).

But if that is true, they cannot possibly assert that they are responsible for revealing to the governors the names of those who spirit themselves away. If the procedure involved an element of risk, those in charge of this business would certainly not irritate those whom they feared by submitting these names, for the obligation they conferred by their subsequent support would not counterbalance their initial offence. So when they claim responsibility for producing that list, they are employing a subterfuge. Moreover in stating that they feared the influence of the opposition, they confess that they are neglectful of their own, for in this they reveal not their innocence of misconduct but the reason for their misconduct. 16. Even cowards who either desert the ranks or do not join them at all could, at their court-martial, use some such argument as, "I was a coward when my mother bore me : I couldn't handle a weapon," or else assert that, though he has done so and joined the ranks, he could not face action and the hurly-burly of fighting. Nor will any who rifles the treasures of the gods or the tombs of the dead lack an excuse for resorting to such actions, but they lament their poverty, as the traitor does, too. But no one is saved by such arguments. As he suffers the punishment, he will come to learn that his sole salvation lies in disproving the charge.

17. So now let no one talk to me of fear, but let him say whether or not he has betrayed the council and revealed himself a rogue. For even if the probability was that he would annoy someone and experience some unpleasant consequences, he ought to think more of doing his duty than of life itself.

475

αὐτῆς. καὶ πολλοὶ πολλάκις εἰδότες τὸν συμβησό-
μενόν σφισιν εἰ μάχοιντο θάνατον ὅμως μάχονται
καὶ μυρίοις θνήσκοντες τραύμασι μετὰ τοῦ χαίρειν
ἀπέρχονται. σὺ δὲ | ποίαν αἰχμὴν ἢ ποῖον βέλος F 4
ἢ ⟨τίνα⟩[1] σφενδόνην ἢ τίνα δείσας ἀσπίδα τὴν τοῦ
R ii. 581 δικαίου τάξιν ἔλιπες; οὐ μέμψεως ἦν ὁ φόβος | καὶ
ῥημάτων ὀλίγων; δῶμεν δ' ὅτι καὶ θανάτου, τί
οὖν; οὐ κέρδος ὁ τοιοῦτος θάνατος; ἢ σύ γε οὐκ
οἶσθα τοὺς λαμπροὺς ἐκείνους θανάτους τοὺς ὑπὲρ
τῶν πατρίδων;

18. Καὶ ταῦτα εἶπον ὡς κίνδυνον ἐνεγκούσης ἂν
τῆς τοῦ δικαίου φυλακῆς. τὸ δὲ οὐχ οὕτως ἂν
ἔσχεν. οὐδὲ γὰρ οὑμὸς πάππος τὸν Ἀργύριον τῆς
βουλῆς εἶναι ποιῶν νέον τε ὄντα καὶ ξένον καὶ μικρὰ
κεκτημένον ἔπαθέ τι κακόν, πρᾶγμα ποιῶν λυπηρὸν τῷ τότε ἄρχοντι, λυπηρὸν δὲ τῷ τότε σοφιστῇ
τὴν πόλιν ἀπὸ νευμάτων ἄγοντι, ἀλλ' ὅμως οὔτε
αἰτούντων χάριν εἶξεν οὔτε ἀπειλούντων ἔπτηξεν,
ἀλλ' ὁ μὲν ἐλειτούργει, τῷ δ' οὐδὲν δεινὸν οὐδαμόθεν ἦν. 19. εἶεν. ἀλλ' ἐκεῖνο μὲν ἀρχαῖον, ἀλλ'
οὑτοσὶ Λητόιος, ἡνίκα ἐβούλευε, φαίη δ' ἄν τις
αὐτὸν καὶ νῦν διὰ τοῦ παιδός, οὐ τρεῖς ἀποδράντας
αὖθις βουλευτὰς ἀπέφηνε, λόχων ἡγησαμένους ἀνθρώπους καὶ στρατιώταις ἐπιτάξαντας καὶ μετ'
ἐκείνων τὸ πολὺ τῆς γῆς ἐπελθόντας καιροῖς καλοῦσιν ὑπακούοντας; καίτοι ταῦτα ποιῶν ᾔδει
κινήσων ἐφ' ἑαυτὸν στρατηγὸν δοῦλον ὀργῆς καὶ

[1] ⟨τίνα⟩ F.

---

[a] Probably Ulpianus, cf. Or. 36. 10 (PLRE 973 (i));
certainly not, as suggested by Foerster, Zenobius.

[b] Argyrius became Syriarch in A.D. 332 (Or. 10. 10). For
his municipal career v. J.H.S. lxxiv (1954), pp. 44 ff.

Many a time and often men have realized that death awaited them if they went into battle, but they go into battle just the same, suffer countless wounds, and gladly depart this life. But you—what spear, what arrow, what slingbolt or what shield were you afraid of, that you deserted the side of the right? Was not your fear that of reproof, of a few mere words? But grant that it was the fear of death; what of it? Is not death in such a cause clear gain? Or have you never heard of all those heroes who have died a glorious death for their country?

18. These comments of mine imply that the defence of the right would have involved danger. But this would not have been the case. My grandfather suffered no harm when he made a councillor of Argyrius, a young foreigner with little property, for all that his action was annoying to the then governor and to the then professor who had directed the city as he liked.[a] Despite this, he did not give way to their requests for favour nor did he cower at their threats. Argyrius went on to perform his civic services,[b] and my grandfather came to no harm at all. 19. Well! That may be ancient history. But what about Letoïus here? When he was a member of the council[c]—and it could be said that, by reason of his son, he still is—did he not re-nominate three absconders as councillors, although they had been battalion commanders in charge of troops and with them had traversed the length and breadth of the world as the needs of the time required? He knew that in doing so he would bring down upon himself a general who was a slave to his temper and full of

[c] Cf. Or. 31. 47, 48. 42 n.

μεστὸν φορᾶς. ἀλλ' ὅμως ἐκεῖνος ἔχων τοὺς ἄλλους πολιτευομένους κακῶς καὶ γράμματα τὰ 'κεί-
νων τῷ μὴ καὶ | τὰ τοῦδε προσλαβεῖν εἶχεν οὐδέν. F 4

R ii. 582 καίτοι διὰ πότου | καὶ τραπέζης αὐτὸν ἐκλύσειν
ἤλπιζε. καὶ ἅμα προπίνων αὐτῷ φιλοτησίαν καὶ
τὸ βιβλίον ᾔτει τὴν προσθήκην, ὁ δ' ἔπιε μέν, δοῦναι δὲ ἃ μὴ καλὸν οὐκ ἠνέσχετο καὶ διετέλεσε μι-
σούμενος μέν, παθὼν δὲ οὐδέν. 20. οὐ τοίνυν οὐδὲ
νῦν φόβῳ ταῦτα συγκεχώρηται οὐδὲ τῷ νομίζειν, εἰ
μὴ βλάψαιεν τὰς βουλάς, ἀπολεῖσθαι, ἀλλ' ᾔδεσαν
αὐτοῖς ἰδίᾳ συνοῖσον τὸ[1] τὰς βουλὰς ἔχειν ὡς ἔχουσιν.
21. Ἔστι τοίνυν αὐτοῖς καὶ τοιοῦτός τις λόγος,
ὡς εἰ καὶ σφόδρα αὐτοὺς βουλεύειν ἀναγκάσουσιν,
ἔστι τὸ λῦσον καὶ πάλιν αὐτοῖς δῶσον τὸ μὴ βουλεύειν ὥστ' αὐτοῖς γέλωτα τὴν περὶ τοῦτο εἶναι
πραγματείαν. ἔστι δὲ πᾶν τοῦτο ψεῦδος. τὸν γὰρ
ἐκ τῶν δικαίων ἃ περὶ τοῦτο ἔστιν εἰλημμένον καὶ
κρίσει καὶ ψήφῳ τῆς βουλῆς γεγενημένον καί, τὸ
ἔτι μεῖζον, τοῖς ὑμετέροις νόμοις τί τὸ λῦσον ἂν
εἴη; ἐγὼ μὲν οἶμαι οὐδέν. 22. εἰ δὲ δεῖ συγχωρῆσαι πάντα ἂν γενέσθαι χρημάτων, τό γε δικαίους
εἶναι περὶ τὴν βουλὴν τούτοις γε ἐσῴζετ' ἄν, εἰ δι'

R ii. 583 αὐτοὺς ἐγγραφέντες | ἑτέρωθεν ἐξηλείφοντο. θή-
ρασον αὐτός, κράτησον, εἰσένεγκε τῇ βουλῇ τὰ
ὀφειλόμενα, γενοῦ χρήστης δίκαιος. ἂν δ' ἀδικῇ
τις ἄλλος, τό γε σὸν οὐκ ἐν | αἰτίᾳ. οὐδὲ γὰρ ἦν F 4
τις ἀρρωστῶν δῆλος ᾗ πάντως τεθνήξων,[2] ἀμελεῖται

---

[1] συνοῖσον τὸ Re., F. : συνοίσοντα Bong. (mss.).
[2] τεθνήξων F. (IBM) : τεθνήσων CAP : τεθνηξόμενος Bong.,
Re. (M marg.).

---

[a] A practice criticized in *Or.* 52. 47 as occasioning corrupt
favours, and banned by Cynegius as ppO.

truculence. And though the general had on his side
the other councillors, who failed in their duty, and
their written recommendations, he still did not get
his way, since he did not have that of Letoïus as well.
He hoped to get him to relent by wining and dining
him, and as he was offering him a toast of friendship,[a]
he requested his letter of commendation as a bonus.
Letoïus drank the toast but refused to make any
improper concession, and so continued to be resented,
but without suffering harm. 20. Nowadays, though,
such concessions are not made from fear nor from
the thought that they will be ruined if they do not
do harm to the councils, but from their realization
that it will be to their own personal profit for the
councils to be in the situation they are now in.

21. But they employ the following argument also,
that however much they compel them to join the
council, there is a means of release that will once
more give them immunity from it, so that to engage
themselves in this business is ridiculous. All this is
a downright lie. What possible means of release
can there be for persons who have been claimed in
accordance with the proper procedure on the matter,
and who have become members of the council by its
judgement and decree and, more to the point, by your
imperial laws? None, surely. 22. But if we have
to admit that money talks in everything, yet these
people could maintain a correct attitude towards
the council if those whom they enrolled obtained the deletion of their names from other sources.
Hunt them out yourself, sir, get hold of them, pay
your due to the council, and honour your debt, and
if somebody is remiss, you at least are free from
blame. If someone is sick and will obviously die in any

μὲν ὑπὸ τῶν ἰατρῶν, ἀμελεῖται δὲ ὑπὸ τῶν οἰκείων, ἀλλὰ καὶ πόνοι καὶ φροντίδες καὶ ἀγρυπνίαι
καὶ φάρμακα, καὶ ὡς μὲν οὐδεμία τούτων ὄνησις
ἔγνωσται, πᾶν δὲ ὅσον ἄξιον πρὸ τοῦ θανάτου πέπρακται. 23. ὁρῶμεν δέ τοι καὶ τὰς ἀσθενεστέρας
τῶν πόλεων τειχιζούσας ἑαυτὰς καὶ ταῦτα ἐπι-
σταμένας ὅτι τῶν μᾶλλον ἰσχυόντων ἐστὶ τὸ πρῶτα
τὰ τείχη κατενεγκεῖν. ἆρα διὰ τοῦτο ζῶσιν ἀτεί-
χιστοι; τί δ᾽ οἱ τῶν ἀφυεστέρων πατέρες οὐχὶ καὶ
τούτους[1] ἐν οἷς οὐκ εἰσὶν ἐλπίδες πέμπουσιν εἰς
διδασκάλων δώσοντας μὲν χρήματα, ληψομένους
δὲ οὐδέν; τί δὴ τὸ πεῖθον; τὸ μὴ βούλεσθαι δοκεῖν ἠμεληκέναι τῶν τῆς φύσεως νόμων μηδὲ
παρέχειν λαβὴν τοῖς ἡδέως ἐπιτιμῶσιν ὅτι ἄρα τὸ
σφῶν αὐτῶν οὐκ ἐποίησαν ⟨οὐχ⟩[2] ὧν ἦσαν κύριοι
παρεσχημένοι. 24. καὶ μὴν τούς γε τῶν οἰκετῶν
κλέπτειν μεμαθηκότας μαστιγοῦμεν καὶ ταῦτα εἰδότες ὡς καὶ ἐν αὐτῷ τῷ τὰς πληγὰς ἰᾶσθαι
χρῶνται τῷ τρόπῳ κἂν τοῖς αὐτοῖς αἱ χεῖρες. ὁ
δεσπότης δὲ εἰ καὶ μὴ τὸν οἰκέτην μετέβαλεν, ἀλλ᾽
αὑτόν γε κατέστησεν ἄμεμπτον ταῖς ἐφ᾽ ἑκάστῳ
R ii. 584 πληγαῖς. τί δ᾽ οἱ τοὺς | ὄνους ὑπὲρ τάχους παί-
οντες οὐχὶ καὶ τῆς βραδυτῆτος μενούσης παίουσιν
ὅμως τὸ δοκεῖν ἐλλείπειν τὰ παρ᾽ αὑτῶν φυλατ-
τόμενοι; |

25. Γίγνου δὴ καὶ αὐτὸς ἡμῖν ὑπὲρ τῆς βουλῆς F 4
ἀνήρ, εἰ καὶ τἠνάλλως πονήσεις καὶ οἱ τὰ τοιαῦτα
μένειν οὐκ ἐάσοντες γενήσοιντο. ἴσως δὲ οὐδὲ
τἠνάλλως ἀκριβεῖ λόγῳ τοῦτό ἐστιν, ὅταν ἐν αὐτῷ
τι τῷ πεπονηκέναι κέρδος ᾖ. οἷον δή τι καὶ τοὺς

---

[1] τούτους F. : τούτων Bong., Re. (mss.).
[2] ⟨οὐχ⟩ F.

case, he is not neglected by his doctors or his family :
they work and they worry, they keep watch at his
bedside and dose him, and though they realize that
there is not a bit of good to be got from all this, yet
everything that can be done is done for him before
he dies. 23. We see even the weaker cities walling
themselves about, though they know full well that
the first thing to be demolished by more powerful
assailants is the walls. Do they therefore live un-
walled ? Why ! don't the fathers of dunces send
them to school, even though they are hopeless, to
pay their fees and to get nothing from it ? What
induces them to do it ? Their refusal to be thought
to have neglected the laws of nature and to allow an
opening to the critics who would readily reproach
them with failing in their duty by not providing
them with what they could have done. 24. Moreover,
we flog those of our slaves who have learned how to
steal, even though we know that under the actual
correction of the lash they keep their character and
their hands will again be engaged in the same activity : and even if the master is unable to reform
his slave, at any rate he has rendered himself blameless by flogging him for each offence. And, as for
the drivers who beat their asses to speed them up,
if their slow pace continues, don't they yet continue
to beat them, guarding against any seeming dereliction of duty on their own part ?

25. So you, too, show yourself for us a man in your
support of the council, even if your labour be in vain
and there be those who will refuse it any permanence.
And perhaps, to be precise, it is not in vain at all,
since there is some profit to be won in the very performance of your labour, as, for instance, we see in

κλύδωνι διαφθειρομένους ἔστιν ἰδεῖν ποιοῦντας.
ἴσασι μὲν ὡς ὁ χειμὼν περιέσται τιθεὶς ὑπὸ τῇ
θαλάττῃ τὸ πλοῖον καὶ οὐδεμία τέχνη τοῦτ' ἐξαρπάσαι δυνήσεται, τὸ δ' ὅ τι δύναιντο βοηθεῖν οὐ
προκαταλύουσιν. ἀλλ' οὐδὲ τὰς μελίττας μέντοι
παύει τῆς ἐργασίας τὸ τοῖς πεπονημένοις τοὺς
κηφῆνας ἐπιτίθεσθαι, ἀλλ' οἱ μὲν ἐσθίουσιν, αἱ δὲ
ὑφαίνουσιν.

26. Ἔτι τοίνυν οὐκ ἐκείνων ἢ τούτων αἱ λύσεις.
ἢν γὰρ δὴ μὴ τούσδε λάβωσι συνεργούς, αἱ 'κείνων συμμαχίαι σκιὰν ἤνεγκαν συμμαχίας. τὸ οὖν
τι τὸν Φίλιππον δύνασθαι παρὰ Λασθένους ἔστι,
παρ' Εὐθυκράτους ἔστι, παρὰ τῶν ἄλλων ὅσοι
δούλας τὰς αὑτῶν ἐκείνου κατέστησαν δώροις, οὐχ
ὅπλοις πολεμοῦντος. δῶρα δὴ καὶ τούτους ἀδικεῖν ἀναπείθει, καὶ μέχρις ἂν αὐτοῖς ἀζήμιον τοῦτο
ᾖ, τρυγῶντες οὐ παύσονται. |

27. Μάστιγι τοίνυν αὐτοὺς ἀμείνους ἀπόφηνον, F 4
R ii. 585 ὅπερ αὖ καὶ τὸν Δία πεποιηκέναι φησὶν | Ὅμηρος,
καὶ ἐπειδὴ μὴ ἑκόντες, ἄκοντες τὰς βουλὰς εὖ ποιούντων. ἃς σὺ μὲν ἀνορθοῖς, οἱ δὲ ἐναντιοῦνται
περὶ μὲν τοῦ πῶς ἂν ἵππος ἵππου καὶ ἡνίοχος
ἡνιόχου καὶ ὀρχηστὴς ὀρχηστοῦ κρατήσειε [καὶ]¹
σκοποῦντες καὶ βουλευόμενοι καὶ παντὸς ἁπτόμενοι καὶ λόγου καὶ ἔργου, τὰ δὲ τῶν βουλῶν ἐῶντες
κατερρυηκέναι δεδιότες μὴ παύσῃς αὐτὰς ἀτυχού-
σας, ἐπαινοῦντες πλοῦς βλαβεροὺς ταῖς ἀθλίαις
νεότητα βεβουλευκότων γενῶν ἄγοντας, τοὺς μὲν

---

¹ καὶ Bong., Re. (mss.), bracketed F.

ᵃ The fifth-columnists who betrayed Olynthus to Philip,
Diod. Sic. 16. 53 f.

the behaviour of those who perish in shipwreck.
They know that the storm will win and will sink
their vessel beneath the waves and that no device
can rescue it, but they do not cease making every
possible effort before that happens. Nor yet do the
honey bees cease their activity because the drones
attack what they have toiled upon, but the drones
feast, and they work away.

26. Moreover, the remissions are due not so much
to those intriguers as to these members. If they did
not have these accomplices, the support obtained
from them would be but a shadow. So Philip's domi-
nation is due to Lasthenes, Euthycrates [a] and all the
rest who reduced their states to slavery while he
fought with bribes, not arms. And it is bribes that
induce these people to betray their trust : while
ever they get away with it scot-free, they will not
cease to collect their pickings.

27. So let them be seen as reformed by your lash,
just as Homer says was done by Zeus,[b] and let them
work to their council's good, if not willingly, then
against their will. While you try to reform the councils, they oppose them, and their attention is reserved
for how one horse, one driver,[c] one dancer can beat
another : this is the object of their deliberations and
to this end they apply their every word and action,
and they let the councils collapse in ruins and are
afraid that you will put a stop to their disastrous
plight : they commend the travels overseas which,
disastrous to the wretched councils, export young
men of families that were once their members either

---

[b] Διὸς μάστιγι δαμέντες, Homer, *Il.* 12. 37, 13. 812.
[c] *Cf. Or.* 48. 9.

εἰς Φοινίκην, τοὺς δὲ εἰς Ἰταλίαν, οὐχ ὡς ἐπὶ καλλίω τῶν παρ' ἡμῖν[1] πεμπόντων ἐκεῖσε τῶν γονέων,
ἀλλ' οὐκ ἀγνοοῦσι μὲν τὴν τούτων εὐγένειαν, ἀπαλλαγὴν δὲ βουλῆς ἐν ἐκείνοις ὁρώντων. 28. ἐφ' οἷς
οὐδεὶς τούτων τὸ ὦ Γῆ καὶ Ἥλιε λέγει οὐδ' εἴργει
καταβαίνοντας εἰς λιμένα οὐδ' ἃ τὰς βουλὰς ἐλε-
ούντων ἦν λέγει, ἀλλὰ καὶ συγχαίρουσι καὶ συν-
εύχονται καὶ προπέμπουσι. καὶ τοσαῦται μὲν
πρεσβεῖαι, φροντὶς δὲ ἐλαττόνων, τῶν τηλικούτων
δὲ οὐδεμία.

29. Καίτοι γε οὐκ ἦν τῆς σῆς ἀνάξιον, ὦ βασιλεῦ, φύσεως θεῖναι νόμον μὴ τοιαῦτα τοὺς τοιούτους μανθάνειν ἀφ' ὧν αὑτοὺς ἔξω τῶν βουλῶν
ποιήσουσιν, ἀλλ' ἀφ' ὧν τὴν τῶν προγόνων ὁδὸν
ἥξουσιν, οἷς ἦν | ἀρκοῦν εἰς φιλοτιμίαν ἀπὸ τῆς F
Ἑλλάδος φωνῆς ταῖς πατρίσι βοηθεῖν. καὶ οὐδὲν
δεινὸν ἔπασχε Φασγάνιος ἐκεῖνος δι' ἑρμηνέων τοῖς
ἄρχουσι συγγιγνόμενος οὐδ' ἰλιγγιῶν ἑωρᾶτο, οὐδ'
οἱ τῶν Ῥωμαίων ἄκροι τῷ μὴ τὴν Ἰταλῶν γλῶτταν εὑρίσκειν παρ' ἐκείνῳ χεῖρον τῇ πόλει τὰ
πράγματα ἔχειν ἔφασκον, ἀλλ' οὕτως ἀνεῖχε τὴν
βουλὴν καὶ τὴν πόλιν καὶ προϊὼν ἐνδοξότερος ἐγί-
R ii. 586 γνετο καθ' ἑκάστην | ἡμέραν, ὥστ' οὐδεὶς τῶν
ἀρχόντων οὐχὶ Φασγάνιος μᾶλλον ἢ ὅσπερ ἦν ἤθελεν εἶναι. καὶ γάρ τοι μᾶλλον ἐκεῖνοι τοῦτον
ἐπανελθόντες ἢ ὅδε ἐκείνους μένων ἐθαύμαζε.

30. Δότωσαν τοίνυν οἶδε δίκην, ὦ βασιλεῦ, τῆς
πολλῆς εἰρωνείας καὶ μαθέτωσαν μὴ τὰ αὑτῶν

---

[1] ἡμῖν Re., F. : ἡμῶν Bong. (MSS.).

[a] For training in law and Latin cf. Or. 1. 214, 40. 7,
43. 3 ff., 48. 22, 28 ff., 62. 21.

[b] A common expression of indignation in Libanius, cf.
Or. 50. 16, 42. 6.

to Phoenicia or to Italy,[a] not because their parents among us send them there for their improvement but because, well aware of their respectable origin, they see in such measures a means of being rid of council membership. 28. None of them exclaims, " Good heavens above !" [b] at this, nor does he try to stop them as they go down to the harbour, nor does he utter any word of pity for the councils. Rather, they congratulate them, wish them well and escort them on their way. And for all their embassies, their concern is for lesser matters : for things like this, it is non-existent.

29. Yet it would not be unworthy of you, Sire, to legislate that such people should not learn such things as will put them outside the council's reach, but rather such studies as will ensure that they follow in their ancestors' footsteps. Their ambitions were satisfied by assisting their home town by the Greek language. The renowned Phasganius [c] was not adversely affected by conversing with governors through interpreters, nor was he ever seen at a loss : nor yet did leading Romans assert that the administration of the city was less efficient because they found in him no acquaintance with Latin. His support of the council and the city and the daily increase of his fame, as time went on, was such that no governor but wished to be in Phasganius' position rather than his own. In fact, they on their return home felt more admiration for him than he, staying here, had for them.

30. So let these people, Sire, be punished for all their double-dealing. Let them learn how to pro-

[c] Libanius' uncle, cf. Or. 1. 13, 86 ; 2. 11 ; 10. 11 ; 53. 4 ; 62. 30 (Seeck 234).

ἀδίκως, τὰ δὲ κοινὰ τῶν πόλεων δικαίως αὔξειν.
νῦν μὲν γὰρ ἀσφαλῶς πονηρευόμενοι πολεμοῦσι
τοῖς συμφέρουσι τῶν πατρίδων,¹ δόντες δὲ δίκην
παύσονται τοῦ τὰ τοιαῦτα πωλεῖν. 31. πρώην τις
ἤγγειλέ μοι τὸν αὐτὸν ἄνθρωπον ἐν μικρᾷ τινι πόλει τά τ' ἔνδον καὶ τά [τε]² τῶν τειχῶν ἔξω δι-
οικεῖν καὶ πολλὰς ἔχειν τὰς τάξεις καὶ προσηγορίας εἰσπράττοντα, τοῖς ἑαυτοῦ χρήμασι λοῦσθαι
τοῖς ἐκεῖ παρέχοντα, τὸν δ' αὐτὸν ἀμφορέα λαβόντα
βαλανέα γενέσθαι, καὶ τῷ ἄρχοντι θαῦμα τοῦτο
ἐνεγκεῖν ὁρῶντι τὸν πολιτευόμενον καὶ | ταῦτα ἐρ- F 4
γαζόμενον. τούτῳ τοίνυν ἐξῆν ἂν ἔχειν κοινωνοὺς
οὐκ ὀλίγους καὶ πρὸς τούτῳ ταυτὶ τὰν τῷ βαλανείῳ διαφυγεῖν, εἰ μὴ κέρδος ἦν αὐτῷ τὸ μεμονῶ-
σθαι. νῦν δ' ὁ μὲν ἄρχων ἐγέλασε, τὸ κακὸν δὲ
ἔμεινεν, ἡ πόλις δὲ εἰς κώμης σχῆμα κατέβη. δι-
όπερ ἐπαινεῖν ἔχω τὸν νῦν τοῦτον ὕπαρχον τρεῖς
τινας ἀπὸ δικαζόντων τῶν³ θρόνων εἰς βουλὴν
μετενεγκόντα, μᾶλλον δὲ οὐ τὸ πᾶν ἐπαινῶ. τῇ
γὰρ ἀρχῇ τὸ τέλος οὐχ ὡμολόγησεν. οὐδὲ γὰρ
R ii. 587 τρεῖς ἂν ἑωράκει μόνους τῷ | δικαίῳ συναγωνιζό-
μενος, ἀλλ' οὐδὲ ἔστιν εἰπεῖν ὅσους.
32. Σὺ⁴ τοίνυν ἀνθ' ἁπάντων γενοῦ ταῖς βουλαῖς,
ὦ βασιλεῦ, ταῖς οὐκ ἐλάττονος σπουδῆς ἀξίαις ἢ
ὅσης αἱ δυνάμεις. αἱ μέν γε ταῖς πόλεσι τὴν σωτηρίαν φέρουσιν, αἱ δ' εἶναί τι ποιοῦσι τὸ σωτηρίας
ἄξιον. τῶν βουλῶν δὲ ὡς ἐδείκνυον διακειμένων

¹ πατρίδων Re., F. (C) : πατρίων Bong. (other mss.).
² καὶ τὰ F. : καὶ τά τε Bong. (mss.) : τά τε Re.
³ τῶν F. (I) : transposed to ἀπὸ τῶν Re. : om. Bong. (other mss.). ⁴ ὅσους. σὺ Re., F. : ὅσους οὔ. Bong. (mss.).

ᵃ Recapitulates Or. 2. 34 ff.
ᵇ Tatianus, ppO A.D. 388–392 : cf. § 1 n. His curial
486

mote not their own unjust advantage, but the just and universal prosperity of the cities. For now they misconduct themselves with impunity and wage war against the interests of their countries, but if they are punished they will stop such venality. 31. Recently I was told of one and the same person who, in a small town, undertakes the administration of affairs both inside and outside the city limits, and holds many ranks and titles [a] : he is collector of the revenue ; at his own expense he has the duty of maintaining the baths for the local inhabitants, and, in his own person, he picks up the jug and becomes the bath attendant. The governor was much surprised to see the town councillor engaged on this task too. But he could have had plenty of partners, and moreover he could have avoided this job in the baths, if it were not to his advantage to be all on his own. As things are, the governor burst into laughter, the situation remained without remedy, and the place was reduced to the level of a village. Hence I can commend our present prefect [b] for transferring three individuals from the magistrates' bench to the council, but my commendation is not without qualification, for the outcome did not match the beginning. If he supported what was right, he would not have seen just three but numbers beyond telling.

32. So, Sire, become the sole saviour of the councils, for they deserve no less support than do the armed services. These indeed bring protection for the cities, while the councils ensure that there is something that deserves protection. But when the legislation is as prolific as that of Cynegius (*v. C. Th.* 12. 1. 119-127).

οὐδ' ὑπὲρ ὅτου καλὸν κινδυνεύειν ἔνι. τοσοῦτον ἐντεῦθεν αἶσχος κατακέχυται τῶν πόλεων τῆς ἐκεῖθεν ἀμορφίας ἐπὶ πᾶν ἀφικνουμένης. ποίησον δὴ πάλιν λαμπρὰ μὲν τὰ θέατρα τῷ πλήθει παρὰ τῶν διδόντων, λαμπρὰς δὲ τῷ αὐτῷ τούτῳ τὰς ἐπιδείξεις τῶν λόγων, ὡς νῦν γε οἱ μὲν οὐδ' εἰπόντες πορεύονται στένοντες, οἱ δ' ὅτι εἶπον ἑαυτοῖς ἐπιτιμῶντες, καὶ μήν, ὃ μέγιστόν | ἐστιν ἁπάν- F 4⁣⟨ των, τὸ τῆς ῥητορικῆς σθένος, ᾗ καὶ τὸ πραχθῆναι προσῆκον εὑρίσκεται καὶ τὸ πραχθὲν ἐγκωμιάζεται. ταύτῃ τοίνυν μετὰ τῶν βουλῶν ἀπολωλέναι καὶ διεφθάρθαι συμβέβηκεν, ὥσπερ, ἡνίκα ἦσαν μεγάλαι, καὶ ταύτῃ τετιμῆσθαί τε καὶ πολλοὺς ἔχειν τοὺς ἐραστάς.

33. Βουλοίμην δ' ἄν σοι τὴν βασιλείαν μὴ μόνον στρατείαις[1] κεκοσμῆσθαι καὶ μάχαις καὶ τροπαίοις καὶ νίκαις, ἀλλὰ καὶ τῇ παιδεύσει καὶ τοῖς λόγοις, ὧν ἡ Ἑλλὰς μήτηρ, ἤ, εἰ βούλει γε, ὧν πατέρες οἱ παῖδες τῆς Ἑλλάδος. ὡς οὖν ἐν τῷ ταῖς βουλαῖς βοηθεῖν βοηθήσων καὶ τοῖς νῦν ἀπερριμμένοις βιβλίοις, τῇ κατὰ τούτων οἷς βραχὺ τῶν δικαίων μέλει κολάσει δεῖξον ἄμφω τὴν ἰσχὺν ἀπειληφότα, τά τε βουλευτήρια τά τε διδασκαλεῖα.

---

[1] στρατείαις F. : στρατίαις Re. (CAPI) : στρατιώταις Bong. (BM).

councils are in the situation I have described, there is nothing worth taking risks for, and in consequence such disgrace overwhelms the cities, since the degradation spreads from the council to every part of the community. So once again restore the prestige of our lecture rooms among the people by reason of the orators, and by this same act restore the prestige of the displays of oratory, for nowadays some people go their ways lamenting that they have not uttered a word, others reproach themselves that they have. And, most important of all, restore the power of rhetoric, whereby the right course of action is discovered, and the action praised. For it has been the lot of rhetoric to suffer ruin and destruction along with the councils, just as, when the councils were great, it too was held in honour and had many devoted to it.

33. My desire is that your reign should be renowned not merely for campaigns and battles, trophies and victories, but also for education and for the eloquence of which Greece is the mother, or, to put it in another way, the sons of Greece are the sires. Therefore, in aiding the councils, proffer aid also to the literature that is now cast aside and, by your correction of those who have scant regard for what is right, demonstrate that power has been recovered by both council chamber and school room.

ORATION 47
ON PROTECTION SYSTEMS

INTRODUCTION

In this oration Libanius, himself a victim of the practice, inveighs against the recent and rapid growth of an organized system of protection run by army officers among the local peasantry. This he saw as detrimental to the established order of land tenure, fiscal obligation and judicial administration.

The activities of such officers are directed, first, against the big villages, evidently *vici publici*, which are occupied by free small-holders. These, relying upon military support, institute a reign of terror among their neighbours, intimidating the rural constabulary, and in consequence patronage becomes nothing more than an encouragement of wrong-doing, rather than a deterrent to it. The decurions responsible for the collection of the village tribute, unable to perform this duty, are forced to sell their estates to make up the deficiency. With such decurions lost to the order, the stability of the social order is prejudiced (§§ 4-10).

Secondly, estates owned by a single landlord fall under their influence. Here the tenants are finally induced to resist the master's demands after learning by experience that he is impotent to protect them, and they are assured of the support of this intrusive patron should the landlord resort to law to secure redress. This Libanius had discovered for himself

493

in the case of his Jewish tenants. The traditional system of land tenure is upset and, with it, the dispensation of justice, since in the inevitable court cases the civil governor connives with the military patron. To remedy this abuse the intervention of the emperor is necessary (§§ 11-18).

Libanius does not protest against patronage as such, but for him it must be based not on this new-fangled and illegitimate encroachment of the military, but on the traditional patron-client relationship of master and tenant. The landlord is the traditional patron and recourse to a military patron is a denigration of this status ; only if he is incapable of fulfilling the duty should there be such recourse, and then by the landlord himself. With him as the middle man, the dangers of direct contact between the army and the peasantry are removed, the rights of property remain undiminished and, while the peasant is satisfied, a potential conflict between soldier and civilian is avoided (§§ 19-24). Sharply contrasted with the rapacity of present-day soldiery is the self-discipline of those of an earlier time, as Libanius proves by citing the example of his uncle by marriage, an eminent soldier who left the service as poor as he entered it. In the past, the military did not deliberately purpose the ruin of the established gentry,—a far different situation from that of the present day (§§ 25-34). The only remedy is for the emperor to enforce a law which he had himself ordained in the past to curb the depredations of these military " protectors."

Several problems arise. First, the military patrons of the free peasants, as Libanius explicitly remarks (§ 4), receive as reward for their activities possession, not of the land itself, but of its produce.

Also, in the case of the second type of village, they do not appear as the purchasers of the estate. There is no question, therefore, of any transfer of property to this patron who appears oddly content with produce in kind. However, the decurions are clearly the losers in both cases : in the first case, they must sell their estates to reimburse the treasury for the tribute, for the collection of which they are made personally responsible by their fellow decurions : in the second, they are deprived of the revenues of their own estates, and again are faced with the compulsion to sell. The question thus arises as to who the purchasers were. If the military are ruled out, as they certainly are, the only other sections of society with the fortune and interest to make such acquisitions of property are the *honorati* and the *principales*, who are closely allied to each other in the prejudices of Libanius. These are the real villains of the piece. It is their acquisitiveness which upsets the structure of the decurionate, as related in the *Orations on the City Council* and in *Oration* 62, and the activities of the military patron are a good stick with which to beat them. Hence his hostility towards the peasantry in this oration. Not only does he show resentment towards his own rebellious peasants for their treatment of himself, but he extends it towards others of the same kind whose recourse to the patronage of the military, so he asserts, finally results in the reduction in curial numbers. They are thus serving the ends of civilian potentates also, and these he detests almost as much as the military. Thus compassion for the oppressed peasant, whether imprisoned by the governor acting in collusion with these grasping potentates, as in the *De Vinctis*, or suffering his arbitrary imposition of the corvées required by this select group, as in the *De Angariis*, is here quite absent. There they had been victimized by this class, and almost automatically assured of Libanius' support; now, they act in such a way as to serve its ends, and therefore incur his hostility.

Again, there is a note of *parti pris* in his account of the nature of patronage. His civilian outlook can conceive of no more justified patronage than that of the curial *dominus* over his *coloni* or that of the decurion over the freeholder. A plurality of patronage is, as he remarks, a contradiction in terms, so that the intrusion of an external patron, whether military, as here, or civilian, as that of " Mixidemus " in *Oration* 39, is a threat to his established order. He quite ignores the fact that the decurions, whose patronage he eulogizes, while far less effective in the support of their dependants than the intruders whom he censures, were in fact every bit as rapacious in their demands (*cf.* Salvian, *De Gub. Dei*, 5. 8). Moreover, the tartness of his comments, and especially those upon the excesses of his Jewish tenants, would seem to indicate that the consequences of this military intrusion had only recently been borne in upon him, and only then because of his personal discomfiture.

A further question which has been hotly debated concerns the status of Libanius' Jewish tenants. Zulueta regarded the phrase ᾿Ιουδαῖοι τῶν πάνυ in ethnic terms and found the locality of the estate in Palestine, since he traced a correlation between Libanius' description of them and the terms of *C.J.* 11. 51. 50, where the status of the *colonus* there was

brought into line with that of other provinces.[a]
Juster rejected this correlation, and interpreted the
phrase " proper Jews " as denoting a religious difference. Harmand's view that it is merely a deroga-
tory term, occasioned by mortification at their impudent activities, is, however, the most obvious and
the most acceptable. Moreover, in view of Libanius'
poor health in these years, there is no question of
finding the location of this estate outside the territory
of Antioch.

Finally, there is the intractable problem of identifying the imperial constitution for the enforcement
of which Libanius appeals (§ 35). Zulueta had regarded this as *C. Th.* 5. 17. 2 [b] of A.D. 386, and had dated
the speech to the years A.D. 386–389. Unfortunately,
this does not deal with patronage—only with fugitive
coloni. Martroye (supported by Foerster III, 403 n.)
identified the constitution with that of *C. Th.* 11. 24. 2
of A.D. 368/70.[c] Here the overriding objection is
that the law, though applicable to patronage, was
passed by Valens, whereas Libanius makes Theo-

[a] *C.J.* 11. 51. 50 : addressed to Cynegius, ppO (A.D. 384–
388) ". . . sancimus ut etiam per Palaestinas nullus omnino
colonorum suo iure velut vagus ac liber exsultet, sed exemplo
aliarum provinciarum ita domino fundi teneatur, ut sine
poena suscipientis non possit abscedere. . . ."
[b] *C. Th.* 5. 17. 2 : " quisquis colonorum iuris alieni aut
sollicitatione susceperit aut occultatione celaverit, pro eo qui
privatus erit sex auri uncias, pro eo qui patrimonialis libram
auri cogatur inferre."
[c] *C. Th.* 11. 24. 2 : " abstineant patrociniis agricolae
subiugandi supplicio, si talia sibimet adiumenta commentis
audacibus conquisierint. ii vero, qui propria patrocinia
largiuntur, per singulos fundos, quotiens repperti fuerint,
xxv auri libras dare debeant et non quantum patroni
suscipere consuerant, sed dimidium eius fiscus adsumat."

dosius responsible for it. Tillemont, followed by
Paul Petit, looked to *C. Th.* 1. 29. 8 of A.D. 392,[a]
which he interpreted as the emperor's response to
the arguments put forward in this speech—but an
objection which appears insuperable is presented
by the phrase νόμου πάλαι περὶ τούτων κειμένου (36),
clearly to be identified with the Theodosian law of
the previous section. Harmand, in view of this
phrase, looked elsewhere, to find the solution in *C.
Th.* 9. 33. 1 of A.D. 384 [b]—but unfortunately there is
no mention here of any patronage, despite his best
efforts. It appears that none of the surviving legislation can be equated with the legislation to which
Libanius here appeals ; and although it may be
tempting to regard *C. Th.* 1. 29. 8 as the reaction of
the government to Libanius' appeal, the case remains
unproven.

From the internal evidence, the oration is to be
placed in the reign of Theodosius and, from the
reference to the settlement of the Gothic problem
and the suppression of the usurpation of Maximus
(§ 35), to the period after A.D. 388. The possibility
of its attribution to the reign of Valens, canvassed
by Gothofredus and Reiske, becomes more remote
when the references to the emperor and his relations
with the author are considered (*e.g.* §§ 38 ; 16).
The commentators, with singular unanimity, would
place it between A.D. 386 and 392, generally pre-

[a] *C. Th.* 1. 29. 8 : ". . . removeantur patrocinia quae
favorem reis et auxilium scelerosis inpertiendo maturari
scelera fecerunt."

[b] *C. Th.* 9. 33. 1 : " si quis contra evidentissimam
iussionem suscipere plebem et adversus publicam disciplinam
defendere fortasse temptaverit, multam gravissimam sus-
tinebunt."

ferring an occasion, imprecisely defined, between A.D. 389 and 392. Significantly enough, the year A.D. 392 provides examples of imperial legislation upon the problems of patronage (*e.g. C. Th.* 1. 29. 8 : 12. 1. 128).

MANUSCRIPTS AND BIBLIOGRAPHY

Manuscripts number seven only, consisting of CAPIBM with the addition of Urbinas 125, itself closely allied with B and M. Short extracts are also preserved by Planudes and Macarius. The *editio princeps* was that of Gothofredus (Geneva, 1631), reprinted in his *Opera Juridica Minora* (Leiden, 1733), later editors being Reiske and Foerster. The oration has received the closest scrutiny, first from the point of view of the history of the colonate, from Gothofredus himself, Zulueta, *de Patrociniis Vicorum* (Oxford Studies in honour of P. Vinogradoff, 1909), Heitland, *Agricola*, Martroye, *Les Patronages d'agriculteurs et de vici aux IV*[e] *et V*[e] *siècles* (Rev. hist. de droit, 4th series, 1928), Pack, *Studies in Libanius*, Petit, *Vie municipale*, and Liebeschuetz, *Antioch*. An edition, with translation and detailed commentary, is given by L. Harmand in Libanius, *Discours sur les patronages*, Paris, 1955.

XLVII

ΠΕΡΙ ΤΩΝ ΠΡΟΣΤΑΣΙΩΝ

1. Εἰ μή σε ἑωράκειν ἐν πολλῷ μὲν χρόνῳ,
μυρίοις δὲ πράγμασιν, ὦ βασιλεῦ, χαίροντά τε τοῖς
τῶν ἀρχομένων ἀγαθοῖς καὶ βουλόμενον μηδένα
παρὰ μηδενὸς ἀδικεῖσθαι, τάχα ἂν ἐμαυτῷ παρή-
νεσα τὴν ἡσυχίαν ἄγειν καὶ τὸν οὐχ ἡδέως ἀκουσόμενον οὐκ ἂν ἐλύπουν οὐδ᾽ ἠνώχλουν· ἐλπίδας δέ
μοι τοῦ σοῦ παρέχοντος τρόπου καὶ χαριεῖσθαί μέ
σοι[1] τοῖς ῥηθησομένοις καὶ πείσειν καὶ δόξαν εὐ-
νοίας | οἴσεσθαι χαίρων τε καὶ προθύμως ἐπὶ τὴν
συμβουλὴν ἥκω τὴν σὴν μᾶλλον ἢ ἐμὴν δόξουσαν
εἶναι τοῦ τὴν ἰσχὺν τοῖς εἰρημένοις δεδωκότος τῷ
προσθεῖναι τὸ ἔργον, οὗ χωρὶς μάταιος ἂν ἦν ὁ
λόγος. 2. τοὺς μὲν οὖν | χαλεπανοῦντας, οὗτοι δέ
εἰσιν οἱ τοῖς τῶν ἄλλων κακοῖς τὰ αὑτῶν μείζω
ποιοῦντες, οἶδα, βασιλεῦ, πολλούς τε ὄντας καὶ
δύναμιν ἔχοντας, ἐγὼ δὲ ὀργιεῖσθαι μὲν αὐτοὺς καὶ
ζητήσειν παρ᾽ ἐμοῦ τιμωρίαν οἶμαι, λήψεσθαι δὲ
οὐδέποτε τῆς σῆς κεφαλῆς σωζομένης παρὰ τῶν
τὸν σὸν βίον τεθαυμακότων θεῶν. οὔτε γὰρ ἐθε-
λήσειν σε προδοῦναι τὸν σύμβουλον οὔτε βοηθεῖν

---

[1] μέ σοι conj. Re., F. : μοι Gothofred., Re. text (mss.).

---

[a] This deferential introduction is most closely paralleled
by that of *Or.* 52.

500

ORATION 47

ON PROTECTION SYSTEMS

1. Had I not seen in the long space of time and in countless matters, Sire, your joy in the well-being of your subjects and your desire that none should suffer wrong at the hands of anyone, I would perhaps have counselled myself to keep silence and would not seek to upset or inconvenience my reluctant hearer.[a] However, your good nature inspires me with the confidence that, by the remarks I am about to make, I will please you, carry conviction with you, and win for myself a name for loyalty, and so it is with pleasure and eagerness that I have come to outline a policy which will be regarded as yours rather than mine, since you give force to any words uttered by translating them into action, and without that argument would be in vain. 2. I am well aware, Sire, that the reaction of many influential persons will be hostile—persons who have achieved success by means of other people's misfortunes—, but I believe that, though they will be angry and will seek to revenge themselves upon me, they will never succeed in this, since your person is under the protection of the gods who have observed your career with admiration, for you will refuse to betray your counsellor and, if you try to assist me, you will not

πειρώμενον οὐκ ἀρκέσειν. τί οὖν δεῖ σιωπᾶν τηνάλλως φοβούμενον ἐν ἀσφαλείᾳ τοσαύτῃ;

3. Εὖ πράττειν μὲν οὖν βουλοίμην ἂν καὶ τοὺς
τῶν ὅλων ἄρχοντας δυνάμεως καὶ τοὺς ὑπὸ τούτοις
μερῶν καὶ ζῆν ἐν εὐθυμίᾳ καὶ τούτους κἀκείνους,
R ii. 501 οὐ μὴν | οὔτε κακὰ κερδαίνειν οὔτ᾽ ἄλλοις τοῦ
πάντα τολμᾶν αἰτίους εἶναι. οἷα πολλὰ δρᾶται νῦν.
ἄκουε δή,[1] βασιλεῦ, καὶ διδάσκου.

4. Εἰσὶ κῶμαι μεγάλαι πολλῶν ἑκάστη δεσποτῶν. αὗται καταφεύγουσιν ἐπὶ τοὺς ἱδρυμένους
στρατιώτας, οὐχ ἵνα μὴ πάθωσι κακῶς, ἀλλ᾽ ἵνα
ἔχωσι ποιεῖν. καὶ ὁ μισθὸς ἀφ᾽ ὧν δίδωσιν ἡ γῆ,
R ii. 502 πυροὶ καὶ | κριθαὶ καὶ τὰ ἀπὸ τῶν[2] δένδρων ἢ
χρυσὸς ἢ χρυσίου τιμή. προβεβλημένοι τοίνυν τὰς
τούτων χεῖρας οἱ δεδωκότες ἐώνηνται τὴν εἰς ἅπαντα ἐξουσίαν. καὶ νῦν μὲν κακὰ καὶ πράγματα
παρέχουσι τοῖς ὁμόροις γῆν ἀποτεμνόμενοι, δένδρα
τέμνοντες, ἁρπάζοντες, θύοντες, κατα|κόπτον- F
τες, ἐσθίοντες. εἶθ᾽ ὧν μὲν ἦν ταῦτα, κλάουσιν
ὁρῶντες, οἱ δ᾽ εὐωχούμενοι γελῶσι καὶ τοσοῦτ᾽
ἀπέχουσι τοῦ δεδιέναι μή τις ταῦτα πύθηται, ὥστ᾽
ἀπειλαὶ προστίθενται τοῖς πεπραγμένοις καὶ τὸ
μηδὲ τῶν ἄλλων ἀφέξεσθαι. 5. δεινά σοι ταῦτα
φαίνεται, βασιλεῦ, ἀλλ᾽ οὐ τὰ μέγιστα ἀκήκοας,
εἴπερ αἰγῶν τε καὶ προβάτων μεῖζον αἱ θυγατέρες,
ὧν οὐδὲ αὐτῶν ἀπέχονται. τί οὖν ἔτι δεῖ λέγειν
πληγὰς[3] καὶ ὕβρεις καὶ ὡς γυναῖκες γυναῖκας[4]

---

[1] δή F. : δέ Goth., Re. (mss.).
[2] τῶν F. (mss.) : om. Goth., Re.
[3] λέγειν πληγὰς Re., F. (M) : λέγειν· (; Goth.) πληγαὶ Goth. (other mss.).
[4] γυναῖκες " num delendum et λαβόμενοι scribendum ? " F. : γυναῖκας om. Goth.

prove incapable. So why should I hold my peace through idle fears in the midst of such security ? [a]

3. For your commanders in chief [b] and for the officers of the regiments they command, both one and all, my wish is for them success and a happy life, but without making any illicit gain or causing others to behave with complete lack of scruple—misconduct such as is rife at present. Listen, Sire, and learn.

4. There exist large villages, belonging to many owners. [c] These have recourse to the soldiery stationed in them, not so as to avoid trouble but so as to be able to cause it. And the payment comes from the produce of the land—wheat, barley, the fruit of the trees, or else bullion or gold coin. So, protected by their arms, the donors have purchased for themselves complete licence. And now they inflict toil and trouble upon their neighbours by encroaching on their lands, cutting down the trees, looting, slaughtering and butchering the cattle, and feasting themselves on it. When the one-time owners bewail the sight, they make merry and laugh at them, and so far from showing fear that anybody should get to know of it, they cap their misdeeds with threats and the promise not to refrain from anything else at all. 5. A sorry tale this, Sire, you think : but you have not heard the worst of it yet, at least if their daughters are more important than goats or sheep— for they don't keep their hands off them either. So what need, then, to mention the beatings and the

[a] For the risks attendant upon publicizing such abuses *cf. Or.* 48. 1, 52. 1. Libanius himself had been threatened with violence even under Julian when he pleaded the cause of the council, *cf. Or.* 1. 126. [b] The *magistri militum.*
[c] These are villages of free peasant small-holders, at odds with others in neighbouring villages.

LIBANIUS

ἕλκουσι λαβόμεναι τῶν τριχῶν, καὶ ὡς φρέατα
ἄχρηστα καθιστᾶσι τοῖς ἔχουσι τοῖς ὑφ᾽ αὑτῶν
ἐμβαλλομένοις καὶ ὡς ποταμῶν ἀποστεροῦσι καὶ
διὰ τούτων ⟨καὶ⟩[1] κήπων, τρέφοντες στρατιώτας
οἱ μὲν πλείους, οἱ δὲ ἐλάττους ἐν μέσαις ταῖς κώ-
μαις καθημένους τὰ πολλὰ καὶ κοιμωμένους ἐπ᾽
οἴνῳ πολλῷ καὶ κρέασιν, ὅπως εἴ τις τῶν ἀδικουμένων ἀλγήσας ἀμύνοιτο, πληγὴ δ᾽ εἰσέλθοι καὶ
R ii. 503 ἐπὶ στρατιώτην, εἶτα τοῦτ᾽ ὄλεθρος εἴη τῷ | πατά-
ξαντι μηδαμόθεν ὄντος αὐτῷ μηδενὸς λόγου; δεῖν
γὰρ αὐτὸν ὑποσχεῖν ἐν ἁπάσῃ μέθῃ στρατιώτῃ
πάντα ἀνεχόμενον καὶ μηδὲν ἐνταῦθα εἶναι τοὺς
νόμους. 6. τοῦτο καὶ λῃστὰς γεωργοὺς ἐποίησε,
τοῦτ᾽ αὐτῶν εἰς τὰς χεῖρας ἐνέθηκε σίδηρον οὐ τὸν
τῇ γῇ φίλον, ἀλλ᾽ ὃς ἀποκτίννυσι. | τοῦ δύνασθαι F 4⟨
γὰρ αὐτοῖς αὐξομένου διὰ τῶν ἐγκαθημένων στρατιωτῶν καὶ τὸ τολμᾶν ἐπίδοσιν λαμβάνει τῶν φυ-
λάκων τῆς χώρας κατὰ τὴν παροιμίαν τοὺς τοιούτους ὁρώντων καὶ οὐχ ὁρώντων, ἴσασι γὰρ ἐπὶ
πολλῷ βοηθήσοντες τοῖς κειμένοις διὰ τὸν προ-
στάτην. καὶ γὰρ δὴ καὶ τοσούτοις κακοῖς τοὔνομα
τοῦτο ἔθεντο, πρέπει δέ, οἶμαι, τοῖς δικαίαις[2] ἐπι-
κουρίαις ἐξαιρουμένοις εἰς ἄδειαν ἀδικουμένην
ἀσθένειαν.

7. Ἡ προστασία δὲ αὕτη πᾶν τοὐναντίον ποιεῖ.
R ii. 504 ῥώμην δίδωσιν | εἰς τὸ κακοῦν ἑτέρους. ὧν εἰσι

---

[1] ⟨καὶ⟩ conj. Re., F.
[2] δικαίαις Re., F. : δικαίοις Goth. (mss.).

---

[a] The excesses of the military here may be compared with
those of the monks in *Or.* 30. 8, but with the important
difference that, while the activities of the monks are spon-
taneous, those of the military are occasioned by other people.
[b] The rôle of this village police in Syria is unknown. For

insults, how the women grab women by the hair
and ill-treat them, how they make wells useless for
their owners with the stuff they throw into them, or
how they rob them of their flow of river water, and by
this means of their gardens too, while they maintain
soldiers, some more, some less, in the midst of their
villages, and these for the most part loll about or
doze after their fill of wine and meat, with the result
that if any of the victims loses his temper or defends
himself, and one of soldiers happens to be hit too,
then it is death for the one who struck him, and not
the slightest chance of an excuse for him. He must
knuckle under to a soldier, however drunk, and put
up with anything ; and the laws in this instance are
a dead letter.[a] 6. This is what has turned peasants
into brigands ; this is what has put into their hands
the steel—not the steel beloved of the land but that
which kills. For, as their power grows by means of
the military billeted among them, their recklessness
also increases, and the local police [b] turn on such as
these the proverbial blind eye,[c] since they know
that if they help the down-trodden victims it will
cost them dear because of their protector. This in
fact is the term they apply to those many rascals,
though it is properly applicable, I feel, to those who,
in the provision of legitimate assistance, succour the
wronged and helpless, and make them secure.

7. This kind of protection, however, produces results exactly the reverse. It provides the motive
force for injuring others—among them the collectors

its counterpart elsewhere *cf.* Johnson and West, *Byzantine
Egypt*, p. 98.
[c] This proverb is not found in the Corpus, though well
known enough from N.T. (Matthew 13. 13).

καὶ οἱ τὸν φόρον εἰσπράττοντες. οὓς ἐβουλόμην ἐνταῦθά μοι καὶ παρεῖναι καὶ βοᾶν οἷα πεπόνθασι.
πάντως δ᾽ ἂν τοῦτο μετὰ δακρύων ἐγίγνετο παρ᾽
ἀνδρῶν πενήτων ἐξ εὐδαιμόνων γεγενημένων. πῶς
γενομένων δέῃ μαθεῖν, ὦ βασιλεῦ; ἔρχονται ἐπὶ
τὰς κώμας ταύτας τὰς διὰ τῶν στρατηγῶν τετει-
χισμένας οἱ κομιούμενοι τὸν φόρον ἔργον τοῦτο
ἔχοντες καὶ λειτουργίαν. εἶτ᾽ ἀπαιτοῦσι τὴν μὲν
πρώτην πράως καὶ βραχυτέρᾳ τῇ φωνῇ, καταφρο-
νούμενοι δὲ καὶ καταγελώμενοι μετὰ ἀγανακτή-
σεως ἤδη καὶ μεῖζον φθεγγόμενοι καὶ οἷον εἰκὸς
τοὺς τῶν δικαίων ἀτυχοῦντας. εἶτ᾽ ἠπείλησαν[1]
τοὺς ἄρχοντας, μάτην | ἐλάττους ὄντας[2] τῶν τὰς
κώμας καρπουμένων. εἶθ᾽ ἥψαντο καὶ ἐπεσπά-
σαντο. οἱ δ᾽ ἔδειξαν ὡς εἰσὶν αὐτοῖς λίθοι. | 8. λαμ-
βάνοντες οὖν οἱ πράκτορες ἀντὶ καρπῶν τραύματα
ἀναστρέφουσιν εἰς ἄστυ τῷ περὶ τοῖς ἱματίοις αἵματι δηλοῦντες ἃ πεπόνθασι. καὶ τὸν μὲν θυμού-
μενον οὐκ ἔχουσιν, ἡ γὰρ τοῦ τὸν μισθὸν εἰληφότος
δύναμις οὐκ ἐᾷ, ἀκούουσι δὲ οἱ δυστυχεῖς ὅτι χρὴ
καταβάλλειν ἢ μαστιγουμένους ἀπειπεῖν. οἱ δὲ
οὔσης μὲν ἀνάγκης τοῦτο ποιεῖν, τὰ δὲ παρὰ τῶν
ἀγρῶν ἀπεγνωκότες καὶ δεδιότες ἕτερα τραύματα,
χρυσίου δ᾽ οὐκ ὄντος οὐδ᾽ ἀργυρίου πωλοῦσι μὲν
θεραπαίνας θρηνοῦντες, πωλοῦσι δὲ ἀκολούθους,

R ii. 505

F 40

---

[1] ἠπείλησαν Re., F. : ἠπείλησε Goth. (mss.).   [2] ὄντες Re.

[a] The decurions, who were appointed by the city council
and were personally responsible for the collection of the
tribute and its delivery to the governor.

[b] In A.D. 387 the *magister militum* (the στρατηγός *par
excellence*) had his H.Q. in Antioch (*Or*. 21. 7, 22. 17). The
term στρατηγοί here is therefore used as a general term for

of taxes, too.[a] I wanted them here to support me
and to complain of their sufferings. It would certainly be to the accompaniment of the tears of men
who have been reduced from wealth to poverty.
Do you want to know, Sire, how this comes about ?
Well, those whose task and duty it is, go to collect
the tribute to these villages which are fenced and
defended around by generals.[b] Then they present
their demands, nicely at first and in a tone of restraint, but, being met with contempt and ridicule,
with increasing anger and raised voice, as is to be
expected when people do not receive their proper
due. Then they threaten the village headmen, but
to no purpose since such are inferior to those who
exploit the villages.[c] Then they lay hands on them
and arrest them, but the villagers reveal their
armoury of stones. 8. So the gatherers collect
wounds instead of tithes and make their way back
to town, revealing what they have suffered by the
blood on their clothes. They have none to take
up the cudgels for them, for the influence of the
person who has taken the protection money forbids
this, and the poor devils are told that they must pay
up or be flogged until they drop. Since they are
forced to do so, and despair of any revenue from
their estates and fear more wounds, and since they
have no ready supply of gold or silver, they tearfully
offer for sale their maidservants, their attendants, the

his subordinate officers : the *dux* may be the chief of these
but, from the nature of the day-to-day contact, these would
most commonly be the commanders of the individual garrison
units stationed in Antiochene territory.

 [c] The villages of Syria were renowned for size and prosperity, *Or*. 11. 230 ff. On the question of their administration *cf*. Liebeschuetz, pp. 119 ff.

τροφέων υἱούς, ἀντιλαμβανομένους τῶν τοῦ πω
λοῦντος γονάτων. 9. ἔρχονται δὲ καὶ εἰς ἀγρούς,
οὐχ ὡς πρότερον μετὰ τῶν τέκνων, ἀλλ' ἀποδω
R ii. 506 σόμενοι μετὰ τῶν | ὠνησομένων. καὶ τράπεζα αὐ
τοῖς κοινὴ παρατίθεται, τὴν τιμὴν δὲ τῆς γῆς
φόρον ὁ πεπρακὼς γιγνομένην ὁρᾷ. ἐξιὼν δὲ τῶν
πατρῴων, ἔστι δ' οὗ καὶ παππῴων, βλέπων εἰς
τοὺς ἐκείνων τάφους καὶ τιμῶν τοῖς διὰ τῶν χειρῶν
φιλήμασι συγγνώμην ἔχειν ἀξιῶν ἀπέρχεται. εἶτα
φροντὶς ὑπὲρ τροφῆς αὐτῷ τε καὶ γυναικὶ καὶ
παισίν, εἶτα οὐδαμόθεν φαινομένης ἡ τοῦ προσαι
τεῖν ἀνάγκη. 10. οὕτω βουλευτὴς βουλῆς ἐξ
αλείφεται οὐ σπόγγου γράμματα ἀφαιροῦντος, ἀλλ'
οὐκέτ' οὔσης οὐσίας. ταῦτ' ἐλάττους ποιεῖ τὰς
βουλὰς ἀντὶ μειζόνων, ταῦτ' ὀλίγους τοὺς καθ'
ἑκάστην ἀντὶ πλειόνων. | ταυτὶ δὲ ζημία πόλεως F
ὅλης. καὶ γὰρ ἂν τοῖς ἄλλοις εὖ πράττῃ, τούτῳ δὲ
R ii. 507 χωλεύῃ τῷ μέρει, μικρὰ τὰ | ἄλλα καὶ μικρὰ ποιεῖ
τῆς βασιλείας τὰ πράγματα. διὰ γὰρ τῶν ἀρχο
μένων ἐκείνη καὶ αὔξεται καὶ τοὐναντίον. οὐκοῦν
βλάπτονται μὲν αἱ βουλαὶ ταῖς καλαῖς προστα
σίαις, βλάπτονται δὲ ταῖς βλάβαις τῶν βουλῶν αἱ
πόλεις, πάλιν δὲ αὖ ταῖς[1] τούτων οἱ μάχιμοι. ὧν
οὐκ ἀμελητέον σοι, βασιλεῦ, δι' ὧν ἔνι καὶ κρατεῖν
καὶ μὴ κρατεῖσθαι καὶ φοβεῖν καὶ μὴ φοβεῖσθαι.

---

[1] αὖ ταῖς Re., F. : αὐταῖς Goth. (mss.).

---

[a] Foster-brothers, even though of servile station and commonly employed as personal attendants, formed a respected

sons of their foster-parents,[a] while they grasp the knees of the seller in entreaty. 9. They go to their farms, too, not, as before, with their children in family parties, but with the prospective purchasers to sell them. A common table [b] is set out before them, but the seller sees the price of his land turn into tax money. On leaving his father's, sometimes his grandfather's estates, he gazes back at their tombs, kisses his hand to them in a final gesture, begs their pardon, and so departs. Then his concern is for the maintenance of himself, his wife and his children, and when none is anywhere forthcoming, the need to beg ensues.[c] 10. So a councillor is erased from the council : no sponge wipes out his name : he no longer has the property. This is what reduces the councils instead of increasing them, and makes the numbers in every one less instead of more. And this is a loss to the whole town. Indeed, if it is otherwise successful, but things go wrong in this respect, all else suffers and especially the fortune of the empire, for its well-being or its ruin depends upon its subjects. So the town councils suffer harm because of this fine protection-system and the towns suffer harm because of that done to their councils, and the fighting forces again because of that done to the towns. And the fighting forces you must not ignore, Sire, for it is through them that you can inflict and not suffer defeat, inspire and not feel fear. So suppress such

and valued part of the family, which is here seen in a state of disintegration.

[b] A bitter play on κοινή—the table common for family parties becomes the table common to the two participants in this transaction.   [c] *Cf. Or. 2. 54.*

ἄνελε δὴ¹ τὰς τοιαύτας προστασίας ἃς εἶναι παρ' ἡμῖν βούλοιντ' ἂν οἱ πολέμιοι.

11. Τὸ δὲ ζητεῖν προστάτην οὐ μόνον ἐκείνων ἐστὶ τῶν ἀγρῶν οἳ πολλῶν εἰσι τῶν ἐχόντων ἑκάστου μέρος οὐ² πολὺ κεκτημένου, ἀλλὰ καὶ οἷς εἷς ὁ δεσπότης. καὶ οὗτοι τὸν μισθωτὸν προστίθενται τῇ τοῦ δεσπότου ζημίᾳ τὸν μισθὸν πορίζοντες καὶ διδόντες ἐξ ὧν ἀποστεροῦσι. καίτοι καὶ τῶν ἐπιφανῶν εἰσιν αἱ κῶμαι καὶ τῶν οἵων τε ὄντων χεῖρα ὀρέξαι λυπουμένοις. ἀλλ', οἶμαι, τὸ κακῶς ποιεῖν διώκοντες, οὐ τὸ παθεῖν φεύγοντες δυνάμεις τινῶν ὠνοῦνται, αἷς χρώμενοι πολλοῦ χρόνου προϊόντος R ii. 508 καὶ | πρὸς τοὺς | αὐτῶν κυρίους³ τοῦτο τῆς γῆς F 41 βουλομένης ἄγριον ἔστησαν ὀφθαλμὸν ὡς ἀνάγκης μὲν ὄντες ἔξω, γνώμῃ δὲ ἐργαζόμενοι καὶ οὐχ ἁψόμενοι τῆς γῆς, εἰ μὴ πείθοιεν αὐτούς.⁴ 12. οἱ δὲ πρῶτοι ταῦτα τετολμηκότες ἔσχον ταχέως πολλοὺς τοὺς ἀκολουθήσαντας κακοῦ παραδείγματος γενομένους μιμητάς. εἶθ' οἱ μὲν γράφονται καὶ κατηγοροῦσι, τοῖς δ' εἰσὶ βοηθοῦντες καὶ λόγῳ.⁵ καὶ πλέον τῶν νόμων ἤνεγκεν ὁ βοηθῶν, ὥστ' εἶναι τὸ ὁρώμενον θέαμα ἐλεεινόν. τί τοῦτο; βοαὶ τῶν περὶ τὴν γῆν ἐχόντων, γλῶτται θρασεῖαι, πλῆθος συνδίκων, ἀγῶνες, δίκαι, νῖκαι. καὶ ὁ μὲν εἰς

---

¹ δὴ conj. Re., F. : δὲ Re. text (mss.).
² μέρος οὐ Re., F. : μέρος τοῦ Goth. (mss.).
³ αὐτῶν Re., F.: αὐτῶν Goth. (mss.). | κυρίους ⟨ἐπισπέρχοντας⟩ conj. Re., F., Harmand.
⁴ αὐτοὺς Goth., Harmand (AP): αὐτοὺς Re., F. (other mss.).
⁵ καὶ λόγῳ ⟨καὶ ἔργῳ⟩ conj. Re., F. (M) : om. Goth., Harmand (other mss.).

a system of protection as this which our enemies would want us to have.[a]

11. But the quest for a protector is not peculiar to those estates which belong to many landowners who each possess a small area, but also to those who have a single owner.[b] These too have recourse to the hireling and pay the price, but at the owner's cost, and they provide their gifts from what they deprive him of. Yet these villages belong to men of standing, too, people capable of offering a protecting hand to the distressed. But, to be sure, it is in quest of committing mischief, not in avoidance of suffering it, that the villages buy the aid of certain individuals. They employ it over a long period of time, even against their landlords, though the land needs working ; they look on them with wrathful eye, as if they work as they like, are beyond compulsion, and will not put a hand to the soil, unless they persuade themselves. 12. The first to behave with such impudence soon have plenty of followers to imitate their bad example. Then, the one party begins proceedings and files charges, but the others have protectors, even in argument. And the protector is more influential than the laws, so that what is to be seen is a pitiful spectacle—protests from the peasantry, the bandying of high words, a crowd of lawyers, legal arguments, decisions, and the winning of the case. And off goes the owner with head

---

[a] Cf. Or. 30. 10 ff., where a similar combination of imperial self-interest and financial justice is adduced.

[b] The inhabitants of this type of village are *coloni*, the landlords only too often decurions. The development of patronage of this kind seems to have been comparatively recent.

γῆν κύπτων ἀπῆλθεν, οἱ δὲ ἕπονται τωθάζοντες.
οἷον δή τι καὶ τὸ περὶ ἡμᾶς, βασιλεῦ, γεγένηται.

13. Ἰουδαῖοι τῶν πάνυ γῆν ἡμῖν πολὺν ἐργα-
R ii. 509 ζόμενοι χρόνον, γενεὰς | τέτταρας, ἐπεθύμησαν μὴ
ὅπερ ἦσαν εἶναι καὶ τὸν παλαιὸν ἀποσεισάμενοι
ζυγὸν ἠξίουν ὁρισταὶ τοῦ πῶς ἡμῖν αὐτοῖς χρη-
στέον εἶναι. ταῦτ' οὐκ ἐνεγκόντες χρώμεθα δικαστηρίῳ. καὶ μαθὼν ὁ καθήμενος τίνες ὄντες εἰς
τίνα παροινοῦσιν ἐν τίνι τὰς ἐλπίδας ἔχοντες, τοὺς
μὲν ἔδησε διπλῷ δεσμῷ, τῷ τε οἰκήματι καὶ σι-
δήρῳ, τοὺς δὲ τὰ ὄντα φράσοντας ἐκέλευσεν ἄγε-
σθαι. καὶ ταῦτα εἰπὼν καὶ χαλεπήνας | πρὸς ἐμὲ F
μνησθέντα λύσεως ᾤχετο ἀπιὼν ἑτέρωσε, οἱ δ' ἐπὶ
τὸ τῶν πολλῶν πάλαισμα, τὸν οἶκον τοῦ στρατηγοῦ,
R ii. 510 καὶ τὴν ἐναντίαν τοῖς | δικαίοις ἀσπίδα. καὶ κρι-
θαὶ καὶ σῖτος καὶ νῆτται καὶ χιλὸς ἵπποις. 14. καὶ
ὁ μὲν προσέταξεν ἐᾶν[1] τοὺς λιπόντας τὴν τάξιν, ὁ
δὲ ὑπήκουσέ τε καὶ ὑπέσχετο. καὶ ὁ δικάζων ὃ
μὲν οὐκ ἦν, ἦν, ὃ δ' ἦν, οὐκ ἦν, ἀντὶ δικαστοῦ
συνήγορος. τοιγαροῦν εἷλκεν ὑπὸ τὴν ψῆφον ἡμᾶς
καθ' ἑκάστην ἡμέραν πέμπων ἄλλον ἐπ' ἄλλῳ, τὸ
ἤδη βουλόμενος, τὸ μήπω μεμφόμενος, σπεύδων
ἐπὶ τὴν ἐχθρὰν τοῖς θεοῖς χάριν. καὶ οὕτως ἦν
δῆλος τὸ δίκαιον προησόμενος τῇ χάριτι, ὥσθ' οἱ

---

[1] προσέταξεν ἐᾶν Re., F.: προσέταξε κᾶν Goth. (mss.).

---

[a] Harmand (p. 192) assumed that the court hearing took
place in the village. But disputes between landlord and
tenant were conducted before the governor (*Or.* 45. 3 ff.),
and the court was therefore held in Antioch. It may be
presumed that the general's quarters were there, too. For

downcast, and they follow, jeering at him,—an experience, Sire, such as I personally have experienced.

13. For a long time now, four generations in fact, we have had as tenants working on land some real, proper Jews. They conceived the desire not to remain as they were, and, casting off their long-established yoke, they presumed to define how I should employ them. I refused to accept this and had recourse to the courts.[a] The president of the court learned who they were, who was the victim of their insolence and who it was on whom they placed their hopes, and he had them arrested in a double bondage—in prison and in chains, and he commanded the summoning of witnesses to relate the facts. After making this pronouncement and losing his temper with me when I made mention of their release, he packed his bags and went off elsewhere. But they resorted to the usual trick and made for the general's quarters, their shield against the claims of justice. Then came the presents of barley and corn, and ducks, and fodder for the horses. 14. And the general ordained the release of these who had deserted their post, and the governor obeyed and promised to do so. And there the judge became what he was not and ceased to be what he was : instead of judge he became advocate. Anyway, day after day he tried to hale me into court, sending one messenger after another, demanding my presence immediately, reproving me for my non-attendance, zealous in promoting an unholy piece of favouritism. It was so obvious that he intended to sacrifice justice for influence that people

problems concerning Libanius' Jewish tenants *cf.* Introduction, p. 496 f.

νυκτὸς ἐξιόντες παρ' αὐτοῦ τῶν ἡμῖν ἐπιτηδείων
οἷς συντυγχάνοιεν ἔλεγον κεκρίσθαι μοι τὴν δίκην
καὶ τὸ κράτος ἔσεσθαι τῶν ἀντιδίκων. 15. καὶ ὡς
τοῦθ' οὕτως εἶχεν, ἐδείχθη τῆς ἐπιούσης. οἱ μὲν
R ii. 511 γὰρ μεθ' ἡμῶν ὄντες ῥήτορες ἤκουον ὅτι | δεῖ
σιωπᾶν ἐν ἀφθονίᾳ τῶν ἰσχυρῶν, τῶν δὲ σὺν ἐκείνοις οὐδὲν ἦν ἀσθενὲς ἐν σκιαῖς τοῖς ἅπασι. τῆς
ψήφου δὲ τεθείσης οἵαν τὸ κράνος καὶ ὁ θώραξ
ἤθελεν, αὐτὸν[1] ἐδίωκεν ὁ ἐψηφισμένος, οὐ γὰρ εἴα
τὸ συνειδὸς ἠρεμεῖν, καὶ πρὸς τοὺς εἰσιόντας οὐδὲν
αἰτιωμένους ὤμνυ πάντας ὅρκους ἦ μὴν ὀρθὴν πε-
ποιῆσθαι | τὴν κρίσιν. ἧττον γὰρ ἡγεῖτο κακὸν τὴν F 4
εἰς τοὺς θεοὺς ἀσέβειαν ἢ τὸ φθέγξασθαί τι τούτων
ἃ σιγᾶσθαι βούλοιτ' ἂν ὁ στρατηγός. 16. ὃν
ἠξίουν ἔγωγε μᾶλλον δεδιέναι τὸ λυμαίνεσθαι τοῖς
δικαίοις ἢ τὸ πυθέσθαι τινὰς ὡς αὐτὸς ταῦτα κελεύ-
σειεν. ἃ εἰ μέν ἐστι δίκαια, τί ἂν αἰσχύνοιτο; εἰ
δὲ ἄδικα, τί τῶν τοιούτων ἐπιθυμεῖ; εἰ δ' οὐδὲ ἐμοὶ
τὸ δίκαιον ἐσώθη τῷ πλεῖστα δὴ περὶ λόγους κάμ-
νοντι καὶ γράμμασι δὴ παρὰ σοῦ κεκοσμημένῳ καὶ
τὴν τῶν πεφοιτηκότων ἔχοντι λύπην, τί χρὴ περὶ
τῶν ἄλλων οἷς οὐδὲν τούτων ἔστιν ὑπολαμβάνειν;
R ii. 512   17. Ταυτὶ | μὲν οὖν εἰς ἀπόδειξιν εἴρηταί μοι τοῦ
ταῖς ἀποστροφαῖς[2] ταυταισὶ ταῖς τῶν γεωργῶν
πολλοὺς οἴκους διασείεσθαι. καθ' ἑκάστην γὰρ δὴ
πόλιν τοιοῦτοι μὲν γεωργοί, τοιαῦται δὲ θύραι,[3]

[1] αὐτὸν Re., F. : αὐτὸν Goth. (mss.).
[2] ἀποστροφαῖς Re., F. (A) : ἀποτροφαῖς Goth. (other mss.).
[3] θῆραι Harmand (M corrected).

[a] These would be the official visitors, *honorati* like
Libanius or *principales* at least, and would see this piece of
chicanery as a precedent contrary to their own interests.
514

who left him one night told the friends of mine whom they met that my case had been decided and that my adversaries would gain the day. 15. And that this was the case was demonstrated next day, for the lawyers on our side were told that they must keep mum, however strong their arguments, and that my opponents' supporters had a watertight case, though in every particular it was sheer humbug. The verdict went as the helmet and cuirass dictated, but the judge who had given this verdict became his own accuser, for his conscience gave him no peace, and to his visitors,[a] though they made no accusation, he tried to swear all kinds of oath that he really had given a straight verdict. His notion was that impiety towards the gods is less of an evil than the utterance of anything that the general would want hushed up. 16. I, for one, felt that the general showed more disquiet at the perversion of justice than at the spread of the news that it had been done at his order. But if it is justified, why should he feel ashamed ? If it is not, why be so eager for such things ? And if justice has not been preserved for me even, despite my long labours in the service of education,[b] despite the receipt of honours by letters from yourself,[c] and the support I shall have in the annoyance felt by my ex-pupils, what must be expected in the case of others who have none of these advantages ?

17. Now, I have mentioned this as a demonstration of the damage done to many families by these desertions of peasants, for in every city there are such peasants, such doors to receive them, such pay-

[b] Libanius' favourite form of self-commendation.
[c] The honorary prefecture, *Or.* 2. 8, 30. 1, 45. 1 and notes.

τοιοῦτοι δὲ μισθοί, τοιαῦται δὲ συνθῆκαι, τοιαῦτα
δὲ κέρδη, τοιαῦται δὲ ζημίαι, τοιαῦται δὲ εὐφρο-
σύναι, τοιαῦται δὲ κατήφειαι. καὶ γὰρ ἐκ τῶν
ἄλλων ἀγρῶν οἷς ὁδὸς οὐκ ἔνι τὰ τοιαῦτα ὑβρίζειν, γυναῖκας καταλιπόντες οὐκ ὀλίγοι καὶ τέκνα
φέρονται πρὸς τοὺς ἰσχύοντας ἐκείνους, τοὺς
τοιούτους πύργους, ἀπολαύσοντες τῆς παρανόμου
δυνάμεως. κἂν ὁ κατηγορῶν γένηται τῶν τοῦ
στρατηγοῦ τις, αὐτῷ μέλειν εἰπὼν | τοῦ κατηγο- F 41
ρουμένου καταπαλαίσας τὸν αἰτιασάμενον ἀπῆλθε.
18. τίνος δὴ ⟨παῦσαι⟩[1] ταυτασὶ τὰς διαδύσεις[2]; τίνος τηρῆσαι τοῖς ἐκδεξαμένοις[3] τοὺς ἀγρούς; σόν,
R ii. 513 βασιλεῦ, τὸ ἔργον. | παρὰ σοῦ προσήκει τὸ δῶρον
ἐλθεῖν. σὸν καὶ παθεῖν τι καὶ ἰάσασθαι καὶ μὴ τὸν
ζῆλον ἕρποντα περιιδεῖν. μᾶλλον δὲ πολὺν μὲν ἤδη
τοῦτο περιῶπται χρόνον, δεῖ δὲ αὐτό που καὶ
στῆναι.

19. Ἐρήσεται τοίνυν μέ τις ὑπὲρ τῶν γεωργῶν εἰ
μὴ ἐξέσται βοηθείας ἑαυτοῖς πορίζειν. τὰς μὲν οὐκ
ἀδίκους φαίην ἄν, τὰς δὲ κακὰς οὐδαμῶς. πρώτην μὲν τὴν παρὰ τῶν θεῶν, ἣ γένοιτ' ἂν εὐχαῖς
τε καὶ θεραπείαις· ἔπειτα τὴν δι' ὑδάτων βλαπτόντων μὲν ἀπωθουμένων, μελλόντων δὲ ὠφελεῖν
ἐπαγομένων. ἔστι καὶ τοὺς κυρίους τῶν κτη-
μάτων πρὸς αὐτοὺς[4] ποιῆσαι φιλανθρωποτέρους,
ὡς τὰ μὲν ὀφείλουσιν ἀφεῖναι, τὰ δὲ καὶ δοῦναι,
ἤν τ' αὖ δίκης που πρὸς ἀλλήλους δέωνται, τοῦτον

---

[1] ⟨παῦσαι⟩ F. : ⟨ἀποφράττειν⟩ conj. Re.
[2] διαδύσεις conj. Re., F. : διαλύσεις Goth., Re. text (mss.).
[3] ἐκδεξαμένοις conj. Re., F. : ἐκλεξαμένοις Goth., Re. text
(mss.).   [4] αὑτοὺς Re., F. : αὐτοὺς Goth. (mss.).

ments, such agreements, such gains and such losses, such transports of joy and such depths of despair.[a] Moreover, from the other estates those who do not have their way clear for such excesses, many of them deserting their wives and children, scuttle to those persons of influence, such towers of strength, to enjoy their illegal power to the full. And even if the accuser be a member of the general's train, he tells him that he will deal with the offender, and off he goes, leaving the accuser floored. 18. Whose job is it, then, to put a stop to evasions like this? and whose to preserve their estates for those who inherited them? The task is yours, Sire. It is proper that this bounty should come from you. It is for you to feel some concern and to provide the cure and not to ignore the growing spread of spite. In fact, this has already been ignored for long enough already; a stop must surely be put to it.

19. Well, I may be asked on behalf of the peasants, aren't they to be allowed to get help for themselves? Certainly, would be my reply, provided it is not illegal, but never any that is evil. First there is that from the gods, which may be gained by prayers and acts of worship. Then there is that from water: if it does harm, it is shut off, but if it is likely to be of assistance, it is let in. They can even make their masters more kindly disposed towards them, so as either to allow a remission of debts, or even to offer a grant and again, if they ever need to have recourse to law between each other, they should approach the

[a] The father of the recent *consularis* Eutropius (*PLRE* 318 (3); Seeck 153 (v)) had been such a fugitive *colonus*, which adds spice to the statements here. For legislation concerning these *coloni cf. C. Th.* 5. 17.

R ii. 514 εἰσιέναι,[1] πλὴν εἴ τι δέοιτο μείζονος. | 20. πάσαις δὲ ἐπικουρίαις οὐ χρηστέον, κἂν ὦσιν οὐ κατὰ νόμον κἂν[2] ποιῶσί με τῶν ἐμῶν ἄκυρον. εἰσὶν ἡμῖν, ὦ βασιλεῦ, πόλεις ἐπὶ τῶν ὁρίων τῶν πρὸς τοὺς βαρβάρους. ἢν οὖν ἔριδι καὶ φιλονεικίᾳ τινὶ πόλις ἐλαττουμένη πόλεως καλέσῃ συμμάχους τοὺς γείτονας βαρβάρους, ἀνεκτὸν ⟨ἢ⟩ καλὸν | τι[3] ποιή- F σει καὶ ἐπαίνων, ἀλλ' οὐ τιμωρίας ἄξιον; ἐμοὶ μὲν κἂν κατασκαφῆναι δοκεῖ καὶ τοῖς πολίταις γενέσθαι τάφος, ἵνα μὴ τοιαῦτα νικῶῃ. εἰ γὰρ καὶ κρατεῖν ἔδει προσθήκῃ τινί, ταύτην ἔνδοθεν ἔδει καὶ παρὰ τῶν οἰκείων εἶναι. 21. οὐδὲ γὰρ οἰκέτην ἄξιον δίκης ἐφ' οἷς ἔπαθεν ἀξιοῦντα τυχεῖν εἰς τὸν δεῖνα καὶ τὸν δεῖνα βλέπειν καὶ παραστάντα ἱκετεύειν τὸν οὐ κύριον ἀφέντα τὸν δεσπότην. οὐδὲ γὰρ ἅπας ἔτ' ἂν εἴη τοῦ δεσπότου, ἀλλ' οὐκ ἂν μικρὸν μέρος τοῦ βεβοηθηκότος ποιοῖ[4] μερίζων μὲν τὴν εὔνοιαν, μερίζων δὲ τὰ τοῦ σώματος. καὶ γὰρ καὶ τοῦτον ἐχρῆν λαμβάνειν μὲν δίκην, λαμβάνειν δὲ διὰ τοῦ δεσπότου· τὸ δὲ δι' ἄλλου κἂν ἀποστερῆσαι τοῦ δούλου πολλάκις τὸν δεσπότην καταπεφρονημένον ἐκ τῆς παρ' ἄλλου βοηθείας.

22. Τί οὖν, φησίν, εἰ τῆς χρείας ἐλάττων ὁ τὸν

---

[1] εἰσιέναι F. : εἰδέναι Goth., Re. (mss.).
[2] κἂν F. : καὶ Goth., Re. (mss.).
[3] ⟨ἢ⟩ conj. Re., F. : ἀνεκτόν τι καὶ καλὸν Harmand (I marg.): καλὸν om. IBM.
[4] ποιοῖ conj. Re., F. : ποιεῖ Goth., Re. text (mss.).

---

[a] A prime need of the peasantry, besides that of protection from outside aggression, involves the security of their irrigation rights (contrast § 5). Yet another is the reasonable settlement of disputes. Indebtedness of peasant to landlord (Jo. Chrys. *Hom. in Matth.* 61, *P.G.* lviii. 591 ; Salvian, *de Gub. Dei*, 5. 8, *P.L.* liii. 101 ff.) is an economic factor

owner, unless some higher authority is required.[a]
20. But they must not have recourse to assistance
of every type, the illegal, for instance, or that
which robs me of what is mine. We have cities on
our frontier, Sire, facing the barbarians : if one city
is worsted by another, and out of rancour or spite
calls the near-by barbarians to be its allies,[b] will its
conduct be supportable or right, and will it deserve
praise and not punishment ? In my opinion, it would
deserve to be razed to the ground and become a
tomb for its citizens, so as not to win a victory of
this kind. If it had to gain the day by some additional support this ought to have come from within
and from its own people. 21. Nor again is it right
for a slave, if he demands justice for wrongs suffered,
to look to any Tom, Dick or Harry, and to present
himself before anyone who is not his owner and im-
plore his aid, while ignoring his master. For he
would no longer belong entirely to his master, but
he would present his protector with the lion's share
in any division of his loyalty and personal services.
Certainly, it is right that he should secure justice,
but he should secure it through his master. To do
so through somebody else often means the master
losing his slave altogether, since he is despised as a
result of the assistance rendered by another.

22. " Well," it may be said, " what happens if

most prominent at this time because of fiscal pressures
exerted by the government, and is here skated over. Libanius'
conception of the landlord (=decurion) as patron bears little
relation to the facts.
    [b] A not impossible idea, canvassed by Themistius, *Or.* 8.
115 c, and at the level of the individual reiterated by the
Greek fugitive at the court of Attila, Priscus, fr. 8 (*F.H.G.*
(ed. Müller) 4. 86-88), and Salvian, *loc. cit.*

ἀγρὸν ἔχων εἴη καὶ δέοι δυνατωτέρας κεφαλῆς; ὁ
R ii. 515 μὲν λεγέτω πρὸς ἐκεῖνον, ἐκεῖνος | δὲ πρὸς τοῦτον,
καὶ σὺ μὲν ἐκείνου, τούτου δὲ ἐκεῖνος δείσθω. καὶ
σύ τ᾽ ἂν ὠφελοῖο ταύτῃ βλάπτοιτό τ᾽ ἂν οὐδ᾽ ἐκεῖνος πεπηγυίας τῆς περὶ ταῦτα τάξεως. οὐ γὰρ δὴ
τοῖς μὲν περὶ τὴν γῆν τούτοις καὶ πόρρω τῶν
πόλεων καὶ βουσὶ συζῶσιν ἐπείθοντ᾽ ἂν καὶ συνέ-
πραττον, τοῖς δὲ ἐκείνων κυρίοις οὐκ ἂν προσεῖχον
οὐδ᾽ ἂν τὸ μὲν παρ᾽ ἐκείνων λαβεῖν ἡγοῦντο καλόν,
| τὸ δὲ παρὰ τούτων οὐ καλὸν καὶ ταῦτα ἴσον ὄν. F 41
ἔστι δ᾽ οὐχ ὅμοιον τοὺς δεσπότας ὑπὲρ τῶν ἐργα-
ζομένων δοῦναι τοῖς δυναμένοις ἢ τοὺς ἐργάτας ἐπὶ
τοῖς δεσπόταις. τὸ μὲν γὰρ βεβαιοῖ τὰ ὄντα τοῖς
ἔχουσι, τὸ δ᾽ οὐκ ἐᾷ θαρρεῖν ὡς ἐπὶ σαθροῖς. 23.
ἔτι τοίνυν ἔστι παρ᾽ οὐκ ὀλίγοις τούτων καὶ τὸ
δύνασθαι παρ᾽ ὅτου καὶ τὸ βοηθεῖν ἄλλοις ἔστι.
πῶς οὖν οὐχ ἱκανὸν[1] αὐτοῖς, μᾶλλον δὲ καὶ τούτοις
R ii. 516 καὶ τοῖς τούτων | πράγμασιν [ἱκανὸν][2] οἱ στρα-
τηγοὶ κτώμενοι δι᾽ αὐτῶν[3] τὴν πλεονεξίαν; εἰ γὰρ
δὴ διὰ τῶν δεσποτῶν, οὐχὶ καὶ κατ᾽ αὐτῶν τὰ
αὐτῶν ἕξειν ᾤοντο. βουλομένοις δ᾽ ἦν κατὰ πρώτων, ἔπειτα καθ᾽ ἑτέρων μυρίων, ὅπως ἐξείη δρᾶν
ἃ πρότερον διῆλθον. διὰ τοῦτο τοὺς τὴν καλὴν
μέν, ἄοπλον δὲ κεκτημένους δύναμιν οὐδὲ ζῆν νο-
μίζουσιν.

24. Οὐδὲν δεινόν, φησί, προσλαβεῖν κηδεμόνας.

---

[1] οὐχ ἱκανὸν Re., F. : οὐχὶ κἂν Goth. (CAP) : οὐκ ἂν IBM.
[2] πράγμασιν ἱκανὸν MSS. : ἱκανὸν om. Cobet, Harmand,
bracketed F.
[3] αὐτῶν Goth., Harmand (MSS.) : αὑτῶν Re., F.

---

[a] Reiske confessedly found the whole of the preceding
section difficult to understand, and not without reason.

the landlord is incapable of doing the job, and some more powerful personage is needed ? " Then let the peasant tell the master, and he tell this other. You, my man, make your request to him, and let him pass it on. You would get help in this way, and he would suffer no harm, since the order of precedence in such matters remains firmly fixed. It would surely not happen that officials would listen to and act in collusion with these farm-workers, these country bumpkins who have their oxen for company, and would pay no attention to their masters, or think it improper to take from the master and proper to take from the man, even though it amounts to the same thing. It is a different matter for the masters to make a contribution to these mandarins for the sake of their tenants and for the tenants to do so to their masters' hurt. In the first case, the possessors are confirmed in their position ; in the second, their confidence is undermined and it is as though the rot has set in. 23. Moreover, not a few of these landlords have influence, too, and from it they can even assist others. Then how is it that it is not sufficient for them, or rather for both the tenants and their estates, for the military commanders to attain their pre-eminence by their agency ? For, surely, if they attained it by means of the landlords, they never thought to employ their possessions as weapons against them too. But it was possible for them, when they wished to do so against the leading citizens, and then against a host of the rest, so as to be able to act in the manner I have described above. Hence they regard the possessors of a notable but non-military influence as simply non-existent.[a]

24. No harm is done, so I am told, by acquiring

521

καὶ μὴν οὐ τοῦτ' ἐν[1] τῷ λόγῳ τῷ περὶ τῶν οἰκετῶν ἐδείκνυτο. ταὐτὸ δέ μοι καὶ περὶ τῶν γεωργῶν εἰρήσθω. καὶ γὰρ εἰ λίαν ὦν εἰσιν ἀφήρην-
ται παρὰ τοῦ θεοῦ τὸ δύνασθαι, βέλτιον ζῆν ἐν τῇ
'κείνων ἀσθενείᾳ καὶ ἀνέχεσθαι τῆς τύχης ἢ τοι-
αύτην ὠνεῖσθαι | δύναμιν καὶ τοὺς κεκτημένους F 41
R ii. 517 ἐλέγχειν, | ἐπεὶ καὶ γυνὴ δυοῖν ἀνδροῖν οὖσα δυνα-
τωτέρα ἂν εἴη, ἀλλ' οὐκ ἂν συνησθείης ἐχούσῃ τὸν
μὲν γάμῳ, τὸν δὲ μοιχείᾳ. καίτοι καὶ πλουσιώ-
τερον ἔστιν εἶναι τὸν μοιχὸν πολλαχοῦ, παρ' οὗ
πλείω τῇ γυναικὶ γένοιτ' ἂν ἢ τοῦ λαβόντος αὐτὴν
μεθ' Ὑμεναίου. ἆρ' οὖν οἰσόμεν λεγούσης ὡς οὐκ
ἴσον εἷς καὶ δύο οὐδὲ μέγας καὶ βραχὺς οὐδὲ
ὡραῖος καὶ ἄμορφος; οὕτω μὲν ὃ μάλιστα συνέχει
τὸν βίον, ὁ περὶ τοὺς γάμους νόμος, οἰχήσεται.

25. Ἐρεῖ τοίνυν τις τοιοῦτον τῶν τὰς ἀρχὰς
κολακευόντων λόγον ὡς ἐλάττω πρόσεισι τοῖς στρατηγοῖς, εἰ τοῦτ' ἐπισχήσει τις τὸ ῥεῦμα. καὶ τί
δεινὸν εἰ τὰ νῦν προσιόντα κακῶς παύσεται; οὐ
γὰρ τοῦτ' ἔστιν[2] ἄξιον σκοπεῖν, εἰ ἐλάττω λή-
ψονται, ἀλλ' εἰ δικαιότερον ἐκεῖνο τοῦ νῦν καὶ εἰ
πονηρᾶς δόξης ἀπαλλάττει τοὺς ἐπὶ τοῦ στρατηγεῖν. τὸ γὰρ αὐτὸ καὶ τοῖς ἀδικοῦσι κέρδος καὶ
τοῖς ἀδικουμένοις, τοῖς μὲν μηκέτ' ἀδικεῖσθαι, τοῖς[3]
δὲ μηκέτ' ἀδικεῖν.

26. Ἀθυμήσουσιν οἱ στρατηγοὶ κωλυόμενοι ταῦ-
τα θερίζειν. καὶ γὰρ οἱ κλέπται καὶ οἱ τοιχω|ρύχοι F 41

[1] τοῦτ' ⟨ὂν⟩ ἐν F.   [2] ἔστιν edd. : ἔνι mss.
[3] τοῖς conj. Re., F. (CIBM) : τοὺς Goth., Re. text (AP).

---

[a] Cf. § 21.

fresh protectors. But it is not this that was demonstrated in my argument about the slaves [a] ; and let me make the same demonstration about the peasants, too. Suppose those, to whom they really belong, by will of the god are deprived of their power, it is better that they should live their lives in their masters' weakness and endure their lot rather than purchase such a power as this and show up the owners. Take the case of a woman : if she belonged to two men, she would have more influence, but you would not welcome her having one in marriage and the other in adultery. Yet it is often possible for the adulterer to be the richer man, and the woman might get from him more than she could from the man who took her in the bonds of matrimony. Are we going to let her get away with it, then, if she says that there is a difference between one and two, between the short and the tall, between the handsome and the ugly ? If we do, the most binding link of society, the tie of marriage, will vanish.

25. Some of the toadies of the officials will put forward some such argument as this, that there will be a loss of income for the military commanders if this source is stopped. Well, what is wrong in stopping these present dishonest gains ? What we ought to consider is not whether they will get less but whether such a situation is more honest than the present one, and whether it rids the generals of their ill repute, for there will be the same profit for the wrong-doer as for his victim—the discontinuance of wrong-doing, whether it be suffered or inflicted.

26. Another objection is that it will be bad for the morale of the generals not to be allowed to reap this harvest. Thieves too, burglars, pick-pockets,

καὶ οἱ βαλαντιοτόμοι καὶ οἱ τῶν τάφων ἁπτόμενοι
καὶ οἱ τῶν ἱερῶν χρημάτων πάντες οὗτοι διὰ τὰς
ἐφ᾽ ἑκάστῳ τιμωρίας ἄχθονται. ἀλλ᾽ οἱ μὲν ἄχθονται, οἱ νόμοι δὲ βοῶσιν ἃ ληφθέντες πείσονται.
καὶ τὸ μὲν τολμᾶν οὐκ ἀναιροῦσιν ὅλως, αὐτοῦ δὲ
τοῦ τολμᾶν οὐ μικρόν. καὶ οὐδεὶς οὕτως ἀπο-
νενοημένος ὅστις ἂν εἰπεῖν ὑπομεῖναι ὅτι, ὦ βασι-
R ii. 518 λεῦ, | τοὺς κωλυτὰς τῶν ἀδίκων τούτων ἀνέλωμεν
νόμους, ἵνα μὴ λυπῶμεν τοὺς ἀπὸ τούτων οὐκ ἐω-
μένους πλουτεῖν μηδ᾽ εὐποριῶν δοκῶμέν τισι φθονεῖν.

27. Μὴ τοίνυν μηδὲ τοῖς στρατηγοῖς ὁδὸς ἀνε-
ῴχθω κερδῶν κακῶν μηδὲ τὸ μὲν τούτων ὁράτω
τις, τῆς δὲ τῶν ὀλίγα κεκτημένων μερίδος ἀμε-
λείτω, οὐδὲ γὰρ τοῦτο σώζει Ῥωμαίοις τὴν ἰσχὺν
καὶ τοῖς πολεμίοις τὸν[1] φόβον, ἐὰν καθ᾽ ἡμέραν τε
καὶ νύκτα καινῶν δέῃ κιβωτῶν τοῖς στρατηγοῖς διὰ
τὸν ἐπιρρέοντα πλοῦτον, οὐ γὰρ πλούτῳ γένοιτ᾽ ἂν
στρατηγικώτερος, ἀλλ᾽ ἀρετῇ καὶ τέχνῃ καὶ δόξης
ἔρωτι καὶ τῷ μᾶλλον ψόγον δεδιέναι θανάτου.
28. οὐδ᾽ οὗτος ἂν εἰκότως ταύτην ἄρχοι τὴν ἀρχήν, ὅτῳ πλῆθος ἔνι ταλάντων ἐξαριθμεῖν, ἀλλ᾽
ὅτῳ λαφύρων καὶ αἰχμαλώτων καὶ τροπαίων, οἵους
τοῖς πατράσιν ὑπῆρχεν τοῖς ἡμετέροις ὁρᾶν. ὧν ὁ
πλεῖστον μὲν χρόνον, πλείστων δὲ ἡγησάμενος
στρατιωτῶν ἕνα μὲν μόλις ἀγρὸν ἐπρίατο, ἔτι[2] δὲ
τῶν οὐκ | ἐπαινουμένων, οἰκέτας δὲ εἶχεν ἔνδεκα, F 4
ἡμιόνους δώδεκα, τρεῖς δὲ ἵππους, κύνας δὲ Λα-
καίνας τέτταρας, ἀλλ᾽ ὅμως δέος μὲν αὐτοῦ ταῖς
τῶν βαρβάρων ἐνῴκει ψυχαῖς. τηθίδα δ᾽ ἐμὴν |
R ii. 519 ἔγημεν ἐπὶ μεγίστῃ προικί, ἕδνα δὲ ἦν τὸ κλέος.

[1] τὸν before τοῖς Goth., Re. (CAP): transposed F.: om.
IBM.

grave robbers and the riflers of temple treasures all resent being punished for their respective offence, but for all their resentment, the laws proclaim what their punishment will be, if caught, and this, though it does not entirely remove the tendency towards crime, removes no small part of it. No one is so senseless as to venture to say " Sire, let us do away with the laws that check these rascalities, so as not to annoy those who are prevented from enriching themselves thereby, nor yet to appear to begrudge people their prosperity."

27. Not even for military officers should the way to base gain be opened, nor should we keep an eye on their interests while ignoring the class of small proprietors. This is not what keeps the Roman empire in safety and its enemies in fear, if day and night alike our commanders require fresh strongboxes because of the money that pours in upon them. A commander becomes no more of a commander because of his wealth, but because of his ability and skill, and love of glory, and his fear of dishonour rather than death. 28. Nor yet would the man who can count his fortune in millions be the proper man to hold this command, but rather one who can list spoils of war, prisoners and trophies,—the sort of people our fathers had the good fortune to behold. One such, after commanding large forces over a long period, was hard put to it to purchase a single farm, and not one that was much esteemed, either. He had eleven slaves, a dozen mules, three horses and four Spartan hounds, but, for all that, the fear he inspired dwelt deep in the hearts of the barbarians. He married my aunt : she brought him a large dowry,

---

² ἔτι Re., F. : τί Goth. (MSS.).

ὁ δὲ γήμας οὐδὲ δειπνῶν ἐμεθύσκετο, οὐδὲ γὰρ ἐν
τῷ στρατηγεῖν οὔτε καλῶν οὔτε καλούμενος, ἀλλ᾽
ἦρχε καὶ τῆς γαστρὸς οὐχ ἧττον ἢ τῶν στρατιωτῶν. τοὺς δὲ νῦν καὶ αὐτὸ τοῦτο διαφθείρει τὸ
ζῆν ἐν τοσούτοις ποιοῦν αὐτοὺς φιλοψύχους ἀντὶ
φιλοτίμων καὶ πεῖθον φεύγειν ἀπὸ τῶν καλῶν κινδύνων ἐπὶ τὰ παρέχοντα τρυφᾶν. 29. διὰ τοῦτο
πάντας ὑμᾶς[1] οὐ πλούτου πορίζειν ἔδει τοῖς στρατηγοῖς ἀφορμάς, ἀλλ᾽ ἔργων μεγάλων ἐπιθυμητὰς
ἀποφαίνειν. νῦν δὲ ἐν βλέπουσι,[2] χρήματα, καὶ
πᾶσα πρόφασις τοῦτο δυναμένη ταχέως ἁρπάζεται,
καὶ τηλικαῦτά σφισιν ἔνδον ὄρη χρυσοῦ καὶ ἀρ-
γύρου προστιθεμένων ἄλλων ἄλλοις ἀναβέβηκεν,
ὥστ᾽ ἀπιστεῖν ἀκούοντας τῶν ἐπὶ τούτῳ ταγ-
μένων, εἰ ἔστιν αὐτοῖς ὅσον ἔστιν. ἐν δὲ τοῖς ὑμετέροις[3] θησαυροῖς, οὓς ἔδει γέμειν μᾶλλον τῆς
ἀρχῆς ὄντας ἢ ⟨τοὺς⟩[4] τῶν ἐπ᾽ αὐτοῖς | ὄντων, F 41
R ii. 520 μικροῦ τοὔδαφος | ἅπαν ὁρᾶται, τὸ κρυπτόμενον
δὲ ὀλίγον. ὑμεῖς δὲ ἀμφότερα εἰδότες οὐδὲν ἐκείνων ἐπὶ τοὺς πολέμους[5] ἕλκετε, ἀλλὰ κειμένων ἀπ-
έχεσθε καὶ ταῦτα ὄντος λογισμοῦ τοῦ παραινοῦντος
ἅπτεσθαι. 30. ἡδέως δ᾽ ἂν ἠρόμην αὐτοὺς ἐναντίον τοῦδε τοῦ θρόνου τί καὶ βούλεται τὸ πλῆθος
αὐτοῖς τούτων τῶν χρημάτων καὶ τίς ὁ νοῦς τῶν
σωρῶν. οὔτε γὰρ θυγατέρας λέγοντες λέγοιεν ἂν

---

[1] ὑμᾶς conj. Re., F. : ἡμᾶς Goth., Re. text (mss.).
[2] ἐν βλέπουσι Cobet, F. : βλέπουσι conj. Re. : ἐμβλέπουσι Goth., Re. text (mss.).
[3] ὑμετέροις conj. Goth., Re., F. (BM) : ἡμετέροις Goth. text (CAPI).   [4] ⟨τοὺς⟩ conj. Re., F.
[5] πολέμους Goth., F. (AP) : πολεμίους Re. (CIBM).

---

[a] On this unexpected family connection of Libanius *cf.*
Pack, *Studies*, pp. 8 f.

but his bride-gift was his fame.[a] After marriage, he
did not go in for drinking, even at dinner ; nor did
he do so in the course of his command, either on issue
or on receipt of an invitation, but he kept control of
his belly no less than of his men. As for the generals
of today [b]—what ruins them is precisely this life of
plenty, which causes them to have more regard for
their lives than for their reputations, and induces
them to shun noble ventures and to make for what
provides the means of loose living. 29. Hence you
should not all [c] present the commanders with op-
portunities for making money, but you should show
yourselves as desiring great deeds from them. As it
is, they have eyes for one thing only—money ; any
excuse which can provide it is eagerly seized, and
such are the mountains of gold and silver mounting
up for them at home, with one piled on top of another,
that, upon being told by those in charge of this
business, they hardly believe that they have as much
as they do have. But in your treasuries, which, as
being those of the state rather than of the officers
in charge of them, ought to be full to overflowing, one
can see practically the whole floor bare, and the
amount contained is paltry. You are well aware of
both facts, and yet you take from those people
nothing for your wars : you keep clear of their
deposits, even though commonsense demands that
you should seize them. 30. I would like to ask them,
here before your throne, what is their idea in amas-
sing such fortunes, and what is the intention behind
their piles of treasure. If they talk of their daughters,

[b] *Cf. Or.* 2. 37 ff.

[c] Emperors in general, including Theodosius. An appeal
to imperial *esprit de corps*, as in *Or.* 24.

527

τι οὔθ᾽ υἱοὺς οὔτε γάμους ἢ ᾽κείνων ἢ τούτων οὔτε
καιρὸν εἰς ὑπάτους ἄγοντα οὐδ᾽ ἄλλην ἄμεμπτον
δαπάνην οὐδεμίαν. ἀναγκάζετ᾽ οὖν ἐπ᾽ ἐκείνην
ἰέναι καὶ τὸν οὐ βουλόμενον, ἣν οὐδὲ ὄναρ ἐννοεῖν
ἀσφαλές. οὕτως εἴ τις ὑμᾶς ἐν ἐλάττοσι ποιή-
σειεν, εὐεργέτης ἂν εἴη μᾶλλον ἢ εἰ πάντα δοίη.
31. εἰ δ᾽ οὐκ ἂν δύναιντο μὴ λαμβάνειν, ἀλλ᾽
ἀνάγκη νοσεῖν, πολλοὶ κρουνοὶ τούτοις ῥέουσιν ἀπὸ
R ii. 521 πολλῶν | τῶν πηγῶν ὁρμώμενοι καὶ πολλάκις ἕκα-
στον Μίδαν ποιοῦντες καὶ Κινύραν καὶ τὰ τούτων.
τοσοῦτον μέν ἐστι τὸ παρὰ τῶν περὶ αὐτοὺς τῶν
διδόντων, ὅπως αὐτοῖς ἐξείη λαμβάνειν, τοσοῦτον
δὲ τὸ παρὰ τῆς τροφῆς[1] τῶν λόχων. οἷς ἔνι ζῶντα
ποιεῖν τὸν οἰχόμενον ἐσθίειν τε αὐτοῖς ἐν τῷ τοῦ
τεθνεῶτος ὀνόματι. 32. ὄντων δὲ τούτων μεγάλων
εἰσὶ Πακτωλοὶ μείζονες, χρυσὸς ὁ δικαίως μὲν ἂν
μείνας ἐν ταῖς χερσὶ τῶν στρατιωτῶν, μεθιστά-
μενος | δὲ ἐπὶ τὰς τῶν στρατηγῶν, ᾧ πένης τε καὶ F 420
ἀθυμότερος ὁ μάχιμος γίγνεται μέρη τε ὑποδη-
μάτων φορῶν καὶ χλαμύδος εἴδωλον. πολλάκις δὲ
καὶ ἀπὸ τῆς γαστρὸς ἡ φορά, ὥστ᾽ ἄγουσιν ἐπὶ τὰς
R ii. 522 μάχας πεινῶντα σώματα. | 33. ἐξεύρηται δὲ καὶ
ἄλλα σοφίσματα χρυσίτιδος γῆς οὐ χείρω. βραδυ-
τὴς τῆς βουλῆς περὶ τιμὴν οὐκ ἀρχαίαν μέν, εἰσελ-
θοῦσαν δὲ ὅμως, εἶτα τοῦτ᾽ ὀργὴν ἐποίησεν, εἶθ᾽ αἱ

---

[1] τῆς τροφῆς conj. Re., F. : τῇ τροφῇ Goth., Re. text (mss.).

---

[a] Along with Croesus and Midas, Cinyras of Paphos,
king of Cyprus, was one of the legendary millionaires of
Greece : cf. Or. 1. 273, 25. 23 ff., 55. 21 ; Homer, Il.
11. 20 f.
[b] Pactolus, the Lydian " river of gold," cf. Or. 21. 24,
62. 66.

or their sons, or the weddings of either, or the career preliminary to the consulship, or any other type of legitimate expenditure—these would be mere nothings. So even if anyone baulks, force him to undertake an expenditure that he would not even dream of without alarm. So, anybody who brings you people down a peg or two would be doing us more of a good turn than if he gave us everything. 31. But if it is impossible to keep them from taking their pick, and if they needs must err, then there are many springs flowing for them, starting from many a source, which time and again turn every one of them into a millionaire.[a] First, there is all that which their dependants offer so that they too can take their pickings. Then, there is what they can get from the regimental ration returns : here they can keep the dead alive and themselves draw rations in the dead man's name. 32. These are big enough, but there are bigger Bonanzas [b] still—the gold that should properly stay in the hands of the men but yet finds its way into those of the commander. As a result the fighting man is pauperized, his morale lowered, as he wears his scraps of boots and his ghost of a uniform. And quite often the contribution he makes is from his belly, so that they lead into action starving bodies. 33. Other dodges too have been devised—each as good as a gold mine. The city council is slow with some honorarium which, though not of long standing, has yet made its début.[c] This results in resentment, and the consequent

[c] τιμή, payment (so Reiske), rather than prestige (as Harmand, pp. 42, 159), seems to be the point here. The refusal by the council to make this new-fangled contribution results only in further extortion.

LIBANIUS

καταλλαγαὶ χρήματα. χρήματα δὲ κἀκεῖθεν· στρατιώτης ἀγοραῖον ἐρεθίζει σκώπτων καὶ κνίζων
ῥήμασι καὶ λαμβανόμενος καὶ ἕλκων καὶ ἐπισπώ-
μενος. εἶθ᾽ ὁ μὲν ἅπτεταί πως καὶ αὐτός, τῶν πεπραγμένων δὲ οὐκ ἴσων εἶναι δοκούντων, μὴ γὰρ
εἶναι φωνὴν ἢ χεῖρα τοῖς τοιούτοις ἐπὶ τὸν στρατιώτην, ἁρπάζεθ᾽ ὁ κατηναγκασμένος ἀλγῆσαι καὶ
ἔστιν ἐν τοῖς σημείοις καὶ τὸ μὴ τυπτόμενος ἀποθανεῖν ὠνεῖται.[1] πολλὰ τοιαῦτα καθ᾽ ἑκάστην
ἡμέραν καὶ σπείρεται καὶ θερίζεται μικρὰ πρὸς τὸ
ῥηθησόμενον. τὸ δέ ἐστιν αἱ τιμαὶ τῶν ἀρχῶν,
ἄργυρος, ἄχθος καμήλων. καὶ παραλείπω τἀκ τῆς
ὑμετέρας οἰκίας εἰς τὰς ἐκείνων καθ᾽ ἕκαστον ἐνιαυτὸν ἰόντα. 34. τί οὖν δεῖ μετὰ τοσοῦτον ὄμβρον
λημμάτων ἀθλίους ποιεῖν ἀνθρώπους οἷς οὐδὲν ἔνι
R ii. 523 πλὴν τῶν ἀγρῶν; τί δ᾽ ἀσεβεῖ πόρῳ τὰ | αὐτῶν[2]
ἐπὶ μεῖζον | ἄγουσι συμπράττειν; μᾶλλον δὲ πολ- F 42
λοὶ μὲν ἄδικοι, οὐδὲ γὰρ οἱ παρὰ τῶν δυνάμεων
δίκαιοι, πολλῷ δὲ οὗτος ἀδικώτατος.[3] πατήρ μοι
κατέλιπεν ἀγρὸν ἢ μήτηρ ἢ οἱ τούτους τεκόντες ἢ
ἐπριάμην αὐτός, ἐν ᾧ γεωργοὺς εἶχον σωφρονοῦν-
τας τὴν Τύχην ἐν ταῖς παρ᾽ ἐμοῦ φιλανθρωπίαις.
εἶτα σὺ τούτους λαβὼν ἐκμαίνεις καὶ κινεῖς ἀνελ-
πίστους πολέμους καὶ ποιεῖς ἀνθρώπους εὐγενεῖς
ἀπόρους.

[1] ὠνεῖται conj. Re., F.: ὤνηται Goth., Re. text (mss.).
[2] αὐτῶν Re., F.: αὐτῶν Goth. (mss.).
[3] ἀδικώτατος conj. Re., F.: ἀδικώτερος Goth., Re. text (mss.).

---

[a] The situation is now different from that preceding the
riots of A.D. 387. A military garrison is now found stationed
in Antioch.

reconciliation in cash. Cash also comes from the following sources : a soldier provokes a market trader, employing abuse and verbal insult : he lays hands on him, manhandles and ill-treats him.[a] Then he too perhaps has hands laid on him, but there apparently is no comparison between the actions : such persons must raise neither voice nor hand against the soldiery, and so this wretch, who is doomed to suffer, is arrested and thrown into the guard-room and purchases the right not to be flogged to death. Every day there occur plenty of such seed-times and harvests, but these are minor matters compared with the next item—the sale of office,[b] the silver and the camel-loads in kind, not to mention all the sums that pass every single year from your palace to theirs. 34. After such a deluge of takings what need is there then to make unbearable the lives of such people who have nothing but their farms, or to act in concert with those who seek to increase their fortunes by unholy means ? Not just that ! There are rogues in plenty, for not even the representatives of the authorities are just, but this fellow is far and away the biggest rogue of all. My father or mother, or their parents before them, left me an estate, or I bought it myself, and there I had decent, respectable tenants [c] who had some pious regard for dame Fortune in the services they received from me, and then you get hold of them, and enrage them, and stir up conflicts unimaginable, and reduce gentlemen to penury.

[b] The generals recommend promotions only after massive bribery.
[c] A generalization which includes Libanius' own position as regards his Jewish tenants.

35. Ἀλλ᾽ οὗτοι μὲν ἑκόντες οὐκ ἄν ποτε χαλινώσαιεν τὴν ἑαυτῶν ἀπληστίαν, τῆς σῆς δὲ δεῖται τὸ πρᾶγμα, βασιλεῦ, καὶ φρονήσεως καὶ τύχης· σὺ γὰρ μόνος ἂν ἰατρὸς κατασταίης ἕλκους οὐ φορητοῦ. καὶ μήτοι νομίσῃς ἀκούσεσθαι παρ᾽ ἐμοῦ περὶ νόμου τοὺς μὲν ἐπισχήσοντος, τοῖς δὲ βοηθήσοντος. ἔστι γὰρ καὶ γέγραπται καὶ κεῖται νομοθέτην ἔχων τὸν σβέσαντα μὲν τυραννίδα, στήσαντα δὲ Σκυθικὴν φλόγα, καὶ μέγιστόν ἐστί μοι κατὰ

R ii. 524 τῶν πραττομένων | ὅτι μου συναγορεύει τῷ λόγῳ διὰ τοῦ νόμου βασιλεὺς θεοείκελος, εἶπεν ἂν Ὅμηρος, τῇ ψυχῇ μᾶλλον ἢ τῷ σώματι.

36. Τί οὖν νῦν ἐσπούδακα νόμου πάλαι περὶ τούτων κειμένου; οὐ τὸ τεθῆναι νόμον, γελοῖον γάρ, ἀλλὰ τὸ μὴ γεγράφθαι μάτην. μάτην γὰρ δὴ γέγραπται, μάτην, ὦ βασιλεῦ, ὄντων μὲν τῶν προσιόντων, ὄντων | δὲ τῶν δεχομένων καὶ τῶν μὴ F 422 ζητούντων τοὺς συναγωνιουμένους καὶ τῶν τοῦτο ποιούντων. ἃ γὰρ ἂν ἑδρᾶτο μηδενὸς νόμου κωλύοντος, ταῦτα κωλύοντος γίγνεται καὶ τό τε ἔργον πολὺ τό τε ὄνομα πανταχοῦ. 37. δέομαι δή[1] σου κυρῶσαι τῇ τῶν οὐ πεισθέντων τιμωρίᾳ τὸν νόμον. ἢ τί τὸ κέρδος τῶν γραμμάτων, ὅταν μηδὲν διαφέρῃ τῶν γεγραμμένων ἀνθρώπων παρ᾽ ὧν γένοιτ᾽ ἂν οὐδέν; τουτὶ δὲ ζημία μὲν τοῖς βασιλευομένοις, οὐ καλὸν δὲ τῷ θέντι τὸν νόμον τοῦ δόξαντος ὄντος

---

[1] δή F. (B) : δέ Goth., Re. (other mss.).

---

[a] On this legislation cf. Introduction, p. 497 f.

[b] Theodosius himself, cf. Or. 50. 14 ; the usurper is Maximus, cf. Ep. 845. For the triumph over the Goths in A.D. 379 cf. Or. 24. 16 (Vol. I, p. 503 n.). A further triumph was celebrated in A.D. 386.

35. But these people would never of their own free will bridle their insatiable greed. It is a matter, Sire, that requires the intelligence and position that you possess, for you can be the only healer of an unendurable wound. And do not think to hear from me talk of a law [a] to restrain them and to assist their victims. It has already been drafted and is on the statute book, and its author [b] is the one who has suppressed tyranny and quenched the flame of Gothic ravages, and my greatest encouragement in the face of these malpractices is that, by means of the law, my speech has the support of an emperor who is, in Homer's words, " like unto a god," [c] not so much physically as spiritually.

36. Then why have I gone to so much trouble when there is a law long since laid down upon this matter ? Not to ensure the passing of a law, for that would be ridiculous, but to ensure that one has not been enacted in vain. For it is enacted in vain—I repeat, in vain, Sire,—while ever there are people to make advances and people to receive them, and while there are those who seek no such partisan support and those who do. For all that would have occurred if there were no law to prevent it, is occurring when there is ; the action is common-place, and its name is everywhere. 37. Then I beg you to enforce the law by punishing those who disobey it. What value is there in engraving laws when they are no different from the graven images of men,[d] from which no action can come ? It is harmful to the subjects and discreditable to the legislator for

[c] Cf. Or. 16. 18 (Vol. I, p. 222 n.), Ep. 1492. Homer, Il. 9. 485, Od. 8. 256.

[d] For a similar pun cf. Or. 35. 22.

ἀκύρου. ἀλλ' ὁ μὲν τὸν τοῦ δεῖνος ὑπερβὰς νόμον δώσει δίκην, ὁ δὲ σὸν ἀθῷος ἄπεισιν; καὶ τοῖς μὲν ἄλλοις ἐμμενεῖ τοῖς σοῖς, τούτου δὲ κρείττων R ii. 525 ἔσται τῆς αὐτῆς καὶ γνώμης ὄντος καὶ | πορφύρας; 38. δὸς δὴ νεῦρα τῷ νόμῳ καὶ ποίησον αὐτὸν ὡς ἀληθῶς νόμον ἀντὶ ψιλῆς προσηγορίας. εἰ δὲ οὐκ ἐθελήσεις, ἐξάλειψον. τοῦ γὰρ κείμενον ὑπερορᾶσθαι βέλτιον τὸ μηδὲ κεῖσθαι. ἀλλὰ μήποτε τοῦτ' ἐπίδοιμι γιγνόμενον, ἀλλ' ἐκεῖνός τε ἀθάνατος μετὰ τοῦ σοῦ σπέρματος μένοι καὶ τῇ τῶν ἠδικηκότων δίκῃ τὰ λοιπὰ βελτίω γένοιτο.

---

[a] σὸν confirms § 35, that this law is of Theodosian origin.
[b] Compare the terms in which he wishes for hereditary successors to Julian (Or. 13. 53, 18. 294), and of his lament (Or. 17. 32).

his decree to be invalidated. Is a man who transgresses the law ordained by some Tom, Dick or
Harry to be punished, while any who transgresses
a law of yours [a] gets off scot-free ? And while he
abides by the rest of your laws, is he to put himself
above this one, although it emanates from the same
resolve and the same imperial purple ? 38. Put
sinews into the law, then, and make it a real law
instead of an empty title. If this is not your wish,
then rescind it. Rather than having an existing law
flouted, it is better for it not to exist at all. But I
trust I may never see this happen, but that it, and
your seed together, may last for ever,[b] and that, by
the punishment of the guilty, the future may be
mended.

INDEX OF PROPER NAMES: A

(Includes those contemporaries of Libanius to whom reference, whether by name or allusion, is made in the text. Numerals in brackets indicate identifications proposed. Arabic numerals = *PLRE*, Roman numerals = Seeck, *B.L.Z.G.*)

INDEX

INDEX OF PROPER NAMES: B

(Names derived from religion, mythology, classical history and literature)

INDEX

Printed in Great Britain by R. & R. CLARK, LIMITED, *Edinburgh*

THE LOEB CLASSICAL LIBRARY

VOLUMES ALREADY PUBLISHED

LATIN AUTHORS

AMMIANUS MARCELLINUS. J. C. Rolfe. 3 Vols.
APULEIUS: THE GOLDEN ASS (METAMORPHOSES). W. Adlington (1566). Revised by S. Gaselee.
ST. AUGUSTINE: CITY OF GOD. 7 Vols. Vol. I. G. E. McCracken. Vol. II. W. M. Green. Vol. III. D. Wiesen. Vol. IV. P. Levine. Vol. V. E. M. Sanford and W. M. Green. Vol. VI. W. C. Greene. Vol. VII. W. M. Green.
ST. AUGUSTINE, CONFESSIONS OF. W. Watts (1631). 2 Vols.
ST. AUGUSTINE: SELECT LETTERS. J. H. Baxter.
AUSONIUS. H. G. Evelyn White. 2 Vols.
BEDE. J. E. King. 2 Vols.
BOETHIUS: TRACTS AND DE CONSOLATIONE PHILOSOPHIAE. Rev. H. F. Stewart and E. K. Rand. Revised by S. J. Tester.
CAESAR: ALEXANDRIAN, AFRICAN AND SPANISH WARS. A. G. Way.
CAESAR: CIVIL WARS. A. G. Peskett.
CAESAR: GALLIC WAR. H. J. Edwards.
CATO AND VARRO: DE RE RUSTICA. H. B. Ash and W. D. Hooper.
CATULLUS. F. W. Cornish; TIBULLUS. J. B. Postgate; and PERVIGILIUM VENERIS. J. W. Mackail.
CELSUS: DE MEDICINA. W. G. Spencer. 3 Vols.
CICERO: BRUTUS AND ORATOR. G. L. Hendrickson and H. M. Hubbell.
CICERO: DE FINIBUS. H. Rackham.
CICERO: DE INVENTIONE, etc. H. M. Hubbell.
CICERO: DE NATURA DEORUM AND ACADEMICA. H. Rackham.
CICERO: DE OFFICIIS. Walter Miller.
CICERO: DE ORATORE, etc. 2 Vols. Vol. I: DE ORATORE, Books I and II. E. W. Sutton and H. Rackham. Vol. II: DE ORATORE, Book III; DE FATO; PARADOXA STOICORUM; DE PARTITIONE ORATORIA. H. Rackham.
CICERO: DE REPUBLICA, DE LEGIBUS. Clinton W. Keyes.

1

THE LOEB CLASSICAL LIBRARY

CICERO: DE SENECTUTE, DE AMICITIA, DE DIVINATIONE. W. A. Falconer.

CICERO: IN CATILINAM, PRO MURENA, PRO SULLA, PRO FLACCO. New version by C. Macdonald.

CICERO: LETTERS TO ATTICUS. E. O. Winstedt. 3 Vols.

CICERO: LETTERS TO HIS FRIENDS. W. Glynn Williams, M. Cary, M. Henderson. 4 Vols.

CICERO: PHILIPPICS. W. C. A. Ker.

CICERO: PRO ARCHIA, POST REDITUM, DE DOMO, DE HARUSPICUM RESPONSIS, PRO PLANCIO. N. H. Watts.

CICERO: PRO CAECINA, PRO LEGE MANILIA, PRO CLUENTIO, PRO RABIRIO. H. Grose Hodge.

CICERO: PRO CAELIO, DE PROVINCIIS CONSULARIBUS, PRO BALBO. R. Gardner

CICERO: PRO MILONE, IN PISONEM, PRO SCAURO, PRO FONTEIO, PRO RABIRIO POSTUMO, PRO MARCELLO, PRO LIGARIO, PRO REGE DEIOTARO. N. H. Watts.

CICERO: PRO QUINCTIO, PRO ROSCIO AMERINO, PRO ROSCIO COMOEDO, CONTRA RULLUM. J. H. Freese.

CICERO: PRO SESTIO, IN VATINIUM. R. Gardner.

[CICERO]: RHETORICA AD HERENNIUM. H. Caplan.

CICERO: TUSCULAN DISPUTATIONS. J. E. King.

CICERO: VERRINE ORATIONS. L. H. G. Greenwood. 2 Vols.

CLAUDIAN. M. Platnauer. 2 Vols.

COLUMELLA: DE RE RUSTICA, DE ARBORIBUS. H. B. Ash, E. S. Forster, E. Heffner. 3 Vols.

CURTIUS, Q.: HISTORY OF ALEXANDER. J. C. Rolfe. 2 Vols.

FLORUS. E. S. Forster; and CORNELIUS NEPOS. J. C. Rolfe.

FRONTINUS: STRATAGEMS AND AQUEDUCTS. C. E. Bennett and M. B. McElwain.

FRONTO: CORRESPONDENCE. C. R. Haines. 2 Vols.

GELLIUS. J. C. Rolfe. 3 Vols.

HORACE: ODES AND EPODES. C. E. Bennett.

HORACE: SATIRES, EPISTLES, ARS POETICA. H. R. Fairclough.

JEROME: SELECT LETTERS. F. A. Wright.

JUVENAL AND PERSIUS. G. G. Ramsay.

LIVY. B. O. Foster, F. G. Moore, Evan T. Sage, A. C. Schlesinger and R. M. Geer (General Index). 14 Vols.

LUCAN. J. D. Duff.

LUCRETIUS. W. H. D. Rouse. Revised by M. F. Smith.

MARTIAL. W. C. A. Ker. 2 Vols.

MINOR LATIN POETS: from PUBLILIUS SYRUS to RUTILIUS NAMATIANUS, including GRATTIUS, CALPURNIUS SICULUS, NEMESIANUS, AVIANUS, with "Aetna," "Phoenix" and other poems. J. Wight Duff and Arnold M. Duff.

2

THE LOEB CLASSICAL LIBRARY

THE LOEB CLASSICAL LIBRARY

Virgil. H. R. Fairclough. 2 Vols.
Vitruvius : De Architectura. F. Granger. 2 Vols.

GREEK AUTHORS

Achilles Tatius. S. Gaselee.
Aelian : On the Nature of Animals. A. F. Scholfield. 3 Vols.
Aeneas Tacticus, Asclepiodotus and Onasander. The Illinois Greek Club
Aeschines. C. D. Adams.
Aeschylus. H. Weir Smyth. 2 Vols.
Aliciphron, Aelian and Philostratus : Letters. A. R. Benner and F. H. Fobes.
Apollodorus. Sir James G. Frazer. 2 Vols.
Apollonius Rhodius. R. C. Seaton.
The Apostolic Fathers. Kirsopp Lake. 2 Vols.
Appian's Roman History. Horace White. 4 Vols.
Aratus. *Cf.* Callimachus : Hymns and Epigrams.
Aristides. C. A. Behr. 4 Vols. Vol. I.
Aristophanes. Benjamin Bickley Rogers. 3 Vols. Verse trans.
Aristotle : Art of Rhetoric. J. H. Freese.
Aristotle : Athenian Constitution, Eudemian Ethics, Virtues and Vices. H. Rackham.
Aristotle : The Categories. On Interpretation. H. P. Cooke ; Prior Analytics. H. Tredennick.
Aristotle : Generation of Animals. A. L. Peck.
Aristotle : Historia Animalium. A. L. Peck. 3 Vols. Vols. I and II.
Aristotle : Metaphysics. H. Tredennick. 2 Vols.
Aristotle : Meteorologica. H. D. P. Lee.
Aristotle : Minor Works. W. S. Hett. "On Colours," "On Things Heard," "Physiognomics," "On Plants," "On Marvellous Things Heard," "Mechanical Problems," "On Invisible Lines," "Situations and Names of Winds," "On Melissus, Xenophanes, and Gorgias."
Aristotle : Nicomachean Ethics. H. Rackham.
Aristotle : Oeconomica and Magna Moralia. G. C. Armstrong. (With Metaphysics, Vol. II.)
Aristotle : On the Heavens. W. K. C. Guthrie.
Aristotle : On the Soul, Parva Naturalia, On Breath. W. S. Hett.

4

ARISTOTLE: PARTS OF ANIMALS. A. L. Peck; MOVEMENT AND PROGRESSION OF ANIMALS. E. S. Forster.

ARISTOTLE: PHYSICS. Rev. P. Wicksteed and F. M. Cornford. 2 Vols.

ARISTOTLE: POETICS; LONGINUS ON THE SUBLIME. W. Hamilton Fyfe; DEMETRIUS ON STYLE. W. Rhys Roberts.

ARISTOTLE: POLITICS. H. Rackham.

ARISTOTLE: POSTERIOR ANALYTICS. H. Tredennick; TOPICS. E. S. Forster.

ARISTOTLE: PROBLEMS. W. S. Hett. 2 Vols.

ARISTOTLE: RHETORICA AD ALEXANDRUM. H. Rackham. (With PROBLEMS, Vol. II.)

ARISTOTLE: SOPHISTICAL REFUTATIONS. COMING-TO-BE AND PASSING-AWAY. E. S. Forster; ON THE COSMOS. D. J. Furley.

ARRIAN: HISTORY OF ALEXANDER AND INDICA. 2 Vols. Vol. I. P. A. Brunt. Vol. II. Rev. E. Iliffe Robson.

ATHENAEUS: DEIPNOSOPHISTAE. C. B. Gulick. 7 Vols.

BABRIUS AND PHAEDRUS (Latin). B. E. Perry.

ST. BASIL: LETTERS. R. J. Deferrari. 4 Vols.

CALLIMACHUS: FRAGMENTS. C. A. Trypanis; MUSAEUS: HERO AND LEANDER. T. Gelzer and C. Whitman.

CALLIMACHUS: HYMNS AND EPIGRAMS, AND LYCOPHRON. A. W. Mair; ARATUS. G. R. Mair.

CLEMENT OF ALEXANDRIA. Rev. G. W. Butterworth.

COLLUTHUS. Cf. OPPIAN.

DAPHNIS AND CHLOE. Cf. LONGUS.

DEMOSTHENES I: OLYNTHIACS, PHILIPPICS AND MINOR ORATIONS: I-XVII AND XX. J. H. Vince.

DEMOSTHENES II: DE CORONA AND DE FALSA LEGATIONE. C. A. Vince and J. H. Vince.

DEMOSTHENES III: MEIDIAS, ANDROTION, ARISTOCRATES, TIMOCRATES, ARISTOGEITON. J. H. Vince.

DEMOSTHENES IV-VI: PRIVATE ORATIONS AND IN NEAERAM. A. T. Murray.

DEMOSTHENES VII: FUNERAL SPEECH, EROTIC ESSAY, EXORDIA AND LETTERS. N. W. and N. J. DeWitt.

DIO CASSIUS: ROMAN HISTORY. E. Cary. 9 Vols.

DIO CHRYSOSTOM. 5 Vols. Vols. I and II. J. W. Cohoon. Vol. III. J. W. Cohoon and H. Lamar Crosby. Vols IV and V. H. Lamar Crosby.

DIODORUS SICULUS. 12 Vols. Vols. I-VI. C. H. Oldfather. Vol. VII. C. L. Sherman. Vol. VIII. C. B. Welles. Vols. IX and X. Russel M. Geer. Vols. XI and XII. F. R. Walton. General Index. Russel M. Geer.

THE LOEB CLASSICAL LIBRARY

DIOGENES LAERTIUS. R. D. Hicks. 2 Vols. New Introduction by H. S. Long.

DIONYSIUS OF HALICARNASSUS : CRITICAL ESSAYS. S. Usher. 2 Vols.

DIONYSIUS OF HALICARNASSUS : ROMAN ANTIQUITIES. Spelman's translation revised by E. Cary. 7 Vols.

EPICTETUS. W. A. Oldfather. 2 Vols.

EURIPIDES. A. S. Way. 4 Vols. Verse trans.

EUSEBIUS : ECCLESIASTICAL HISTORY. Kirsopp Lake and J. E. L. Oulton. 2 Vols.

GALEN : ON THE NATURAL FACULTIES. A. J. Brock.

THE GREEK ANTHOLOGY. W. R. Paton. 5 Vols.

THE GREEK BUCOLIC POETS (THEOCRITUS, BION, MOSCHUS). J. M. Edmonds.

GREEK ELEGY AND IAMBUS WITH THE ANACREONTEA. J. M. Edmonds. 2 Vols.

GREEK MATHEMATICAL WORKS. Ivor Thomas. 2 Vols.

HERODES. *Cf.* THEOPHRASTUS : CHARACTERS.

HERODIAN. C. R. Whittaker. 2 Vols.

HERODOTUS. A. D. Godley. 4 Vols.

HESIOD AND THE HOMERIC HYMNS. H. G. Evelyn White.

HIPPOCRATES AND THE FRAGMENTS OF HERACLEITUS. W. H. S. Jones and E. T. Withington. 4 Vols.

HOMER : ILIAD. A. T. Murray. 2 Vols.

HOMER : ODYSSEY. A. T. Murray. 2 Vols.

ISAEUS. E. S. Forster.

ISOCRATES. George Norlin and LaRue Van Hook. 3 Vols.

[ST. JOHN DAMASCENE] : BARLAAM AND IOASAPH. Rev. G. R. Woodward, Harold Mattingly and D. M. Lang.

JOSEPHUS. 9 Vols. Vols. I-IV. H. St. J. Thackeray. Vol. V. H. St. J. Thackeray and Ralph Marcus. Vols. VI and VII. Ralph Marcus. Vol. VIII. Ralph Marcus and Allen Wikgren. Vol. IX. L. H. Feldman.

JULIAN. Wilmer Cave Wright. 3 Vols.

LIBANIUS : SELECTED WORKS. A. F. Norman. 3 Vols. Vol. I.

LONGUS : DAPHNIS AND CHLOE. Thornley's translation revised by J. M. Edmonds ; and PARTHENIUS. S. Gaselee.

LUCIAN. 8 Vols. Vols. I-V. A. M. Harmon. Vol. VI. K. Kilburn. Vols. VII and VIII. M. D. Macleod.

LYCOPHRON. *Cf.* CALLIMACHUS : HYMNS AND EPIGRAMS.

LYRA GRAECA. J. M. Edmonds. 3 Vols.

LYSIAS. W. R. M. Lamb.

MANETHO. W. G. Waddell ; PTOLEMY : TETRABIBLOS. F. E. Robbins.

6

THE LOEB CLASSICAL LIBRARY

MARCUS AURELIUS. C. R. Haines.

MENANDER. F. G. Allinson.

MINOR ATTIC ORATORS. 2 Vols. K. J. Maidment and J. O. Burtt.

MUSAEUS: HERO AND LEANDER. *Cf.* CALLIMACHUS: FRAGMENTS.

NONNOS: DIONYSIACA. W. H. D. Rouse. 3 Vols.

OPPIAN, COLLUTHUS, TRYPHIODORUS. A. W. Mair.

PAPYRI. NON-LITERARY SELECTIONS. A. S. Hunt and C. C. Edgar. 2 Vols. LITERARY SELECTIONS (Poetry). D. L. Page.

PARTHENIUS. *Cf.* LONGUS.

PAUSANIAS: DESCRIPTION OF GREECE. W. H. S. Jones. 4 Vols. and Companion Vol. arranged by R. E. Wycherley.

PHILO. 10 Vols. Vols. I-V. F. H. Colson and Rev. G. H. Whitaker. Vols. VI-X. F. H. Colson. General Index. Rev. J. W. Earp.

Two Supplementary Vols. Translation only from an Armenian Text. Ralph Marcus.

PHILOSTRATUS: THE LIFE OF APOLLONIUS OF TYANA. F. C. Conybeare. 2 Vols.

PHILOSTRATUS: IMAGINES; CALLISTRATUS: DESCRIPTIONS. A. Fairbanks.

PHILOSTRATUS AND EUNAPIUS: LIVES OF THE SOPHISTS. Wilmer Cave Wright.

PINDAR. Sir J. E. Sandys.

PLATO: CHARMIDES, ALCIBIADES, HIPPARCHUS, THE LOVERS, THEAGES, MINOS AND EPINOMIS. W. R. M. Lamb.

PLATO: CRATYLUS, PARMENIDES, GREATER HIPPIAS, LESSER HIPPIAS. H. N. Fowler.

PLATO: EUTHYPHRO, APOLOGY, CRITO, PHAEDO, PHAEDRUS. H. N. Fowler.

PLATO: LACHES, PROTAGORAS, MENO, EUTHYDEMUS. W. R. M. Lamb.

PLATO: LAWS. Rev. R. G. Bury. 2 Vols.

PLATO: LYSIS, SYMPOSIUM, GORGIAS. W. R. M. Lamb.

PLATO: REPUBLIC. Paul Shorey. 2 Vols.

PLATO: STATESMAN, PHILEBUS. H. N. Fowler; ION. W. R. M. Lamb.

PLATO: THEAETETUS AND SOPHIST. H. N. Fowler.

PLATO: TIMAEUS, CRITIAS, CLITOPHO, MENEXENUS, EPISTULAE. Rev. R. G. Bury.

PLOTINUS. A. H. Armstrong. 6 Vols. Vols. I-III.

PLUTARCH: MORALIA. 17 Vols. Vols. I-V. F. C. Babbitt. Vol. VI. W. C. Helmbold. Vol. VII. P. H. De Lacy and

THE LOEB CLASSICAL LIBRARY

B. Einarson. Vol. VIII. P. A. Clement, H. B. Hoffleit.
Vol. IX. E. L. Minar, Jr., F. H. Sandbach, W. C.
Helmbold. Vol. X. H. N. Fowler. Vol. XI. L. Pearson,
F. H. Sandbach. Vol. XII. H. Cherniss, W. C. Helmbold.
Vol. XIII, Parts 1 and 2. H. Cherniss. Vol. XIV. P. H.
De Lacy and B. Einarson. Vol. XV. F. H. Sandbach.
PLUTARCH : THE PARALLEL LIVES. B. Perrin. 11 Vols.
POLYBIUS. W. R. Paton. 6 Vols.
PROCOPIUS : HISTORY OF THE WARS. H. B. Dewing. 7 Vols.
PTOLEMY : TETRABIBLOS. *Cf.* MANETHO.
QUINTUS SMYRNAEUS. A. S. Way. Verse trans.
SEXTUS EMPIRICUS. Rev. R. G. Bury. 4 Vols.
SOPHOCLES. F. Storr. 2 Vols. Verse trans.
STRABO : GEOGRAPHY. Horace L. Jones. 8 Vols.
THEOPHRASTUS : CHARACTERS. J. M. Edmonds ; HERODES,
etc. A. D. Knox.
THEOPHRASTUS : DE CAUSIS PLANTARUM. G. K. K. Link and
B. Einarson. 3 Vols. Vol. 1,
THEOPHRASTUS : ENQUIRY INTO PLANTS. Sir Arthur Hort.
2 Vols.
THUCYDIDES. C. F. Smith. 4 Vols.
TRYPHIODORUS. *Cf.* OPPIAN.
XENOPHON : ANABASIS. C. L. Brownson.
XENOPHON : CYROPAEDIA. Walter Miller. 2 Vols.
XENOPHON : HELLENICA. C. L. Brownson.
XENOPHON : MEMORABILIA AND OECONOMICUS. E. C. Mar-
chant ; SYMPOSIUM AND APOLOGY. O. J. Todd.
XENOPHON : SCRIPTA MINORA. E. C. Marchant and G. W
Bowersock.

VOLUMES IN PREPARATION

GREEK AUTHORS

ARRIAN I. New version by P. Brunt.
LIBANIUS II. A. F. Norman.

LATIN AUTHORS

MANILIUS. G. P. Goold.

DESCRIPTIVE PROSPECTUS ON APPLICATION

CAMBRIDGE, MASS.	LONDON
HARVARD UNIV. PRESS	WILLIAM HEINEMANN LTD